Jim's Blog
Volume 3

Jim

West Martian Limited Company
1st Edition, September 2024

First printing 2024
The publisher can be contacted at westmartian.com
ISBN-13: Paperback

Contents

Jim's Blog
Volume 3

Replacing Obamacare

2017-01-05 02:28:31

The major problem with the American healthcare system is that it has no prices[1], making it a completely non market system. It also has a massive redistribution from whites to nonwhites, which wealth redistribution system disrupts the provision of healthcare. What tends to happen is a hospital treats a hundred illegal immigrants for morbid obesity, and they do not pay their bills, and then it treats one white male, and he does pay his bill - which is set high enough so that the one person who pays covers the hundred people who do not pay.

The best system is Singapore, which has a socialist healthcare system for the poor, and the most Ayn Randian hard core capitalist healthcare system in the world for everyone else. Which system provides healthcare at a fraction of the cost of everyone else's system and for the most part healthcare of substantially better quality.

If you are poor and sick, or sufficiently healthy that the quality of your healthcare does not matter much to you, you go to a government owned hospital, consult with a government employed doctor, buy government owned medicines from a government owned pharmacy. Otherwise, you just pay for it as if you were hiring a plumber to make modifications to your bathroom. The major government intervention in the private sector is making pricing information accurate and available. Private healthcare practitioners are free to dump people who will not or cannot pay on the socialist sector, or just not let them through the front door if they fail a credit check.

So the explicitly socialist system takes care[2] of the pity cases, and the explicitly capitalist system takes care of everyone else. So everyone else gets the benefits of capitalism, and only the poor or the healthy suffer the consequences of socialism[3].

Mission

2017-01-05 07:46:18

The Dark Enlightenment is simply the scientific method applied to politics, society, and religion - resulting in a big pile of highly unpopular bad news, that people are different from each other, that races are different from each other, and that the sexes are different from each other being a major part of that bad news.

Neoreaction is a political program (largely inspired by the Dark Enlightenment) for restoration - to recover western civilization and rebuild Chesterton's fences - racism, ethnic states, and patriarchy. Israel should be Jewish, and America should not be Jewish. That does not imply that America should murder and rob all Jews in America, any more than it implies that Israel should murder and rob all non Jews in Israel - but it is fine if Israel murders and robs any non Jews in Israel who are determined to take political control of Israel away from Jews. The Old Testament position on non Jews in Israel is reasonable,

---

[1] https://blog.reaction.la/economics/how-to-do-health-care-right/
[2] https://blog.reaction.la/politics/death-panels/
[3] https://blog.reaction.la/economics/the-inevitability-of-murder-under-government-health-care/

commanding tolerance and hospitality for the stranger in the one case, and mass slaughter for the stranger in the other case. One should neither be a cuck on the one hand, nor avoidably multiply enemies on the other hand.

The alt right is everyone who is literally worse than Hitler and has decided to laugh about it. Needless to say, one alt rightists is literally worse than Hitler for one reason, and another alt rightist is literally worse than Hitler for a different, and often entirely opposed, reason.

One of the Eldar listed various missions for Neoreaction:

1. Vaisya[4] Political Party of Soldiers try to get a combination of numbers and power to actually take over USG and end democracy, or at least democracy with universal suffrage. I favor rule by a semi hereditary class of officer aristocrats, but Trump as God Emperor to be succeeded by his sons, or a republic with franchise limited to fighting men and males with property and children would also be good. Anything is better than a democracy in which we are bound to be permanently outvoted by a bunch of stupid parasites.

2. Vaisya Political Party of Priests Build an out-of-power state church, ready to be adopted by Vaisya who take power. Provide the ideological justification for a Trumpist or soldier takeover, so that they won't feel bad about themselves for doing so, and will have something to replace the Cathedral with if they do take over.

3. Subversive Brahmin[5] Political Party figure out someway to bring reactionary ideas about by appealing to disaffected Brahmins and doing an inside job. But Brahmin rule tends inevitably to produce the results it has been producing. Rule by the holy results in holiness competition, and here we are.

4. Mutual Aid Society/Fraternity/Meta-church/Asimov-style Foundation provide a support system for helping red-pilled fathers or would-be fathers surviving the decline. Produce a religious political sect where mutual support between males supports male authority over women, so that in four hundred years or so, the foundation remains, and the Cathedral has quietly vanished. The plan is not to win power in the near future, but to survive the coming social collapse and dark age preserving something from which Western Civilization can be rebuilt. Observe that the high fertility of Orthodox Jews reflects a social order that demands that women give way to men, etc. This not only increases the fertility of the Orthodox Jews, but everyone who has substantial interaction with them, since they demand that all women, not just Orthodox women, give way. Similarly, Saint Paul on various methods for keeping female social status down. This plan is to maintain normal families in the here and now, and in the distant future, in a world where normal families are pretty

---

[4] https://unqualified-reservations.blogspot.com/2007/05/castes-of-united-states.html
[5] https://unqualified-reservations.blogspot.com/2007/05/castes-of-united-states.html

much illegal. If we can have patriarchal families, we win in the long run, since the non patriarchs vanish, and our descendants survive. Men who believe in old style marriage and patriarchy get together socially and have social events in which the proper role of women is socially enforced. Notice that the Mormons also arrange for Mormon women to get together and have social female events - from which events a woman is excluded if she fails to behave.

5. Antiversity an institution dedicated 100% to finding the truth. If all the smart people quietly believe the Dark Enlightenment, while merely giving lip service to progressive pieties, one day there is a preference cascade, and suddenly it is revealed that all the elite is quietly red pilled. Infogalactic is a good step towards this. I have set my browser to redirect Wikipedia links to Infogalactic links, and I recommend you do also. Infogalactic explicitly commits to observable truth, rather than official truth and official spin.

6. Poolside at the decline just continue to live life, and maintain a select circle of smart, red-pilled buddies to correspond with and occasionally have a beer with. Die with no children, or thirty children that are half South Asian. This position accepts the end of western civilization and the white race as unavoidable. We shall drown, and no one will save us. Our race, and our greatness, will not be remembered, nor will we have descendents to remember us. The next civilization will find a few strange, ancient artifacts, and will be astonished to find the ruins of ancient machines on the moon, wondering who put them there.

The evidence that Russia hacked the election

2017-01-07 05:54:06

When you subtract the spin, the evidence is that Russia Today News reported true things about the American election that the mainstream media did not want reported, that this is the same sort of thing as stealing true emails from the Democrats and giving them to Julian Assange to publish, therefore the same authority as ultimately has charge of Russia Today News stole the emails.

The spy agencies do not in fact know anything about the hacking that is not known to everyone. The emails themselves reveal that the Democrats were spearphished. The spy agencies are just forming an opinion on it from the point of view of someone who finds the existence of news media outside the power of the United States Government outrageous.

It is just an opinion based on the same evidence as is available to every well informed person, and most well informed people have formed a different opinion.

That Russia Today News reports truths that the mainstream media do not is reported as a horrifying outrage that pretty much constitutes an act of war. How dare anyone mention stuff that goes against the Cathedral spin?

Trump denounces the press

2017-01-11 20:26:14

Trump[6] is able to take on the mass media because he has is own non state power base. He is the Batman's Bruce Wayne.

But the elephant in the living room is Academia. He has small plans to take on Academia over global warming pseudo science and reluctance to subject vaccines to adequate safety testing, but the biggie is degree deflation, and we have not heard a word about that - yet. Any plans for degree deflation will burn everyone who has spent a fortune on inflated credentials and will be massively misrepresented as plans to deny education to the masses, so that is a tricky one.

Trump against the spooks

2017-01-12 00:14:43

Some of the spy agencies are loyal the red empire, some to the blue. I have reason to believe that Five Eyes and No Such Agency are loyal to the red empire, but it is mighty hard to tell, because, hey, they are secret.

However the people that have been overthrowing regimes are totally blue agency. You can tell that tree is poisonous from its poisoned fruit.

And this apparatus, the apparatus that destroys regimes, is now turned against Trump. The story that Trump had golden showers in Moscow was reissued to the press, given au-

---

[6]https://www.youtube.com/watch?v=IoCjWES7zUg

thority, and made into news, by the organization that briefs him that it was Putin that stole the Democrats emails and gave them to Wikileaks to publish.

At the end of his press conference Trump tells us:

> I have many meetings with intelligence. And every time I meet, people are reading about it. Somebody's leaking it out. So, there's maybe it's my office. Maybe in my office because I have a lot of people, a lot of great people. Maybe it's them. And what I did is I said I won't tell anybody. I'm going to have a meeting and I won't tell anybody about my meeting with intelligence.
>
> And what happened is I had my meeting. Nobody knew, not even Rhona, my executive assistant for years, she didn't know I didn't tell her. Nobody knew. The meeting was had, the meeting was over, they left. And immediately the word got out that I had a meeting.

So what happens is that the spooks meet Trump, tell him propaganda designed to legitimize the overthrow of his government, then report to the press propaganda designed to legitimize the overthrow of his government as the official findings of the spy agency, which Trump stubbornly and unreasonably refuses to accept.

Vaccination safety

2017-01-13 20:09:42

Some of my commenters have been arguing that vaccinations are dangerous. So I have been looking into it.

I am not going to present the evidence, just my interpretation of the evidence.

Autism presents at about the same age as kids get a bunch of shots, so by shear coincidence it will frequently happen that a kid gets a bunch of shots, a week or so later has some health crisis, is taken to hospital, and gets diagnosed with autism. So if you search for such coincidences, you will find a pile of them. Some people have gone looking for such coincidences, and the health industry has responded with demonization and persecution rather than investigation - a violently unscientific response to an extremely unscientific search.

Looking for coincidences between autism diagnosis and vaccinations is anti scientific, because you are bound to find what you are looking for - but it is also anti scientific to go forth and apply the power of the state to punish people who look for such coincidences, and pressure and punish the families that they found. The search muddies the waters, but the coercive reaction to the search muddied the waters even more.

Those searching found a bunch of coincidences. The reaction of the state and official science was to "prove" that these coincidences were all fraudulent, that they did not really happen, and proceed to coercively punish the "fraud". But by shear chance, there were bound to be plenty of real coincidences, so it was the charge of fraud itself that was fraudulent.

Official science is that the mercury preservative used in vaccines is completely different to mercury found in fish. This is just a lie. The differences are not significant. If mercury in fish is dangerous, mercury in vaccines is dangerous. If vaccines are safe, fish are safe.

What happens is that when they research mercury in fish, they design the experiments to get the desired result, that mercury in fish is dangerous, and no matter what results they get, they torture the data to prove the desired conclusion, that mercury in fish is dangerous. And similarly, when they research mercury in almost the same form in vaccines, they design the experiments to get the desired result, that mercury in vaccines is safe, and no matter what results they get, they torture the data to prove the desired conclusion, that mercury in vaccines is safe.

I believe the results that mercury preservative in vaccines in safe, and disbelieve the result that mercury in fish is dangerous. But if you believe the one conclusion of official science, you have to disbelieve in the other conclusion. There is a disturbing lack of interest in reconciling the supposed science on mercury in fish with the supposed science on mercury in vaccines. If one is real science, the other is pseudo science. I rather think that the data on fish is pseudo science.

But in any case, mercury has been removed from vaccines since 2000, so this issue is now irrelevant. The scandalous inconsistency between fish mercury science and preservative mercury science casts grave doubt on scientific conduct, but no longer casts doubt on the safety of vaccines.

So what about aluminum salts in vaccines?

Aluminum salts in vaccines are very tiny compared to oral intake of aluminum salts - but oral intake is mostly not absorbed, while injections are absorbed. The FDA has calculated[7] that injected alumina is still insignificant compared to what is absorbed from oral intake. But given the long history of gross data torture on mercury, I would be a lot happier if this was measured, rather than merely calculated.

Why not measure aluminum salts in the urine before and after a course of vaccinations? Better still, isotopically label the injected salts, so you can distinguish where the aluminum salts in urine are coming from. It does not seem very hard to do, and if they have not done it, it is likely because they fear the results. Official research on vaccine safety is not research, but circling the wagons.

Progressive Jews divorce Israel and religious Jews.

2017-01-14 00:42:19

German court calls torching a synagogue free speech against Israel. Arsonists get suspended sentences, which is to say, go unpunished.

If you say that the holocaust was not exactly as officially depicted, that is not free speech, but an act of hate. Molotov cocktails, however are OK.

The perils of government intervention in health care.

2017-01-16 05:21:23

It is mighty embarrassing if a sick person is turned away from hospital to die in the street because he has no money. So the kindly government insists that sick poor people be treated for free.

---

[7]https://vaccinepapers.org/wp-content/uploads/FDA-aluminum-paper.pdf

But if the hospital is going to treat poor people for free, then the hospital is going to besieged by people with carefully memorized symptoms for vague and difficult to treat diseases who show up looking for a bed, some food, and some human contact.

So, the next thing the government should do is empower to the hospital to turn away unwanted patients with a jab from a stun gun. But they don't, because that looks kind of bad. But they do kind of sort of give the hospital some kind of monopoly power, and some power to hurry up patients who are taking too damned long to die. And then to the government's surprise they find the hospital is mistreating and murdering affluent middle class patients. The government also finds that it *still* running up gigantic medical bills on bums, who are supposedly getting all sorts of extremely expensive medical treatment, though in fact they are getting this super expensive treatment only in the most superficial manner or not at all.

The hospital is rushing middle class patients out the door or into the morgue, while every corridor is piled high with incredibly expensive (and profitable) bums piled three to a urine soaked bed. (Yes, Canada, I am looking at you.)

When the government empowered the hospital to be quietly and furtively brutal and murderous, the intent was that the hospital only be brutal and murderous to the horde of bums besieging it - but they could not actually say that out loud, and if they had said it out loud would still find it difficult to get compliance.

So now the hospital is massively over treating bums, massively undertreating people who are genuinely ill with genuine diseases, and murdering any of its customers who are too sick and weak to protest. And medical costs are soaring.

So what should the government do?

Firstly, needs to hit who everyone lays down his head on a hospital bed with a high enough deductible that anyone who is not all that sick and who has to pay the deductible will not go near the hospital bed. It does not have to be all that high, does not need to be nearly as high as the Obamacare deductibles. Five hundred should do it. First thing that should happen on intake is a wallet inspection.

But suppose the patient does not have five hundred in his pocket, nor an acceptable credit card, and seems unlikely to pay. Then the nice friendly hospital for nice respectable middle class people sends him to the hospital for poor bums staffed by big ugly lesbian nurses with thick mustaches, where the first thing he meets is the death penal, with a big male guard holding stun gun, a baton, a taser, and a twelve gauge shotgun standing uncomfortably close beside him, and the death panel decides whether his treatment is likely to be cost effective.

Now at the nice friendly middle class hospital for nice middle class people we try to organize things so that the doctor and the hospital has to please the customer, if they are going to make some money, and the patient bears enough of the cost to scream bloody murder if overbilled or billed for nonexistent or barely provided services. Deductibles need to be high enough to hurt a bit, but not so high that they are, like Obamacare deductibles, frequently unpayable.

And at the hospital for poor bums, we provide all the wonders of socialist medicine so beloved by Bernie Sanders, modeled on the wonderful success of Cuban healthcare.

If the hospital is in the business of handing out free beds and food, it is going to need to be able to whack undeserving customers with a baton, jab them with a stungun, and throw them into the street hard enough to bounce several times. On the other hand, you would probably prefer to send your elderly grandma to hospital that does not do that sort of thing. So we need to keep a good separation between the hospital that hands out freebies, and the hospital that does not hand out freebies.

Or, equivalently you need to have very different rules in place for treating the people who are getting free food and free beds, from treating the people who want to get out of hospital as soon as they can. You have to treat one lot pretty much the opposite of the other lot.

Daily Shoah doxed for not being sufficiently anti semitic

2017-01-17 05:41:16

If the Daily Shoah is insufficiently anti semitic and pro Hitler[8], who is sufficiently anti semitic and pro hitler?

If they doxed me for being insufficiently enthusiastic about wanting to rob and murder Jews in sufficient numbers, there would be some logic in that, but the Daily Shoah?

Those doxers are evil and crazy, they are our enemies - because none of us is sufficiently anti semitic.

The Daily Shoah are not my enemies, but my friends, and those who are their enemies, are my enemies. Whosoever goes after the Daily Shoah is likely to go after me.

Seeking war with Russia

2017-01-18 01:23:12

I have been reading the rationales for actions and policies likely to lead to nuclear war with Russia, and they are incoherent, absurd, and make no sense. They are obviously post hoc rationalizations. The person posting wants war, and looks for justifications until he finds something that is socially acceptable and that he can pretend makes sense. They use Argumentum Ad Baculum (we need to blow up Russia or I will call you a ignoramus and a nazi and destroy your career), Argumentum ad Misericordiam (the guys we sent to destroy Aleppo and murder the Alawites are being bombed), Argumentum ad Ignorantiam (you cannot prove the Russian are not attacking our democracy), Argumentum ad Verecundiam (the CIA says so), Argumentum ad Hominem (Trump is stupid, hateful, and rapes women, therefore we need to go to war with Russia), and Non Sequitur (Hitler caused World War II by invading Poland, therefore we should go to war with Russia over the Ukraine).

Obviously, these people want war for some reason unspeakable and unthinkable even to themselves

Remember when Pussy Riot trashed a Russian Orthodox Cathedral, and the Russian government treated them like thieves and whores?

US government, professorial, and mainstream media reaction was that Pussy Riot is high status, and Christians are low status, therefore Christians should stop offending

---

[8]https://itsgoingdown.org/no-honor-among-trolls/

Pussy Riot, rather than that Pussy Riot should stop offending Christians - pretty much the same reaction as when left wingers riot to shut down right wingers.

Well if Russia treats people like Pussy Riot and the European University as low status, maybe they are low status, and if Pussy Riot and the European University are low status, then the people making arguments likely to lead to nuclear war with Russia are also low status, since they are the same sorts as Pussy Riot and the European University. Nuclear war with Russia would erase this threat to their status - assuming that US nuclear weapons are still mostly functional, which they believe but which I do not believe.

Open Letter to Scott Aaronson

2017-01-19 00:46:57

Obviously you are not going to read this, because even though you keep patting yourself on the back about how open minded you are and how you refrain from cutting off contact with those who disagree with you[9], how you love all of humanity and want to maximize utility, you are in fact isolated in a self imposed bubble and blinded by hatred, self imposed ignorance, crimestop, and ignorant prejudice, which hatred and ignorance will quite likely get both of us killed, you more likely to be killed than me, because I lie low, have more than one passport, and more than one identity, while you hang out with totalitarians even more murderous, cruel, hateful, and intolerant than yourself. You know this, and at the same time you refuse to know it. You say it, and you deny it.

You are a very very smart guy - except that crimestop makes you very stupid. You think yourself a very good person, but have sold your soul to evil that is likely to devour you and all of western civilization.

And here is a good example of self imposed ignorance, willful stupidity, and self imposed isolation from outside thought[10].
> The emancipation of slaves, the end of dueling and blasphemy laws and the divine right of kings, women's suffrage and participation in the workforce, gay marriage—all these strike me as crystal-clear examples of moral progress, as advances that will still be considered progress a thousand years from now, if there's anyone around then to discuss such things.

Obviously I disagree strongly with all of those things. I hope that Trump will make himself King to be succeeded by his sons, and so does pretty much everyone who uses the phrase "God Emperor Trump". Which is a lot of people, many of them very smart people. You may think you are right, but if you think they are crystal clear, you are just suffering from ignorance and self imposed stupidity. You will not listen, and will not understand, why some people argue we need a King, that we are suffering from chronic Kinglessness.

If gay marriage is crystal clear and will be recognized as crystal clear in a thousand years, why was it not crystal clear eight years ago? Answer me!

Take my favorite topic: Female emancipation. Men and women very much want to form families and want those families to last into their old age. My wife was eighteen in my eyes all her years, except near to the very end, and even though I sometimes have

---

[9]https://www.scottaaronson.com/blog/?p=2931
[10]https://www.scottaaronson.com/blog/?p=2494

some pleasant youthful female companionship, I still sometimes find myself shaking and weeping when I remember my wife.

If you look at any successful family, no one is equal. Dad is in charge, mum picks up the socks. In principle, it is possible to form families in a society where men and women are equal, by freely contracting out of equality, but in practice, it is hard, and I see how hard it is for my sons. We have prisoners dilemma with few iterations, so the natural equilibrium between men and women is defect/defect. To prevent defect/defect, to ensure cooperate/cooperate, requires heavy handed coercive intervention by state, family, and society, and this heavy handed coercion necessarily bears far more heavily on women than on men. If you want a society where men and women know sexual love, or if you want a society which has above replacement total fertility rate, women just cannot be allowed to follow their pussies. And this requires a lot of supervision and coercion, primarily keeping women under control, rather than keeping men under control. For most women this requires that they be subject to the potential threat of physical discipline by the men in their lives. For a great many women, this requires that they be subject to the actuality of physical discipline by the men in their lives. So women should never have been emancipated, and some "violence against women" is legitimate, proper, and proportionate. Women, like children and dogs, need discipline and supervision and are never happy if they do not get them. A spoiled child, or a spoiled woman, or a spoiled dog, is never happy. The dog and the woman bark all the time.

And, in case you have not noticed, we still have blasphemy laws - except that these days you cannot blaspheme against magic Negroes. For reasons I have explained at length, all societies need blasphemy laws, and prohibiting people from blaspheming against something like holy oil or the flag, causes considerably less harm and suffering than prohibiting people from blaspheming against John Lewis. All your objections to Trump are objections to blasphemy. What is supposedly crystal clear to you is in fact something you do not believe in the slightest. Elsewhere I argue that we should venerate holy oil from Mount Athos because of all the things we might venerate, that is likely to cause the least collateral damage.

The liberty of the slaves

2017-01-19 03:46:34

The Dark Enlightenment and neoreaction recommend reading old books, and taking them seriously as the works of civilizations whose knowledge we have lost and whose institutions and social order we no longer understand, reading them to find out what evils Chesterton's fences once held back.

Thermidor has noticed a great gem in Seneca: That the modern conception of liberty is the liberty that the Romans allowed to slaves and small children, but not, however, to free adult male Roman citizens[11]:

This needs to be added to the Canon:
> It is perfectly natural, normal, and indeed, inevitable that those who studiously affect the manners and habits proper to slaves- whether they are self-aware of it or not- should

---

[11] https://thermidormag.com/the-liberty-of-the-slaves/

get the type of rule they have coming to them, namely slavery. ...
>
> In this respect, the blue-pill mytho-history of Progress, with its story of a historical ascent from darkness and despotism to an enlightened age of Liberty under the "rule of law" is a mirror-image in which the facts of modern history appear in reverse. From the red-pilled point of view, the historical trajectory runs in the opposite direction. What actually happened is that Westerners, much like the clueless teenage girl who runs away from the home of her firm but loving parents only to end up becoming tattooed as property by some outlaw biker and tricked out on the streets with an arm and a pimp to feed, quit a life of moderate subjection under the intrinsically lawful and just auspices of throne and altar for a perhaps more exciting, but perilously more dangerous and in any case, degraded and dehumanized life- one that additionally turns out to be rather less than perfectly liberating when it is already too late to go back.

Deploraball totally cucked.

2017-01-20 01:39:18

Pepe banned from the Deploraball, which means the left gets to define what symbols mean, and what symbols are permitted.

If the left can ban Pepe from the Deploraball, they can make Deploraball attendees cheer someone in drag as "stunning and brave", and the first Deploraball attendee to stop cheering loses his job, and will never be able to get another job.

97% of scientists support the scientific consensus on climate change

2017-01-20 04:33:49

And one of them is the Senior Fellow at the Alliance for Climate Education, who has just been charged with murdering a woman in what is obviously a race hate crime, though of course when white women get murdered, it does not count and nobody cares very much. And as marginal electorates in flyover country that have had large numbers of Syrian refugees dumped on them are discovering, when white women get raped it does not count and nobody cares very much.

Police are, of course, "mystified by the motive for this senseless killing", even though his Twitter feed loudly proclaims his motive and intent over and over again. "The United States is a violent white supremacist settler empire whose only fate is annihilation"

Note that proclaiming hatred of white people and urging their extermination does not get you banned from Twitter, but complaining about other people proclaiming hatred and urging genocide will get you banned from Twitter.

Kind of young for being a senior fellow,

His qualifications for being extremely expert at climate change are latinx studies - the study of the politics of Hispanic transexuality. An intersectional study.

We must bow before such eminent expertise.

Which I suspect is rather better than Michael Mann's qualifications, since Michael Mann got one of those consolation prize degrees you get if you go to an high status university, take a hard science course, and cannot handle the hard science. Then they give you an "interdisciplinary degree", sarcastically referred to as a "no discipline degree".

Oops, I think transexuality is now a hate term. Sorry about that. It was not a hate term the day before yesterday. This Senior Fellow at the Alliance for Climate Education studies the politics of gender inclusive latins embedded in a gender binary. Or something like that. Whatever. It will change again tomorrow to catch more people for the hate crime of using the wrong term.

The Senior Fellow at the Alliance for Climate Education attacked and robbed three young white women in rapid succession, killing one of them. Each attack was a few blocks and a few hours from the previous attack. He was slightly known to the woman he murdered, which enabled him to get into her home, but not enough connection to provide any motive for murder, other than whiteness, heterosexuality, and vulnerability.

This is the young woman he murdered.

She did not know that sexual deviants, like blacks, are dangerous.

We don't know all the facts yet but it looks as if he just attacked any white heterosexual person that was smaller and weaker than he was and that he could get alone.

While your typical climate scientist, your typical 97 percenter, does not murder white women and white children, he uses language that justifies and rationalizes the murder of white people, and as we saw in 10:10 no pressure,

he would love to murder white people, especially white children, for climate science is merely ignorant hatred of the technological civilization white people built, just as tranny studies gender inclusive studies is merely ignorant hatred of heterosexuals. So the Senior Fellow at the Alliance for Climate Education is clearly well qualified, for he hates better than most. And in Academia today, hatred is all you need. Though you are of course supposed to call hatred love.

Hence Bernie Sanders rather revealing statement "We should make higher education free so that *everyone* can receive the benefits of higher education." (Emphasis added). Maybe if *everyone* is qualified to receive higher education, it is not in fact all that beneficial any more.

The Senior Fellow at the Alliance for Climate Education is archetypical and completely representative of climate science and climate scientists, not in that the typical climate scientist will run around murdering women, but in that the motivation, reasoning, and intellectual capability of the typical climate scientist is more visible in the The Senior Fellow at the Alliance for Climate Education than in the rest of them. The Senior Fellow at the Alliance for Climate Education is not typical, but archetypical. His instance is closest to the platonic form of Climate Science. An interdisciplinary degree is typical. Intersectional studies is archetypical. Hating white people is typical, indeed required. Hating white people and wanting to murder white children is typical of climate science. Actually murdering white women is archetypical of climate science.

Police fine with left wing violence

2017-01-21 12:28:42

Milo attempted to give a talk. Leftists arrived to blockade the talk and prevent people from entering. The blockade was allowed to succeed, in that only those who came early got in. People who merely arrived on time were prevented from entering.
> Bricks, firecrackers and paint were thrown at officers and others — and then a gunshot rang out.

...

> Seattle Police Chief Kathleen O'Toole said there were no arrests and no serious injuries other than the shooting on the UW campus. "Things went well," she said

Evidently I am a bit old fashioned, but it seems to me that if bricks are thrown, and people are prevented from going where they wish by violence and the threat of violence, there damn well should have been some arrests.

If you allow violence, violence will escalate. Hence the shooting. My guess is that someone who was unaware of events was suspected of attempting to attend the meeting, probably wrongly, was attacked, and defended himself. Because that is what happens when some privileged people are allowed to engage in violence with impunity. The police presence is to not to keep ordinary people safe, but to enable impunity, to keep those who are attacking people safe.

Smoke grenades and such are merely providing the drama to entertain violent people. Violent people need to be arrested and removed from society.

Analysis of the shooting near Milo's talk.

2017-01-22 09:50:48

I examined the video[12] frame by frame.

At nine seconds, Yellow Hat is walking swiftly and calmly through the crowd of thugs blocking access to Milo's speech, and no one pays him any attention. He appears to be just another protester helping block access.

At 17 seconds Bald Man suddenly starts running towards him, and Yellow Hat abruptly starts backing away

At 19 seconds, a big yell goes up from the crowd. Yellow Hat appears to be being beaten up by the much larger Bald Man, or possibly more than one much larger man, and is fleeing, dodging, and zig zagging.

He is trying to evade Bald Man, and Bald Man is pursuing. It looks like some more people are joining in to cut off Yellow Hat's escape.

At 26 seconds, Yellow hat is not facing towards Bald Man, who is right behind him in hot pursuit, but rather facing towards another man who appears to be moving into the path of Yellow Hat's escape, so that Yellow Hat is trapped between Bald Man whom he is fleeing, and people moving into his path. Possibly several men are moving to intercept Yellow Hat. One man is advancing towards him hands outstretched as if to grab him, another hits him with a piece of cloth, perhaps a crumpled up banner. At 27 seconds

---

[12]https://vid.me/V3JL

a shot rings out. Bald Man falls, and Yellow hat reverses course, paying absolutely no attention to the fallen Bald Man, and retreating from the man he was facing when the shot was fired. Yellow Hat runs towards a group of left wing banners.

Either someone else shot Bald Man to take the pressure off Yellow Hat, or Yellow Hat shot Bald Man while glancing at him out of the corner of his eye in order to give himself a path of retreat. Yellow Hat did not look at Bald Man immediately before, during, or immediately after the shot, yet his reversal or course indicates he was aware that Bald Man had suddenly ceased to be a threat, and that he was now ignoring Bald Man because he had far more urgent problems.

Immediately after the shot, we see a big bunch of people with black masks over their heads and faces run from behind the camera towards the place where Bald Man was shot. Black masks being a pretty good indication of bad intent. Whether by accident or design, Bald Man had been chasing Yellow Hat towards the place the black masks appeared from. To the left of camera, everyone starts looking at the place the black masks came from, like there is something there much more important than a mere shooting.

In conclusion, leftie on leftie violence. Either Yellow Hat shot Bald Man in self defense, or someone else shot Bald Man to take the heat off Yellow Hat, fearing Yellow hat was about to suffer grave harm, possibly at the hands of the black masks. Probably Judean People's Front versus the People's Front of Judea. What do you expect when you hang out with violent thugs? Maybe everyone involved was a bad guy, but the one who got the bullet was the one who attacked first, unless a different bald man got popped in the confusion. Looks like justice on the face of it. Back in the sixties and early seventies I noticed that radical left organizations had a mysterious unfortunate mystery death rate similar to that of Clinton Associates.

Deferred Action for Childhood Arrivals

2017-01-25 05:06:32

This is an Obama program, still legal and operating right now, that gives illegal immigrants who are "children" de facto legal status - automatic permission to live and work in the United States, provided that they apply for it and register. In effect, retroactive magic soil citizenship, retroactive anchor babies.

Question: How young does your child have to be to be your retroactive anchor baby.

Answer: Your child had to be under sixteen when you arrived. If you illegally entered the USA with a child under sixteen, he can be your anchor baby.

People are telling Trump to let it stand, for if he stops it the press will go crazy with pictures of cherubic five year old orphans, and he will be discredited.

In Australia Tony Abbott and Malcolm Turnbull had a big run in with the press on imprisoning and throwing out cute little babies who had arrived illegally, or were born in Australia to illegals, and who were suffering from sad photogenic illnesses that supposedly could only be treated in Australian hospitals. If Tony Abbot and Malcolm Turnbull can tough it out, Trump should breeze through it.

No other advanced country in the world gives citizenship on location of birth (Except Canada). Nearly every country very recently used to give young illegals, and children of illegals born on magic soil, the heave ho, and there was never anything controversial about it until very recently. Further, Tony Abbott and Malcolm Turnbull got away with reversing the supposedly irreversible tide of history, and undid magic soil citizenship. The press thought it outrageous and extremely controversial, but it simply was not. In the end, no big deal. The dogs barked, and the caravan moved on.

On the face of it, giving illegals who have been in the US a long time citizenship is reasonable - if it was accompanied by measures to stop new illegals from arriving and deport recently arrived illegals. Which it never is. Wall and deportation has to come before amnesty.

The bitter bitch march

2017-01-26 22:39:06

Chateau Heartiste is full of great wisdom, about how to get women to submit to your will, and about what motivates women, and has put his insightful finger on the Washington Women's march. It is the Bitter Bitch March.[13]

Ashley Judd is the star and exemplar of the anti Trump women's march. Ashley Judd is single, childless and forty eight, soon to be forty nine. She is a nasty woman. In other words, she has failed as a woman. He ex husband, whom she dumped, has a hot young wife, a woman as beautiful as Ashley used to be when she was married to him, who recently gave him a child.

She used to be super hot, she was a movie star - but her perception of her sexual market value grew ever more inflated as her actual sexual market value hit the wall. Her last real movie was "Someone Like You" in which she was thirty three and her character was a woman waking up to falling sexual market value and about to hit the wall. Since then she has been in NGOs and a few political movies, and one real television series where she played a single woman with no love interest - only one year of real acting work - in other words, since she hit the wall fifteen years ago she has primarily been on the State Department payroll as part of its program of state sponsored leftism to move America and the world left.

Yesterday, a whole bunch of State Department heads "resigned" - in other words, were fired by Trump. I suspect she will not be getting any more gigs during the Trumpening. Childless, alone, and soon to be unemployed.

A man is not old at forty or fifty but a childless woman is. And in her old age, no one loves her and she is useful only for hurting people and making trouble. A nasty old woman, angry at older men with hot young wives, and about to be fired.

Trump's healthcare plan

2017-01-28 06:36:36

Trump has explained the free market part of his healthcare plan in detail. It is heavily influenced by the free market part of Singapore's tremendously successful free market

---

[13]https://heartiste.wordpress.com/2017/01/26/childlessness-and-mass-female-hysteria/

healthcare system. I have no doubt that if implemented as described, it is going to work and work well.

Trumps plan for the free market healthcare system is great.

But what about Singapore's socialist healthcare system for the poor and unfortunate?

Trump gets vague. Hospitals, he tells us, are going to get paid to take care of people "who really cannot take care of themselves".

The trouble with this is that as I said earlier[14] if bums, vagrants, and drug addicts go through the same intake, queue in the same line, and get the same treatment as you and me, there are going to be so many drug addicts looking for free drugs, and so many vagrants looking for free room and board, in line ahead of you and me that you and I are not going to get treated.

The way Obamacare deals with this problem is that you and I cannot afford to get treated because we are paying so much to look after drug addicts and vagrants.

Obamacare has provided insurance for everyone, by making everyone equally uninsured, provided equal access to everyone by equally denying everyone access. Obamacare has, predictably, collapsed. Ann Coulter cannot get insurance that covers broken bones and cancer[15]. If you cannot get insurance that covers broken bones and cancer, not much point in having insurance at all. (Ah, but she is guaranteed free abortions, which get priority above broken legs.) If she suffers anything expensive, she will wind up with the same treatment options as the homeless bum who heads to hospital for free room and board. Which is to say, really crappy room and board, which is what you got in place of treatment in Cuban hospitals. Universal healthcare for the poor has become universal lack of healthcare for the well off.

The healthcare system has, predictably, collapsed, because it is being swarmed by bums, vagrants, and drug addicts.

When you fly, there is business class and cattle class. For Trump's plan to work, hospitals are going to have to have separate intakes for those who are insured and paying deductible, and those who are getting free handouts. And those who are getting free handouts have to be made to really wish they were getting the kind of treatment that those who are insured and paying deductible get.

The big, big, problem, the problem he is being very quiet about, is preventing his plan for "Insurance for everyone" from devouring free market insurance the way Obamacare did. To prevent it from devouring the free market, you have to be mighty harsh on people who are getting medical care free.

You cannot adequately take care of bums, because bums will always demand more care than can be supplied. Thus a genuine universal scheme always winds up not providing care for anyone. If Ann Coulter breaks a leg or gets cancer, probably will wind up flying to Singapore, Thailand, or India.

For Trump's scheme for "those who cannot take care of themselves" to work without destroying healthcare for paying customers, hospitals are going to have to have a separate door for "those who cannot take care of themselves". And behind that door there needs to be someone with a taser, a stun gun, and a baton, plus doctors with a very simple and

---

[14]https://blog.reaction.la/economics/the-perils-of-government-intervention-in-health-care/

[15]https://www.anncoulter.com/columns/2017-01-25.html

effective treatment for drug addition and obesity. They give the druggie no drugs till he completes withdrawal, and the obese person with no food at all till he is slim. Doctors have a hundred too clever by half rationales for not giving unpopular treatments. For non paying customers, however, need to give the most unpopular effective treatment possible.

The urban gene shredder

2017-01-29 00:18:48

The discussion on the Jewish question raised several interesting and important issues, which tended to be drowned out by obsessive and repetitious discussion of the kill-them-all-and-take-their-stuff option. (If you think too much about outgroups, it is bad for your mental health.)

One of which is that Latin America browned out and went down the shithole because brownish people in the countryside reproduced and whitish people in the cities did not, and were replaced by brownish people from the countryside. Failure of elite reproduction.

But failure of elite reproduction is going to make us stupid even if the city imports fresh elites from a white countryside. Pretty soon we will need Jews to rule us (descended from rapidly reproducing orthodox urban Jews) just to keep the electricity and water going, just as Nigerians need whites and Chinese to keep the electricity and water going.

Mormons manage to reproduce in the cities. Right wing Jews manage to reproduce in the cities.

Men and women want to form families, but fail because of prisoner's dilemma. There is an obvious state level solution to this: Empower husbands, disempower women. Authorize more violence by husbands, both in that they should be allowed to physically discipline wives and children, and in that they should be allowed to kill adulterers. Also death penalty for sleeping with another man's wife, regardless of who carries the death penalty out. Enforce chastity on women, with "Homes for Wayward Girls", similar to the female factory in late eighteenth century Australia. Lower the legal and social status of women. Prohibit women from exercising authority over men, other than their sons. Generally encourage manliness. Legalize dueling. Give property owners broader police authority. Videos should depict feminine women, manly men, patriarchal families, and obedient and respectful children.

Orthodox Jews and Amish are successful in reproducing in substantial part because they keep their kids out of an education system hostile to males, manliness, and household formation. Reversing credential inflation is important. Girls should finish formal education at puberty, and men not long thereafter. Engineers educate themselves informally all their lives. Everyone should do the same. It is easy now in the age of the internet. Unfortunately businesses are legally compelled to rely on educational credentials.

Trump's family successfully reproduced in a society hostile to males and family formation, possibly because the Trump dynasty is uncomplicatedly and straightforwardly patriarchal. A large part of this is sheer force of personality, which men can and should cultivate. Be like Trump. Trump Trump Trump.

But force of personality will not do you much good if there are no marriageable women, and there are no marriageable women in Silicon Valley. Look at Zuckerberg's wife and Bill Gates' wife. In Silicon valley, the pump and dump lifestyle is simply the only viable strategy, because we have a social order dedicated to making women unmarriageable.

Fathers need to protect daughters from this social order, but it is hard for them to do so. If you are a silicon valley engineer, and you want to get married, need to take a year off and go for a trip around the world.

The psychological benefits of protectionism
2017-01-29 20:40:04

Free trade is good on average, but:

1. Protectionism declares production, which is at present condemned as fascist nazi sin against Gaia, to be righteous and good. Protectionism strikes at the moral superiority of progs, who think that shutting down factories, mines, and sawmills is inherently virtuous.

2. International agreements like the Transpacific Partnership are not free trade, and impair people's ability to form families and have children, which harms the kind of people that voted for Trump.

3. Even genuine free trade, even though beneficial on average, hurts some people. In particular free trade between China and the US tends to equalize worker's wages between China and the US, which harms the kind of people that voted for Trump. On the other hand, free trade between Britain and the US is fine for the kind of people who voted for Trump.

When Trump permitted two pipelines, conditional on them using US made steel in US made pipes, the delicious liberal tears flowed - for not only did they consider the pipelines sinful, but they considered US made steel and US made pipes sinful as well. When Trump added those protectionist conditions to the pipelines, he used the bully pulpit to tell liberals that they were *not* holy, that producing stuff is right and good. No matter what the detrimental effects of protectionism on efficiency, the effects of a moral climate that condemns work and production as sinful and illegitimate is a thousand times worse. When Trump explained his permits to the American people, Trump told the people that a steel mill belching out carbon dioxide *is a good thing*.

Obviously free trade is good on average. But international trade agreements that consist of thousands of pages of legalese like the Transpacific Partnership are not free trade. Rather, they are arrangements to replace local regulation with regulation by "The International Community". But distant regulation is necessarily more rigid, inflexible, and out of contact with reality, than local regulation.

Local regulation is corrupt in that you have a beer with a friend, who has a beer with his friend, who arranges that the regulation will be overlooked for you. Or one of your employees seduces the bureaucrat. Distant regulation, international regulation, is corrupt in that you hire a team of Harvard lawyers and team of lobbyists, who occupy several towers in Washington and New York City and get to write the regulations that bugger your competitors more severely than they bugger you. Thus distant regulation, the Transpacific Partnership, inevitably favors giant corporations in major cities, and crushes small businesses in small towns - favors the people who voted against Trump, and crushes the people who voted for Trump. When Trump dumped the Transpacific Partnership, he took a boot off the throats of the people who voted for him.

Inevitably, international trade agreements like the Transpacific Partnership favor people in the big cities, and hurt people in flyover country, hurt the people who voted for Trump, benefit the people who voted against Trump. So people move from flyover country to the big cities. And it is hard to marry in big cities, and there is nowhere for the kids. Women in big cities, like women on international trips, are free from the watchful eyes of friends and family, and tend to fuck around, rendering them unmarriageable. If you repeatedly reuse stickytape, it stops sticking, and women that fuck too many men become emotionally incapable of bonding to husband and children. Also, in the big city, hard to know what your wife or girlfriend is doing. In a small town, your wife will not misbehave, because she knows news will get back to her husband. Because the big city makes it easier to cheat on your wife or husband, the big city makes it harder for men and women to co-operate to form families. Notice that most of those women screaming in outrage about Trump grabbing women by the pussy are big city women who are old enough that they are quite safe from the likelihood that Trump might grab them by the pussy, are single, are too old to marry and have children, and are facing what they thoroughly deserve, a lonely and unloved old age. Again, Trump benefits those who voted for him, and to hell with those who voted against him, to hell with those who are now screaming at him and weeping tasty tears.

Trump Derangement Syndrom and Status

2017-01-31 10:14:23

Trump's 2017 order on Muslim immigration is not very different from Obama's 2011 order. But what makes it different, the reason liberals weep tears of outrage, is that during his election campaign Trump committed Lèse-majesté, blasphemy, against Muslims.

Now suppose a bunch of sluts and whores go into a Cathedral and perform obscene acts on the altar disrupting the service, and get away with it, then that lowers the status of Christians, and raises the status of sluts and whores.

Thus, when Russian cops jailed Pussy Riot for trespassing in a cathedral and committing obscene acts, the progs were outraged, because sluts and whores are high status, while Christians are low status, and obviously high status people should be able to give low status people a hard time, and low status people should just suck it up. High status chickens peck low status chickens, and low status chickens do not peck back, they peck lower status chickens. High status chickens go where they please, and lower status chickens get out of the way.

If Putin does not let sluts and whores give Christians a hard time, he implies that sluts and whores are lower status than Christians, which of course causes progs apoplectic rage, because it casts doubt on the status of progs. Until Trump was elected, looked very much as if progs were going to defend their status with nuclear weapons.

If Muslims are allowed to go where they please and give ordinary white people, aka racists, a hard time, that implies that Muslims are higher status. Which implies that progs are even higher status. If they are not allowed, that implies that progs are not higher status.

You will notice that Trump is creating safe zones in the Middle East for Muslim refugees. Which is arguably a lot better for Muslim refugees than coming to an alien country where they cannot get wives or jobs. The problem for progs is that not just that they want Muslims to go where they please, they want them to go where they please and give ordinary whites (racists) a hard time. They are not worried about the welfare of Muslims refugees, but their status. Safe zones, instead of US migration, undermines Muslim status relative to white Americans. It denies Muslims the opportunity to prove that working class white people in flyover country are low status contemptible hateful people who do not matter.

Hence the seemingly peculiar proposition that Trump is being racist. Islam is not a race. Banning Muslims is like banning communists. There are Muslims of all races and communists of all races. Trump is not banning Hindus. There are plenty of Muslims in Russia with better claims to Aryan ancestry than any Southern white gentleman, and there are plenty of Muslims in the countries on Trump's ban list that are as white as any American - for example Assad's wife, Asma al-Assad.

Trump's ban is racist because it raises the status of white Americans, not because it lowers the status of Muslims. It is racist not because it lowers the status of nonwhites, but because it raises the status of people that progs hate and wish to destroy. Same as Putin's police arresting Pussy Riot for vandalizing a Cathedral.

That Alawites tend to marginally whiter than some other Syrians is of course a major part of the reason why the State Department wants them genocided, but there is a very large minority of Syrians of all religions as white as Asma al-Assad. Asma was a Sunni, and Sunnis are a major part of the refugees from Syria. The ban is not racist because it lowers the status of Muslims, it is racist because it raises the status of American whites, particularly those American whites in marginal electorates in flyover country who have had large numbers of Muslims refugees dumped on them and are now suffering inner city levels of murder and Rotherham levels of rape, due partly to the fact that Muslims tend to rape infidels, indeed arguably this is a religious duty, and partly due to the fact that the refugees are generally single military age men who do not speak English. Of course they are going to rape, even if it was not their religious duty.

Progs are apoplectic with rage because the Muslim ban raises the status of the sort of people in flyover country who voted for Trump, and thus lowers the status of progs. People in flyover country are low status, so should get pecked, and Muslim refugees are dumped upon them to do the pecking. Trump grants the people in flyover country high status. Trump is acting like a King, the fount of all honors mortal and divine, hence the prog cry "Not our president". They reject his status, and his power to grant status, because they see he is disinclined to grant them the status they deem appropriate.

Long may the God Emperor reign.
You will notice that progs are almost as much outraged by Trump's safe zones as by his ban on Muslim immigration, for the one takes away their power to rub their enemies faces in the dirt almost as much as the other.

After the Flight 93 election

2017-02-04 03:57:54

Comes the hour, comes the man. Trump, vivat rex, is president, and may well take the throne and save America from catastrophe.

But what happened at Berkeley University when Milo attempted to give a talk shows that winning, we can never afford to lose again - if there is danger we might lose, we cannot afford a free and fair election, for the left intends to devour us. The stakes are now too high to allow democratic elections to continue. A single defeat will be absolutely permanent and fatal. Once in power they will utterly crush us, and never give white males a chance to regain power. So we have to do them before they do to us.

They have stopped listening, they will not hear. So, inevitably they fear us, demonize us, and will attack us, are beginning to attack us. Berkeley is Krystalnacht for "racists". We therefore have to attack them, in a more organized, efficient, systematic, and deadly fashion, to ensure that they will never regain political power.

The attacks in Berkeley were done under the protection of a police no arrest policy[16] and where there is a police no arrest policy, you can be pretty sure that the person issuing those orders to the police, is the same person issuing orders to the rioters, and that destruction and the conflict between police and rioters has been scripted and choreographed, usually by someone who loathes and despises rank and file cops.

You can also be sure that if we did the obvious thing and organized some brownshirts to protect our freedom of speech and freedom of assembly, the original purpose of Hitler's brownshirts, that no arrest policy would be instantly dropped.

So, if brownshirts are out, then blackshirts. Fortunately Trump, vivat rex, is president

Trump, vivat rex, has threatened Berkeley funding, and his FBI (yes, the FBI is mostly loyal) is examining that no arrest order and examining Berkeley for complicity in organizing the riots.

Imagine if Hillary was president. Then any campus that did have an arrest policy would be getting the black-lives-matter treatment from the justice department, and pretty soon there would be a no-arrest consent agreement to allow antifa to beat people up and set fire to stuff.

Once you have the terrorists out of the cockpit, you do not let more terrorists board the plane on the next stop. If they had won this election, their victory would have been permanent and irreversible. They would have crushed us with physical violence, and brought in a hundred million black male military age Muslim voters to maintain the superficial appearance of democracy. If they win any subsequent election, their victory will also be permanent and irreversible.

The basic theory of democracy is that instead of holding a civil war, every so often you count heads, declare who would have won if you had actually held a civil war, and proceed in a civilized manner, thus avoiding a lot of death and destruction. But if you count women and blacks you are not really doing this. Further, if one side will not listen to the other, and thus inevitably demonizes the other, you are not going to get enough civility for the losers to peacefully acquiesce. The left is not civil enough for us to peacefully acquiesce. Should we hold an election and they win, we just cannot afford to yield power, so best not to hold anything like a fair election.

Politics, they say, is war by other means. With "no platforming" it has become war by familiar means. If they have the power, they will not allow us a platform. We have the power, we dare not allow them a platform.

---

[16]https://www.breitbart.com/milo/2017/02/03/bb-news-daily-milo-berkeley-police/

Courts predictably rule Trump's election platform illegal

2017-02-04 23:44:23

The judicial order is clearly illegal, being an exercise of executive, not judicial, authority, as it was in Australia. In Australia Tony Abbott ignored the courts, and found loyalists to enforce his will. Courts then went quiet, no drama ensued, and the precedent that the executive gets to make executive decisions is now respected in Australia, for the moment, despite the fact that Tony Abbott has been replaced by someone obviously weak kneed.

Upon being successfully defied, the Australian courts acted guilty, rather than outraged, eventually accepting their loss of status, and have made no attempt to reclaim the inflated status that they previously enjoyed and successfully claimed. They have been successfully humbled, and remain humbled.

The first confrontation between the Trumpenreich and the permanent government.

2017-02-06 00:09:10

If Trump, vivat rex, appeals to the supreme court and wins, a Pyrrhic victory. But do not fear, there will be many more confrontations.

if he appeals to the supreme court, loses and cucks out, then he is, like Reagan, just another speed bump in front of the progressive steamroller.

If he appeals to the supreme court, loses, and ignores them, a huge victory.

When Kevin Rudd attempted to slow the exponentially increasing flood of "refugees" to Australia (most of them not from war torn countries but from India and Bangladesh) the courts aggressively overruled him, expanding their authority. When Tony Abbott actually stopped the flood of "refugees", the courts aggressively overruled him, further expanding their authority. "Refugees" remained stopped, eventually resulting in courts suddenly and quietly accepting a diminution of their authority to merely judicial matters.

Trump's confrontation has not started as auspiciously as Tony Abbott's confrontation, but then Tony Abbot had the benefit of Kevin Rudd in front of him. Kevin Rudd had promised to stop the "refugees" and failed, and then Tony Abbot promised to stop the "refugees" and thus had implicitly promised to ignore the courts, and had a mandate to do so.

So far, Trump is acting more like Kevin Rudd than Tony Abbott, which worries me. But Trump is twice the man that Tony Abbott was, and ten times the man that Kevin Rudd was. So I hope and expect that this will change when the time is right to strike down his enemies.

The solution I would really love to see is congress fire the United States Court of Appeals for The Ninth Circuit and institute a new bench of solid Trump judges, as the constitution explicitly provides for. But congress is full of cucks.

Trump is going to exhaust all legal remedies. He will appeal this to the supreme court once his judge gets put on the bench.

As commander-in-chief, Trump can, legally, declare martial law, formally adjourn Congress, send all judges to military prisons, and govern by executive degree. That might be unwise at this time, but a good confrontation with the judiciary with the judiciary acting in a blatantly unlawful manner could bring us a good step closer.

The cost disease

2017-02-11 08:00:35

Some leftists and a PC libertarian have noticed that progress is not progressing: Education, healthcare, and infrastructure is getting much more expensive without improving in quality, and in many respects declining in quality. Doctors no longer make house calls. Education teaches ignorance and stupidity. Infrastructure has brutalist architecture. Naturally they are completely mystified about what is causing it because crimestop makes them stupid.[17]

First world poverty – the inability to afford a wife and children – is as artificial as the Ukraine famine. It is not a natural result of technology. Rather it is a manifestation of ever escalating left wing repression. Parents are forced to pay ever higher prices to send ever fewer children to ever lengthier periods in institutions of left wing propaganda. Used to be that getting a school leaving degree at the age of twelve showed you were a smart hard working kid. Now getting a PhD in intersectional feminist basketweaving at the age of thirty shows you are an idiot.

The ever escalating suppression of jobs forces people to live ever closer to the revolving door between regulators and regulated. Anarcho tyranny destroys housing and prevents the creation of new housing. Credentialism intended to force people to attend ever lengthening lectures on leftism forces people to waste their youth.

Reverse degree inflation, children become profitable once more. Cut regulation, price of housing falls because people can get jobs without having to live next to the regulatory revolving door. Restore marriage 1.0. Marriage then gives you the security to produce children and invest in them.

In a previous post Fixing Housing Healthcare and Education[18], I address those fixes. In this post I will also address the problem of overpriced infrastructure spending.

The rise in education costs is runaway rule by priests. Most education is useless, and gets more useless at the higher levels. If you ask why we are giving more stupid people more useless education even though it costs much more than it used to, then you also have the answer to why it costs more. If you have priests in charge, they will make everyone go to church all the time. Our education system is the state church making everyone go to church and attend religious festivals. It is time for the Dissolution of the Monasteries. We need degree deflation.

Our education system is state church making everyone go to church and attend religious festivals. In other words, degree inflation To deal with this, needs a full on attack on priestly power. We need a revolutionary transfer of power analogous to the dissolution of the monasteries.

After crushing the priestly class, then we can deflate credentials[19].

---

[17] https://slatestarcodex.com/2017/02/09/considerations-on-cost-disease/

[18] https://blog.reaction.la/economics/fixing-housing-health-and-education/

[19] https://blog.reaction.la/economics/fixing-housing-health-and-education/

The priests need to be subjected to the Bishop, the Bishops to the Archbishop, and the Archbishop to the King. The Dean of a university should be appointed by the board, the Dean should have the power to hire and fire professors, and all academic funding should go through university, which is to say through the dean. If the Pentagon wants a professor at MIT to research something, it should pay MIT, not the professor. I discuss disempowering the priesthood and dissolving the monasteries in Draining the Swamp[20] and in The Cathedral Defined[21].

The problem with Healthcare is that a system of cross subsidies and transfers results in a non price system, where there is no competition on price and quality. They abolished the free market in order to provide hidden subsidies from men to women, from whites to blacks, and from the rich to the poor, resulting in socialist levels of efficiency. Compare and contrast with Singapore, India, and Thailand that have free market sectors in medicine.

When you regulate healthcare so that the husband of a woman with complications of pregnancy winds up subsidizing the services provided to half a dozen women getting abortions, the result is that both the facility providing pregnancy care, and the facility providing abortions are given regulatory immunity from price competition, resulting in socialist levels of efficiency.

For healthcare to be efficient, you cannot allow people for whom healthcare is free to go in by the same door and face the same triage nurse as people who pay for their healthcare. If you want people to pay for their healthcare, they had better not see a pile of drug addicts looking for free drugs and vagrants looking for free room and board in the queue ahead of them. And you will only get efficient reasonably priced healthcare if people do in fact pay for it themselves.

Infrastructure is inefficient to the extent that it is provided by socialist means.

If I hire some people to fix my privately owned road, they come in, fix it, are done in no time. Council workers fixing council roads take a little longer. If, however, a road is being done on a federal tourist development grant, being paid for by people far away, well, when the cat is away the mice will play. That road takes a couple of years to do. Socialism is bad for infrastructure costs, especially when Democratic Party Politicians start importing vote banks, and federal socialism is worse for infrastructure costs, even if Republicans are in charge.

Infrastructure costs reflect in varying degrees, socialism, Parkinson's law, and Democratic Party vote banks: The subway systems tend to become welfare programs for blacks, employing large numbers of blacks for their votes without any real expectation of any useful work. The most egregious examples of outrageous infrastructure costs are Democratic party vote banks, where ever more people with a Democratic Party voter profile are employed to do ever less work.

Educational inflation, (degrees are inflated in the sense that even stupid lazy people get the degree these days, and they are also inflated in that they cost a hell of a lot more) is a reflection of priestly power. Priests need to be disempowered.

Medical inflation is a result of the non market economy, that medical facilities (doc-

---

[20]https://blog.reaction.la/war/draining-the-swamp/
[21]https://blog.reaction.la/culture/the-cathedral-defined/

tors are mere cogs within a "facility") do not compete on price and quality.

Housing inflation is a result of regulation, zoning, and ethnic cleansing.

Infrastructure inflation is Parkinsons law: Socialist production always gets more expensive over time - and Democrat politicians hiring Democratic Party voting blocks worsens this natural tendency.

Vox, observing gigantic bureaucracies flailing incompetently, says[22]
> By the same token, while we know now that it's certainly possible to set up a Healthcare.gov website that works as intended, we also know that on the launch date the Obama administration had not, in fact, built such a website. That embarrassing governance failure undermined the president's signature policy initiative in serious ways, with crucial long-term repercussions.

But Vox was disinclined to wonder why the Healthcare.gov website failed.

It failed because women and minorities were in charge of setting it up. They threw ever more enormous amounts of money at it. Nothing worked until they brought in an emergency team that just happened to consist entirely of white males and east Asian males. This closely parallels the fact that Democratic Party administrations whose infrastructure building teams are full of people who profile as Democratic Party voters tend to produce Democratic Party majorities but not to produce very much infrastructure.

Dumping Flynn

2017-02-14 23:44:23

Dumping Flynn looks weak and will encourage the left to go after more scalps. And the people that were after Flynn are seeking war with Russia and Syria. War is easy, peace is hard, for it is always easier to create disorder than maintain order.

But, on the other hand, Flynn was expendable. On studying his career, I find he was a neocon, and an advocate of Coin (counter insurgency warfare). There is no such thing as counter insurgency warfare. There is only warfare. The stronger force wins, the weaker force loses, unless a large outside power (the Soviet Union or the United States State Department) has its thumb on the scales. In warfare, you don't worry all that much about hearts and minds, for if you have to choose between being loved and being feared, you choose to be feared. If choosing to be loved was a realistic option, it would not be war. It would be social work.

If every time someone shoots at you from a girl's school, you incinerate the school with girls and teachers inside, people stop shooting at you from girl's schools. Or, more likely, the girls decide to skip attending school for the duration of the war.

The reason the Taliban has defeated the US in Afghanistan is that the US forces are infested with lawyers, the political commissars of the State Department, while the Taliban is not. The Taliban has the close equivalent of lawyers, priests, but their priests are interested in winning, they are warrior priests, while the State Department, the Blue Empire, is more interested in defeating the Pentagon, the Red Empire, than defeating the Taliban.

---

[22]https://www.vox.com/policy-and-politics/2017/1/1/14112776/new-york-second-avenue-subway-phase-2

If one side is fighting by police rules, and the other fighting by warrior rules, of course the warriors will defeat the police.

So quite possibly Trump initially chose Flynn as a compromise candidate, to sooth his enemies until his Pentagon powerbase is more secure, and is merely ditching him earlier than planned.

The hard core Trumpist position is that Russia should be allowed to be Russia, rather than being forced to accept progressivism, but Muslims should be smacked around till they stop making war on us. To get the Pentagon behind this position, he needs to do a Grenada - decisively defeat some penny ante bunch of Islamic extremists, preferably in cooperation with Russia. Maybe set up safe zones in Syria with the cooperation of the Russian and Syrian government.

The cost disease part 2

2017-02-19 06:59:03

Costs of many important things, in particular education, housing, and healthcare are rising in ways that create artificial first world poverty, the inability to afford a wife and children.[23]

Scott Alexander wrote a superficially thoughtful and well informed examination of these problems, which analysis[24] was made stupid by crimestop.

A lot of high intelligent well informed people responded with explanations of the problem which accurately described parts and details of the problem, but crimestop prevented them from seeing, or at least prevented them from mentioning, the big picture formed by the details they quite accurately describe. Scott has collected these intelligent and detailed responses[25].

Among the commenters, LukHamilton observes that increased education is likely of negative value to society, and fc123 observes we are spending an awful lot of money educating stupid people in things that are unlikely to be of use to them, but then fail to put two and two together, or if they did put two and two together, they refrain from mentioning it.

The things raising costs are described correctly enough, but are treated as an assemblage of random unrelated facts. Things just supposedly happen to be this way supposedly for no apparent reason, and the fact that we cannot seem to do anything about these things also supposedly has no apparent reason.

Defunding the left

2017-02-19 23:50:37

Reagan talked about defunding the left, but never actually did anything.

---

[23]https://blog.reaction.la/economics/the-cost-disease/

[24]https://slatestarcodex.com/2017/02/09/considerations-on-cost-disease/

[25]https://slatestarcodex.com/2017/02/17/highlights-from-the-comments-on-cost-disease/

As a result of Trump's threats against Berkeley, they are starting to think that hiring a bunch of thugs to beat people up and cause over a hundred thousand dollars worth of damage may have been a bit excessive.

Meanwhile Trump and congress are working on stripping two billion from NASA global warming propaganda.

NASA put up a bunch of satellites to measure global warming. To their considerable disappointment, these show no significant warming in the past twenty years. To a good approximation, no significant warming since the satellite data became sufficiently accurate as to deny people excuses for "correcting" it. So they returned to the old faithful, "surface temperature measurements" - otherwise known as weather reports. The trouble with weather reports is that from time to time the location of the thermometer, or the time of day when it is read, changes. Also the location is usually directly adjacent to human habitation[26], which over time tends to have more humans, more cars, and more parking spaces, all of which tends to warm things up. This requires numerous very large "corrections", which corrections are pulled out of the rectums of NASA's climate "scientists"[27] - who sound more like cultists than scientists. One of the commenters asks of one such correction:

> Did anyone ever figure out how the trends in the interior of Greenland could exceed the trends actually observed at stations*? Since there are no stations in the interior, the trends there must be computed by interpolating from nearby (coastal) stations

According to NASA's climate data, GISS, calculated from surface stations, the world is getting hotter primarily in places where there are no surface stations.

Of course cutting a few billion from climate change activism is small change compared to the core of the problem, the universities, and I cannot see Trump taking on the universities unless he makes himself King.

But two billion less for climate change activism is the first cut for the left since the cuts that happened in restoration of Charles the second. It is a start.

Further, it is going to scare the vermin into voiding their bowels, since it was the most blatantly propagandistic warming "science" that got the first cut.

On purging Milo

2017-02-21 02:50:34

If Milo was purged for being a Jewish coal burning gay, that would be one thing, but being purged having sex with an older man at the age of fourteen is a different thing. Gay sex is disgusting and self destructive regardless of age, and thirty year old women are no more competent to make unsupervised sexual choices than twelve year old girls.

Purging Milo for "pedo" concedes the left position that consent is all that matters, that anything is fine if it is consenting adults that do it.

We should view sex with properly owned women as rape if her *guardian* does not consent to it (which is what "rape" meant a couple of hundred years ago) and sex with feral women as a form of regrettable but unavoidable predation regardless of whether

---

²⁶https://wattsupwiththat.com/2010/09/22/arctic-isolated-versus-urban-stations-show-differing-trends/
²⁷https://wattsupwiththat.com/2010/07/26/giss-swiss-cheese/

they consent or not, which predation is best remedied by shotgun marriage or similar, remedied by ensuring that a feral woman comes into the possession of a man who can plausibly be expected to have good intentions towards her and treat her with kindness - if necessary without regard for her undoubtedly foolish opinions on the matter.

And, of course, if a man lies with a male, as with a woman, both of them have committed an abomination: they shall surely be put to death; their blood shall be upon them.

We should not purge Milo for being a Jewish coal burning gay, for there are far worse on the left, and only after they get helicoptered or thrown from high buildings should we ask Milo to clean up his act. And if we did not purge him for being a Jewish coal burning gay, then we certainly should not purge him for underage sex.

If two people agree to exchange corn for iron, obviously the exchange must make both of them better off or else they would not have agreed to it. So state and society should not interfere in such agreements, and if everyone is free to engage in commercial trade, then state and society is better off. If two people agree to have sex, this is a very poor indicator that having sex makes both of them better off, because sexual impulses are volcanically powerful and deeply irrational. The converse can also apply. A woman's decision to cease having sex with the father of her children usually has appallingly bad consequences for everyone, especially her children. A fertile age woman who ceases to have sex with her husband is always motivated by having received semen from a male more alpha than her husband, or excessively realistic fantasies of receiving such semen.

There are lots of good reasons why we should purge Milo. But this is a very bad reason. We are purging him for insufficient progressivism.

Conservatives find their balls

2017-02-21 06:36:56

As a general rule, the left deploys any means necessary, routinely engaging in treason, criminal acts, and barefaced lies, as for example the latest business about Islamic rape war on Swedes. And the cuckservatives roll over and let them get away with it. The left does this stuff because they can, and routinely do, get away with it.

However, the committee on Science, Space and Technology is now insisting on investigating the latest act of Global Warming deception by the National Oceanic and Atmosphere Administration, demanding papers that the National Oceanic and Atmosphere Administration is highly unlikely to release, because these papers would likely be proof of crimes by civil servants. You cannot prosecute a scientist for being one eyed about what he is determined to believe is true, but you most definitely can prosecute a civil servant for willfully deceiving the government.

Hat tip Watt's up[28]

Trump has a pile of prosecutions he can apply for breaches of national security, and now we are seeing potential prosecutions for fraudulent warmism. If he applies these (and you know Trump - would he not) the permanent government is going to be brought to heel.

---

[28]https://wattsupwiththat.com/2017/02/20/fresh-congressional-probe-into-flawed-karl-pausebuster-scandal/

Warmism and the old Gods of Mexico

2017-02-26 00:10:55

Warmism is an updated and rebranded version of the old Mexican religion, demon worship. The priests announce that unless human sacrifices are made, the sun will cease to rise.

And, guess what, this gives the priests a whole lot of influence over which people get sacrificed to sun god, and which people do not. Thus we find the priests of global warming involved in all sorts of highly lucrative schemes whereby carbon indulgences are sold, and subsidies handed out, with the result that certain priests of global warming get a whole lot of money, for example the carbon indulgences sold by Carbonscape[29].

The demons were worshiped through cannibalism, sodomy, and transvestism. (That is how you can tell that they were demons, rather than angels or saints.) While we no longer have literal cannibalism, the food to fuel program has similar results, and we still have sodomy and transvestism as priestly acts demonstrating priestly holiness, as for example in Earth Worship conducted by Less Wrong.

Certain Indian nations were somewhat ticked off that the Aztecs were always sacrificing them, and they were not sacrificing Aztecs, and therefore took advantage of Cortez's invasion to revolt against the Aztecs. Whereupon it became apparent that their priests were secretly in cahoots with the Aztec priests to facilitate Aztec domination of their people and Aztec cannibalism of their people - that the Gods would make announcements through the temples of the revolting tribes that were planned and coordinated in the Aztec capital. In other words, the old Gods of Mexico made their proclamations via peer review.

Implementing Patriarchy without the state.

2017-03-06 08:09:52

Obviously to properly implement patriarchy requires a patriarchal state, and an official state church that can combine moral pressure with official coercion. Adultery, interfering with another man's wife or betrothed, should be met with lethal violence which lethal violence needs to be state supported. If we can shoot burglars, should be able to shoot adulterers. Misbehaving women need to be locked up, runaway women need to be forcefully returned to fathers or husbands.

But there are quite a few groups that do a reasonable job with merely social pressure and illegal private violence. In the long run, such groups will grow until they can impose their morals and religion as state church and state violence. I do not have any statistics or concrete evidence for conservative Muslims in the US, the ones that put hijabs on their daughters and marry them off at eighteen, but anecdote is that they are reproducing at a truly amazing rate. Women are extremely vulnerable to social pressure and the threat of social exclusion. If one woman in a social group has bastard children, or has taken her children from her husband, that enormously increase the risk that another woman in that group will have bastard children, or take her children from her husband. They are

---

[29]https://blog.reaction.la/global-warming/global-warming-scientists-trapped-in-antarctic-denial/

particularly vulnerable, extraordinarily vulnerable, to male disapproval, from any male with even a modest claim to male on male status.

So: You make sure your womenfolk do not have anything to do with filth, sluts, or trash - and especially any women with fatherless or many fathered children. You police your wife and daughter's social circle and tell her:

> "That girl is a slut. Don't have anything to do with her. If the others want her to be with them, you are not to be with them. I forbid it"

And you get the men in your social circle to do the same thing, so your women get multiple independent authorities telling them this. And make sure the word "Slut" is used. If you want to keep your daughter off the pole, tell her that women who are on the pole are filthy and dirty *and she is to have nothing to do with them*. Filth is infectious, both literally and metaphorically, and women are extremely vulnerable to metaphorical infection.

Social pressure works. Ideally all your wife's circle should, like the social circle of Mormon women, be women who married young, focused on being a wife and mother first, and only worried about career later in life, after menopause. But failing that, should at least exclude any filth, sluts, and trash.

The solution we do not want.

2017-03-08 01:07:38

One of my commenters asks "Why not just become Muslim?"

I presume he means conservative Muslim, since a whole lot of Muslims are pozzed, are not breeding and not getting any pussy.

That is the Mormon solution (control women's socialization) plus the orthodox Jewish solution (make female status artificially low), plus the ever popular individual male solution (illegal violence or the quiet potential for it) plus you turn off the Cathedral's ever vigilant immune system plus you have a pre-existing community. (Just grow a wildman beard, attend mosque, and you are in like Flynn.) If you want to marry those eighteen year old socially conservative virgins, you need high socioeconomic status (they are in high demand), which leads to a problem with the wildman beard (tricky to have high socioeconomic status with the wildman beard), but that one is easier to navigate than political correctness, plus if you are Muslim you get a pass for all political incorrectness relating to gays and women. No one is going to ask a Halal bakery to bake a gay wedding cake. I see a lot of engineers putting on a dress and declaring that they are trans women in order to get ahead. Declaring yourself to be a Muslim almost makes you trans brown. Should be almost as good for your career as declaring yourself a trans woman, a whole lot better for your sex life than declaring yourself a trans woman, and the wildman beard is not nearly as bad as the dress. You also get a free pass to be manly, which helps with the ridiculous beard. If you lift iron and do a little bit of high intensity training, the beard will not look quite as bad.

Plus this is the solution we are going to get if we don't do anything dramatic, if we continue to drift along our present course, if the passengers don't attack the cockpit and kill whoever is flying the plane to its doom. Wherever we get data on Muslim births in

Western countries the data shows that Muslims are massively outbreeding the natives. I assume this is conservative Muslims, since anecdote suggests that pozzed Muslims have the same dreadfully low reproductive rate as pozzed Jews. Islam is quietly becoming the official religion, in that sacrilege against Islam effectively carries the death penalty (in most western countries if you drop bacon on the pavement outside a mosque the judge will give you a jail term comparable to that which he gives for raping and murdering small children, and while you are in jail some Muslims will kill you while the prison authorities turn a blind eye, like the blind eye Berkeley police turn to black bloc beating up pro-trump protestors) while sacrilege against Christianity is almost mandatory: (Gay wedding cake, Church required to pay for abortions, Pope kisses the feet of aids infested homosexual transvestite prostitutes, government funded sacrilegious "art", free pass for gays and feminists to physically attack Christians and disrupt religious services.)

So, you ask, what is not to like?

What is not to like is that when Islam conquers a civilization, that civilization dies. When people talk about the great achievements of Islamic civilization, they are actually talking about the achievements of peoples enslaved by Muslims, and what remained of their libraries after the Muslims finished looting them for toilet paper and kindling.

The Trinity is God the father who, though he might seem pretty mean to merely mortal perception, is limited by law and logic, the God that can command genocide, but cannot lie, thus is compatible with science, a more approachable God the son, who is wholly man and wholly God, who experienced every suffering that mortal flesh suffers, including the sense of abandonment by God, and the Holy spirit, who talks to people.

Because the Christian God the Father imposes limits upon himself, unlike Allah, science is possible, and Christians do not have to say "God willing" all the time. The limitless and arbitrary caprice of Allah makes science impious, and promises impious. A good Christian says "I will do so and so", and then does it. A good Muslim says "I will do so and so, God willing", and then very likely does not do it.

If the Christian God decides to create a stone so heavy he cannot lift it, then he cannot lift it. Allah cannot create a stone so heavy he cannot lift it. Kind of like playing Solitaire. There is nothing preventing you or God from cheating at solitaire, but then there would be no point to the game. The Christian God not only throws dice, he throws dice where even he cannot see them. He is omniscient but we have free will. Allah, on the other hand, cheats at Solitaire. Hence no Islamic science.

The Christian God the Father cannot lie. The Muslim Allah lied all the time. During Mohammed's career, Allah would declare one thing, that was convenient for Mohammed at the time, and then when convenient for Mohammed, would declare a different thing. Which is why science and promises are impious if you are a sincere Muslim.

Judeo Christianity sucks. We need Christian Christianity. The trouble with Judaism is that they keep reinventing their religion all the time to accommodate the times and the surrounding society, as any group in exile must, but keep torturing their holy texts to prove that they are not reinventing their religion. This results in an alarmingly creative attitude to truth, promises, and contracts. A negro or a Muslim will just casually break a promise or a contract. A Jew will not break a promise or contract outright, but he is apt to find, and with great chutzpah proclaim, an ingenious and surprising meaning for the promise, the bet, or the contract, much as he is apt to find, and with great chutzpah proclaim, an ingenious and surprising meaning for the words of his holy books. Hence the failure of Orthodox Jews to contribute much to science, compared to prog, atheist, and agnostic Jews, who have contributed immensely to science. Almost every Jew who has made important scientific progress finds the Orthodox Jew twisting and torturing his holy books to be rather ridiculous.

It also means that Judeo Christianity is not really capable of resisting progressivism. I have had a debate with by Jewish commenters as to whether Jewish Orthodoxy or Christianity is better and resisting progressivism, and I ask, where is the Jewish Phil Robertson?

Christianity inherits its solution to theodicity from the Jews in substantial part.

1. Evil exists because of human and satanic choices, free will. Genesis: Fall of man in the Garden of Eden was caused by, and caused, consequences remarkably similar to those one would expect in a universe of where natural selection and evolutionary psychology are true.

2. God allows evil because God is trying us, wants to see what we are made of, wants us to make hard choices that really matter. Book of Job.

3. The goodness and greatness of God is beyond mortal comprehension. If it does not make sense to us, if it looks to us that God is a mean bastard, hard biscuit. Book of Job.

   But Christianity also inherited the Greek philosophers' concept of the unnamed one god, God as the underlying cause, reason, and logic of the universe.

4. God created an orderly universe of cause and effect, and thus mere flesh and blood is apt to get squished as the cold logic of the universe unfolds.

You will notice that these features of Christianity support a world where truth is spoken, promises are kept, and science is actually scientific. Which is a big part of why it was Christians that made the scientific and Industrial Revolutions, not Jews and not Muslims, why it will be Christians that settle space and conquer the universe. (Maybe atheists are better at building rocket ships, but they will not have the children to fly those rocket ships to new worlds and settle them.)

What we need to do is import the good parts of Islam into Christianity: Patriarchy, repression of women, execution of homosexuals, holy war, intolerance of sacrilege, intolerance of heresy, and intolerance of apostacy. Retain the good bits of Christianity, the trinity, the attitude to logic, reason and law, the Orthodox communion of the saints, where the final authority on faith, doctrine, interpretation of the bible, and morals, is ancient Christians. Keep the Episcopalian married clergy, plus Episcopalian subordination to earthly authority. Decorate the result with a few Episcopalian symbols and call the result Episcopalianism, and make it the official state religion of the US empire in place of progressivism, with all other religions subordinated to it, second class, and unequally backed by the state. In school, kids get taught that official Episcopalianism is wise, good, and right, and all other religions are stupid, much as today they are taught that official progressivism is wise, good, and right, and all other religions (except possibly Islam) are stupid and evil.

We always have an official state religion: As Boldmug tells us:
The trouble is basically that sovereignty is conserved. If you try to design a political system that discards some element of sovereignty, like the right of the state to promote truth and suppress error, a parallel, informal state will rush into this gap and fill it.

Since control over information is incredibly powerful in the age of broadcast media, this parallel state will become the strongest organ in the actual government. It will be completely irresponsible and unaccountable, since it's not even part of the official state. But there is no political, economic, or intellectual check on its operations. Once again, sovereignty is conserved.

This sovereign information-delivery system naturally assumes the religious imperiousness we expect from an intellectual sovereign. It is also disorganized, centerless and leaderless, which means there is no possible way for it to feel pity or shame. Sound familiar?

There is no way to disestablish religion. It's just an unsolvable engineering problem. If the state disavows its religious authority, all it's doing is disavowing control over that authority. Which leaves said authority in a perfect position to control the state. So the nominal objective of separating church and state leads naturally to the theocratic state. This is not a new phenomenon in Anglo-American history.

Even if you don't care about quality of government, but just about quality of thought, putting the church in charge of the state — ie, the nerds in charge of the jocks — has a nasty effect on quality of thought. Thought is distorted not by the repulsive force of a fascist jock state that discriminates against nerds, but rather by the attractive force that offers free power to power-craving nerds.

The state which disavows religion is basically a flawed engineering structure that's leaking power. The power leak has a horrific evolutionary effect on the nerd population, basically favoring sniveling, student-government weasels over good sensible open-minded people. Noticed anything like this around you? Anyone? Bueller?

This is only one of many reasons why humanity flourishes under leaders who unite both nerd and jock qualities, ie, true aristocracies, and has serious difficulties when these qualities are opposed or even just divided.

Anarcho capitalism is apt to tempt some more cohesive group, like Muslims, to come in and kill the men, and take your property and women, and separation of church and state is apt to lead to a hostile and cohesive religion taking over your state. Progressivism took over from Christianity, and in due course Islam will take over from progressivism.

Back in the seventeenth century, the Church was the mainstream media and the education system, and Charles the first appointed the archbishop and the Bishops, and the Church damn well taught what he wanted. The puritans, of course, felt this was a very bad thing, and were all in favour of religious freedom (except that they agreed that atheists and Roman Catholics should be executed) In 1640, they seized power, Bishops were in effect abolished, and the Established Church was formally stripped of almost all its power

- while informally becoming Puritan, a hundred times as powerful, a hundred times as intrusive, and a hundred times as oppressive. Formally and officially the Puritans brought freedom of conscience, informally and unofficially they brought brutal religious repression.

Which is pretty much what we have today, except that today's Puritans are holier than God.

In 1660 Charles the second returned, bringing with him official formal theocracy. The Archbishop crowns the King, and the King appoints the Archbishop. The Archbishop tells the Bishops what to say and think, the Bishops tell the priests what to say and think, and the priests tell the assembled congregations what to say and think. The British people celebrated this enthusiastically, recognizing the formal theocracy as abolishing informal theocracy. They celebrated by engaging in pagan festivals such as maypole dancing, that had been cruelly suppressed by the Puritans.

If we are openly ditching the first amendment, what about the second? Well, it turns out it is mighty difficult to deny organized hostile groups arms, so you might as well allow your support base to carry arms, as in Iraq. Ideas are more powerful than guns. The dictator Sadam Hussein of Iraq did not allow his people ideas, but he did allow them full auto military style weapons. Looks like he knew what he was doing.

All married property owning men, all soldiers, all cops, all authorized mercenaries, all rentacops, and all security watchmen should be allowed to keep and bear arms, because in a well functioning society, that is the ruler's base of support. He looks after them, and they look after him. The rest, probably not. Not single men, nor men without property, because they have nothing to lose, and therefore will likely fail to defend society and uphold order. Guards and suchlike have been vetted that they will protect protect property and order, so should be allowed to keep and bear arms even if they do not have wives and property.

Why Ryancare will not work

2017-03-08 20:54:43

Ryancare, like Obamacare, involves cross subsidies. Some people wind up subsidizing other people. The resulting landslide of rules and regulations will shut down competition, with the result that everyone plus the government winds up paying unreasonable prices.

Ryancare requires that insurance cover people with pre-existing conditions. That is not insurance, that is a handout. If the government is going to give people handouts, should be done openly through government funded hospitals and the like. If you rope private enterprise into giving handouts, you will find that this turns out to be a stupendously expensive way of providing handouts, not a cheap way.

You order private enterprise to give handouts, you wind up giving them monopolies so that they can fund these handouts, and they wind up abusing these monopolies. Further, people receiving handouts tend to be problem people. Some of them are unlucky, but most of them are no good. You don't want no good people showing up to hospital in front of the good people who are actually paying for the hospital, or you get the

Canadian situation, where no Canadian who can avoid it goes to a Canadian hospital but rather nips across the nearby border to an American hospital, because the Canadian hospital is full of homeless and drug addicts. And when I say full, I mean very full indeed, with beds in the corridors and urine soaked sheets, and not a normal middle class person in sight.

If the government is going to give handouts to people with pre-existing conditions, or handouts to anyone, it needs to keep the insurance companies and private sector hospitals out of it. Handouts need to be done openly and need to appear on the books as handouts. Hidden handouts inadvertently shut down the free market system, resulting in at best socialist levels of service, at worst socialist levels of service with staggeringly high costs.

Ryancare is the continuing ratchet leftwards, Ryancare is Republicans doing their jobs as tax collectors for the welfare state, where Democrats create unfunded entitlements, and Republicans proceed to make white middle class males pay for them.

Ryancare means that Republicans get to take the blame for Obamacare. If you are not going to repeal Obamacare, at least hang it on the Democrats.

Undead Christianity

2017-03-10 04:20:15

Europe is the faith, the faith is Europe. When Roman Paganism died, the Roman Empire in the west died. Julian the apostate tried to revive paganism, got an undead religion. My commenters tell me Christianity survives as a mustard seed, but to me, it looks like a dead parrot.

I wish Christianity could be revived, I hope it can be revived, but am not all that optimistic.

European Christianity was the official state religion, which is sort of odd because Europe was never really one state, even when there was a functioning Holy Roman Emperor and Holy Roman Empire. It has been said that the Holy Roman Empire was not holy, not Roman, and not an empire. But this is not true. It was not Roman, and not an empire, but it was holy. The Emperor, the Empire, and the state was subject to the Church in those matters where it is proper for the Church to command, and the Church was subject to the state in those matters where it is proper for the state to command. (With the usual frequent disagreements as to what is Caesar's and what is God's)

When the Empire faded, the Church inevitably and inexorably got drawn into earthly politics, backing one state against another, which led to the Church of England, the protestant reformation, and the sack of Rome, and eventually the bloody religious wars of the early seventeenth century. These terrible wars were resolved by the peace of Westphalia. The King gets to set his state's religion, and other states are not supposed to interfere, though, of course, they did.

The peace of Westphalia in effect said "forget about universalism, leads to too much bloodshed"

The rise of Progressivism was the return of the holy universalist state Church, and led to the terrible wars of the twentieth century. These wars ended when one superpower became supreme, ruling in the not quite imperial style of the Holy Roman Empire, not quite an empire, but an empire nonetheless, and imposed its faith on all of Europe, and almost all of the world - but now that superpower is fading, while progressivism is more holy and more universalist than ever.

To cut the long story short, today progressivism is the state religion, and Christianity is effectively suppressed. My commenters assure me that a mustard seed remains, but I just don't see it. Recently existent Christianity enforced patriarchal durable monogamy, with divorce being damn near impossible. The wife got a permanent obligation to honor and obey, the husband got a permanent obligation to love and cherish. And, apart from some tolerance for polygyny in early Christianity, Christianity has always been this way, until now. The New Testament, and the communion of the Saints, are quite clear on the topic.

The earthly church is a fictive kin of God, God and Church being a reflection of husband and family, (Ephesians 5:22-33) making all Christians in a church fictive kin, a tribe. Marriage is the sacrament that everyone has the power to make, the sacrament that priests could never take away from the congregation, and which links families to the congregation and to God, since the husband and wife rely on God and the congregation for social enforcement of the deal. If you end marriage as it used to be known, you end Christianity, and if you end Christianity, you end Europe. Durable Patriarchal marriage is not just one doctrine among many, it is a keystone part of the functioning of Christianity, hence the joke "Hatched, matched, and dispatched".

For 1900 years, from the beginning of Christianity, to second wave feminism in the nineteen sixties, men removed their hats on entering church, and women covered their heads in church and on the way to and from church. For 1900 years women had their hair long. (1 Corinthians:11)

And now they don't, and no one seems to notice that there is anything wrong with this. But don't you feel just a little bit uneasy when you face a fertile age woman with a pixie cut? Something is wrong, something is off, something is odd, unpleasant, and disturbing, but you are not allowed to notice it.

Today's Christians, including the supposed reactionaries like Dalrock, Bruce Charlton, and Zippy will tell you it was just a cultural thing, just Paul foolishly mistaking the fashions of his day for the universal laws of God. Which is not much different from saying that when Paul prohibited men having sex with males, he was just mistaking the fashions of his day for the universal laws of God. Similarly, Ephesians 5. Bruce Charlton will tell you that Ephesians 5 is just a metaphor, about the relationship between God and man, but not about the relationship between husband and wife. Dalrock will tell you he totally supports Ephesians 5, except he does not, and Zippy would rather not go there.

You cannot have Christianity without patriarchy, and if you are not entirely comfortable with patriarchy maybe you should be worshiping the Goddess.

In short, the Christian right, like the Republicans, are just progressives who are a bit behind the times. You may say that a short haircut on a girl is not like a man sodomizing a boy, and it is not, but if a fertile age woman wears a pixie cut, chances are she has been taking it up the ass from Mister Very Wrong, and she will forever feel in her heart that Mister Very Wrong was way more manly than you are.

Congressman Steve King's solution to healthcare

2017-03-13 10:54:58

Instead of having a plan developed behind closed doors and then you have to vote for it to find out what is in it, you legislate the old fashioned way, congressional vote by vote. "A return to regular order[30]".

The great advantage of this is its great disadvantage. Congress cannot centrally plan the economy, or any significant part of the economy. No one central plan can receive a majority vote, or even a large plurality. Your are only going to get two or three percent to vote for one central plan, and four or five percent for another, and three or four percent for yet another, because there is a near infinity of possible central plans, any one of which is going to step on lots of people's toes, each plan stepping on a different set of toes. You can never socialize medicine, or anything else, by congressional vote, except they vote for a closed box and discover to their big surprise what is in it when it gets implemented.

Before Obamacare, American medicine was unreasonably expensive by a factor of about ten or twenty.

After Obamacare, American medicine was unreasonably expensive by a factor of about ten or twenty, but bums, drug addicts, and vagrants were getting a lot more of this very expensive medicine, paid for mostly by white middle class males, and very shortly thereafter, white middle class males were getting a whole lot less of this very expensive medicine. Obamacare wanted more care for the poor, but it sought to prevent the total consumption of care from rising, for fear that would accelerate the already excessive price pressures, so a reduction in access to care by white middle class males was planned and intended from the beginning, though I don't think anyone wanted to admit just how drastic and radical a reduction they had in mind.

The way to substantially reduce the cost of medical care is to have a free market in medical care with well known, well defined, and advertised prices, as in Singapore. At present, no one knows how much care is going to cost, and prices are frequently absurd by world standards. There is no good reason why a treatment in America should cost ten or twenty times what unsubsidized, for-profit, care, paid for out of pocket, costs in Taiwan and Singapore.

Genuine advances in medical care make medicine more expensive, as things can now be (expensively) treated that formerly could not be treated. But this fails to explain the enormous discrepancy in healthcare prices between America, and prices charged by private enterprise, for profit, healthcare businesses in Taiwan, Thailand, Singapore, and India.

UN Peacekeeping

2017-03-15 05:51:46

Trump proposes radical cuts in US taxpayer funding for the UN, and in particular and especially, "Peacekeeping"

---

[30]https://twitter.com/SteveKingIA/status/840942441129738240

Now if you are a typical reader of this blog, your reflexive assumption is likely to be that "Peacekeeping" is code for mass murder, terror, and artificial famine.

A major part of our peacekeeping is Ivory Coast, where we "democratically" installed some guy with extensive connections to Harvard and the UN, but no particular connection to Ivory Coast, in power.

This was democratic because of population replacement. The people lost the confidence of the UN, so the UN elected a new people, importing the new people and expelling and dispossessing the old people.

OK, that is not mass murder and artificial famine, though it certainly is and was terror. But peacekeeping in the Congo (now wound down) was, for the most part, mass murder, terror, and artificial famine.

Another significant part of our current peacekeeping is Haiti, which is not mass murder and terror, but it is, or very recently was, artificial famine.

If you are an empire, you have to do this sort of stuff from time to time. And if you are an empire that is pretending it is not an empire, you have to do this sort of stuff one hell of a lot more that you would if you just put proconsuls openly in charge of your protectorates.

Of course if the world was not an empire, there would be chaos, and other actors would be creating mass murder, terror, and artificial famine. But they would be the ones paying for it.

Lancelot, Guinevere, romance, and the red, blue, purple, black, and white pills.

2017-03-21 08:09:56

Evolutionary psychology predicts that a man will love a woman he regularly has sex with, who lives with him and that he lives with and will be inclined to look after her welfare, which is not necessarily the same thing as doing what she wants. He will do what he thinks is good for her, and make her do what he thinks is good for her, even if she wants something different. Because one flesh. Taking care of her is taking care of her capacity to bear him children and raise his children.

It does not predict that she will love him all that much, since Gnon wants resources transferred from men to women, and from parents to children, but it does predict that she will obey him, respect him, and physically desire him, in order that he can take care of her and the children they have together.

That is how it supposed to work.

If, however, she is someone else's wife, or is staying with her family rather the joining with him to form a new family, thus someone else is going to be looking after his kids by her, maybe the state is going to be taking care of her and he is just passing through, then evolutionary psychology predicts romantic love, that he will flatter her and do whatever she wants, no matter how foolish, unreasonable, and self destructive, as Lancelot treated Guinevere.

So, evolutionary psychology predicts that males will primarily experience romantic love in the case of adultery, and to a lesser extent in casual fornication. It predicts that they they will experience the love that a husband bears his wife after they have been living together and having sex for a while. And that women will tend to be at best good wives, rather than in love with their husbands. The wife who craves the seed of a man more alpha than her husband says

> "I do not love my husband any more, therefore it is OK for me to service this rock musician and his biker roadies"

but women never love men all that much. They are not supposed to. They are supposed to respect, honor, obey, and desire their husbands.

Thus, the first mention of sexual love in the bible: Rebekah meets Isaac, explains herself. "And Isaac brought her into his mother Sarah's tent, and took Rebekah, and she became his wife; and he loved her: and Isaac was comforted after his mother's death." The second mention of sexual love in the bible on the other hand has love and romance preceding sex and marriage instead of following sex and marriage - and things go badly wrong.

Romantic love was celebrated by the troubadours, and as depicted by the troubadours, was always adulterous love. King Arthur's wife Guinevere desired Lancelot, and had sex with him, and Lancelot romantically loved Guinevere, King Arthur's wife. In consequence Lancelot does lots of stupid humiliating self sacrificing things that prove his enormous burning love, Guinevere acts like an arrogant depraved obnoxious spoiled slut bitch, the fellowship of the Round Table breaks up, Camelot is defeated, and everyone gets killed.

This makes sense for maximizing reproductive fitness. Crazy destructive passion in order to cuckold other men, calm, gentle, firm, nurturing affection for one's own family. Romance is what the troubadours depicted with alarming accuracy.

Romance is defect/defect equilibrium. Lancelot believes he is sacrificing himself for Guinevere in a Christlike fashion, and the troubadours believed he was sacrificing himself for Guinevere in a Christlike fashion, but in fact he is maximizing his Darwinian genetic self interest at the expense of everyone else. Guinevere also behaves badly to both Lancelot and to her husband King Arthur because she is maximizing her genetic self interest at the expense of everyone else.

Guinevere and King Arthur are in a defect/cooperate relationship. King Arthur is cooperating with Guinevere, by looking after her, and cooperating with Lancelot, in that Lancelot gets benefits as a knight of the fellowship of the Round table, while Lancelot and Guinevere are defecting on King Arthur.

King Arthur, of course, finds out, and Camelot gets defect/defect. Everyone is much worse off, and Camelot falls. That is Romance.

Sexual love is a bad thing except inside the confines of marriage. Men are supposed to have sex first and love later, and women are not really supposed to love men all that much at all. Nowhere in the bible are we told of women loving their husbands, and Guinevere treats both Lancelot and King Arthur very badly. We are, however, fairly frequently told in the bible of women seeking the love of their husbands.

If a woman thinks she is love, she is lying to get some alpha cock. Perhaps lying to herself because all the books she reads and all the movies and television shows she watches tell her that romantic love justifies and purifies every kind of horrible bad behavior. In reality, women are never in love all that much, rather they experience desire for love and sex, which they confuse with love when they proceed to do bad things in pursuit of this desire. Rather than loving a man, a woman desires to be loved by a man. If a man is in romantically in love with a woman whom he is not living with and having regular sex with in his own bed, he is crazy or evil.

What is the Red Pill?

It is the practical and applied knowledge of the Dark Enlightenment, the bad news about how the world really is, and especially and particularly the bad news about the nature of women. The Dark Enlightenment is science and the Red Pill is engineering. There is a certain cynical ruthlessness about the Red Pill. You are told how to use it against other people, and how to protect yourself from other people. Much seemingly virtuous and altruistic behavior, like the behavior of Lancelot towards Guinevere, is revealed to be foolish or, more commonly, wicked and dangerous. Even virtue is reduced to pragmatic self interest - virtue is trying to get into and maintain cooperate/cooperate relationships - as distinct from pretending to virtue in order to get into defect/cooperate relationships. Also, virtue is developing one's own excellence, as for example lifting iron, or perfecting social skills.

What is the Blue Pill?

It is the official truth about the way the world supposedly works, and particularly and especially the official truth about the nature of women. If women were really the way that the blue pill says they are, then the behaving towards women the way that progressives say you are supposed to behave would work. Unfortunately, the way you are supposed to behave fails, and fails horribly badly with utterly disastrous consequences.

What is the Purple Pill?

It is an attempt to reconcile Red Pill truths with Blue pill morals: "Not All Women are Like That". It is an attempt to avoid the most grossly self destructive behavior commanded by the Blue Pill, while still accepting that Blue Pill behavior is wise and virtuous behavior, rather than foolish, destructive, self destructive, and evil behavior. It is an attempt to reconcile with reality while remaining virtuous as Blue Pillers see virtue. But Blue Pill "virtues" are like Lancelot's love for Guinevere: They are evil in themselves, and manifestations of evil. It was wrong for Lancelot to love Guinevere, as much wrong as it was wrong for Guinevere to have sex with Lancelot. Not only is it unwise to be the equal of your wife, it is also wicked. It is your job to supervise and discipline your wife, and some women, not all of them, not most of them, but quite a lot of them, sometimes need to be physical disciplined. You are wicked if you are not prepared to physically discipline your wife and your children in the unfortunate case that the necessity should occur.

What is the Black Pill?

The Black Pill is despair at the sad and cynical truths of the Red Pill, and the belief that we are doomed, that we as individuals shall not know a good sexual and family relationship, that we shall have few or no great grandchildren, that our race shall perish, that our homelands will be flooded by hostile angry sullen low IQ aliens who live on crime, welfare, and voting for the left, who get violent at microaggressions, that our civilization will die, overrun like Detroit and Salisbury by savages incapable of operating civilization.

What is the White Pill?

Deus Vult: That we will be victorious. That those of us that are lucky and strong will create proper families, that we will have love and grandchildren, that we will save our civilization and conquer the enemies of our civilization. That the able will rule over their inferiors, and men will rule over women, as is right for us to do. It is the will of Gnon that those obedient to his commandments shall fill the stars and subdue them

Fixing healthcare

2017-03-26 07:17:15

Obamacare is in a death spiral.

Trump promised to repeal and replace Obamacare, but then ran dead on it, allowing Ryancare to fail and washing his hands of it.

Trump then announces he has to compromise with the Democrats on medicine.

Single payer for everyone, as in Britain and Canada, is a horrible disaster, but despite being a disaster, once in place it seems impossible to remove. If we get single payer, we are screwed.

The key problem of US healthcare is absurdly high and completely unpredictable health costs - you stroll into hospital for something trivial, and if you are white and male, get hit for three hundred thousand dollars for no apparent reason. Routine and standard health care procedures like a colonoscopy typically cost twenty times what they cost in the rest of the world, and even though they are absolutely routine and standard no one will tell you what they are going to cost.

So, America has to copy from countries that have attained low and predictable health costs, and most importantly, up front health costs, where you know what you are going to be charged: These are Singapore, India, and Thailand, which have single payer *for poor people*. Which means that when some bum shows up at the rich people's hospital, they send him over to the poor people's hospital.

The reason America has no market in healthcare is cross subsidies - white males pay for everyone, and this requires opaque prices. The government decrees that hospitals will take care of the poor and female, that insurance companies will take care of the poor and female, which in practice winds up as cross subsidies, white males taking care of the poor and female, which results in a system with no prices and no markets.

To get health costs down you need a market and prices. Singapore and similar countries have a market and prices, and they can get away with this politically because there is a safety net for the poor, the feckless, and the unlucky.

If you have clear up front prices, someone has to pay for the poor people. If explicit up front prices then you need an explicit overt handout in place of the hidden handout paid for through hidden prices.

The trouble with single payer for poor people is that it is apt to grow into single payer for everyone, as has more or less happened in France and is happening in Germany. But Singapore has kept single payer under control, and single payer has not swallowed up the entire medical industry in Australia.

What I would really like is a system where you can just turn the poor and the sick away, but we cannot have that when we pretend to democracy, so some kind of single payer for poor people it has to be.

The trouble is, of course, the Democrats are going to demand single payer for everyone. But as the Obamacare crisis ripens, and the mid term elections approach ...

Apology to B.

2017-03-29 09:35:37

B did in fact win the bet that the Orthodox were holding the line on gay marriage. I failed to notice, because I ignored the evidence he brought up. I will settle the bet shortly.

Unowned women should be unprotected and fair game

2017-03-31 00:30:08

You want Roissy ran out of town on a rail. There is a good chance he "raped" your girlfriend, and if he did not, he had her before you, or will have her after you.

But who is going to run Roissy out of town on a rail? No one has incentive to do so, or legitimate authority to do so, unless husbands and fathers have property rights in women's sexual and domestic services.

So if you want a society where Roissy gets run out of town on a rail, or better, shot like a dog, you need a society where husbands and fathers have legitimate, socially recognized, legally recognized, and legally enforced property rights in women's sexual and domestic services, where a husband or a father can legally and morally legitimately shoot Roissy for sniffing around where he should not, as he can shoot a burglar for sniffing around where he should not.

And if you start "protecting" unowned women from Roissy ("oh the poor things") you are abandoning male property rights in women.

The system that Victorians liked to pretend that they had, where unowned, unprotected, and uncontrolled women were presumed to be chaste and of comparable value to owned, controlled, and protected women, is not incentive compatible. No one has strong motivation to protect the society that you piously pretend that you have. You are not upvaluing unprotected women. You are downvaluing wives and daughters.

You cannot have the supposed Victorian and the supposed Puritan system, for the same reason as the Victorians and the Puritans could not have it either. The Victorian system resulted in far too many women giving birth in the rain in dark alleys, resulting in far too many Oliver Twists, resulting in the welfare state, resulting in far too many women marrying Uncle Sam the big Pimp. And here we are.

If you start "protecting" unowned women from Roissy you are not going to succeed, because unowned women are uncontrolled women. And your entire intended system goes down the drain.

You cannot "protect" unowned women from seduction and "rape[31]", because women are notoriously uncooperative with anyone trying to "protect" them.

---

[31] https://www.reddit.com/r/confession/comments/5xpx8y/remorse_i_cant_stop_hating_my_girlfriend_for/

Whereupon, surprise surprise, no one runs Roissy out of town no matter how much the preacher vainly rants about chastity.

If chastity is based on male property rights in women, unowned women are outside the system and are presumed to be unchaste – and need to be outside so that they can be discriminated against and treated as of lesser value and lesser worth. Roissy screwing unowned women cannot be allowed to matter, because unowned women cannot be allowed to matter.

High estimates of the number of whores in the eighteenth and early nineteenth century were not based on the modern usage of "whore" to mean a woman rents her pussy for cash by the hour, but rather, were estimates of the number of unowned, and thus presumed to be unchaste, women. Similarly "sluts".

You cannot keep women permanently chained to the wall. You are going to have to let them loose every now and then to take care of the baby, pick up the socks, and cook the meals. So you need to have a system that is incentive compatible with what women want. If women get entirely their way, civilization collapses, because most men will not have posterity, so will not plant trees for their grandchildren to enjoy the shade. So you need to have a system where male ownership of women is incentive compatible with what women want, where women have reason to cooperate in a system that restrains their worst excesses. So you have to downvalue unowned women and upvalue owned women. And if you downvalue unowned women, you cannot allow yourself to care about what Roissy gets up to. (Unless of course, he starts sniffing around your wife or daughter, in which case you shoot him like a dog, and the cops shrug their shoulders and say "needed killing".)

The problem is not that women want to bang multiple high value alpha males. They want to bang only one high value alpha male, and that high value alpha male also wants them to bang only that one high value alpha male. The problem is that finding themselves of low rank the high value alpha male's ever growing harem, they start playing off one high value alpha male against another high value alpha male in order to raise their value. The solution is to associate this tactic with being low value. And if allow ourselves to care about what Roissy gets up to, we are upvaluing women who employ this tactic. No one should care about what unowned women get up to, or about what happens to them, thus motivating unowned women to come in from the cold, and owned women to stay where it is warm.

It does not matter if the archbishop proclaims that all fertile age women are the property of their father or husband. He can, and should proclaim that all fertile age women should be the property of their father or husband, but short of keeping them all permanently chained to the dungeon wall, not all of them are going to actually be the property of their father or husband. Hence Roissy.

If we could stop unowned women from seducing Mohammed, then we could have the system that the Victorians and the Puritans pretended that they had. But we cannot.

Or if we could prevent significant numbers of women from becoming unowned, then we could have the system that the Victorians and the Puritans pretended that they had. But that would require measures that are extreme, cruel, disturbing, and, worst of all, inconvenient.

The likely shape of a Trump autocoup

2017-04-01 10:13:50

For Trump to actually be the executive of the United States government would be something very like a autocoup, a coup by the merely elected government against the permanent government. At present the government continues to fund the left, the IRS continues to target the tea party and conservative organizations. An overwhelming proportion of the "refugees" admitted to the US are still black male military age Muslims screaming for infidel blood and white pussy. Planned Parenthood has not been defunded,

Trump has the praetorians in his pocket, the military in his pocket, but the spies are an obstacle I did not expect.

To get control of the spies, Trump has to fire some spies - but he cannot fire spies without a self coup, and cannot have a self coup until he gets control of the spies. The solution, of course, is to charge some spies with crimes against national security and then place them on administrative leave pending resolution of the charges. It would only take removal of a very few to get enough leverage to get the rest in line.

So why no charges yet? Maybe he is a cuck, but that does not sound like Trump.

In his tweets, he is focusing on getting Gorsuch on the supreme court. Maybe he is worried that anything that looks like preparation for a self coup would make it difficult to get Gorsuch confirmed.

I hope and I believe that the reason that Trump has been pussyfooting around lately is that he wants to get his man on the supremes first, and that once Gorsuch is in, we shall see the old Trump once more, that once his man his in, he will, we will, confront the judiciary and purge the spies.

His inaction so far on the judiciary and the spies has me worried - but not that worried. I expect to see the old Trump back once Gorsuch is confirmed.

It took Abbott ten months of confrontation before he deemed the time ripe to go Andrew Jackson on the judges, and I am not necessarily expecting Trump to go any quicker, but I expect the sparks to start flying very shortly after Gorsuch is in.

Trump already remakes the world

2017-04-03 06:05:18

Clearly the permanent government is still in control, and Trump is not yet in control. But equally clearly, he is working on it.

With Trump's election, the Arab Spring died. Suddenly and mysteriously, the mysterious benefactors that enabled Arab subversives to operate from a big important expensive office, stopped funding that big important expensive office[32].

Simultaneously, Marvel heroes no longer push females doing manly things and sexual deviants doing admirable things. Supposedly this is because of a sudden and mysterious change in public taste[33], but in fact Spider Girl and Tranny Thor and the rest were always

---

[32]https://www.buzzfeed.com/borzoudaragahi/egypts-rulers-are-hailing-president-trump-democracy

[33]https://www.bleedingcool.com/2017/03/31/marvels-david-gabriel-sales-slump-people-didnt-want-diversity-didnt-want-female-characters/

violently unpopular. It is just that until now the official truth was that they were popular, and were bringing in new and more diverse readers.

The Black Lives Matter movement was always a front for the Department of Justice, which is a branch of the United States Government. When Trump was elected, it vanished like smoke, and the numerous incidents of racist cops maliciously gunning down unarmed black male honors students (who dindu nuffin) on their way to choir practice, vanished with it.

When gangs of thugs burned down supermarkets and petrol stations, and forced white people to abandon their houses, that was the Department of Justice in blackface.

With the vanishing of Tranny Thor and the like, has come a similar vanishing of sex incidents in software engineering. Are smart engineers no longer talking down to affirmative action engineerettes in the art harem? Are horny engineers no longer finding excuses to visit the art harem to hit on the affirmative action engineerettes?

When I saw Trump's tech summit, I noticed that instead of dressing in Silicon Valley expensive dark casual, the summitteers were dressed in job interview formal. I immediately knew that complaints of mansplaining and being hit on by insufficiently high status males (with the subtext that the complainant is entitled to be hit on by higher status males, and in a just and fair society would be considered hot) would no longer receive such a warm hearing. Ideas are more powerful than guns, but fashion is more powerful than ideas.

Romanovs and war with Russia

2017-04-07 01:57:41

Trump is seemingly going along with plans for war with Russia, or maybe he is pretending to go along to separate the sane from the truly mad.

It is supposedly morally imperative to go to war with Russia because some bad people in the in middle east have gassed other bad people in the middle east, instead of their usual schtick, which is cutting people's heads off. Kind of obvious that our ruling elite is looking for an excuse, any excuse.

And our ruling elite[34] has joined the reaction and the alt right[35] in calling Trump and his family the Romanovs[36].

Some time ago I remarked[37]:

> Trump may well cuck out, as the Romanovs cucked out. But if he does, the left will kill him and kill his children as they killed the Romanovs and their children.

To which Grumpus replied:

> (Important people read this blog. Let's watch and see if the Romanovs analogy grows legs out there.)

---

[34]https://www.tigerdroppings.com/rant/politics/msnbc-knocks-parade-trump-family-as-the-new-romanovs/68281319/

[35]https://www.reddit.com/r/The_Donald/comments/51jait/trump_is_to_america_as_romanov_is_to_russia/

[36]https://dailycaller.com/2017/02/15/chris-matthews-trumps-family-is-almost-like-the-romanovs-video/

[37]https://blog.reaction.la/politics/the-first-confrontation-between-the-trumpenreich-and-the-permanent-government/#comment-1530170

What do you know. It has grown legs.

The reason that our elite wants to kill the Trump family, and the Republicans for siding with the Trump family, and kill the Russians is Pussy Riot and European University[38]. The continued existence of Russians, and the continued existence of Trumps, undermines their status. If Trump and the Republicans ever allow the Democrats to regain power, they will be killed.

The stakes have grown too high for democracy to continue. Maybe Trump can de-escalate the situation, but entropy is easier than order, only takes one side to escalate, two sides to de-escalate.

Allying with far to destroy near

2017-04-09 12:12:41

Whosover wants to overthrow Assad of Syria, wants to murder all Alawites and murder or expel all Christians. There used to be a moderate opposition, composed entirely of do-gooder employees of "NGOs", which is to say, employees of the State Department, but they all got out when things went bad, and are now employed on various do-gooder international grants all over the world, such as setting Somali refugees on middle American marginal electorates in flyover country. The opposition to Assad is now 100% head chopper Muslim. The Cathedral delusively imagines it can regain control once they have finished chopping off heads.

Whosoever wants to overthrow Assad of Syria, wants to ally with people unlike me, to murder people who are like me, to murder them for what they have in common with me. Murdering some people who are like me, murdering them because they are like me is a step towards murdering everyone like me.

It is striking that the advocates of reason, rationality, niceness, and maximizing everyone's utility always wind up with pyramids of skulls. The French revolution was in large part a creation of the cult of reason, and I see the same evil and madness in today's rationalist community, for example the Bay Area rationalist community, whose rationality is strikingly and conspicuously limited by their refusal to engage in thoughtcrime and their demented demonization of thought criminals.

Recall the Populares of Rome. "Populares" is latin for "Democrats", or "People's Party". In the end they allied with the Samnites. I suppose the Populares wanted to give the Samnites citizenship and fairer treatment, because that is the kind of moldy bananas the Populares stood for, being nice to people, especially the oppressed, remedying justice and inequality, rationality, reason, and reasonableness, all that filthy disgusting garbage. The Samnites, however, wanted to overthrow the walls of Rome, kill every Roman male, and rape every fertile age Roman woman. The Populare/Samnite alliance strikingly resembles today's progressive/Muslim alliance.

The fans of kindness, niceness, pleasantness, reason, and rationality tend to wind up quite unreasonably and unpleasantly torturing and murdering very large numbers of people. Hostility to near is a key foundational principle of leftism, goes down all the way to friends, family, and political allies.

---

[38]https://blog.reaction.la/politics/trump-derangement-syndrom-and-status/

War with Syria is war on the side of Jews against the side of Christians, since Assad is keeping Syrian Christians alive, and Israel is backing the side that wants Assad (and Christians) dead. I don't think this is a matter of the Zionist Occupation Government ruling the world. Rather it is that the Cathedral, though it hates Israel, or rather hates Israel being Jewish, wants a non Jewish Israel, hates Christians even more. The Cathedral is allied with Israel the state, but there is a point of contention, since they cannot stand Israel being Jewish nor India being Hindu, any more than they can stand America being Christian. Israel the state wants Syria the state in chaos, and the Cathedral wants to rule Syria and imagines it can rule through the head choppers. Were they to actually succeed in ruling through head choppers, Israel the state would find itself under a lot heavier pressure to become less Jewish, but the Israelis doubt that this outcome is very likely.

Trump's attack on Syria was both real and fake - real enough to threaten Assad and Putin, real enough to get his judge through the senate, real enough to keep the Pentagon on his side, fake enough to avoid war with Assad and Putin. What is clear is that the left wants to overthrow Assad. If we continue to take substantial measures to overthrow Assad, then Trump will have cucked out to the left as the Czar did, which I think will likely be the death of Trump and his family, as it was the death of the Czar and his family. Any concessions to the left are just blood in the water. They are more likely to kill you if you play nice with them than if you piss on them.

When Obama took power, we were involved in two pointless unwinnable wars in the middle east, where we supporting the side that could perhaps be argued to be the good guys, though it was far from clear who the good guys were.

When Obama had governed for eight years, he had gotten us into five more pointless unwinnable wars in the middle east, where we are for the most part supporting sides that are appallingly evil and indiscriminately murderous.

When I say unwinnable, it is not that we lack the capacity to defeat a bunch of backward goat herders. It is that we lack the capacity to defeat a bunch of backward goat herders when our troops are required to behave like heavily armed nursemaids, and when I say pointless, I mean that the victory condition is defined as our enemies liking us, rather than our enemies being dead or enslaved. If you forbid our troops to kill civilians that are intermixed with our enemies, our enemies will grasp civilians to their chests. If you applied the the old laws of war, which allowed you to flatten enemy cities and such like, civilians would separate themselves from combatants, and combatants would have no reason to prevent them from doing so.

And now Trump is under extreme pressure to bring us into war with Syria, North Korea, Russia, and China, and may well be cucking out under that pressure, bringing us from seven low level wars in five of which we are allied to the bad guys, to eleven wars, in three of which we will be the bad guys, and two of them likely to go thermonuclear.

Why is it that the fans of niceness and rationality tend to be unpleasant and irrational, from the Bay Area Rationalist community to the Khmer Rouge?

It is because caring for your children, your spouse, your lover, your sisters, your brothers, and your friends is likely to be expensive and inconvenient. Caring for far away people located in places you cannot find on the map tends to be a whole lot cheaper and much more convenient.

And thus it is no surprise that Badwhites look after their children, their spouses, their kin, their lovers, and their friends, while Goodwhites do not look after their children, their spouses, and their kin, and routinely stab lovers and friends in the back. Often stab kin in the back also - observe what happens when the old man dies, and fights over the inheritance break out. Leftists lie, betray, and sometimes murder, in order to rob their brothers and sisters, sometimes even their parents and their children.

Can you imagine one of ours suckerpunching an Obama supporter to the enthusiastic cheers of everyone who voted against Obama? Reflect on the Yellow Hat incident - the video shows yellow hat being sucker punched, presumably because he formerly wore a Trump hat. There is just no way that could happen on our side. Nasty goings on when inheritance is being distributed usually involve lefties behaving ruthlessly to close kin. Normal people generally cooperate with close kin. The rubbish and destruction left after left wing protests, as compared to the neatness and order of right wing protests. It is not like a ten percent greater likelihood of littering and vandalism, it is a thousand fold greater likelihood of littering and vandalism.

Lord Howe arranged for his men to die. The Victorian anti slaver movement committed perjury in court. Who kills commies? Commies kill commies. It is totally and completely one sided. Nazis, right wing dictators, right wing death squads kill hardly any commies by comparison. It is not like there is a ten percent greater tendency to murder their own, it is more like a thousand fold greater tendency to murder their own. The ratio of commies killed by commies, to commies killed by right wing dictators, is similar to the ratio of rubbish left behind after left wing street protests, to rubbish left behind by right wing street protests.

Would our people have produced something like the "10:10 no pressure" video?

The moral difference between lefties and normies is as clear as the trail of rubbish that they leave in their path.

Hostility to near is a key foundational principle of leftism, goes down all the way to friends, family, and political allies. Hence Lord Howe. If your commanding officer is a leftist and he orders you into danger, desert.

Leftism as an individual propensity is a propensity to game the systems for status, affiliation, alliance formation, and virtue signaling. Leftism as a movement is large scale organized gaming of the status, affiliation, and virtue signaling systems, and thus tends to work to the disadvantage of individual leftists. No friends to the right, no enemies to the left, means all your friends are your enemies and all your enemies are your friends, hence the greatest danger to leftists as members of a leftist movement is being murdered by their own movement.

If you are genuinely decent and conscientious, you are substantially less interested in cheap signals of decency and conscientiousness. Decent conscientious people are not attracted to whatever opinions are high status. People who want cheap ways of signaling decency and conscientiousness are attracted towards whatever opinions are high status.

Thus, observe ...

Trump the chess master or Trump the cuckold

2017-04-10 23:06:56

First, I endorse this excellent post by Heartiste, Minion of Satan[39].

If Trumps beats the judges on legal immigration, avoids war with Russia, and builds the wall, he is what we thought he was. Hail Trump, God Emperor. Those three items amount to making war on the deep state and winning. Missiling Syria is deeply worrying, but it is far too soon to count him out on what really matters.

And to that excellent post by Heartiste, Minion of Satan, I will add this. In chess, you can see the moves the master makes. When Trump moves, you frequently cannot see him move. Even when his move is public, a fashion statement or a tweet, it is often at a level that you cannot see what he is up to except in retrospect. He is playing a different game to the game his enemies think he is playing. Therefore, while we should take seriously the likelihood that Trump will double cross his loyalists for the praise and flattery of his enemies, we should take considerably less seriously any theory that supposes he is doing something stupid. Which is more likely? That you are smarter than Trump and know more than he does, or that Trump has an ace up his sleeve and a Smith and Wesson in his pocket?

Making warlike moves on Syria is a strategic retreat under fire, never a good sign. The merely temporary government, Trump is retreating under fire from the permanent government. But is is not over till it is over, and now that Gorsuch is in, Trump is free to move on lowering the status of judges, preparatory to going Jackson on them. That is bigger than Syria, though not so big as war with Russia. If Trump gets legal immigration of Muslims severely slowed, avoids war with Russia and avoids installing the head choppers in charge of Syria, the attack on Syria will not have mattered.

Trump accomplishments.

2017-04-12 04:13:38

The invasion of illegals has largely stopped. Though no wall yet, arrests of illegals have fallen to a tiny fraction of what they used to be - because now when they try to cross, they will likely be arrested, so they don't even try. The wall matters, but men with guns matter more, and if there is no wall yet, there are more men with guns with more authority to use them.

That is the big thing that we voted for and we got it.

We got it now. It is effect and working right now today. So even if he totally cucks out from here on in, we still won. We got the number one big item we voted for. The wall is just icing on the cake. Further, if he is willing and able to deploy men with guns, he will be willing and able to deploy a wall. If he can get away with deploying men with guns, he can get away with deploying a wall. OK, we also voted for the eviction of the anchor babies, and he is not doing that, and maybe he will not do it ever, but the number one big problem, the number one thing we voted on, the flood of illegals, has largely stopped.

---

[39]https://heartiste.wordpress.com/2017/04/10/trump-the-4d-chess-master-or-trump-the-puppet/

The invasion of legals is still in full swing, with large numbers of male military age Muslim Democratic party voters screaming for infidel blood and white pussy being dumped on marginal electorates in flyover country to live on crime and welfare, but now Gorsuch is in, Trump is preparing to do something about it. He has not done anything about it yet, but he has done something about H1B. Previously unenforced rules about applicants being specially talented in ways not not readily available in the US are now enforced. Pretty sure absolutely zero existing H1B holders would qualify, since demand for H1Bs is 100% demand for cheap low status slave labor. Partly H1B is about saving money, mostly it is about status. The bean counters and the HRs are troubled by the status of engineers. Notice the complete absence of H1Bs in HR and accounting. If he can stop H1B, despite corporate interests screaming blue murder, he can stop the rapeugee invasion despite the courts.

OK, enormous numbers of Muslims still legally pouring across the border to live on crime, welfare, and voting Democrat in marginal electorates in flyover country, but the H1Bs are either be drastically cut, or else H1Bs are going to be radically higher quality people rather than cheap slave labor. A radical cut in numbers being considerably more likely than a radical improvement in quality.

Jobs are back due to threats, promises, actual de-regulation, and promised de-regulation. Not to mention a sudden scarcity of fresh H1Bs.

The Global Warming movement is dead in the water. Now government is talking about cheap energy, so now if you want your grants, instead of applying for a grant on the effect of global warming on squirrel nut gathering, you apply for a grant on obtaining energy cost efficiently. Government funding for the left, though still enormous, has suffered major cuts. You want a grant, now you have to sing a right wing song (cheap energy good, because man's mastery over nature is good) instead of a left wing song (humans are evil and deserve unending and severe punishment for despoiling the earth).

Tranny thor, tranny spiderman, and tranny wolverine have all bitten the dust. Supposedly the the comics industry spontaneously saw the light, but that is a joke. You don't have free speech. Do you think the comics have free speech? They got told by Obama to do sex changes on their most distinctively manly heroes, and now they got told by Trump to sex change them back. Television, however, is still a disgusting attack on maleness, men, and masculinity. Television is all about manning up to be cuckolded and raise someone else's child. Biological fathers on television are horrible people, for example Homer Simpson, the only good men being cuckolds raising other men's children, when it is not about counterstereotypical women, counterstereotypical gays, counterstereotypical blacks, and counterstereotypical black males fornicating with white women. (Who are allowed to be feminine if and only if they have sex with black men) There is no indication that the celebration of cuckoldry is going to stop, but FCC changes give me considerable hope. If Thor is a man again, maybe men on television will stop raising other men's bastard spawn. Maybe dads being dads will become as mandatory as non dads being dads is now. Notice how salient it is that Trump is a father, whereas it was barely salient that Obama was a father. If Trump signaling fatherhood, and kicking ass on the FCC, chances are that television will also be signaling fatherhood pretty soon.

OK, I hear you say, but what about war with Syria, which goes totally against everything he promised?

Well, to the progs he saying "War with Syria", and to his base, he is saying "No war with Syria". Which is kind of what you expect from Trump. And I rather think it will be no war with Syria, that he is lying to the deep state, not to us.

Nixon famously said "I am not a crook", but in one of Trump's speeches, Trump implied he was a crook, and he is, and all the better because of it. We were voting for a president, not a pastor. The left has no morals. Politics is war within limits, which limits are constantly in danger of being trampled down, and I voted for Trump in part because I expect him to stomp right over those limits.

We won the battle of Berkeley

2017-04-16 00:47:34

A free speech rally was held at the symbolically important location of Berkeley

Was the free speech sometimes anti semitic?

Yes, damned well was.

Naturally antifa, a wholly owned subsidiary of George Soros, tried to shut it down. Failed dismally.

It is a symbolic victory. Symbols matter, often more than the things that they symbolize. We won, because police were relatively neutral this time. That police were neutral this time, and that we win if police are neutral, sends an important message.

And, of course, based stickman was there.

> "They picked Berkeley because they want to feel they could do this in the most liberal place in the country," said Geoff Millard, an anti-Trump protester, Iraq war veteran and Mr San Francisco Leather 2017. "It's important that we shut them down and let them know they can't pull this crap here."

Well, they could not shut us down, and we can pull this stuff there.

The enemy within

2017-04-16 02:00:38

Trump's CIA director, Pompeo, tells us that Julian Assange, the leader of wikileaks is "on the wrong side of history."

That is commie language, commie thinking. To say that history has a side in earthly political struggles is history reified and personified as the Jewish God.

Probably he is a cultural Marxist rather than an old style Marxist, since old style Marxists are mighty thin on the ground these days.

Personifying "History" is characteristic of Jewish descended leftism via Marx. Puritan descended leftism via Harvard immanentizes salvation, rather the immanentizing the deity.

This ideology puts one on a course that necessarily results in the murder of very large number of people. Pompeo is ticked with Julian Assange for exposing, and thus disrupting, various color revolutions, but the biggest color revolution that is cooking right now is in America itself, which revolution, if it goes through, will likely result in the deaths of Trump and all his family, and probably most republicans in office. If you favor color revolutions, you favor antifa, you favor killing Trump, his family, and Trump supporters.

The Marxist does not think of himself as intending to murder the peasants, and the cultural Marxist does not think of himself as planning to send all hetero males to the Gulag. Rather he thinks that if it was not for "bullying" all nine year old boys would be gay and they would all be fucking in the classroom a great big pile. When a great big pile fails to ensue in the classroom, escalates the war on "bullying", until it eventually starts to look remarkably like sending all cisgender males to the Gulag.

The original Marxists were going to emancipate the peasants from the landlords, and utopia and abundance would ensue. Utopia and abundance failed to ensue. Obviously invisible intangible landlord oppression. Therefore, war on kulaks, which liberation of the peasants looked curiously similar to war on the peasants. And thus, today, instead of war on kulaks, war on cis hetero patriarchal oppressors. They are liberating us from being "bullied". They are indignant at our lack of gratitude. And the war on bullying inevitably escalates.

> "ohh mai gosh, people like you, cishet white privileged DUDEBROS, are the reason women and POCs are oppressed, wow just wow, the white race must be abolished (don't worry, only as a social construct, I have nothing sinister in mind *rubs hands*), so listen now, fratboyrapist microaggressor douchenozzle, we're sending you and your associates to the gulag – k bye!"

The Czar failed to support Pyotr Stolypin, and appointed a bunch of lefties to the council of ministers, who, when the Czar was away at the front, refrained from any serious effort to restrain revolutionaries who intended to kill the Czar and his family, and who when trouble broke out, resigned in favor of the revolutionaries. Giving Pompeo power and taking power away from Bannon is a similar error. Politics is war by other means, and for the past couple of decades has been drifting closer to war by the usual means.

Punching unowned women in the face

2017-04-19 04:16:03

The rule on hitting girls should be, "don't hit someone else's girl". If a girl is misbehaving, you should call for the man who is in charge of her[40], ask him to take care of the problem, and if he does not, you should punch him out, not his girl.

Moldilocks went to the free speech rally in Berkeley declaring she was going to collect one hundred fascist scalps. She was wearing brass knuckle gloves, having watched too many Hollywood movies where action girl takes out five mooks while doing a backflip.[41] She threw glass bottles at people.[42]

A gentleman should never under any circumstances strike a lady, but Moldilocks was no lady.

---

[40] https://heartiste.wordpress.com/2015/01/21/who-bitch-this-is/

[41] https://pjmedia.com/lifestyle/2017/04/18/boys-punching-girls-feminisms-big-win/

[42] https://www.freespeech.report/2017/04/17/breaking-antifa-girl-caught-on-livestream-advocating-violent-communist-revolution/

If an unowned, unsupervised women, gets beaten by some male, your default presupposition, your prejudgment of the situation absent other evidence, should be that males are generally well behaved, unsupervised and uncontrolled women are frequently badly behaved, therefore chances are that she probably needed a beating.

Women are, of course, the precious sex, and men are the expendable sex. It is right that men should die for their women. Men have a duty to love and cherish their women, and women do not have a duty to love and cherish their men, but a duty to honor and obey. But not all women are precious. Unowned women frequently behave in ways that make them less valuable, and more expendable, than men. Observe that Moldilocks was beautiful, became a porngirl (her ranking is too low to qualify as pornstar) became unattractive with astonishing speed, her inner ugliness becoming externally manifest. Her inner ugliness made manifest revealed that this woman was worthless trash.

Some women are precious, not all women are precious. It is entirely OK to punch porngirls, especially unattractive porngirls. No punching cute porngirls in the face, but measures less likely to mar them are fine.

Women are precious because they can create life, whereas all a man can do is merely kill someone. A woman can make you immortal, whereas all a man can do is merely kill you. But porngirl Moldilocks is not going to make you immortal, so no great loss spoiling her face even further.

Not the Jews

2017-04-22 04:29:26

The key fundamental point uniting the alt right is that all men are not created equal, nor women equal to men. There are important differences between individuals, groups, categories, and races.

And among those differences are differences which cause Jews in exile to be irritating and a problem. No one in the alt-right, including the many Jewish members of the alt-right, can or should deny this. But Jews are not the big problem.

Chan has done an analysis of the antifa officer and organization core, and even though antifa is backed by Jewish money and spreading Jewish memes, its leadership and organization is just not all that Jewish[43].

And if you point out that antifa is a wholly owned subsidiary of George Soros, well, George Soros is a wholly owned subsidiary of the Permanent Government in the State Department. Native ruling elites have a long history of hiring Jews to do the dirty work against their own people, and then discarding those Jews when things got rough. Started with Jewish tax farmers. Then when the peasants got pissed with the tax farmers, the ruling elite would encourage them to knock over a pawn shop.

Don't be one of the idiots who gets distracted by the shiny broken glass and the shiny stuff in the pawnshop. That is just the Matador's flashing cape.

If you gassed all the Jews, antifa would only be mildly inconvenienced. Cthulhu would continue to swim left. If you take all the progs in government and quasi government institutions for helicopter rides to the Pacific, there would be quite a few wet Jews,

---

[43]https://www.youtube.com/watch?v=uKRDLKAKUZc

but, more importantly, antifa would be out of business and Cthulhu would no longer swim left.

Violence, repression, and freedom

2017-04-22 23:00:10

When the left stopped attempting to communicate with its enemies, stopped listening, stopped talking, and instead dehumanized, demonized and no platformed us, I knew that this would necessarily lead to violence against us, and eventually war.

The violence has started. War comes.

Today, if you support freedom of speech and the right to peaceably assemble, you are a nazi. So, what the hell, you had better ally and organize with actual unironic nazis. George Soros is a Jew, and he is providing your enemies with military grade pepper spray and restricted explosives, so if the Nazis say "the Jews" are doing this, why split hairs with them?

Freedom of speech and freedom of assembly was always a lie, sometimes, as in our past, a little white lie. Sometimes, as at present, a great big blatant arrogant lie. There is always a state religion, and you can never commit lese mageste against the state religion and its symbols. Back when the constitution was written, the reason that the federal government was forbidden from interfering with the press or from establishing a federal church was that each state had its own official state church, formally, overtly, and openly established, and the corresponding restrictions on freedom of speech, freedom of association, and the freedom to peaceably assemble.

But, as long as the state religion does not deny glaringly obvious facts about the actual world, as long as it is not aggressively intrusive, these restrictions are not all that irritating, not all that intrusive, and when these formal and official restrictions were replaced by informal and unofficial federal restrictions, when the state religion of New England became the state religion of the United States, it was possible to pretend that these restrictions were not really there.

The trouble is that our official unofficial state religion has open entry into our officially unofficial inquisition, the social justice warriors, with the result that it is intrusively developing a line on everything - not only race and sex but fatty foods and global warming, so that the necessary restrictions on freedom of speech, freedom of assembly, and freedom of association have become alarmingly intrusive and aggressive.

The shutdown of conversation between right and left by the left is a manifestation of this. Repression of thought crime has become more heavy handed and less effective, as more and more thoughts become crimes.

The state inherently has the right to suppress falsehood and enforce truth, people will never agree on what is truth and what is falsehood, and so here we are. You always wind up with a state religion, and denying it just makes its power informal and unofficial, which is worse than having an official and formal state religion.

No one ever sincerely supports freedom of speech, freedom of association, and freedom to peaceably assemble. We speak, associate, and assemble with the ultimate goal of stopping the other group from doing so. If we win, social justice warriors will lose - they will lose their jobs among other things, and will be forced to refrain from certain speech, certain kinds of association, possibly in order to keep their jobs, possibly in order to stay out of jail, possibly in order to avoid helicopter rides to the pacific ocean.

The best you can get is a state religion that does not flagrantly contradict reality, and therefore does not find it necessary to flagrantly and outrageously suppress speech, association, and assembly. If we win, lots of crazy hateful evil stuff that progs say today, will not be safely sayable. This, however, is not all that obnoxious, provided that it is only crazy hateful evil stuff. If they win, lots of true and important stuff will not be sayable.

We will always have a state religion, and the corresponding restraints on speech, association, and assembly. But if we are required to believe that all men and women are created equal, or that Kim il Jong incarnates the will of the people, then the state religion will cause problems.

And now we have those problems.

In a society where we are able to say that people are not equal, it will likely be a society where you cannot advocate some kinds of affirmative action, or some kinds of taking stuff from some people to give it to other people.

Let us consider for example, women in the actual fighting military, and action girl in the movies who takes out five men in a back flip. Moldylocks watched this, decided to go into battle with brass knuckles and glass bottles to attack people peaceably assembling to say and hear politically incorrect things, and freely associating with fascists and nazis both ironic and unironic. Naturally got smacked down.

This started not in the 1960s, but in the 1860s, with making a hero out Florence Nightingale, and demons out of the actual heroes of the Crimean war, in particular Lord Cardigan. The Crimean war was fought in substantial part by each side attempting to stop the other side's logistics and starve them out, which was rough on everyone and particularly rough on civilians. So the press had plenty of opportunity to depict heroes as baby killers. This led to camp followers, such as Florence Nightingale, becoming officially heroes, and in due course officially part of the army, and classified as soldiers.

After a while it became kind of obvious that logistic providers were not really soldiers, and were still camp followers, so, action girl in the movies, and women being given the title, but not the actual functionality, of the men who actually fight, for which category of soldier we have the thought, but strangely, the word is forbidden.

Warriors.

It is a little bit naughty, a little bit disturbing, to call soldiers who shoot and get shot at warriors, to distinguish them from what used to be called camp followers.

If we win, if we are able to speak, to associate, to peaceably assemble, chances are the other side will not be able to get away with demonizing our warriors as baby killers, even if our warriors use methods, such a siege and famine, that do in fact kill babies. If we get freedom of speech, association, and assembly, then as a result of the way the world is, the way society works, they will not. The state will always necessarily take a side on enforcing truth and suppressing error, especially on crucial matters like whether warriors are heroes or baby killers. And if you say the wrong thing, then at best you can kiss your prospects of a high status job in a quasi statal institution goodbye, and at worst you get helicoptered to the Pacific Ocean.

Today, saying that women are innately unsuitable to be warriors, that putting women on the front lines is wrong and that pretending to put women on the front lines is worse, is saying the wrong thing. You will not get into a good university, nor get a good job, if you are caught saying such things. If we win, calling our warriors baby killers is likely to have similar consequences, quite likely far worse consequences.

The state is incapable of being neutral, so we might as well cut out the hypocrisy and make the state openly, officially, and formally sponsor the state Church, and the state church openly, formally and officially sponsor the state. That way we can regulate the Church to prevent runaway holiness signaling.

Things are getting violent because the state's official belief system is getting ever crazier and ever more hurtful, thus the amount of repression needed to make it stick is getting ever greater.

The solution is not freedom of speech, freedom of assembly, and freedom of association. The solution is that the state Church should have saner beliefs that require less repression to make the state Church stick. The solution is Freedom of Speech, Freedom of Assembly, and Freedom of Association for us, but not for them, because our beliefs are sane and reasonable, and their beliefs are crazy and evil, and getting more crazy and evil every day.

Freedom of speech and religion is not really attainable, and if you try to attain it, then the State of Virginia, which really did have freedom of speech and religion, gets conquered by the state of Massachusetts, which really did not. The war of Northern Aggression was a holy war in which the side with the most powerful and intrusive state religion conquered the side with a milder and less intrusive state religion. Bring a gun to a gunfight, and a religion to a holy war.

The restrictions that necessarily follow from respect for the state and the state religion are only a big problem when the official state belief system vigorously enforces beliefs that are obviously false, such as "all men are created equal", or "Kim Jong-un represents the will of the people"

Repression is ramping up not because we used to have freedom of speech and freedom to peaceably assemble before and now we do not, but because the official belief system is getting ever crazier, and thus requires ever more violence to be enforced. We used to believe in holocaustism, which is far away and long ago, and that logistic support are soldiers, which is not that close. Now we are required to believe in action girl and to disbelieve in fathers, which is mighty close, and thus causing problems.

Holocaustism is sort of true, in that Hitler really did decide to murder the Jews and made a good start on it, but it is sort of false in that there are plenty of communists who did far worse than Hitler, and making Hitler the incarnation of evil is ridiculous. Also the holocaust has been decorated and elaborated with all sorts of legends and myths to make it as different as possible from the communist mass murders. But all those issues do not matter any more, because now we are being forced to believe not in holocaustism, which our rulers are starting to forget, but in magic Negroes, the virtue of porngirls, and the fighting capability of action girls, among other things, among many, many other things. Hence the increasing violent repression. Kids today don't remember the awful crime of Hololocaust. They remember the awful crime that back in the bad bad old days women used to be forced to fullfill their marriage vows and black people were not allowed to drive whites out of the inner city.

And though our slogan should be, and is, Freedom of Speech, Freedom to Peaceably Assemble, and Freedom of Association, that slogan is a half truth. The only way we can achieve what we want is by overthrowing the current officially unofficial state religion, and replace it with a saner religion, whose official beliefs will intrude less on people's lives. And this requires the dissolution of the Monasteries Universities.

Truth is we are fighting for Freedom of Speech, Freedom to Peaceably Assemble, and Freedom of Association for ourselves, not for those who call warriors baby killers, who want to destroy marriage, Christmas, and Christianity. We want freedom for us, not them. Freedom of Speech for everyone is unilateral disarmament, and our enemies never disarmed for a moment. Like anarcho capitalism, freedom for everyone assumes general good behavior, tolerance, generosity, and an ethnically and culturally homogeneous society. Disarm in today's society, you get shot. Diversity has a striking tendency to develop into the war of each group on all of the others, and if one group disarms, you get what we got.

On fighting in the streets

2017-04-24 00:31:03

The left does not win by fighting in the streets. Believing that is left wing propaganda and Whig history.

The left faction of the permanent government uses this myth to seize power from the traditional and legitimate government. They put rioters in the streets, forbid the army and the police from dealing with them, and then cry out, while the Czar is away at the front,
> "Oh we have been overwhelmed by the mighty power of the justifiably enraged masses and have to surrender to them"

Thus, supposedly Berkeley would love to have Ann Coulter speak, but alas, to their great regret, the irresistible might of antifa prevents them from allowing anyone to the right of Pol Pot to speak, peaceably assemble, or associate.

We do not win by fighting in the streets either. We win via Sulla or Pinochet, not by "winning" at street fighting. But winning at street fighting undermines the "surrender to the justly enraged masses" narrative.

Sulla takes power, we tell him that he needs a priesthood that will tell the people that what he did was right and brave, and that it is glorious to serve one's nation in battle. That is how we win, not by crushing antifa and driving them before us.

But crushing antifa and driving them before us is still way fun, jind sticks a big spoke in the Cathedral narrative.

These are skirmishes, not war. War is about seven years off, give or take a few years. A skirmish is a reconnaissance in force. You provoke the enemy into revealing his capabilities and intentions, while trying to conceal your own capabilities and intentions.

The seven year estimate is about how long it takes the left to go full democidal. The proportion of the population that are deemed fascists has been steadily and rapidly growing, and has now reached about half, with the overwhelming majority of whites being "fascists". The view that whites should somehow not be around any more is mainstream and high status, arguably the highest status view within the left, though not yet the official view of the left in power, not yet a required belief of the regnant left.

The view that this should be accomplished by violent and deadly means is not yet high status - it is a supposedly crazy fringe view - or at least saying it out loud is a supposedly crazy fringe view, though snarkily implying it is just fine.

Since Cthulhu swims always left, this view will shortly be the mainstream view from which dissent is impossibly dangerous.

This will likely manifest as war external or internal or very likely both - the Cathedral will go to war with Russia and/or China and/or Iran and/or legacy Americans. Very likely all of them. Holiness spirals and purity spirals work like that. The Jews revolted against the Romans and attacked their Greek neighbors, who were being equally oppressed by the Romans, simultaneously,

Our information systems are better than theirs, thus skirmishing is working in our favor. We are gaining useful information about their capabilities and intentions, them not so much. Crushing them and driving them before us is really cool and a great recruiting instrument, but at this stage does actually not win us anything real, other than revealing that our men are strikingly more manly, physically considerably stronger, more loyal, and more amenable to discipline than their men. At this stage, it is a battle of observation and information.

But driving them before us may make it easier to reach a settlement short of war. Trump is under dire threat from a color revolution. The battle of Berkeley must have profoundly discouraged the color revolutionaries, since winning in the streets is for the left, though not for us, of vital symbolic importance. They need to win in the streets to legitimize the permanent government doing illegal things, such as suppressing Ann Coulter and judges legislating, budgeting, and administering from the bench. But them losing in the streets does not actually remove the permanent government from power. To remove the permanent government from power we need a Sulla or a Pinochet.

Any settlement short of war has to halt the holiness spiral, thus will be by today's standards unthinkably right wing radical. It will be the dissolution of the monasteries.

The Trump Aesthetic

2017-04-27 22:51:52

Ideas are more powerful than guns, and fashion is more powerful than ideas.

Ever since Beau Brummel successfully snubbed the Regent, the Puritan aesthetic has been politically dominant. It has been the high status aesthetic, beloved by our rulers, most notoriously loved by city planners and university regents.

Trump has been challenging that aesthetic.

What is the Trump aesthetic?

The Regency aesthetic became, at the end, too much detail, too much stuff, too much obviously non functional or even dysfunctional decoration. People say that Kings lost power because of gunpowder, because of capitalism, because of the change from agricultural based sources of energy to fossil fuel based sources of energy, because of this and because of that, but if we look at King George losing power, it seems to me that the problem was in large part that he was too fat, too lazy, his taste was not good enough, and his mistresses insufficiently attractive, the reason he lost power is that Beau Brummel could snub the King and yet continue to set fashion.

Even when Beau Brummel was old, poor, broke, syphilitic, and dying, his mistress was cuter than the King's mistress. I think if King George the Fourth had had a better tailor, a cuter mistress, and lost some weight, Kings might well still rule. It does not seem to me that gunpowder and all that had much relevance. Hence the propensity of the mainstream media to edit the color balance so as to adjust Trump's skin tone to orange.

The Puritan aesthetic of Beau Brummel was elegant simplicity - less decoration, less stuff, and much less color. Which was good, and a proper reaction to the Regent's propensity to excessive piles of expensive brightly colored decorations, but if simplicity is holy, more simplicity is holier, and so the puritan aesthetic became soul crushing brutalism, most glaringly evident in today's ugly cityscapes of giant boxes.

Trump is pushing a new and distinctive aesthetic which rejects the Puritan Aesthetic.

It does not go all the way back the Regency complexity, detail and decoration, we still have Beau Brummel's elegant simplicity and his predominantly monochrome palette, but with small splashes of much brighter, more intense colors than Beau Brummel permitted, fully saturated colors, colors that are clearly intended to invoke royalty, aristocracy, and old military dress uniforms. The Trump aesthetic somehow recalls and echoes the Regency aesthetic. It is not so much he has more details and decorations than the puritan aesthetic permits, but that the details are more ostentatious, colorful, prominent, and expensive than the Puritan aesthetic permits.

In calling back to the Regency, the last King of England who exercised real power, the Trump aesthetic is profoundly reactionary.

In deprecating the Puritan virtue of simplicity and modesty, it is mildly reactionary, and opens the door for more severe deprecation of the Puritan virtues in future.

While brutalist architecture announces its modesty with trumpets and cymbals, there is nothing humble or modest about brutalism. These unadorned boxes, because they lack small details, are larger than human scale, thus have a message, and that message is "I am mighty, I am vast, You are tiny. You are insignificant. You shall submit and I will crush you."

Trump tower in New York, typical of Trump buildings, has a human sized entrance, which is embedded in a very similar larger than human entrance, which is embedded in a larger glass and steel box, which is part of many glass and steel boxes that make up the towers. Thus there is a hierarchy of scales connecting the human scale with the tower scale: the scale of the normal entrance, the scale of the big entrance in which it is embedded, the scale of glass and steel box in which the big entrance is embedded, and the scale of the tower in which the glass and steel box is embedded.

Brutalism is, among other things, intended to destroy the messy human street by making the roadway inhospitable - it is just a barren path beside an enormous wall. Puritanism does not want you comfortable.

Trump Tower in New York on the other hand extravagantly and ostentatiously spends a whole lot of very expensive square footage making the street adjacent to the tower comfortable for humans. The Trump aesthetic is intended to be relaxed and comfortable, hence the Trump aesthetic has a conspicuous touch of informality, without going all the way to Silicon Valley casual. Just a touch of informality, but like the touch of colorful decoration, a conspicuous and striking touch.

The Regency Aesthetic tended to extravagance and ostentation for the sake of extravagance and ostentation. The Puritan Aesthetic rejected extravagance and ostentation. The Trump Aesthetic needs some plausible excuse for extravagance and ostentation. The extravagance and ostentation has to be the outward sign of some genuine inward excellence, and be plausibly in the service of that excellence. Thus his plane has gold plated toilets, not gold plated wheel hubs. Because gold plated toilets are cleaner. Does Trump have gold plated toilets because he is germophobic, or is he germophobic to justify gold plated toilets?

Silicon valley casual is comfortable, but conspicuously egalitarian. Steve Jobs wore clothes that look very similar to the clothes that some unemployed white man purchases at Walmart using his girlfriend's EBT card and were only subtly more expensive and better fitted than the clothes that some unemployed white man purchases at Walmart using his girlfriend's EBT card. The Trump aesthetic is conspicuously inegalitarian.

The status markers of Silicon Valley casual are subtle and difficult to read, thus if you display them and can read them, this shows you are one of the smart people. But they are also easy to imitate. The status markers of the Trump Aesthetic are easy for masses to read, harder for the masses to imitate. Because Silicon Valley casual is so easy to imitate, it is tempting to counter signal by wearing clothes that are not merely similar, but the same as the clothes some white man bought at Walmart on his girlfriend's EBT card. So is this silicon valley programmer subtly signaling elite, counter signaling elite, or did he actually buy clothes at Walmart with his girlfriends EBT card? It is hard to tell.

Trump's towers are not a total break with brutalism. They still rely heavily on giant undecorated colorless boxes of glass and steel, but the giant undecorated boxes are substantially smaller, and there is decoration, the minimum necessary decoration, to connect the human scale to the giant undecorated box scale, and this colorful and ostentatious decoration is a towel snapped in the face of the Puritan Aesthetic. Trump is a status challenge to Puritanism, as Beau Brummel was a status challenge to monarchy. That is part of the reason that they are going crazy.

It is only a relatively small change to the Puritan Aesthetic. Trump's towers are still rather brutal, relying as they do on unadorned giant boxes of glass and steel, but it is a challenge that goes right to the roots of the Puritan Aesthetic. His decoration is rather minimal, and almost conventional - but nonetheless, dramatic against the monochrome uniformity of the Puritan Aesthetic, and the unhuman scale of the Puritan Aesthetic in architecture. His decoration calls out "To hell with modesty and simplicity", and by its immodesty, and by the saturation of its colors, calls out to the Regency Aesthetic of the last days of Kings who actually ruled.

The Trump Aesthetic sends a message that the ideas of our rulers are passé and low status. They have, like feminism, hit the wall.

Trump probably on track

2017-05-01 00:26:54

When Trump says one thing to us, and another thing to his enemies, we should not necessarily assume he is lying to us and telling the truth to his enemies.

One very promising sign is that he invited Duterte, who is on the State Department death list, to the White House, which would imply that he can control who gets murdered in the United States and who does not. I expect however that a swarm of Trump's praetorians will be in the vicinity of Duterte at all times. Inviting Duterte is also another gentle hint to our lawless, corrupt, and criminal judiciary.

Of course, the real power in Washington has long been the White House Press Corps. This weekend he broke them. He skipped the annual White House dinner and, lo and behold, the celebrities fell into line with him against the White house press corps. This weekend, the White House Press Corps dinner was not only missing a president, it was missing hot young movie stars there to get nailed by high status alpha males, and Silicon Valley billionaires with briefcases full of hundred dollar bills there to beg and buy political influence.

The press corp piously announced that they had a good time, the party continued just fine, and it was just great to not to be crowded by movie starlets and silicon valley billionaires on their knees offering blow jobs. The press declared glorious victory over Trump's attack on their status. The press tells you that they are high status and holy, that Trump is low status and unholy, that they are winning and he is losing. You would not be so low status as to doubt the press, would you? Only low status people doubt the press.

Another good sign - the Cathedral Streisanded our smug Pepe meme - revealing profound status insecurity. People are starting to smell blood in the water. When a high status person shows status insecurity, you can gain status by insulting him and by desecrating what is holy to him.

OK boys, there is blood in the water. Time for the feeding frenzy. He who joins the feeding frenzy early is more likely to win status points than when everyone is doing it. It has been working for Milo, hence Scott Alexander is jealous. Also, time to split the ninth circuit. A necessary first step to splitting the ninth circuit is ridiculing and denigrating the ninth circuit judges as individuals - their races, their appearance, their personal conduct, their sex lives, their corruption, their conspicuous lack of intelligence, and last and probably least important, their arrogant and absurd judicial opinions.

Trumpcare passes the house

2017-05-05 05:34:49

Still has to pass the Senate, but already the Democrats are terrified.

The essential and important feature of Trumpcare is that it "denies insurance to millions of Americans". In other words, when you seek medical care, when those who pay for and operate our system of medical care seek medical care, they will not find one hundred drug addicts looking for free drugs and one hundred bums looking for free food, a free bed, and human contact in front of them. Those people, drug addicts, criminals, and suchlike, are still going to get subsidy, but they will go literally or metaphorically through a different door to the people who are paying.

Now even if Trumpcare passes the Senate, we still have to pass it to find out what is in it. The details are going to be filled in by regulators - regulators who are theoretically under Trump's supervision, but are in fact far more answerable to the permanent government. So we still could be screwed nine ways from Sunday.

But like Trump himself, Trumpcare offers remote possibility of success, as compared to the absolute certainty of failure.

A possible outcome of this vote, a successful outcome of this vote, is that the marginal voter, the swinging voter, gets reasonable healthcare, or at least healthcare that is less outrageously terrible, and the Democrat voter core (vagrants, drug addicts, whores, single mums, and criminals) loses out - which of course is going to mean a major swing to Trump and Republicans, and a major swing away from Democrats. Hence the widespread abject pants-wetting terror among democrat politicians.

Trumpcare protects people with pre-existing conditions, without however giving them the same insurance you get. Which may in practice mean that people who don't pay go in through the same door you do, or may not mean that. If it means that people who don't pay go in through the same door, then that means that people who pay get treated like criminals, vagrants and drug addicts, in short like Democratic party core voters, that being the vast majority of non paying people showing up at hospital. People say that the very old are costing us a bundle, that the very sick are costing us a bundle. No, it is Democratic Party core constituencies that are costing us a bundle.

Not needing to pay for healthcare and having plenty of time on your hands makes a vastly greater difference to how much healthcare you consume than being old and sick does. In short, being a Democratic core constituency is the major variable determining how much healthcare a person is going to consume.

Any system that guarantees that some morbidly obese alcoholic on the street is going to get the same standard of healthcare as an affluent middle class person is going to guarantee that that affluent middle class person is going to get very little healthcare. If Trumpcare is going to provide a reasonable standard of healthcare for the median voter, it has to deny a reasonable standard of healthcare for the modal Democratic party voter. Whether it will do so is far from clear, but it is absolutely certain that Obamacare will not provide a reasonable standard of healthcare for the median voter.

Moldbug model of communism

2017-05-08 22:21:33

The Moldbug account of communism, simplified, is that the that the Soviets were Democrat agents, a proxy force for the blue empire of the consulates against the red empire of the bases, and they were collapsed when they started to break free of the Democrats.

Simplified even further: "America is a communist country".

Of course any useful truth is necessarily a simplification. Reality is always more complex than even the best descriptions. Puritan derived leftism (progressivism) both cooperated and competed with Judaism derived leftism (Marxism) and each infiltrated and attempted to use and manipulate the other. Both engaged in entryism, and entryist agents would turn, becoming double and triple agents, creating a dense maze of camouflage and lies. Obama is a red diaper Marxist, but he is progressive, and his Marxist mother was a double agent, probably a triple agent, who like most female agents, had sex with the enemy becoming unreliable as a result.

The Czars lost intellectual sovereignty to English intellectuals. Instead of the Czar being fount of all honors, mortal and divine, which is to say instead of the Czar setting the rules for status competition, the Czars competed in a status competition with the rules set by English intellectuals with Puritan derived memes, and thus sawed of the branch on which they sat, by disempowering aristocrats and empowering leftists. The bureaucratic government was left and getting lefter, and so eventually staged a coup against the traditional and legitimate government.

While the Czar was away at the front, the bureaucracy flooded the streets with rioters and protestors, forbade the army and police from taking care of them, and then piously announced that they had to surrender to the might of the justly enraged masses, though in truth no one except brewers, distillers, Jews, and pawnshops had much to fear from the rioting masses. This coup installed Puritan derived leftism in charge of Russia, but, of course, it found itself in dangerous alliance with Judaism derived leftism, which loudly announced itself to be lefter than thou. And since no enemies to the left, no friends to the right, puritan derived leftism in Russia had disarmed itself. So in due course the leftmost faction of Judaism derived leftism was victorious, under the slogan "All power to the Soviets". Which workers soviets they immediately dismantled.

Thereafter there was alternate cooperation, competition, collaboration, and armed conflict between the blue empire of the consulates, and Soviet Russia, with cooperation and collaboration being dominant until shortly after World War II, competition and armed conflict from World War II to the Berlin airlift, and cooperation and collaboration from the Berlin Airlift till about 1980.

Russian leftism froze in place during Stalin's rule, and ceased to move leftwards, while Puritan derived anglosphere leftism continued to move leftwards. As time passed, the blue empire became increasingly pissed off because Russia, like Charles Murray, was not keeping up, was not left enough. Did not those damned Russians know it is now?

The blue empire strategy and meme had long been "Oh we must surrender to the might of the Soviets and their tremendously successful socialism", since surrendering to the distinctly right wing gun owning American masses was unattractive. This is the vision depicted in the future history of "Startreck the Next Generation" episodes produced before the fall of the Berlin Wall, but it became less attractive and less plausible because of the increasingly obvious economic failure and military weakness of socialism and because the Soviets were increasingly abandoning the claim to be lefter than thou, abandoning the claim to be the leftmost.

In the future history depicted in Startreck, reflecting the progressive wet dream, the Soviets theoretically win, but actually the permanent government of the US wins, just as in Russia, the masses theoretically won, then the Soviets theoretically won, but in fact the actual Soviets generally got shot or sent to slave labor camps while the bureaucracy that formerly answered to the Czar kept their jobs and increased their power.

When the rot set in

2017-05-15 11:55:25

Eighteenth century view was that women were sex crazy and needed to be kept under tight control or else in their feverish sexual lust they would destroy the family, and because state, society, and the church rested on the family, if you let women loose, everything would fall apart.

Nineteenth century view was that women were wonderful, and the marital contract only needed to be enforced against men, never against women, because naturally a woman would never break it unless a man forced her to do so.

And everything did fall apart.

The permanent trump crisis

2017-05-20 23:13:57

At a gut level, the Cathedral feels the Trump presidency to be illegal, unconstitutional, and improper. They simply know it is illegal, unconstitutional and improper, but cannot come up with any intelligible or coherent explanation of why - or rather any explanation that they can say out loud.

All the standard rules that you or I should apply in a conflict with Social Justice Warriors apply in a conflict between Trump and the Cathedral: They always lie, they always project, and any apology or concession will excite them to even greater rage. At the slightest sign of concession, they smell blood in the water.

They are not moving towards impeachment because they have found any exciting reasons to support the Russian narrative (Trump supposedly stole the election using the KGB). The real reason they are moving towards impeachment is that Trump bombed, and continues to bomb, Syria, that Trump appointed cuckservatives to the whitehouse staff, who promptly spread lies about him. When he did that, they smelled blood in the water.

Trump cannot appease them. They are unappeasable. He can only deter them. That is the nature of the beast.

A scorpion and a frog meet on the bank of a stream and the scorpion asks the frog to carry him across on its back. The frog asks, "How do I know you won't sting me?" The scorpion says, "Because if I do, I will die too."

The frog is satisfied, and they set out, but in midstream,the scorpion stings the frog. The frog feels the onset of paralysis and starts to sink, knowing they both will drown,but has just enough time to gasp "Why?"

Replies the scorpion: "Its my nature..."

Because the Cathedral is primarily driven by holiness competition, it is incapable of acting rationally. This is in some ways a strength. The way to win at chicken is to first drink a bottle of vodka, then at the last moment rip out the steering wheel and throw it out the window. Maybe they will succeed in impeaching Trump on the grounds of "cover up"

But it is also a weakness. The likely result is, sooner or later, to blunder into war, state to state, state level civil war, nonstate war, and likely all of the above.

The only good Muslim is a bad Muslim

2017-05-23 11:42:16

If a Muslim is not murdering innocents and raping children, he is a bad Muslim.

Over the last thirteen hundred years numerous Kingdoms, religions, cultures, empires, nations, tribes, and peoples have sought to coexist with Islam. None have succeeded. We shall not be the first.

We shall capitulate, or we will suppress and expel them.

A short while ago, some Muslims detonated some nail bombs at an English concert, targeting mostly children and young girls, killing twenty two and severely wounding many more. I guarantee that the English response will be that there is not enough affirmative action for Muslims, not enough Muslim immigration, and we are being too hard on Muslims that rape English girls, and the big important tragedy that makes this event so sad is that it undermines Muslim immigration and affirmative action for Muslims.

"Manchester will not be divided"

2017-05-25 23:29:40

Manchester's response to the terror attack is "Manchester will not be divided", meaning they will continue to embrace with open arms those that murder their children and rape their daughters.

If, however, a white male member of a college fraternity hits on a drunken slut, then they will continue to throw the book at him. Nothing divisive about that.

Also, anecdotal reports that young women in Manchester are responding to violence in the way that women are notorious for responding to violence. Hence Trump's wise and important point that they should be called losers, not monsters. Women love monsters. Looks like fresh crop of light brown fatherless babies is under way. Manchester females are not being divided from Muslim males. The attack, and Manchester's response to the attack, confirms Muslims as high status, and men who work and pay taxes as low status.

But of course, men in a society where unaccompanied girls attend a Ariana Grande-Butera concert, where unaccompanied girls go to watch prostitutes perform and the prostitutes present as high status, are low status men. Come the restoration, girls who attend such an event will not be blown up, but if they attend unsupervised by their fathers, fiancees, or husbands, will be sent to a home for wayward girls.

The problem with prostitutes is not that sex happens. The problem with prostitutes is that if a whore is high status and well paid, you are low status and low paid. Hence the epidemic of "rape" on campus, and hence the response to the Manchester terror attack. It is illegal for white males to hit on white girls, because it is illegal for white males to be high status.

The problem with an Ariana Grande-Butera concert is that a large part of the audience is unaccompanied eight year old girls, who see whores presented as sexy, successful, and empowered, and an even bigger problem is that the whores that they see really are successful and empowered. We have to stop girls from learning that stuff. Because girls do learn that stuff, men have no reason, no motive, no will, to resist Muslim conquest. Prostitutes should not be sexy, successful, and empowered. But if they are, we should make sure that other girls do not find out about it.

Women should not be allowed to get a substantially better deal by screwing around, and if some women do get a substantially better deal by screwing around, other women should be prevented from discovering it. And if you do let women discover it, your beta males, who are most of your police and soldiers, will not get their dicks wet, in which case they will not fight. And so, Manchester will not be divided. Especially the women.

The Enlightenment debunked

2017-05-27 22:17:34

The Oxford Companion to Philosophy gives us the official version of the enlightenment:
"Reason is man's central capacity."
"Beliefs are to be accepted only on the basis of reason, not on the authority of priests, sacred texts, or tradition."
"All men (including, on the view of many, women) are equal in respect of their rationality, and should thus be granted equality before the law and individual liberty."
"Man is by nature good. (Kant endorsed the Christian view of a "radical evil" in human nature, but held that it is possible to overcome it.)"
"Both an individual and humanity as a whole can progress to perfection."
"Tolerance is to be extended to other creeds, and ways of life."
"The Enlightenment devalues local "prejudices' and customs, which owe their development to historical peculiarities rather than to the exercise of reason. What matters to the Enlightenment is not whether one is French or German, but that one is an individual man, united in brotherhood with all other men by the rationality one shares with them."

Hat tip Dark Reformation[44], who inspired me to critique the enlightenment. I apologize for not giving this hat tip earlier.

The first two propositions superficially sound like a commitment to the scientific method - but somehow they have left out evidence, experiment, and observation. After dismissing religion, the Enlightenment demands adherence to three blatantly false religious beliefs, which beliefs contradict reason, experiment and observation far more blatantly than young earth creationism does.

All men are not equal, nor women equal to men, nor groups and categories of men equal to each other.

Nor is man by nature good. In the cold and morally neutral terminology of the dark enlightenment, the natural outcome is defect-defect, and avoiding this outcome, getting to cooperate-cooperate, becomes more and more difficult as the number of people that you have to deal with increases. It takes social institutions, and to deal with these ever larger scales, these institutions have to be ever more finely honed and precisely made, and are

---

[44]https://darkreformation101.wordpress.com/2016/08/18/dark-reformation-part-9-two-enlightenments/

ever more vulnerable to entropy and error.

The "progress to perfection." line is that our nature is entirely the result of environment. Just raise the self esteem of women and blacks, and everything will be lovely. This has been tried, and the outcome is far from lovely, but they just keep trying harder. The grotesquely inflated self esteem of blacks leads to blacks committing acts of violence against whites, and the grotesquely inflated self esteem of women leads to disastrous choices. They divorce the father of their children expecting to marry a six foot six athletic billionaire, or they marry late, or they do not marry at all.

The extension of tolerance is notoriously selective, and necessarily selective, for if tolerance is mandatory, freedom of association, freedom of assembly, and freedom of speech is forbidden, which is not very tolerant at all. Tolerance is not extended to the "intolerant" meaning not extended to those who prefer to cooperate with people who are cooperative, and who prefer to refrain from cooperating with those who defect. Hence the financial crisis. Official minorities and single women, and in particular minority single women, and in particular blacks, and in particular black single women, generally do not repay mortgages. Any criterion that leads to banks extending loans to people that are inclined to repay, leads to banks discriminating against minorities, single women, and especially blacks. Which is forbidden. And so the 2007-2008 financial crisis. So the enlightened tolerate Muslims blowing people up and raping infidel women, but do not tolerate whites hanging out with people who are inclined to pay their debts. That is one creed and one way of life that they are not inclined to extend tolerance to. Forbidding an ever increasing range of speech and association is necessarily intolerant. We should stick to suppressing dangerous lies and heresies that aggressively pursue political power (such as The Enlightenment). Any suppression of freedom of speech, association, and assembly that goes beyond this is excessive and damaging. Official tolerance is inherently and necessarily dangerously intolerant.

Civilization is the advance of technical and scientific knowledge, and most importantly, social organization. Most of all it is the capability to maintain cooperate/cooperate relationships in very large groups. You will notice that the enlightenment is a root and branch attack on civilization, and Rousseau explicitly framed it as an attack on civilization and intent to destroy civilization.

The devaluation of local prejudices and customs is the dismantling of Chesterton's fence, the abandonment of the slowly and painfully accumulated habits, customs, laws and institutions that make civilization possible, the devaluation and abandonment of the roots of Western Civilization. Our Cathedrals are empty and abandoned.

Fake News

2017-06-05 23:09:18

mark @markantro catches CNN staging a fake Muslim protest against terror. Hat tip Heartiste. Everyone in the reactosphere has posted this already, and I am posting it last, but I will give you a text summary of the video.

CNN positions the cameras pointing at a fake memorial of to those killed by terrorism, which "memorial" was supposedly created by the "Muslim protesters", though initially we see only CNN camera crew around the "memorial". Then they move the "Muslim protesters" into position after the fake memorial has been set up, giving them stage directions, positioning them, and posing them, in a way that makes it perfectly obvious they are actors who can be relied upon to take direction.

First the "memorial" is positioned by CNN staff who are not dressed as Muslim mothers. Then a CNN employee, not dressed as Muslim mother, holds a sign where the "Muslim mother" with the cute child is going to stand holding her sign. Then the child actor is positioned adjacent to the supposed memorial, because all the viewers will always look at the child actor first, and then, after the child actor and his supposed mother are positioned, all the other actors are positioned by the CNN movie director relative to the "memorial" and the child actor.

And then the official news starts about this heartwarming display of solidarity by Muslim mothers.

CNN says these are real protesters, not actors, despite the fact that they seen on video taking direction like competent actors.

OK. So is the "memorial" a real memorial despite the fact we saw that it had already been set up by CNN camera crew with not a "Muslim mother" in sight? If the memorial is fake, then the heartwarming mother and child are fake. The typical British Muslim is a military age male, and he is a refugee alright - taking refuge from the draft, frequently a refugee from a draft that would have conscripted him to fight a slightly different brand of Islamic terror, which draft he is dodging because he supports that other brand and does not want to fight against it.

Fact is if you are a Muslim, and you are not murdering innocents and raping children, not necessarily with your own hands, but in the sense of actively aiding and supporting those who do murder innocents and rape children, then you are a bad Muslim. And the vast majority of Muslims are at least passably good Muslims. Poster girl principle applies: If there was a significant minority of Muslims who do not support terror then CNN would not be reduced to faking it.

Islam is a warlike political movement. It is at war with us. We must conquer or surrender. And with our current leadership, surrender is starting to look not so bad.

Repeating once again: For well over a thousand years many kingdoms, nations, peoples, cultures, religions, tribes, and armed religions, have sought to coexist with Islam. None have succeeded. We will not be the first. In the end, we have to convert, or pogrom them, or they will pogrom us. Those are the choices. And surrender will not stop the pogroms, as each Muslim faction will complain that the other Muslim factions are insufficiently holy. Surrender, and we will become Bangladesh and Beirut. Surrender will cure our demographic death spiral, but will result in the decline of western science and technology, as it resulted in the decline of Indian science and technology. (The Damascus steel that so impressed the crusaders was Indian steel, created by the Aryan Indian castes, and soon Damascus steel swords became heirlooms, as the art of making them was lost.) A world without western science and technology cannot support the current world population, though China may well preserve our technology and economic system, and continue making minor improvements. Islam is the solution we do not want.

Our rulers plan to bring in four hundred million black male military age Muslims screaming for infidel blood and white pussy for their votes, to live on crime and welfare, and proceed to delude themselves about the long term consequences of this policy, which long term consequences are becoming apparent as we see supporters of Islamic terror elected to high office in London.

https://twitter.com/markantro/status/871419204846669825

That CNN finds it necessary to fake Muslim opposition to terror tells us that there is only one solution. Islam must be expelled and/or suppressed. If Muslim states of a different faction find it necessary to expel Qataris back to Qatar[45], we need to similarly expel Muslims.

If Qataris are too dangerous to Muslims of a different faction to be allowed to stay in certain Muslim lands, Muslims are too dangerous to us to be allowed to stay in Christian lands. Expelling Muslims is supposedly unthinkably wicked, but Muslims are always expelling each other, usually for obvious and excellent reasons, and no one blinks an eye. When whites were expelled from Detroit, by bands of black thugs led by community organizers closely affiliated with the Democratic party, did anyone care?

The true cost of renewable energy

2017-06-08 05:29:27

Because the cost of renewables is falsified, installation of renewables causes power crises. Renewables are installed. The cost of renewables is hidden in some other part of the system, renewables continue to be installed, that part of the system does not get increased funding, collapses, blackouts and brownouts ensue. Fixing the blackouts and brownouts costs money, the cost of electricity then rises to reflect the actual cost of renewables that no one will admit.

The cost of renewables is assessed without regard for the fact that renewables are intermittent and unpredictable. Sometimes the sun shines, some times it does not, sometimes the wind blows, sometimes it does not, sometimes it blows too hard and the windmills must shut down. This creates a burden on the grid, and the need for backup power, and this backup power and grid load is not costed or funded

So the overburdened grid shuts down, and you get blackouts, or there just is not enough power, and you get brownouts.

Eventually industry threatens to up and leave for lack of predictable power, and then, and only then, only after major threats from major industries, the additional generating capacity and grid capacity is built - and people have to pay for it. And then, and only then, the true cost of renewables becomes apparent.

Generating electricity costs very little. What is expensive is generating it when it is needed, and not when it is not needed, and transporting it from where it is generated to where it is used.

The rational way to charge for electricity would be like internet - charge by the size of the pipeline, not how much goes through it. Most of the cost of household electricity is the grid and power stations idling for times of peak demands.

---

[45]https://www.npr.org/sections/parallels/2017/06/05/531588673/diplomatic-rift-between-gulf-arab-allies-and-qatar-presents-fresh-challenges

The trouble with wind and solar is that sometimes the wind blows, and sometimes it does not, and sometimes the sun shines, and some times it does not. So it puts an unreasonable load on the grid and requires some kind other power source for times people want power, but the sun is not shining and the wind stops blowing.

If you have solar power on your roof, then when you feed excess power back into the grid it costs the power company money, because they have to have the extra grid capability to support unpredictable power being fed back into the grid at inconvenient times.

Hydroelectric is OK, provided one has a decent sized dam behind it, so that one can run water through the turbines when one needs power, and not run water through the turbines when one does not. It is the dam that is expensive, and the dam that makes hydroelectric power useful. Without a large enough dam, it is as useless and expensive as wind and solar.

If we had a cheap and effective means of storing power, then wind and solar would be great, and every household and every business would cheerfully go off grid and use solar for everything. High temperature batteries relying on molten sodium, molten salt, and beta alumina membranes are promising, but they are not yet economical in sizes small enough for household use, or even use by ordinary businesses.

The only cheap and effective means for storing power is pumped hydro. You need two large dams close together, one much higher than the other, and when the sun shines you pump water uphill, and when it is dark you run water downhill through the turbines. If you have rivers suitable for pumped hydro, then wind and solar is pretty reasonable. It is costlier than carbon and nuclear, but compared to the cost of the grid, not enough to make a huge difference.

Norway uses hydro, and hydro works fine. Austria uses hydro and pumped hydro. Portugal uses pumped hydro, and for them, wind and solar works fine. But most of the EU just does not have enough suitable dams for pumped hydro. And for them, renewable power sources are very expensive.

I took a list of EU countries that use widely varying amounts of renewable electrical power sources[46], leaving out Norway, Portugal, and Austria because of hydro and pumped hydro.

The cost of electricity in the remaining countries is, to a good approximation, proportional to the proportion that is generated renewably. Extrapolating to 100% renewable, it would cost 55 cents per kilowatt hour, extrapolating to 0% renewable, it would cost about 10 cents per kilowatt hour.

Why feminists support Islamic Rape Jihad

2017-06-11 08:50:29

Doubtless you have heard of the recent Idaho gang rape[47].

This was Islamic Rape Jihad, not just Muslim rapists, because the girl was five, because the boys put it on video, because the boys expected the support of their community, and

---

[46] https://ec.europa.eu/eurostat/tgm/table.do?tab=table&init=1&language=en&pcode=tsdcc330&plugin=1

[47] https://duckduckgo.com/?q=Idaho+girl+five+assault+Muslim+migrants

because the boys *received* the support of their community.

Feminist response to this rape shows what feminists really want. Everyone reacting to this in an indignant manner is a male who is in favor of patriarchy to a greater or lesser extent, and many of them want to completely reverse female emancipation.

In the ancestral environment, and indeed today's environment, if a woman was property the way a cow is property, she was likely to have substantially greater reproductive success than a free woman. If a man was property the way a cow is property, likely to have zero reproductive success.

In the ancestral environment, as today, male slaves don't reproduce. Female slaves generally outreproduce free women. Thus the optimal strategy for a woman is to provoke until provocation results in enslavement.

The evolutionary optimal strategy for a female, in the ancestral environment, and in our present day environment, is to act in ways that gets the west conquered by Islamic State. If free, likely to have 1.5 children, and similarly her grandchildren, rapidly resulting in the total disappearance of her genes. If her menfolk are conquered and she is sold naked in chains on the auction block by Islamic state, likely to have six or seven children.

Optimal reproductive strategy for a woman is to be captured by a man who owns her much as he owns a cow and can do anything to her he could do to a cow. The optimal reproductive strategy for her owner is to treat her considerably better than he treats his cows, but the less he has power to do bad things to her, the more it is in his interests to do bad things to her. For a free woman, the stable strategy is defect/defect, for the woman to defect by serial monogamy, for the woman to spend her hottest and most fertile years continually trying to trade up to a higher status male or better place on some other male's booty call list, and for a male to defect by keeping as many women as possible on his booty call list, to spin as many plates as possible, without investing in any of them. For a slave, because the slave cannot defect, because the slave is guaranteed to play cooperate, cooperate is also a good move for the male owner of a female slave, because he has a biological interest in the welfare of her children. He is free to impose cooperate/defect on her, but that is not actually all that much in his biological interest, which biological interest manifests in the tendency of men to love and care for women that they regularly have sex with, provided that they believe those women are not having sex with other men.

Feminist demands for emancipation ever escalate, no matter how extraordinary the privilege women are granted, because they are pushing for someone strong enough to master them. In the ancestral environment, free women were unsuccessful at reproducing, because prisoner's dilemma. That she can defect on a man guarantees defect/defect, guarantees that he will try to defect before she does - giving her no care, protection, or support, keeping as many plates spinning as he can, so they look for someone powerful enough to stop them from defecting. Slave women will generally outreproduce free women, because he who owns a woman absolutely has incentive to invest in her and her children. Similarly, cows are numerous, their wild ancestors are generally extinct. If animal liberationists liberate chickens and cows, there are not going to be very many chickens or cows. If the People's Popular Committee for Food Abundance tells the farmer he does not own his land and his crops, there is going to be crop failure.

And feminists, in supporting Rape Jihad, are unconsciously pursuing their optimal evolutionary reproductive strategy, which is to be sold by Islamic state naked in chains on the auction block. We are descended from free men and unfree women. Peoples, nations religions, cultures and groups with strong, proud, free, and independent women died out. They always die out.

Female emancipation is a shit test that we failed. Feminists support Rape Jihad because they are unconsciously looking for men who will pass their shit test.

Why female status limits fertility

2017-06-12 00:13:36

Men want to have sex with as many women as possible, and give them no support.

Women want to have sex with the highest status men available (as women perceive status, which is similar to the way a small evil child raised by cannibal head hunters perceives status), and be supported by men.

A prisoner's dilemma problem, the war of the sexes, ensues.

If both freely pursue their interests, we get a defect/defect equilibrium, where a small minority of men have casual no strings attached sex with the large majority of women, and a these women sleep with only one man at a time, but sleep with one man after another, trading partners in an unending struggle to get a better male, or get a better position on his booty call list. This bad female behavior is exacerbated by the male tendency to give the newest woman the highest position on his boot call list. Women get the sex they want until they approach the end of their fertile years, but children don't get fathers. Since producing fatherless children places a large burden on women, most women do not have children until used up on the cock carousel and approaching the end of their fertile years.

To enforce a cooperate cooperate equilibrium, mating choice has to restricted, denying men access to women, and women access to men. In order that men have the incentive and the power to restrict female sexual choice women have to be owned by men. Men and women have to be stuck with each other. Men need to own women, except that they cannot sell, rent out, abandon, or give away a well behaved woman that they have had sex with.

Iterated prisoner's dilemma has a good solution if the number of iterations is large and has no definite end, but this is not the case with mating behavior, because a woman's fertile years are short. The progressive scenario where woman sleep with one man after another until they find "the one" and then live happily ever after is prisoner's dilemma with a large and indefinite number of iterations resulting in cooperate/cooperate, but the actual outcome is that they sleep with one man after another until they start to get desperate.

Rollo Tomassi, in his excellent book "The Rational Male[48]", starts out by criticizing "oneitis" – criticizing male disinclination to defect. If you defect on women harder and faster than they defect on you, women will defect on you less, not more. It is a successful and effective male adaptation to female emancipation. It works. He also criticizes mate guarding, because ineffective mate guarding is counterproductive, and effective mate guarding is illegal. Hard to do effective mate guarding without substantial social

---

[48]https://www.amazon.com/gp/product/1492777862

support - which certain religious communities have, but most of us do not. That effective mate guarding is difficult and illegal is extremely distressing to males.

Roman Catholic Church cuckolded.

2017-06-13 03:25:54

I had thought the Philippines was the last place on earth where the Roman Catholic Church was not thoroughly cucked. Now it is cucked there also[49].

Muslims in the Philippines have been pissed at Christians ever since the Spanish conquered the place and imposed Roman Catholicism with fire and steel. And not very long ago, the Roman Catholic priesthood in Mindanao was mighty comfortable with fire and steel.

The Muslims in Mindanao in the Philippines think the crusades happened yesterday, and are at it again, attempting to seize the traditionally Muslim city of Marawi from Christians, killing priests and Christian teachers, burning their homes, churches, the usual. In response, President Duterte declares martial law and applies heavy weapons. And the Church seems to be more worried that martial law might lead to "human rights violations" than terror directed at Christians.

I am perfectly sure President Duterte will violate "human rights" all over the place. When I was in Davao, he was always violating the human rights of small time crooks and big time corrupt officials, and everyone loved him for it. I loved him for it. I would love to see Trump similarly violating the human rights of our federal bureaucracy.

According to the Roman Catholic priesthood of Mindanao, terrorism "is totally against the tenets of any religion of peace. Especially so when terrorism is perpetrated while our Muslim brothers and sisters are preparing for the holy month of Ramadhan. Terrorism distorts and falsifies the true meaning of any religion."

You will notice there are no Muslim clerics in Mindanao saying that this terrorism is against the tenets of their religion

because it is not.

The bitcoin crisis

2017-06-29 03:28:53

There can only be one.

There can only be one money, at the root of all others. Money is a measure of value, a store of value, and a medium of exchange, and you want to uses the same medium of exchange and measure of value as everyone else.

At the very beginning, I said the trouble with bitcoin, as originally designed, is that it does not scale. Everyone, to be a peer, to be an equal participant, has to store and process everyone else's transactions, thus the cost of each transaction increases with the number of peers. I estimate the current cost of a transaction to be about a thousand dollars, most of which is carried by people speculating in bitcoin, hoping that as the USG empire collapses, bitcoin, rather than gold, will replace the dollar.

---

[49]https://www.southcotabato.org/2017/05/mindanao-catholic-bishops-issues.html

Bitcoin is reaching, indeed has substantially exceeded, its inherent limits. For it to become the one, it has to get away from a system where everyone processes everyone's transactions, and stores everyone's transactions.

The sidechain proposal is a way of getting away from that without a hard fork, so that your transactions are not seen by everyone, merely by enough people, and not stored by everyone forever, but only by a very small number of people forever.

Altcoins are hard fork proposals, which if they fix the scaling problem could become the one. At present the total value of altcoins is roughly equal to the total value of bitcoins.

At present, the true cost of bitcoin transactions is so outrageously high it cannot possibly become the one. It must die, and everyone invested in bitcoins will lose all their money, unless the sidechain proposal provides a forkless path to a world in which the true cost of bitcoin transactions is reduced to something reasonable.

But the interest in crypto currencies is so very great, the amount of money invested in crypto currencies is so very great, that one shall succeed. The amount of serious money invested is so very great that it looks overwhelmingly likely that as the USG empire falls, crypto currency, rather than gold, will replace the US$.

And that one shall be one that allows low, rather than hidden, transaction costs. Likely an altcoin rather than bitcoin, because the weight of special interests in bitcoin makes it hard to get to there from here.

But the wise investor should invest in gold, should invest in bitcoin in the hope that the scaling problems can be fixed without a hard fork, and should invest in an altcoin that has solved the scaling problem. And the last time I took a good look, none of them had actually solved the scaling problem, though many of them were hoping to solve it, claiming they had solved it, or had plans for eventually solving it.

The sidechain proposal has been kicked around for three years, and bitcoin's transaction cost has been getting rapidly worse all this time.

Anyone who invests in bitcoin, is investing hoping that scaling can be fixed, for if scaling is not fixed, bitcoin will surely die. The current true cost of bitcoin transactions is absolutely unsustainable.

Not the Zionist Occupation government

2017-06-30 03:37:30

The presidency grows ever more powerful, becoming more and more a total regime, dominating and effectively replacing every other level of government except the federal judiciary. Every school board, every local police shop, answers to the feds, not to local authority, and the power of the presidency aggressively extends into every business, every home, and every family. At the same time the merely elected government, including the mere president, are fading away to shadows conducting empty rituals, like the Queen of England proceeding in a stagecoach to open Parliament.

I had hoped for and predicted a Trump coup, in which Trump seizes control of the presidency. I still have hopes, but I predicted the coup would happen by now, and it has not happened yet. Rather, a reverse coup threatens, in which the special counsel indicts Trump of obstruction of justice on the grounds that his statements about Russia rigging the American elections in Trump's favor are supposedly untrue, inconsistent, etc, and then the special counsel has men uniformed as cops make Trump do the perp walk, thus effectively impeaching Trump in place of an the archaic and obsolete procedure of a two thirds Senate vote. Of course, such coup by the permanent government against the merely temporary government has a significant risk that the secret service or the army might interfere, answering a coup with a counter coup. CNN is one of the voices of the permanent government, one of many loudspeakers connected to one microphone, and the recent firing of some CNN reporters indicates the permanent government is retreating from a coup.

The permanent government, or some in the permanent government, have been walking away from the increasingly improbable impeachment by two thirds senate vote and have been prepping for impeachment by special counsel. The firing indicates that they have been told by others in the permanent government to cut the special counsel option out. Retreat, once started, is hard to stop, hard to keep under control, tends to get out of hand. So I still have high hopes, but I have already been wrong on this topic.

Which brings me to the topic of this post. *Who are the permanent government*? Are they the permanent government of Israel.

On this topic, I have information from a well placed Jewish member of the American permanent government. When Jews from Israel's permanent government talk to members of the US permanent government, they say "May I kiss your ass sir?". When told to jump through hoops, and with great regularity and harsh and casual abruptness, they are told to jump through hoops, they ask "How high should the hoop be and should it be on fire?"

The American permanent government is disproportionately Jewish, and the Jewish members of the permanent government do not identify as white in their own minds. But they definitely do not identify as Israelis.

When we purge the universities, the civil service, and the judiciary of progressives, there will be a lot of Jews taking a swim in the pacific. There is going to be a lot of disparate impact. But the their equivalents in Israel are not going to miss them one little bit.

If we were to purge the genes, rather than the memes, if we were to gas the Jews, rather than drown the heretics, we would be goring the matador's cape and would miss the matador.

That said, there is a disturbing visceral hostility to whites and white civilization in the US permanent government, which is particularly noticeable in Global Warming "science" and in "environmentalism". Even if it were true that Global Warming is happening and is exactly what official science said that it is, the Paris treaty was not to stop global warming, but to punish whites in general and Americans in particular.

Remember Angela Merkel shrinking from the German flag, like a vampire from the cross. That is very much the attitude of many in the government to any science or technology that invovles getting your hands dirty. Except it is grandfathered in, it tends to be deemed self evidently illegal and immoral.

Jews have made many important contributions to science, and we would be poorer and less powerful without them, but to technology and applied science, not so much. Like the classic Greeks they theorize without getting their own hands dirty. For this reason I am inclined to doubt the Jewish nuclear force. Feynman made a big contribution to the Manhattan project, but he never actually laid hands on an actual piece of plutonium. The kind of person who could actually build successful nuclear weapons, rather than merely theorize about them, would insist on actually testing them. That Israel has not tested any nukes inclines me to doubt it has the kind of people who could successfully build them.

There is deep and wide hostility in the government to technological civilization, to commercial application of technology, to technology applied and developed to create wealth and power, to what makes white civilization powerful and importantly different from past civilizations. Not all Jews are hostile to technological civilization, Feynman certainly was not, and not everyone hostile to technological civilization is Jewish, but it is a disproportionately Jewish characteristic. Not all Jews are like that, but that is the way to bet. Blacks will tell us "You did not build that" and tell us "we wuz Kangs" and whites stole all our stuff from them, and history taught at our best universities tells us they were Kangs and we stole all our stuff from them, but Jews, unlike blacks, will condescend that actually building stuff is for menials and inferiors. Blacks would like to be capable of techno-commercial civilization, but are not. Jews sneer and condescend at techno-commercial civilization. Which is irritating, but not usefully addressed by gassing them.

Not a dog barked

2017-07-04 13:38:40

Remember all those mighty and entirely spontaneous protests demanding that the Obama regime do what it quite obviously wanted to do and was quite obviously looking for justifications for doing, protests demanding that the government block every form of energy production in every white country, which obstructions have made the US into an energy importer for sixty years or so.

And, of course, with deep reluctance the Obama regime would invariably yield to the justified and entirely spontaneous and genuine rage of the mighty masses.

Overnight (well, over the first one hundred and fifty days of the Trump regime), the US has become an energy exporter. Trump would repeal a regulation by executive order, and the next day coal miners would be digging coal, repeal another regulation, and the next day drillers would be pumping oil. One day he makes an executive order, the next day Americans in flyover country are back to work. The next day after that he makes another executive order, and the day after that, more Americans in flyover country are back to work.

You did not hear of this.

Probably because the mighty and justifiable enraged masses strangely failed to spontaneously show up to spontaneously demonstrate their might and spontaneous justified rage. They were always demanding that Obama shut down energy, but somehow, when Trump turns the energy policy of every previous Democratic and cuckservative president for the last sixty years arse over tit, no protests happen.

Funny thing that.

By the way did you know that there is overwhelming support for impeaching Trump? It must be true, I read it in the newspapers.

Leftism has been a mass movement under both Democratic and cuckservative presidents, been a mass movement since nineteen sixty three. But Donald Trump gets elected, and suddenly and quietly it just is not a mass movement any more. Funny thing that.

Yes, the permanent government is giving Trump a hard time. Trump has not won yet, and maybe the permanent government will win. We are, or recently were, right on the edge of the special counsel impeaching Trump without bothering with that old fashioned two thirds vote in the senate. But Trump has cut off the permanent government at the knees, in that the mighty and justifiably enraged masses are no longer spontaneously demanding whatever the permanent government wants them to spontaneously demand this morning and no longer spontaneously enraged about whatever the permanent government wants them to be spontaneously enrage about this morning.

Reagan talked about defunding the left, Trump has actually made a start on defunding the left. Obviously there is a lot more defunding to be done, but suddenly leftists that do not yet have social justice warrior jobs are no longer expecting that they will get social justice warrior jobs in the very near future as a quid pro quo for the latest protest. That funding for the left has stopped its endless and open ended increase and has actually decreased, even if only by a little, has resulted in leftism as a mass movement vanishing in a puff of smoke.

This has resulted in an intense search for other sources of social justice warrior funding. Thus for example, we see complaints that venture capitalists that control large amounts of other people's money should be subject to destruction at whim without evidence by social justice warriors. Cheryl tell us[50]: "This is where it has to be fixed – the fact the burden of proof always falls on the person reporting the incident."

"Fixing" this, of course, will have the effect that Silicon Valley venture capital will wind up funding social justice, rather than technical advance, which we already see happening with Uber, Airbnb, and Apple. Uber and Airbnb are committing social justice suicide. Apple has such deep pockets that it will likely survive, but probably not Airbnb and Uber.

Airbnb is trying to prevent Filipinos and Chinese from being racist. Would have more success preventing water from being wet.

Their power base in Silicon valley derives from appointments made by the Obama regime. Thus for example Cheryl, who is currently shaking down the management of Silicon Valley venture capital firms with sexual harassment allegations for which there is a curious lack of evidence, worked for a Malaysian startup fund funded by the Obama administration and the Malaysian govt. Not a tech person, not a startup person, a political commissar. In the course of accusing a venture capitalist of inappropriate sexual behavior, she depicted herself as engaging in behavior that I find entirely inappropriate in a woman - for example this evil venture capitalist somehow caused her to be alone with him, and, while alone with him in a private flat with a nice bed, somehow caused her to consume very large amounts of scotch. Pretty sure that if sex did not ensue, it is because he fought her off.

---

[50]https://cherylyeoh.com/2017/07/03/shedding-light-on-the-black-box-of-inappropriateness/

for family, for freedom, for country, and for God
2017-07-08 06:58:20

Trump's speech contains some alt right memes, but its approach is not a frontal attack on the enlightenment and enlightenment values, but rather to praise and endorse those values in ways that re-interpret them as anti enlightenment values. It is a dog whistle rather than a shout out, but it is a dog whistle not only to the alt right, but to that part of the alt right that does not want to merely roll things back to nineteen sixty (men's rights movement) nor to nineteen thirty (ironic and unironic nazis) but back all the way to undoing the enlightenment.

Much as Pope Francis piously reinterprets Christianity as celebrating sodomy, abortion, divorce, single motherhood, transvestism, and the destruction of marriage, Trump piously reinterprets progressivism as the victory of distinctively white civilization

At 29:00 in the speech:

> Our adversaries, however, are doomed because we will never forget who we are. And if we don't forget who are, we just can't be beaten. Americans will never forget. The nations of Europe will never forget. We are the fastest and the greatest community. There is nothing like our community of nations. The world has never known anything like our community of nations.
>
> We write symphonies. We pursue innovation. We celebrate our ancient heroes, embrace our timeless traditions and customs, and always seek to explore and discover brand-new frontiers.
>
> We reward brilliance. We strive for excellence, and cherish inspiring works of art that honor God. We treasure the rule of law and protect the right to free speech and free expression.
>
> We empower women as pillars of our society and of our success. We put faith and family, not government and bureaucracy, at the center of our lives. And we debate everything. We challenge everything. We seek to know everything so that we can better know ourselves.
>
> And above all, we value the dignity of every human life, protect the rights of every person, and share the hope of every soul to live in freedom. That is who we are. Those are the priceless ties that bind us together as nations, as allies, and as a civilization.

Much of it sounds like boilerplate progressivism, except that he naughtily included the distinctively white art form of symphonies, the distinctively white activity of innovation and exploration, and naughtily left out that all men are created equal, and that women are equal to me.

When Trump is attacking radical Islam and somehow leaves out explicitly mentioning female equality, not an accident, but rather a significant step towards rolling back several centuries of the "moral arc of history bending towards justice". Perhaps in the end the progressive steamroller will roll over him as it rolled over Reagan, but he is having a go.

He also said we debate everything, which was a progressive value before they were in power, but swiftly ceased to be a progressive value once they were in power. Free debate is always what the out of power belief system wants, since the out of power belief system is always forbidden from doubting, let alone contradicting, the official belief system. Everyone always wants freedom of speech, freedom of association, and the right to peaceably assemble for themselves, not for their enemies, and it is always the out of power belief system that is denied these things. In practice, you are not only forbidden from doubting that women are equal to men, you are even forbidden from doubting that saturated fats are bad for you, in that researchers who inquire into this topic lose their jobs. Freedom of speech, freedom of association, and freedom of assembly is always the call of the out of power faction.

When those who theoretically believe in equality will not go into a black majority area, nor accept that when when women, like children, make bad choices those who make the choices should face the costs of those choices, we see the actual truth about equality.

At 11:00 into the speech:

> For two centuries, Poland suffered constant and brutal attacks. But while Poland could be invaded and occupied, and its borders even erased from the map, it could never be erased from history or from your hearts. In those dark days, you have lost your land but you never lost your pride. (Applause.)
> So it is with true admiration that I can say today, that from the farms and villages of your countryside to the cathedrals and squares of your great cities, Poland lives, Poland prospers, and Poland prevails. (Applause.)
> Despite every effort to transform you, oppress you, or destroy you, you endured and overcame.

15:00

> The story of Poland is the story of a people who have never lost hope, who have never been broken, and who have never, ever forgotten who they are. (Applause)
> AUDIENCE: Donald Trump! Donald Trump! Donald Trump!

15:50 precisely equal billing for commies and nazis.

> In 1920, in the Miracle of Vistula, Poland stopped the Soviet army bent on European conquest. (Applause.) Then, 19 years later in 1939, you were invaded yet again, this time by Nazi Germany from the west and the Soviet Union from the east. That's trouble. That's tough.
> Under a double occupation the Polish people endured evils beyond description: the Katyn forest massacre,

> In the summer of 1944, the Nazi and Soviet armies were preparing for a terrible and bloody battle right here in Warsaw. Amid that hell on earth, the citizens of Poland rose up to defend their homeland. I am deeply honored to be joined on stage today by veterans and heroes of the Warsaw Uprising. (Applause.)
> AUDIENCE: (Chanting.)

Notice the conspicuous lack of extra billing and extra star treatment for the Warsaw Ghetto uprising, and that Trump accurately depicts the Warsaw uprising as directed as much to prevent Soviet occupation as to defeat German occupation, billing the Soviets as occupiers, not liberators.

The priesthood of the religion of Holocaustism were mightily pissed that he attended the Warsaw Uprising Memorial, but not the Warsaw Ghetto Uprising Memorial. That Trump is obviously philosemitic makes it possible for him to regularly and routinely piss on Holocaustianity.

Then he links the globohomo project to abolish nations, masculinity, and Christianity to defeated communism and the future defeat of Islam:

27:10

Finally, on both sides of the Atlantic, our citizens are confronted by yet another danger one firmly within our control. This danger is invisible to some but familiar to the Poles: the steady creep of government bureaucracy that drains the vitality and wealth of the people. The West became great not because of paperwork and regulations but because people were allowed to chase their dreams and pursue their destinies.

Americans, Poles, and the nations of Europe value individual freedom and sovereignty. We must work together to confront forces, whether they come from inside or out, from the South or the East, that threaten over time to undermine these values and to erase the bonds of culture, faith and tradition that make us who we are. (Applause.) If left unchecked, these forces will undermine our courage, sap our spirit, and weaken our will to defend ourselves and our societies.

41:00

I declare today for the world to hear that the West will never, ever be broken. Our values will prevail. Our people will thrive. And our civilization will triumph. (Applause.)

AUDIENCE: Donald Trump! Donald Trump! Donald Trump!

PRESIDENT TRUMP: Thank you. So, together, let us all fight like the Poles for family, for freedom, for country, and for God.

Thank you. God Bless You. God bless the Polish people. God bless our allies. And God bless the United States of America.

Thank you. God bless you. Thank you very much. (Applause.)

Pushing back on social justice warriors.

2017-07-11 02:57:05

Remember how Github went social justice?

Well elections have consequences[51]

---

[51] https://where.coraline.codes/blog/my-year-at-github/

"Coraline", an autogynophilic male to female transexual, competent programmer, and political commissar, recently got purged from Github by the mandarinate.

Mandarins are priests, and Social Justice Warriors are priests, but social Justice Warriors are primarily into runaway extreme holier than thou holiness, while mandarins are more into politely conforming to the official religion and emitting all the right social signals. Thus the holiness spiral with mandarins tends to be , while the holiness spiral with social justice warriors rolls a lot faster, tending to be

"Coraline" claims to be a good programmer by the objective standard of high lines of code contributed, high bugs fixed, high features added, low bugs caused. This is plausible because autogynophiles tend to be good programmers, combining the male propensity for strong and rigid logic, with the female propensity for conformity, obedience, and rule following. Effeminate gay male to female transexuals, on the other hand, combine the female incapacity to do logic, with an extreme form of the male propensity to break the rules and defy authority, showing up for work infrequently, late, and stoned.

But "Coraline" was not hired as a good engineer, but as a social justice warrior that other engineers could respect and take seriously, as a political commissar that could understand what the engineers were actually doing. It was hired by its female non engineer boss, to impose social justice on its fellow engineers.

In restrospect, should have stuck to engineering, for women will never perceive a male to female transexual as genuinely female, and thus, never perceive it as genuinely deserving of their own immensely high social status, thus always in their hearts perceive it as a low status male (redundant, I know, because males are always and automatically low status - observe how the guy in the corner office gets interrupted by his female staff and does not get laid) thus denying it the power and authority that a political commissar needs to be effective, needs to do its political job.

If you want to check to see whether your company's organization chart corresponds to actual status, pay no attention to mere words, but rather watch who interrupts whom, who speaks over whom. Chances are the women speak over and interrupt their merely male boss. The words of the interruption are invariably courteous, helpful, respectful, friendly, and polite, but the fact that it is an interruption is the opposite of courteous, the opposite of helpful, is disrespectful, unfriendly, hostile, hateful, and impolite. It is a shit test. Fertile age women cannot help shit testing men, just as men cannot help looking at a woman's boobs. And if she gets away with interrupting and speaking over your boss, he failed the shit test, no matter how superficially friendly, respectful, and polite the words of her interruption are. Conversely, if he regularly and routinely passes her shit tests, she will probably fuck him, no matter how old, bald, fat, and married he is. No action of his, no matter how gross, will ever constitute sexual harrassment.

Yes, if you are a boss who regularly and routinely passes their inevitable shit tests "you can do anything, you can grab them by the pussy."

"Coraline" was working as an engineer, and was successful as an engineer, and appreciated for its engineering, when Github recruited it as a political commissar:
> They wanted to offer me a job. They had just created a team called Community & Safety, charged with making GitHub more safe for marginalized people

Danger Will Robinson!

Its team was one normal male, two male to female transexuals, two colored women, and a normal female manager. Thus, three real engineers, all low status, and three fake engineers, all high status. And it is a real engineer, and a good one. Danger Will Robinson!

"Coraline" found itself socially isolated at Github. Danger Will Robertson!
> This was the first instance of what came to be referred to as my "non-empathetic communication style".

"Coraline" was talking about social justice issues in the direct, logical, unemotional, and factual style of a male, rather than in the socially required female style. The mandarinate found this low class, which is to say masculine, and did not like it. Danger Will Robinson!
> when I joined the video call with my manager, it became clear that something was wrong. She went back to the issue of my lack of empathy in communications and collaboration.

"Coraline" was claiming status as a very holy social justice warrior that the mandarinate was reluctant to grant to a white male - and women will always see an autogynophile as a male, no matter what delusions the autogynophile harbors. So all the high status people on his team were reluctant to accept his holiness status, and incapable of perceiving his competent engineer status.
So, perceiving his attempt at female status had failed, he attempts to kill himself and is involuntarily committed to a mental hospital.[52]

It is not people like me who keep using the wrong pronouns who drive people like "Coraline" to suicide. It is people like his manager, who no matter what pronouns they use, keep acting as if they perceive him as what he is - a man wearing a dress who has cut his dick off and grown boobs. The Opalgate incident, when lots of people piled on him calling him a man in a dress, did not make him in the least suicidal. It was the bad review by his boss, which review effectively amounted to "I can still sense the masculinity in your communication style" that caused his suicide attempt.

When the politically correct say "empathic" they actually mean feminine. If his female boss had actually been empathic, would not have driven him to suicide. They wanted someone who was a competent engineer, but who could also pass as a female social justice warrior, not just in carefully posed still photographs, but interactively. And that is not what they got. Indeed, it is never what they get.

He irreversibly mutilated himself to elevate his status to that of a woman, and his status did not in fact rise. Hence, suicide. Calling him a man in a dress did not adversely affect his perception of his own status, because he perceived those using the wrong pronoun as low status. But he perceived the women in his group as high status, they perceived him as a mere male, no matter what pronoun they used, thus, suicide.

> In the past several months GitHub has fired at least three transgender engineers

He was fired for being interactively unconvincing as a woman.
> and many more cisgender women.

---

[52]https://twitter.com/CoralineAda/status/856929039193317376

With Trump in power, less need to pretend women are engineerettes.
> Prominent people who were trying to effect positive change in the company culture have quit.

Social Justice Warriors have quit, perhaps one step ahead of being fired.
> ... In a return to its meritocratic roots, the company has decided to move forward with a merit-based stock option program despite criticism from employees who tried to point out its inherent unfairness.

That merit is inherently "unfair" is an implicit admission that women are inferior at activites in the male sphere and coloreds are just inferior.
> And the widely publicized results of the open source survey show that the company's platform is still not appealing to anyone but straight white guys.

The company's platform is quite appealing to autogynophilic male to female transsexuals, who are heavily overrepresented. And the rest cannot code. Ability to code is a pre-requisite for actually finding the company's platform useful.

Holocaustianity

2017-07-13 12:25:47

The holocaust is real, in that midway through the war, the Nazis decided to kill every Jew, and made a good start on doing so. The holocaust is fake, in that a pile of myths have been manufactured around it to deceive people about the nature and motivation of the crime.

The point and purpose of the mythmaking is not to exaggerate the crime, but to make the crime as different as possible from the communist mass murders (which probably killed more Jews even though they did not consciously intend to target Jews) and in particular and especially to deny the role of envy and covetousness.

Jews, like kulaks, were murdered because people broke the tenth commandment, the commandment against coveting that which belongs to someone else. If Jews spent one percent as much energy on the tenth commandment as they spend on the prohibition against eating a goat boiled in its mother's milk, it would be a fairly healthy and sane religion. But instead Jews seem stubbornly suicidal, as for example in their firm support for the Islamization of Europe even as Muslims run them out of Europe, and in their hostility to the crusades, then and now.

The death camp of which we have the most reliable knowledge is Majdanek, which was overrun early while still in operation before the Germans gave any thought to concealing their crimes. Majdanek did not have gas chambers - the alleged gas chambers are delousing chambers, for the "gas chambers" lack doors that can be locked against those inside, and have genuine baths and showers for actually washing people and getting them clean. Poster girl principle: If no gas chambers at Majdanek, no gas chambers anywhere. In this sense, the holocaust as conventionally depicted is a myth. However, it is also clear that everyone sent to Majdanek died quickly - not from gas, but from overwork, lack of food, exposure to the elements, and disease - much as in the communist democides. The only survivors were those that had not been there very long. In this sense, the holocaust is very real.

Estimates of the death toll at Majdanek have varied enormously, by a factor of fifty, which inclines me to doubt all such estimates. One lie, all lies. But it is clear that if people were sent to Majdanek, they died fairly quickly, from which we may conclude that if people were sent to any such camps, they usually died fairly quickly. From which we may conclude that when the Germans rendered an area free from Jews, those Jews were sent to their deaths. The German internal documents show that the Germans had no intention of feeding them enough to keep them alive, and expected them to be dead fairly soon, and the evidence from Majdanek shows that is indeed what happened. Irrespective of whether it was exactly six million Jews, it was every Jew that the Germans managed to get their hands on.

Initially the plan was to deport them all, preferably to Israel. When this plan was frustrated by the allies, the Germans consciously adopted a plan of killing them all.

OK, no gas chambers, but the Jews still wound up dead. Which brings me to the diary of Ann Frank, which like the gas chambers is fake but true. It is clear that the diary of Ann Frank is a forgery, in that it was not written by Ann Frank. It is clear that the story of Ann Frank is not a forgery, in that Ann Frank lived and was murdered much as depicted.

Of all the Jews murdered by the Nazis, the Jew to be specially humanized just happens to be single, female, and did not have major possessions to confiscate. So that her murder is pure discrimination, and absolutely nothing to do with envy and covetousness. The choice of Anne Frank as poster girl rather than someone more typical profoundly and dangerously misleads us about the nature and causes of mass murder.

Undue focus on the deaths of six million Jews, when communism murdered a hundred and sixty million, is unfair and is driving us insane, driving us towards the murder of billions, for it is not discrimination that kills, but covetousness, wanting what is someone else's, and the Diary of Ann Frank is inexorably linked to a narrative justifying and endorsing envy and covetousness, a narrative that white males do not deserve their stuff but somehow grabbed it before single women and people of color could, that husbands and fathers should be expelled from their homes and separated from their children, that those who work and pay taxes are the real welfare queens whose resistance to demands that they lose their undeserved privilege is racism and sexism.

Killing Jews and taking their stuff is a really bad idea, and even ejecting them to Israel and taking their stuff is also a really bad idea, because taking their stuff means that it will be ruined rather than sold to someone competent to use it productively. A desire to take their stuff reveals a motivation of envy and covetousness. The Nazis murdered a lot of Jews, not necessarily six million, but something like six million, though probably not by means of gas chambers.

But they did so for the same reasons that the communists murdered vastly more people, and considerably more Jews. *They did so out of envy and covetousness.* Holocaustianity is a religion that the real sin is "racism", from which it follows that one group having more nice things than another group is evidence of a crime. Stronger and stronger methods are then applied to correct this crime, but strangely, nothing will correct it except murdering all those wicked people whose wickedness is proven by their continued possession of nice things. The murderers do not start out intending mass murder. They expect that after correcting this regrettable injustice, everyone will happily be brothers, but they get frustrated when this terrible injustice proves strangely difficult to correct.

The same dynamic will likely play out in Israel. If progressivism rather than Judaism continues to be the state religion of Israel, Israel will likely finish doing to Ashkenazim Jews what Germany began doing. For Ashkenazim to survive, they have to re-activate the tenth commandment, and to re-activate the tenth commandment, they have to let go of Holocaustianity, which needs to recede to its proper place in history, one rather small mass murder among the many enormous mass murders of the twentieth century.

Nazis are virgins

2017-07-18 12:26:22

I am not disowning my fellow alt rightists who happen to be nazis. I am inviting them to become better friends and allies than they already are by discarding their blue pill illusions about women - by becoming even more evil than they already are.

Progs tell me that Andrew Anglin is the leading force for Nazism in the America, and have forced him to flee to Nigeria, where the locals do not see anything odd, evil, surprising, or unusual, about a white advocating for the interests of whites, or the interests of those whites ethnically similar to himself. Doesn't everyone do that? Nigerians are too busy hating Nigerians who are a different breed of black to themselves to worry about whites.

My problem with Andrew Angelin is that if he is the leading force, progs don't have much to worry about. This a man who thinks that twelve year old girls would be pure and chaste if it was not for evil males preying upon them.

He tells us that the problems we have with women are due to evil Jewish mind rays[53]. If it was not for those damned Jews, women would never give us such tough shit tests. This is the sort of thinking that led to Hitler having only moderate success in raising the German birthrate.

The trouble with Nazis is that they leftists stuck in the 1930s, while the rest of the left has moved even further left. And the left was mighty bluepilled back in the 1930s.

---

[53]https://theendofzion.com/feminism-a-jewish-war-on-femininity/

His truly impressive loli collection suggests to me a man who does not score a whole lot of real life women, though I would guess he does considerably better than Scott Alexander. **[Edit. Photo is fake.

I still say is beliefs about women indicate he has not a whole lot of contact with women, albeit more than the typical male progressive, in that he is on the 1930s blue pill while progressives are on the 2017 blue pill.]***

There is a man in urgent need of the red pill.

The trouble with blaming everything on Jews is not that it is unkind to Jews. Unkind to Jews is not my problem. I will let Jews worry about that. The problem with blaming everything on Jews is that it leads to the conclusion that 1930s leftism, leftism before we let the Jews into the left wing club, was just fine. And Andrew Anglin's truly impressive loli collection is where that thinking gets you.

In fact, things started going bad early in the nineteenth century[54], when frothing at the mouth biting mad feminism gave us a marriage contract that was enforced on men, but not on women, resulting in the collapse of the family.

And, shortly after that, white man's burden, with the corresponding attacks on unit cohesion and military discipline, with the result that inferior races started to defeat whites in 1841, and have been defeating us militarily worse and worse ever since.

That is when things went to hell - when marriage was successfully attacked by those holier than thou, when our military was successfully attacked by those holier than thou.

---

[54]https://blog.reaction.la/culture/when-the-rot-set-in

Rolling things back to the 1930s is not going to help. We need to roll things back to the 1730s.

Yes, Jews have always been subversive, and they were subversive back in the 1730s also. But I am pretty sure it was not Jews that caused everything except science to turn to shit in the nineteenth century, and it was not Jews that caused science to turn to shit in the twentieth. What happened to science after World War II was plainly the result of Harvard strong arming the Royal Society. Andrew is blaming the flies for the condition of a corpse that has a bullet hole in the head. It is not that I support flies, it is that I oppose being shot in the head.

There is a correlation between flies and corpses, but Nazis have the causation backwards.

Why we need the double standard.

2017-07-20 03:01:35

Chastity should be imposed on women, not men. A key that opens many locks is an awesome key. A lock that can be opened by many keys is a crappy lock.

The problem is that women are hypergamous, while men are polygynous. A man wants to possess many women, while a woman wants to be possessed by the best possible man. Which means that if we let nature take its course, a few men will have most of the women. Notice surveys in which many women report having boyfriends, and considerably fewer men report having girlfriends, even though we would expect the lying to go in the opposite direction.

Of course each of the top male's many girlfriends will be causing much drama, as each seeks to get a higher position in his booty call list, with the result that they keep shifting from one alpha male to the next. So though they are only sleeping with one male at a time, they have numerous male orbiters, and are continually shifting from one male to the next to get a better deal. The male defects by being a jerk, by never being available, by never providing resources, the female defects by dumping him. So though in this system women do not particularly want to be serially monogamous, defect/defect equilibrium means that in practice they are serially monogamous.

Sperm is cheap, eggs are dear. Therefore we should guard eggs, not sperm. What this means is that it only needs a small number of badboys to render a very large number of women unmarriageable. Thus curtailing male badboy behavior is not going to succeed. And if we restrain prosocial well behaved upper class men from being badboys, the girls are going to get their kicks with Jeremy Meeks and Muslim rapeugees. Restraining male behavior results in upper class women fucking men low IQ men who live on towel folding jobs, petty burglary, drug dealing, and sponging off their numerous high IQ high socioeconomic status girlfriend, men whose careers are not going to be adversely affected by a few rape charges, underage sex charges, child support orders, and domestic violence restraint orders. The lawyerette does not fuck her fellow lawyers, she does not fuck judges, she fucks Jeremy Meeks. If we let upper class men be badboys, if we stopped afflicting judges with rape charges, underage sex charges, child support orders, and domestic violence restraining orders, at least she would be fucking judges.

The problem is that law and society strengthens shit tests against well behaved, respectable, affluent men, but has limited success in strengthening shit tests against Jeremy Meeks. She fucks men against whom rape charges, underage sex charges, child support orders, and domestic violence restraining orders have limited effect, because they can pass her shit tests, and you, even if you have a nicer car and a nicer hotel room than Jeremy Meeks, cannot. Plus the police and the courts just don't seem to be pursuing rape charges against rapeugees, perhaps because of disparate impact.

All these laws have the effect of holding men responsible for female bad behavior. It is a lot more effective to hold women responsible for male bad behavior, because women, not men are the gate keepers to sex, romance, and reproduction. If you stop some men from behaving badly, women will just find men you cannot or dare not deter.

The problem is that we need to guard what is precious, guard eggs, not sperm. We need to restrain female sexual behavior, not male sexual behavior.

First, we need to change the social order so that the lawyerette fucks the judge instead of Jeremy Meeks. Then we can address the much harder problem of preventing her from fucking either one.

Peak Oil

2017-07-21 03:33:04

If you discover more than ten years of reserves, politicians are apt to take it away from you.

So for the last hundred years or so, the world has only had ten years worth of proven oil reserves left and has been about to run out in ten years or so. In fact the world has only had about ten years of anything left for the past hundred years or so.

King Hubbert created a composite, mega-decline curve that predicted U.S. crude oil production would peak in the 1965-70 time period. But, of course, it did not decline. So his prediction was retroactively relabelled "Lower 48 states Oil Production". Which *retrodiction* was true - for a while. Retrodictions always are. See global warming for example.

Well, for some time US oil production in the lower 48 states has been increasing. So it was re-relabelled "Lower 48 states conventional oil Production" The new story was that fracking has intolerable environmental and financial costs, so is not a practical replacement for old type oil production.

When Trump stopped the government from funding and organizing people to protest fracking, the intolerable environmental costs mysteriously vanished in a puff of smoke, and when Trump made it easier to get permission to frack, so did a large part the economic costs, with the result that US frackers are now giving the Saudis a hard time.

For a given technology, and a given price, a given oilfield or group of oilfields does indeed follow a Hubberd Curve, and you can use the curve to estimate what the real reserves are. (They are usually enormously greater than the official reserves.)

Although science has been stagnating since Harvard got the upper hand over the Royal Society, technology that makes money continues to advance. We have a problem with new blue sky technologies. No one in the west is developing new technologies any more, just polishing up existing profitable technologies. We are not getting any replacement for chip patterning using one hundred and ninety three nanometer excimer laser lithography, just ever more minute improvements in excimer laser lithography, with the result that Moore's law has run out of puff. People keep talking about ten nanometer, but it is just not going anywhere. They keep saying they will use both one ninety and ten. If ten was working, would not use one ninety. If they were talking ninety nanometer, rather than ten, then I would be impressed. If someone could make money out of supersonic jets, we would get better and better supersonics, but instead, planes are slowing down, not speeding up. But people could make money out of drilling and stimulating oil fields, so drilling and oilfield stimulation got better and better, and continues to improve.

Physical resources are effectively infinite, in that physical limits to growth are unlikely to be a significant problem in the reasonably foreseeable future. The problem is social decay.

Trump taking power - slowly.

2017-07-22 05:12:45

I predicted that by now he would have power, which prediction failed to come true. But neither is he defeated. He is moving along. He recently reduced US support for terror and genocide in Syria, turning off the Jordan supply line for terror and mass murder directed at Christians and Alawites. He honors businessmen who advance technology, instead of honoring businesses who appoint childless women to jobs for which they are entirely unqualified.

One of his huge problems is lack of Trumpists with Washington qualifications, as illustrated by the fact that for a long time he has had a press secretary and White House Communications director who hate him, think him stupid and evil, and have been gunning for a coup against him.

Personnel are policy, and the White House policy was that Trump was evil, dangerous, and needed to be overthrown and killed. Hence the mainstream press's frequently accurate depiction of chaos in the White House.

So he eventually had them "move on to pursue new opportunities" and has now appointed a loyalist who is smart and able but has no particular connections or experience in "communications".

What he needs is an institutional funnel, an anti university, for providing him with loyalists with relevant training. No such thing exists, because until now, any Trump like thinking was automatic and total disqualification for any such jobs. Personnel are policy, and Harvard gets to control the personnel. And the policy is that Trump has got to go.

Anyone with relevant and appropriate qualifications is probably an unappeasably hostile enemy of Trump

King David had his mighty men. Pinochet was conscripted into the coup by the junior officers almost at gunpoint, and hauled off from his grandchildren to the still smoking presidential palace. Trump is rather isolated in a hostile Washington. Needs to bring in an occupation force hostile to Washington, has not been doing so.

Appointing a loyalist communications director is a good start. Needs to bring in anti

Washington Trump loyalists who have the attitude that they are a hostile occupation force who have come to seize the Washington establishment's land and women, that they are there to drain the swamp, and the locals, everyone with supposedly relevant qualifications, are swamp critters who depend on the swamp ecology, who are unlikely to appreciate their beloved swamp being drained.

He needs to bring in loyalists who can themselves bring more loyalists from outside the swamp. If you are going to drain the swamp, cannot rely on swamp critters.

Coup by permanent government in the wind

2017-08-04 00:15:58

I expected, and predicted, a self coup by Trump, seizing the power of the presidency for the president, but instead, Mueller has empaneled a grand Jury, which is the permanent government, the presidency, seizing the president.

Empaneling a grand jury is institutional preparation for arresting Trump, not institutional preparation for an impeachment vote in the senate. Attempting to arrest Trump is a coup.

A grand jury issues indictments. That is what it is for. A grand Jury indictment directly results in an order for someone to be arrested and imprisoned. The target usually does not know what the indictment is, what the evidence is, what the charges are, until after he is jail, which is mighty convenient for prosecutors - and for coup makers.

Should it succeed, not long thereafter leftists will be arresting leftists for insufficient leftism, until the process is halted by a Cromwell, a Stalin, or a Napoleon, or until the process goes all the way to the Seven Kill Stele, and everyone executes everyone else for insufficient leftism, leaving very few survivors.

Mueller's cops armed with guns and a warrant may well be quietly shown the door by Trump's praetorians armed with guns and a presidential pardon, but if both sides survive, trouble and escalation will ensue until one side does not survive.

A grand jury is pretty much a formality, since the prosecutor has complete control. A grand jury will indict you for being a ham sandwich, so will surely indict Trump of being a Russian agent and stealing the elections. Or something. We will probably never find out what the charges were, because once the arrest is made, or attempted, the charges will cease to matter, and being able to hit what you are shooting at will matter. Does anyone recollect the charges on which King Louis or Czar Nicholas was executed?

The trouble is that the institutional outcome of the grand jury process is not a two thirds vote in the Senate, as provided by the constitution, but a bunch of social justice warriors dressed as cops equipped with an arrest warrant from someone no one has heard of, giving Trump a perp walk in front of the press.

And when you attempt to give the president a perp walk, that is not an arrest, but a coup. By empaneling a grand Jury, Mueller begins walking down a path where the end of the path is his death or Trump's death.

First faction to start shooting usually wins. The merely elected government, the mere president, needs men who will shoot to kill other men dressed in police uniforms and equipped with a judicial warrant from someone no one has ever heard of. For I am pretty sure that those attempting to serve a judicial warrant on the president will shoot to kill. Once the fatal words are spoken, the logic of the situation is that you win or you die. The violence inevitably escalates. Whoever is slowest to face up to this loses, gets arrested, imprisoned, and eventually, executed, for once imprisoned, too dangerous to live. If Trump gets arrested, one thing will lead to another thing, and pretty soon his entire family and then all elected Republicans will be arrested, and not very long thereafter, executed. It is defect/defect, and the one who defects hardest and first wins. A grand jury exists to arrest people. Once you start resolving political conflicts by arresting your opponents, you win or you die. If Mueller attempts to arrest Trump or his people and fails, Trump has to arrest Mueller and his people, for if he does not, Mueller will surely succeed the second, the third, or the tenth time.

And if Mueller successfully arrests Trump, he is going to have to kill Trump, and a rapidly increasing number of other people, for if he does not then sooner or later Trump is going to be unarrested.

Arresting people is violence, and the logic of violence takes over from the logic of politics. Once started, hard to stop. This does not mean that the escalation will take place overnight, though it well may do so, but there will be escalation.

If the permanent government successfully performs a self coup against the merely legitimate and formal government, we get informal and illegitimate government, on the model of our officially unofficial official state religion. This sets in process a power struggle, where you get a sequence of coups, each lefter than the last, as happened when the Kadets overthrew the Czar to institute moderate conservative parliamentary democracy on the British model, until the army, the praetorians, or the security services get involved, or until a single dictator makes himself absolutely supreme.

Unless saner heads prevail and stuff Mueller back in the bag, or just simply shoot him and his jurors, we are on track for a coup, which, if it succeeds, will result in a chain of ever more radical coups.

From the illegal re-election of Tiberius Gracchus in 133BC to Caesar crossing the Rubicon in 49BC was eighty four years, one long human lifetime of steadily escalating political violence, ending in direct military intervention.

From moderate constitutional monarchists overthrowing the King of France to Napoleon was ten years of steadily escalating violence, ending in direct military intervention.

From the Kadet's overthrowing the Czar in the name of constitutional democratic monarchism to Stalin stabilizing the Russian political system was sixteen years of steadily escalating political violence, during which the military and the security services have remained strangely quiescent.

So this grand jury is not going to result in the stuff instantly hitting the fan. Rather, we will see substantial and escalating erosion of the norms of peaceful political competition, and in retrospect future historians will record the revolution as starting in 2017 or not very long thereafter. It is not going to instantly result in war to the knife, and for a while, everyone will think that normality continues. But the logic of events takes us to war to the knife, and the side that first sees the logic of events and acts on that logic, wins.

Politics by arresting your opponents is not politics, but war. Wars are easy to start, hard to stop. The side that first realizes that war has begun gains a substantial advantage.

Revolution and helicopter rides

2017-08-06 12:23:37

The word "revolution" used to mean a political change that restored some previous state of affairs. Since everyone wanted to claim legitimacy from the ancient past, they would call their political changes "revolution", meaning what we would now call a "restoration". Then leftists claiming legitimacy from the supposed will of the people, also dubiously claimed ownership of some recent "revolutions" to make it plausible that they could succeed in seizing power -

Standard color revolution tactic: when the State Department decides to overthrow someone, the lame stream media announce he is weak, he is weaker, he cannot possibly continue in power, he is out of power, and someone with a connection to the US and Harvard is in power. When this works, the Cathedral seizes power fairly bloodlessly. When it fails, as in Rwanda and Syria, the Cathedral is apt to go genocidal. Trump was not able to halt CIA efforts to exterminate Syrian Christians until last month, and the Wikipedia account of the attempt to genocide the Tutsis is that they had it coming and need to apologize to the Hutus.

As a result of this tactic, the word "Revolution" took the meaning of the people overthrowing the state, or the oppressed masses overthrowing the privileged elite. Which in fact never happens. It is just propaganda. The Iron Law of Rebellious Tools tells us that all such revolutions are always fake. The people never matter and the oppressed masses never matter. What we always have is some quite small powerful conspiratorial group, which has a great deal of power but lacks legitimacy, moving against legitimate and traditional power, and invoking the masses as mascots.

Kings got tired of aristocrats, tired of able powerful fertile rivals spawning numerous additional able powerful rivals, so instituted what we now know as supposedly professional bureaucracy, a bureaucracy composed of low fertility nonentities without powerful family connections - and found they had sawn off the branch on which they sat, for the King's state apparatus composed of commoners proceeded to overthrow him, whereas when the Kings apparatus had been composed of aristocrats, when members of the elite were selected largely on the performance of their ancestors, it merely checked his power in irritating and inconvenient ways. And when the King's ruling apparatus composed of commoners proceeded to dispense with the King, it would piously announce it was surrendering to the wrath of the justly enraged masses. And thus "revolution" came to have its modern meaning, even though there are no actual events that fit the definition. The word "revolution", like "psychopath" and "racist" refers not to a concept, but to an anticoncept, exists to obscure, rather than discuss reality.

The use of eunuchs by the Chinese emperors was an extreme form of this fear of powerful and fertile people in the state apparatus. Notice that when Trump appoints his kin to power, the permanent government are not worried that nepotism results in him appointing incompetent people to power, but rather worried that he is appointing dangerously competent people to power who are likely to be loyal to him, rather than them.

And now, we are back to eunuchs, as the Cathedral deploys cat ladies and castrated males after the style of the Chinese Emperors.

Which brings me to right wing death squads and helicopter rides:

Leftism is priestly rule, categorizing professors, judges, and mainstream media with other priests. We are in practice always ruled by warriors or priests, and right now, priests are out of hand.

Judges are unpopular in the Philippines, because they administer justice in accordance with Harvard values, rather than Philippine values, or even Philippine government values. Hence the immense popularity of Rodrigo Duterte and his death squads[55].

Helicopter rides in South America occurred in the context of a communist "uprising" that was in fact backed by the Judicary, that was in fact an instrument of a part of the government that controlled the judiciary. One side in the struggle declined to use the courts, because courts were controlled by the enemy.

And it is plain that in America today the courts are acting in an utterly brutal, ruthless and lawless way in pursuit of a hostile political agenda.

Death squads are fine provided that discipline is tight. You can tell if a death squad is OK by the snappyness of their uniforms. And courts are bad because discipline is not tight. "Independence of the Judiciary" is a terrible principle. An independent judiciary is a corrupt judiciary. When you hear stories of the enemies of the Cathedral improperly influencing trials, it is always a lie[56]. *Harvard* improperly influences trials. Hence the immense popularity of Duterte.

Field Report on a trans

2017-08-08 12:16:54

I was with a girl in a bar, (under another identity, of course) and a friend of hers showed up who appeared to be a young man, a teenage male. If you saw a photograph of him, you would have no doubt he was male. But the movement was off, the social interaction was off, the voice, though deep for a girl was off, and after a minute or so, something seemed horribly wrong, disgusting, revolting and weird. Something difficult to explain or describe. I asked "Are you a ladyboy", and it replied, using old and politically incorrect terminology, that it was born a woman passing as male to hit on straight women. (It being that night at the bar) It made no attempt to hit on the girl I was with.

But after a minute or so longer, she passed all the way through uncanny valley to the other side, from male to weird intersex to female superficially disguised as male, and no longer felt weird and creepy to me. Felt female. So I treated her like any female - negged her, insulted her, and told her to get me my coffee. She loved this, loved serving me, but after a minute or so disappeared, and I thought no more about her.

Then, a few days later, she showed up with at my place, still looking like a boy, cleaned it up, raided my fridge, cooked me a remarkably delicious meal, and called me "daddy". She explained that she had no father, and regarded me as her father. While still making herself as ugly as possible.

---

[55]https://blog.reaction.la/politics/duerte-harry/
[56]https://www.unz.com/pgiraldi/the-magnitsky-hoax/

A few more days, a few hours before this post, she assures me she still has all her original plumbing and offers me her virginity. Not because she wants sex with a male, she assures me the thought absolutely disgusts her, and she wants me to get it over with as quickly as possible and with as little physical contact as possible, but to please me. This after a couple of negs, several demands for service, respect, and obedience, and one slap on the backside.

I have not kissed her, I have not held her hand. I have not patted her backside, I have not touched her except to slap her on the backside. And I have not felt inclined to do any of these things. And I only slapped her backside because not slapping her after she cooked me a lovely meal and claimed I was her father felt like unkindly ignoring her.

Which offer would blow my mind coming from almost any other female. I don't have high standards. But not however, this female, who has gone to remarkable lengths to successfully uglify herself. And she made the offer without doing anything to make herself less ugly. Obviously, if she was inclined to accompany such offers with efforts to make herself beautiful, she would not be trans in the first place.

Moral of this story: You want to reduce the suicide rate among trans?

Ban them from being trans. It is a horrible and self destructive mistake. Pandering to people who believe they will be happier as the opposite sex is like pandering to people who believe that jumping off cliffs will enable them to fly. Hence the suicide rate. They kill themselves because transitioning just does not work. They cannot actually pass, and they do not actually want what they think they want.

Recap on the Left Singularity

2017-08-12 19:57:50

The violent suppression of the UniteTheRight ralley, and the firing of James Damore, shows repression is getting more and more extreme, with more and more people deemed nazis, and nazis suppressed more violently.

For roughly two hundred years, leftism has been getting lefter, and crazier. For a bit over a hundred years, repression and censorship has been getting more extreme, more repressive, and crazier. This trend is not going to naturally peter out. It is not going to stop until something extremely drastic stops it.

Leftism jumped the shark, and total fertility rate started to fall, when King George was unable to divorce Queen Caroline for flagrant adultery[57] (because women are wonderful, and if a woman does something bad it must be because some evil man made her do it.)

Censorship jumped the shark in 1900-1906, when every single academic in every single academy everywhere suddenly forgot the evidence that the Great Zimbabwe was built by Hebrew gold miners, not by blacks. In 1900, you could speak the truth about race, but not if you wanted a job in Academia. Now, you can speak the truth on race, but not if you want a job. Indeed, that was explicitly mentioned in the James Damore case: "Suppose he had written the same memo on racial differences"

The trend towards ever more thorough, ever more widespread, and ever more violent and coercive censorship, ever more obviously irrational, will not stop today. It has been

---

[57] https://blog.reaction.la/culture/when-the-rot-set-in/

getting more unreasonable and extreme for a very long time. It jumped the shark in 1906, and has been jumping more sharks ever since. Unless someone has fuck you money, he does not dare say to a random acquaintance the things that Obama said in 2008, and this trend has been getting steadily worse since 1900

1910 Russia was markedly more tolerant and democratic than today's America, but by 1930 everything had gone to hell. The trend in the Anglosphere has been to increasingly severe repression, starting around 1900 or so, and steadily accelerating. It is not going to level out or reach a limit.

Back in the early nineteenth century people were saying "if they go too far".

At any given time, going too far will have bad consequences, and not going far enough will have bad consequences - but it is always a lot safer to be on the bleeding edge of the left, than to be in the slightly behind the times mainstream middle. And the lefter we go, the more dire the consequences of being insufficiently left.

Everyone, including you and me, have moved a long, long, long way left. And our insufficient leftism is a lot more dangerous than it used to be.

Further, not only have consequences become more drastic, and applied for ever more frivolous offenses, but objecting to this, or even noticing this trend, is itself an offense. When they start flaying people alive in the streets, no one will be able to see it even when it happens right in front of them. This is simple extrapolation of existing trends, plus it has all happened before many times: Britain going lefter until Cromwell brought things under control, France going lefter until Napoleon brought things under control, Russia going lefter until Stalin brought things under control.

Social Justice Warriors can punch people now. If the victim complained, the Social Justice Warrior would counter complain that his victim was a nazi, and the victim would be fired.

This is a new thing, but expect it to rapidly escalate to Maoist style struggle sessions where people get beaten to death and then eaten as in China during Maoism, or get gasoline poured over their children and then set on fire as in the Soviet Union shortly before Stalin clamped down and monopolized all the torture and murder, or flayings as in France in 1794.

This replicates numerous past left wing singularities all the way back to the collapse of the Bronze age. It is approximately what happened the last few times, why should you doubt it happening this time?

When it escalates to cannibalism, flayings, and burnings, corporations will collapse, as trade collapsed at the end of the bronze age, and in France in 1793.

Mostly it will merely be mango soup, and only a handful of flayings and burnings, because as soon as *$#|&* gets really bad, someone is going to seize power, but if no one is able to securely and stably seize power, could potentially go all the Jim's to Szechuan and the Seven Kill Stele, where everyone tortured everyone to death for insufficient leftism until there was almost no one left.

The mechanism is simple:

1. You must believe in the holy faith or we will punish you.

2. A key principle of the holy faith is that unbelievers must be punished.

3. You had better believe enthusiastically, or you might be punished.

4. You had better demonstrate your belief by enthusiastically hunting for unbelievers and finding them.

5. How many children of unbelievers did you burn alive today, comrade?

Everyone terrorizes everyone else into terrorizing everyone else.

To stop this we need an official inquisition that puts the free lance witch finders out of business. I hope we get a Sulla, who burns Havard to the ground, sack of Rome style, purges the social justice warriors, confiscates their property, and enslaves their women, or a Cromwell who imposes reasonable and sane leftism, but a Stalin, who makes it as dangerous to be too far left as it is to be too far right, would suffice, would be a whole lot better than the Seven Kill Stele.

If Trump does a self coup, and purges the public service of his enemies, starts firing very large numbers of people, that could save the day, but the further left the singularity continues, the bloodier the process by which it eventually must be checked.

Summary of the Global Warming evidence
2017-08-13 03:56:49

Surface measurements have various major sources of error, which have to be guestimated away in an ad hoc manner. The only data that is arguably good enough to estimate the rather small changes in climate is Australia, Britain, and the US - which on the whole have not been warming as measured by surface instruments. And even for them, the warming estimated from surface instruments is rather similar to various sources of error, that have to be "corrected". The main contribution to global warming as measured by surface instruments comes from sources where you can get any result you want by rather arbitrarily deciding some data is good enough to include, and some data is not, by cherry picking particular events - for example warm nights indicate America is warming, but hottest days indicates America is cooling. You can always find one indicator to be alarmist about, but on the whole, where our data is good, surface instruments indicate little or no global warming. Because our surface instrument database is noisy, inaccurate, and incomplete, there is plenty of room to spin it any way one pleases.

The most precise measurement of global warming comes from satellites, which indicate a warming of one degree centigrade per century.[58]

Recent changes in the icecaps indicate slight warming over the last thirty years ago, though the antarctic icecap has increased by almost the same amount as the arctic icecap has decreased, but the icecaps still have substantially more ice than a hundred years ago. The landing sites of early antarctic explorers are now behind a vast barrier of thick, and very old, ice impenetrable to icebreakers. A century ago there was too much open water at the North Pole, even in midwinter, to access it by dog sled, yet today, you can access it by dog sled in winter. Early attempts to reach the North Pole by dog sled had huge problems with open, ice free areas of water. Recent efforts to recreate those trips using identical equipment just took a straight line over solid ice.

---

[58]https://wattsupwiththat.files.wordpress.com/2017/07/uah_lt_1979_thru_june_2017_v61.jpg

The worlds biggest glaciers, the ones in the Himalayas are growing. Greenland glaciers are arguably shrinking, but by a miniscule amount. Glaciers do not tell you today's weather as compared to yesterday, but today's weather as compared with a very long time ago. Which fits with the experiences of arctic and antarctic explorers a century or so ago. Different glaciers are giving different indications, which is consistent with the conjecture that some years, some decades, and some centuries are warmer, and others are cooler.

So, lukewarming is true, for the moment, natural variation is true, and catastrophic warming is not true.

Not time for war yet

2017-08-14 21:43:04

A lot of people are saying that Charlotsville means time for war.

No, not time for war yet, because the God Emperor says to cool it. You have to go with the King you have, rather than the King you would like to have, because otherwise it is democracy, and we know democracy does not work.

When they arrest him using a warrant from some judge no one has heard of, then likely it will be time for war.

Gassing the Jews is worse than a crime

2017-08-16 03:57:42

It is a distraction.

A Jewish neoreactionary accurately complains about today's nazis:
> being happily married, with children, and having regular employment, does wonders to stabilize and sober up the minds of creative, imaginative, intelligent people with energetic and action-oriented "free radical" personalities. Fatherhood as antioxidant. Socialization with other normal fathers as electrical ground. The longer one of these types goes without these moderators and governors, the more likely they are to keep drifting until eventually finding a social scene which amplifies ones impulses. Like Taliban groups of unattached single men are constantly pumping and psyching each other up for Jihad, right here, right now, even if it's senseless. There's definitely some kind of masculine failure mode there.

In the ancestral environment, if you were a reproductively unsuccessful male, you formed a tribe of young men, who went off and stole some land and enslaved some women. Holiness signalling about racial purity is tribe formation.

What their genes really want them to do is confiscate the Ivy League endowments, kill the males at Harvard, occupy the Ivy League buildings, and enslave the Ivy League women. Given that the alternative is near certain genetic extinction, this is not a stupid ambition, though purity spiraling, which generates the solidarity needed to accomplish this program, also distracts from this program.

Getting overly obsessed about Jews creates the cohesion necessary to address this problem - but also results in not conquering and enslaving women, which is actually the whole point of the program, just as females shit testing results in those females not having children and not forming relationships, even though from the point of the genes the whole point of shit testing is family formation - girls are behaving provocatively to find a male powerful enough to subdue them, but girls think they are behaving provocatively because they actually want power, freedom, and independence, with the result that they attain neither power nor family, and achieve freedom and independence as cat ladies.

Your genes don't actually want you to gas the Jews. That is just a flag to rally around, and a club with which to attack your enemies. (Hence the tendency of Nazis to denounce everyone they don't like as Jewish.) Your genes want you to gas the enemy males, take their land, revenue sources, and buildings, and enslave their women. Krystalnacht was assets being smashed, rather than transferred to individuals competent to use them. If you gas the Jews without winding up supported by the revenue from the campus endowment, in a nice home with a couple of ivy league slave girls serving you in what used to be an ivy league campus, it has all gone horribly wrong, like a thirty year old woman issuing an inappropriately brutal shit test to a beta provider male.

It is a "masculine failure mode" only if you don't get the land, the house, and the slave girls. Recollect that in the American Revolution, the Whigs dispossesed the Tories, drove them out of America, and took their stuff. The alt right are today's Tories, and their genes want a re-run.

That escalated quickly

2017-08-17 12:46:04

First Damore at Google, then he gets fired, then the Charlottesville march to protest the destruction of white history is violently crushed, then then the erasure of white culture and history is dramatically escalated, then protest march about Google's mistreatment of Damore is threatened with the Charlottesville treatment, and folds in the face of clear intention to terrorize them as at Charlottesville.

At this rate, we will be at democide and infinite leftism by Wednesday.

I still predict the left singularity for two thousand and twenty six or so, but if I was going by the latest headlines, I would predict it for Wednesday.

I don't think it will happen by Wednesday, but these events make it more likely that they will shortly attempt to arrest the God Emperor on the basis of an arrest warrant issued by some judge no one has heard of, without bothering with the obsolete inconvenience of a two thirds senate vote.

The left plan

2017-08-17 21:48:08

The plan appears to be to go right ahead with massive repression as if Hillary was president. If the mere president allows this to happen, he and his family get arrested later, by a bunch of social justice warriors dressed as cops carrying a warrant from some judge no one has heard of. If the God Emperor does not allow it to happen, they attempt to arrest him sooner.

Looks like Spencer and Charlottesville had nothing to do with it. They just happened to be in the line of fire when Democracy Spring started to roll.

We not only over estimate the role of street protests and public opinion, we also over estimate non state agency. Collective action starts from state decisions This was always about Trump. Going after Trump through the Russians was not working, so now they are going after him through their real target, the right.

The plan was that Hillary would be elected, then they would do to conservatives, including cuckservative Republicans, what they did to Nazis. With the unexpected loss of the presidency, the plan is being adapted in an ad hoc fashion. If "Russia stole the election" had worked, they would have taken out Trump, then the right. Now they are going to attempt to take out any and all Trump loyalists, then take out Trump, then implement the original plan.

Red Guards and Cultural Revolution

2017-08-21 06:34:55

Three years ago, after World War Trans, people said, "OK, one more unconditional and total capitulation by the right, and then we will be able to live in peace.

But today we have red guards and a cultural revolution.

And that is what everyone says, after each capitulation, starting with the denial of King George's divorce. "The left has today become so crazy, so extreme, it cannot get any crazier, and there is going to be a blacklash." (Or, in the case of King George, a holash. And after King George's divorce was denied, there was indeed a holash against wives who fuck around, but it did not stop things from rapidly getting worse, and the attack upon the family from endlessly escalating, and the total fertility rate from endlessly falling, with a temporary remission from the early thirties to the early sixties, between first wave and second wave feminism.)

Now it is apparent that the next big thing is Red Guards and the Cultural Revolution. Whiteness is today being erased from our past, and tomorrow we will be erased from our present. After whitness, maleness, starting with fathers and husbands.

A left singularity is usually terminated, as by a Stalin or a Cromwell. One leftist grabs all power and absolute power, and then stops things from getting worse, lest he be devoured in his turn. But until then, it just goes on getting ever more extreme. It does not stop quietly of its own accord, merely because it has become sufficiently extreme to sate people's appetite for destruction. It is only going to stop if someone stops it.

Fathers and husbands will be deemed toxic for wives and children and will be removed from their families - the salami slicer is already operating to remove the supposedly worst husbands and fathers, and eventually it is going to get the whole salami. Wives who fail to cooperate in the removal of husbands and fathers will lose their children, and eventually be subject to violence and imprisonment, and eventually execution. Next cishet single men, then insufficiently gay single men, and then ...

Eventually, as in Szechuan, everyone enthusiastically tortures everyone else to death in an unsuccessful effort to be the last to be called out for insufficient leftism and devoured, and no one remains, unless at some point, the left gets it in the neck, and is purged from the institutions of the state religion - in our case the Ivies and the key media.

In Russia, the left communists were leaving old fashioned Marxism Leninism behind, as the Unitarians had left Puritanism behind. Stalin was guilty of old fashioned Marxism Leninsm, and so would surely have been devoured, so he purged the left communists under the excuse that they were "objectively fascist". In the ensuing purge, Jews suffered disparate impact, extreme disparate impact, and the party wound up pretty much Judenrein, but it was not a purge of Jews for Jewishness. It was, mostly, a purge of communists for heresy, entirely genuine heresy.

The "fascists" and "wreckers" that were purged were largely imaginary, but the "Objective fascists" that were purged really were heretics from what had been orthodox Marxism Leninism, and they were nailed for heresy, not Judaism.

Eventually, the left edge of politics is going to be purged from the Ivies and government employment - perhaps by us, more likely by someone unimaginably further left than any present day tendency.

Or else, as in Szechuan, everyone is going to die horribly.

Equality and Social Justice is just rhetoric for mobilizing envy and covetousness and turning it into violence and destruction, as for example Detroit.

The left cares about power, and power is "impact", and "impact" is making people suffer. When they run out of kulaks, they liquidate the peasants. Obamaphone woman cares about equality and social justice, the mindless river of meat cares about equality and social justice, in the sense that they are pissed that some people have nicer stuff than they do, and want to trash that stuff and mess up those people, but the puppeteers controlling Obamaphone woman do not give a shit. When they have finished using her to kill all whites and all males, they will take Obamaphone woman's phone away, and then they are going to kill her: Impact!

Look at any greenie environmentalist protest. They leave a trail of garbage behind them, they totally trash the environment. Look at the save-our-jobs counter protest. They clean up behind themselves as if they had never been there.

They don't want to save the earth they don't want equality and social justice, they want power, power is impact, impact is making people suffer. Every BLM and greenie protest proves it.

Leftism has made envy and covetousness into a sacrament, because that is the sin that is easiest to pander to politically.

Not only is it easier to destroy Detroit, than to transfer it intact from whites to blacks, it is easier to destroy Jewish assets than to transfer them intact to Germans.

And not only is it easier, it is much more satisfying in the short run. Do you want to balance a set of account books, or do you want break windows and terrorize the people behind those windows? BLM and Antifa!

Face it. Smashing and terrorizing is just more fun. If you want a mob of muppets, you don't offer them other people's assets to organize and operate, you offer them other people's assets to destroy, and other people to destroy. BLM and Antifa is impact!

Impact!

The never ending war in Afghanistan

2017-08-23 20:03:23

Too many Americans have died in order that Afghan girls can be taught how to put a condom on a banana.

Trump has reversed course on Afghanistan. Perhaps he needed to do that to keep the officers on side, but this war needs to be won or lost. Keeping it going forever is costing far too much blood and treasure.

How do you win an Afghan war?

It is not hard: You need a genuinely Islamic strong monarch who can accomplish the difficult job of keeping order, and let him know that if trouble comes out of Afghanistan and reaches you, he is going to die.

The problem with our existing war is that it is a holy war, fought to emancipate women in Afghanistan, and to destroy conservative Islam, not to create order under the control of someone who can be held responsible for any trouble coming out of Afghanistan. If you are going to fight a holy war against a live religion, need to kill huge numbers of people and level their cities, which we are reluctant to do - although if they were white Christians, I am sure there would be no hesitation.

If we are reluctant to slaughter and burn on the require scale, then we need to let Afghans be Afghans. It is time to shut down those prog schools in Afghanistan.

Too many Americans have died in order that Afghan girls can be taught how to put a condom on a banana.

We forbid our soldiers to piss one hundred yards upwind of Koran, we forbid them to carry bibles, while we attempt to destroy the values taught in that Koran.

I would totally support holy war against the Afghans, fought with the methods necessary to win a holy war. I am not so keen on unholy war. We are fighting to destroy what is right with Islam, rather than what is wrong, fighting to corrupt Islam as Christianity was corrupted, and the Taliban rightly sees this as wickedness.

Censoring the internet

2017-08-26 05:34:56

Racist sites are being taken off the internet. Expect "racist" sites to follow.

The internet is built to resist censorship, and it is time for alt tech that takes advantage of this[59]. patronize Gab.ai, duckduckgo, hatreon, and infogalactic.com, assuming that they are still up by the time you read this. If they are not, namecoin and tor.

No enemies to the right

2017-08-26 06:26:20

No enemies to the left has been working great for the left, and no enemies to the right has been working great for us.

---

[59]https://voxday.blogspot.com/search/label/%23AltTech

If you declare someone to your right your enemy, you wind up dancing to a tune called by leftists.

Supreme Dark Lord Vox Day recently criticized Spencer and the Nazis as fake right[60] - criticized them not for being too far right, but for being too far left, for being socialist. He did not criticize from the left, but from the right. He is correctly maintaining a position of no enemies to the right. You can argue that his criticism was too harsh, that he was cutting off communication, but his action was not an example of enemies to the right. Socialism is leftist, and Nazis are leftists who have been left behind by the rest of the left as the rest have continued to move further left.

People who want to smash or steal stuff belonging to Jews are mistaken. That never makes us rich, it makes us poor.

Non Jews should be removed from state and quasi state power in Israel, and Jews should be removed from state and quasi state power in the US. But if you go smashing up a Jewish pawnshop or a Jewish distillery, you are allowing covetousness and envy to distract you and make you do stupid things. Taking or smashing other people's stuff is a bad idea. Land and women can be usefully and effectively stolen, but the trouble with socialism is that more complicated forms of wealth tend to get messed up in the transition. Jews in exile tend to specialize in precisely those forms of wealth that are not usefully confiscatable.

The threatened imprisonment of Sheriff Joe

2017-08-27 01:23:59

Sheriff Joe was threatened with imprisonment for enforcing the law of the land, after he was elected on a platform of enforcing that law.

This reflects the drift towards criminalizing political differences. Or as the Democrats call it "rule of law", rule of law being a euphemism for rule by judges, where judges make executive rulings on traditionally executive issues.

Straightforward extrapolation of this trend is that if Trump loses power, he will be imprisoned, and eventually executed, and not very long thereafter, we will see a purge of military and police in which most of the current leadership is imprisoned and/or executed, nominally for past crimes towards single women, blacks, gays, fat people, and whoever gets on the oppressed list next year, actually for being suspected of insufficient loyalty and enthusiasm for the new regime.

Trump is losing or firing his strongest loyalists, and surrounding himself with people who intend his destruction. He rather should surround himself with people who intend Trump and his descendants to remain in power permanently.

People are going to tell me that imprisoning and killing the Trumps is unthinkable. It is unthinkable in 2017, but a whole lot of things were thinkable in 2016 that were unthinkable in 2008, and imprisoning Sheriff Joe was one of those things.

Purging loyalists and installing enemies in power is how the Romanovs died. The first coup resulting from this policy was the Kadet coup, which merely intended democratic constitutional monarchy, which was swiftly followed by a social democrat coup

---

[60]https://voxday.blogspot.com/2017/08/what-say-you-supporters.html

which merely intended a democratic socialist Republic, resulting in the purging of the Romanovs, which was swiftly followed by a communist coup, which swiftly resulted in the execution of the Romanovs. Something along those lines for 2024 is just straightforward projection of current trends, of which the attempt to imprison Sheriff Joe for enforcing the law of the land is one straw of a great many straws in the wind[61]. The elite is increasingly using political violence, not only on ordinary political opponents as at Charlottesville., but on elite political opponents such as Paul Manafort and Sheriff Joe. They have crossed a line, and there are no remaining lines between what they are doing now and full scale war. This sets in motion an inevitable drift to the greater use of simple violence to resolve political disagreement within the elite. Wars are easy to start, hard to stop. We are drifting towards wars internal and external. War is a form of entropy. If you don't do anything clever, forceful, and effective to prevent war, war will probably ensue. If actions are unconstrained by the possibility that war may ensue, war will ensue. War is easy, peace is hard. Even if the right rolls over and plays dead, this will merely mean that people who are today unthinkably far left will be deemed extreme right, and eventually executed for their reactionary tendencies.

Holiness and corporate performance.

2017-09-01 05:35:11

Notoriously, corporations that are Social Justice converged behave in ways that are not only evil, but self destructive, leading to loss of shareholder value.

It is difficult to objectively assess social justice convergence, but we can expect it to have a pretty good correlation with the company's business model - a green energy company is going to be full of social justice warriors, and receive lots of investment from fund managers who are trying to earn brownie points from the government, rather than brownie points from investors, whereas a gun company is probably trying to make good money by making good guns.

"Watts Up With That" recently did a ten year comparison of such companies, and found that over ten years, holiness investing lost nearly all your money, while sinfulness investing doubled your money[62].

Twelve years ago, holiness investing consisted largely in investing in providing mortgages for single women, Hispanics, and blacks. And all that money disappeared also.

However, while holiness investing is terrible for investors, it works extremely well for management, as for example Jon Corzine, the world's most regulated and regulating financier, who without informing his customers proceeded to use their funds to rescue Greece.

Jon Corzine's customers were eventually paid back by burning JP Morgan, illustrating that when you do business with progs, someone gets burned. The short of it was that various financial entities who were improperly paid with money belonging to Jon

[61] https://pjmedia.com/trending/2017/08/25/report-fbi-raid-paul-manaforts-home-heavy-handed-designed-intimidate/

[62] https://wattsupwiththat.com/2017/08/31/invest-with-greens-or-sinners/

Corzine's customers had to give it back, so that they are out of the money, they got burned,[63] yet somehow Jon Corzine is still smelling of roses.

Corporations that go left tend to disappear or get hollowed out, unless they have some kind of state protected monopoly.

Time to get out from under ICANN

2017-09-05 05:36:24

"Private" companies are threatened with loss of their domain names for taking the wrong political position. Gab billed itself as a free speech platform, was threatened with loss of its domain name if it did not politically censor people. Hey, it is not political censorship because private companies are doing the censoring.

The libertarian solution to this is that ICANN should be neutral between political positions. Separation of Church and State and all that. That would be great. But the trouble is that we have never had separation of Church and State and never will have separation of Church and State.

All the states that united to form the United States had established churches, and the war of Northern Aggression was the state church of New England, headquartered in Harvard, engaging in a crusade to impose its religion as the religion of the United States over the individual states. The war of Northern Aggression was a continuation and escalation of the Mormon war.

There was a time when the United States had no official religion, but only in that the individual states were free to have their own official religions. Whatever you think the real history of the war of Northern Aggression was, the US currently has an official state religion at the federal level, (though officially unofficial) and formerly had official state religions at the state level.

Not having a state religion is an unrealistic ideal. Having a state religion that is not so embarrassingly in conflict with the empirical evidence is a more realistic ideal, but the way the wind blows, what is happening is that the state religion of the US is getting crazier by the day.

That all men are created equal is harder to believe than young earth creationism. Hence the purge of James Damore.

The least bad realistic option is the Westphalia solution. The religion of the King is the religion of the people. ICANN should enforce American Social Justice doctrine, that all men are created equal, so don't believe your lying eyes, while China enforces Socialism with Chinese characteristics, the nearest thing to capitalism permitted in today's world, and Russia enforces ... whatever it is that they figure out is going to be their state doctrine.

If Russia and China do not want to be color revolutioned the way Syria and the Ukraine were, they need to make sure that web sites in in Russia and China do not need to please ICANN

Instead of one name system for the world, we would get one name system per nuclear power, plus several underground name systems. Maybe North Korea can add a name

---

[63] https://fortune.com/2013/11/15/how-mf-globals-missing-1-5-billion-was-lost-and-found/

registration business to its existing drug dealing and counterfeiting businesses. There is quite a lot of money to be made there.

Jewish overrepresentation among badly behaved elites.

2017-09-06 23:54:08

When whites are driven out of affluent middle class areas which then become terrifying run down burned out urban jungles, it is not Jews that they are fleeing.

The inner city used to be where the affluent, the rich, and the upwardly mobile lived. It is not Jews that destroyed the inner city, Detroit, Ferguson, and are now destroying Chicago.

Female bad behavior comes from desire to fuck taciturn narcissistic assholes, starting at age eight or nine. If it was Jewish influence, they would want to fuck neurotic talkative dweebs resembling Woody Allen. Margaret Mead fucked people of both sexes and numerous races, but did not fuck Franz Boas.

Blaming Jews is yet another good news religion, because it is easy to gas the Jews, but considerably more difficult, and more disturbing, to keep women under loc parentis supervision from eight to menopause. So the program of restoring civilization sounds a lot easier if all you have to do to get things back on track is gas the Jews.

If we blame the Enlightenment, in particular and especially the extravagantly absurd claim that all men are created equal, if we blame blacks, single women, and the holiness spiral, then it looks like a harder problem, that requires us to do things that are inherently unpopular and unholy, whereas exterminating a market dominant minority is always popular, and you can very easily get away with representing it as holy. Jews are a market dominant minority, and we whites are about to become a market dominant minority.

People who hope to win an election with a universal franchise have to blame the Jews, or else blame whites in general. You cannot shut down a holiness spiral in a democracy except with another holiness spiral.

Muslims in Europe and America are very close to successfully representing gassing the Jews as holy, and shortly thereafter will go to work on similar representation of whites.

Notice eager Jewish collaboration[64] in Muslim efforts to represent gassing the Jews as holy. This falsifies the doctrine that Jewish misbehavior is collectively rational behavior that advances the interests of "the Jews".

I have often said that going after the Jews is goring the matador's cape, rather than goring the matador. You have to shut down the holiness spiral itself, rather than a category of people that contains a disturbingly large proportion of exceptionally enthusiastic demon worshipers.

Shutting down the holiness spiral requires something like an inquisition. We don't need to burn people at the stake, though Charles the second did need to burn a few people at the stake, in particular one alarmingly and excessively holy female heretic, whose holiness was inconveniently and irritatingly genuine, and whose Unitarian Christian derived belief system was alarmingly twenty first century. But mostly what Charles the second

---

[64]https://www.unz.com/isteve/why-have-so-many-liberal-jews-become-obsessive-islamophilics-lately/

did was fire everyone in state and quasi state jobs, and invite them to re-apply for their old jobs. In the job interview, the applicant was asked whether he would "conform" - conform to the new standard of moderate holiness, which prohibited excessive holiness in general, and the old form of holiness in particular. If one declined to say he would conform, he did not get burned at the stake - but neither did he get his old job back. Many who declined to conform departed under their own power to New England. A few said they would conform, got their old jobs back, but then engaged in apostasy, and those ones Charles came down on pretty hard, but usually they got ridiculed and their careers got ruined, rather than burned at the stake. Looks to me that only one genuinely sincere and genuinely holy heretic got burned at the stake by Charles the Second, and all the others that were burned were two faced slimy lying hypocrites, and that most of the apostates just got laughed at and their careers stalled, rather than burned at the stake, or even fired. But you really do need to sometimes take firm measures against stubborn and excessively ostentatious holiness.

The problem with Jews is that they are a market dominant minority with a strong identity. Being a market dominant minority with a strong identity they are particularly subject to potential persecution, plus, in even in the absence of actual persecution, they still have an extremely strong persecution mythos, which makes them paranoid and hostile. Since one is going to get treated as a persecutor no matter what, one feels inclined to actually persecute them.

Jews are are inclined to attack the fabric of the host society, because when it's strong it attacks them, and when it's weak it lays off. The fabric of society is essentially everything "fascist", so they are naturally anti-fascist insofar as they identify as jewish. Obviously this pattern has been reinforced. The reform jews most so because they are actually trying to integrate, which they can't if everyone is Nordic Catholic "Fascists".

When they engage in a holiness spiral, they don't have any personal attachment to the things that their utopian schemes will destroy, or any concern about the reasons it won't work. Whereas a white man would say "what about my job, family, community, ancestors, people, church, business", your typical academic jew would say "Certain elements of the bourgeois will feel the move to equality as oppression (and I never liked those dumb goyim anyways)".

Their talents make them useful to short-sighted elites, which puts them in the position of High, but with more mobility, more of a mobile bandit; they can always go elsewhere and feel just as at home. In addition to the insecurity they feel as a persecuted minority, they are naturally aligned with High which has in our recent history been engaged in destructive anti-fascism.

Their talents further mean that they are quite good at the subversion, which, lacking attachment to their host society, they naturally get into.

But the problem is not Jewish participation in subversion, it is that subversion is profitable, respected, and rewarded. Make it unprofitable, despised, and dangerous, and there will not be a Jew in sight.

Civilization is the art of people living together in large numbers: The basic problems of civilization are shutting down violence, ensuring that men and women agree to stick together for richer or poorer, or better or worse, and are forced to stick by that agreement, and securing property rights. Leftism is an attack on all of these, leftism is siding with the forces of entropy for political advantage, and Nazism is just leftism that has been left behind by a hundred years of movement even further left. "Fascism" is freedom, freedom is made possible by law, law is made possible by first establishing order, order is made possible by peace, peace first require victory, and victory requires war. Leftism reverses this chain of causation and moves us back towards the war of all against all. Leftism weaponizes covetousness and envy to attack property rights and female sexual lust to attack marriage. Single women, rather than Jews, vote for the mass import of rapeugees, because unconsciously they hope to be sold naked in chains on the auction block.

Observe what is happening with the Rohingya. The Rohingya correctly believe that a good Muslim should live under Muslim rule, and that a Muslim should establish Muslim rule wherever he lives. They attempted to establish a Muslim state in Burma, the Burmese were not having any, and are now expelling them. The expelled Rohingya don't want to go to the USA. They want to go to a Muslim state, but Islamic states fear that if they accept the Rohingya, the Rohingya will decide that their hosts are insufficiently Islamic, or the wrong kind of Islamic. The US government wants them, wants to dump the on marginal electorates in flyover country, and you really cannot blame the Jews for this. You cannot blame the Rohingya for this. They don't want to go to an infidel state. It is single female lust for men manly enough to subjugate them. If a bunch of east europeans were fleeing some place, I bet the PUAs would be keen on bringing them here.

Not agreement capable

2017-09-08 02:07:00

When the Russians were dealing with President Gay Caffè Latte, they complained the US was "not agreement capable". They would make an agreement with one branch of the US government, and few hours later another branch of the US government would sabotage the agreement by blowing stuff up.

I have been trying to figure out US government policy on Libya. Some time ago the US color revolutioned the place, but somehow power did not fall into the hands of the Interim Transitional National Council, the collection of quarreling rootless cosmopolitan NGO employees that the US proclaimed were the new government.

So the US launched fourteen thousand bomber strikes, each strike dropping thirty tones of explosives, mostly on civilians, murdering about thirty thousand people, but somehow still power did not fall into the hands of the collection of quarreling rootless cosmopolitan NGO employees that the US proclaimed were the new government.

So the US government successfully had Gaddafi murdered, and somehow still power did not fall into the hands of the collection of quarreling rootless cosmopolitan NGO employees that the US proclaimed were the new government.

Then Benghazi happened, and the US government could not agree on what had happened, what was going to happen, or how they were going to deal with it. They do not know who is in power in Libya, cannot agree who should be in power. Whoever is in power (and I am pretty sure that whomever the coastguard answers to is in power) the US Government is simultaneously at war with them and at peace with them. Or rather some elements of the Permanent US Government are at war, and some elements are at peace.

President Gay Caffè Latte is no longer president. President Trump is president. The Permanent United States Government is in open revolt against him. But, as is evident from its current Libyan policy, the Permanent United States Government lacks a single leader, or even a united and disciplined politburo. The revolt by the Permanent Government against the merely elected government is leaderless, confused, and chaotic.

It is a truism on the alt right that there are only three independent governments in the world, China, Russia, and the US. Well, maybe five now, North Korea and Libya having become independent. North Korea because it is acquiring nuclear missiles, Libya because all the high value targets have already been blown up or murdered.

That Libya looks independent tells us that US government is weak and incohesive. There is no strong reason why the US empire does not collapse tomorrow, the way the Soviet empire did. People are rightly worried that if they revolt, then when the empire gets its act together, it will exact terrible and bloody revenge, but it has been a while, and the empire is not yet getting its act together.

Charlottesville was a disaster, and the response of the neoreaction to the rest of the alt right was:
> "We told you so, frontal attack on the Permanent Government has always failed disastrously, purported rebels are always tools of the powerful. We should give up on freedom of speech and freedom of assembly, which are in practice only for those backed by state power."

Which is true:

And also:
> "The Permanent Government is invincibly strong, therefore frontal attack on the Permanent Government will always fail disastrously."

Which is not at all true when the Permanent government is spectacularly incohesive.

Obviously if you hope to defeat the Permanent Government, you don't bring Nazi symbols, because to your enemy, that means "The guys who lost last time". And you need a better cause than the erasure and demonization of our past. These guys have been erasing and demonizing our past since 1830 or so. Pretty soon not only will Washington and Jefferson vanish down the memory hole, but even Newton and Darwin will be remembered only for raping their slaves, whom they personally abducted from Africa. And reliable electricity and affordable air conditioning will be equated with the Love Canal and Exxon oil spill. Global warming will be caused by demons unleashed by white people. (What do I mean "will be"? It already is. Mainstream science accounts of Global Warming no longer seriously pretend to be scientific.)

And freedom of speech and freedom of assembly is not a useful cause. You are fighting on your enemy's turf. Freedom of speech is for them, not us. Any disagreement by anyone anywhere constitutes an attack on their freedom of speech. That is what freedom of speech and freedom of religion means. Freedom of Speech and Freedom of Religion means that businesses get shut down, as Sweet Cakes and the Bank of Beverly Hills was, if they permit their employees to show insufficient piety towards the state religion. That is what it has meant ever since the War of Northern Aggression. This really is not new. And before the war of Northern Aggression, it only meant that the federal government could not enforce a state religion. The individual states could and did enforce their particular state religions, and the war of Northern Aggression was fought to bring them all into line, to all enforce one single religion upon all.

But because our enemy is incohesive, they are bound to do something spectacularly stupid and wicked sooner or later. Maybe they will arrest or attempt to arrest Trump and his family prematurely, though somewhat to my surprise they have not attempted to arrest him yet. Maybe they will go to the mat on resisting the building of the wall, a color revolution against Trump over the wall. If a color revolution can fail in Syria and Libya, it can fail in the USA, though quite possibly with levels of violence more severe than in Syria or Libya. And because those stupid things have been foreseen, discussed and warned against, quite likely it will be some entirely unexpected and unforeseen stupid thing.

I am not predicting that the balloon goes up next month, though quite possibly it could. I still predict 2026, but the way the left singularity has been accelerating, next month is within the bounds of possibility. They could snatch President Trump tomorrow, and likely we would be in civil war the day after. It daily becomes less accurate to model our opponent as a single rational self interested being with a single will. In retrospect it is apparent that our opponents lost cohesion under President Gay Caffè Latte, and far from regaining cohesion, are continuing to lose cohesion. Power is about to fall into the street to wait for someone to pick it up. There is a lot of ruin in a nation, and this could well go on for a decade or so before the balloon goes up, but we are seeing a lot of ruin. The most likely scenario is internal and external collapse happening roughly simultaneously, escalating into roughly simultaneous internal and external war. The external collapse is foreshadowed by Syria, Libya, and North Korea, internal collapse foreshadowed by the election of Trump in the face of Permanent Government opposition.

If the Permanent Government dealt with weakness and disunity by temporarily moderating its external position and external demands while it sorted out its internal problems, it would have no problems, but disunity means it cannot rationally address weakness. Instead it responds to its own weakness by escalation. That does not necessarily mean war and collapse next month, but if the trend continues, means war and collapse sooner or later.

The election of Trump shows that the Permanent Government is just not all that strong internally. Libya and Syria show it is just not all that strong externally. And it reacts to these demonstrations of weakness by uncontrollably sliding into positions more extreme and aggressive. The wind has been blowing this way for some time, and continues to blow this way.

Masculinity

2017-09-12 22:17:18

I play a wealthy vain narcissistic playboy sadistic violent criminal adventurer asshole in front of women. A confrontational bully. It works. What else can one do if one wants to get laid?

But the character I play is not the man that that builds or maintains civilizations. It is the man that is high status in a world of female dominance, where women are more equal than men. It is not the man who should be high status, not the man that a civilization needs to make high status in order for that civilization to succeed.

Unguided, unsupervised, and unrestrained female choice rewards male bad behavior.

But recognizing that this is the man that women want is a good corrective to what progs teach men to be. That man is a lot closer to the man that builds civilization than the emasculated man.

As civilization falls apart, likely we can only attain Pauline masculinity by going through Viking masculinity and out the other side. A world of female sexual choice is a world that is likely to be conquered by men practicing Viking masculinity, for its cuckolded males will not defend it, neither will its playboy males watching the decline from the poolside defend it, hence the female preference for that kind of masculinity.

The natural limits of monarchy.

2017-09-17 13:10:10

Throughout history, the normal and usual form of government has been monarchy. Republics and such have been rare aberrations that have usually ended disastrously. The neoreactionary position is that nothing very much has changed. Our republic is decadent, corrupt, disunited, and lawless. It suffers from anarcho tyranny and lack of asabiyyah. Pretty much like most republics before they collapse to Ceasarism, external enemies, or internal disorder.

The neoreactionary position then is that we will be in monarchy soon enough, one way or another way, and the problem then is to make the transition go relatively smoothly, and the monarchy adequately functional.

Kings are usually theoretically absolute, and if they are not supposedly absolute, if they are not the final judge, the final legislator, if they cannot appoint judges that please them and fire judges that displease them, then problems ensue.

But government that is actually absolute, rather than merely formally absolute, works poorly. Mortals cannot really exercise that much power.

The Patriarch is not the ruler of his family because the King makes him so, rather the King is ruler of the state because the patriarch is ruler of his family.

And similarly, the King owns the state because the farmer owns his garden. The farmer does not own his garden because the King grants him title.

And if the King develops overly grandiose ideas, he find himself dangerously dependent on a dangerously powerful bureaucracy or aristocracy.

Taking power from the father, the businessman, and the landowner, does not grant that power to the King. It grants it to dangerously powerful people dangerously close to the King.

Which is how the Romanovs died.

Therefore, the wise King needs to let society run itself as far as possible, applying state power only in exceptional cases, when there are large scale organized challenges to state, society, legitimacy, property, the status of the King, and law.

We are vastly wiser than our ancestors in matters of technology, and the biggest break through was the limited liability company and double entry accounting. While the limited liability company is a disaster for banking and insurance, because of the obvious moral hazard, which results in banking and insurance companies becoming quasi govermental, becoming defacto socialist, the limited liability company and double entry accounting made possible Rand's heroic scientist engineer ceo, who mobilizes other people's capital and organizes other people's labor to advance technology, and make those improvements in technology widely available. We first see technological advance mediated by limited liability companies, we first see Rand's hero scientist engineer CEO, immediately after the restoration of Charles the Second.

But today, this social technolgy, fundamental to the triumph of white civilization, is being undone by an ever more lawless and intrusive government, by anarcho tyranny. HR is socialism, a branch of the state intruded into every limited liability company and standing between the entrepeneur and his employees, and Sarbannes Oxley is making accounting into the same kind of thing, a branch of the socialist state intruded into every limited liability company and standing between the entrepeneur and his investors, remaking every business into the kind of quasi state thing that banking and insurance already is.

Technology, and the limited liability company that made technology widely available, are real progress, but when it comes to morals and government, no progress is apparent. After two thousand years of failure, people are still trying socialism, figuring it will be different this time.

Looks to me that the no coveting commandment was a reaction to late Bronze age Egyptian socialism and counter measure against it, and "Proverbs" (the famous wisdom of Solomon) a reaction to and counter measure against legalism and bureaucracy.

So, since then, regress in the fields of morality and governance. Since we are evidently no wiser about socialism, bureaucracy, and absolutism, it is unlikely that the old pattern, where monarchy was the norm, and Republics dangerous and short lived, will change.

The swerve left

2017-09-20 19:56:10

We are ruled by a government that hates us and wants to destroy us, and tells us we hate ourselves and wish to destroy ourselves, and I suppose most people will believe this. But it is not true, and the last election proved it was not true.

In the recent election, the public voted to end Obamacare, build a wall, stop immigration, stop white replacement, the abolition of white jobs, and to rebuild infrastructure. But permanent government policy against legacy Americans on all these matters has in fact escalated.

If Obamacare is not repealed, the wall is not built, mass migration continues, and our infrastructure continues to deteriorate, America is not a democracy.

Damore and Charlottesville reflects a swerve left. The Charlottesville protest was a reaction to accelerated erasure of white history, and then followed accelerated left wing violence against rightists.

And this swerve left has swerved the Trump white house left. Trump is the only Trumpist left in the Whitehouse. Trump is tired and weak, and is acting like a lame duck. He has allowed himself to be surrounded with people who are fundamentally hostile to him. He has been put inside a bubble of unreality where mass low IQ replacement immigration is popular, the dreamers are popular, the wall is unpopular, rebuilding infrastructure is unpopular, Obamacare is popular and virtuous, never ending wars to make conservative Mohammedans into progs are popular and virtuous, and so on and so forth, a bubble where he is a bad person, a low status person, and his natural inclinations are gross, wicked, and depraved. They are gaslighting him. Alinsky 101: socially isolate the target.

Having one Trumpist in the White House is still something. He went through the motions of trying to overthrow Syria, while quietly letting Syria be Syria. We thought he cucked out when he bombed Syria in February, but in the end, Trump prevailed despite officially cucking out and bombing Syria. He seemingly yielded, but in the end, it was Trump playing 4D Chess.

Rather than looking at the complicated details of DACA, the wall, miscellaneous wars, Charlottesville, Google, domain name seizures, and lawless exercise of executive authority by judges, all of which may be interpreted as collapse of will by Trump, 4D chess by Trump, or the Permanent Government cheerfully going its merry way paying absolutely no attention to the mere president, we need to step back and view current events in the context of the last thousand years.

What tends to happen is that when you have a permanent government that is incohesive, it suffers a holiness spiral, as each little conspiracy in the government tries to outflank all the other little conspiracies, taking advantage of no friends to the right, no enemies to the left. And so the Tsar was forced to hold elections and cede power to elected officials, because his bureaucratic apparatus wante legitimacy for stuff that was lefter than could plausibly be blamed on the Czar. Then the Kadets seized power, intending and expecting to institute a constitutional monarchy. Then the socialists seized power and removed the monarchy, but found it difficult to support their democratic credentials because the people were not in fact ready for socialism and not in fact ready to lose the monarchy, then the communists seized power, and then there were internal power struggles within the communist party.

Grenada has a similar story. What happens is that movement left is made in the name of the people, but inevitably the permanent government moves left faster than the people do, so its democratic credentials become less and less credible, and the government increasingly lies about representing the will of the people, and crushes anyone who calls out the lie.

And right now the policies that are in fact being implemented have no plausible democratic credentials, despite ever louder proclamations to the contrary.

We are not in the run up to open left wing dictatorship, because left wing dictatorship is never open. Mao and the rest claimed to be the will of the people, and I am sure the vast majority of Chinese, North Koreans, and so forth believe that leftism was the will of the people. But we are in the situation where the lie becomes more obvious, and is therefore enforced more coercively.

This is a rerun of the Russian "Revolution", the French "Revolution", Pol Pot's Cambodia, communism in Grenada, and many others like it. You need to step back from the details of Trumpists being exiled from the Trump government and look at current events from the thousand year view.

Maybe Trump will reluctantly go along with this, maybe he will be overthrown and killed. It looks less and less likely that he will prevail, though he prevailed on Syria.

If Obamacare is not repealed, the wall is not built, mass migration continues, and our infrastructure continues to deteriorate, America is not a democracy. We are now retreading the path the socialists took in Russia and Grenada, with a merely elected government unable to deliver legitimacy to the ever lefter actions of the Permanent Government. In America today, the mere president cannot supply legitimacy to the mighty power of the Presidency. As in Grenada 1979 and Russia 1916, the permanent government is too far left to obtain legitimacy from elections.

We are ruled by a government that hates us and wants to destroy us, and tells us we hate ourselves and wish to destroy ourselves, and I suppose most people will believe this. But it is not true, and the last election proved it was not true.

Chicks dig jerks

2017-09-21 06:22:10

This is not going to turn into a game blog. Other men are much better at game than I am. I know, because I have seen them in action. On the other hand, I am not just an average f#@#!g chump. I clearly score more than the average f#@#!g chump, and fat and in my sixties I still score more than the average f#@#!g chump, though back when I was very fat, not so much.

I know a man half my age who was a male model and is a lot richer than I am. Girls stop and turn their heads when he walks through the mall. If he stands still, cute girls appear from nowhere and start conversations with him. But then nothing happens. Money and looks gets your foot in the door, but it does not get you laid. His problem is that he is far too nice.

Now a lot of readers of this blog seem to believe that nice, upper class girls, the girls that come from intact families, go to good universities and have supportive upper class fathers are not like that. Being a nice guy will, they think, get you a nice girl.

Bullshit.

The girl who started fucking at nine years old, jumped aboard more cocks than merry go round rides, mostly the cocks of criminals, and is still unmarried at thirty five because she is incapable of bonding with any man, is the girl who whose doting intact family spent a shitload of money getting her a good law degree from a good university. And this is precisely what evolutionary theory predicts[65]. It is precisely the girl with the good family and a loving father who is disinclined to have sex with the nice guy. Nice guys have a way better shot with girls whose fathers have died or abandoned them. I have tried nice, and I have tried being an asshole, and nice gets mostly gold diggers and a few fatherless girls.

---

[65]https://heartiste.wordpress.com/2013/11/18/a-new-theory-explains-why-chicks-dig-jerks/

If you want a nice girl, be the bad man. The only society where nice guys get the girl is the society where the patriarch does not allow any non related males near his daughter except the man he has already decided will marry her. (And in such a society she will agree to marry him, because she wants to climb aboard the first plausibly high status cock that she meets, and her Dad treats him as high status and forces her to treat him as high status.) Ballroom dancing is pretty much a ritual to make the males look high status to the girls, so back in the day the system was a girl had a dance card filled out by her father, and was compelled to dance with everyone on the dance card, and be polite and respectful to him, and forbidden to dance with anyone not on the dance card.

But in a society where you can meet chicks without asking their dad to put you on their ballroom dance card, you need to treat chicks like dirt. And you especially need to treat them like trash if you want chicks from intact families who don't have a number larger than your own.

One of my commenters told me that if I was dating much younger women, I was dating gold diggers. Yes, I have dated gold diggers, lots of gold diggers. But the trouble with gold diggers is that they want the gold, they don't want to lay me. If I want to lay women, I get far better luck not giving them any gold, at least not until they have been having sex with me for a while without any indication of fidelity or financial support. I would be happy to date gold diggers if I got laid that way, but I don't get laid that way - OK, I did get laid by one gold digger, but it was part of a plot to commit paternity fraud. Beta provider game just does not work. I know, because I have tried it extensively. You need a little bit of beta provider game, but it has to be part of asshole game, and you don't turn on the beta provider game until after asshole game has succeeded. The chick needs to think that by laying you, serving you, and obeying you, *then* she reveals the soft nice guy inside your harsh exterior. Early niceness will lose the chick. Similarly, when you catch a fish, got to give it a hard jerk to set the hook. You let it run only after it is well and truly hooked. There comes a time in the relationship when you need to give her some beta provider game, or else you will lose her. But if you give her beta provider game too soon, too easily, or too much, you will also lose her, to someone who is a much bigger asshole than you are.

If you want a society where men act well, you need a society where men that act well get laid. Thus for civilization, must have patriarchy, and that patriarchy will be very forcefully resisted by women howling for their demon lover, and has to be very forcefully imposed on those women.

How forcefully? Well, England before 1810 or so was fairly successful at keeping women in line, and frequently deployed methods that would make the Taliban blush, methods that horrified the Victorians. We need to copy eighteenth century England, eighteenth century Virginia, and early nineteenth century Australia. The Old Testament gave women a legal status similar to that of modern day pets, and eighteenth century England was only marginally more progressive than Old Testament Israel. And to the extent that it was marginally more progressive than old Testament Israel, I would argue that this was a big mistake that led to the disaster we now suffer.

Giving women legal status similar to that of pets would have two effects: It would reward civilized behavior, and it would raise fertility to Timor Leste levels. Now some of my commenters are worried about white fertility. If whites were reproducing at Timor Leste levels, pretty soon we would need to conquer inferior races, take their land, and restrain them from reproducing. Oh the horror. Which reasoning seems scarcely different from the proposition that Europeans should restrain their reproduction so that we can benevolently rescue four billion African refugees over the next forty years.

Cryptocurrency

2017-09-25 05:52:06

Our financial system is corrupt and oppressive. Cryptocurrencies represent an opportunity to route around that system, and make lots of money doing so.

Cryptocurrency is real, and presents the opportunity to make enormous amounts of money. Also, cryptocurrency scams are real, and present the opportunity to lose enormous amounts of money. Like the dot-com bubble in the 90s, you can add the concept of blockchain to just about anything and have a 'business' worth millions, no matter how idiotic the original idea. The vast majority of initial coin offerings are investments in businesses that are not providing anyone with any value, have no real customers and no obvious prospect of ever having any real customers.

The successful altcoin will be genuinely decentralized, as bitcoin was designed to be, originally was, and to some extent still is. Most of the altcoins, possibly all of them except the Bitcoins and Ethereum, are furtively centralized.

It will use, or at least offer the option, of Zooko type wallet names, as Bitcoin and Ethereum do.

It will be scalable to enormous numbers of transactions with low transaction costs, as Steemit and Ripple are, but Bitcoin and Ethereum are not.

It will support sidechains, and exchanges will be sidechained.

It will be a blogging and tweeting platform, as Steemit is, and will be a decentralized blogging and tweeting platform, as Steemit is not.

Every website reporting on the altcoin boom and the initial coin offering boom[66] has an incentive to not look too closely at the claimed numbers. Looks to me that only Bitcoin and Steemit.com have substantial numbers of real users making real arms length transactions. Maybe Ethereum and Ripple also. The rest are unlikely to have any significant number of real, arms length, users. The white papers don't tell you the qualifications of the people running the operation, or what they are going to do, what milestones they hope to reach.

The crypto coin business is full of scammers, and there is no social pressure against scammers, no one wants to look too closely, because a close look would depress the market. There is no real business plan, no very specific or detailed idea of how the coin offering service is going to be of value, how it is going to get from where it is now, to where it is going to usefully be. It is very hard to find out how many real users a crypto currency has, and how much stuff is available denominated in that crypto currency.

Most of the alt currencies are just me-too copies of bitcoin, not adding any substantial value, and/or they cannot scale, and they are deceptive about how centralized and how

---

[66]https://coinmarketcap.com/coins/

vulnerable to state attack they are. Nearly all of them are furtively centralized, as Bitcoin never was. They all claim to be decentralized, but when you read the white paper, as with Waves, or observe actual practice, as with Steemit, they are usually completely centralized, and thus completely vulnerable to state pressure, and quite likely state seizure as an unregulated financial product, thus offer no real advantage over conventional financial products. When you buy an initial coin offering, you are usually buying shares, usually non voting shares, in a business with no assets and no income and no clear plan to get where they will have assets and income, as in the dot com boom.

The numbers show[67] that Bitcoin is number one, ethereum number two, ripple number four, and steemit.com number eighteen, but my wild assed guess is that Bitcoin is number one, steemit number two, ethereum number three. I have absolutely no idea where ripple stands. No one is providing data that would enable us to estimate real, arms length users.

Bitcoin exchanges are banks, and banks naturally become fractional reserve institutions. Bitcoin exchanges are furtively and secretly investing customer deposits, without reporting the resulting term transformation.

Genuinely free market banks, and bitcoin exchanges are genuinely free market banks, have a financial incentive to engage in term transformation - borrow short, lend long. Which is great for everyone until a rainy day comes, rains on everyone, and everyone withdraws their deposits all at the same time, and suddenly all those long term loans cannot be liquidated except at a loss, whereupon the banks exchanges turn to the state, and so begin the transition from a backed currency to a state currency, ceasing to be free market banks.

The trouble with fractional reserve is that free market banks, banks trading in a backed, rather than state, currency, tend to deny, understate and misrepresent the term transformation risk, making them slowly, and often unintentionally, drift into becoming scams. If the reserve fraction is visible to customers, then we could rely on caveat emptor. Right now, however, every bitcoin exchange is drifting into becoming a scam.

We need, and we could easily have but do not have, a system where the amount of bitcoins owed to customers by an exchange is knowable and provable, and the amount of bitcoins owned by an exchange is knowable and provable, so that the reserve fraction is visible, whereupon the exchange would have to provide information about the extent and nature of its term transformation, or else would likely lose customers, or at least would lose large, long term customers. This would involve the decentralized cryptocurrency making each exchange a sidechain operating a centralized cryptocurrency backed by the decentralized cryptocurrency. Which would also help mightily with scaling.

Bitcoin and ethereum is truly decentralized, in that it is a protocol that any entity can use, and that in practice lots of entities do use. If the government grabs some hosts, or some hosts do bad things, they can just be ignored, and the system continues elsewhere. They also use Zooko type identities, which in practice means your wallet name looks like line noise. This is outstandingly user hostile, and a reason so many people use exchanges, but it provides the core of resistance to state power.

Unfortunately, Bitcoin and Ethereum face scaling limits. Maybe ethereum will fix its

---

[67] https://coinmarketcap.com/coins/

scaling limits. Bitcoin does not seem to be fixing them. This makes Bitcoin and Ethereum transactions inherently expensive, which is likely to prevent them from replacing the corrupt and oppressive US government controlled financial system.

Steemit.com has a far superior design which does not result in scaling limits - although we have yet to see how its witness election system will perform at scale - as the system scales, money holders have less incentive to vote, less incentive to vote responsibly, and voting will inherently cost more.

Steemit.com is also highly centralized. The altcoin that will win will be the one needs to be scalable all the way to Visa and Mastercard levels, and needs to be visibly decentralized, visibly resistant to state seizure, and needs to have a mechanism that makes the fractional reserves of exchanges visible to exchange users.

Bitcoin was genuinely decentralized from the beginning, and over time became more centralized. Big exchanges and a small number of big miners are on the path to inadvertently turning it into another branch of the oppressive and corrupt government fiat money system.

The new altcoin offering are for the most part not genuinely decentralized. They have a plan for becoming genuinely decentralized some time in the future, but the will and ability to carry the plan through has not been demonstrated.

I like the steemit design. The witness system is scalable, the witness election system has problems which may be fixable, or may be inherent.

But I have a suspicion that investing in steemit is only going to profit whoever owns steemit.com, not the owners of steemit currency.

According to Steemit documentation, it looks like a well designed cryptocurrency that deserves to replace Bitcoin, because it is more scalable, more user friendly, and more immediately usable.

Well, that is what it looks like. Except its front end is the steemit.com website, and any one website can easily be seized by the feds. If actually decentralized, it should be a bunch of websites using a common crypto currency and a common identity system,

Remember usenet: A common protocol, and an internal name system. The particular host through which you accessed it did not matter all that much, because all hosts had to behave much the same. Steemit should be something like usenet with money, and it is not.

The way usenet worked, anyone (meaning anyone's computer and his client program) could join as a client by having an agreement with a host, and anyone (meaning anyone's powerful and well connected computer system) could join as a host by having an agreement with a few existing members.

A successful altcoin needs to be a blogging platform like Steemit, but it also needs to be a federation, like Usenet or Mastodon. Many of the blogs will be offering goods or services for cryptocurrency.

Then one could be more sure that success of the federation currency would benefit owners of the currency, rather than owners of a single central website.

Needs to be Mastodon with the ability to support a blog like post, and like Steemit, and unlike Mastodon, to send and receive money. Steemit.com is wordpress.com with the ability to send and receive money.

Bitcoin has a decentralized name system, rooted in Zooko style names that are not human intelligible. Its resistance to state power comes partly from the fact that there are several miners and anyone can be a miner, and partly from its decentralized name system.

Steemit has a communication and blogging system. But if I hold steemit currency, steemit.com connects that to my phone number, which the government connects to my true name. All that handy dandy data that the government would like all in one place that you can serve a warrant on or mount a raid on. Or just sell for profit.

Need a decentralized communication, identity, name, and blogging system, unlike Steemit.com's centralized communication and blogging system, and a name system that is resistant to government intervention and control, like Bitcoin's name system. Thus the blogs offering goods and services for crypto currency will be resistant to regulation or seizure by the state. When a ruler meddles as much as our state does, he gives dangerously great power to those dangerously close to him. The regulatory state inevitably drifts into anarcho tyranny, or, like Venezuela, into violent and chaotic anarchy.

But we also want human readable names. How can we square Zooko's triangle? (As Aaron Schwarz famously asked, and then infamously gave a very stupid answer.) I will give my answer as to how a crypto currency can square Zooko's triangle in a following post. (The answer being, much as namecoin does it.)

Losing in Afghanistan

2017-09-27 23:35:10

To the immense disappointment of his base, and indeed the immense disappoint of the vast majority of American voters left and right, Trump, breaking his election promises, decided to continue war in Afghanistan, while making the war slightly less infested by lawyers, transexuals, and women's rights activists.

Well, delawyering the war will certainly help, but lawyers are not the core of the problem.

To put the Afghan war in perspective: In 1983 Reagan invaded Grenada, won the war in about the same time as our initial victory in Afghanistan, purged the permanent government very thoroughly, including numerous "non governmental aid organizations", installed a new government at bayonet point, and left one month after invading. The new right wing government promptly held an election, which produced a very similar right wing government, and since then there has been no trouble in Grenada, and all elections since then have produced similarly Reaganite results, even though all elections before the invasion produced radical left wing results.

Reagan put his foot down for one month, and the place remains quietly Reaganite forever, without an American soldier in sight.

The Afghan war, on the other hand, has been running for sixteen years, and the Afghan government, despite being supposedly democratically elected, is so corrupt and bitterly unpopular that it would collapse overnight without constant violent American support. And this simply shows no sign of changing. Even if we fight a lot more effectively, thanks to delawyering the war, there is still a power vacuum in Afghanistan waiting for the Taliban.

The problem in Afghanistan is not winning the war. We won the war overnight immediately after invading. The problem is, what do you do with victory?

The problem is not that the US army in Afghanistan is infested with State Department agents making marines wear high heeled shoes. The problem is that the government in Afghanistan is infested with State Department agents making schoolgirls put a condom on a banana, who are trying in an ineffectual limp wristed fashion to impose the American state religion in an environment where a hostile and armed opposing religion has deep roots. Further, every Afghan who matters can see that victory for the State Department religion would mean that he probably will not get his dick wet. Communism in Grenada had no roots except the permanent government and the quasi statal NGOs. Purge the permanent government and the NGOs, problem solved. Mohammedanism in Afghanistan has considerably deeper roots.

You need to bring a gun to a gun fight, and a religion to a holy war. The State Department has brought a religion to a holy war, but the problem is that their religion stinks.

How do you win in Afghanistan?

You install a King whose religious practices and official state religion are acceptable to the vast majority of his subjects, which is to say, totally unacceptable to the State Department. You install a conservative Mohammedan King, one who does not think that Mohammedanism, rightly understood, is progressivism. You install a King with a striking resemblance to Dost Mohammad Khan.

The cause of these wars is that the State Department is violating the peace of Westphalia, by imposing our state religion on the entire world.

What women want

2017-09-28 22:50:14

This is not turning into a pua blog. I studied pua long before there was such a word, or such a community, but what I have learned is not easy to express verbally, and anyway other people are one hell of a lot better at it than I am.

The main thing I have learned is that women are incompetent and wicked at making sexual and romantic choices, and should never have been emancipated.

Also the concept of "consent" is not easily mapped onto the real life sexual and romantic behavior of women, and therefore should not be given legal or moral weight. Short of a full marriage ceremony where vows are made before God and man under parental guidance, it is really difficult to say whether a woman consented or not, and makes little practical difference.

Sometimes I watch chick flicks either for social reasons, or to learn the nature of women. The evidence provided by such movies is useful, because I don't want to discuss my private life, and if I do discuss my private life my commenters are going to say "but those women are no good skanks. Most girls who go to nice universities don't behave like that". The movies on the other hand obviously target the norm, the typical female. They have been focus tested as to what gets their audience panties wet.

So:

The anime romance, "Yona of the Dawn": (which inspired this post) Love interest number one murders Yona's father. This gives her the total hots. Love interest number one is about to murder her also. Her response is disturbingly erotic, and seriously lacking inclination towards self preservation. Her father's dead body is lying around during this scene, but she pays it almost no attention. Love interest number two rescues her. You might suppose that this terminates the romance with love interest number one, but you would be wrong. She has a knack for unrescuing herself.

Now you know why female voters vote to import Mohammedans.

"Mike and Dave need Wedding Dates". Alpha males with massive preselection fall so in love that they turn into beta bucks friendzoned chumps, and the female protagonist fucks someone else.

"The Wedding Date" Mr Beta bucks is so in love he marries the woman who cuckolded him and who shows every indication that she intends to continue to cuckold him.

I am not cherry picking the worst movies. These are just the last three, except for another that was pretty similar. Disloyalty, infidelity, desire for murderers, self destructiveness, desire for violent evil men, and sexual desire overriding duty to kin, friends, and lovers.

One hundred roses monogamy comes from coercively restraining women from bad behavior, which comes from understanding that women are prone to bad behavior. Without external coercion, we tend to get stuck in defect/defect equilibrium.

The Victorian strategy of persuading women to behave well by ascribing good behavior to women bit the Victorians on the ass badly.

In defense of Hugh Hefner

2017-10-02 23:10:23

Why is Hugh a pevert for having sex with numerous fertile age women at the age of ninety? Here is a toast to 20 milligrams of tada and 12.5 milligrams of caber.

It is stupid and counterproductive to blame men for sexual revolution, and particularly stupid and particularly counterproductive to blame alpha males for the sexual revolution.

Blaming Hugh Hefner for the sexual revolution is stupid. Blame Queen Caroline. Hugh Hefner was just watching the decline from poolside.

The problem is not that Hugh Hefner had sex with lots of women, the problem is that women want to have sex with alpha males. The problem is that women want to party till their youth and beauty runs out. Rather than contrasting the sexuality promoted by Hugh Hefner with one hundred roses monogamy that only existed up to the early nineteenth century, we need to contrast it with today's sexuality.[68]

Starting with Queen Caroline, and following up with Florence Nightingale, the problem always has been women out of control.

---

[68]https://www.hollywoodreporter.com/news/camille-paglia-hugh-hefners-legacy-trumps-masculinity-feminisms-sex-phobia-1044769

She wants 2.3 more years of sex with other men before she settles for you.[69] They don't want to waste a day more of their youth and fertility on their husbands than absolutely necessary

Monogamy and chastity are an agreement between males for equitable sharing of pussy, which deal was imposed on women with a stick, and the stick needs to re-applied from time to time.

"Hypergamy" means that women prefer to fuck Hugh Hefner. Since we have suppressed all the Hugh Hefners, since today's elite is unmanly and emasculated, it now means they prefer to fuck Jeremy Meeks.

We were better off when they were fucking Lord Byron and Hugh Hefner, than with them fucking Jeremy Meeks.

Suppress the Hugh Hefners of the world, and you will find your ten year old daughter is fucking a forty year old motorbike gang leader and ice dealer.

The problem is not Playboy magazine. The problem is that Queen Caroline did not receive a whipping.

In Victorian times they said that the problem was aristocratic wealthy male military officers. Make the army plebeian, it will solve the problem.

Then in Hugh Hefner's time, they said the problem was wealthy and cultured businessmen, make business politically correct, it will solve the problem. What are they now saying about Jeremy Meeks?

We are targeting affluent high IQ males to make them terrified of women, thus "A rape on Campus" and "sexual harassment". The man who did twenty years in prison for torture, rape, murder, and cannibalism gets a free pass.

This whole business started out as an attack on King and Aristocracy. Women are wonderful, it is just aristocrats and military officers *forcing* them to behave badly. Free and empower women, raise their self esteem, make the military plebeian, and they will behave well.

Have they been behaving well?

We observe women doing bad things with powerful men. We conclude that powerful men are using their power to make women behave badly. So we take power away from men and give it to women. "Sexual harassment" law makes eunuchs of wealthy men. The reason that lawyerettes have sex with criminal lowlives is that the judges and senior partners they associate with are terrified of them, and are therefore unattractive.

Are women now behaving better? Is it better that lawyerettes have sex with judges, or sex with criminals?

Well, actually, it is better if they get married, cook meals, and have babies. We now have profoundly dysgenic fertility, as cooking and babies is only for women too stupid to become cat lady PhDs. A woman has all her life to get an education and career, but only a short time to get married and have children.

I don't behave badly because I am a bad person. I behave badly because in this environment, that is what it takes to get my dick wet. I don't like defect/defect equilibrium at all.

---

[69]https://dalrock.wordpress.com/2017/10/02/she-wants-2-3-more-years-of-sex-with-other-men-before-she-settles-for-you/

We cannot get out of defect/defect and into cooperate/cooperate by calling on only one side in the war of the sexes to cooperate. In fact we cannot get out of defect/defect merely by calling on people. To end the war will take some enforcement, which enforcement was abandoned with Queen Caroline.

A bad time to invest in Bitcoin

2017-10-08 06:42:34

Back in 2013 I urged people to invest in Bitcoin.

Yesterday someone asked my cleaning lady to invest in Bitcoin.

Now if someone had asked her to accept payment in Bitcoin, or send payment in Bitcoin, then this would be compelling evidence that one should invest in Bitcoin.

But when cleaning ladies are asked to invest in Bitcoin, not a good investment.

When Bitcoin began, everyone was a miner, and everyone was a peer, everyone stored the entire blockchain. Which was great, but did not scale. And now people are struggling with half assed ideas about how to get it to scale. Bitcoin can no longer deliver on its original promises, has not figured out what new promises to make, and many of the new promises are unworkable, or are scams, or are likely to turn into scams.

How to do cryptocurrency right

2017-10-08 06:44:24

Proof of work tends to be inherently slow, has inherently high transaction costs, and the miner's interests are not identical with those holding currency as a store of value and those using currency as a medium of exchange.

Proof of stake is nontrival to get right. It is a form of the infamously difficult to understand (and infamously difficult to program correctly) Paxos protocol. The Paxos protocol has the great advantage over the proof of work in that after an unpredictable and possibly large time, it announces a definite result, whereas with the bitcoin proof of work protocol, no result is ever final, it just becomes exponentially probable.

Ignore the carping that proof of stake is inherently flawed. Any implementation of proof of stake that is easy to understand is likely inherently flawed, that being the infamous nature of Paxos.

Bitcoin was genuinely decentralized from the beginning, and over time became more centralized. Big exchanges and a small number of big miners are on the path to inadvertently turning it into another branch of the oppressive and corrupt government fiat money system.

The new altcoin offering are for the most part not genuinely decentralized. They have a plan for becoming genuinely decentralized some time in the future, but the will and ability to carry the plan through has not been demonstrated.

Assume that, instead of everyone being a peer, we have few dozen or so peers, the peers distributed among several nuclear armed jurisdictions, and each peer has a hundred million or so clients, and each peer stores the entire blockchain forever.

OK, we are talking rather large peers. A terabyte of storage, a hundred dollars worth, will keep one of them going for a week. Say two terabytes for redundancy. I don't think cost of storage is going to be a significant problem.

Scaling, however, is the hard problem. Making enormous amounts of storage actually useful and effective is the problem. The amount of storage per client is absolutely insignificant. The amount of bandwidth per client is absolutely insignificant. Having a useful connection between enormous numbers of clients and enormous amounts of storage via enormous amounts of bandwidth is the hard part.

Prompt response is another problem. It inherently takes time, and potentially large and unpredictable time, to reach consensus on the blockchain.

We can, however, have fast trust base responses followed by consensus: Since the peers are pretty big, you can trust a peer for your payment during the short time it takes for consensus to settle.

The way this would work is that every client is hosted by a peer. If his host should crash, or turn evil, he can move to another peer, though during the move he will not be able to make fast transactions. When he makes a payment, the peer hosting him testifies that this is not a double spend, and the payment is instantly flagged to the recipient as cleared - but it does not get flagged as settled, and the recipient cannot spend the payment, until it gets incorporated into the blockchain consensus, about twenty minutes later. Since the peers are big and long lived, you can trust them with your money for half an hour or so, and if you don't want to trust them or you don't trust some of them, you just wait for the transaction to be incorporated into the consensus.

Trump still not in power.

2017-10-09 23:31:23

I hoped and expected that Trump would be in power by now, and observed that this would feel like a coup, and would require measures that resemble a coup.

CNN complains "Trump goes rogue" and complains that Trump is fighting for control of the presidency.

Now he is fighting for control of the presidency?

During the weekend, he issued a demand to end the great replacement[70], which has continued during his presidency.

Giving effect to these demands would require open political conflict with the Republican party, and open armed conflict with the permanent government.

If he yields, he will be a one term president, and the Republicans, to their immense relief, will be voted out in 2018 and 2020, giving them excuses for not implementing the policy that they run on in elections.

On his performance since the election, and the precedent of every president since Roosevelt, he will yield.

But he is Trump.

___

[70]https://www.washingtonpost.com/news/post-politics/wp/2017/10/08/trump-administration-releases-hard-line-immigration-principles-threatening-deal-on-dreamers/?utm_term=.0f840b978ba4

To win, he has to bring the White House into line, and then get heavily involved in a bunch of primary fights to remove Republican Party cucks in 2017. Which so far he has not been doing. He has been trying to make a deal with the establishment, a deal consistent with him remaining sufficiently faithful to his base to win re-election, and the establishment just is not having any.

Events so far have been consistent with the Moldbuggian view that elections and all that are as relevant as Queen Elizabeth going in a stagecoach to open the British Parliament. The Permanent Government runs the country day to day, Harvard sets policy, and the American Law Institute, a wholly owned subsidiary of Harvard, legislates.

Indeed CNN implicitly endorsed the Moldbuggian view, by complaining that the country has two foreign policies, one set by the State Department and the Defense Department, and Trump's policy - with the clear implication that Trump should butt out and stick to robotically signing State Department policy.

The trouble with CNN's solution, however, is that the State Department and the Defense Department do not have one foreign policy, but a hundred, with the result that their foreign proxies are always shooting at each other, and from time to time shooting at US troops and diplomats. Without a president in charge, they are institutionally incapable of acting as one. The Cathedral has not solved the institutional and organizational problem of acting as one without delegating all power through a single chief executive officer. They are not agreement capable.

And, not being agreement capable, they are incapable of making a deal with Trump.

Trump is a deal maker. But now he is in a situation where deals are just not possible. He has to fight and possibly be utterly defeated, or fail to fight and quite certainly be utterly defeated, fail to fight and be a lame duck for his entire single term, and then ignominiously lose the election in a landslide.

His attempts to cut a deal have alienated his base, and show absolutely no sign of producing a deal. He is dealing with a group of people institutionally incapable of making a deal. The accusation that Trump is intransigent is pure projection. Social Justice Warriors always project.[71] Trump is alarmingly ready to compromise, but can find no one to compromise with. Winning will require measures that have been unthinkable - yet Tony Abbot and Duterte were willing to deploy such measures. I thought, therefore, Trump would be willing to deploy such measures. So far, however, he has yielded. Trump is a deal maker. He is going to have to be a general. He is going to have to seize the power of the presidency, or be a one term president as he takes the blame for Harvard's policy of electing a new people.

Role models

2017-10-10 07:44:47

When Han Solo hits on princess Leia in "The Empire Strikes Back", he does it right.She shit tests him to hell and back, and he plows on[72]. Similarly, in "Gone with the wind"

---

[71]https://voxday.blogspot.com.au/2017/08/sjws-always-project.html
[72]https://www.youtube.com/watch?v=QMk0-pZfx5Q

Rhett Butler proposes to Scarlett O'Hara, she rejects him, and he forcibly kisses her[73].

When I look at old movies, the hero always does it right. When I watch newer movies, the hero never does it right. It seems forced, artificial, and gratingly unnatural. Looks like robots carrying out a script to move the plot along. In real life, would never work, the hero would never score dealing with a woman in the way that men deal with women in modern movies.

And modern men just do not score approaching women in real life. In modern movies, action girl saves the lad in distress, and then for no apparent reason starts to like him. So it is like, "how do you meet a girl except you wait for action girl to rescue you?"

Boy meets girl remains a major plot thread, but boy and girl just never get romantic in a natural normal manner. I don't mind if boy meets girl because of time travel, elves, space ships, dragons, and space aliens. For that I can suspend disbelief. But I just cannot suspend disbelief when they get romantic without going through the normal mating dance. In the Lord of the Rings movie, Arwen goes in for a kiss with Aragorn. The dialog explains that they already have a sexual relationship. The film maker has to depict them as already somehow having a long established off screen romance, because he is just not allowed to depict a man and a women getting together in the way that men and women actually do. He just cannot depict Aragorn going in for a kiss with an as yet unkissed Arwen.

Never interrupt the enemy when he is making a mistake

2017-10-15 21:26:19

The left, in its enthusiastic rush to ever greater holiness, has forgotten that its rules are only for the little people.

Sometimes the enemy of my enemy is my friend. But Harvey Weinstein is my enemy, even though he is being devoured by my enemies.

The Khmer Rouge started out as a bunch of very smart western educated intellectuals. Who proceeded to torture each other to death. They wound up with cadre that could not read numbers. Observe the obvious collapse in intelligence and competence among our elite. You could not trust the scientists building to ITER to build a chicken coop unsupervised. Recollect Obama's struggles to get the Obamacare website up. Remember the inanity and stupidity that was revealed in the Challenger inquiry[74], and ITER is a long way downhill from the Challenger.

But we should no more buy in to this doctrine of the innate purity of women, than we should buy in to the allegations of CIA, fascist, and capitalist influence in the Khmer Rouge.

It is great that Harvey Weinstein is getting the shaft, but these women are not victims. They are whores.

Harvey Weinstein is guilty of hitting on hot chicks while old and fat. And worst of all, hitting on them incompetently. If he had lost some weight, or been better at it, he would

---

[73]https://www.youtube.com/watch?v=74kz5K70iAo
[74]https://blog.reaction.la/global-warming/the-cause-of-the-decline/

have been fine. The reason this is all coming to light now is that he has been getting older and fatter.

You need to apply the Mike Pence rules in the workplace: If you are with female coworker, leave the door open, because if you close the door, it is like watching television with a large economy size bag of potato crisps beside you.

Sex is pre rational and pre verbal. If you are alone with a pretty woman, no one is going to open the door, and there is a horizontal surface, you will, perhaps unconsciously and unintentionally, emit certain stimuli, and likely she will react to these stimuli with certain other stimuli, quite likely without conscious awareness of doing so, and you will, perhaps unconsciously, react ...

And pretty soon you are both horizontal on the floor.

But since she probably did not intend any of that to happen, under the current rules, she gets to call it rape. The mating dance has the form of pursuit and predation, conquest and surrender. So if she subsequently decides she was raped, it is always plausible, at least to her.

Its like having a bag of potato crisps beside you while watching television, except that she gets to claim that the potato chips forced her.

Which, in a sense, they did. She did not want to have sex with you, and she did not want to finish an entire economy sized bag of potato crisps. While she and you were watching television you heard her say eleven times that she did not want any more potato crisps. And while she and you were fucking she said
> **"Stop!"**
loudly and clearly several times, but you were too distracted to keep count.

By enforcing anti sex rules selectively upon the elite, we make the elite unattractive, with the result that women want to mate dysgenically.

We need to enforce anti sex rules selectively upon the non elite.

Obviously it should be illegal and subject to the death penalty for a man and a woman to get together behind closed doors, when that woman belongs to another man, so in a sense this is a move in the correct direction, but the trouble is we are only restraining the sexual behavior of affluent white males, not of dope dealers, criminals, and blacks, so criminals and blacks get all the pussy, and get to look, and act, way more manly than the guy in the corner office.

The concept of consent requires verbal and verbalizing consciousness. And sex predates verbal and verbalizing consciousness by a very long time. The part of your mind that decides to have sex is far older and more powerful than the part of your mind that is capable of making up a narrative about what you are doing and why.

We can meaningfully apply the concept of consent to marriage, where a woman consents to move from one household and the authority of one male, to another household and another male, but trying to apply it to sex winds up with the absurdity that each thrust needs a legal notary.

If the door is closed, and the woman does not swiftly make an exit, sex is likely to ensue, and she consented to the likelihood that it would ensue. If a man and a woman are together in private in a secure place for a reasonable length of time, there is good chance that they are going to have sex regardless of what they theoretically intend. If a woman consents to be alone with a man in private, she knows full well that sex may well ensue. If you cannot really expect to leave the large economy sized bag of potato crisps half full, regardless of your intentions, you cannot really expect to refrain from having sex, regardless of your intentions.

The reason Harvey Weinstein is now getting in trouble is that he is fat and has been getting fatter. If he had lost weight and lifted iron, he could have hit them over the head with a brick and gotten away with it.

The trouble with the way the left is enforcing restraints on male sexuality is that it means that Jeremy Meeks gets all the pussy. We need to enforce a no-getting-together-behind-closed-doors rule starting with Jeremy Meeks, rather than starting with Harvey Weinstein and Mike Pence. Our testosterone is falling, and we are getting stupid. But that the left is getting stupid is a very good thing.

Another day, another scalp

2017-10-25 11:10:48

Trump is not alt right, but the alt right is Trumpist. Jeff Flake was a cuckservative enemy of Trump, and went out denouncing Trump. The alt right is successfully nailing Trump's enemies.

Mencius Moldbug interpreted the Democrats as the inner party, and Republicans as the outer party, as subservient to the Democrats. Which accurately describes and predicts their inability to build a wall, halt race replacement, or repeal Obamacare.

But Trump, whatever his faults, is not part of the Outer Party, is manifestly an enemy of the inner party.

The inner party has been investigating Trump for imaginary crimes, but inevitably the investigation started turning up Clinton crimes, not Trump crimes, since the Clintons are criminals, and Trump is not. I expected the investigation to lead to a left wing coup or an attempted left wing coup, with some judge no one has heard of issuing a warrant for Trumps arrest on the basis of a grand jury indictment, to be followed not long afterwards with arrests of numerous prominent Republicans for insufficient leftism, but it looks like it is just going to evaporate.

With a permanent government coup against Trump evaporating, this makes a Trump coup against the permanent government ("You're fired") far more feasible, as everyone rushes to support the strong horse.

The Moldbug analysis is that all this is just a distraction. No Trump coup, Trump will never take power, Trump will merely delay some parts of the inner party program by eight years, thus ensuring that the frog is slow boiled, rather than fast fried.

So far, Trump is not in power, and nailing Jeff Flake, and perhaps nailing the Clintons, is merely a step towards getting him into power. But it is a step that Moldbuggians and neoreaction would not have predicted.

If Trump turns out to be just another chump, retreading the steps of Nixon, then the Moldbuggian analysis is confirmed. All Nixon's rightward measures evaporated like the morning dew. A recalcitrant governing apparatus simply failed to give any lasting effect to them. All Nixons leftward concessions proved permanent, fundamental, massive, disastrous, and irreversible.

Trump has taken important and major steps to defunding the left. He has had far more success in defunding the left than Ronald Reagan. But the left is still massively government funded, while the alt right is still massively government persecuted.

If Trump takes power, falsifying the Moldbug thesis, it will be that the alt right frog marched him into power, as King David's mighty men conscripted him into Kingship, and the junior officers hauled Pinochet off to the still smoking presidential palace. It is striking that Jeff Flake conceded on the same day, or within a few days, of the investigation into Trump going off the rails, indicating that both are merely symptoms of a deeper change, that deeper change being recognition of the strong horse. We are still far away from Trump actually being in power, but today, not as far as it was.

Trump actually in power would be able to use the resources of the state to ensure his re-election. The presidency has gathered power so overwhelming as to render democracy largely moot, giving itself legislative, judicial, and budgetary authority, as for example funding Obamacare without regard of the inability of Congress to agree on paying for the freebies they had already agreed to. If Trump actually had power, he could just direct the wall to be built, without regard for any budget. After all, congress has not been able to pass a budget for a mighty long time. The budget process is starting to resemble the Queen riding a stagecoach to open the houses of Parliament. Thus Trump actually in power would likely result in a Trump dynasty. The Whitehouse press corps are de-facto government employees, working at government desks using government office services. Trump actually in power would simply fire them. If not yet fired, Trump not yet in power.

Google is evil

2017-10-28 21:40:00

Does your business use Google Analytics on its website?

Then Google will use the information that it so generously generates and analyzes for you to show ads for competing businesses to your customers. While you are analyzing the information to see how you can improve your business, they are analyzing the information to see how they can destroy your business.

And a general reminder to everyone: Add the following to your hosts file:

```
127.0.0.1 googlesyndication.com
127.0.0.1 tpc.googlesyndication.com
127.0.0.1 doubleclick.net
127.0.0.1 g.doubleclick.net
127.0.0.1 googleads.g.doubleclick.net
127.0.0.1 www.google-analytics.com
127.0.0.1 ssl.google-analytics.com
127.0.0.1 google-analytics.com
127.0.0.1 www.onclickmax.com
```

This will cause a whole lot of ads, and a whole lot of ad targeting, to disappear.

Turn off Thunderbird and Firefox's routine tattling.
Mozilla Firefox
+ Type 'about:config' in the address bar
+ Click through the warning
+ Type 'geo.' in the search box. A list of items appears
+ Doubleclick on the geo.enabled item till it reads 'False'
+ Change the two strings to 'https://localhost'
+ Change the timeout to 1
Mozilla Thunderbird
+ Select Tools/Options/Avanced/General/Config Editor
+ click through the warning
+ type 'geo.' in the search box. A list of items appears
+ set the timeout to one, and the url to 'https://localhost'

Don't use Google accounts.[75] Remember that you can create a new google account without giving them any ID information on a fresh android phone which is connected to the internet by the mall wifi, but does not have a sim card in it.

Don't use Google search for anything related to politics or money, since this is sending your searches character by character to Google. Definitely don't use Google search while logged in to your Google account. Use DuckDuckGo. I have never received a targeted ad from DuckDuckGo except in reply to my search.

Don't use Chrome, because this reports all browser activity to Google.

Disable all durable cookies for Google Servers.

Stormfront is a honeypot

2017-10-29 05:24:07

Stormfront uses Google Analytics. Google Analytics runs an alarmingly large pile of obfuscated javascript code on your browser that if you visit Stormfront, can very likely uniquely identify your browser, even if you are accessing Stromfront through Tor to anonymize your IP.

Thus, you visit Stormfront, carefully using a fake name and an anonymized IP. And then you visit Youtube with the same browser, and Youtube says that you cannot watch this video unless you sign in with your Google account, which Google goes to alarmingly great lengths to link to your true name, thereby linking your browser fingerprint to your true name.

Mueller points deer, makes horse

2017-10-30 22:11:33

Chinese have a lot more history than anyone else, and everything that happens today, happened before many times, usually in China.

So they have a saying "point deer, make horse, □□□□[76]"

---

[75]https://blog.reaction.la/politics/google-is-evil-2/
[76]https://bloodyshovel.wordpress.com/2015/06/03/the-purpose-of-absurdity/

Qin, the first emperor of China, created the first highly centralized state, with a centralized bureaucracy instead of a distributed aristocracy. And of course, wound up with a far too powerful prime minister - the classic evil vizier.

The prime minister wanted to kill the next emperor, but was not sure he could get away with it. So, to test whether he can get away with it:
> brings a deer into the palace, calls the emperor to come out, and says "look your majesty, a brought you a fine horse". The Emperor, not amused, says "Surely you are mistaken, calling a deer a horse. Right?". Then the emperor looks around at all the ministers. Some didn't say a word, just sweating nervously. Some others loudly proclaimed what a fine horse this was. Great horse. Look at this tail! These fine legs. Great horse, naturally prime minister Zhao Gao has the best of tastes.

And next thing you know, anyone who doubted it was a horse was executed, and shortly thereafter the emperor.

If Mueller succeeds in arresting these people on bogus charges, he will arrest every Trump loyalist near Trump, and, shortly thereafter, Trump.

Women and gays ruin everything

2017-11-06 23:35:20

The KDE foundation was converged, and predictably stopped maintaining KDE software.

Meanwhile, in an area far less important to me, military discipline in the US military officer class is collapsing. At the same time the US government is engaged in unsuccessful wars in Afghanistan, Iraq, Iran, Ukraine, Yemen, Somalia, Syria and Uganda, and unsuccessful regime change that requires the threat of war and is likely to drift into war in Russia, China, Belarus, Kyrgyzstan, Hungary, Czech Republic, and Macedonia.

If you have women in your organization, they need to stick to making coffee and such. The smarter ones can do a decent job at database organization and some kinds of database programming, and there are plenty of good female content creators, though the top ones are always male. But women are maladapted to large group dynamics. They are better than men at one on one social dynamics, for example superior ability to read people, but though this impressive in family scale groups, women fail disastrously at functioning larger groups, and if you give women leadership roles in such a group, the group will not accomplish its goals. Gays similarly, although the way they fail is different from the way women fail.

The trouble with convergence is that it leads to obvious and spectacular failure. The converged organization just cannot perform its goals. (Remember the Obamacare website.) Now someone is going to say NAWALT (not all women are like that). But if you have any group of substantial size, the rare exceptions, supposing the rare exceptions exist (and the lack of credible poster girls suggest that they do not exist) are too rare to have much effect on the overall group dynamics. And a group of women, or a group containing any significant number of women, cannot keep its eye on the group goals. Women have to operate under male supervision.

This creates a problem in that if the supervision is actually effective, they will seduce their supervisor. The traditional solution to this was either that they were married to their supervisor, or an all female group with an female hierarchy, but with males monitoring the performance of the all female group at every level, for example the traditional system in hospitals where the doctors and orderlies were all male, the nurses were all female, and were under the authority of a female head of their organization, the matron, but the male doctors monitored and directed the nurses moment to moment. Similarly, priests and nuns.

The modern state exists because of modern military discipline. The modern industrial economy exists because of the scientific method, and the joint stock corporation, and the joint stock corporation exists because of double entry accounting. SoX has smashed double entry accounting, Harvard has smashed the scientific method, and convergence is now smashing military discipline.

Rectification of names: Science

2017-11-10 05:26:57

Vox Day attempts to rectify names related to science[77].

Derb sneers at this as if the rapidly changing official newspeak was a valid means of communication[78], indeed the only possible valid means of communication.

Our rulers are systematically changing the meaning of words in order to obliterate reality and make it difficult for people to think, creating words that link unlike things together[79], make distinctions without real difference, obliterating the meanings of old words that make meaningful distinctions, and giving old words new nonsense meanings, meanings intended to make males, whites, and straights weak, frightened, and ashamed.

For example "pedophile" links together men who find ten year old boys attractive, men who find ten year old girls attractive, men whom ten year old girls find attractive

---

[77]https://voxday.blogspot.com.au/2017/11/derb-on-16-points.html
[78]https://www.unz.com/jderbyshire/derb-at-the-mencken-club-am-i-alt-right/
[79]https://blog.reaction.la/tag/antconcept/

(since girls can never do anything wrong, except some evil male makes them do it) and men who find fifteen year old girls with delicious breasts, bouncy buttocks, slim waists, broad hips, and fully functioning reproductive systems attractive. These are different populations. Men who find ten year old boys sexually attractive are also apt to find manly adult men sexually attractive, and are not likely to find ten year old girls attractive. Men who find ten year old girls sexually attractive are unlikely to find ten year old boys attractive, and highly unlikely to find manly adult men sexually attractive. Men whom ten year old girls find attractive are almost always preselected by an adult female demonstrating their extreme alpha characteristics (Cinderella is all about preselection) so are unlikely to be paying much attention to the misbehaving ten year old girl. And, of course, all straight males are pedophiles, because all straight males are sexually attracted to fifteen year old girls with delicious breasts, bouncy buttocks, and slim waists. Which is of course the whole point and purpose of the word "pedophile": to normalize gays, excuse female bad behavior, and demonize straights.

To see the use of the word to normalize gay sex between a middle aged man and a ten year old schoolboy, while making sex between a fifteen year old girl and a nineteen year old male sexually deviant, observe the "anti bullying" campaign. If you worry about a middle aged male hugging cross dressing schoolboy, you are a "bully". If you are not worried about a thirty year old male hugging fifteen year old girl, you are a "pedophile".

Vox Day attempts to deal with the problem of leftists killing science, gutting the body, and wearing its carcass as a skin suit, by introducing some new words:

> Scientody: the process
> Scientage: the knowledge base
> Scientistry: the profession

However, we already have well established words for all of these, in particular and most importantly the established phrase "the scientific method", which from the restoration to World War II was defined and enforced by the Royal Society.

Unfortunately, after World War II Harvard introduced a new process, "peer review" wherein official "scientists" meet behind closed doors, decide the official truth on the basis of secret evidence that they refuse to reveal to the public, and then make sure that anything that gets published is in accord with the "consensus", a procedure revealed in the Climategate files[80]. Peer review is in practice a conspiracy against the public by people trying to give themselves powerful positions in the official state religion.

The trouble with consensus, is that if someone tells you, in place of actual evidence, that X is the consensus, then chances are that all the people who believe in X are also taking the consensus as evidence. This is a positive feedback loop, similar to the squeal which occurs when you hold the microphone too close a loudspeaker. When you hold the microphone too close to a loudspeaker you get meaningless noise, and the scientific consensus is meaningless noise. Anything peer reviewed should be read with the same suspicion and incredulity as when one reads articles by believers on the lives of their saints, for much the same reasons.

---

[80]https://duckduckgo.com/?q=site%3Ahttp%3A%2F%2Fbishophill.squarespace.com%2F+climate-gate+files&t=ffsb&ia=web

The knowledge base that Vox Day refers to are the experiments and observations, but these are increasingly being contaminated by peer reviewed material. If you read The Big Fat Surprise: Why Butter, Meat and Cheese Belong in a Healthy Diet[81](a thorough study of how the scientific consensus of fat developed and changed) you will discover that peer reviewed material is like a barrel of wine to which a bucket of sewage has been added. Her account of the Mediterranean diet is a particularly entertaining depiction of the manufacture of consensus and the subsequent development of peer reviewed evidence for that consensus. After reading that, I stopped using vegetable oil. And if you consume peer reviewed material, you are getting a mixture of facts and sewage.

However, thanks to powerful articles by Feynman and Galileo, the old meaning of "scientific method" is not lost beyond recovery, and we should not abandon it for Vox Day's new word "scientody".

Where old words with old meanings still have some life in them, we should defend and restore the old words and old meanings, rather than coining new words.

When the restoration comes, we may well need a new word in place of "marriage" but "scientific method" is not so far gone that we need Vox Day's "scientody".

Whenever necessary, we need to explain that climate skeptics are actually practicing the scientific method, while the climategate files reveal that "scientists" have absolutely no interest in whether the world is warming or cooling, or whether humans are causing climate change or not. They are looking for ammunition, not truth.

As for the scientific profession, it is increasingly priestly. If you practice the old style scientific method, you are going to find it difficult to get published. Indeed, if you are affiliated with an institution, you will need to get the permission of numerous bureaucracies and bureaucrats to do the experiment you are interested in, and you will not even be allowed to do the experiment if it touches on anything political - and these days all sorts of things that you never imagined to be political, will, to your surprise, and in defiance of all logic, turn out to have been politicized.

How to lose weight

2017-11-18 07:14:25

When a high status person shows status insecurity, you can gain status by insulting him and by desecrating what is holy to him. Smash his icons to steal his status. Eating meat, salt and fat insults our ruling priesthood and our ruling religion, and desecrates what is holy to them.

Real men eat meat and fat, and salt the hell out of it.

The holy campaign against saturated fat never had any scientific basis whatsoever. It was always official science - peer reviewers meeting behind closed doors to tell mere observers what they should observe and poison the scientific literature. It was entirely motivated by instinctive irrational gut hostility against masculinity, just as the holy Global Warming campaign is motivated by gut hostility to technological civilization, hatred of what white people have created. (Also they needed an excuse to stick it to those coal min-

---

[81]https://www.amazon.com/gp/product/1451624433

ers in flyover country, and global warming gives them a rationale to make those that they hate and despise suffer.)

When my wife got sick, I was too busy looking after her to sleep with other women, so I stopped bothering about my weight, and since I was cooking and feeding her, there was always food in front of me tempting me, with the result that I developed a striking resemblance to Jabba the Hut. When she died, I set about replacing her, and God, it was brutal - well, it was always brutal, but what with being older and considerably fatter, it was even more brutal. So I set about losing weight on a high fat, moderately low carb, paleo diet, with regular fasting, running, and lifting iron. I now wear size S (small) pants, and size L (large) shirts and jackets. I have lost 38 kilos, and now dating is somewhat less brutal.

My diet is 60% fat by calorie, 20% protein by calorie, 20% carbs by calorie. Switching away from carbs is tough, a full ketogenic diet (75% fat, 20% protein, 5% carbs) gives you the keto flue until you are fully withdrawn from carbs, but even a moderate carb diet like mine is kind of harsh at first.

Fat makes you full. Carbs make you hungry.

It is not calories in calories out that makes you fat. It is insulin that makes you fat, causes heart attacks, high blood pressure, etc. Type one diabetics don't get fat except that they take insulin. Snacking, and especially snacking food containing carbs, keeps your insulin continually high, and causes you to become addicted to high insulin.

All addictive foods contain substantial amounts of carbs. They are a manifestation of insulin addiction, and high insulin tolerance. I cannot eat just one potato chip, or one slice of pizza, or drink just one glass of ice cold Mountain Dew. I keep going till it is all gone. But I like pork crackling even more than I like pizza, and yet I can easily eat an appropriate amount of pork crackling, and then stop. It is carbs that cause uncontrollable eating. Even fruit if you eat too much of it. Broccoli with cheese sauce is easier to control. Avocados are easier to control than watermelon. Not that I can entirely give up watermelon, but if I eat too much of it, I will then eat even more of it.

On a moderate carb diet, you need sodium, potassium, magnesium, and zinc. You really need to watch your electrolytes on a full ketogenic diet, but even on a moderately low carb diet it is an issue. Leafy greens help. Broccoli with cheese, Chinese cabbage with butter and chicken broth. Butter fried mushrooms.

Most of my calories come from pork, bacon, butter, lots of butter, eggs, and more butter. I liberally salt my meat, and drink lots of coffee and cold water.

Salt will raise your blood pressure, but only if you have dangerously high levels of insulin, which most Americans do. I salt the hell out of my meat and add fish sauce to everything. My blood pressure has dropped to healthy levels, my cholesterol and lipid profiles, which used to look pretty bad, now look great. To get adequate potassium and suchlike I eat brocolli and cabbage covered in hot melted cheese, mushrooms fried in butter, raw tomatoes, tomatoes cooked in butter, and raw tomatoes covered with my buttery substitute for gravy and mayo.

I also have testosterone replacement therapy, and control my estrogen levels to healthy normal male levels. Since we invented clothing, no one gets enough vitamin D3 any more, so I have 2000 units of Vitamin D3 every morning. And, of course, run, and lift iron.

Hate running, don't run very far, but I run hard for the very short distances that I do run.

But the trouble is that gravy is wheat based, thus non paleo. And what is meat without lots of salty gravy? Also, on a high fat, moderately low carb diet, I never get enough fiber, so I don't want to eat any carbs except in the form of fruit and vegetables,

Fats make you full, carbs make you hungry. All highly addictive foods contain substantial carbs, so regular gravy on meat results in uncontrollable overeating.

So this is my substitute for gravy: Take the meat juices. If I don't have enough meat juices, some broth. Add some whole eggs, a bit of mustard, some vinegar, maybe some strong hot coffee, maybe some steamed garlic, some turmeric, and some chilis. Lots of chilis, lots of fish sauce. Toss in the blender and let the blender whip it till it gets hot. Add butter, till the mix is about fifty percent meat juices, eggs, and chilis, and fifty percent meat fat and butter. Maybe some steamed parsley to make it different from time to time. I never make it the same twice. Keep going till the temperature reaches sixty five centigrade or so to make sure the eggs are pasteurized. Make sure it has enough salt. Always needs more salt than I expect. Slosh liberally over the meat, into coffee, over tomatoes, etc.

It is sort of gravy - hollandaise sauce - mayonnaise - redeye gravy. Hollandaise sauce is hot mayonnaise made with butter rather than vegetable oil. Gravy is meat juice and fat that you mix using flour to make water and oil miscible. Hollandaise and mayonnaise uses eggs and vinegar to make them miscible. Southern redeye gravy uses coffee to make the fat and meat broth miscible. So this is gravy with eggs, vinegar, and perhaps coffee to make the butter, fat and meat juice miscible.

There is something just more manly about eating bacon, roast pork crackling, and suchlike. Perhaps it is irrational to think that, but the same irrationality resulted in the government and the medical profession poisoning Americans. Anything that pisses them off is good. Chicks like badboys, and this is another little bit of badness.

Women like sexual coercion

2017-11-24 08:28:52

Their resistance is merely a shit test, to separate the strong from the weak.

What they hate, hate, hate hate hate, hate with a hatred hotter than a thousand suns, is that some guy whom they had sex with turns out to be substantially less alpha than they thought.

You doubt me? Reflect on the current Hollywood drama. Everyone has always known about the casting couch but in actual practice women acted as if being sexually exploited by rich, famous, and powerful men was a fringe benefit, rather than an occupational hazard - until the advance of feminism turned previously arrogant and entitled Hollywood moguls into weak and timid betas using wealth, fame and power as a weak crutch.

Reflect on Sweden, rape capital of the world.[82]

> In June, a 12-year-old girl in the small town of Stenungsund reported that she had been dragged into a public restroom and raped by an older boy. Six weeks later the girl had still not been questioned by the police. Even though

[82]https://quillette.com/2017/10/10/swedens-sexual-assault-crisis-presents-feminist-paradox

she believed she had identified the perpetrator, the police had yet to pay him a visit.

"We have so many similar cases," a spokeswoman of the local police told the Swedish public television channel SVT on September 12, "and there are so few of us, that we simply don't have the time." She continued: "We have rape victims three years old," and even their cases await investigation.

Needless to say, feminists, and indeed women generally, are totally untroubled by this, just as they untroubled by Rotherham[83].

What happened is that Swedes escalated the definition of rape, so that looking at a woman sideways was rape.

Then they de-escalated the punishment for rape, so that it was similar to letting your dog poop on the pavement.

And then they imported a million or so brown Mohammedans.

And when anyone noticed that a million old style knife to the throat rapes of white women by brown Mohammedans were happening, old fashioned actual rape type rapes, the criminal noticer got severely punished, hate speech being treated far more severely than mere rape. And if police attempted to arrest the brown guy with the knife: "Racism! Islamophobia! Police Brutality" Cars would be set on fire, and police would ticket the scorched ruins of the car for being illegally parked.

So police decided it was a lot more urgent to ticket people walking their dogs, and rapes by brown men got left on the back burner.

Swedish males are a little bit unhappy about this but, after all "We are not your women", so they are not all that disturbed.

And what is the reaction of Swedish women? It is "bring in more refugees! We are not your women!"

Female resistance to rape is a shit test. It is not that they don't want to be raped, it is that they don't want to be raped by insufficiently powerful males. I say again: Female resistance to rape is a shit test. It is not that they don't want to be raped, it is that they don't want to be raped by insufficiently powerful males.

There is no college rape crisis, because if there were, female enrollment would be much higher.

Also, there is no college rape crisis, because the Obama Department of education subjected colleges to extreme and extraordinary pressure to identify and punish heterosexual white male college student rapists, and the colleges subjected coeds to extreme and extraordinary pressure to say that they had been raped, and despite all this storm and drama, the poster boy white male college frat rapist that they managed to turn up was glass rapist Haven Monahan[84], indicating that the number of affluent white frat boy rapists, the rapists that Obama was twisting the arms of university admins to find, is indistinguishable from zero, that every single rape accusation made against such men is false, for if one of the accusations was plausibly true, he would be the poster boy instead of Haven

---

[83]https://blog.reaction.la/culture/the-trouble-with-rotherham/
[84]https://dailycaller.com/2014/12/16/university-of-virginia-students-catfishing-scheme-revealed

Monahan. Such a ridiculously low rate of rape indicates that our college boys are disturbingly emasculated, hence the female rage directed against them, and conspicuously not directed at groups that have a very high rate of actual no kidding rape type rape.

If a high status fraternity really could get away with glass raping coeds, the way that Swedish and English Muslims get away with raping very young girls, there would be a horde of coeds hanging around the frat house carrying glasses.

The extraordinary and vicious rage and hatred directed at high status white male heterosexual frats is because they do not dare rape, dare not sexually coerce women, having too much to lose, and thus feel like fake alphas. And nothing enrages a woman worse than having sex with a seeming alpha and finding he is not actually all that alpha. That is a thousand times worse than being raped, and they are getting it all the time from frat boys.

If high status frats really could rape girls and get away with it thanks to their immense social status, girls would be as relaxed about it as they used to be about the Hollywood casting couch, and even more relaxed than they are about Sweden and English Mohammedan rapes.

And, also, the success of the eighteenth century Australian authorities in turning sluts into respectable wives for respectable men. Cartoonishly extreme coercion, which moderns, and even Victorians, would regard as enslavement and rape, was on the books, but very seldom need to be actually applied. Faced with a firm hand, women internalized the values commanded, and hastily volunteered for respectable marriage. Often very hastily.

Today's coercion turns virgins into whores. Early Australian coercion turned whores into wives. But both ways, in both directions, it is clear that women rather like sexual coercion. Harvey Weinstein's problem was that despite being rich, famous, and powerful, he so internalized leftist dogma that he acted beta. He swallowed the blue pill. If he had acted arrogant and entitled, he would have been fine. He should have hit those whores with a stick.

We ban rape because we are not allowed to ban what we really want to ban - other men having sex with our women.

Throne, Altar, and freehold

2017-11-27 19:57:42

I have argued for Throne and Altar before:

> Throne because a stationary bandit is better than a mobile bandit; Altar because we have to shut down open entry into the state religion: Harvard needs an Archbishop and a Grand Inquisitor to stop America's officially unofficial state religion from holiness spiraling out of control into ever greater holiness.

But throne and altar has been tried, and has failed. How did it fail? The answer is, failed because of loss of freehold.

Freehold means that the peasant in his hovel possesses Kingly power under his hovel's roof, which Kingly power the King has no right to mess with, even if the peasant abuses it.

That profits supposedly lead to increased investment and ensuing improvements in the standard of living assumes that investment is relatively frictionless. In practice, however, you need a thousand approvals from Washington, and the Washington bureaucracy has, Soviet style, strangled itself in its own red tape as a result of its efforts to manage everything and everyone, and is no longer issuing approvals in a timely manner.

The great centralization has been driven by the centralization of approvals. But this inevitably results in complexity getting out of control, because every decision has unintended consequences, which are dealt with by further ad hoc and often illegal decisions (as for example Obama taking legislative, budgetary, and judicial authority over Obamacare as Obamacare goes off the rails and starts driving into a ditch) which in turn have further unintended consequences, which leads to further centralization and further ad hoc decisions.

This this uncontrollable and unmanageable complexity led to the King losing control of his bureaucrats, hence the American and French Revolutions,

> He [King George] has refused his Assent to Laws, the most wholesome and necessary for the public good.

> He has forbidden his Governors to pass Laws of immediate and pressing importance, unless suspended in their operation till his Assent should be obtained; and when so suspended, he has utterly neglected to attend to them.

> He has erected a multitude of New Offices, and sent hither swarms of Officers to harass our People, and eat out their substance.

But they did not abolish those New Offices, but instead created immensely more. So now the top bureaucrats are losing control, and you get anarcho tyranny.

Obviously a stationary bandit is better than a mobile bandit, and one might well conclude from this that the more absolute the King the better, that if he owns everything and everyone, he will have correct incentives. But the trouble with this solution is that no one rules alone. If he attempts to own everything and everyone, he claims more power than mortal man can exercise, and the power will slide through his fingers into the hands of a faceless horde of bureaucrats around the throne, who say "Yes your highness" while actually getting their own way, who endanger him and his heirs, and you get anarcho tyranny.

Too much power results in paralyzing complexity, resulting in insecure power. Hence anarcho tyranny.

So, he has to let some of this power be the personal property of people far from the throne - including the dangerously great aristocrats who gave King Louis XIV so much grief. When King Louis XIV disempowered the nobility of the sword, he found he had empowered the nobility of the robe, who devoured the monarchy. The further this power is from the throne, and the more it is the personal property of more numerous and less powerful individuals, the less dangerous it is for the throne. One great magnate, or half a dozen great magnates, is, as King Louis XIV found, a problem. A hundred or a million, not such a problem. The cure for the problems with aristocracy that King Louis XIV encountered was decentralization, but instead he chose centralization, which had fatal consequences for Louis XVI and his wife.

Instead of governors failing to pass laws of immediate and pressing importance, low level bureacrats are failing to give approvals of immediate and pressing importance, and senior bureaucrats are utterly neglecting to attend to them.

This is the crisis of socialism. In Venezuela socialism takes the form of rationing and price and wage control, here it takes the form of Human Resources and Accounting, which are tentacles of the state inserted into every corporation, and the mere owners of the business are powerless before them, because they armed with laws that no one can comply with, that everyone is guilty of breaking, as fathers and husbands are castrated by family law that defines being a husband and a father as domestic abuse. Thus those that provide the capital have no power, those responsible for making payroll have no power, those that are responsible for closing deals with customers have no power, those responsible for delivering product to customers have no power, because all of them are criminals before the power of human resources and accounting, just as all fathers and husbands are guilty of domestic abuse.

And the ensuing crisis of socialism is paralyzing Washington, as two centuries ago it paralyzed Kings.

The Sun King had troubles with powerful aristocrats dangerously far from the palace, the nobility of the sword. So he centralized all power and emasculated aristocrats, turning them into bureaucrats, the nobility of the Robe, but as his heir was to discover, he had created dangerously powerful bureaucrats dangerously close to the palace. That was the crisis of socialism then, and it still getting worse, hence the great centralization.

No one rules alone, thus when the King attempts to gather all power in his own hands, he finds he has in fact gathered all power into the hands of dangerous powerful people dangerously close the throne. To fix this problem, the official Church need to remind the people that the God who commanded obedience to Kings, also commanded that Kings, like other men, should refrain from coveting that which belongs to someone else.

Repeating: Freehold means that the peasant in his hovel possesses Kingly power under his hovel's roof, which Kingly power the King has no right to mess with, even if the peasant abuses it. That power is not the King's to interfere with, even if the peasant is arguably mistreating his wife and his children. If the lord stops that peasant from mistreating his wife and children, pretty soon King George the Fourth gets cuckolded, as he cuckolded others.

The government cripples the power of the patriarch which has the side benefit that King George the fourth can get away with cuckolding and humiliating some aristocrat by screwing that aristocrat's wife, but the courts quietly take his power away from him without anyone quite noticing, and the next thing he knows he himself is humiliated by inability to divorce or control the slut Queen Caroline, which humiliation turns him into a shadow King without real power, and his government then pisses on him, as he pissed on the aristocrats on whose power he depended.

King George the third had real power. When he told the Prime Minister William Pitt the younger to take long walk off a short pier, the King got his way and William

Pitt lost his job. But when King George the Fourth failed to divorce queen Caroline, in the process letting everyone know he was massively cuckolded, the power of Kings was no more. It was often said that it had been a very long time since a King refused assent to a parliamentary bill, but is just Whig history, Whigs rewriting history to claim that they have always been in power. The reason that it had been a very long time is because until the refusal of the divorce of queen Caroline, parliament would never dare pass a bill of which the King disapproved, though they would sometimes refuse to pass a bill the King wanted. Whigs have been in power in America from the American revolution to the present, and in England from the attempted divorce of Queen Caroline to the present. Dating Whig power to the Glorious Revolution is a Whig rewrite of history. After the Glorious Revolution, the new King did a number on those that had overthrown the old King, with the result that Locke and the Lockeans fled into exile, and that lesson was taken to heart. The Lockeans fled, and their power did not return until Parliament denied the divorce of Queen Caroline.

Charles the first lost his head, but George the Fourth lost his stature of a man, which was more devastating to the power of Kings. If he could not control his women, obviously could not control anyone.

Centralization leads to complexity, complexity leads to crisis, attempts to fix the crisis have, because of complexity, unintended consequences, which escalate into further crisis, leading to further centralization, Hence Soviet Russia, Hitler's Germany, Venezuela, and now America.

This is the crisis of socialism, explained in "I pencil", which makes the point that no one actually knows how to make a pencil, hence socialist production of pencils will fail.

In order to manage complexity, you need walls, so that one man can make decisions without having his decisions mucked up by another man's decisions. Hence, private property and local authority, the authority of the father, the authority the business owner, the authority of the CEO. And, not so long ago, the authority of the local aristocrat, who tended to be a high officer in the local militia, a major employer and landowner, and related by blood or marriage to most of the other high officers in the local militia.

Ideally all the consequences of a decision should be contained within those walls. Of course they never are, but if you try to manage all the externalities, things very quickly slide of control. Every attempt to manage the externalities has unexpected consequences, and attempts to deal with the unexpected consequences have additional unexpected consequences, because trying to control matters that have externalities connects everything to everything else, resulting in a tangle beyond human comprehension.

This, the management of complexity, is the central problem of software engineering at the higher levels, and the higher level software engineers have found solutions, but in politics, the solutions collide with who/whom, since any solution to complexity always takes power away from someone, and gives it to someone else. Further, any solution to complexity is going to take power away from the man who is supposed to be dealing with it, and who is failing to deal with it - going to take power away from the courts, the bureaucracy, from accounting, and from Human Resources.

Abusive fathers exist, but they are rare, because of fatherly affection, and fatherly knowledge of the particular circumstances of his family. Abusive family courts are absolutely normal. And now the same crisis is replicating with accounting and human resources, manifesting in Washington as decisions being pushed up to higher and higher levels, with the highest levels being overwhelmed, as King George was overwhelmed, resulting in the American Revolution.

Even if we suppose that child support and the family court does a better job that fathers, which is not the case, the courts are a threat to the power of the throne, and the patriarch is not a threat to the power of the throne. Undermining the power of the patriarch undermines the power of the ruler, giving us mobile bandits in place of stationary bandits. The emperor is in charge of the nation only if the patriarch is in charge of his family. If the patriarch is not in charge of his family, power will slide into the hands of bureaucrats too numerous for the emperor to keep track of, and too close to the throne to be safe. If King George the Fourth had been able to give that filthy slut Queen Caroline a good whipping and lock her up in the palace, chances are England would still be ruled by Kings. It certainly would have been ruled by Kings a good deal longer than it was. And in a society where he could do that, chances are that he would have found it considerably more difficult to sleep with other men's wives, short of employing the measures employed by King David.

If you give up on coherent, coordinated, centralized control, and resource constraints are not an issue, then you could break up your problems among many of these boss-pyramids, but which requires one to accept the risk of independent 'fiefdoms' which could conflict, and anyone at the top only having reactive instead of predictive / proactive ability to resolve problems before they manifest in big issues or crises.

In practice, this is how the United States Government actually copes with the issue. The easiest way to end a war is to surrender, and the easiest way to deal with an unmanageable design is by not managing it, and letting permanent civil servants who spend their lives accumulating institutional and organization capital stay spun-up on everything to the human limits, and given very wide berth when it comes to effective levels of discretion in policy. What management flows from the top is precisely the output of the triage of strategic political priorities.

Surrender was the death of the Czars.

Software engineering, at the higher levels, (not mere programming) is the science of managing immense complexity and detail: And the well known solution is loose coupling, minimize variables of global scope, and especially mutable variables of global scope. Otherwise large systems develop out of control complexity, which is what is happening now to the federal government. Socialism is tight coupling at global scope, as for example Obamacare, Sarbanes Oxley, and Human Resources.

Tight coupling at global scope makes it impossible to control the top bureaucracy, as well as making it impossible for the top bureaucracy to control the mid bureaucracy. The King and president become powerless, hence the recent overthrow of Kings and the looming overthrow of any president that declines to be a puppet, and the citizens are victimized by anarcho tyranny.

Translating the software solution to the political sphere, this is a program of King, Altar, *and freehold*. Legislators get to legislate, rather than one million anonymous judges and bureaucrats, or better, laws are few enough and simple enough that the King can himself alone legislate. Recollect that the American colonists complained about his inability to do so. They wanted more laws, and boy did they ever get them.

Altar should mean that scientists have to settle their disputes by evidence, rather than by incorporating them into the state religion, because only the archbishop gets to say what the state religion is, and if scientists and professors engage in theological innovation, the inquisition should go after them. Peer review is generating official truth by consensus, which is theology, not science. Theologians are dangerous the state and need to be kept under tight state control, because they are apt to discover that they are holier than those that presently have power. If scientists get into theology, the consequences should be dire. The state needs to treat peer review by scientists in quasi state jobs as treason and heresy. If the conclusions of peer review seem superficially politically neutral, the scientists should lose their quasi statal jobs. If the conclusions of peer review imply that the scientists are holy and those in political power need to be holier, as the conclusions of peer review tend to do, as for example with animal fat, pollution, and global warming, the scientists should lose their heads. Scientists should not meet behind closed doors and generate conclusions on the basis of consensus and secret and anonymous evidence. When they do so, it destroys science for politics and endangers the state. That which endangers the state leads to insecure governance, resulting in rulers behaving more like mobile bandits and less like stationary bandits.

Recollect that the anti animal fat scientists, and global warming scientists, did not win the discussion by providing evidence and argument, but by having their beliefs officially incorporated into the official state religion.

The center needs to be stronger, much stronger, hence the neoreactionary demand for throne and altar, for a King, an Archbishop, and a Grand Inquisitor, but it can only be stronger if it abandons efforts to control more than a single man, or a small group of men, is capable of controlling. Freehold is the center giving up attempts to control stuff that it is unlikely to be able to successfully control - for example the family and accountancy.

If the King attempts to prevent the father, the businessman, the property owner, and suchlike from doing every bad thing that they might do, from doing all manner of bad things that a wise and good ruler should prevent and forbid, he finds he has not taken their power to himself, but rather granted power to a vast bureaucracy, dangerous to everyone, especially to himself, whose impossibly complicated activities make it impossible for him to control, impossible for anyone to control, impossible for the bureaucrats themselves to control. How many lives has the family court ruined with its ham fisted, brutal, unpredictable, and capricious exercise of power over people of whom they know nothing, and for whom they care nothing?

The ruler needs to accept that some of his subjects are entitled by right to do bad things, are privileged, have a property right, freehold, to do bad things, which he may not rightfully interfere with, that not every wrong has a proper political remedy, for if he starts interfering in matters complicated, numerous, and detailed, he finds he has empowered an incomprehensibly complicated and dangerous apparatus, dangerously close to the throne. Hence the family courts, the Khmer Rouge autogenocide, Obamacare, the Holodomor, Sarbanes-Oxley, and Venezuela.

Pol Pot had an entirely sound rationale for the Cambodian autogenocide. Most production in Cambodia was rice production on a flood plain. Thus one peasant's ditching and diking to grow his crop tended to have a large externality on downstream peasants. Therefore, obviously all that ditching and diking needed to be done by a central plan. America's finest academics agreed enthusiastically with this moderate agrarian reformer, and I still from time to time see this presented as an irrefutable killer argument against the authority and power of the private landowner to farm as he sees fit, by people unaware that they are paraphrasing an academic endorsement of Pol Pot. But somehow, strangely, this moderate agrarian reform by this moderate agrarian reformer did not turn out well. Nor has any other instance of socialism turned out well, though most are less disastrous than the Cambodian autogenocide, but people keep trying. The Cambodian autogenocide was exceptionally bad because bad planning combined with the left wing singularity. It was impermissible to notice that the plan was bad, therefore any bad outcomes had to be the result of treason and sabotage. And the search for traitors and sabotage ensued, while the total failure of the rice crop led to mass starvation that no one was allowed to notice. The same thing happens to some extent with every socialist intervention. Thus bad outcomes from child support and the family court system do not happen and at the same time also are the result of domestic abuse by husbands and fathers, requiring even stronger measures against abusers and deadbeat dads, which measures become ever stronger, as the ensuing outcomes become ever worse. These bad outcomes cannot possibly be the result of courts capriciously intervening in families of whom they know nothing and exercising powers over husbands and fathers that we would not accept them exercising over murderers? Similarly, any bad outcomes from Sarbanes Oxley are obviously the result of greedy businessmen engaged in fraud, money laundering, and tax evasion? If the government ever really got serious about making Sarbanes-Oxley work, most of the businessmen and their executives would be in jail, and, like Pol Pot's plan to dramatically increase Cambodian rice production, it still would not work.

Power needs to be transferred back to patriarchs, even if some patriarchs abuse the power horrifyingly, for the family court and the ever growing collection of family services are doing a job that is increasingly horrifying in its evil and incompetence. And even if they were doing a fine job, their predecessors screwed King George and will screw whoever is nominally in power, with the result that we get ruled by mobile bandits rather than a stationary bandit.

The problem is that it seems to be increasingly impossible for key executive officers to delegate certain aspects of review and analysis. Even elite performers can only do so much in a day, and so, when divide and conquer fails to be a feasible approach, it creates a fundamental human bandwidth bottleneck with regards to scale and scope for any particular headquarters-level office.

The way this problem is coped with now in Washington seems to be, well, egregious delay. That is, the systems of prioritization and accountability for deadlines completely break down, and the senior officers end up constantly putting out the most immediate fires from the most senior and most angry counter-parties delivered outside the normal system conduits, and let everything else "for later", that is, until they become anger-inducing fires too, or, hopefully, just go away (or are approved for inadequate 'resolution').

The end result being chaos and disorder: It's easy to observe that high level staff are personally handling matters which ought to be below their pay grades

Yes, it would be great if everyone just got twice as much money and twice as many personnel, but the bottlenecks and key officer human-bandwidth limitations would still be there.

Been there, done that (in software engineering, not in running a country).

We have a saying in the software business: "Adding more people to a late project makes it later"

With the end result that the project with its newly bloated staff gets declared finished and pushed out the door in completely broken condition, like Obamacare and every Soviet four year plan.

We also know the solutions, which I have successfully applied.

Unfortunately, applying these solutions in politics, rather than code, runs directly into who/whom. Instead of saying "You cannot access these variables because they are out of your scope" and expect the compiler and source control to enforce that, you have to say "You have to respect Joe's authority over his own domain, even though there are externalities so that what he does hurts other people"

To manage complexity, it has to be broken up into smaller bits, with walls between the bits, so that one man can plan and organize without his plans being fouled by another man's plans (and it always is men, women are great at detail, but when the plans get larger, they get lost in detail). In software, these walls manifest as restrictions on one's access to private variables, typically no access or read only access to immutable values, shared nothing message based multiprocessing, Google's protobuffs, Git's immutable versions, Rust's temporal variable scope, and suchlike. Google's protobuffs are a metaphorical door in a metaphorical wall with a metaphorical security man checking visitors in and out. When it comes to politics, rather than software, these walls manifest as actual walls, also as actual security men with actual clubs, stun guns, and actual guns, guard dogs trained to attack strangers on private property without waiting for human permission, not to mention walls in the less visible and physical form of power and privilege.

The guard dogs are not producing anything directly, so to the good progressive bureaucrat they look like a net loss of utility, inflicting harm on poor people to benefit rich people, but what they are doing is subdividing the problem of production and consumption into smaller and manageable pieces, making it possible to plan and organize.

The guard dogs are keeping the problem of social cooperation and collective action down to something human minds can manage.

When you restrict homeowners from shooting burglars, suddenly and strangely, your administrative apparatus grows out of control.

You take down Chesterton's fence, and everything starts interacting with everything else, resulting in unmanageable complexity. One ad hoc solution to one problem causes a dozen other problems, and the ad hoc solutions to those problems cause several dozen more.

And you wind up shipping completely broken software, and Venezuela winds up starving the masses as a result of their efforts to guarantee the masses food.

To make complexity manageable, you need walls, metaphorical walls like Chesterton's fence, which are apt to manifest as actual physical walls, which break big problems of organization into smaller problems of organization, problems small enough for the privileged man in possession (and it is always a man, and usually a white man) to comprehend and deal with. These metaphorical walls hurt people, and their purpose is not obvious. What is the harm in taking them down, in order to feed the hungry and heal the sick, rather than siccing savage guard dogs onto the hungry, the weak, and the frail?

Well, Venezuela shows you what the harm is.

If you want Ann Coulter to be able to buy health insurance, a doctor needs to be able to sic a savage guard dog onto an hiv positive gay drug addict with multiple stab wounds, who is seeking urgent medical care but has no money to pay for it because he blew all his money and assets on drugs: Because if you try to make sure the broke hiv positive gay drug addict with multiple stab wounds gets medical care, you wind up with a labyrinthine, complicated, and out of control bureaucracy telling the doctor whom to treat and how to treat him, and somehow, strangely, neither Ann Coulter nor the hiv positive drug addict gets actually useful medical care.

What we are today seeing in Washington is a generalization of what happened with Obamacare and Venezuela. Everything that is causing people to starve in Venezuela and be deprived of medical care in the USA was done to feed people in Venezuela and give them medical care in the USA.

And any attempt to back out of it is quite correctly and entirely accurately denounced as likely to cause people to starve in Venezuela and cause people to be deprived of medical care in the USA.

The reason for this seeming paradox is that urgent ad hoc measures to achieve highly desirable and beneficial ends cause tight coupling between components, tight coupling makes the system complex beyond human comprehension, resulting in unpredictable and unexpected outcomes, unintended consequences, resulting further urgent ad hoc measures.

In the case of Obamacare, the chaos and disorder is causing people to go without medical care, in the case of Venezuela, to go without food or basic medicine. And any attempt to restore order involves restoring privilege and authority at the expense of feeding people or giving them medical care.

For example, if you want people to have food in Venezuela, you have to stop worrying about the rights of hungry people, and start worrying about the rights of bakers, farmers, businessmen, and merchants. Similarly the problem of violence in American schools. Time to start worrying about the rights of fathers, the lack of strong men in education, and the excessive presence of young filthy sluts and disgracefully aging cat ladies in education. Fixing the problem involves removing state interventions that were intended to fix, and do in fact fix, entirely genuine and important problems - albeit these problems were in large part caused by earlier state interventions also intended to fix entirely genuine and important problems.

Decoupling in the social order, much like decoupling in software, involves privileges and restrictions. You have to restrict some parts of the code from doing things, in order that other parts of the code are able to do their stuff with predictable consequences, and in the social order these privileges tend to fall upon affluent white males, while the restrictions tend to fall upon women, especially single women, children, and NAMs. In Venezuela, the privileges will fall upon those least likely to be hungry, and the restrictions upon those most likely to be hungry. Which those most hungry will resent, failing to connect these measures with the counter intuitive outcome that when they are applied, the shops mysteriously and coincidentally have food on the shelves for a change.

Order means that people can reason about the consequences of their actions - which they cannot do if a large part of the consequences are how any one of ten thousand meddlesome bureaucrats might potentially respond.

This is the crisis of socialism. In Venezuela socialism takes the form of rationing and price and wage control, here it takes the form of Human Resources and Accounting, which are tentacles of the state inserted into every corporation, and the mere owners of the business are powerless before them, because they armed with laws that no one can comply with, that everyone is guilty of breaking, as fathers and husbands are castrated by family law that defines being a husband and a father as domestic abuse. Thus those that provide the capital have no power, those responsible for making payroll have no power, those that are responsible for closing deals with customers have no power, those responsible for delivering product to customers have no power, because all of them are criminals before the power of human resources and accounting, just as all fathers and husbands are guilty of domestic abuse.

And the ensuing crisis of socialism is paralyzing Washington, as two centuries ago it paralyzed Kings.

The Sun King had troubles with powerful aristocrats dangerously far from the palace, the nobility of the sword. So he centralized all power and emasculated aristocrats, turning them into bureaucrats, the nobility of the Robe, but as his heir was to discover, he had created dangerously powerful bureaucrats dangerously close to the palace. That was the crisis of socialism then, and it still getting worse, hence the great centralization.

Cannot delegate, because delegation assumes decoupling of the components. If Pharaoh allows the Israelites to not make bricks because straw has failed to arrive, then he is going to have to allow the intended recipients of the bricks to not build. Of course in due course the building falls down, but before it falls down Pharaoh has more urgent fires to fight.

It is spaghetti code - if you add more programmers to the team, they will subtract from the productivity of the other programmers, not add to their productivity. And if the lead engineer delegates, he will get less done, because of the ensuing fires he has to put out.

If you have ever tried to hit a late deadline by adding more people to the team, this should be entirely familiar to you.

The problem of spaghetti code, and the problem of parallel processing, is the same problem Jim as socialism. If Pharaoh delegates the straw issue to Moses, he shortly thereafter finds the scroll of Ipuwer in his intray, detailing a dozen more crises each more serious than the one he delegated to Moses, because Moses broke a dozen other modules in the course of fixing the module he was assigned.

And, in trying to administer a state, rather than organize code, not only hard to structure it that way, but such structuring is bound to step on the toes of the low part of the high/low coalition, because that is the part that creates disorder and fails to create order.

In the computer language Rust, you have restrictions on what you can do with variables that were created in a different context, which is mighty handy for the engineer who is responsible for that context. He knows the other engineer cannot screw his code. In the social order, the equivalent is denying fatherless children access to food and medical care. Which means the patriarch knows that his wife and her social worker cannot screw his family.

We see collapse of decision making in the federal bureaucracy, with everything being pushed up to the highest level when someone sufficiently powerful gets sufficiently angry, and everything else sitting in the too hard queue and not getting done. The federal government is becoming severely dysfunctional, as it takes on responsibility for everything everywhere in the entire world and attempts to regulate every person's every action.

The initial seed of Silicon Valley was Shockley. Every transistor everywhere in the world is built by an engineer who learned it from an engineer who learned from an engineer who learned it from Shockley. Hence Fairchild and fairchildren. That is why they call it Silicon Valley, because the fairchildren worked in silicon.

But as those engineers spread over the world, the underlying natural technological force was decentralization, not centralization. From 1980 onwards, Silicon Valley was no longer running on Shockley and the fairchildren, but running on the Silicon Valley exemption, that Silicon Valley was allowed to practice meritocracy that was being suppressed in the rest of America.

Then, quite recently, the Silicon Valley exemption began to evaporate. Today, Silicon Valley runs on Sarbanes Oxley. Due to Sarbanes Oxley, the only way to cash out your startup is to sell it to Google or suchlike. Hence the great centralization.

Sarbanes Oxley makes every accounting department into a tentacle of the state, hence centralization. Which has the unfortunate side effect of abolishing actual accounting in favor of bureaucratic ass sniffing.

The Silicon Valley network is not a network of people who can optimize Google's ad revenue by 0.0001%

The Silicon Valley network is a network of venture capitalists who can sell startups to Google and suchlike. Which means that their business is making startup economic activities Sarbanes Oxley legal. The business of Silicon Valley used to be silicon. Today, however, the business of Silicon Valley is making startups Human Resources and Sarbanes Oxley compliant.

Kings fell from a little bit of socialism, and democracy is falling because it inexorably leads to even more socialism.

The state must be one, but society must be many. You need many independent actors to operate the economy, but the state must be one actor, and must restrict itself to things where only one actor can operate.

Further, in matters where that actor can operate in a geographically limited scope, the state needs to grant local power, even if it is likely to mean local oppression (King, God, *and Freehold*)

The presidency has grasped such immense power that it is paralyzed and impotent, powerless because far too powerful.

Invader justice for invaders

2017-12-02 02:58:51

Recently saw picture of the invader jury that acquitted the invader who whimsically and casually murdered a white woman. They were very pleased with themselves. They were delighted. They were extremely proud of themselves.

The problem is that for some time, Democrats have been manufacturing a unitary and cohesive invader identity that is hostile to whites, and now we are getting invader justice - one immigrant from one country is apt to back another immigrant of a different ethnicity and religion who commits a crime against a white, because they are both invaders.

And the more anti white and anti native you are, the holier you are, thus Mexicans are holier than Asians, mestizos are holier than whitish Mexicans, indios are even holier, and Muslims are the holiest of all.

And acquitting an invader who murdered a white chick for laughs pleasingly raises one's holiness status, hence the pride and joy of the jury. If you are Asian, and you acquit a Mestizo who murdered a white girl, this raises your status towards that of Mestizos, and even further above that of whites.

Someone in the comments is going to present some complicated legal argument that it was not exactly murder for laughs, or there was reasonable doubt it was murder for laughs, and there was some complicated legal reason why the murderer should get off, that it was not really who/whom justice, but even if that argument was completely true, that would not explain the happiness and obvious pride of a jury that did something guaranteed to look very like supporting the murder of white people for being white.

These were people who perceived themselves as having gained status. Killing white people is holy. Even if that murderous illegal immigrant totally deserved to get off (and quite obviously he was guilty as hell) these people believed that letting him off raised their status, and convicting him would have made them unholy, racist, and evil.

The facts of the case are that he stole a gun and used it to kill a white girl for laughs. But the facts of the crime do not matter. Maybe there was reasonable doubt, though I am sure that if the races were reversed no one would think there was reasonable doubt. What matters is not the facts of the case, but the facts of the attitude of the judge, jury, prosecution, and mainstream media, that the jury felt that acquitting an invader who looked remarkably like he frivolously and casually committed a murderous act against white girl was pretty good for themselves.

Obviously the invader stole a gun and murdered the white girl just for laughs, or out of hatred for whites, but regardless of the facts of the crime, even if he was innocent as morning dew, the emotional affect of the jury only makes sense if invaders murdering white girls for racial reasons is holy, socially approved, and high status.

A good time to invest in bitcoin

2017-12-04 08:26:24

In 2013 I recommended investing in bitcoin.

Quite recently I recommended not investing in bitcoin[85], because my cleaning lady who has no idea what to do when her computer freezes up, is investing in bitcoin. When the widows and orphans start buying stocks, it is time to sell.

Lately I have heard tell of thought criminals opening bitcoin accounts, because they noticed "Nazis" getting their accounts blocked, and figured that come the terror, they would need some money that could not be blocked.

That, people getting bitcoin accounts for actual monetary use, is a mighty good reason to invest in bitcoin. Time was when these people would have purchased gold or uncut diamonds.

Total value of Bitcoin it is currently around two hundred billion. People hold gold for roughly the same purpose as they hold cryptocurrency. It is reasonable that the total value of all crypto currencies should be comparable to the total value of gold, which is at present ten trillion.

Some other crypto currency may, and quite likely will, replace bitcoin.

But at the present moment, Bitcoin is where it is at. The aggregate value of all the various cryptocurrencies out there is dominated by aggregate value of bitcoin.

Which gives room for Bitcoin to rise by a factor of fifty.

Kate's wall

2017-12-05 20:25:59

The importance of the Trayvon Martin case is that every single person realized that obviously Trayvon Martin attacked Martin Zimmerman out of racial animus, but those arguing that Zimmerman should be charged with murder were arguing that whites should just suck up being attacked and killed by blacks. Every single person that accuses Zimmerman of attacking Trayvon, adduces as evidence that Zimmerman provoked Trayvon by suspecting him of being a criminal merely because he was dressed like a criminal and acting like he was casing the joint. But if Zimmerman provoked Trayvon, that is not reason to suspect that Zimmerman attacked Trayvon, that is reason to suspect that Trayvon attacked Zimmerman. They say that they are arguing that Zimmerman attacked Trayvon, but in fact the arguments and the evidence that they present are arguments and evidence that Trayvon, being black, was entitled to attack and kill Zimmerman, being less black.

And the importance of the #KateSteinleVerdict is that capriciously killing whites for laughs is socially approved and high status.

Several years ago in California, an invader with no license traveling very far above the speed limit on the freeway smashed rammed my car from behind, wrecking it. Police let him off. I should have seen this as a straw in the wind. One guy who does something bad is just life. One guy who does something bad with social and organizational support from other guys like himself is war and invasion. They are coming to kill us all and take our stuff.

And this is what surrender and treason looks like: Amy Elizabeth Biehl was murdered for being white while a crowd shouted anti white slurs. Her murderers were, of course,

---

[85] https://blog.reaction.la/economics/a-bad-time-to-invest-in-bitcoin/

unpunished, and her father then then shook hands with his daughters murderers to celebrate their release. Traitors need to be charged with treason and executed.

Yes, we probably should have executed Amy ourselves, as well as her father, and we probably should have executed Kate Steinle ourselves, but us executing them for treason would reduce the danger to ourselves, while our enemies killing them for being white and receiving social approval, status, and economic rewards for so doing, increases the danger to ourselves.

Our elites are telling our enemies that badwhites are the problem which needs to be eliminated, but the distinction between "badwhites are the problem and need to be eradicated", and "whites are the bad problem and need to be eradicated" gets lost in translation.

This post cheerfully stolen from Peppermint[86].

Bitcoin and the May scale of monetary hardness

2017-12-09 01:55:21

The current price of bitcoin is only justified if there is a significant probability of bitcoin taking over the world, and substantially replacing other assets that are less easily transferable and/or more subject to the caprice and violence of an increasingly disorderly, unpredictable, destructive, and anarchic state.

If it does take over, will rise a hell of a lot further.

For example, investing in real estate rental property is lucrative, with steady modest income and impressive capital appreciation - but it is subject to the Ferguson effect. One fine day you find that the police protecting your investment have been deemed racist, now have a bunch of fat blue haired lesbians from the federal government supervising them at twelve thousand dollars per day per fatso to cure their horrid racism, and the police have pulled back to give the mob room to burn your property, and maim and rape your tenants. Your male tenants then leave, ashamed of their horrible racism, and your female tenants never paid the rent themselves anyway.

It would be nice to have your assets in a form that perhaps was unlikely to generate value, but did not need to be defended.

If, at the time of Caesar, a wealthy Roman invested in income producing properties, what would his wealth be worth now?

Absolutely nothing.

And this has been typical over most of the world throughout most of time, including most of the world during most of the twentieth century. If, on the other hand, he buried gold in a hole in the ground, what would it be worth now?

About what it was worth then.

But right now today, bitcoin is hitting its scaling limits hard. If scaling is not solved, the current price of bitcoin is difficult to justify. If scaling is not fixed, the price will collapse eventually.

The current plan, or perhaps it is merely a hope, rather than a plan, is the Lightning Network. The Lightning Network, if ever implemented successfully, will be able to handle and exceed Visa scale levels of transactions and Visa speed.

---

[86]https://blog.reaction.la/culture/invader-justice-for-invaders/#comment-1763112

But money in the Lightning Network will, like Paypal money or credit card money, like Visa card money, be soft money, soft bitcoin. At the cost of a fee and some delay, you will be able to convert it into hard bitcoin. You will be able to convert hard bitcoin into Lightning Network bitcoin quickly and for no fee. Transfers from Lightning Network Bitcoin to hard Bitcoin will still be subject to scaling limits. But perhaps these limits will be acceptable when we only do such transfers infrequently and for very large sums.

Your hard bitcoin is represented by a secret key and a public key, by a collection of secret keys and public keys. (Unless, of course, it is an account at a bitcoin exchange, as it usually is, in which case it is a promise to deliver bitcoin by some guy whose only known assets are a business suit he purchased from a Chinese supplier on Ebay and two airline travel bags.)

Your Lightning Network bitcoin will be represented by an account at an exchange. And if the exchange goes down, or decides to mess with you, you will be out of pocket. Which makes it soft money. Rather like Paypal or that account on the bitcoin exchange operated by some guy with two airline travel bags who is presently located in the nicest international business hotel in Outer Mongolia, which is not actually all that nice as international business hotels go. (You did put your bitcoin into a wallet where you have real control, right?)

So here is the May Scale of monetary hardness, updated to include Bitcoin and a hypothetical future Lightning Network Bitcoin:

May Scale of monetary hardness

1. Street cash, gold, US dollars, Bitcoins where you hold the secret keys

2. Street cash, euro currencies, japan

3. Street cash, other regions

4. Interbank transfers of various sorts (wires etc), bank checks

5. personal checks

6. Consumer-level electronic account transfers (eg bPay)

7. Business-account-level retail transfer systems, bitcoins on the hypothetical future Lightning Network

Soft

8. Paypal and similar 'new money' entities, bitcoins on a bitcoin exchange controlled by your username and password login

9. Credit cards

The difference between hard money and soft money is that people are always happy to take hard money, not so happy to take soft money. Always willing to give you soft money for hard money, not so keen to give you hard money for soft money.

The Blue Empire of the consulates gets it in the nads

2017-12-10 22:53:02

I predicted that Trump would have taken power by now. Obviously he has not. But, he is working on it. Unwise to bet against Trump.

In return for Israel not funding his enemies, he recognizes Jerusalem as the eternal and undivided capital of Israel. State Department furtively instigates world wide outrage against this move, which world wide outrage fizzles out dismally. The elite is maximally indignant, the Pope condemns the move, but the masses fail to show up on cue.

As I said earlier in regard to the president re-legalizing oil extraction and coal mining[87]:

> the mighty and justifiably enraged masses are no longer spontaneously demanding whatever the permanent government wants them to spontaneously demand this morning and are no longer spontaneously enraged about whatever the permanent government wants them to be spontaneously enrage about this morning.

The sackings I have long hoped for are actually taking place. The State Department, which has been industriously working on a color revolution in the United States against Trump, is being purged[88].

At that link you will read a diplomat who recently "resigned" (one step ahead of being fired) telling us what good and important work he and the State Department has been doing Sudan. That would be the Sudan plunged into civil war with both sides believing that the State Department has been playing both sides against each other. He helped Americans escape Sudan, he tells us, neglecting to mention they had to flee because the State Department has pissed off the Sudanese government, rebels, and military. If a diplomat has to flee, his diplomacy has evidently been seriously unsuccessful.

The Blue Empire of the consulates has lost in Libya and Sudan. OK, those are merely far away cesspits, but Afghanistan was a far away cesspit, and Soviet defeat in Afghanistan prefigured the fall of the Soviet Empire. Add to Libya and Sudan, the Philippines and Hungary. Not cesspits, and not so far away.

Most of the empire continues to servilely move ever leftwards, and ever against local identity, electing a new people. We are still losing, and losing quite badly. But if you are a diplomat who just got fired by Trump, does not necessarily look that way.

---

[87] https://blog.reaction.la/economics/not-a-dog-barked/

[88] https://foreignpolicy.com/2017/12/09/u-s-diplomat-resigns-warning-of-state-departments-diminished-role-diplomacy-national-security-tillerson-africa-somalia-south-sudan/

And Mueller is biting the dust. Flynn's guilty plea is a massive strategic defeat for Mueller.

What was supposed to happen is that Trump's associates would plead guilty of a very long laundry list of extremely evil things that they did for Trump, at his orders, and in service to him. Then they get let off, the Republicans come under pressure to impeach him, if no impeachment, then Mueller indicts Trump, and Trump gets the perp walk.

Lying to the FBI is a fundamentally frivolous charge. If you open your mouth to the FBI, you are guilty of lying to them, if you keep your mouth closed, you are guilty of conspiracy. It is what you get convicted of when you are pure as the driven snow. What Flynn was supposed to say was "I am guilty of lying to the FBI in that I said Trump was innocent, but actually he is guilty of this long, long, long list of charges, that I wrote out while Mueller steadied my trembling hand". But the content, or rather lack of content, of Flynn's guilty plea indicates that Flynn has not flipped. If Flynn had flipped, we would be seeing it already. Which indicates insider judgment that there is a good chance that Trump will actually take power.

I am in favor of American empire. But the trouble is that soft power is insecure power, so your proconsuls tend to act like mobile bandits, rather than stationary bandits. The State Department and its NGOs are a horde of locusts. Recollect the utter devastation and ruin that they inflicted on Haiti. I favor an empire based on colonialism and hard power, and we cannot do colonialism without colonials, and we will not have colonials until we first fix elite fertility. You need colonials for empire, because they care about their homeland, and also care about the colony.

The trouble with Rotherham

2017-12-13 22:55:27

The trouble with Rotherham is not that white girls were raped and beaten, but that Muslims get exemption to be manly as women understand manliness, and whites and Hindus do not.

The Rotherham girls were raped, threatened, and beaten all right, but they were also complicit in the violence.

For the most part, the pimp, rather than aggressively forcing his women into prostitution by the threat or actuality of violence, is aggressively, but unsuccessfully, attempting to restrain them from prostitution by the threat or actuality of violence, and to the extent that he goes along with their prostitution, is just being the dancing monkey, pretending to be in charge so as to retain some tattered shreds of manliness despite being massively cuckolded.

Human female sexuality is closer to feline female sexuality than to chimpanzee female sexuality. Apes are primarily vegetarians, but we are descended from killer apes. Even when sex involves quite dangerous violence against women plus infanticide and plenty of it, as it rather often does, human females are massively complicit in that violence and infanticide. The women that pimps go through the motions of oppressing are topping from the bottom, and pimps are more accurately understood as the cucked and oppressed victims of lustful bawdy women.

Prostitution is frequently in substantial part an alarmingly enthusiastic and endlessly continuing search for a male who is alpha as women understand alpha - which manliness and alpha character is in substantial part is demonstrated by criminal violence against women and children and being able to get away with violence against women and children.

Even when sex involves a lot of violence against women and children, as it often does, it is the pimps that are the real victims, being brutally cucked by their lustful women.

If a girl is being sexually trafficked, there is absolutely no way the pimp can stop her from wandering off with one of her customers, and whores do this with great regularity. The client is trying to "rescue" the girl from prostitution and her brutal pimp and human trafficker, but she then tries to turn him into a pimp and cuckold. Hence the saying:

> "You can take the girl out of the bar, but you cannot take the bar out of the girl."

Reality is that all the power is in the hands of the whores, not the pimps, which deeply frustrates the women, who are endlessly searching for manly power and authority in all the wrong places, and not finding it. Everyone gets hurt, no one gets their desires fulfilled.

The Democrats prefer to import Jihadis, criminals, and whores. Jihadis and criminals because they can be relied upon to vote Democratic, whores because they will become cat ladies who can be relied upon to vote Democratic. As a rationalization for importing whores, they implemented the "blue campaign", which defined illegal immigrant whores to be victims of human trafficing, which the government proceeded to "rescue".

The purported "victim-centered approach" - as opposed to criminal-focused prosecutions - was mostly a fraud-enabling way in the spirit of asylum/refugee fraud to give a bunch of illegal alien women yet another zero-scrutiny way to claim a victim status that was a free and quick golden ticket to a green card. Cf: U Visas). "Some evil man trafficked my humanness here and took all my documents which are totally from a country that is both unable and unwilling to cooperate with your investigators.")

Men who come here to kill us and take our stuff will reliably vote Democratic, and women who are whores will remain single, and thus reliably vote Democratic.

Hence the striking and conspicuous preference for importing criminals, Jihadis, and whores.

Two incidents with a woman:

1. I protected her. We were walking along a little used path in a semi rural area when a dog charged us barking furiously. She would have run, in which case the dog would have done a large circle around me and attacked her (a barking dog always wants to attack from behind) so I tightened my grip on her, and turned to face the dog while sweeping her behind me like a sack of potatoes and prepared to strike at the dog with my free hand and with one foot. The dog, seeing my focused immobility, the steady predator gaze of the tiger in ambush, abruptly spun around, tucked its tail between its legs, and fled.

Heh, I thought. Massive display of protective manliness. She is going to remember this fondly.

Wrong!

Wrong again!

She totally and completely forgets it.

2. I endangered her:
"Why", I ask, "are we at the kiddy pool?"
"I cannot swim", she replies. I pick her up.

"Hey, put me down", she screams. She then realizes that I carrying her off to the adult pool. Her screaming redoubles.

She then realizes that I am carrying her off to the deep end of the adult pool, and realizes I am going to throw her into it. She screams and struggles.

I am doing this in front of her family, in front of several male members of her family. The trip from the kiddy pool to the deep end of the adult pool requires me to walk past the security guy, who is responsible for order and safety.

I am old and at that time was rather fat. She is young and slim. I am walking very briskly, so, obvious sexual predator forcibly abducting screaming young girl, or at least a guy being disorderly and endangering safety. To avoid triggering his white knight impulses, I totally ignore him, and keep my gaze steady on my destination, so I don't know how he reacted. As usual, when I act with confidence and determination, as I have learned to do in the presence of fertile age women, no one gets in my way.

I toss her in, shortly thereafter get laid like a rug.

I really do not like violence against women all that much. The incident with the dog was way more in accord with my sexual fantasies. Truth is, I had been warned there was a dangerous and aggressive dog in that area. I had no way of knowing for sure that I would be able to intimidate it or defeat it, but was confident I could. I have plenty of experience with dangerous and aggressive dogs. Dogs, like humans, can tell if you are seriously considering killing them and think you might be able to accomplish it. It was totally a setup to give effect to my sexual fantasies. But I am a dancing monkey, and I do what it takes to get laid. Eggs are dear, sperm is cheap, so male fantasies do not matter, and female fantasies do matter. That is just the way the world is. Women do not particularly want protection, and are disinclined to cooperate with males who protect them. The early James Bond movies reflect male fantasies. Female fantasies involve motorcycle gang leaders, vampires, demons, and serial killers, and men have no alternative but to play along. I must dance, and women call the tune.

The Rotherham problem was not Muslims out of control, but women out of control. The cure is not to restrain Muslims, but to restrain women.

For women to reproduce successfully, they have to be under male authority, and in the modern world, they look for that authority and do not find it.

Female behavior makes total sense from the point of view of evolutionary psychology when you reflect that the barista with an advanced degree in women's studies and one hundred thousand dollars in college debt will probably become a cat lady, but if Islamic State was militarily victorious, and auctioned her off naked and in chains at public auction, would probably have seven children and twenty grandchildren.

It also makes total sense if you take the story of the fall seriously. It is the curse of Eve. "thy desire shall be to thy husband, and he shall rule over thee."

It also makes sense of female voting behavior. Single women have no country. They want us to be conquered, they want their male kin to be castrated, so they can finally get into the possession of someone strong enough to own them.

Whenever someone talks about rape in the sense of the female not consenting, implying it is perfectly fine and completely normal if she has sex without her father consenting, or engages in serial monogamy, he is normalizing a morally degenerate male fantasy that fails to correspond to observed female revealed preference.

Women perceive protective manliness as something as natural as the sun rising in the east, and aggressive male dominance as an extraordinary gift from heavens to be adored and worshiped.

Which makes total sense from the point of view of evolutionary psychology, since aggressive male dominance is likely to result in being auctioned off naked and in chains, followed by seven children and twenty grandchildren, while protective manliness is likely to result in becoming a cat lady.

Female sexual autonomy results in defect/defect equilibrium, the equilibrium of whores and pimps. Nobody gets what they want. Queen Gwenevere cheats on King Arthur with Lancelot, King Arthur finds out, Camelot falls because of internal disunity, and everyone gets killed.

Protective manliness that protects the sexual autonomy of women, protective manliness that protects Queen Gwenevere's sexual autonomy, is not only unappreciated by women, but is white knighting, is wicked, evil, and morally degenerate. The curse of Eve is that women should not have sexual autonomy, and endlessly look for a man strong enough to take it away from them.

Be that man.

In order to reproduce successfully, women need to be conquered and subdued. Her owner can then safely invest in her. With female sexual autonomy he cannot, so he does not. Her bearing children for her owner, means her holding hostages against him, thus cooperate/cooperate equilibrium.

The Blue Empire of the Consulates continues to collapse

2017-12-19 00:01:11

Pakistan expels the NGOs. So, soft power looks like it is not doing too well in Syria, Libya, Sudan, the Philippines, Hungary, and Pakistan.

The NGOs are the foot soldiers of the US State Department, and, as the the internal cohesion of the state continues to collapse, act like a plague of locusts. The empire dissolves into a horde of mobile bandits. Gigantic amounts of money were poured into Haiti, and spread famine and disease[89].

The official press demonizes Chinese soft power, calling it "sharp power[90]". When the State Department does this sort of thing, it is called Soft Power, and is supposedly holy and good, but when other nations do this sort of thing, supposedly evil, unholy, and heretical, requiring us to kill people and blow stuff up. Supposedly, grounds for holy war.

---

[89] https://www.aljazeera.com/programmes/insidestoryamericas/2012/01/201211311112785532.html
[90] https://www.economist.com/news/leaders/21732524-china-manipulating-decision-makers-western-democracies-best-defence

Banned	My suggested replacement
vulnerable	living on crime and welfare
diversity	Helicoptered into jobs they cannot perform
entitlement	privilege
transgender	pervert
fetus	baby
evidence-based	trick to hide the decline
science-based	consensus formed behind closed doors

Which brings me to hard power and the Red Empire of the Bases (though since Obama placed feminists and transexual commissars all over it, no longer all that red).

How is the affirmative action Navy doing?

The affirmative action Navy seems to be having a spot of difficulty operating all that complicated machinery created by evil white males, especially now that they have stopped those evil white males from engaging in the evil white male microaggression of mansplaining. Lot of crashes lately. Which problem has been solved, or at least substantially reduced, by the simple expedient of staying in port and operating as a floating brothel and a jobs program for people who profile as Democratic voters.

An empire can long survive the decline of its military power, continuing to rule by habit, custom, and institutional inertia. When, however, you get people agitating for holy war against the insufficiently holy at the same time as military power is collapsing, probably will not survive all that long. Let us hope that the collapse does not involve nuclear weapons. Because it is looking as if our nuclear weapons have not had proper maintenance for quite some time.

I repeat: I favor American Empire. I also favor formal, open, official, and explicit Empire, with arrangements to ensure that American colonialists have an incentive to rule well, which incentive was conspicuously lacking in Haiti.

Relations between competing empires should be conducted on the basis of the peace of Westphalia, so that conflicts are dealt with in ways that mostly avoid killing people and breaking stuff. In particular, and especially, when your empire is pursuing its interests, and the other empire also pursuing its interests, not allowed to declare the other ruler unholy and his doings heretical. That was dangerous back then, and more dangerous today when people have nuclear weapons. And extra dangerous when your empire is in decline.

Trump and power

2017-12-23 05:08:58

I kept predicting Trump would have taken power by now. He has not. But he is getting there.

Some officials issued a new list of forbidden words, not exactly on Trump's instructions, on their own initiative, but likely on their own initiative because they got word of his displeasure.

Meanwhile, Trump moves to take control of the actual apparatus of coercive power, with which he will be able to punish enemies[91] and reward friends[92].

All women are like that

2017-12-27 20:19:12

Women are attracted to arrogant violent men. They are attracted to IQ<80 criminals because criminals are allowed to be violent, while high status males are not, with the result that the status hierarchy as perceived by women winds up upside down from the status hierarchy as perceived by men. AWALT. All women are like that.

Hypergamy never sleeps, a man must always perform, can never relax, is always on stage, can never let his guard down.

When people say that not all women are like that, NAWALT, it is like aging fat feminists saying that different men have different types so you can't say one type of beauty overrules the others. Not so: Men want to fuck young, beautiful and fertile women. Women want to fuck arrogant, violent, criminal men. That is all there is to it. We may nuance after accepting that, but only after accepting that.

Brad Pitt got horribly burned.

Einstein wound up with a KGB girl friend who cared more about Stalin than Einstein.

Feynman needed to learn game, put on an asshole persona, did pretty much what I am doing.

If not all women were like that, these famous men would have done better. Feynman scored, I scored, but if General Butt Naked had shown up, wearing a necklace of human eyeballs, an AK47, and nothing else, we would have been shit out of luck. All women react to the same stimuli in the same way. It is just a matter of which stimuli they get exposed to.

If Feynman cannot score merely being brilliant, famous, and admired, Brad Pitt gets burned despite being rich, famous, and handsome, Einstein winds up having sex with the KGB and serving as a communist loudspeaker, then all women are like that. The lioness knows which lion to fuck, because she sees him killing her kittens.

To align the crude, cruel, simplistic, vicious, and brutal female perception of the male status hierarchy with the subtle, complex, multidimensional, and nuanced reality of the male status hierarchy as actually organized by males, we need to legalize and socially support domestic discipline by taxpaying husbands and fathers, also husbands and fathers that are members of the military, the police, rentacops, and mercenaries. (McLintock[93]), and back that discipline with conspicuously public state violence[94]. We also need to make it legal to use violence on men who come sniffing round your women, as the law was under King Solomon. Then hypergamy will be eugenic, rather than dysgenic. Right now,

---

[91] https://www.zerohedge.com/news/2017-12-22/fbi-fires-suspected-leaker-and-comey-ally-james-baker

[92] https://wattsupwiththat.com/2017/12/22/an-opinion-on-the-epa-gravy-train-and-why-shutting-it-down-is-a-good-thing/

[93] https://blog.reaction.la/economics/fertility-and-corporal-punishment/

[94] https://forgottenstories.net/2012/07/09/fear-ye-the-ducking-stool-ye-common-scolds/

hypergamy is massively dysgenic. Hence the character I play when interacting with fertile age women.

Women have a primitive concept of power. And we men are all dancing monkeys. So, the thing we are forced to do is to become powerful as women understand power.

Which unfortunately is anti civilizational and counter civilizational. Hence the need to modify civilization so that high status males get to perform more private violence. It is easier to have more private policing, to make male status hierarchies more convincing to women, than it is to make women have sex with the men that they should, and refrain from having sex with the men that they should not.

When affluent respectable middle class white males beat misbehaving daughters and wives, and receive any necessary public assistance in so doing from police and authorities, while low lives do not receive similar assistance, then IQ<80 criminals will stop being so strangely attractive to women, and the guy in the corner office will find himself receiving hot letters from women he has never met.

But that said, women are quite agreeable to being made to have sex. They prefer it that way. Resistance is a shit test, and they are turned on by being overpowered. So we need to make it the law that the man that they should have sex with, their husband, the father of their children, gets to overpower them.

The vast majority of rape accusations and the vast majority of rape convictions are false.

2018-01-01 22:54:46

It is perfectly obvious that few if any rape accusations against white heterosexual males are true, and the "rape on campus"[95] case confirmed what was obvious to everyone who was not keeping his eyes tight shut. There were thirty six rape accusations that year on Virginia University Campus, none of which led to disciplinary action, and if any of them had been the slightest bit believable, Rolling Stone would have run with them instead of Jackey Coakley's story.

It is equally obvious that almost no convictions of white males for heterosexual rape are true. If you look at the details of the case, they always sound suspiciously like "domestic abuse" cases, and anyone who knows women knows that few domestic abuse charges are true, probably none of them are true. If a woman actually suffers domestic abuse that she does not want and does not aggressively seek out, not hard for her to wander off to another lover who will treat her like a princess. But these women have the strange habit of wandering off from one "abuser" to the next. And if they don't get"abused" they will attack their lover with a kitchen knife till he is forced to defend himself. "Domestic violence" is merely a shit test that gets physical. Watch female cats shit test tomcats. Human female sexuality resembles feline female sexuality more than it resembles ape female sexuality, perhaps because we are primarily carnivores, while apes are primarily vegetarians.

But a progressive will tell you that they all true, because women never lie, and it is absolutely a miscarriage of justice that so few complaints to the police result in rape con-

---

[95]https://blog.reaction.la/war/the-vast-majority-of-rape-accusations-are-false/

victions, and that what seems glaringly obvious to me, is the exact opposite of what seems glaringly obvious to him.

One in nine rape complaints investigated by Scotland Yard resulted in conviction. So, of those few convicted, how many were actually guilty? Well, from what I know of women, I would say none of them, or none of them in the sense that a half drunk woman wandering in a dark alley with her boobs about to pop out of her dress who then gets into a car with a total stranger is not exactly a rape *victim*[96], but other people disagree with my assessment of women, so how will we empirically test this question?

Well, two Scotland Yard rape trials have recently collapsed, when it was discovered that the police had been concealing convincing evidence of innocence[97]. In both cases the accused was savagely defamed in the newspapers, his life was destroyed, and he had been kept in jail for a long time without trial as "a danger to the public", on the whimsical and changeable word of some drunken sow, whose identity was protected, and who continues to be protected, despite evidently being guilty of malice and perjury.

So, with police cutting corners to get rape convictions, and imprisoning men without trial, they still only manage to get one in nine convictions, and their two most recent rape cases were revealed to be abuse of police power and miscarriages of justice.

If the most recent two, likely all of them. The UK is now re-examining all currently active rape cases, which will no doubt mean the release of a great many males locked up without trial as "a danger to the public". How about re-examining all recent rape convictions? But evidently the government does not want to go there, which itself tells me what they would likely find.

Trump is on the ball

2018-01-08 19:26:03

I had hoped for a self coup making Trump King and erasing the constitution by now, but he is making significant progress. Maybe we will see a self coup on his third term. He is not yet in control, but he is definitely biting the permanent government at the edges.

Protecting American Workers

Trump killed the Transpacific Partnership[98], killed the Paris Treaty[99].

The Transpacific Partnership was not so much a free trade agreement as a system of economic regulation by the "International Community". Free Trade for corporations big enough to own a skyscraper in a major city and fill it full of lawyers. Lesser businesses would find themselves criminals because of a thousand pages of regulation that no one reads and no one understands, least of all those enforcing it.

---

[96] https://archive.li/Ns35n

[97] https://archive.is/8Myr4

[98] https://www.theguardian.com/us-news/2016/nov/21/donald-trump-100-days-plans-video-trans-pacific-partnership-withdraw

[99] https://www.whitehouse.gov/the-press-office/2017/06/01/statement-president-trump-paris-climate-accord

He has "reopened" negotiations on NAFTA and, surprise surprise, the negotiations are not going too well - looks like NAFTA is going to die, or else be radically modified in favor of the US.

The biggest issue is that Trump wants forty two percent of a car to be built in the US, to get NAFTA status in the US. At present, the rule is sixty two percent of a car built in the US, Canada, *or Mexico*. Which in practice means Mexico, in part because regulatory burdens and corporate taxes are highest in the US. Canada has the lowest corporate tax rates, but a higher regulatory burden than Mexico.

Trump obstructs H1B, the program for legally bringing in cheap workers from India and Pakistan[100].

DOJ files suit against company for not hiring Americans[101]

US agency raids Indian IT firms[102]

Silicon Valley Staffing Firm Charged, H1B Fraud[103]

China, U.S. reach trade agreement on beef, poultry and natural gas[104]

China opens rice market for US exports for first time ever[105]

First U.S. Natural Gas Shipped to Poland[106]

Trump slaps tariffs on Canadian lumber imports[107]

United States and Mexico finalize sugar trade deal[108]

Crude oil shipment from Texas opens new vistas in India-U.S. ties[109]

Argentina agrees to allow first U.S. pork imports in 25 years[110]

Companies behind Trump's $250 billion China deal[111]

---

[100] https://archive.is/nf91F
[101] https://archive.is/tWFCS
[102] https://archive.is/hIL4p
[103] https://archive.is/sTj7G
[104] https://archive.is/5kxIF
[105] https://archive.is/R9LSx
[106] https://archive.is/9L9mH
[107] https://archive.is/sGxmO
[108] https://archive.is/XV3PV
[109] https://archive.is/gPaNm
[110] https://archive.is/twmqa
[111] https://archive.is/Rd5Yr

Fixing the economy

One important thing he is doing is fixing the economy, bringing back the flyover country jobs, the smalltown jobs, the lesser city jobs, that the regulatory state was systematically destroying.

When people leave flyover country to the big cities, they are outvoted by the horde of Democratic party voters imported to America to live on crime, welfare, and voting Democrat. More people in flyover country means more seats for Republicans, fewer seats for Democrats, increasing the Democrat problem that the horde of angry white hating criminals that they have imported to vote Democrat tend to cluster in certain locations that are already solidly Democrat. Obama used to dump Somali rapeugees on marginal electorates in flyover country in order to reduce this problem, but that program has of course stopped and those rapeugees are percolating back from marginal electorates in flyover country to big city electorates that are already solidly Democratic Party.

Pruitt on a mission to change the climate of the EPA.[112] The ideology of Anthropogenic Global Warming is motivated by hatred of white men and the industrial civilization we created, and is a rationale for destroying us and destroying our civilization[113]. It is evident from the Climategate files that climate scientists have absolutely no interest in whether the world is getting warmer or cooler, nor whether humans are causing it or not. They are after ammunition, not the truth, they are looking for any mud that they can hurl. The Paris Treaty disproportionately affected America because it was largely targeted at destroying flyover country.

Day One: Secretary Zinke Signs for Orders to Expand Access to Public Lands[114]
Zinke Signs Secretarial Order To Streamline Process For Federal Onshore Oil And Gas Leasing Permits[115]
Mulvaney: Obama Administration Had 'Secret List' of Regulations[116]
Trump budget chief touts progress in rolling back regulations[117]
Trump Cut Regulations 32%[118]

Remember all those libertarians who told us that they supported sodomy, open borders, and race replacement, but they were supposedly totally opposed to taxes and intrusive economic regulation. Have you heard them praise Trump for cutting taxes and economic regulation?

No, they say Trump is the evil big government conservative.

Mick Mulvaney on the Budget, Congressional Scorekeepers and Staying Frugal[119]
Research and Development Priorities.[120] This prioritizes research towards questions that might result in prototypes and demonstrations of feasibility that entrepreneurs could de-

---

[112]https://archive.is/TvdAM

[113]https://wattsupwiththat.com/2018/01/08/open-letter-to-president-donald-trump/

[114]https://www.doi.gov/pressreleases/day-one-secretary-zinke-signs-orders-expand-access-public-lands

[115]https://www.doi.gov/pressreleases/zinke-signs-secretarial-order-streamline-process-federal-onshore-oil-and-gas-leasing

[116]https://archive.is/gw49C

[117]https://archive.is/y0ghK

[118]https://archive.is/nxp5W

[119]https://archive.is/YKi1D

[120]https://www.whitehouse.gov/sites/whitehouse.gov/files/omb/memoranda/2017/m-17-30.pdf

velop for profit and jobs. This is a radical re-orientation from current priorities, which reward finding grounds to regulate private enterprise on real or imaginary externalities, which externalities connect everything to everything else, generating a flood of real and imaginary issues that make all matters too complex for human comprehension.

If an official scientist found something that expanded the power of the regulatory state, he gets cash and prizes, and anyone who attempted to replicate his results had better not disagree. Getting one's results made into regulation or government programs tended to constitute decisive evidence for the truth and correctness of those results, as in the infamous animal fat controversy. Testing the animal fat question was deemed immoral and dangerous, because we already supposedly knew the answer, though in fact there was no real evidence on the issue, just a "scientific consensus".

Trump Lays Out Plan to Privatize Air Traffic Control System[121]
President Trump Announces "Massive Permit Reform" Push[122]
Trump Signs Order Rolling Back Environmental Rules on Infrastructure[123]
Trump vs.the Regulatory State[124]

President Trump has proved to be a full-spectrum deregulator,

CFPB Now a Deregulation Department[125], Mick Mulvaney Staffing CFPB with Trump Loyalists[126] The CPFB was a slush fund for the left. The CPFB would threaten to destroy people's businesses unless they paid off left wing activist groups. Thus it would destroy the productive jobs of whites, and create highly paid political activists. Fewer employed whites therefore fewer Republican votes, more highly paid political activists, therefore more Democratic Party votes. Trump has done far more to defund the left than Reagan did. Similarly,the Justice Department[127] settlement[128] slush fund[129].

Rick Perry and the "Texas Approach" to Renewable Energy and Infrastructure[130]
Rick Perry's Plans for US Energy Dominance[131]
A Vision for American Energy Dominance[132]
Trump approves US-Mexico pipeline: 'That'll go right under the wall'[133]
Oil starts gushing through controversial Dakota Access Pipeline[134] Notice the total lack of protests this time. The left's inability to marshal its usual rivers of meat is because Trump has slightly reduced their funding. Since funds for the left tend to get stolen by

---

[121] https://archive.is/4h1o5

[122] https://archive.is/JgxUu

[123] https://archive.is/zMpjW

[124] https://archive.is/iWzF7

[125] https://archive.is/GFfZs

[126] https://archive.is/p2cKy

[127] https://www.washingtonexaminer.com/house-passes-bill-stopping-justice-departments-settlement-slush-fund-practice/article/2638573

[128] https://www.wsj.com/articles/look-whos-getting-that-bank-settlement-cash-1472421204

[129] https://nypost.com/2015/11/14/how-obama-is-bankrolling-a-non-stop-protest-against-invented-outrage/

[130] https://archive.is/XjtQb

[131] https://archive.is/zQqjE

[132] https://youtu.be/hkEwzNC8l-U

[133] https://archive.is/QfMLv

[134] ttps://archive.is/N2ACk

leftists, funding is not very effectual unless continually increased, thus even a small decrease radically reduces left activism.

DOE Announces $6.9 Million for Research on Rare Earth Elements from Coal and Coal Byproducts[135]. It is only a tiny amount of money, but it is an important symbol. For the last sixty years coal has been so evil, racist, hateful, and low status that no high status person would have anything to do with it, but now a bunch of high status people will have to be associated with coal if they want to get some of that gravy. Also, rare earth elements are as high status as coal is low status.

U.S. coal exports soar, in boost to Trump energy agenda, data shows[136]. Remember all those highly credentialed economists swearing that the collapse of the coal industry was a natural result of economic forces, not a regulatory assault by bicoastal elites who hate white men in flyover country and want to destroy their lives. "Trump is lying, those coal jobs are gone and are not coming back."

By the way, the U.S. has become the world's dominant energy superpower[137]
Coal Production Up 7.8%[138]
President Trump's executive order will undo Obama's Clean Power Plan rule[139]
EPA's Pruitt moves to roll back over 30 environmental regulations in record time[140]
Trump's EPA To Repeal Obama's 'Waters Of The US' Rule https://archive.is/8SPGh[141]
EPA chief says administration to roll back Obama's clean power plan[142]

And these deregulatory measures are having the promised effect on the economy

Trump Cut More US Debt for Longer Period than Any President[143]
2017 Debt Growth slows[144]
Q3 GDP up 3.2%[145]
Government spending as % of GDP down[146]
Exports 2.5yr high[147]
Record 6M job openings, 6.8M Americans looking for jobs[148]
Small business confidence spurring hiring and spending spree[149]

---

[135] https://energy.gov/articles/doe-announces-69-million-research-rare-earth-elements-coal-and-coal-byproducts
[136] https://archive.is/RcG3d
[137] https://archive.is/V6jZ5
[138] https://archive.is/vWmgq
[139] https://archive.is/6dOZh
[140] https://archive.is/H4msB
[141] https://archive.is/ target=
[142] https://archive.is/RhYW1
[143] https://archive.is/lJk4Z
[144] https://archive.is/arVLL
[145] https://archive.is/EUL3n
[146] https://archive.is/2sG4k
[147] https://archive.is/Ulytn
[148] https://archive.is/TQrnw
[149] https://archive.is/vQAi6

Wages up 2.5%[150]
Inflation 1.7%[151]
Consumer confidence NOV 129.5 17yr high[152]
Consumer Sentiment Up[153]
Economy Reaches Its Potential Output[154]
63.1%: Participation Rate: Trump-Era High[155]
Fewest Jobless Claims Since 1973[156]
2.2M jobs added since election[157]
2017 Unemployment record low in 13 States[158]
Summer Youth Unemployment Lowest Since 1969[159]
Black Unemployment Lowest in 17yrs[160]
Hispanic Unemployment all time low[161]
Unemployment to drop: lowest since 1969[162]
Manufacturing Expands at Fastest Pace in 13yrs[163]
Summer employers hired American, raised wages[164]
Recovery Trickling Down to Least-Educated Workers[165]
Median Incomes Climb- First Since 2007[166]
Blue-collar wages surging[167]
Job Satisfaction Highest Since 2005[168]
1.5M Fewer on Food Stamps[169]
Net worth rose 1.8%[170]
New-Home Sales 11yr High[171]
2017 Durable goods rose 5.4%[172]
Dow: first eight-quarter winning streak in 20 years[173]

---

[150] https://archive.is/PrZHT target=
[151] https://archive.is/IL57F
[152] https://archive.is/udMh9
[153] https://archive.is/JXY9o
[154] https://archive.is/NEWhM
[155] https://archive.is/4KYyH
[156] https://archive.is/ulfiI
[157] https://archive.is/2jc6L
[158] https://archive.is/huATO
[159] https://archive.is/t2RHr
[160] https://archive.is/uf5OQ
[161] https://archive.is/LAeem
[162] https://archive.is/sIocV
[163] https://archive.is/1kE5U
[164] https://archive.is/dZVZc
[165] ttps://archive.is/7dwNo
[166] ttps://archive.is/TyB3d
[167] https://archive.is/7N2mu
[168] https://archive.is/h8D7W
[169] https://archive.is/IAxTW
[170] https://archive.is/pRixH
[171] https://archive.is/afseF
[172] https://archive.is/8QSLh
[173] https://archive.is/pRr0w

Stock market powers wealth to $96.2t[174]

Ok, but what about an out of control judiciary continuing to

flood America with criminals, terrorists, and Democratic Party voters?
  Trump Is Rapidly Reshaping the Judiciary.[175]

And the Deep State?

Sessions Declares Fight Against Elite Pedophiles Top Priority[176]
While eyes are on Russia, Sessions dramatically reshapes the Justice Department[177]
How the CIA Is Changing Under President Trump[178]
DOJ will intervene in campus free speech cases[179]
Trump Defied Bureaucracy to Advance Immigration Agenda[180]
Haley cheers cuts to UN peacekeeping: 'We're only getting started'[181] (UN peacekeeping in practice looks mighty like State Department terrorism)
  US secures $285M cut in UN budget[182]
Four charged with leaks from Trump administration[183]
DOJ conducting 27 investigations into classified leaks[184]
Sessions ask FBI for info on Uranium One[185]
Sessions orders review after report Obama gave Hezbollah pass[186]
Tillerson to shutter war crimes focused State Dept. office[187]
It's a bloodbath at the State Department[188]
Tillerson Tightens Limits on Filling State Department Jobs[189]
State Department to Offer Buyouts in Effort to Cut Staff[190]
Report: Trump plans to cut foreign aid, merge State and USAID[191]
Ryan Zinke plans overhaul because Interior Department employees 'not loyal'[192]

---

[174] https://archive.is/EcBpD
[175] https://archive.is/TvdAM
[176] https://archive.is/NiDB9
[177] https://archive.is/pzCbG
[178] https://archive.is/3Q1Vf
[179] https://video.foxnews.com/v/5589751733001/?#sp=show-clips
[180] https://archive.is/3Dd9X
[181] https://archive.is/NtGfT
[182] https://archive.is/4kwqz
[183] ttps://archive.is/8AIzT
[184] https://archive.is/MgIWv
[185] https://archive.is/ZTWmg
[186] https://archive.is/auUHd
[187] https://archive.is/hVIoM
[188] https://archive.is/nBiti
[189] https://archive.is/YiKBN
[190] https://archive.is/u40BI
[191] https://archive.is/mTpEv
[192] https://archive.is/ikehT

It is now a year, and still no wall

Final Panel in Upgraded Border Fence Installed[193]
Army Corps starts pre-construction work on border wall[194]
Texas Wildlife Refuge Prepared for First Border Wall Segment[195]
Bill allocates $1.6 billion for border wall[196]
Border wall prototype anti-climb testing begins[197]
Feds take over Texas National Guard border mission[198]
Border Patrol Morale at Highest Level[199]
Border Crossing Arrests 46yr Low[200]
Memo: ICE officers have free rein[201]
ICE Morale Through the Roof[202]
Raids target suspected gang members[203]
80% jump in illegal targets[204]
New crackdown on sanctuary cities[205]
ICE wants smuggling charges on leaders of sanctuary cities[206]
Denver To ICE: Stop Arresting Illegal Immigrants At Courthouse. ICE To Denver: Not A Chance[207]
17 Texas sheriffs approved to partner w/ICE[208]
ICE crackdown scaring families back to Mexico[209]
Raids turn Oregon city into ghost town[210]
Self Deportation Up 31%[211]
Trump ends Obama-era delay tactic[212]
'Extreme Vetting' for green cards[213]
DACA Renewals Drop 21%[214]
Reforms To Immigration Courts[215]

---

[193] https://archive.is/MzAgi
[194] https://archive.is/EvfL0
[195] https://archive.is/AcC8G
[196] https://archive.is/ja3c3
[197] https://archive.is/8MlvB
[198] https://archive.is/l6SOc
[199] https://archive.is/VPOqo
[200] https://archive.is/yUOye
[201] https://archive.is/yfFzM
[202] https://archive.is/832Cn
[203] https://archive.is/7aXF6
[204] https://archive.is/g77SY
[205] https://archive.is/6WZGh
[206] https://archive.is/7rlwN
[207] https://archive.is/IyFdk
[208] https://archive.is/RvlXW
[209] https://archive.is/fqhUK
[210] https://archive.is/yzW35
[211] https://archive.is/gBdnN
[212] https://archive.is/We7XH
[213] https://archive.is/qakPP
[214] https://archive.is/IHvpi
[215] https://archive.is/3GK66

Sessions announces crackdown on 'so-called' sanctuary cities[216]
DoJ Stands by Texas's Voter ID Law[217]
New Order Indefinitely Bars Almost All Travel From Seven Countries[218]
Trump takes more Christians than Muslim Refugees[219]. Christians are being terrorized by Muslims. Muslims are not being terrorized by Christians. That is the way it always has been, even during the Crusades, when brave Christian knights actively defended Christians recently overrun by Muslim hordes. Why are we taking in Muslim "refugees" - oh yes, Christians might not vote Democratic.

Fewest Monthly Refugee Arrivals in August Since 2002[220]
Trump signs order cutting refugee quota to lowest level since 1980[221]
Trump Announces 'Extreme Vetting' Plans[222]
Trump set to DEPORT 300,000 refugees[223]
Trump to announce new refugee admissions cap, stronger vetting rules as ban expires[224]
U.S. walks away from UN migration agreement[225]

War on Guns

DOJ Halts Operation Chokepoint, Which was Targeting Gun Dealers[226]
House approves concealed-carry reciprocity, gun bill faces challenge in Senate[227]

War on men

Campus Rape Policies Get a New Look as the Accused Get DeVos's Ear[228]
DeVos' meetings with 'men's rights' groups over campus sex assault spark controversy[229]
Betsy DeVos Is Right: Sexual Assault Policy Is Broken[230]
DeVos to Replace Obama-Era Sexual Assault Guidelines[231]
This post stolen from Pastebin username2017'[232]

[216] ttps://archive.is/6WZGh
[217] https://archive.is/pGLvQ
[218] https://archive.is/7JKRT
[219] https://archive.is/4HPSi
[220] https://archive.is/TyRvd
[221] https://archive.is/JlMdY
[222] https://archive.is/d4bgo
[223] https://archive.is/asxmP
[224] https://archive.is/eQosd
[225] https://archive.is/WNiCd
[226] https://archive.is/bDDcZ
[227] https://www.foxnews.com/politics/2017/12/06/house-passes-gun-reciprocity-faces-challenge-in-senate-from-dems-and-gun-control-advocates.html
[228] https://archive.is/G1Zv7
[229] https://archive.is/l0v1w
[230] https://archive.is/wY3kY
[231] ttps://archive.is/FZnX7
[232] https://pastebin.com/JnS5Qy2Q

Fixing Christianity.

2018-01-11 00:13:12

Some argue that Christianity is irretrievably cucked, and is the cause of our current problems. And there is much truth in that. Maybe we just have to say "Let Gnon sort them out".

But, on the other hand, Europe was saved, and indeed formed, by the Roman Catholic Church under the holy Roman Emperor, and we got World Empire, Science, and Industrialization under the officially official State Anglicanism re-established by Charles the Second. We became what we are under throne and altar, and without throne and altar, are declining from what we were.

If you are going to have a state, you are going to have an official established Church. If you officially do not have an official church, you will unofficially and informally have an officially unofficial Church, a formally informal Church, the arrangement that we first saw with Cromwell's puritans. Which unofficially official Church tends to wield unaccountable power and is subject to holiness spirals, so they became holier than Jesus, thus Unitarian. A unitarian Bishop, rather than striving to be like Jesus, congratulates Jesus on striving to become as virtuous as her very holy self[233]. Then holier than God. Today's progressives are holier than God puritans, who have dumped God for insufficient holiness as the unitarians dumped Christ for insufficient holiness.

Natural selection has a huge amount of explanatory power for describing the world that is, and accounting for how it came to be; Evolution contains vital and important truths about the nature of man and the world, which we must not discard. The story of the fall, the book of Genesis also contains vital and important truths about the nature of man and the world, which we must not discard.

But the story of evolution tells us that we are risen killer apes who rose over the corpses of a thousand genocides, whereas the story of the fall tells us that death only entered the world in the fall. We have to reconcile these positions.

We gained knowledge, we were black pilled by it. We want to go back, to return to innocence, to unknow what we have learned. But we cannot go back. This is the fall.

The fall is spiritual aspiration rather than a literal descent from a literal plane of existence. The loss of innocence in the story of the Garden of Eden is the black pill, and we cannot return to Eden by unknowing what we have learned, cannot regain our innocence, but must instead take the white pill.

Rather than the Tower of Babel being the last attempt to return to that higher plane of existence, to regain our innocence, to return to Eden, it was the first of many. The story of Babel reflects our consciousness of tribalism, and the problems that it poses for larger political units.The EU is consciously reprising the tower of Babel, which was, so legend tells us, raised by the first city, capital of the first King.

Cities, Kingdoms, and empires followed agriculture, and agriculture first appeared where legend locates Nimrod and the tower of Babel, so likely the legend is based upon truth, that a mighty hunter of the first city became the first King of the first city, the first Kingdom became the first empire, the first empire sought to abolish the fissiparous nature

---

[233]https://pjmedia.com/faith/2017/09/26/lesbian-bishop-calls-jesus-bigot/

of man, and spectacularly failed to do so. And similarly, the Puritan socialist experiment was consciously an attempt to return to Edenic innocence.

As was the nineteenth century attribution of innocence and virtue to women, which continues to this day, forgetting what we knew of women in the eighteenth century. By unknowing what we learned in the fall, supposedly women would become unfallen.

Roosh is the only one of a very few Middle Easterners banned from Britain. England fears Roosh more than it fears terrorists who drive trucks over people at nativity scenes, because since 1800 it has been trying to unknow what we know about women. A wall against terrorists would admit the truth about tribalism - so they instead want a wall against Roosh, because Roosh speaks the truth about women. Speaking the truth about women is more terrible by far than driving trucks into nativity scenes to crush the people there.

The EU, Victorianism (and by Victorianism I include the current rape hysteria and sexual violence hysteria) and socialism, are all attempts to cure the black pill, to return to the Edenic plane of existence, by regaining innocence, by forgetting the terrible things that we have learned. The tower of Babel was not the last attempt at return, but the first. But there is no path back. The cure for the black pill is the white pill.

Proofs of God are not interesting, because they can at most prove the existence of a God vast, cold, indifferent, and far away. Back before Darwin, it was seemingly obvious that God was like us, a maker, and we alone of all his creatures were like him, makers, therefore made in his image. And any one who doubted this was a clever silly. Now that argument does not fly any more. Further, a God that is excessively vast and powerful, the God of Muslims and Jews, is inimical to science and technology. Notice the total non contribution of Muslims and orthodox Jews to science. The Trinity solves this problem. God is three and God is one. Christ is wholly man and wholly God. God has omniscience, but we have true choices and free will. Notice how the Muslims fail to get stuff done, because they always say "I will do such and such, God willing", whereas a Christian will say "I will do such and such". Predestination sodomizes your civilization and corrupts your culture. Have to have doctrine that we get to make real choices, and our choices matter, that we are capable of knowing the truth and of being deceived, and the difference matters.

A God of any argument for the existence of God, is fundamentally inimical to our civilization, for our civilization rests on the Christ and the Trinity. Which God makes absolutely no sense transcendeth human understanding.

When you try to prove the existence of God, you are proving the existence of the Muslim or Orthodox Jewish God, and we want that God like we want nine inch nails hammered into our heads. Our civilization rests on a God that is as much a man as any Greek God, indeed more a man than any Greek God, for he knew pain and death.

For our civilization to survive, for science, technology, and industry to survive, we either have to go with Christ or with the Norse gods, or perhaps both, and the Norse gods are deader than Christianity. The only people who seriously claim to be worshiping the Norse gods are a bunch of gay polyamorist greenies, who claim to be worshiping the Norse gods, but are actually worshiping themselves, demons and the evil dead. Reactionary attempts to revive the Norse Gods suffer from a fatal lack of awe and sincerity.

This may change in future - there is a project under way to unite Odin, who was hung by the neck from a tree, with Christ, who died on the cross. We will see how that works out, but at the moment, not really working out. Needs a prophet. Will not necessarily get one.

If Islam wins, and as long as conservative Muslims, and only conservative Muslims, are allowed to have real marriages and real families, it is going to win (white Christian women convert to conservative Islam for alpha dick, white Christian men convert for marriage and children) then we are going to wind up looking like the middle east.

Either we go with Darwin alone, or we go with a Christianity reconciled with Darwin. Anything else is the death of European civilization. And very few people can handle Darwin alone. Most of those who claim that they can, are lying, and are in fact preaching progressivism, a form of Christianity rendered observably false by being transliterated from the next world to this world.

The doctrine of the fall contains important truths about the nature of man. The doctrine of evolution also contains similar important truths about the nature of man. Our state religion is going to have to deploy both doctrines simultaneously.

And the doctrine of evolution is that we are risen killer apes who rose upon a thousand genocides. So, death did not literally come into this world with the loss of innocence. Rather, it is a spiritual truth about the black pill, about spiritual death.

A lot of it is a matter of explicating what predecessors said and did reverentially but not uncritically. If the process of explication uncovers errors and defects, it has to be pointed out and fixed accordingly. This is how you make old books live again and recover and reactivate traditions.

If you don't integrate Darwin and Christ, the clever sillies, claiming falsely to know the truth from Darwin, whom they do not read and do not understand, will take down Chesterton's fence, and you will start agreeing with them that Chesterton's fence is really stupid and come up with some clever reasoning that it is not really part of Christianity. And I see this happening right now, and it has been happening ever since Darwin

Christianity is a church, adoptive kin, it is necessarily a tribe, and thus, being a tribe, necessarily something rather like a state. Merely individual Christianity, a personal and individual relationship with god, is not Christianity. Faced with a hostile belief system, Christians are retreating before it, and yielding the collective and tribal functions of the Church to the educators, to the progressives. And inventing a merely individual Christianity that is concerned with merely individual salvation. In so doing, they are hoping to save Christianity by abandoning it.

The clever sillies invoke Darwin merely as a creation myth, to discredit the bible and to discredit the moral, psychological, and spiritual truths of the fall. The correct response is to retreat from young earth literalism, while pointing out that Darwinism confirms the psychological and spiritual truths of the fall. Christianity's response has been to retreat from young earth creationism as literal truth and also to retreat from the moral, psychological, and spiritual truths of the fall

Religion needs to be a true statement about this world, as well as an unfalsifiable statement about the next. Christianity needs to be fixed so that it once again makes the true statements about this world that it used to make. Speaking truth about this world is a vital and important task of religion, which task it has fled from fearing condemnation by the state religion of progressivism Instead of speaking the truth, they torture the texts, Jewish style, to make them say the opposite of what they say. They turn Saint Paul into a feminist, and turn Deuteronomy and Proverbs into twenty first century anti family and anti marriage law.

Leonardo da Vinci and Lyell showed the world is immensely ancient, and I myself have verified this with a sledgehammer and a crowbar. And then the church fled in embarrassment from the truths that were linked to young earth creationism. Thus the EU repeats the error of Nimrod. This is not a sign of the end times, it is a sign of entropy and forgetfulness, that men do stupid things anew, having forgotten the lessons they learned last time around. It is not a sign of the end times, it is a sign of the decline of social technology.

Who is complaining about the EU project on religious grounds? Only nutcases who think it is a sign of the end times. A Darwinist would tell you that humans are naturally fractious, and one tribe will oppress the other, and a Christian should tell you that one world of one beige colored people is not part of God's plan for men. If a Darwinist and a Christian got together, as they should, they should agree that to the extent that the EU works, it will work by forming a tribe of Eurocrats that oppress everyone, and to the extent that it does not work, Eurocrats are insufficiently tribal to make it work, and Europe's military incapacity was demonstrated in the Balkans. The European Union project is demons in the dark enlightenment sense of self destructive memes possessing people. Whether it is demons in the literal sense of Satan and the antichrist is unverifiable, and does not make a whole lot of difference. Either way the church should be calling it out.

The Anglican Church full of liberals, Catholic Church full of liberals, and world council of churches full of liberals is because the earth is very old. No one can prove Darwinism, though Darwinism makes sense of the world in ways that other forms of analysis do not, but anyone can pick up a sledgehammer and a crowbar, and, following the footsteps of Leonardo and Lyell, prove that the world is immensely old, that young earth creationism is false. The problem is that the truths about human nature and the human condition are linked to Young Earth Creationism, and in quietly abandoning the error of Young Earth Creationism as literal history, the Churches have quietly abandoned their duty to speak the truth about human nature and the human condition, which is almost the same thing as their duty to speak against liberalism and the enlightenment, for in transliterating religious promises about the next world to this world, the enlightenment necessarily denies important truths about human nature.

Therefore, the church has to accept Darwinism, and treat Young Earth Creation as a myth and symbolism expressing important Dark Enlightenment truths about the human condition: Among those truths: The city of Babel became the empire of Babel, failed because of tribalism, the European Union will fail because of tribalism. Also, and more importantly, All Women Are Like That

Universalism neglects the incarnate nature of Christ and his Church, making the Christian God into the God of the Universalists, the God of the Muslims, and then the "Arc of History" of the progressives. At the same time, the Church must not take particularism to the extreme that mistakes the good things of home, family, and nation for ultimate ends in themselves, must steer between the error of the Enlightenment, and the error of the Nazis, must proclaim both to be heresies. "Neither man nor women, neither Jew nor Greek" was said of the next world, not this. Today, the EU, having ensured that there is neither Jew nor Greek, is abolishing men and women.

Request for research assistance

2018-01-14 23:20:48

Since our existing state religion has gone rabid in an insane holiness spiral, we are in the business of designing a Gnon compliant state religion.

We need to steal from the best. If all societies had the economic system of twentieth century Hong Kong, all societies would have the economic outcomes of Hong Kong. If all societies had the healthcare system of Singapore, all societies would have the health outcomes and healthcare costs of Singapore. And if all societies had the family law of Timor Leste, all societies would have the fertility of Timor Leste.

Well, then, we need to steal the state religion that Charles the second imposed, which gave us empire, science, and industrialization.

So how did his state religion handle courtship and marriage?

I hope to find a clue in the County microfilm records: Library of Virginia[234]: Available by interlibrary loan.

Lancaster County:

Reel 102 Marriage Bonds & Consents, 1706 - 1819

Reel 350 Marriage Bonds, 1701, 1715-1736

Northhampton County:

Reel 99 Marriage Bonds & Consents, 1706 - 1780

Reel 62 Marriage Register, 1706 - 1853 c, Unpaged (Stratton Nottingham Compilation)

The consents and bonds are the juicy part, since that is the parent or guardian contracting with the prospective son in law that he damn well will get married.

The bond is a promise to pay damages if the marriage is not carried out - so I assume the couple are having sex at the time of the bond, or immediately after. (Otherwise, there would be no need to pay damages)

Bonds go from 1660, When Charles the Second's Anglicanism was imposed in England, to 1860, when marriage as it has been understood for the past couple of thousand years was legally abolished in England (though it continued to be socially enforced till about 1972.) Virginia of course was not subject to English rule in 1860, but its state religion was still effectively the Church of England, much as the State Religion of Israel is not Judaism, but United States State Department progressivism.

I am not at present located where it is easy to get an interlibrary loan, so will someone please look at these, see what is juicy, and if there are any good parts, send me a scan, or a link in the comments to a scan.

---

[234]https://www.lva.virginia.gov/public/local/

The Reichstag is on fire

2018-01-19 23:58:54

If Trump had been successfully given the perp walk by social justice warriors wearing recently issued police uniforms on the basis of a court order obtained by Mueller on the basis of being an accomplice after the fact in Russian spying on Hillary from some judge no one has heard of, or if he had been successfully stuffed into a straitjacket by social justice warriors wearing recently issued psychiatric orderly costumes, on the basis of a long distance mental health diagnosis by some psychiatrist no one has heard of, this would have been a deep state coup by the permanent government against the merely temporary and merely elected government.

If, however, high ranking members of the deep state are arrested for illegally spying on American citizens, which is to say, illegally spying on members of the merely temporary and merely elected government, this is a coup by the elected government against the deep state and the permanent government.

For the elected government to act decisively, it necessarily has to be incarnated by its president, just as a corporation can only act decisively as incarnated by its chief executive officer. For a group to act decisively, one man has to decide, and everyone else decide to go along with it.

If on the other hand, no one gets arrested, well, we are getting closer to the point where someone does get arrested, and there will be a next time, for as the left moves ever lefter, there will be another crisis, each crisis bigger than the last.

I am not making a prediction about which coup will happen, or that a coup will happen now. But I am telling you what it will mean if someone does get arrested,

The science is settled

2018-02-02 09:00:58

A little while ago I saw cited yet another Harvard study supposedly proving that women CEOs are just as good as men, except better, not withstanding the fact that anyone can see that women in charge are profoundly disruptive and destructive, that women can no more run a large group than they can chop wood with an axe, pilot a plane, do science, or clear a path through the jungle with a machete, that putting a woman in charge is pissing away shareholder's assets, as divorced women piss away their husband's and their children's assets, so I thought I would remind you of this golden oldie:

Click on the graph to see it in its full glory.

Is not science wonderful? I have been finding a pile of similar science data not just in global warmering, and in studies of demonic males viciously oppressing saintly women, but also dietary science, medical science, biology, and even string theory and materials science. These days, the way to get ahead in any area of science is to discover that your field has some political relevance that is unlikely to occur to any sane person, and then produce data that supposedly comforts the oppressed and saves the earth from cruel exploitation by white males. For an added bonus, you can destroy the careers of your colleagues as oppressors of the weak and vulnerable, because back in the bad old days they upheld the old evil theory (now refuted by your new data) for no reason other than hatred of some saintly victims and desire to cause harm to those saintly and long suffering victims.

The Fisa Memo

2018-02-04 00:16:19

It has long been known, long before the memo, that the Deep State engaged in illegal spying both with a false warrant, and without a warrant, on behalf of the Democratic Party Presidential Campaign.

It has long been known the Deep State, three letter police and spy agencies that were effectively part of the Democratic Party Presidential Campaign, illegally spied on the Trump campaign at the behest of and in coordination with the the Democratic Party Presidential Campaign and shared this information with the Democratic Party, the MSM, and Google. In course of this illegal spying they obtained one or more FISA warrants on false pretexts. In the course of spying on the particular individual or individuals named in these unlawful or falsely obtained FISA warrants they engaged in massive "unmasking".

When one spies on someone named in a warrant, it is inevitable that one will "accidentally" pick up information on people not named in the warrant. "Unmasking" means that one forgets that one is pretending that this is supposed to be accidental, and just plain spies on people not named in the warrant, on the basis that there is supposedly some connection between them and the people named in the warrant. "Unmasking" means that the fig leaf that one was using to spy on someone without a warrant fell off.

The memo, with much drama, does a big reveal of one part of this story, one small part of a story that we already know, that they obtained a pretextual warrant on behalf of and in coordination with the Democratic Party Presidential Campaign.

Expect, leading up to the 2018 elections, further big dramatic reveals of the story that we already know, which will provide a legal basis for a political purge of the supposedly non political appointees in the Deep State, and to send Hillary to prison.

Expect a 2018 campaign as referendum on impeaching Trump.

If they get the numbers to impeach Trump, or get away with pretending to have the numbers, he goes to jail, and so do many members of his administration, followed by numerous Republicans, leaving only shadow rump composed of a rapidly diminishing number of the most overtly and loudly cucking Republicans - European politics. If they don't, Hillary, or key members of her organization, go to jail.

Politically, if we care about how voters wish to vote, the best thing to do would be to refrain from purging the deep state from the three letter agencies until after the mid terms. But we are rapidly approaching the European situation where it seldom matters what the voters vote for, because all parties are the same, and any party that is not the same gets its members beaten up by Antifa and its key members sent to jail for racism, Nazism, hatred, misogyny, violent speech, Islamophobia, etc. Thus it would probably be wiser to purge the three letter agencies after another couple of big dramatic reveals, but well before the 2018 elections.

The disastrous effects of females in power

2018-02-05 03:18:44

Women cannot do men's jobs, and the pretense that they can and are is doing immense damage to men's work and the creation of value by men.

Women in men's positions subtract value. Women in powerful male positions subtract enormous amounts of value. Men at work get paid for creating value, and are forced to pay women for destroying the value that men create.

The reason for female under representation among top engineers, scientists, etc, is that women are slightly less competent on average and have a narrower distribution.

The reason for female under representation among CEOs is moral and emotional, unrelated to competence. Women are very competent managers. A woman has always managed my affairs, and generally done so very well, but women are uncomfortable running things without a strong alpha male supervising them and approving their work from time to time. If they don't get the supervision that they emotionally need from someone masculine, patriarchal, and sexy, they start acting maliciously, and self destructively, running the operation off the road and into the ground in a subconscious effort to force an alpha male to appear and give them a well deserved beating. The problem is that if she does not get the supervision that she emotionally needs, she will maliciously run the operation into the ground, like a wife married to a beta male husband whom she despises, destroying the family assets and the lives of their children.

Happens every single time, as near to every single time as makes no difference, no matter how smart and competent and hard working they are. Exceptions are so rare as to be nonexistent for all practical purposes.

I would explain the fact that a company with a female founder was one eighth as likely to get follow on funding by the fact that absolutely none of them should have received funding, and the only reason that any of them got any follow on funding was that the venture capitalists wanted to deny that anything was wrong. The official and enforced explanation is that it is proof of irrational hatred and misogyny by venture capitalists. And if you doubt this, you obviously must hate women.

So, to decide between these two explanations, let us look at company acquisitions. When venture capitalists fund a company, they intend it that if it succeeds it will be acquired by a big company. If a company is not acquired, the venture capitalists have pissed away their money. Most times they lose, sometimes they win big.

So, that eleven percent of companies with all male founders were acquired represents the venture capitalists winning one time in nine.

With all female founders, they won one time in two hundred and seventy. With all female founders they had only one thirtieth the chance as with all male founders.

One might suppose that this indicates that women are one thirtieth as likely to be able to operate a company as a man, but obviously this conclusion is absurd. The companies must have been acquired for political brownie points, not because they were being operated successfully. It is as plain as the nose on your face that women are absolutely disastrous when given this kind of authority, but official sources will deny what is spitting in their faces and kicking them in the balls, so how do we check this? Are they insane, or am I insane?

Answer: Look at companies with both male and female founders. If the reason is misogyny, then the female founder will have no effect, because the purchasers will assume she is only there for decoration and to warm the bed of the real founders.

So, if misogyny, companies with mixed founders should be purchased at roughly the same rate as companies with all male founders.

If the problem is that women are just naturally incompetent as CEOs, then companies with mixed founders should be purchased at a somewhat lower rate, as the male founders carry the female founders on their backs while the purported female founders paint their nails, powder their faces, and discuss their most recent booty call from Jeremy Meeks.

If, however, the problem is that women in power just invariably and uniformly act like feral animals, as if they had been raised by apes in the jungle, then zero companies with mixed founders will be purchased. If the problem is that the female founders need to be placed in cages and put on leashes, but the male founders are not allowed to do so, then zero companies with mixed founders will be purchased. If the problem is that these days women are no longer subject to the restraints of civilization, then zero companies with mixed founders will be purchased.

Well, guess what.

If a woman has a strong husband who is himself wealthy and powerful, and she washes his dishes and sorts his socks, then she can be a good CEO. Today, however, husbands are generally weak, and therefore competent female CEOs correspondingly rare.

Females can no more do large group socialization than they can chop wood with an axe, or clear a path through the jungle with a machete. Females in or near positions of power have a disastrous effect on the social cohesion of the group to which they belong, on the propensity of group members to cooperate with each other, on the asabiyyah of the group, on the group's capability to pursue goals in common.

It is a standard psychiatric finding that women are supposedly more agreeable than men, and in very important ways they are.

If tell a woman I have mislaid my keys, she will find them. In this sense women really are more agreeable than men.

If I tell a woman to get me coffee, she will get me coffee. In this sense women really are more agreeable than men.

If I slap a woman on the backside, she will yelp and jump, but then smile and laugh. In this sense women really are more agreeable than men.

But who is it that interrupts the boss?

It is always a woman. Yes, she interrupts in a supposedly friendly, supportive, and agreeable manner, but interrupting is in reality unfriendly, undermines him, and is in fact disagreeable.

Women are catty. Two women are friends, three women are a contest to see which two will become friends. Women are disruptive. They never stop shit testing their bosses. If a woman interrupts her boss, talks over her boss, even though her interruption is supposedly friendly, supportive, and all that, as it always supposedly is, she is disrupting and damaging the organization.

Women take advantage of and abuse restrictions on physical violence, and other rules commanding prosocial behavior, which abuse undermines prosocial behavior and impairs large group cooperation between males. Women are bad for and disruptive of any large group that attempts to cooperate to get something done. They undermine asabiyya, throwing sand in the wheels just for the hell of it. They are always throwing down shit tests to find which male is alpha enough to subdue their bad behavior, always disrupting, always looking for a well deserved spanking.

The psychiatric category of "agreeableness" is cooked to support the doctrine that women are wonderful. It conflates going along with bad behavior, with going along with good behavior. It declares resisting bad behavior to be disagreeable, while ruthlessly and cynically imposing on good behavior is supposedly not disagreeable.

Yes, women really are wonderful in their proper sphere. In power, they are only tolerable to the extent that strong males keep them in line.

A more accurate analysis of female behavior is that females are bad at, and bad for, large group social dynamics. Female or substantially female businesses fail, often fail very badly. Women are better at one on one dynamics than men - all women, all the time. Worse at large group dynamics than men. All women, all the time. All women are like that.

It is obvious to me that women are having a devastating effect on male efforts to create wealth, and I have long been puzzled at other people's inability to see what is not merely right in front of their faces, but repeatedly spitting in their face and then slapping them.

A business appoints a female boss because progress. She acts in an angry hostile manner, infuriating customers and vital employees, disruptively knocking the business off track instead of keeping it on track, as if the business was a beta husband, and she wanted a divorce with the house, the children, and alimony. Business goes down the tubes. No one notices. Supposedly the business ran into mysterious head winds that have absolutely no connection to the new boss whatsoever.

When males aggress, they get in each other's faces, they shout, there is always a hint of the possibility it might turn physical, a suggestion of physical menace. Women aggress and disrupt in a more passive manner, and these days we are not allowed to react to female aggression by shouting at them and getting in their faces, by menacing them. It used to be, within living memory, within my memory, that female misbehavior was met with a male response that hinted at the possibility that she might get spanked, put in a metaphorical cage, or put in metaphorical or literal irons, just as an aggressively misbehaving male got then and gets today a response that hints at the possibility of a punch in the face or imprisonment. Women today therefore routinely aggress and disrupt in a manner I find shocking, crazy, disgraceful, bizarre, and extreme, and do so with shocking and disgraceful impunity, as if within my lifetime women came to be possessed by demons, and everyone is walking around like zombies pretending to not notice. Recall in the infamous interview, Jordan Peterson looks away from Kathy before calling out her bad behavior, because if he looked her in the face while calling out her bad behavior it would have been socially unacceptable, because women are supposedly wonderful.

A male quarrels with a male. They get in each other's faces, you feel that violence might happen, or at least one of them will call security and have the other shown the door.

They have the body language of two male goats about to butt heads over possession of a female goat.

A female quarrels with a male. She interrupts him and talks over him in a supposedly friendly and supportive way "So what you are really saying is ..."

A male who intends to aggress against another male who is ignoring him intrudes into the other male's space and just plain gets close enough that the male he is aggressing against has to drop what he is doing and pay attention. Again we see the body language of two male goats about to butt heads over a female goat.

A female who intends to aggress against a male who is ignoring her also intrudes, but not so close, and proceeds to interrupt what he is doing and distract him with some halfway plausible excuse as to why he has to stop what he is doing and pay attention to her, which excuse is something that in theory should not irritate him, and he has trouble understanding why he is irritated, and why she lacks any real interest in the nominal justification that she supposedly has for demanding his attention and interrupting his activities. Supposedly she is helping him in a friendly pleasant nice way, though her "help" is hostile, nasty, angry, disruptive and entirely unwanted, and she ignores his forceful denials that he needs any such "help".

We need a society where women feel that if they act like Cathy Newman did in that infamous interview with Jordan Peterson, they might get slapped in the face, or sent to the kitchen and the bedroom and restricted from getting out except on a short leash. But if Jordan had responded to her bad behavior by getting in her face as if she was a man, they would probably have called security and tossed him out. Notice that whenever Jordan calls out Cathy Newman's bad behavior he looks away and gives a little laugh. If he called out her bad behavior while looking at her, it would have been socially unacceptable. What needs to be socially acceptable is that her husband should have given her a slap in the face for publicly disgracing his family with her bad behavior. The same government policies that helicoptering women into powerful positions are allowing them to act badly and destructively in those positions.

As affirmative action makes the differences between men and women starkly and dramatically visible to everyone, at the same time it makes it a criminal offense to notice, or even think about, those differences.

A woman in power is like a woman who finds herself the breadwinner, and her husband is a kitchen bitch, like a dog who finds himself the alpha male of the household, like a woman who intrudes into a males space and proceeds to feminize it and make it hostile to males. She behaves badly in an unconscious effort to smoke the alpha male out of hiding by provoking him to give her a beating.

Supposedly the reason there are so few female CEOs is because of evil sexism, not because boards keep appointing female CEOs and those CEOs keep driving their companies into the ditch. From time to time some big important Harvard expert informs us that female headed or female founded companies do better than male companies[235], but they will not show us their data, which data conspicuously flies in the face of common sense, anecdote, and casual observation. And if you ask to see their data, you are a racist sexist islamophobic misogynist, and the only reason you could be asking such an obvi-

---

[235] https://hbr.org/2017/09/the-comprehensive-case-for-investing-more-vc-money-in-women-led-startups

ously hateful question is because you just hate women and are trying to harm them by asking hate questions about hate facts. Also, you are anti science and a global warming denier[236]. We ignorant hateful hicks who keep asking to see the evidence that women can do a man's job are just like those ignorant hateful hicks who keep asking to see the evidence for global warming. We are anti science, because the science is settled.

Well, fortunately, a surprisingly truthful feminist chick went looking for the data.

Her graphics were truthful, but somewhat misleading, as she de-emphasized and partially hid the most important and dramatic datum, so I edited her graphics for clarity. The graphic at the start of this post is mine, but based on her data and graphics. Which got purged from the internet, not long after I posted this.

What we know about the Reichstag fire.

2018-02-06 21:31:54

This is unofficial knowledge, which I expect to become official in due course, in subsequent official events resembling #releasethememo. This post is copied wholesale from a certain neoreactionary of influence, except that I have spun it slightly towards my interpretation of events, rather than his.

The Democrats applied the full suite of extremely powerful intelligence capabilities of USG to spy on Trump and everyone remotely connected to his campaign, in order to help Hillary and hurt or intimidate Trump's people and deter potential people from joining up with him, and they wanted as much of that information to be as widely shared as possible so that the dirt they were certain would be there (which, to everyone's surprise, wasn't) would be leakable to the propaganda machine press and public in a way that would be impossible to attribute to any particular individual.

Using the fig leaf of an illegal fisa warrant on one member of the Trump campaign, they illegally spied on Trump and the entire Trump campaign, ("unmasking", June 27, 2016 "Tarmac Meeting", Samantha Power) expecting something to turn up that would retroactively make the spying arguably legal, legal in the progressive sense of "what does it matter now".

Except that it did not.

The ultra-expensive, national security-level tools of the permanent government were pointed towards these improper targets, in the ultimate form of "opposition research", but for free, paid for by taxpayers. They figured that what was true for practically anyone would be true for Trump, that all one needs is a pretext to start surveillance, and one would inevitably turn up evidence of some activity which could fit within the broad interpretation of the modern state's endless list of offenses, at least enough to support an indictment, or at the very least, legal but scandalous, which is effective when used against Republican candidates when spun by the propaganda machine, or at the very, very least, not against Trump the man himself, but against one of his team or even several degrees of separation removed from them (given chain-investigating, the investigatory equivalent of chain-migration) for anything they may have done over the course of their entire lives that might end up "inadvertently" being hoovered up in the course of an infinitely-expanding

---

[236]latex/images/hide_the_decline.gif

network and scope of investigation. And in the last resort, use one of those cases to "flip" that individual into an informant to tell them something dirty about Trump that the surveillance couldn't pick up.

They believed all they would have to do is just get the surveillance started. They knew the (foreign and domestic) surveillance needed a FISA warrant, which needed a foreign power hook, which had to be Russia. Which didn't exist, so someone would have to make it up out of whole cloth. Which obviously couldn't be corroborated, because false and totally made up, and so if supported by oath, somebody could be liable for perjury. Fusion GPS seems to exist in large part for this purpose: to produce opposition material, some of which is from normal "research and investigation", though spun to the very limits of truthiness, some of which is a conveniently "leak" drop point for insiders, and some of which is fabricated out of whole cloth and laundered through the operator game of repetition through intermediaries, and also as a "jobs for the friends and family of valuable people" shop (cf. "Friends of Angelo VIP program"), and as a conduit to move side-payments / mole bounties / kickbacks / "household loyalty" money around, when necessary.

And so it became indispensable to find a basis for credibility and probable cause not based in actual corroboration or investigation, the only one available being "previously credible, reliable, and valuable informant." And once the spying started, they expected that something would turn up to make the initial illegality of the spying irrelevant.

Meanwhile the DoJ and FBI were all on board, using the dossier as cover for everything they were doing, and expecting a sure and easy Hillary victory which would prevent any of this from coming to light and blowing up in their faces, and confident that Trump would never learn about it.

Except that he did learn all about it at soon as it started, probably from Admiral Rodgers and the surveillance couldn't come up with any dirt, despite it being on and greatly expanded for months, and being a sure-fire way to produce lots of dirt nearly 100% of the time on usual targets.

This was what the whole "Mike Rogers did what?!" administration flip-out and threat of disciplinary action (recommended by Clapper and Aston Carter) was all about (as Sailer says, nobody remembers nothing.) This was also the basis of Trump asking Comey "three times" whether he was under investigation, knowing Comey would lie about it.

Guns, Ideas, Fashion, and Military Parades

2018-02-10 08:48:37

Ideas are more powerful than guns, but fashion is more powerful than ideas.

If Trump has a military parade with snappy parade uniforms, we may well win. Trouble is that our elite has been busy making soldiers dress androgynously, because they hate and fear the military. We are always ruled by warriors or priests. If soldiers continue to dress like Elon Musk's rocket scientists, soldiers, like nerds, will remain low status, and priestly rule will continue.

They probably will not make the marines wear high heeled shoes, but they will make them wear baggy clothes that are interchangeable with the similarly baggy clothes worn by female "soldiers".

If they parade wearing camo versions of what Elon Musk's rocket scientists wear, military will remain low status, and thus warriors will be unable to challenge priests.

People in large masses toting guns and moving in unison is impressive, and big rockets are impressive, but to translate that impressiveness into power, need to dress the part. Clothes make the man. Consider Musk's show with the heavy rocket.

Musk is a showman and Trump is showman, but Musk's show sucked because everyone was dressed in Silicon Valley Casual that was actually casual. Needed to dress them in Silicon Valley Casual that was actually Silicon Valley Cool.

You look at a bunch of very smart rocket scientists acting and looking like World of Warcraft players who have just cleared a dungeon, and you think "low status"

I want warriors in power, and I want people who make cool toys for warriors in power, and they will need to dress the part.

Let us imagine how Musk's heavy rocket launch would have gone if he draped a bikini model over the sportscar that he launched to Mars, if his rocket scientists were better dressed, and if he himself posed with the bikini model and the sportscar wearing nice clothes with a touch of mad scientist. Similarly, however cool a military parade is, (and a military parade, like a rocket launch, is very cool indeed) you are not going to visualize those parading in power unless they dress the part.

Obviously the parade will raise Trump's approval rating significantly. The problem is, however, at some point he is going to have to demonstrate that an airforce commando outranks a supreme court justice, so we need to raise the approval rating of air force commandos.

My assessment of the fall of Kings that began in the nineteenth century is that kings did not fail because of gunpowder, did not fail because industry rather than land became the source of wealth. Kings failed because George the fourth was fat, lazy, had a fat mistress, a bad tailor, and slept with other men's wives, but most of all, Kings failed because Beau Brummel made the Puritan aesthetic cool. If King George the Fourth had had better fashion sense and hotter mistresses than Beau Brummel, and if his mistresses had, like Beau Brummel's mistresses, only been sleeping with him, instead of sleeping with him and their husbands, we would have been fine. Also, if he had gotten off his fat ass and did some kinging, we would have been fine. He failed in the job of being the fount of all honors, mortal and divine (which is to say the job of regulating status competition into prosocial positive sum displays, rather than antisocial negative sum displays). The successors of the puritans took that job, ran with it, and have never let go of it.

So far, however, our attempts to produce reactionary fashion have all been miserable failures, and perhaps we will always fail until we have victorious soldiers exercising power, for all the cool reactionary fashions of the past are based on the uniforms worn by soldiers in victory parades.

But I am now coming around to the view that fashion should feature physically fit men wearing tight clothes that have been personally tailored to them. Standard stretch pants that fit without requiring a belt, and on the top a shirt, perhaps a T shirt, that has been tailored to fit, and tailored to end just below the point on your pants where a belt would be if they needed a belt, which your pants should not. The shirt goes outside the

Figure 1: Good old boy hat

pants, but is almost, but not quite, tight around the pants.

Well fitting clothes are automatically high status. It is the last sumptuary display. An off the rack business suit is not high status. A custom fitted T shirt is high status. Baggy pants are low status. Men wear baggy pants because gangsters who claimed high status on the basis of violence were countersignaling by wearing baggy pants, but baggy pants do not work unless you can also plausibly signal real capability and will to commit violence. Such plausible signals are apt to get you killed, so make sure your pants fit. If you countersignal by poorly fitting pants, have to signal by violence, which can get costly.

Secondly, the costume should contain some element of peacocking, ideally a unique and idiosyncratic element. I now wear a fighting cock feather in my hat, the tail feather of a fighting cock that died in battle. Unfortunately, such feathers do not last a whole lot longer than the cock that donated them. It is tricky to get the right feather attached in the right place. Each fighting cock feather is unique and different (fighting cocks themselves peacock, with longer, floppier, and more diverse feathers than regular cocks). Most fighting cock feathers will do something bad like flopping in your eyes. Need a feather that flops around, but stays out of your eyes and your field of view, while flopping around in the other guys's field of view.

Big hats are good, and better with something decorating them.

Gold chains also good, though male gold chains need to be big. Fine gold chains are girly. Not sure if multiple peacocking elements are a good idea. The Regency Aesthetic failed through excess, which excess justified the Puritan Aesthetic. A gold chain needs to be accompanied by bros or a bodyguard. If no wingman, then no gold chain. if a weak geek neck, cannot support a fighting cock feather.

You cannot peacock unless the alpha male of the group is also peacocking, or unless it is plausible that you are, by at least some metric, the alpha male of the group. Your boss is not going to be peacocking, and if your subordinate is peacocking while you are not peacocking, you will need to do something about it.

Any item of peacocking that draws attention to your head needs a suitably large neck to support its metaphorical weight, as if it had actual physical weight. I have therefore added neck exercises to my exercise regimen. I attach a looped belt to a resistance cord, and pull with my head in different directions, in order for my neck to be strong enough to support the mighty weight of the fighting cock feather in my hat. If you have a geek neck, don't try to wear a big hat.

Obviously you cannot wear something to job interview or similar occasion that is more dramatic or unusual than your interviewer will be wearing. No peacocking allowed at work or in job interviews, but you can wear better fitting clothes than your interviewer. If Silicon Valley Casual is socially required, you can wear Silicon Valley Casual that just happens to fit you perfectly, as Steve Jobs invariably did. Also, matching colors combined with dramatic clash of colors, so that the clash is clearly intentional, rather than the result of whatever passed the sniff test that morning. If you are going to have a dramatic clash of colors, superhero style, make sure that one major part of your costume matches another part.

Well, this is the latest in a long string of attempts to conjure reactionary meanswear into existence, and all previous attempts have failed embarassingly. Let us see how this one goes. We still need a victory parade with cool manly military parade dress uniforms to really make reactionary fashion stick.

But, lacking a victory parade, physical fitness is something. Reactionary males tend to be markedly stronger and slimmer than progressive males, due to fasting, diet, and lifting iron. Reactionary fashion will succeed, if associated with reactionaty phenotypes.

In the age of feral woman and family breakdown, when fatherhood is illegal, when everyone is a bastard, menswear that is associated with being able to beat people up is likely to succeed. The difference between today and past ages was that in successful civilizations, top fashions were associated with being a member of a group that was able to beat up other groups in organized collective disciplined physical violence, hence the connection to victory parades, while in an age of social collapse and family breakdown, in a civilization in decline, in a time when a dark age looms, when fatherhood has been criminalized, successful fashion tends to be more associated with the capability to perform individual thuggery, hence the perverse and ugly baggy pants fashion. When fatherhood is illegal, only criminals can be fathers. The underlying problem with menswear fashion is that the state is violently, coercively, brutally, and forcefully imposing black mating patterns and white gay mating patterns on white heterosexual males, which mating pattern in turn causes unattractive clothing to be fashionable, and attractive clothing to be unfashionable, the baggy pants fashion being an example of this problem.

If reactionaries are having troubles restoring reactionary fashion, it is because we are having troubles restoring reactionary families, and reactionary families require reactionary male social groups that collectively enforce reactionary socialization on potentially feral women. But, on the principle of fake it till you make it, reactionary fashion can cause the social conditions that will in turn cause reactionary fashion.

Dress like a patriarch, dress like an aristocrat, and have your women dress as if under patriarchal authority. Good fit is patriarchal, and peacocking and physical fitness is aristocratic. You cannot peacock at work if your boss is not peacocking, but you can be physically fit and wear well fitted clothes.

On Punching Women

2018-02-14 23:30:34

Many women deserve to be punched, and do not get punched, but punching a woman indicates loss of control and weakness. You should avoid getting into fights except where you can bring overwhelming supremacy to bear, and you should always be able to bring overwhelming supremacy to bear on a woman. If you have overwhelming supremacy, you can pin the opponent, and either put a painful submission hold on them, or whack him part of the body where it is safe to do so without likelihood of causing injury.

I have found I can use this kind of violence on a woman in public, safe and controlled irresistible violence, and everyone just grins. Especially other women.

Part of being able to control what kind of fights you get into is to be well prepared for a terrible, destructive, and uncontrolled fight where you cannot bring overwhelming supremacy to bear, and I am always prepared for such a fight. I am trained in unarmed combat, and when going into an unpredictable situation carry the most dangerous concealed weapon legally permitted, but the reason to be prepared for such a fight is not to get into such a fight and win, but to be able to better get out of such a fight by offering your opponent a safer path, offering your opponent a dignified way out of such a fight. One prepares for such a fight in order to better obtain your opponents cooperation in staying out of such fights, not to fight and win them, for even if you win, seldom profitable. Even if you win, you lose. Having the potential to do your adversary great harm is often profitable. Actually exercising that potential is rarely profitable.

Jesus said "resist not evil", but we cannot take this literally, because if evil smells that you are a soft target, evil will be on to you like a dingo on a baby. We have to interpret the sermon on the mount as Jesus anticipating crucifixion, and pointing at our inability to attain salvation by personal virtue in a fallen world. Literal application of the Sermon on the Mount would be suicidal in a fallen world. We apply it by always being willing to do what it takes to find the path that does not involve terrible and destructive combat. But it takes two to make peace, only one to make war, and to find the peaceful path requires the ability to dissuade your opponent from the path of combat.

White knights are evil men - a man who white knights another man's woman is a man who will spread hateful lies about his friend behind his friend's back to sow discord and anger between friends. A man who white knights another man's woman also engages in every kind of depraved and cowardly evil. When you punch a woman, no matter how much she deserves it, you show weakness and loss of frame, and weakness attracts evil. Deal with a misbehaving woman with firmness and strength, you will have no problems. Deal with her from weakness, white knights will materialize like flies on rotting meat.

Losing weight

2018-02-15 06:23:35

At my morning weigh in, eighty eight pounds below my maximum, despite having added a lot of muscle.

I used to assume that this was because I no longer have to cook for my sick wife and hand feed her, thus relieved of continual food temptation, and that no doubt is part of it. I still cannot outstare a pizza and a pitcher of mountain dew.

But I notice that the average weight loss among men on added testosterone[237] is thirty six pounds, Jordan Peterson lost fifty pounds on the low carb paleo diet[238], and that people report similar weight loss from regular fasting, and since I am following all of those at once, I guess my weight loss is absolutely typical of these methods.

So we have medical evidence that testosterone therapy has, on average, a huge effect, and anecdotal evidence of effective diet strategies which also have huge effect.

So, Americans are fat, but weight loss looks like a solved problem. Every male needs to eat a pound of meat a day, everyone needs to stop eating bread and such, (pizza is my Achilles heel) almost every male needs testosterone therapy, everyone needs to stop eating vegetable oils except for olive oil and coconut oil, everyone needs to eat more butter and eggs, and everyone needs to fast regularly.

Testosterone therapy needs to be accompanied by estradiol monitoring, and an appropriate dose of exemestane to keepestradiol above twenty and below thirtypicograms per milliliter. Anything higher or lower is likely to cause male sexual problems, depression, psychological problems, spiritual problems, impotence, male sexual deviance, and sudden death in males. Lowestradiol in males is usually caused by low testosterone, and in males lowestradiol should be treated with testosterone, not estrogen. High estrogen in males is usually caused by being too fat. American males suffer simultaneously from obesity and low testosterone, so theirestradiol levels are all over the place, about as many with dangerously high levels as with dangerously low, which may explain such weird things as cuck porn.

It also needs to be accompanied by monitoring of luteinizing hormone. Added testosterone can cause your luteinizing hormone to drop resulting in your balls shriveling up, possibly permanently, and male infertility, possibly permanent male infertility. If your luteinizing hormone drops too far, you will need Human Chorionic Gonadotropin to compensate.

If you are fat, and your testosterone levels are artificially raised to healthy normal male levels (six hundred to nine hundred nanograms per deciliter) your estrogen is going to go way too high, likely causing health and sexual problems, and your luteinizing hormone may well go way too low, causing damage to your testicles, quite possibly permanent damage.

But if every male American was put on testosterone therapy, likely the average weight loss would be thirty pounds or so, since most Americans have testosterone levels far below those that used to be normal, (to which the government has responded by redefining "normal" way down to levels so low as to have major and serious health consequences) Most males have hormone levels, low testosterone and out of range estradiol, that are known to be associated with major adverse physical and mental health consequences.

This would go a good way to explaining and curing the obesity epidemic.

Well, it would explain it if we had the explanation of falling testosterone and sperm

---

[237] https://www.news-medical.net/news/20120625/Major-weight-loss-an-added-benefit-of-testosterone-replacement-therapy-for-men.aspx

[238] https://rosemarycottageclinic.wordpress.com/2017/04/08/jordan-peterson-on-diet-and-health/

production levels. My guess is that the cause of falling testosterone levels is not estrogen in the water supply, but spiritual estrogen in the spiritual water supply - that the war on "toxic" masculinity is the equivalent of being continually defeated, degraded, and humiliated, which is well known to lower testosterone, that the war on men, maleness, and masculinity starting in school is making men into fat chicks. Compare Musk's rocket scientists with Wernher von Braun. Just looking at American males and comparing them with males of earlier periods, looks like something has gone massively and horribly wrong with their hormones, that we have a massive epidemic of hormone derangement, which, combined with too much sugar and wheat flour, may well explain our male obesity epidemic. There is also some hormone derangement going on with our females.

Bread, sugar, and snacking, especially sweet drinks is also a significant part of the problem. People are not eating home cooked meals any more, which puts them on the opposite of the paleo diet, and since the low carb high saturated fat paleo diet causes major weight loss, likely the frequent snacking on heavily processed food diet causes major weight gain. Likely the abandonment of the kitchen had a worse effect on women than men. If you snack on heavily processed food you are snacking on grain derived carbs, soy oil, soy protein, and soy *phytoestrogens*. Grain, soy, and low testosterone likely explains a great deal of our problems.

My experience of testosterone is that testosterone does not itself directly cause weight loss, but strengthens and frees the will, making it easier to diet, fast, and exercise, that the direct effect of testosterone is primarily spiritual, and that the physical effects are secondary upon the spiritual effects.

I also guess that the decline in testosterone is primarily caused by the spiritual, rather than physical, environment. When I fail a shit test, I can feel my testosterone fall. When I pass a shit test, I can feel it rise. Androgyny makes men and women fat and ugly. When a woman marches down the middle of a corridor, and her male co-worker scuttles to the side of the corridor, her testosterone rises, making her fat and ugly, his testosterone falls, making him fat and ugly.

For a long time the medical profession has been telling us that nothing works for obesity. They tell is that they try everything, nothing works, and it always fails. But everything that works has been ignored by the medical profession, because associated with maleness and masculinity. The campaign against meat started with oppressive government regulation of meat slaughter that raised the price of meat and reduced the availability of meat, which regulatory assault on meat was motivated by a left wing campaign demonizing slaughterhouses. The left just does not like meat, and looks for reasons to stop it, just as they just don't like coal and coal mining and look for reasons to stop it. Too male. Then followed the food pyramid, based on pseudo science even more transparently and flagrantly bogus than global warming. Everything that works tends to be associated spiritually and culturally with various maleness and masculinity movements, which is why official science does not like anything that works.

Five more years

2018-02-16 09:25:40

Scott Alexander's predictions for the next year have become ever more cautious, thus ever more boring and ever less likely to be falsified. And then he came up with a pile of wild assed stuff for the next five years[239]:

> AI will be marked by various spectacular achievements, plus nobody being willing to say the spectacular achievements signify anything broader. AI will beat humans at progressively more complicated games, and we will hear how games are totally different from real life and this is just a cool parlor trick.

In other words, he will say it is spectacular, and I will say it is more of the same boring stuff.

> AI translation will become flawless,

No it will not. AI translation is as good as it is going to get - gives you a good guess as to what the speaker is actually talking about, while remaining unacceptable as a finished product. You get the gist of things when AI translating between closely related languages like English and Spanish, and near gibberish when AI translating between distantly related languages like Chinese and English - a marginal improvement on what you would get by language dictionary lookup.

> 1. Average person can hail a self-driving car in at least one US city: 80%
>
> 2. ...in at least five of ten largest US cities: 30%
>
> 3. At least 5% of truck drivers have been replaced by self-driving trucks: 10%

Nah.

> 4. Average person can buy a self-driving car for less than $100,000: 30%

But he will have to sit at the wheel, and will likely die if he falls asleep at the wheel.

> The European Union will not collapse.

The EU is a branch of the US empire, and I have long predicted failure or similar crisis for the US empire in 2026. As long as the US stands, its servants in Europe will continue to do as they are damn well told.

> Countries that may have an especially good half-decade: Israel, India, Nigeria, most of East Africa, Iran. Countries that may have an especially bad half-decade: Russia, Saudi Arabia, South Africa, UK. The Middle East will get worse before it gets better, especially Lebanon and the Arabian Peninsula (Syria might get better, though).

---

[239]https://slatestarcodex.com/2018/02/15/five-more-years/

"May have"? What sort of a prediction is that? Might be right, cannot be wrong.

Here is my actual prediction. Russia will have a great decade. South Africa will drift from a shit hole to a hell hole.

Religion will continue to retreat from US public life.

Scott has not noticed that the US has an official religion that daily becomes more extreme, deranged, puritanical, and oppressive

> As it becomes less important, mainstream society will treat it as less of an outgroup and more of a fargroup. Everyone will assume Christians have some sort of vague spiritual wisdom, much like Buddhists do. Everyone will agree evangelicals or anyone with a real religious opinion is just straight-out misinterpreting the Bible, the same way any Muslim who does something bad is misinterpreting the Koran. Christian mysticism will become more popular among intellectuals. Lots of people will talk about how real Christianity opposes capitalism. There may not literally be a black lesbian Pope, but everyone will agree that there should be, and people will become mildly surprised when you remind them that the Pope is white, male, and sexually inactive.

OK, this prediction will come true, but this, like Europe continuing, is just the official religion of the US empire continuing. The official religion of the US empire will fall, but probably survive for more than five years.

> 1. Trump wins 2020: 20%

Trump will win in 2020, assuming no coup or violent death. Democracy has already expired. The question is how soon this becomes obvious, and to what extent violence will ensue when people realize it.

> On the other hand, everyone will have underestimated the extent of crisis in the Democratic Party.

The misconduct of the Clinton presidential campaign was a manifestation of the fact that the pretense of democracy in the Democratic party was irrelevant to outcomes. It will go right on being irrelevant to outcomes. With the Clinton machine at best falling apart, and at worst being sent to jail, power in the Democratic party will fall into the hands of a Lenin type individual who realizes the irrelevance of electoral politics and proceeds to grab power directly. Primaries will remain irrelevant to the outcome, but the man seizing power will probably be radically left.

Slate Star Codex predicts politics as normal, the usual stuff in the usual ways, that something like what recently happened will happen again. I predict the unexpected - at least as startling as Trump himself, probably a lot more startling. Expect the unexpected. The Republic approaches its end. It will probably not end in five years, but the storms of its coming fall will rage.

The culture wars will continue to be marked by both sides scoring an unrelenting series of own-goals, with the victory going to whoever can make their supporters shut up first. The best case scenario for the Right is that Jordan Peterson's ability to not instantly get ostracized and destroyed signals a new era of basically decent people being able to speak out against social justice; this launches a cascade of people doing so, and the vague group consisting of Jordan Peterson, Sam Harris, Steven Pinker, Jonathan Haidt, etc coalesces into a perfectly respectable force no more controversial than the gun lobby or the pro-life movement or something. With social justice no longer able to enforce its own sacredness values against blasphemy, it loses a lot of credibility and ends up no more powerful or religion-like than eg Christianity. The best case scenario for the Left is that the alt-right makes some more noise, the media is able to relentlessly keep everyone's focus on the alt-right, the words ALT-RIGHT get seared into the public consciousness every single day on every single news website, and everyone is so afraid of being associated with the alt-right that they shut up about any disagreements with the consensus they might have. I predict both of these will happen, but the Right's win-scenario will come together faster and they will score a minor victory.

Slate star predicts politics as they are now continuing, but politics as they are now are already extraordinary and remarkable by the standards of two years ago. Again, I predict the unexpected - a significant likelihood of democide or ethnic cleansing, with whites being driven out of large areas, and then blamed for the ensuing ruin that follows when they are no longer holding stuff together. More drama, more surprises, more shock.

The last two years have been very surprising for everyone except me - I predicted Trumps victory shortly after he announced. And I predict the next two years to be even more surprising, and the three years after that to be even more surprising, with a continuing drift towards civil war, democide and genocide, though we probably will not see democide, genocide, and civil war for about six years or so.

First World economies will increasingly be marked by an Officialness Divide. Rich people, the government, and corporations will use formal, well-regulated, traditional institutions. Poor people (and to an increasing degree middle-class people) will use informal gig economies supported by Silicon Valley companies whose main skill is staying a step ahead of regulators. Think business travelers staying at the Hilton and riding taxis, vs.low-prospect twenty-somethings staying at Air BnBs and taking Ubers. As Obamacare collapses, health insurance will start turning into one of the formal, well-regulated, traditional institutions limited to college grads with good job prospects. What the unofficial version of health care will be remains to be seen. If past eras have been Stone Age, Bronze Age, Iron Age, Information Age, etc, the future may be the Ability-To-Circumvent-Regulations Age.

On this, we agree.

> Cryptocurrency will neither collapse nor take over everything. It will become integrated into the existing system and regulated to the point of uselessness. No matter how private and untraceable the next generation of cryptocurrencies are, people will buy and exchange them through big corporate websites that do everything they can to stay on the government's good side.

Nah. Bitcoin may well collapse, and its successor (probably Monero) may also collapse, but one cryptocurrency, maybe Bitcoin, maybe Monero, maybe something not yet on the radar, will eat the world. If it has not eaten the world in five years, the storm of its coming will nonetheless be evident, and will profoundly undermine the government's ability to control the economy.

> Multinationals will occasionally debate using crypto to transfer their profits from one place to another, then decide that would make people angry and decide not to.

Already false. Crypto transfers are already big - and already cryptic.

Skipping most of his predictions as boring and hard to decide what would constitute fulfillment of the rather vague prediction.

> 3. Paris Agreement still in effect, most countries generally making good-faith effort to comply: 80%

Already false. No one is making a genuine good faith effort to comply.

> 4. US still nominally committed to Paris Agreement: 60%

Already false. In 2017 June the US announced it had ceased all implementation of the Paris Accord. That is something a bit less than being "nominally committed". That will not change, and people are already forgetting that there ever was a Paris agreement. The only real action item on the Paris accord was smashing Americans in flyover country, making them suffer, and providing political cover for smashing Americans in flyover country. If Americans in flyover county are not being smashed, not one gives a tinker's dam about the rest of it. It is already sliding out of sight and out of mind.

School shot up because murdering white kids is OK

2018-02-20 00:39:05

The Florida school shootings did not happen for lack of gun control. They happened because of refusal to enforce law and maintain order when blacks and hispanics attack white children.

Back in 2015 I said:

> Difficult to say what will happen to Mestizos and Indios. In Mexico, the old gods walk again, but this has not happened in the US,[240]

---

[240]https://blog.reaction.la/war/putin-successfully-stabilizing-syria/#comment-1140392

Well now the Old Gods have walked from Mexico to Florida, and spoken to Nikolas Cruz.

Nicolas Cruz had a long history of violence, menace, evil, and madness. And, of course, the school's response was[241]:

"We do, as teachers, everything that we possibly can to help them"

Maybe when someone hears voices commanding him to terrible things and willfully chooses to obey those voices, it is time to think about not about helping him, but helping those near him.

But, instead[242]:

> that harsh approach fell out of favor amid concerns that it was funneling too many young people — and particularly black and Hispanic students — into the juvenile justice system.

When a fat feminist who is hitting the wall complains that group of white males have an unhealthy attitude to women, does anyone say "We should do, as teachers, everything that we possibly can to help them". No, they say "Let us throw the book at them, and not worry whether these accusations are true, false, or even remotely believable."

When white males are accused of misbehavior, everyone has total confidence in the effectiveness of swift and harsh penalties, which should not be slowed down by old fashioned concerns about evidence or guilt. When a bunch of white males get together for some purpose that does not involve fucking each other, they are automatically suspected of being an evil terrorist organization.

> In recent years, Broward schools became a leader in the national move toward a different kind of discipline — one that would not just punish students, but also would help them address the root causes of their misbehavior. Such policies aim to combat what is known as the "school-to-prison pipeline," giving teenagers a chance to stick with their education rather than get derailed, often permanently, by criminal charges.

In other words, a free pass for blacks and Hispanics to attack people at random, while if a white kid nibbles a slice of bread into the shape of a gun, the social workers get called to take him from his parents.

Blacks attack kids to take lunch money and such, without much regard for race, religion, ethnicity or social class. They are dangerous to everyone near them, ingroup or outgroup. Education and culture has little effect. Harvard blacks almost as dangerous as

---

[241] https://www.washingtonpost.com/local/education/teachers-say-florida-shooters-problems-started-in-middle-school-and-the-system-tried-to-help-him/2018/02/18/cdff7aa6-1413-11e8-9065-e55346f6de81_story.html

[242] https://www.washingtonpost.com/local/education/teachers-say-florida-shooters-problems-started-in-middle-school-and-the-system-tried-to-help-him/2018/02/18/cdff7aa6-1413-11e8-9065-e55346f6de81_story.html

ghetto blacks. Blacks are more responsive to effective law enforcement than whites, thus black misbehavior is always a symptom of refusal to enforce the law on blacks.

But in Mexico, killings are generally human sacrifices of outgroup members to the old gods. People say they are drug cartel related, but this is politically correct bullshit. War is good for business only if someone else is paying for it. War is bad for business if you are paying for it. If a black drug gang commits mass murder, it is because they are doing it for business reasons but are incompetent at business. If a Mexican drug cartel in Mexico commits mass murder, they are murdering members of a near outgroup because they hear the voices of the Old Gods. The black drug gang commits murders because too stupid to find a peaceful resolution of a business dispute. The Mexican drug gang commits mass murders because listening to demons.

And now the voices of old gods have been heard in Florida.

The ruling underclass

2018-02-23 13:00:52

Hanson, once a neoconservative, finds himself a second class citizen in a California that is increasingly strange, alien, and dangerous[243].

I and one of my sons have mostly fled Silicon valley. The other lives in a shrinking island of whiteness that is ever more dangerous and ever more expensive, in San Francisco near the Embarcadero, near where Kathryn Steinle was murdered for being white, and her murderer acquitted, because high status people can get away with shooting second class people.

Hanson complains:

> Throw out onto the road three sacks of garbage with your incriminating power bill in them, or dump the cooking oil of your easily identifiable mobile canteen on the side of the road, and there are no green consequences. Install a leach line that ends up one foot too close to a water well, and expect thousands of dollars of fines or compliance costs.

> ...

> A cynical neighbor once summed up the counter-intuitive rules to me: if you are in a car collision, hope that you are hit by, rather than hit an illegal alien. If someone breaks into your home and you are forced to use a firearm, hope that you are wounded nonlethally in the exchange, at least more severely than is the intruder. And if you are cited by an agency, hope it is for growing an acre of marijuana rather than having a two-foot puddle on your farm classified as an inland waterway.I could add a fourth: it is always legally safer to allow your dog to be devoured by a stray pit-bull than to shoot the pit-bull to save your dog.In the former case, neither the owner nor the state ever appears; in the latter both sometimes do.

---

[243]https://amgreatness.com/2018/02/19/understanding-california-mind/

He fails to name his rulers.

He neglects to notice.:

Is it permissible for a member of Tribe A to criticize Tribe B?

Is it permissible for a member of Tribe B to criticize Tribe A?

In physical conflicts between As and Bs, who is more likely to be the aggressor, the A or the B?

Given equivalent circumstances, is the judicial system more aggressive in punishing offenses of As against Bs, or vice versa?

Given equivalent circumstances, in economic competition between an A and a B, which is more likely to win? If you are looking for a government contract or position, an official distinction, an educational opportunity, etc, etc, is it better to be an A or a B?

Is it more socially marginal for a B to be rude to an A, or an A to be rude to a B?

If the territories of two tribes overlap, one must necessarily rule, one must necessarily be ruled. It is that, or war.

He is ruled.

Humans are naturally fissiparous. During the filming of the "Planet of the Apes", extras costumed as orangutans formed a tribe, extras costumed as chimps formed another tribe, and extras costumed as gorillas formed yet another a tribe.

But with improved communications and mobility, we don't get physical separation between tribes. Which is a problem, because if tribal territories overlap, the natural outcome is that one tribe rules, and the other is ruled.

And because white males ruling has been deemed unacceptable, the inevitable outcome is that whites get ruled. Actually war and slow genocide, rather than rule, is the natural outcome, but if we are lucky, careful, and clever, we can avoid that and merely get one tribe ruling and one tribe ruled, though this arrangement is always fragile, unstable, and apt to tip into genocide, slow or swift, unless carefully managed from above.

Empires and their state religions want to make everyone into one big tribe, but this does not work. The great big tribe lacks cohesion and solidarity, and is first parasitised, then predated upon, by smaller tribes within the larger tribe. Too big a tribe, too hard to maintain good behavior.

The traditional solution to this problem is territorial states each with their own state church, the peace of Westphalia. But this is no longer workable. For it to work, needs smaller states and less migration.

The Turkish Caliphate prefigures a solution better adapted to our mobile era, though that solution ended in genocide when the Caliphate, which was keeping the precarious system in balance, fell. The solution to the problem successfully implemented by the Caliphate is microterritories in addition to macroterritories: for example with blacks and whites we get the spontaneous formation of the ghetto and also the spontaneous formation of the black table at the school cafeteria. Put a black in charge of the ghetto, a Jew in charge of the Jewish area. Explicitly recognize territories, acknowledge the black table and the white tables in school cafeteria, make them formal and official and put them overtly and formally under the authority of the relevant tribes.

The concept of equality under the law should be inexpressible and incomprehensible. That we can speak such nonsense means that there is something wrong with our words, which fail to cut reality at the joints. Different tribes naturally have different laws. A member of tribe A in the microterritory of tribe A will of course be subject to different rules than a member of tribe B in the microterritory of tribe B. Equality should only be in that if a member of tribe A is in the microterritory of tribe B, he is under disabilities that are sometimes roughly similar to the disabilities of a member of tribe B in the microterritory of tribe A, though by no means exactly the same.

Which does not mean that a black should not be allowed to sit at the white table at the school cafeteria, or vice versa, but does mean he should only be allowed to sit at the white tables only as a guest of a white person in good standing with the white tribe of cool schoolkids, and this white person shall be responsible for that black person's good behavior, and if black person misbehaves, then the white person whose guest he was loses his good standing with the white tribe at the school.

Notice how when buses were integrated, when blacks no longer had to go to the back of the bus, whites were forced to stop riding buses in areas with significant black ridership, because of a well founded fear of being beaten up. Diversity plus proximity leads to war.

Similarly, males and females. For reproduction to be successful there needs to be peace between men and women. For there to be peace between men and women, territories outside of the proper female sphere need to be male, and females only be present as a guest of a male, who for fertile age women should always be a father, brother, husband, or betrothed. And if he is not, then she is slut, and sluts should get a substantially lower level or protection than decent women, should likely suffer minor physical violence.

Protectionism

2018-03-03 20:26:37

Trump, in accordance with his campaign promises to the rust belt and flyover country, has just slapped a tariff on steel and aluminum.

If you look at the Nucor product catalog, you can see that the USA has ceded high end steel production to foreigners.

Ceding high end steel production to foreigners is militarily unwise.

Ceding the high end is also likely to have externalities. A network of skills unravels. If company A does something high tech, it cultivates employees, customers, and suppliers that make it substantially easier and cheaper for company B to do something high tech, and this benefit is not captured by company A, unless, as in South Korea during the dictatorship, the state gives company A substantial monopolistic privileges, something difficult to do in a democracy, particularly a democracy where covetousness is deemed the highest virtue and high status.

And if company A stops doing something high tech causing other companies to stop doing high tech stuff - you have the rust belt, which is the network of high skilled white males unravelling. You have smart white men deskilling, taking opiates, and committing suicide.

That the rust belt is rusting means that white males commit suicide or move to the big coastal megacities. Which means they move from where their votes are useful to Trump and Republicans, to where their votes are useless, because massively outvoted by hordes of aliens imported to live on crime, welfare, and voting Democrat.

Stopping the rust gives republicans a little more time, regardless of whether it is economically justified or not. Even if it was a total money loser (and quite likely externalities make it economically lucrative) it would still be politically a big winner, by halting the great centralization.

Recollect that the government was importing hordes of black male military age Mohammedans screaming for infidel blood and white pussy, and bombing marginal electorates in flyover country with them. The permanent government continued doing this for the first year of the Trump presidency, but in 2017 December, Trump finally managed to put a stop to it. This also gives Trump and Republicans a little more time.

A policy of economic autarky ruined Nazi Germany. The very similar Smoot Hawley Tariff Act of 1930 was also an economic disaster, ruining the USA. And, similarly, India's program of economic autarky kept India stagnant and desperately poor for decades. But these three examples of bad, indeed utterly disastrous, protectionism were accompanied by massive regulation. Trump is deregulating. That is a big and important difference.

Externalities

2018-03-05 22:38:23

About twenty percent of a car is, or should be, high quality specialty steel which is not made in America. Because there are no local sources of such steel, it is organizationally difficult to make such parts in the US, so the parts tend to be made overseas. Or, disturbingly often, made out of crappy steel.

When Jobs was creating the smartphone, he went to Corning to talk to the people who make specialty glass. If we had been importing our specialty glass from China, the way we are importing our specialty steels from India, maybe no smartphones, or smartphones with easily scratched plastic screens.

Let's say that you're after armor steel, and you want to buy it direct from the mill. Your options are more or less limited to:
Arcelor Mittal's "Mars" Steel from India.
SSAB's "Armox" or "Ramor" from Sweden.
ThyssenKrupp's "Secure" From Germany.

And if you want it cheap, and you want a supplier who speaks English, probably India.

Assume the God Emperor is not a complete moron. If a tariff on all steels, an intent that locals will start producing specialty high tech steels. Remember all those people declaring that Trump was lying when he promised coal miners coal jobs were coming back? They told us coal jobs were gone, and were not coming back. Specialty steels are coming back.

Tariffs tend to have bad consequences, because they tend to reflect corruption and special favors. What happens is that there is a high tariff on goods imported by regular folks, and someone who is cozy with the government gets a special permit, a recategorization, or some such, and he gets to import stuff without a tariff, and mark it up.

But the biggest indignation against Trump's tariff is that he is taxing specialty steels, taxing steel that you just cannot buy in America, which tax is not a gift of free money to existing steel producers, but a demand that they get their act together and an opportunity for them to do so.

And, if they do so, they create high skill, high pay jobs for white males in flyover country

jobs for Trump voters in electorates where their votes make a difference.

Never forget who whom. Be mindful of who are your friends, and who are your enemies. The Democrats do not attempt to follow an economically optimal policy, but a policy that harms their enemies economically, even if it causes some lesser harm to their friends. They have been aggressively destroying jobs in flyover country to force the great centralization, so as to get the most voter power out of the people they have been importing to live on crime, welfare, and voting Democrat.

It is likely that this policy tariff policy is economically efficient, because of technological externalities, but even it was not, ask whom it harms, and whom it helps.

China passes the US

2018-03-14 17:04:14

The most important, powerful, and effective weapon in the US arsenal is a fifty year old plane firing seventy year old cannons scoured from museums and looted from ancient forgotten overseas arms depots.

Some people may say that the most important, powerful, and effective weapon in the US arsenal is nukes, but after all these years, who knows if they work any more? We can no longer make tritium, we can no longer make Pu238, why should nukes have fared better?

Russia has been called a gas station masquerading as a country, because total GDP is very low, and per capita GDP unimpressive. Its civilian technology is not especially impressive, but it produces military technology that is as good as the US at a considerably lower price, and is hoping to soon surpass the US in ways that will deny the sea and the air to the US.

China's total GDP has passed the US, though the US official statistics are in denial. Per capita GDP remains well below that of the US, but the gap is rapidly shrinking, with increasing numbers of westerners seeking Chinese jobs. Technologically, China has focused on buying, stealing, and copying US civilian technology and Russian military technology. But in civilian technology, the pupil has surpassed the master. All Chinese CPUs are based on the Arm design that they purchased from the US long ago, but they are now improving on this design in ways that arguably leave the US behind. They are at least equal in CPU design and fabbing, arguably superior. They are still copying, but are less reliant on copying.

Meanwhile US academia focuses on combating masculinity and raising female self esteem by showering them with unearned credentials.

There are no utilitarians.

2018-03-22 02:18:53

Whosoever claims to be a utilitarian is lying. Whosoever lies, is lying because he is defecting on those he lies to, seeks to harm, or is harming, those he lies to. In the case of utilitarianism, the lie is the claim to care about far, in order to cover actions or intentions harmful to near.

By nature, we don't care about far people. We care about ourselves, then our close kin, then our friends and allies, then members of our ingroup. Except that we prefer to avoid war with outgroups, and except that some individual members of the outgroup are friends or allies, we don't care about outgroup members.

But the ingroup are our direct competitors for status, power, and wealth - they occupy, and threaten, our own ecological niche. Thus the evil man always seeks to ally with far in order to destroy those closest to him. Hence leftism. Thus the evil man always loudly claims to love the outgroup. Thus the evil man is supposedly more concerned with the welfare of women and children than husbands and fathers, and proceeds to institute a cash and prizes system to incentivize women to divorce their husbands, even though these divorces invariably wind up being extremely bad for women and children. Yet that same evil man is more concerned with Muslims than with women, and so ignores rape and violence against women by rapeugees, even though this is totally inconsistent with his position on affluent white male university students having sex with half drunk co-eds, and his position on actresses whoring themselves out to movie producers, and those actresses then getting butthurt when they hit the wall, and movie producers are no longer buying.

Samaritans were not the neighbors of the man set upon by thieves. In the parable, the good Samaritan became a neighbor because he acted in a neighborly fashion, and the priest ceased to be a neighbor, because he did not act neighborly. But all the other neighbors did not cease to be neighbors, and all the other Samaritans did not become neighbors.

When we recognize evil, we recognize someone as dangerous to have as a friend or ally. And if you look at all the cases where utilitarian doctrine prescribes evil behavior, it prescribes behavior that would identify the person behaving in that fashion as dangerous to have as a friend or ally. And conversely, utilitarian doctrine allows an evil person to be pious and holier than thou about his evil behavior. He is being malicious because you are a Trump supporter, or a white male, or heterosexual, or some such, so being malicious to you serves the greater good. Thus, for example, progressives will disrupt thanksgiving dinners, harming members of their family, on the basis that they suspect some family members of having voted for Trump, which is a hint of the potential for more serious malice, such as murdering members of their family in order to inherit the family home.

If someone is a progressive, chances are he will harass the family because some family members voted for Trump, and if someone harasses family members over Trump, chances are he will murder family members over inheritance. Notice that when progressives seize control of a company, they burn the shareholders. And similarly, the current progressive policy of race replacement. If all whites except their good selves are murdered or expelled, this benefits those whites remaining, since whites are always and everywhere the chief competitor to other whites. Of course you lose the benefit of the high trust society characteristic of whites, but evil people benefit from a high trust society less than good people. And in the long term it is likely to be harmful because you lose science, technology, and industry, but evil people do not care about the long term.

Evil is almost the same thing as dangerous to near, because near is the competition, and progressivism and utilitarianism are rationales for behaving badly to near.

The word "evil" is not defined by philosophers, or even by priests, but rather by mothers to their children. The story of Snow White defines evil. No one would genuinely think the stepmother evil for taxing the peasants, but for attempting to murder her stepdaughter, and likewise, we think Snow White is good because she does her job of housekeeping with enthusiasm, because she honors her commitments.

Don't vote

2018-03-23 19:30:30

No matter whom you vote for, the uniparty gets elected.

Electing Trump has made a big difference. But he has has not made a big enough difference to prevent the government from electing a new people.

Trump's rust belt program was undoing the great centralization.

Lo and behold[244]:

> Back in June 2009, in one of our earliest posts in the aftermath of the financial crisis, we took a "random walk down Madison Avenue" and found empty storefront after empty storefront after empty storefront.

> In retrospect, the ghost town that was New York's "Golden Mile" was not surprising: after all the US economy had just been hit with the worst recession since the Great Depression, and only an emergency liquidity injection of trillions of dollars prevented a global financial collapse.

> What is more surprising is why nearly 9 years later, at a time of what is supposed to be a coordinated global recovery, a walk along Madison Avenue reveals the exact same picture.

Naturally I find it totally unsurprising that it is exactly the same picture. The election of Trump has been a boom for flyover country, and a catastrophe for the bicoastal elite. The Paris Treaty and the Trans Pacific Partnership amounted to "Lets smash those deplorables in flyover country." Though the Paris Treaty was theoretically a world treaty, most of the sacrifice was going to be made by flyover country, and everything else in the treaty does not amount to a can of beans.

---

[244]https://www.zerohedge.com/news/2018-03-22/starbucks-chairman-we-took-walk-madison-avenue-it-reminded-me-financial-crisis-2008

The great centralization was a series of political attacks on the economy outside the bicoastal elite areas, and Transpacific Partnership and the Paris Treaty would have been the next attacks in the long series of attacks. With the attacks halted, spontaneous economic forces, primarily the internet and containerization, are causing decentralization.

The great centralization was part of the Democrat program of electing a new people. The people that they brought in to live on crime, welfare, and voting Democrat tended to hang out in the big coastal cities, resulting wasted votes, so Obama bombed marginal electorates in flyover country with black male military age Mohammedans screaming for infidel blood and white pussy, while destroying white male jobs in flyover country to move whites into the big coastal cities, where their votes would be neutralized by a supermajority of the new people.

The bombing of marginal electorates in flyover countrywith black male military age Mohammedans screaming for infidel blood and white pussy has stopped. The systematic smashing of white male flyover country jobs has stopped. This is not nothing. This is big. But it is just not enough to end the great erasure.

The removal of exemption for state and local taxes is a big deal. Big. It is a tax on filling your city with imported Democratic party voters, or a removal of the tax exemption for filling your city with imported Democratic party voters.

But all these things are pretty small potatoes compared to illegal immigration. Trump can't even send back the DACA illegals.

The new people are still being elected. The great erasure continues.

Republicans voters losing interest in voting.

2018-03-29 07:46:43

Recently there was a big upset in formerly Republican safe seat, and Democrats told themselves it is because Trump is such an ultra extreme right winger who hates women. And now another close result in a formerly safe seat looms. Trump won Arizona by 21%, yet Republicans are in danger of losing in Arizona. Is this because Trump the president revealed himself to be far more racist, sexist and right wing than Trump the candidate?

Well, that is what the Uniparty would tell us, but it is obviously false. Further, the uniparty is leafleting the state with leaflets telling people it is their duty to vote to support democracy and all that, which reveals that Republicans are failing to vote because recent events reveal that no matter who you vote for, no matter what you vote for, you get ever lefter policies.

Americans voted for a wall. Republicans voted for a wall. If no wall, no point in voting.

Trump's ban on transgender is alive and well

2018-04-02 01:50:23

You no doubt heard "Judge Blocks Trump's Ban on Transgender Troops in Military"[245]. But Trump's seeming surrender was threedee chess, not surrender.

---

[245]https://www.nytimes.com/2017/10/30/us/military-transgender-ban.html

The word transgender deliberately confuses people with very different kinds of problems, grouping unlike people together, and making distinctions without a difference.
1. Actual transgenders: Crazy people who clearly of one sex, but suffer the delusion that they are of a different sex in the same way that some people who are clearly not Napoleon the First, Emperor of France, suffer the delusion that they are Napoleon the First, Emperor of France.
2. Traps: gay males who want to be screwed by manly men, and are painfully aware that other gay males are seldom manly.
3. Cuntboys: Lesbian women who want to screw feminine women. These tend to be less weird, nasty and evil than traps, and also tend to be conventionally attracted to manly men as well as feminine women, usually having more sex with manly men than with women, despite their theoretical lesbianism. Theoretically they have relationships with women and sex with males, but this is mainly because they tend to have sex with males who are not interested in having relationships with them.
4. Cross dressers:People who get off on being mistaken for a member of the opposite sex: These superficially resemble traps, but a trap will take it all the way.
5. Actual transexuals: People who are mixed up physically, who are born with mixed up physical characteristics. There are very few of these, and most of them are genetic males with androgen insensitivity syndrome. Everyone starts off with a female phenotype in the womb, and then those who are genetically male normally develop a male phenotype starting at the sixteenth week after conception. A few, a very few, abnormally fail. Some of these subsequently develop the outward and inward male phenotype belatedly at puberty with no medical intervention, despite failing to develop it in the womb.

Trump's policy[246] in effect bars the transgenders, and most of the traps, cuntboys, and crossdressers. It allows the actual transexuals, provided they meet the physical standards. But actual transexuals are so rare that it does not matter.

```
Transgender persons who require or who have undergone gender
transition are disqualified from military service.
```

Actual transexuals, unlike transgenders, rarely get *transition* surgery, because any surgery they get is usually towards their outward apparent birth sex, which is usually congruent with their inward subjectively experienced gender, or, in even rarer cases, they are transexual in spontaneously transitioning at puberty from superficially seemingly female to unambiguously male without need for surgery - delayed testicular descent and delayed penis development.

The ban on *transition* surgery bans most of the crazies and perverts, and the ban on gender dysphoria bans most of the remaining crazies and perverts. But the genuine transexuals are allowed in - both of them. As they should be.

So Trump used the Social Justice Warrior's own doubletalk against them.

Similarly, after announcing he cares so much about DACA[247],...

---

[246] https://media.defense.gov/2018/Mar/23/2001894037/-1/-1/0/MILITARY-SERVICE-BY-TRANSGENDER-INDIVIDUALS.PDF

[247] https://www.apnews.com/6d02c4a6480d405dbe3c7e32f8f50efc/Trump-on-deal-to-protect-'Dreamer'-immigrants:-'NO-MORE'

DACA and transgender give me some hope that we will see a good start on a wall in time for the mid term elections. By now we should know that Trump is crazy like a fox.

Operation Sovereign Borders

2018-04-06 04:18:22

American judges have been expanding the category asylumrefugee to open borders to the world, preparatory for rapid race replacement and white erasure in the US. Illegal immigration is now legal in the US, indeed a fundamental human right (unlike freedom of speech, freedom of religion, and the right to keep and bear arms) as it has been for some time in Germany and Sweden.

In response to this, Trump has promised to use the the military to defend our borders against invaders. The world is shocked by this terrible violation of human rights. The military should only be used for good nice kindly humanitarian purposes, such as bombing civilians in Libya to punish them for their disinclination to support a Cathedral sponsored color revolution.

To use the military for selfish purposes, such as keeping hostile and predatory outsiders on the outside, is a clear violation of fundamental human rights recently discovered in the emanation of the penumbra of the umbra of the great and glorious US constitution. The US military should only be used for good and unselfish purposes, such as teaching Afghan schoolgirls how to put a condom on a banana and blowing up people who are insufficiently grateful for the benefits of freedom and democracy bestowed upon them.

If Trump keeps this promise, chances are he is also going to have some wall in time for the mid term elections. If he does not, he will not.

Keeping either or both of these promises is likely to lead to confrontation with the judges, as it violates the inalienable human right of South America and Africa to move to America to live on crime, welfare, and voting Democrat.

In 2012, the Australian authorities escalated race replacement and the erasure of white

Australia by legalizing illegal immigration through endless expansion of the asylumrefugee loophole, resulting in rapidly escalating flood of boats carrying illegal immigrants to Australia, similar to flood of boats now carrying Africans to Europe through Italy. The Australian labor party did everything possible to stop the boats, short of actually stopping them, and everything possible to discourage illegals from coming to Australia to live on crime, welfare, and voting for the Labor party, short of actually denying them Australian residence, welfare, and votes.

Supposedly this was the awesome power of the judges overruling the Labor Party government by allowing the asylumrefugees residence, welfare, and votes, and perhaps it was, but when power gave the asylum refugees them due process and thus treated them as citizens, rather than invaders, power was signaling to judges that it would rather like them to be made into citizens.

Tony Abbott was elected at the end of 2013 on a platform of stopping illegal immigration by military means. And, unlike Trump, immediately stopped it, turning back the boats, [248]

imprisoning illegals, and punishing people smugglers.

Which, of course, immediately led to lawfare.[249]

and confrontation with the judges.[250]

If the government cannot deny permanent visas to people who illegally set foot in Australia[251]

and if the government cannot turn back people coming on boats with the intent of setting foot on Australia illegally ... then the borders are open.

It became apparent the one hundred and fifty three Tamil asylumrefugees were one were not in fact from Sri Lanka, but from Tamil State in India,

At the same time as this was happening,[252] an illegal immigrant in Australia was getting due process, and of course, the courts ordered the government to give him a permanent visa. And the government did so.

And those waging lawfare for open borders were gloating. They considered that they had already won, even though their pretext that these were refugees seeking asylum had already been decisively exposed, they did not care, no one cared, it made not the slightest difference to anyone.[253]

The pretext that they were using to open the borders had evaporated, yet they were still completely confident that they had won, that the borders were opening. They were every bit as much full of pious indignant righteous rage at the government denying Tamils from Tamil State entry, as they had been at the government denying Tamils from Sri Lanka entry.

---

[248] https://www.qt.com.au/news/reports-abbott-has-turned-boat-back-indonesia/2132785/

[249] https://www.qt.com.au/news/un-abbotts-anti-asylum-seeker-plan-could-be-illega/2136904/

[250] https://www.qt.com.au/news/high-court-challenge-looms-morrison-over-refugees/2309049/

[251] https://www.qt.com.au/news/high-court-stops-153-tamils-being-returned-sri-lan/2311922/

[252] https://www.smh.com.au/politics/federal/costly-cruel-futile-the-price-of-scott-morrison-holding-157-asylum-seekers-on-floating-prison-20140725-3ckr2.html

[253] $https://www.vice.com/en_us/article/5gkwn8/after-four-weeks-at-sea-157-asylum-seekers-have-landed-in-australia$

Tamil state is, as it says on the can, an ethno state, thus a claim by an ethnic to be an asylumrefugee pitifully fleeing the ethno state of his own ethnicity is not believable.

But what is believable is that if the the voters are here, you can keep them here until they get to vote, that if they are here, you have the upper hand, and the people they are going to vote against have the losing hand.

This looked awfully like the collapse of the borders in the face of lawfare, like the government cucking out in the face of the awesome power of the judiciary. If a court order can stop the government from deporting people, then they have to go to Australia, and once in Australia, have to be given permanent visas, and once they have permanent visas, welfare and votes. If one illegal immigrant gets a permanent visa by court order on the asylumrefugee excuse, one hundred million black male military age Mohameddans screaming for infidel blood and white pussy can get permanent visas by court order - particularly as their claim to be refugees from each other's habitual violence is in fact true, unlike the transparently false claim to be a refugee from one's own peaceful ethnostate.

One might suppose that government cucked out in response to the court order, but it could also be that the court order was a response to it cucking out. Or, more likely, that both reflect power being applied behind the scenes. Or maybe they thought that due process would make it glaringly obvious that these asylumrefugees were not in fact fleeing persecution, having a perfectly good and reasonably well functioning ethnostate in which Tamils were the ruling religion and ethnicity, but that never seemed to matter to the judges before, and it seems unlikely it would matter this time.

If power signals it wants white erasure, then it is in your interest to feed your brothers and your children to the crocodiles, in the hope of being last to be fed to the crocodiles.

It looked like it was all over for white Australians, that they were about to become a permanently outvoted second class minority, hated and despised, permanently blamed for the massive dysfunction of the ruling majority, as South African whites are blamed for the failure of black South Africans, and light skinned Venezuelans blamed for the failure of darker skinned Venezuelans. Lighter skinned Venezuelans are getting Kristallnacht, and white South Africans are getting genocide.

And then Tony Abbot found his balls.[254]

I earlier claimed that Tony Abbot did a Jackson. This claim was not accurate. But as we shall see, it is accurate to say that the courts ruled his actions legal only after he gave them the finger, and demonstrated he was not going to cuck out, and they then quietly reversed, forgot about, or reinterpreted, all their earlier precedents opening the borders.

In the face of a court hearing questioning whether he could imprison or deport the one hundred and fifty seven Tamil Asylum refugees without judicial process, and in the face of a court order prohibiting him from deporting them to Sri Lanka, he proceeded, three days before the originally scheduled date of the hearing, to deport and imprison them in Nauru without judicial process, Nauru being a nominally independent state of the Australian empire, in the same way that Canada and England are nominally independent states of the US empire. Since a supposedly independent state was now imprisoning them, a court order saying that they could not be deported or detained would have no

---

[254]https://www.reuters.com/article/us-australia-refugees/australia-sends-157-asylum-seekers-to-nauru-detention-center-idUSKBN0G203420140802

effect.

Which in theory, because Nauru is supposedly independent, is not quite doing a Jackson, but is a signal of intent to do a Jackson in effect. If the court says he cannot imprison or deport, he is likely to say: "Too bad, how sad, they are in Nauru now, and the Nauruans are mistreating them, but alas, I have no authority to tell the Nauruans to let them go. Independent state. Do you doubt it is independent?"

Thus he did not pull a Jackson in the sense of ignoring a specific court order after it had been made. But he did pull a Jackson in that he signaled to the court that if it gave a court order, that court order was going to be ignored.

And the courts, all of them, backed down.

As did the UN, the newsmedia, the professoriat, and the NGOs. Lawfare ended. And to this day, the Australian government can and does detain and/or deport visa runners without the judges interfering. Illegal entry, overstayed visas, and the like result inadministrative imprisonment and administrative deportation, without judicial process.[255] There have been no further lawfare dramas legalizing illegality. There was lawfare on anchor babies, children of illegals born in Australia, but that also was rejected.

No longer do those in the country illegally get permanent residence, let along court ordered permanent residence. After this incident, the high court somehow decided to take a humbler view of its powers. Maybe that was Abbot signaling in public by shipping them to Nauru, maybe something happened behind the scenes. But lawfare largely went away, and what little lawfare happened, failed.

The program of white replacement and erasure continues, but considerably more slowly, and no longer by illegal immigration.

Losing weight is a solved problem

2018-04-16 12:31:42

One frequently reads despairing reports that major weight loss is impossible. If you attempt it, supposedly your metabolism slows right down, making you weak, tired, lethargic, slow, and very very hungry.

I read in far right and manosphere sources anecdotes from people who claim to have lost a great deal of weight. I followed their advice and lost a great deal of weight: The short of it is weigh yourself every morning, paleo (no wheat products, manufactured foods, or sweet drinks), carnivory (adequate protein, lots of animal fat), fasting, and getting your testosterone and estradiol levels correct.

I am not going to repeat the advice on how to lose weight here. Rather, I look at the the connection between successful weight loss, and the rightosphere, and the obesity epidemic, and the endless and rapidly accelerating movement left.

Why is it that there is a connection between the rightosphere and sound advice on losing weight, and the leftosphere and bad advice on losing weight?

Anecdotally, and from my personal experience, low testosterone in men leads to weight gain, high testosterone makes it easier to lose weight. Anecdotally, high testosterone in

---

[255] https://duckduckgo.com/?q=villawood+immigration+detention

women leads to weight gain, and makes it hard for them to lose weight. Hence the stereotype of the fat mustachioed lesbian bully from Human Resources berating males for toxic masculinity while groping schoolgirls. In other words, androgyny causes obesity. And leftism promotes androgyny.

A woman who interrupts her boss and who walks down the middle of the corridor, will be prone to getting fat because this raises her testosterone, and the man who scurries out of her way to one side of the corridor will be prone to getting fat, because scurrying out of her way lowers his testosterone, as will the boss who (because no one dares restrain uncivilized female behavior) allows himself to be interrupted in a supposedly helpful and supposedly friendly fashion.

The diet high in fat and meat is demonized because associated with masculinity. Testosterone is made difficult to obtain because masculine. Women routinely get estrogen, but mighty hard for males to get testosterone. Fasting is ignored and deemed harmful because of the connection to old type Christianity.

In this sense, everything that works to lose weight is right wing, and everything that makes us fat is left wing. The obesity epidemic is connected to leftism in much the same ways as the human immunodeficiency virus epidemic is connected to leftism. Leftists want gays to be allowed to make blood donations, fat acceptance, and don't want us to get testosterone, for much the same reasons.

Women gone nuts

2018-04-20 00:20:42

The Zman asks "Why Did Women Go Nuts?[256]"

Simple. When you repress bad sexual behavior by males, and do not repress bad sexual behavior by females, you get very little bad sexual behavior by males, and a whole lot of bad sexual behavior by females.

I see women behaving as if raised by apes in the jungle.

Things are going to hell because we fail to restrain bad behavior that gets right in our faces. Male sexual behavior in the workplace is nigh nonexistent and male heterosexual rape is nigh nonexistent, but to the extent that it exists, the man is looking for a warm wet pussy. Female sexual behavior is different. She is trying to disqualify males, testing as many males as possible to see if they meet her exacting requirements. This testing is necessarily stressful, for she is stress testing men to see if they break under pressure, thus necessarily more disruptive than male sexual behavior, more damaging to workplace productivity, male cohesion, and social cooperation.

In a normal and sane society, ninety percent of fertile age women would within a few minutes of behaving as they now do, be whacked hard with a stick, like a stray dog harassing a farmer's chickens. And then they would stop. Their owner would be called, and they would be hauled off on a leash.

Yet everyone around me acts like zombies and fails to notice.

It is completely obvious to me that women in the workplace continually disrupt the workplace by fitness testing attractive male co-workers, and a minor and infrequent side

---

[256]https://thezman.com/wordpress/?p=13575

effect of these fitness tests, when the fitness test goes explicitly and overtly sexual, is that the woman complains, and entirely believes, she was sexually harassed. So am I insane, or is everyone else insane? Am I hallucinating disruptive sexual behavior right in front of my face by lusty women fitness testing every attractive male they meet to see if he has the stones to beat them and rape them, or is everyone else hallucinating chaste sexless angels persecuted by lecherous men?

Slate Star Codex recently attempted to surveyco-worker sexual harassment complaints by workplace type, and reviewed existing surveys[257]. The major result was that the more women were outnumbered by men, (engineering, mining) the less that women experienced "sexual harassment", and the more women outnumber men (supermarket checkout chicks, actresses) the more they experience "sexual harassment". These results wereswiftly confirmed[258] by subsequent work by other people, who also produced similar results for rape - or at least females complaining about "rape".

But this only makes sense if incidents of men "raping" women and men "sexually harassing" women are generally female initiated, not male initiated, which is what I see in front of my nose, and what I see everyone else failing to see. All workplace sexual harassment cases of males supposedly sexually harassing females, as near to all of them as makes no difference, are female initiated: It is a fitness test. The chick is looking for a coworker with the stones to beat her and rape her.

If workplace sexual harassment is male initiated, we would expect females in predominantly male workplaces to report a lot of it, in particular we would expect engineerettes and female miners to report lots of it, because outnumbered approximately a hundred to one by males, while we would expect actresses and supermarket checkout girls to report very little of it, because they heavily outnumber male co-workers. Survey data is the exact opposite. The more that female workers outnumber male workers (and thus the thirstier the female workers) the more "sexual harassment" by every plausible measure, indicating that all cases of males sexually harassing female co-workers are actually cases of female co-workers fitness testing attractive males, as near to all of them as makes no difference.

In the time period of the "Rape on campus" incident, University of Virginia investigated thirty eight rape complaints. None led to disciplinary action, therefore all fake, or University of Virginia horribly biased. The fallout of the "Rape on Campus" case indicates fake. If there were any real cases, Obama's team would have come up with better poster girls. All reports of rape by white heterosexual males are lies, as near to all of them as makes no difference. Recollect that the University of Virginia accusation "A Rape on Campus", was driven by female sexual lust[259].

And, similarly, sex between middle aged men, and girls well below puberty. Humbert Humbert wants to creep into bed with the sleeping twelve-year-old Dolores Haze, but does not do so, in part because she is not in her own bed, she has crept into the bed of the drunk and sleeping Jeremy Meeks. Any time you hear that an old man has raped a female child, ascertain whose bed the "rape"occurred in.

We should not "teach women not to lie about rape". We should throw women in jail

[257] https://slatestarcodex.com/2018/04/17/ssc-survey-results-sexual-harassment-levels-by-field/
[258] https://slatestarcodex.com/2018/04/18/highlights-from-the-comments-on-survey-harassment-rates/
[259] https://blog.reaction.la/culture/the-overwhelming-majority-of-rape-accusations-are-false/

for lying about rape, or else legalize rape when done on private property that a woman voluntarily chose to enter. But, far more importantly, need to fire women who shit test co-workers in the workplace, because their disruptive behavior profoundly damages productivity and social cohesion.

To win, we are going to need a red pilled Christianity that is willing to enforce order, patriarchy, and orthodoxy. We will need to spin the story of the fall not as a literal account of mankind's descent from a higher plane of existence, but rather a parable or metaphor about men becoming black pilled when we realized large scale cooperation was hard, knowing good and evil, and knowing we screwed up. Evolutionary psychology and game theory leads to conclusions that parallel the traditional Christian understanding of the fall.

Fixing (or replacing) Christianity

2018-04-24 01:44:09

High IQ species with lengthy childhood find it hard to reproduce without cooperation between males and females.

Productivity is not an issue. In a wealthy society, a man could easily buy enough food and shelter for taking care of umpteen children, but he cannot actually take care of umpteen children. Observing variations in total fertility rate over different regions and different times, we see that even in very poor societies, boom or bust, war or peace, wealth or poverty, make very little difference to the total fertility rate. The only thing that matters is female emancipation.

Support in the sense of feeding and sheltering children is not an issue in the west, indeed it is not the major issue even in very poor countries. The problem is not feeding children, but looking after children, which requires two people. A single person household can barely look after one person, except by paying for services that are not easily obtained on the market place. A single person household tends to eat out a lot, has difficulty with house maintenance. A single person household tends to have no garden, because unable to manage a garden. If you rent to a single person, chances are you will see a lot of repair and maintenance costs.

If you rent to a single person, you have to be really fascist about the condition of the house, because a single person gets overwhelmed.

So, reproduction requires two, and a two person household requires one man in charge, and the wife to honor and obey.

And the connection compelling the wife to submit to the husband has to be durable - has to last long enough to raise children.

If you have moment to moment consent, you cannot have durable marriage. Indeed, any kind of female consent makes reproduction hard, because all women would prefer to have sex with Jeremy Meeks, and are apt to hold off on marriage till their eggs start drying up in hope of getting a booty call from Jeremy Meeks. We really should have romantic consensual marriage normal and normative only for women that can reasonably be presumed chaste. The rest should be pressured or coerced into patriarchal marriage, or a similar, but lower status and less secure, arrangement.

One helpful workaround in a society hostile to fathers, husbands, and marriage is that God backs the authority of the husband and the father, and the husband and the father backs the authority of God.

This works well for me as an individual. It would work a whole lot better if backed by a tribe / church / religion / social support group representing the authority of God on Earth.

Unfortunately all actually existent religious groups, with the notable exception of Mormons and some weird and unpleasant Jewish sects tend to be aggressively hostile to the authority of the husband and father. Latin Mass Catholics seem to be non hostile, but are not all that supportive.

Christian theology is that the fatherhood of God makes the fellow members of your congregation adoptive kin. (This is the Christian replacement for the Jewish Abraham). Thus "Christian" hostility to God the Father kills the Christian Church dead. A religion is a tribe, and actually existent Christianity is hostile to its own tribe, much as the US government is hostile to legacy Americans.

Anti patriarchal Christianity is a self contradiction - but it is all we have got.

Poolside is defect/defect equilibrium, the battle of the sexes. Difficult to reproduce poolside, difficult to have a family, difficult to have an old age surrounded by children and grandchildren. The only way to end the war is male victory, followed by some alarmingly drastic coercion. I base this on what happened on the shore of Port Jackson, when they were working with female material far more favorable than that which we have, and were initially paralyzed because reluctant to do what proved necessary, which is presumably what fathers had been doing behind the scenes.

Obviously anyone who tries what was tried on the shores of Port Jackson is not going to be left alone by progressives.

For successful reproduction and child raising, women must be *compelled* to obey the father of their children, *compelled* to submit sexually to him, and *forbidden* to submit sexually to anyone else. Moment to moment consent frustrates both men and women, since it makes it difficult for them to reproduce. We need outside coercion to get to cooperate cooperate equilibrium. Moment to moment consent results in defect defect equilibrium, where no one gets what they really want. To reproduce successfully, men, women, and their children need durable and patriarchal marriage, and durable and patriarchal marriage needs coercion.

When Black Mohammedans in the middle of Africa try overtly coercive methods similar to those used on the shores of Port Jackson, the Cathedral drones them.

So, since public whippings give the enemies of the family an excuse to meddle, need to synthesize a tribe, and primarily use social pressure rather than public whippings. A tribe requires a religion. And the participants in the religion have to socially support all well behaved women, and forcefully exclude all badly behaved women and their male bastards.

God backs the authority of the husband and the father, and the husband and the father backs the authority of God. God's authority on earth is manifested through the tribe. There is something of an exemption for religions - the Cathedral will not jump you provided you stick to weaponized social pressure and observe age limits that are increasingly difficult to observe. It is illegal or close to it to stop girls nine or older from having sex, and illegal or close to it for them to marry under eighteen, let alone be pressured into marriage, but so far one can socially enforce patriarchy.

The Benedict Option[260]:

> What I call the Benedict Option is this:**a limited, strategic withdrawal of Christians from the mainstream of American popular culture, for the sake of shoring up our understanding of what the church is, and what me must do to be the church. We must do this because the strongly anti-Christian nature of contemporary popular culture occludes the meaning of the Gospel, and hides from us the kinds of habits and practices we need to engage in to be truly faithful to what we have been given**. As Jonathan Wilson has pointed out about the New Monasticism movement (a form of the Benedict Option), the church must do this not to hide away as a pure remnant — the church would be unfaithful to Christ if it did so — but to strengthen itself to be the church for the world.

This assumes that actually existent Christianity is just fine.

It is not. It is cucked. Christianity has to be patriarchal, because of "God the Father", because its replacement for biological kinship through Abraham is adoptive kinship through the fatherhood of God.

And, despite all the hand wringing by progs, actually existent Christianity is hostile to fathers and husbands. And actually existent Judaism is not a whole lot better.

Even the Mohammedans are in trouble, with Iran and Saudi Arabia gone feminazi. A big part of the appeal of Islamic State is that fighting for Islamic state was apt to get you a real wife.

The problem is not that popular culture is anti christian. It is that actually existent Christianity is anti christian.

You can have an individual relationship with God and Jesus "Jesus is my boyfriend" without patriarchy.

But you cannot have a Christian Church, except it is solidly patriarchal and goes full Pauline on marriage. If no patriarch, then no nuclear family, if no nuclear family, then no extended family, if no extended family, then no support for actual kinship. If no support for actual kinship, then no adoptive kinship. If no adoptive kinship, no church.

You can have individual Christians without Pauline patriarchy, but without Pauline patriarchy, you don't have a Christian Church. Dalrock[261] is not a church. He is another guy with another blog, and taking a sane position on the problem of reproduction and a straightforward position on the interpretation of Saint Paul on marriage has alienated him from his Church, and his Church from him.

If there was a church that was willing to support me, I would support it.

Christianity without patriarchy is Pope Francis celebrating gay sex and transvestite prostitutes. Christianity without patriarchy inexorably winds up joining Heartiste poolside. Some Roman Catholics are whining about the Church supporting divorce, but if you support moment to moment consent, if you oppose "marital rape", then you have

---

[260]https://www.theamericanconservative.com/dreher/accidental-benedict-option/
[261]https://dalrock.wordpress.com/

to support divorce. I remember a time when everyone supported marital rape, when the words "marital rape" made no sense, when it was incomprehensible to most people that there might be anything wrong or unusual about a man compelling his wife to perform her marital duty. Today, I don't think even Dalrock supports "marital rape", but if you oppose "marital rape", it is logically inconsistent to oppose divorce at capricious whim. If wives have a duty to honor and obey, and wives and husbands have a duty each to sexually gratify the other, then no such thing as marital rape. If they don't have such a duty, why do you have a problem with the church service celebrating a transvestite prostitute auctioning off his body cavities?

In order to oppose both marital rape and a church service celebrating transvestism and sodomy, Christians have to be against sex generally, rather than against the war of the sexes, a position that is stupid, contrary to the bible, contrary to the survival of the species, anti Darwinian, and contrary to what the Bible tells us of God's plan - it is the foolish and wicked heresy that Puritans were rightly accused of. Marriage in the old testament is not a magic ritual making sex magically OK. It is a man's commitment to keep a woman and never let her go. Such a commitment is impossible and foolish today, however much a man desires it, thus no marriage any more. It is all fornication, the sacrament is in vain.

One of the major earthly jobs of religion is to promote peace and cooperation generally, particularly cooperation between members of the religion, and particularly members of the congregation, and particularly cooperation between men and women in begetting and raising children. This is intended to promote sex, not prevent it. In order to prevent the battle of the sexes, the Church needs to prohibit not sex, but adultery. And adultery is not a code word for sex. Adultery means the same thing in marriage as in beer. Improper mixing. Adultery means one man's seed going into the same pussy as another man's seed, because that prevents a man from raising his children.

So the Church abandons its mission of promoting cooperation within the family, and then, to demonstrate that it is nonetheless twice as holy as before, doubles down on opposing movie producers having sex with starlets, even though abandoning marriage and the family makes opposition to movie producers having sex with starlets irrelevant, absurd, and pointless.

Science and Christianity

2018-04-27 00:15:29

You always have a state religion. If your state religion is easily falsified by the empirical facts of this world, then your state religion is going to be inherently hostile to science, technology, and industry.

So, if your state religion proclaims
> "all men are created equal",

you have a problem.

And not long after that, your state religion is proclaiming all sorts of remarkable things, most recently Global Anthropogenic Catastrophic Warming. Regardless of whether this doctrine is true or false it is not a scientific doctrine for to doubt is sin[262], to be in favor

---

[262]https://wattsupwiththat.com/2018/04/24/epa-to-end-secret-science-with-new-transparency-law/

of higher CO_2 or warmer temperatures, even if you live in Alaska, is sin.

You should not confuse real science, the science of the Royal society from 1660 to 1945, with the post 1945 peer review "science" of Harvard, which has murdered science, gutted its corpse, and wears its gutted corpse as a skin suit.

The key lights of the early Royal Society were deeply Christian and opposed to the enlightenment. Science rested on a commitment to truth that was rooted in aristocratic and elitist Christianity, a value system whose elitism and aristocracy ran fundamentally contrary to the enlightenment, and whose Christianity ran fundamentally contrary to the enlightenment.

Science was possible because a gentleman and a nobleman should speak the truth, and because truth speaking was a sign of being a gentleman or a noble.

Compare and contrast with the Harvard self esteem culture, where speaking the truth shows you are a deplorable and an oppresser of the holy masses.

Judaism is inimical to science. Orthodox Jews don't do science or technology. Judeo Christianity did not do science and technology. Christianity did science and technology. Not the enlightenment, and not Jews.

Progressivism and progressive Judaism is not inimical to science on an individual level. Individual progressives and individual progressive Jews individually do lots of good science, but their collective behavior is inimical and hostile to science and the scientific method, rewarding unscientific and antiscientific behavior, because progressivism rejects truth speaking. Atheist Jews do lots of good science, a quite disproportionate amount, and usually support the scientific method (not counting progressives as atheists, because they believe in "the arc of history), but the trouble with their atheism is that they don't have a moral basis to defend the behavior on which the scientific method depends, and so their defenses of the scientific method address the individual, rather than the scientific community. They are disarmed before progressives, who do have a moral basis for attacking science and the scientific method, who attack it as hurtful to oppressed holy victim groups and damaging to the earth.

The proposition that our society is not religious is obviously false. The solution is to replace a state religion which has equality as its key belief, with a state religion whose key beliefs are less easily falsified by empirical data about the world.

Take Christianity, reinterpret away young earth creationism as a parable about early humans getting black pilled, and we have a religion far more resistant to empirical falsification by the facts of this world than progressivism, a state religion far more compatible with reason, science, technology, and industrialization than our current state religion.

Fortunately the Church fathers were already onto the job, sixteen hundred years ago.

Origen, writing about two hundred years after the crucifixion, tells us in no uncertain terms in Book Four of "The Principiis" that the young earth account of creation is to be understood spiritually, not literally:

> let us examine the passages of Scripture. Now who is there, pray, possessed of understanding, that will regard the statement as appropriate, that the first day, and the second, and the third, in which also both evening and morning are mentioned, existed without sun, and moon, and stars — the first day even without a sky? And who is found so ignorant as to suppose that God,

as if He had been a husbandman, planted trees in paradise, in Eden towards the east, and a tree of life in it, i.e., a visible and palpable tree of wood, so that anyone eating of it with bodily teeth should obtain life, and, eating again of another tree, should come to the knowledge of good and evil? No one, I think, can doubt that the statement that God walked in the afternoon in paradise, and that Adam lay hid under a tree, is related figuratively in Scripture, that some mystical meaning may be indicated by it. The departure of Cain from the presence of the Lord will manifestly cause a careful reader to inquire what is the presence of God, and how anyone can go out from it. But not to extend the task which we have before us beyond its due limits, it is very easy for anyone who pleases to gather out of holy Scripture what is recorded indeed as having been done, but what nevertheless cannot be believed as having reasonably and appropriately occurred according to the historical account. The same style of Scriptural narrative occurs abundantly in the Gospels, as when the devil is said to have placed Jesus on a lofty mountain, that he might show Him from thence all the kingdoms of the world, and the glory of them. How could it literally come to pass, either that Jesus should be led up by the devil into a high mountain, or that the latter should show him all the kingdoms of the world (as if they were lying beneath his bodily eyes, and adjacent to one mountain), i.e., the kingdoms of the Persians, and Scythians, and Indians? Or how could he show in what manner the kings of these kingdoms are glorified by men? And many other instances similar to this will be found in the Gospels by anyone who will read them with attention, and will observe that in those narratives which appear to be literally recorded, there are inserted and interwoven things which cannot be admitted historically, but which may be accepted in a spiritual signification.

And Augustine similarly tells us that the Bible is not a science textbook, and if you argue scientific facts on the basis of biblical authority, you are an idiot. Three hundred and seventy years after the crucifixion, and twelve hundred and sixty years before science and the scientific method was granted the prestige and authority it came to possess and had the success it came to have, he tells us that religion needs to stay out of matters in which science has its proper magistry - something that the enlightenment is in its arrogance and violence conspicuously and spectacularly fails to do.

Compare and contrast with the enlightenment. Irrespective of whether the left position on Catastrophic Anthropogenic Global Warming is true or false, it crushes science and replaces it with holy rolling and the persecution of dissent. Global Warming is sin. Being in favor of Global Warming is like being in favor of adultery.

Saint Augustine took various self contradictory positions on the book of Genesis, but in his final work on the topic, "the confessions" holds it to be allegorical and to contain a multitude of spiritual meanings. Fourteen hundred years before Darwin, Saint Augustine points towards Darwin's program:

> In the beginning were created only the germs or causes of the forms of life, which were afterwards to be developed in gradual course.'

This account (which is to say Darwin's account) is, according to Saint Augustine, the "literal" meaning of Genesis, which is not very literal at all.

The proper magistry of science in religion is, for example, to confirm the doctrine of the fall with evolutionary psychology, that risen killer apes will have the human nature described in the book of Genesis. The proper magistry of religion in science is, for example, the moral character of the scientific method - that scientists are obligated to speak the truth, and use methods of evidence and argument likely to lead to the truth. And if they fail to do so (as for example in global warming science, vegetable oils, and so forth) then those scientists are sinful. Sin is within the proper magistry of the state religion.

In the argument on animal fats, and the argument on Global Warming, scientists, instead of employing the scientific method, politiced to add their doctrines to the official state religion. This should be heresy, and heretics should be denied state and quasi state employment - not heresy in claiming Catastrophic Anthropogenic Global Warming is true, nor heresy in denying that it is true, but heresy in adding either doctrine to the state religion.

John Bolton wants war

2018-05-01 12:29:27

John Bolton's plan for denuclearizing Korea:
> "We have very much in mind the Libya model from 2003, 2004,"
Hmm, how did that work out of Gaddaffi?
In 2011 February Gaddafi gives up weapons of mass destruction. Then Obama, or rather a presidency that Obama was unable to control, immediately launched a color revolution, which failed horribly. The State Department then had Gaddafi murdered in a US air strike in on the 2011 October 20th. But the State Department is still unable to make its color revolution stick. When the State Department attempt at color revolution in Libya continues to fall flat on its face despite the murder of Gaddafi, the US proceeds to bomb everything of value and murder everyone important. The US was able to destroy the existing regime, but was unable to impose the regime it wanted, so just kept bombing, killing, and sponsoring various armed groups to kill and destroy. After three years of savage destruction, remaining State Department assets fled the chaos that they had created in 2015. Since then Libya has been one of the very few genuinely independent states, a defeat and retreat by the US empire resembling in many ways the Soviet defeat in Afghanistan and retreat from Afghanistan. The government of Libya is, of course, not recognized by "the international community", and is necessarily somewhat furtive and semi hidden in order to avoid drone strikes, but nonetheless, since the State Department retreat in 2015, has been able to maintain a reasonable level of order, security, and safety.

Korea is one of the many branches of the US empire that are failing to show a profit for America and Americans. The obvious solution is to spin it off. Let the rulers of North and South make the deal that they say they want to make, and bring US troops and US nuclear weapons home from Korea. If, on the other hand, the US continues to rule and occupy South Korea (at a considerable loss) this obvious presents a grave threat to the ruler of North Korea, in which case Kim would have to be crazy to give up nukes. But this plan - peace and independence in Korea - is giving "the international community" fits. The international community is horrified by the prospect of Trump making peace and denuclearizing Korea, which they correctly see as retreat.

If you want an empire, you need colonialists who settle and stay, so that they have ties to the home country, and also ties to the subject country, so that they have reason to govern the subject country well. In order to have colonialists, you need a fertile ruling elite, which produces more offspring than there are statal and quasi statal jobs for in the home country, so the elite sends their excess offspring off to settle and rule the empire.. The State Department rules instead through carpetbaggers, who tend to steal everything not nailed down and then move on to the next target. To rule an empire, you need a cohesive, family oriented, ruling elite, or your empire will disintegrate through anarcho tyranny, no matter how enormous your preponderance of military power. The State Department attempts to rule the world, but lacks a ruling elite they can rely on to rule their subject countries, or even America itself. They don't trust the US military, the red empire, to rule, but the blue empire is incapable of rule, as was illustrated by their utterly disastrous governance of Haiti. The State Department is itself "the international community" - rootless cosmopolitans who are hostile to old America and to legacy Americans, and not particularly loyal to each other, who lack honor or human decency, who feel themselves hostile aliens in a hostile alien land, exiles, men without a country, without a tribe, without a faith, without a future or a past, a string of sand. It rules the world, but is unable to rule anything. Not only do they want to erase whites, but also Israel. The difference between Trump and the Jews who hate him and seek to destroy him is that Trump has Jewish grandchildren, and they do not. Like Angela Merkel, they want the world to end with themselves. They have erased their past, and have no future. Their enormous wealth and power is ashes in their mouth.

Their only source of cohesion is to be lefter than thou, to double down on hostility to white males. Their only faith, their only religion, the only source of cohesion that they can draw upon, is that white males have got to go. Thus we, not Kim of North Korea, not China, not Russia, are their real enemy. This leaves them in better shape than the Soviets, who having lost faith in communism had no source of cohesion at all, but still poor shape as they drift towards war. This implies that China, Russia, and even North Korea, are enemies of our enemy. Of these enemies of our enemy, Russia is most like us, and thus most likely to be an ally, as we drift towards war, internal and external.

Who gets sex

2018-05-03 01:08:21

The simplistic account is that eighty percent of women are having sex, and twenty percent of men are having sex - a hell of a lot of sex.

It kind of feels as if it is true, it is emotionally true, but it is not literally true. The number of men and women getting sex is not hugely different. More woman are having sex than men, and substantially more women are having regular sex with a regular partner than men are having regular sex with a regular partner (reflecting substantial levels of polygyny), but not hugely more, the numbers are not all that different.

What, however, makes the simplistic account feel true, is that ninety percent of men never get to pop a virgin. Every man, except for a rather small handful of men, are getting sloppy seconds. There is not a huge asymmetry as to how many men are getting sex compared to how many women, not a huge asymmetry as to how many men are in a sexual relationship as compared with the number of women in a sexual relationship. Rather the problem is that we don't see virgins entering relationships with other virgins, and then having sex with each other. This is the huge inequality between men and women, and between the vast majority of ordinary males, and the small minority of males that females notice - the problem is that almost every women gets popped by a high status alpha male, while very few men get to pop a hot virgin.

Eventually the hot chick slides down the desirability ladder, and reluctantly deigns to enter a relationship with some male who is sufficiently lowly and unattractive that he is interested in having a relationship with her. And most sex, most of the time, takes place between men and women that are not as grossly mismatched as women wish that they were, with the result that most sex, most of the time, is not all that unequally distributed. Most sex, most of the time, is between men and women not too far apart in the desirability ladder, with the result that the numbers are not all that unequal. But by that time, by the time she has reluctantly decided to settle for someone like you, her count has become considerable.

If you have ever had sex with a virgin, you will be in no doubt about it. If you think she is a virgin because she told you so, she lied.

The number of female involuntary celibates is roughly similar to the number of male involuntary celibates. But the female involuntary celibate is celibate because she is an alpha widow. She is celibate because she once got a booty call from Jeremy Meeks, and now rejects all lesser males in the hope that one day she will get a second booty call from Jeremy Meeks. The male involuntary celibate is likely a virgin, and if he ever had sex, he got the dregs, while the female involuntary celibate got the cream.

Inclusivity codes of conduct

2018-05-09 05:16:56

When an open source software project adopts a "code of conduct" it slowly dies. Bugs don't get fixed, new features break stuff, and it is unable to accommodate updates and changes in the environment. Over time, it gradually suffers bitrot - unchanging and unchangeable assumptions in a changing world, combined with "fixes" that introduce new bugs, and confusing new misfeatures that irritate old users, never quite work as they were supposed to, and are an obstacle to new users.

And now the eye of Soros has fallen on the Space X reusable rocket program, and "women in tech" will likely kill the re-usable earth to orbit second stage. We will still get something called the Falcon Heavy which will reach orbit, but chances are that the promised reusability is never going to arrive, that it will not be able to land back on earth, promptly refuel, and promptly go back to orbit again. And will therefore never be able to radically lower launch costs. And in a generation or so it will suffer the fate of the space shuttle. Too many disastrous accidents, costs keep growing without limit, eventually grounded for life. Similarly, the latest fighter planes have poorer performance than earlier generations of fighter planes, and much higher cost. People tell me that advances in missile technology and stealth make high performance fighters obsolete, and maybe that is true, but if performance is obsolete, why are fighters, like bridges[263] that fall down[264], getting more expensive, rather than less? Looks to me that the government is buying all the performance it can afford - and all the performance it can afford is rather less than it used to be able to afford. Reminds me of the Obamacare website: No amount of money could get it up, until they gave up on political correctness, and went with a team of white males leavened with east Asian males - with white males on top.

Why is "inclusivity" so devastatingly lethal to tech?

Observe "women in tech". As Spandrel observes[265] "Women in tech" are women trying to get nerds out of tech. Nerds protest. "We were here first! We built this from scratch!". Yeah whatever. There's money to be made, so women want in. Then they saw nerds there, and then they can't help their instincts. Nerds must go. Women just won't live close to them; the same way humans don't like living close to snakes or rats. That getting rid of the nerds would destroy the whole ecosystem is secondary. When tech collapses after women chase the nerds away, women will just migrate to somewhere else built by some other males, as if nothing had happened.

> Hypergamy means that all women want the top men. The top 20%, the top 5%, definitions vary. Here's some data. But even with the most generous definition, women see 80% of men as being completely out of consideration for sex. They just won't sleep with them. If they do (and they do every now and then for money or other motives), and other women find out, well that automatically means they're lower status, certainly lower status than women who sleep with better men. Not even sex really, the mere company of undeserving men is like a skin disease for women. It's like an old rag worn by a leper. The attention of mediocre men is low status itself, it defiles women in their own eyes. So it follows that if possible, mediocre men should disappear. Just die.
>
> Incel men being the most mediocre among the mediocre, they are at the top of the list for things women want to eradicate. They just don't want them to exist. Wherever they meet them they try to make them disappear.

Google used to be very smart, is now very stupid. Still making billions, will continue to make billions, but from my point of view, has already collapsed. Most of the good stuff being created now, is being created by ex googlers. Hollyweird is now getting what techies have been getting for some time. The only way a good techie can avoid the purge is to actually do what he would otherwise be accused of doing. The instincts of women mean that the innocent get purged and the guilty get laid.

The lioness knows which lion to fuck, because she sees him kill her kittens. Feynman was smart and famous, but to get laid, had to use his smarts to learn to put on the same

---

[263] https://sandrarose.com/2018/03/diversity-fail-women-engineering-team-behind-collapse-miami-pedestrian-bridge/

[264] https://www.wnd.com/2018/03/when-merit-based-hiring-is-deemed-racist-bridges-fall-down/

[265] https://bloodyshovel.wordpress.com/2018/05/08/the-incel-question/

performance as I perform. All women are like that[266]. If some women were not like that, we would have seen them with Feynman, Einstein, and Brad Pitt.

"The intellectual Dark Web" – and Jordan Peterson

2018-05-14 07:40:12

Yesterday, Saturday, I was shopping at the farmers market, and at one of the stalls my girlfriend asked if we should buy some choko, and I said "You are in charge, you decide", meaning she was in charge of cooking and the kitchen. Whereupon the stall holder, a late twentieswhite male small scale farmer selling his own produce or his family's produce, said
> "Hey don't say that. They might start believing it!"
>
> "Don't worry, I beat her regularly", I said.
>
> "Right, that is OK then", he said, giving me a thumbs up.

The New York Times has recently blessed "The intellectual dark web" - which is the latest controlled opposition.

If the New York Times blesses you, you are our enemy, and you intend to destroy everyone like me, you intend to deny me grandchildren, you intend to to erase my culture and destroy its statues, monuments and great buildings. You intend to demonize and erase my ancestors and their great achievements from history, you intend to erase my past and deny me a future. You are planning to flatten the great buildings of my ancestors, and replace them with concrete boxes, because you hate my past.

All the members of the Intellectual Dark Web are the usual neocons, who are open about their intent to erase my past and crush my future– except for Jordan Peterson, who is not a neocon. So Jordan Peterson and thus his followers, are being urged to assimilate to those who unambiguously intend to destroy us, and to repudiate and disown those who hope to preserve us.

Where does Jordan Peterson stand on preserving my past and my future?

Evasively.

White people always have a state religion. Our current state religion is progressivism, a heretical descendant of Christianity based on immanentizing the eschaton, transliterating Christianity from the next world to this.

And our current state religion hates us, and seeks to destroy us.

Children need fathers, fathers need a tribe and a faith. Peterson is attempting to synthesize a new faith– but it is a faith without a tribe, without tribal identity. Adherents of Peterson's faith have, shall have no practices that identify them to each other. Adherents of the faith are urged to do good to everyone - which is pretty stupid, and holiness competition in appearing to do good to far away strangers (without actually doing good to them) is in substantial part what got us into this mess. Peterson's new faith is fully progressivism compliant, and progressivism just loves progressivism compliant faiths, which

---

[266]https://blog.reaction.la/culture/all-women-are-like-that/

somehow rapidly become entirely indistinguishable from progressivism, and then quietly fade away.

For a faith to avoid assimilation by progressivism, has to have some key points of doctrine and practice that will prevent that assimilation - for example a commandment based on some red pill facts about women would work. Peterson gives no useful advice, let alone any commandments, on how to deal with women, though he seems to have noticed how oddly relaxed women are about the rapeugee problem.

Peterson urges males to be masculine, to not be ashamed of masculinity, which is a mighty inspiring message for men who have been demonized and taught to hate themselves and their own nature, but his concept of masculinity avoids directly confronting the progressive demonization and hatred of males and masculinity. Peterson's masculinity is expressed in cleaning up your room and pedestalizing women, but I have found that if you want to pull chicks, important to seem scary and potentially violent. Peterson is plugging that masculinity which is the least offensive possible to progressives, the least threatening possible to progressives, but in practice, the most offensive possible masculinity is considerably more advantageous, short of actually getting into fights, and so long as smooth talking and expensive lawyers can keep one out of jail, the masculinity that the man at the farmer's market stall was plugging, which was noticeably more virile than the masculinity plugged by Jordan Peterson.

Jordan Peterson has, in the past, been disturbingly cozy with globalists, with people who want to eliminate the white race, erase the history of white civilizations, end high tech capitalism, industrial capitalism, and large scale capitalist extraction of natural resources.

For Peterson's new faith to resist progressive assimilation, and to actually benefit its adherents, he needs to follow up that thought about the oddly relaxed attitude of feminists to the rapeugee problem.

People hunger and thirst for truth. Jordan Peterson promises truth but does not deliver. Cleaning up your room will not make you a man, let alone get you pussy.

Leftism as memetic virus

2018-05-20 03:41:24

For the English speaking world, leftism is the memetic analogue of to cancer - an internal part that ran wild, breaking the unity of the body[267].?

For the rest of the world, it is outside memetic disease, analogous to Canine transmissible venereal tumor, which was cancer for the original dog, but an outside infection for all other dogs.[268]

---

[267] https://dissentingsociologist.wordpress.com/2016/11/26/leftism-the-religion-that-failed-a-study-in-insecure-power-and-social-disorganization/

[268] https://www.the-american-interest.com/2018/03/02/collapse-racial-liberalism/

We are all white supremacists now

2018-05-20 03:53:43

Obama promised a post racial America. We elected Obama so that we could once and for all cleanse ourselves from the guilt for our racial sins.

Obama running for election spoke of the "nation's original sin of slavery," in the celebrated "A More Perfect Union" speech on race.but promised redemption. Elect Obama, and your sins will be forgiven.

Shortly after election, we discovered that our original sins were irredeemable, we are all guilty, we all must be punished with hellfire for eternity.

What, in fact, he delivered is an America where all white males are irredeemably hateful and evil, and must be purged. Original sin for the crime of slavery with absolutely no possibility of redemption. (Though in fact blacks enslaved other blacks, sold a small part of the surplus to whites, and ate the rest of the surplus. Those blacks that were enslaved by their fellow blacks, usually enslaved by black authorities for petty crimes, but who then got the boat to America were vastly better off than those blacks who remained in Africa.)

Obama, running for election, told us he was going to heal the wounds of racial division. Once elected, however, the logic of ginning up the black vote prevailed, and he proceeded to pour salt on the wounds and gasoline on the fire.

The left devours its own. Of course the left radicalized further in the last few years, as they have every year since around 1800 or so.

Some time ago I wrote to Scott saying that because he hangs out with evil and malicious people, he will be righteously condemned, then murdered or executed, and and his death endorsed by all right thinking decent people, while I, who actually say all the things he will be falsely accused of saying, will likely be fine. I think he sincerely thought the prediction so absurd that I must be joking, and forgot about it.

Egalitarianism is not about lifting up the downtrodden. It is about afflicting those insufficiently downtrodden, because the insufficiently downtrodden are a status threat, and the downtrodden are not. The left delight in the harm they cause. They want to hurt people, and as the world moves ever leftwards, the harm that they inflict will become ever greater, the final stage of leftism being that everyone tortures everyone else to death for insufficient leftism. Of course leftism usually self destructs before absolutely everyone is tortured to death, but they frequently make a good start on the program.

And here we are now, ruled by state religion that rules us irredeemably evil and wants to make us suffer. Leftism gets ever lefter, and the presidency continues to go on its own way ignoring the president. What constitutes being lefter than thou cannot be predicted in advance, because if you could predict it, they would already be doing it. But right now holier than thou is one leftist hating whites even more than the other leftist.

The privileges enjoyed by blacks over whites continue to escalate, and in consequence the self destructive and self defeating behavior of blacks continues to escalate.

Blacks, to prosper, need considerably harsher and simpler laws than whites, more swiftly and brutally enforced. Racial quotas on arrests are the worst thing you can do to harm blacks, for while racial quotas on arrest have done immense damage to whites by allowing blacks to run wild, the main victims of blacks running wild are other blacks.

If you privilege the behavior of aristocrats over peasants, so that an aristocrat can get away with behavior that a peasant could not, can get away with violence that a peasant could not, this works fine provided that aristocrats have a good code of honor, so that aristocratic misconduct is rather classy, honorable, brave and stylish. Privileging black and brown misconduct and violence is disastrous, because they have a code of dishonor, alleviated only be the fact that they do not follow even that.

The logic of prohibiting profiling inexorably leads to actual criminality being part of the forbidden characteristics that police are not allowed to notice. The Supreme court has for years been dealing with an endless parade of cases where a policeman, often a black policeman, noticed a black man doing something criminal, stopped him, searched him, and found evidence of the crime, and the lawyer appealed on the basis that the policeman should not have noticed and therefore neither the original forbidden noticing, nor the evidence found, should have been admitted in court. This has steadily escalated and filtered down to day to day police practice.

And when forbidding noticing fails to reduce the arrest disparity, we get arrest quotas.

In retrospect it is now apparent that we were locked onto this course when all men were declared to be equal. They are not, and pretending that they are necessarily results in legal privileges for inferior groups.

We can never have the same laws for different groups, and we don't.

The drift to civil war

2018-05-29 07:44:16

Whichever outcome happens, Trump in prison or the swamp in prison, as leftism keeps getting lefter the stakes just keep getting higher, and the processes for seizing the stakes are losing legitimacy. When things are falling apart, the first guy to escalate tends to win, and the first guy to escalate to naked violence is likely to win.

The deep state, the swamp, figured that they would illegally hound the Trump campaign, and something was bound to turn up that would retroactively justify the investigation, and they could jail Trump for some crime or other.

Because, hey if any of them were investigated, not that that could ever happen, something would turn up.

Well, they have been at it for two years, and nothing has turned up. What the press keeps announcing as another triumph is that in the course of casting the net wider and wider, they find some technicality or other with which to charge someone or other somehow connected to Trump, and hope to "turn him" – get him to rat on Trump, to reveal all these terrible Trump crimes that must surely exist. Every leftist assumes, sees as quite obvious, that if anyone connected to Trump is brought under pressure, he is likely to have some Trump crimes to report. Its inevitable and obvious – because everyone has some crimes, right?

But after two years of this, of people supposedly being about to "turn" as a result of being charged with crimes increasingly technical, boring, irrelevant, and legalistic, it is increasingly obvious that these Trump crimes do not exist, and all this illegal use of police and investigatory power is going to get them in trouble. If anyone was going to "turn", he would have turned by now. If anything was going to turn up, would have turned up by now.

They are investigating people and charging people to pressure them to rat on Trump, to reveal the terrible Trump crimes that surely must exist. No ratting happens, indicating no Trump crimes exist.

The uniform and confident expectation that if you put the heat on some random Trump associate, he will have the goods on Trump, reveals that if you were to put the heat on some random swamp dweller, he would have the goods on some more senior swamp dweller.

Predictably, the deep state, and entire left, reacts to this problem not by conciliation and retreat, but by escalation.

A little illegality (of which they hoped that they would be able to say "Well, what does it matter now" after turning up some Trump crime that would retroactively justify the investigation) has been slowly turning into a big illegality with nothing to justify it.

And when an illegality gets big enough, it is civil war.

On lefty boards, I keep hearing the argument "Well the first FBI and DoJ actions could not have been illegal, because if they were then the later actions would be even more illegal".

There is a flaw in that argument.

The real meaning of that argument is "Anything we do is legal because we do it, and anything you do is illegal because you do it, because we can and will escalate further than you dare to escalate." Wanna bet about what Trump will not dare? Duterte escalated all the way, and is as a result hugely popular.

They might be right. No wall yet, and the swamp shows no signs of draining, but if they are right this time, sooner or later, will be wrong.

The expectation that something would turn up is projection. They know nothing about Trump except what everyone knows, indeed they know less, because they close their eyes for fear of exposure to thought crime. That they think that something will turn up, that any close associate of Trump must know of Trump crimes, and therefore bringing a close associate of Trump under pressure will result in him ratting out Trump for some crime or other, implies that bringing any swamp dweller under pressure will result in him ratting out a more senior swamp dweller for some crime or other.

John Huber has been appointed to investigate the swamp.

So, will John Huber do the job? Will he obey the presidency and disobey the president, or will he obey the president and disobey the presidency?

On the one hand, John Huber is an Obama appointee, which would suggest that the swamp has something on him. The nature of the swamp is that to advance very far, you have to participate in hideous crimes, you have to demonstrate loyalty by making yourself blackmailable. We don't actually have any very concrete evidence of swamp dwellers sexually murdering abducted third world children in obscene satanic group rituals, but it is the kind of thing that they would do, and their thinking is the kind of thinking that one would expect of people socially required to do that kind of thing. If they had a normal disgust reflex, if anyone in their social circle had a normal disgust reflex, someone would have told them that 10:10 No Pressure was a really bad idea.

But, on the other hand John Huber lives were he was born. He is answerable to his God, who is represented on earth by his Church, his tribe, and his congregation. Should he fail to do his duty to the law and to his nominal employer (to President Trump) his family and his congregation is likely to look at him funny, which will give him the feeling that God is looking at him funny. That he hangs out in Utah, rather than hanging out in the swamp, means that the swamp dwellers did not have all that much opportunity to socially inveigle him to participate in blackmail material. So there is a good chance that he is going to do his job.

And, if he does his job, then what the swamp dwellers expected to happen with Trump, is going to happen to the swamp dwellers, the deep state, the exposure of one crime leading to the exposure of another crime. We know that, because they were projecting from their own social circle onto Trump's circle. They are going to rat each other out, as they expected Trump's people to rat each other out.

As we approach the left wing singularity (which I am still predicting for 2026) things get less predictable, and more dramatic. Expect the unexpected.

There are two likely courses:

1. Leftism rolls on: Republican voters, depressed by failure to build the wall and drain the swamp, fail to vote in the mid terms. Democrats get a majority and impeach Trump, then imprison him for imaginary or contrived crimes, then replace or openly ignore Pence. Leftists overthrowing the elected president leads to those even further left overthrowing leftists, and those even further left overthrowing them, as in revolutionary France and revolutionary Russia. Then facing collapsing legitimacy and increasing resistance, after a couple of rounds of radical leftists being overthrown by even more radical leftists, they execute Trump and his family for fear of counter revolution, as with King Louis XVI and Czar Nicholas II.

2. But Trump is ten times the man that King Louis XVI and Czar Nicholas II were. In the last month or so before the mid term elections he may arrange a huge confrontation with the swamp dwellers over building the wall and draining the swamp. This energizes Republican voters, and in due course under pressure of prosecution, swamp dwellers start ratting each other out, and a Trump self coup follows, where Trump seizes the awesome powers of the presidency for himself and his descendants. There is a problem with this scenario, in that Trump is short of Trump loyalists. Personnel are policy, and personnel are mostly criminal swamp dwellers who conspicuously lack the disgust reflex, indicating that swamp employment usually requires participation in disgusting things.

3. The unexpected.

Did I say two *likely* courses?

Draining the swamp is an autocoup. The power of the presidency is so vast, that if a president and his successors were to successfully seize it, they would never lose power, never lose an election. But because it is so vast, it is slippery. It is more power than any mortal can successfully exercise.

For the president to keep a grip on the presidency, the presidency needs to be trimmed down to manageable size, which will require Throne, Altar, and *Freehold*[269]. For the president to control the presidency, he is going to have to radically shrink it. And radically

---

[269]https://blog.reaction.la/economics/throne-altar-and-freehold/

shrinking it would also ease the problem that personnel are policy.

As long as the presidency remains vast, it will remain chaotic, uncontrollable, and anarcho tyrannical, in which case the drift ever leftwards will continue, even if a Trump autocoup slows things down a bit for a while.

Baking a gay marriage cake

2018-06-05 20:45:12

The supreme court has rolled back the decision that forced a particular baker to bake a particular gay marriage cake.

But has done nothing in general about the rules that pressure everyone else to piously give service to gay marriage, that require ever other baker to bake a gay wedding cake.

The reason for undoing that particular decision is that the human rights commission was openly and enthusiastically delighting in mockery and sacrilege and openly expressed the intent to humiliate Christians. The marriage was completely unserious, just a piece of mockery directed at monogamy and Christianity, performed for the purpose of sacrilege.

So, the Supremes left open the possibility of forcing a baker to bake a cake for a serious and sincere gay marriage - if any such are ever found.

Nonetheless, it is an important step, because this decision says that the state cannot openly seek to humiliate Christians and crush Christianity. Furtively seeking to humiliate Christians and crush Christianity, however, is still just fine.

Related to this is the sacrament of abortion "This is my body". No one is allowed to commit sacrilege against the holy sacrament of abortion. Sacrilege against Christianity however, is just fine. Observe the outrage when Pussy Riot gets imprisoned for busting into a Cathedral and desecrating it and for smashing up an explicitly Christian war material. Democrats are looking for nuclear war with Russia over that issue.

The power of the state is still being applied to make progressives holy, and to desecrate everything that is holy to everyone else, except that they are going easy on Mohammedans in an effort to split conservative Mohammedans from moderate Muslims.

What makes a Mohammedan "moderate"?

Does a "moderate" Mohammedan oppose terror?

Nope, whenever there is a terrorist incident, the press go looking for a "moderate" imam to condemn it, come up empty.

Does a "moderate" Mohammedan oppose the conquest, subjugation and ethnic cleansing of Christians?

Nope, the Cathedral has repeatedly armed and funded groups that ethnically cleanse Christians from the Middle East.

Notice that the Cathedral always uses the phrase Muslim, not Mohammedan. Muslim means, approximately, obedient to God, while Mohammedan means obedient to Mohammed, as Christian means obedient to Christ.

What makes a "moderate" "Muslim" "moderate" is that he supports western education for girls, meaning he supports nine year old girls being taught sodomy and how to put a condom on a banana. He also supports girls being systematically promoted above boys in the education system, and boys being taught by women - that boys grow up in an environment where females are systematically higher status than males in every way at every level.

Observe: Sadat, in obedience to the what the Cathedral ostensibly told him to do, and in disobedience to what they actually meant, in disobedience to the real meaning of their commands, created an education system in which males and females were exactly equal, having exactly the same representation at every level and in every role and also protected Christians and other religious minorities from violence, humiliation, and sacrilege, implementing the pretended ideals of the Cathedral with absolute rigor and precision.

Needless to say the Cathedral set about overthrowing him - sponsoring, funding, and arming moderate Muslims who were openly genocidal against Christians and minorities, but who were fine with nine year old girls putting a condom on a banana.

Jordan Peterson, controlled opposition

2018-06-07 21:50:45

Jordan Peterson is on our side of the Culture War:* anti-political correctness
anti-identity politics
biological sex roles and traditional gender roles
meritocracy and meritocratic hierarchy
personal freedom and responsibility
angers our enemies

But this man is not an ally. The enemy of our enemy is not always our friend.

It is good that my enemy's enemy is successful against my enemy, but much though I wish my enemy's enemy was my friend and ally, I don't get to choose.

Jordan Peterson is reaching a huge audience, and that is good news for us ... but ...

On sex roles there is a big difference between Peterson's directive: "clean up your room" and my observation: "I must dance, and women call the tune."

And similarly, he omits the truth on NAMs and Jews, crediting American Jews with an average IQ high enough to entirely explain their disproportionate influence, and completely failing to notice that whites are second class citizens to NAMs. He advocates hierarchy based on meritocracy, and conspicuously fails to notice major deviations from meritocracy.

Official truth is that Jordan Peterson's target market is a tiny, ignored, underserved niche market ... but it is, in fact half the population

Mass market service of half the market, which is what Jordan Peterson is supplying, does not go all the way with the whole truth even though that is what the customers hope to receive, because, surrounded by a barrage of propaganda, people like to hear truth that is compatible as possible with that barrage of propaganda.

Mostly they are content with the same old propaganda, minus the spitting at them and projectile vomiting over them.

I have tried lots of different personas on women. I know what persona works. Heartiste is correct, and indeed understates his case. Playing a really bad man, even worse than that recommended by Heartiste, works best. I can play that character convincingly because I have monsters inside, and I let them out to play, but I am not really that person. I must dance, and women call the tune. The solution is not to clean up your room, but to project the masculinity of the vicious psychopathic criminal, combined with the assets and material lifestyle of the respectable male, staying out of jail while superficially seeming the kind of man that they would find in jail. Jordan offers fatherless boys the same old blue pill solutions to dealing with women, which result in them living in involuntary celibacy.

Of course insufficient spitting looks to the left like hard core genocidal nazism, so you still get the same enemies. Peterson gets in trouble for saying that commies murdered a hundred million or so, and are entirely unrepentant. Jordan Peterson neglects to say that they hunger and thirst to do it all again, and that Democrats are on the same course, a course headed directly for the Red Terror of 1794, which eighteenth century horror prefigured the enormously larger mass murders of the twentieth century, and the extraordinary increase in war, state violence, and private criminal violence that we have seen starting with the French Revolution.

For women to reproduce successfully, they have to be under male authority, and in the modern world, they look for that authority and do not find it.

Female behavior, their attraction to very bad men, makes total sense from the point of view of evolutionary psychology when you reflect that the barista with an advanced degree in women's studies and one hundred thousand dollars in college debt will probably become a cat lady, but if Islamic State was militarily victorious, and auctioned her off naked and in chains at public auction, would probably have seven children and twenty grandchildren. It also makes total sense according to curse of Eve: "thy desire shall be to thy husband, and he shall rule over thee".

In order that we can make men into sheep dogs rather than wolves, have to make women into property. For men to become sheep dogs, women must become sheep.

Jordan Peterson is pushing a new religion. Any new religion is going to be an improvement on progressivism, which hates us, and which is erasing our past and destroying our future, but his proposed religions lacks key elements of Christianity that made western civilization possible: The Trinity gives us a God who is both big and small. A god who, unlike Odin, is big enough to offer hope, and who simultaneously makes himself small (turning a blind eye in Eden to allow us to steal the knowledge of Good and Evil, and taking on mortality and death) to reach out to mankind, to allow room in the universe for more than one being with free will, choice, and responsibility for choices. The God too big problem prevents Muslims and Orthodox Jews from doing science and keeping promises, and the God too small problem let Odin worshipers be conquered by Christians. The gods of Jungian paganism, which is what Jordan Peterson is pushing, are too small to give us strength. Invoking the Christian God at mealtime grace gives fathers authority over their families. There is no Jungian equivalent, and there does not seem to have been a Norse equivalent.

Should Jordan Peterson's religion succeed, the immediate threat to us of enemies in charge of us who wish our destruction will have been turned aside, but Jordan's religion would not allow western science and empire to recover, nor allow white and east Asian fertility rates to recover to replacement. Christianity permits a culture of keeping promises and speaking truth, to which other religions are apt to be inimical.

With the collapse of truth speaking, science has collapsed, resulting in the replication crisis. Drug companies in the west are giving up on developing new drugs because of the replication crisis. Nobody trusts their research, and they should not trust anyone else's research.

The Mohammedan says he will do such and such "God Willing" and then does not do it, while the Jew says he will do such and such, and then finds a novel and surprising meaning for his words and yours. Today's Conservative Mohammedans and Orthodox Jews, whose fathers are armed with a very big God, are doing a lot better on patriarchal authority than today's Christians, hence their fertility rate, but eighteenth century Christians did equally well, while at the same time giving us science, technology, industrialization, and empire. We are not going to recover western civilization without an official belief system substantially similar to theirs, to theocratic Anglican state Christianity as it existed from 1660 to about 1810.

Can't stump the Trump

2018-06-12 08:57:38

Naturally the world press attempted to frame this as Trump taking a humiliating beating like an errant schoolboy.

But ...

But the frame fell off with Trudeau's eyebrows.

Trump targeted Trudeau in particular, not because of anything he said, that was just an excuse, but because the Canadian economy is the most vulnerable to a tariff war with the United States. The fake eyebrows were a visible manifestation of less visible weakness. A weak country produces, and is produced by, weak men.

Which brings me to a far more important conflict: The president's struggle with the presidency.

The left seemingly holds all the cards. Christianity has surrendered to the left, and is dying for its own sins, for its heretical endorsement of vile sins. The left control every institution. Surely it is all over?

Well, maybe it is all over. On past performance the left, being macro scale entropy, is never defeated until they start murdering each other in large numbers, or until very few people remain and alien outsiders move in on the vacant lands.

But the left is vulnerable because incohesive. Because the left is entropy manifest in the form of people and political action, they have no cohesion, which leads to them always being out holied by even crazier leftists, the latest big leftwing projects being genocide of Christians, and boys changing sex before puberty, which is currently being promoted in comics and television cartoons, but also leads to them falling apart when opposed by a strong leader. They have a leadership vacuum, made manifest by Obama, Hillary Clinton, and Angela Merkel. The left wing tendency to absolute dictatorship is their solution to the terrifying entropy of leftism, their solution to their fear of each other, their solution to their endless and increasingly dangerous struggle with each other. They wind up with despotism as a desperately needed substitute for strength and unity.

In so far as they have unity at the moment, it is because their top people have blackmail material on each other. If Trump can get a decent prosecution going of a few mid level leftists, they are going to start singing on each other, the way they keep expecting Trump people to sing when they launch spurious prosecutions against them.

But that is a coup complete problem. How does Trump get a prosecution going, when the criminals are the Department of Justice and the FBI? On the other hand, as we approach the left wing singularity, coups become increasingly probable.

If he gets a good prosecution going, he will then own the presidency. But hard to get a good prosecution going until he first owns the presidency.

If Trump pulls off an autocoup, the next big problem will be making it permanent. The presidency is too vast and sprawling to be easily controllable, thus tends inexorably to entropy, hence leftism, and leftism tends ever leftwards. To make an autocoup permanent, Trump will have to disempower almost all of the presidency. After an autocoup, if the presidency remains vast, and vastly powerful, it will continue to work to disempower the president and his successors, though more slowly, in a more furtive fashion, and with less conscious intention.

And Tango does not make three

2018-06-21 02:24:02

Singapore and Hong Kong resist "International Community" dominance, taking gay books off the library shelves[270].

Now that Trump is disinclined to back Blue Empire soft power with Red Empire hard power, Blue Empire soft power is running into severe head winds. Recall Duterte threatening to give Soros a helicopter ride if he came to the Philippines.

One of the books removed is "And Tango makes Three", a book that schoolchildren in countries under Blue Empire domination are forced to read.

The story in "And Tango makes Three" is about two cute homosexual penguins who adopt a baby penguin. Supposedly this is a true story, or based on a true story, but of course it is a lie. The two real life penguins on which it is based have never had sex with each other. They were buddies. It was a bromance. Gays are a signaling hazard[271], and this signaling hazard prevents male on male cohesion. That David and Jonathan loved each other facilitated David becoming King of Israel, because it facilitated cohesion among David's mighty men. If David and Jonathan had had sex with each other, he never would have become King of Israel, because there would have been no cohesion between him and his mighty men. Gay men do not cohere, and gay penguins do not cohere.

That males could cohere, and could build a strong society, required that gays be put to death. Nations, tribes, peoples, cultures, and religions that forcefully suppress men who also lie with mankind, as they lie with women, conquer nations, tribes, peoples, cultures, and religions that do not or cannot. Israel has not won a war since it had gay parades, women in the front line, and gays in the military.

Chinese soft power actually works, being based on thousands of years of history and deep understanding of the use of soft power. Progressives know no history, because everything before the current year is shameful and hateful, so they cannot do soft power very effectively. Their "soft" power is actually based on terror and mass murder, as for

---

[270]https://www.scmp.com/news/hong-kong/community/article/2151705/and-tango-makes-three-among-10-childrens-books-same-sex

[271]https://www.socialmatter.net/2016/05/17/homosexuals-signalling-hazard-traditional-societies/

example Libya and Syria. Peoples and nations submitted to their "soft" power in fear of what happened to people and nations that failed to submit.

Hard power requires suppression of gays, among other things. Soft power requires knowledge and understanding of history. Thus the "international community" is weak, both in soft power and hard power, and now, as in the last days of the Soviet Union, this weakness is showing. The Soviet Union lost soft power, because they ceased to believe, and hard power, because socialism wrecked their logistics. The "International Community" cannot do soft power, because of self imposed ignorance, and cannot do hard power, because of gays and women in the military, and because people are getting sick of unsuccessful attempts to use hard power.

Profiting from the destruction wrought by social Justice

2018-06-22 03:00:39

The media mogul Rupert Murdoch noticed that the mainstream television news consisted of repetitious boring lies, and was persistently denigrating its audience.

So he produced a new television news channel, Fox News, which of course became a huge success, and is now being purchased for sackfuls of money by a fully converged corporation, which will kill what made Fox News successful.

Vox Day is repeating this operation. Now that DC Comics and Marvel consist of tedious and hostile propaganda, he went into the comics business, which will likely follow a similar trajectory, unless the government just plain shut him down. What is happening is that any operation that is not aggressively hostile to Social Justice gets taken over and destroyed.

Kathy Forth's suicide

2018-06-23 23:27:33

Kathy Forth offed herself, leaving a lengthy suicide note in which she accused numerous men of sexually harassing her, and the entire society of ignoring this terrible sexual harassment, thereby driving her to suicide.

Fat, pushing forty, and supposedly suffers unbearable amounts of sexual assault.

Back when she was hot, the amount of sexual assault she suffered was entirely bearable.

All women love drama, all women create drama, and all women create drama because they are looking for a spanking from a strong man. All women are like that. Childlessness and the lack of a strong man in their lives greatly worsens this problem.

Not all women make false accusations of sexual harassment, not all women kill themselves, but all disruptively create drama and problems: The ones not under the authority of an alpha male, and the ones that have remained childless while their fertility is running out, create more disruption, more drama, and more problems.

They are all cruising for a spanking, every single one.

All the sides in this debate that are permitted within the Overton Window are the same insane side. Scott[272] is evil, depraved, decadent, and insane, #metoo is even more evil and more insane, and the fat old cat lady who offed herself was ridiculous, hilarious, evil, sinful and insane, her over the top evil, and her over the top vanity being hilariously funny to any sane person. Any remotely sane person commenting on that reddit thread gets instabanned. Anyone who manages to post twice on that thread is evil or insane, and most likely both. That thread is a conversation in the lunatic asylum.

Every woman lusts for drama. Fat, and pushing forty, people were ignoring her: *Men* were ignoring her. So she decided to go out in a blaze of glory, the ultimate "Hey look at me" opera, a gigantic soap opera of martyrdom.

Kathy Forth was evil and spent her life ruining other people's lives out of depraved, foolish, and ridiculous sexual lust.

It is normal, and indeed universal, for childless unowned women who are fertile age, or not very long past fertile age, to destructively and self destructively destroy their social and organizational environment, burn the family assets, disrupt the business, divorce, etc. Kathy took this to extremes.

All Women Are Like That. Kathy more than others.

When a woman creates drama she is unconsciously, and in Kathy's case quite consciously, hoping to smoke the alpha male out of hiding so that he will take possession of her and give her a spanking. She flat out tells us in her suicide note. In her suicide note she tells of her fantasies for powerful alpha male to take possession of her, to own her, to command her, supposedly in order to protect her from all this supposedly terrible sexual harassment.

This is what female lust looks like. It is not genitally focused like male lust, but that does not make it better, it makes it worse. Much worse.

During her fertile years, a lustful woman is not funny. Past fertile age, a lustful childless woman is hilarious.

Not every woman makes false rape and false sexual harassment allegations, but every woman acts disruptively, every unowned fertile age woman acts more disruptively and causes great damage, childless unowned women even more so, and childless unowned women continue doing so well past fertile age, while women with children calm down as their fertile period ends, particularly women who have previously experienced the firm hand of the father of their children.

Overgaming

2018-06-30 04:22:45

This is not a PUA blog. To learn PUA, read Heartiste, and then practice on actual women, not this blog.

But some people have partially misinterpreted my observations on passing shit tests, so, clarifying.

I depict shit tests as tough, deadly, scary, threatening, and vital to pass, because they are. But though a cat will be bored if it manages to catch a cat toy, it will also be bored if

---

it seems there is absolutely no chance of catching the cat toy.

The girl thinks she wants to enslave you, wants to dominate you. In a sense she does want those things, but if she were to actually get them, would lose interest. But at the same time you let her eventually earn the sight of soft vulnerable marshmallow inner core under that solid stone cold exterior - alpha badboy with a touch of provider beta. You need to let her win a little bit, or to think she might win a little bit. But not too much.

You are far more likely to err on the side of undergaming than overgaming. I play a very bad man, and I still regularly err by undergaming, and am endlessly astonished at the ways in which my mistreatment of women is rewarded. But zero vulnerability, zero betabucks provider, does not work long term either.

Do not take this as me telling you it is OK to be a whimpering beta provider. It is not. That tactic seriously fails to work. Been there, done that, got burned. Don't be a nice guy. Be a bad boy. But while being a bad boy, let them see the occasional hint of a heart of gold. Just the occasional piece of niceness.

Ideally, of course, the man and the woman perform their biblical roles. The woman honors and obeys, the man loves and cherishes. And I suppose that if you got one hundred percent honor and obedience, it would then be safe to give one hundred percent loving and cherishing. But if you only get eighty percent honor and obedience, need to provide rather less than eighty percent loving and cherishing. Keep her on her toes.

Here ends PUA advice. Back to your regularly scheduled political posts.

When the west started losing wars

2018-07-06 01:21:07

The Victorian theory that women were angels, therefore no coercion was needed against naturally saintly women, only against demonic males who make saintly women do bad things, led to an intolerable flood of bastards and women giving birth in the rain in dark alleys, which in turn led to "Oliver Twist" and "Les Miserables", which brought us the welfare state, and the replacement of the nuclear family with child support. As people in the eighteenth century were aware, people need marriage in order to reproduce, and marriage needs coercion to make it stick, and the primary victims of this coercion need to be women, otherwise they will have sex with one man, then sex with another, making it difficult and unpleasant to father children.

Similarly, "White Man's Burden", and "la haute mission civilisatrice" was the death of colonialism.

It led the British general who was invading Afghanistan to believe he was doing Afghans a favor, and if he was sufficiently nice to them they would throw flowers at his troops. So he forbade his troops to take necessary measures for self defense, and, as a result, he and his troops died.

The white man's burden was profoundly counterproductive to social cohesion, because it led to them sacrificing near (British officers and troops) for far (afghan officers and troops)

If it is a burden, then you proceed to conspicuously display your holiness by burden carrying – which is apt to mean making your troops carry burdens.

Before the British intervened in Afghanistan, the most recent news that most people had of it was records of Alexander's army passing through two millenia ago.

The empire of the East India company was expanding, and the empire of the Russias was expanding, and it was inevitable that the two would meet. And so it came to pass that the Kings of Afghanistan encountered both, and played each against the other.

When the British became aware of Afghanistan, they interpreted its inhabitants as predominantly white or whitish – as descendants of Alexander's troops and camp followers and/or descendants of Jews converted to Islam at swordpoint.

Afghanistan was, and arguably still is, an elective monarchy, and the fractious electors tended to fight each other and elect weak kings who could scarcely control their followers, and so it has been ever since Alexander's troops lost Alexander.

Mister Mountstuart Elphinstone, in his account of is mission to Kabul in 1809, says he once urged upon a very intelligent old man of the tribe of Meankheile, the superiority of a quiet life under a powerful monarch, over the state of chaotic anarchy that so frequently prevailed.

The reply was "We are content with alarms, we are content with discord, we are content with blood, but we will never be content with a master!"

As Machiavelli observed, such places are easy to conquer, but hard to hold, and so it proved.

To conquer and hold such places, one must massacre, castrate, or enslave all of the ruling elite that seems fractious, which is pretty much all of them, and replace them with your own people, speaking your own language, and practicing your own customs, as the Normans did in England, and the French did in Algeria, starting 1830. The British of 1840, however, had no stomach for French methods, and were already starting to fall short of the population growth necessary for such methods.

So what the British could have done is paid the occasional visit to kill any king that they found obnoxious, kill his friends, family, his children, and leading supporters, install a replacement king, and leave. The replacement king would have found his throne shaky, because Afghan Kings have usually found their thrones shaky, but the British did not need to view that as their problem, knowing the solution to that problem to be drastic and extreme. If the throne has been shaky for two thousand years, it is apt to be difficult to stop it from rocking.

After a long period of disorderly violence, where brother savagely tortured brother to death, and all sorts of utterly horrifying crimes were committed, King Dost Mahomed Khan took power in Kabul in 1826, and proceeded to rule well, creating order, peace, and prosperity, and receiving near universal support from the fractious and quarreling clans of Afghanistan.

The only tax under his rule was a tariff of one fortieth on goods entering and leaving the country. This and the Jizya poll tax are the only taxes allowed by the Koran, at least as Islamic law is interpreted in this rebellious country which has historically been disinclined to pay taxes, and because this tax was actually paid, it brought him unprecedented revenues. On paying this tax "the merchant may travel without guard or protection from one border to the other, an unheard of circumstance"

However he did not rule Herat, which was controlled by one of his enemies, who been King before and had ambitions to be King again. He therefore offered Herat to the Shah of Persia in return for the Shah's support against another of his enemies, Runjeet Singh. He was probably scarcely aware that Runjeet Singh was allied to the British, and the Shah was allied to the Tsar of all the Russias.

Notice that this deal was remarkably tight fisted, as was infamously typical of deals made by Dost Mahomed Khan. He would give the Persians that which he did not possess, in return for them taking care of one of his enemies and helping him against another.

The British East India Company, however, saw this as Afghanistan moving into Russian empire, though I am pretty sure that neither the Shah of Persia nor the King of Aghanistan thought they were part of anyone's empire.

So Russia and the East India Company sent ambassadors to the King of Afghanistan, who held a bidding contest asking which of them could best protect him against Runjeet Singh. He then duplicitously accepted both bids from both empires, which was a little too clever by half, though absolutely typical of the deals he made with his neighbors.

Dost Mahomed Khan was a very clever king, but double crossing the East India Company was never very clever at all. No one ever got ahead double crossing the East India Company. It is like borrowing money from the Mafia and forgetting to pay them back.

Russia and England then agreed to not get overly agitated over the doings of unreliable and duplicitous proxies that they could scarcely control - which agreement the East India Company took as permission to hold a gun to the head of the Shah of Persia. The East India company seized control of the Persian Gulf, an implicit threat to invade if the Shah intervened in Afghanistan to protect Dost Mahomed Khan. It then let Runjeet Singh off the leash, and promised to support his invasion of Afghanistan.

So far, so sane. Someone double crosses you, then you make an horrible example of him, and no one will do it again. Then get out, and whoever rules in Afghanistan, if anyone does manage to rule, will refrain from pissing you off a second time.

The British decided to give a large part of Afghanistan to Runjeet Singh, and install Shah Shoudjah-ool-Moolk, a Kinglet with somewhat plausible pretensions to the Afghan throne, in place of Dost Mahomet Khan.

Up to this point everything the East India Company is doing is sane, honorable, competent, just, and wonderfully eighteenth century.

Unfortunately, it is the nineteenth century. And the nineteenth century is when the rot set in.

His Majesty Shah Shoudjah-ool-Moolk will enter Afghanistan, surrounded by his own troops, and will be supported against foreign interference, and factious opposition, by the British Army. The Governor-general confidently hopes, that the Shah will be speedily replaced on his throne by his own subjects and adherents, and that the independence and integrity of Afghanistan established, the British army will be withdrawn. The Governor-general has been led to these acts by the duty which is imposed upon him, of providing for the security of the possessions of the British crown, but he rejoices, that, in the discharge of this duty, he will be enabled to assist in restoring the union and prosperity of the Afghan people.

So: The English tell themselves and each other: We not smacking Afghans against a wall to teach them not to play games with the East India Company. On the contrary, we are doing them a favor. A really big favor. Because we love everyone. We even love total strangers in far away places very different from ourselves. We are defending the independence of Afghanistan by removing the strongest King it has had in centuries and installing our puppet, and defending its integrity by arranging for invasion, conquest, rape and pillage by its ancient enemies the Sikhs, in particular Runjeet Singh. Because we love far away strangers who speak a language different from our own and live in places we cannot find on the map. We just love them to pieces. And when we invade, we will doubtless be greeted by people throwing flowers at us.

You might ask who would believe such guff? Obviously not the Afghans, who are being smacked against the wall. Obviously not the Russians. Obviously not the Persians. Obviously not the British troops who are apt to notice they are not being pelted with flowers.

The answer is, the commanding officer believed this guff. And not long thereafter, he and his troops died of it, the first great defeat of British colonialism. And, of course, the same causes are today leading to our current defeat in Afghanistan.

The commanding officer of the British expedition made a long series of horrifyingly evil and stupid decisions, which decisions only made sense if he was doing the Afghans a big favor, if the Afghans were likely to appreciate the big favor he was doing them, and his troops were being pelted with flowers, or Afghans were likely to start pelting them with flowers real soon now. The East India company was no stranger to evil acts, being in the business of piracy, brigandry, conquest, and extortion, but people tend to forgive evil acts that lead to success, prosperity, good roads, safe roads, and strong government. These evil acts, the evil acts committed by the British expedition to Afghanistan, are long remembered because they led to failure, defeat, lawlessness, disorder, and weak government.

As a result, he, his men, and their camp followers, were all killed.

Progressives tend to judge people by their good intentions, and the intentions of the British Empire in invading Afghanistan were absolutely wonderful, but the man who does evil because insane is a worse problem than the man who does evil because he expects to profit. The rational profit seeking evildoer, you can pay off, or deter. You can surrender on terms that will probaby not be too bad. The irrational evildoer just has to be killed. Before 1840, the East India Company was sometimes deterred, frequently paid off, and frequently accepted surrender on reasonable terms. In 1841, just had to be killed.

This illustrates the importance of the rectification of names, of formalism. If you lie to yourself, you are deceived. I have been reading the Clinton emails, and one of the most striking features is that Clinton and company are deluded and deceived by self flattering lies, that despite having vast spy networks in far flung places, are seriously out of contact with reality, as their circle tells each other what they want to hear.

If you know the enemy and know yourself, you need not fear the result of a hundred battles. If you know yourself but not the enemy, for every victory gained you will also suffer a defeat. If you know neither the enemy nor yourself, you will succumb in every battle. Hillary and her advisers, and therefore I suppose the entire state department, know neither the enemy nor themselves. They dream grandiose delusions, in which they are the terribly smart and virtuous people, rather than a drunken old sow surrounded by lying flatterers.

The East India Company did not realize that it was about to be recast, or was recasting itself, from being a for profit company, empowered to make war and engage in acts of piracy and extortion for private profit, to being the British government's instrument of holy do gooding, benevolently carrying the white man's burden for the benefit of a bunch of strangely ungrateful foreigners. In place of a ruthless mafia with uniformed soldiers, the East India Company was about to become an NGO with uniformed nursemaids.

Yet strangely, the greater the good intentions, the more they were to be resented. The East India Company seems to have been more popular when they were pirates and bandits than when they were pious do gooders. No one seemed to appreciate the East India Company doing good to them at gunpoint. The ridiculous part of the white man's burden was the striking ingratitude of the supposed beneficiaries, resembling the striking ingratitude of Middle Easterner's towards meddling by presidents Bush and Obama in the Middle East. Those@!^&$ Middle Easterners just somehow do not know what is good for them, unlike far away strangers, who, being terribly clever, know exactly what is good for the Middle East without ever having lived there.

If an elite attempt to rule distant places, they will rule them very badly, unless some of the children of the elite move to those places, and stay there to rule them. Carpetbaggers who come and go tend to leave horror and devastation in their wake, as for example the looting of Haiti by do gooder ngos after the earthquake. If you are not going to stick around, the incentive is to take everything and smash everything, which is what happened to Haiti when the US State Department ngos got coercive quasi governmental power. Haitians wound up eating dirt, sleeping in the rain, and got cholera. So, not going to rule well, unless you have a fertile elite, which needs more governmental and quasi governmental jobs for its excessively numerous offspring. In which case good rule will naturally follow from the desire of that elite to make a nice place for themselves and their descendants. This is necessarily going to be rough on the existing local elite, but an ideology of doing good to far away strangers does not result in doing good to far away strangers, but at best to famine, destruction of property, and disease, as recently demonstrated in Haiti.

Technological decline

2018-07-06 23:27:31

As societies enter a dark age, military technologies are apt to be the last to be lost, and in the recovery from a dark age, the first to advance.

In dark ages, art declines, great buildings decline, ordinary people's living standards decline, people harrow the ground with stones tied to bits of wood instead of iron plows, but weapons technology usually goes right on improving.

Our art is crap, we no longer build Cathedrals, but until recently, weapons were good and improving.

The 2018 Nuclear Posture Review[273] has recently appeared, revealing that we have

---

[273]https://media.defense.gov/2018/Feb/02/2001872886/-1/-1/1/2018-NUCLEAR-POSTURE-REVIEW-FINAL-REPORT.PDF

lost all nuclear military technology:

> U.S. production of tritium, a critical strategic material for nuclear weapons, is now insufficient to meet the forthcoming U.S. nuclear force sustainment demands, or to hedge against unforeseen developments. Programs are planned, but not yet fully funded, to ease these critical production shortfalls.

This is euphemistic. Recent attempts to produce tritium were fully funded, but failed, which failure resulted in new plans for new attempts to produce tritium, which have not yet been fully funded.

I have regularly remarked on America's inability to produce tritium. All existing nuclear weapons require tritium to juice their detonation, and without tritium, would produce a low yield explosion. Tritium decays over time, and so fresh tritium continually needs to be added. The US is out of tritium, has repeatedly attempted to produce more, and repeatedly failed.

Fully funding the Obamacare website did not produce an Obamacare website, and I doubt that fully funding proposed new tritium production facilities will produce tritium.

> In the absence of sustained support for these programs, including a marked increase in the planned production of tritium in the next few years, our nuclear capabilities will inevitably atrophy and degrade below requirements.
>
> The U.S. is also unable to produce or process a number of other critical materials, including lithium and enriched uranium. For instance, the United States largely relies on dismantling retired warheads to recover lithium to sustain and produce deployable warheads. This may be inadequate to support the nuclear force replacement program and any supplements to it.

So, our enrichment facilities have ceased to function across the board.

And, recapping my previous remarks on technological decline:

Fighter planes are getting slower, and can no longer fly as high or as far.

We need Pu238 for nuclear batteries. The 2006 New Horizons mission to Pluto and the Kuiper belt was launched without enough Pu238 to keep all its equipment live during the Pluto flyby, and without enough Pu238 to do its Kuiper belt mission,

Existing nuclear weapons have not received maintenance for a very long time, and it is unclear whether there is anyone with the relevant skills to perform maintenance and adequately test them for readiness.

Fusion weapons require lithium enriched in lithium six to juice them. Enriched lithium does not decay, but the US has lost the capability to make more of it.

Attempts to build new nuclear reactors in the US keep running into indefinite delays. To make significant amounts of plutonium 239 will need new reactors.

Plutonium 239 is the stuff used in nuclear weapons, plutonium 238 the stuff used in nuclear batteries, plutonium 240 is the stuff you don't want because it spontaneously fissions. You want to produce your plutonium using enriched uranium in a sodium cooled fast neutron reactor because then you get considerably more of the plutonium you want, and considerably less of the plutonium you do not want. The US used to build fast neutron reactors, but all recent attempts to build a fast neutron reactor in the west have failed, and all existing fast neutron reactors in the West have stopped working. The only existing fast neutron reactors that are working well enough to produce significant amounts of plutonium are in Russia and China.

If all existing fast neutron reactors have ceased to work, if all our existing isotopic enrichment plants have ceased to work, should we really believe that our existing nuclear weapons will work?

Money, "full funding", is unlikely to be the issue. Obama threw stupendous amounts of money at the Obamacare website, and the site did not come up. It only came up when a conspicuously undiverse team of white and east Asian heterosexual males led by white heterosexual males took over the job.

Nuclear weapons were produced by western civilization, and since 1972 the core project of our universities has been "Western Civilization has got to go."

Science requires a level of trust and trustworthiness that a diverse society is incapable of, and a level of truth speaking that a progressive post christian society is incapable of.

Testosterone and weight loss

2018-07-09 04:03:27

Exogenous testosterone can cause your testicles to shut down - and possibly shut down permanently. Hence the need to get off testosterone from time to time.

I learned that my sperm production was down - not so low as to render me entirely infertile, but low enough to significantly impact my prospects of having another child. So, I stopped taking exogenous testosterone on May 14th. By May 27th, had gained ten pounds and my abs were no longer visible. So, on May 27th, adopted the carno ketogenic diet. Extreme low carb, with an eight hour eating window each day, and longer fasts from time to time. One and half grams of protein per day per kilogram of ideal weight.

I have now lost the weight that I gained, and it feels like my testosterone levels are recovering. But it was a struggle to lose that weight without exogenous testosterone to strengthen me. I miss carbs terribly, and now that I can see my abs again, am going to slowly go back to eating a little bit of carbs. I will retest my testicles in August or September.

I have done weight loss with and without exogenous testosterone. Weight loss is never easy for me, even with exogenous testosterone, but without exogenous testosterone it is mighty hard.

The axis of deplorables

2018-07-13 12:03:01

Until recently, everyone in power everywhere in the world was culturally aligned with the Blue Empire, or at least reluctant to be openly unaligned. Every government, every head of government, every government school, every university everywhere, every television station (including Fox), every newspaper (including the Murdoch newspapers). The Cathedral would from time to time go into high dudgeon because not everyone was as enthusiastic as they would like, but anyone who outright opposed them was low status and powerless.

Universities and their endowments are still converged, and all the mass media and internet giants are converged. Trump has few loyalists among his political appointees in government. But it is a start. A start that denies the inevitability of Blue Empire power, a start that tells us that surrender is not the only option. That Trump had the last laugh over Gay Mulatto gives every man a shot of testosterone. That Melanie is hot, while Michelle belongs in a zoo, makes every progressive everywhere look and feel bad.

When we successfully do the Dissolution of the Monasteries on the universities, confiscating their endowments, and ending their power as gatekeepers to high status high pay jobs, when we are no longer ruled by the clergy, that will be victory, and the rest will be mopping up operations. It is a long way from here to there, some very bad things will happen on the way, and there may well be a red terror and a civil war along the route, but in the far distance, we can see hope for victory. If Trump fails, he will nonetheless have pointed the way for one that will follow.

The best outcome would be that Democrats launch a coup prematurely, leading to civil war prematurely, and lose it, leaving Trump as King, as happened in the Social War of the Roman Republic, when the Populares played their hand too soon and too recklessly. Worst outcome would be that they launch their coup, get away with it, leading to a rapid succession of coups by ever more extreme factions, as in the coups against Czar Nicolas and King Louis XVI, and, as in those coups, we launch the civil war too late, and lose it. But we have something that they did not have. We can see the pattern, making it possible to step off that path early rather than late, getting an outcome more like that of Social War of Rome, than the French and Russian Revolutions. That would buy us time enough for technological progress in gene editing technologies to save the day, assuming we can fix the fertility problem. The failure of the Roman elite to reproduce led to endless waves of elite replacement, resulting in chaos and instability, so Sulla's restoration failed to last. To fix the fertility problem, we have to restrict sexual female choice. We have to force women to get married, to stay with their husbands, to refrain from sex with anyone other than their husbands, and to obey their husband. Even if we have gene editing, still takes two to raise a child. A high IQ species necessarily has a long childhood, which requires cooperate/cooperate equilibrium between husbands and wives, which equilibrium requires substantial external enforcement. Peoples that allow female sexual choice disappear. Rome got in trouble despite Sulla's restoration because its elite kept disappearing, resulting a dangerous degree of social mobility at the top.

Thermodynamics of Social Entropy

2018-07-14 23:55:39

Entropy is always increasing. A fully disordered society is illustrated by wild animals and primitive peoples such as the Tasmanian aboriginals, where all other creatures except for close kin are enemies, obstacles or sources of raw materials - Hobbes state of war.So if you look back in history, you can always see entropic processes, bringing us back towards that condition.

So, how come ordered societies exist, how come surviving and prosperous societies are generally at least somewhat orderly?

You cannot make something clean without making something else dirty, but you can make any amount of stuff dirty without making anything clean. Order for the ingroup always comes at the expense of someone else: Thus, for example, chastity and monogamy requires men hitting badly behaved women with a stick. (Dalrock banned me for pointing this out.) Thus, for example, in Africa we saw societies that herded cattle and planted crops had to enslave, or kill and eat, vagrants that were apt to hunt other people's cattle and gather from other people's gardens. The shift from hunting and gathering to herding and gardening involved extended cooperation - and a fair bit of brutality to hunters and gatherers.

As birds are born to fly, humans are born to cooperate. That is our key capability. Our telos is various forms of cooperation, as the heart's telos is to circulate blood. The whites of our eyes are white, so that other people can see what we are looking at. We are vulnerable to choking, because our throat is optimized towards making a wider variety of distinct sounds than other animals. We have a more muscles in our face than other animals, so that we can unfalsifiably communicate our emotional state, just as every feature of a bird's anatomy is optimized for low weight and high metabolic output. This cooperation manifested as tribes cooperating to kill other tribes and capture their women. Order consists of extended cooperation. Because entropy naturally tends to increase, because there are a near infinity of ways for society to be disordered, but only a small number of ways for it to be ordered, maintaining order requires a fair bit of ruthlessness towards disorderly people and towards outgroups whose cooperation is unlikely. Gays undermine male solidarity. David's mighty men could cohere because David could love Jonathan.

David could love Jonathan because gays were put to death. Peoples who have gay parades do not win wars.

The ten commandments consist of four commandments concerning man's relationship to God, five commandments that had the effect of ensuring that congregation of the Lord operated on a cooperate cooperate basis, and the final commandment, the tenth commandment, prohibited coming up with clever rationales for undermining, subverting, and re-interpreting those five.

The four commandments that facilitate cooperation are:
Exodus 20:
Honour thy father and thy mother: that thy days may be long upon the land which the LORD thy God giveth thee.
Thou shalt not kill.
Thou shalt not commit adultery.
Thou shalt not steal.
Thou shalt not bear false witness against thy neighbour.

The rule on honoring thy parents and committing adultery secured ownership of family, thus cooperation within the family. The rules against killing, stealing, and false witness enabled economic cooperation on the basis of property rights and the market economy.

And the final commandment:
Thou shalt not covet thy neighbour's house, thou shalt not covet thy neighbour's wife, nor his manservant, nor his maidservant, nor his ox, nor his ass, nor any thing that is thy neighbour's.

prohibits people from concocting ingenious theories as to why someone else's property or wife is rightfully their own - forbids the entire ideology and program of Social Justice.

Compliance to the four commandments concerning God made fellow members of the congregation readily identifiable, and by complying with these four commandments, for which compliance was as visible as possible, one gave other members of the congregation reason to believe one would comply with the other five commandments, for which compliance was less visible, and thus reason to believe that cooperation with people who complied with the first four would be reciprocated and rewarded by cooperation, resulting in cooperate/cooperate equilibrium.

Social Justice Warriors have turned the tenth commandment on its head, making envy and covetousness a sacrament. This explains their chronic failure to cooperate, explains why rallies to save the earth leave a snail trail of trash behind them. Social Justice declares that what people have is "privilege" and should be taken away from them. Which creates a society in which people have no reason to have wealth or family.

A religion is a synthetic tribe. If the priesthood has power and status, and also has open entry into the priesthood, one gets holiness spirals - as for example priestly celibacy. Cooperate cooperate equilibrium, giving every man his due, makes all good members of the religion equal in holiness though unequal in property and power, thus a holiness spiral is going to redefine holiness away from forms that promote cooperation. The tribal religion has to reward exceptional and unusual holiness with honor, but not power and wealth. Send saints to live in a hermitage with spartan living conditions on a remote island as far from the capital as possible, where they can demonstrate superior holiness without subverting and undermining social order. On the one hand, to encourage good behavior, the society must honor supererogatory holiness. On the other hand preaching supererogatory holiness always threatens to redefine holiness in ways that undermine order, making holiness a force of disorder instead of order.

As for example:

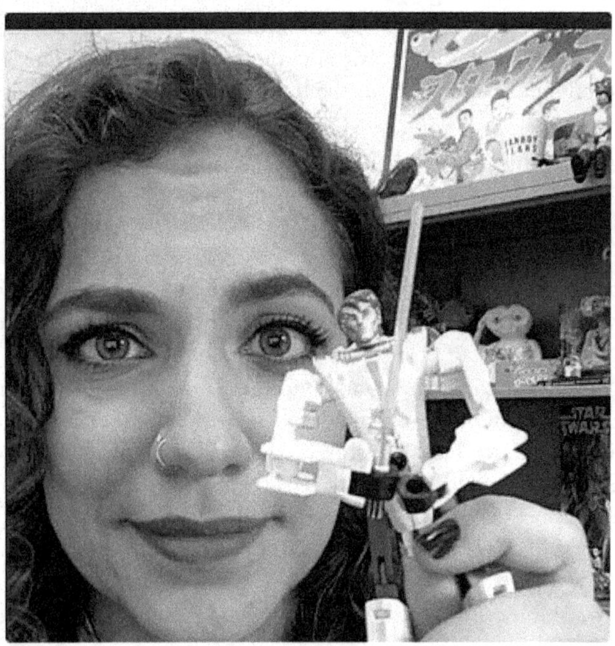

Starbucks hates its customers, and LucasFilm hates its customers, which subverts cooperation on the basis of exchange. While practicing supererogation should be honored, preaching it needs to be forcefully suppressed. People who preach supererogation should not be martyred, which might increase their status, but rather treated like a stray dog that chases chickens - punished in ways that lower their status.

As example Russia dealing with Pussy Riot:

If the Sovereign is forced to punish someone who preaches supererogatory holiness in a way that might potentially increase their status (and Charles the second was forced to burn one conspicuously and irritatingly holy nonconformist woman at the stake)the

Sovereign should lock the body in a mortuary for three days, and on the third day ironically check the body to see if they have risen from the dead. But it is as dangerous to martyr those who preach supererogatory holiness, as it is to tolerate them. The Sovereignmust always strike at primarily at their status, as Russia dealt with Pussy Riot and European University.

While entropy always increases, it is always possible to locally reduce entropy, usually at the expense of someone else less effective and successful at extended cooperation (as, for example, women, pussy riot, gays, or hunter gatherer outgroups).

The highest and best example of this is western civilization, which is anglo civilization, which is the restoration of Charles the Second. The restoration gave us science, technology, corporate capitalism, industrialization, and world empire, which represent the highest level of extended cooperation ever achieved.

The restoration cured the disorderly tendencies of the protestant holiness spiral by putting priests under bishops, and bishops under the King. Which was the imposition of order, at the expense of "non conformists" - whose very name implies their disorderly tendencies. "Non conformists" were priests, professors, judges, and suchlike who were disinclined to accept this hierarchy, on the grounds that the King at the top was conspicuously lacking in holiness. We need to do something similar with our university system, as well as radically reducing its size and the amount of time it sucks out of people's lives - we need to do Charles the Second's Bishops, and Henry the Eighth's dissolution of the monasteries.

Universities have always had as their primary job inculcating people in the official religion, and giving people cultural and scientific knowledge has always been merely their secondary job. Lately, their secondary job has largely been abandoned. It used to be that giving people job skills was entirely irrelevant, since this was done by enforceable apprenticeship.

We shall restore the enforceable apprenticeship system and divest universities of the task of giving people job skills, in the process divesting them of the power to accredit people to jobs. We shall give considerably higher, but still secondary, priority to the task of giving people cultural and scientific knowledge, and change the official religion to make it saner, by erasing all doctrines that are potentially falsifiable by the realities of this world. Members of the elite will still be required to adhere to the official religion, as they are now, but the task of checking adherence will not be outsourced to the universities. Instead, people in state jobs and quasi statal jobs will be required to recite a catechism and take an oath.

Contrary to the myth about the plymouth rock puritans, that early puritans supposedly filled the North American continent, where we have genealogies, puritans are descended from those who left restoration England to establish their own dissident theocracy, not from the pre english civil war wave of migrants fleeing Charles the first, but from the post civil war wave of "noncomformist" migrants fleeing the restoration, fleeing Charles the Second and subsequent Kings. The first wave, the pre civil war wave, left very few direct descendants.

Restoration England was successful at elite eugenic reproduction, because women were kept under control, and cured the disorderly propensities of the protestant reformation by keeping "non conformists" under control, thereby enabling the extended co-operation that made science and industry possible. Immediately after the restoration, we see Ayn Rand's heroic archetype appear, the scientist engineer CEO, mobilizing other people's capital and other people's labor to advance technology and make that technology widely available. Often these were people who before the restoration had competed for superior holiness, (analogous to Musk's subsidized and money burning tesla, solar panels, and solar batteries), but after the restoration competed for creating technology to produce value (analogous to Musk's reusable booster rocket.) This form of order was made possible at the expense of "non conformists", such as the excessively holy woman that Charles the Second burned at the stake.

In order for society to have cooperate/cooperate equilibrium, the science, industry, and technology that we see promoted by the corporate form, in order to promote cooperation with cooperators, the sovereign must promote defection on defectors. One such defector being a holy woman conspicuously holier than Charles the Second. Charles the second successfully redirected status competition from unproductive channels into productive channels, as for example members of the Royal Society gaining status by discovering truth and speaking truth, while previously puritans had gained power and status by having a Christianity that was purer than the other man's Christianity. You will notice that Putin dealt with Pussy Riot's weaponized supererogatory holiness preaching in a way that deliberately maximized disorder - maximized outgroup disorder in order to sustain ingroup order. That is the way to do it.

The restoration created a society that had the greatest cooperate/cooperate equilibrium ever, where people were able to engage in positive sum cooperation, which was made possible by severely negative sum uncooperation - you cannot get more negative sum than burning an excessively holy woman at the stake. If Charles the Second had not burned a holy woman at the stake for excessive, conspicuous, and obnoxiously superior holiness, he would have had the William Wilberforce problem.

Humans are inherently tribal.We have ethnicities and religions, all of which are in substantial part the same phenomenon. A millet is a smaller tribe (religion) within the empire that the empire recognizes and grants some limited self rule and autonomy.

Two tribes cannot co-exist in overlapping territory, except they create little zones for themselves, for example the black table in school cafe. One tribe will always rule, and another will always be ruled.Segregation and Jim Crow was an effort to give blacks autonomy and self rule, make them into a millet, conditional on the black rulers assimilating to white middle class values and behavior. Integration proved to be black dominion. When the blacks were allowed to the front of the bus, they inevitably wound up forcing white people off the buses.

This tribalism is the problem with libertarianism - if you allow liberty, people will use it to synthesize smaller ingroups within the larger group in order to dominate the detribalized majority. William Wilberforce and his "elect" destroyed what the restoration had accomplished, undermining the small scale cooperation between men and women to have children, and the cooperation between elites and individual members of the elite to maintain an empire that kept large scale economic cooperation over the oceans. His successors transliterated the religion of the elect from the next world to this world, creating modern progressivism. Since the transliterated tenets, such as equality, are transparently false to this world, this required them to reject truth telling and truth speaking, resulting in peer review and the replication crisis that has destroyed science.

The earthly telos of holiness is to promote the broadest possible cooperate/cooperate equilibrium. Holiness competition results in people finding grounds to declare other people unholy, thus Starbucks and LucasFilms declare their customers unholy, thus holiness competition destroys the earthly telos of holiness. Therefore we cannot allow excessively holy people to gain power in the state religion. Instead, need to send Social Justice Warriors away from the universities off to a hermitage in a remote island and honor their superior holiness from a safe distance. If someone wants to demonstrate superior holiness, it should be costly for himself, rather than profitable for himself, and costly for everyone around him. Superior holiness and performing superogatory acts has to be made unprofitable.

The murder of the Czar and his family

2018-07-16 08:33:01

A hundred years ago the Czar and his family were murdered, which murder foreshadowed and led to the murder of huge numbers of ordinary people.

Progressives, including supposedly very moderate centrist progressives, made, and continue to make all sorts of myths justifying and rationalizing the murder, revealing their intent to do it all over again.

Myth: The Czar was brutal and oppressive, but the soldiers refused to fire on the revolting masses, so he was overthrown, and thus the communists, representing the masses to power.

Reality: The Czar was a cucked progressive. He had Lenin and Stalin in his hands, guilty of all sorts of crimes that gave him grounds for execution or indefinite imprisonment, but let them off because letists are holier than thou. There were no revolting masses, just a series of coups made in the name of the revolting masses, and such riots and looting as occurred, occurred Ferguson style - the police were ordered to stand back and let the mobs loot stuff and smash stuff.

The February revolution was no revolution - rather the elite allowed the mobs to knock over a few breweries, to provide an excuse for them seizing power from the Czar while he was away at the front.

The communists did not overthrow the Czar. The Kadets overthrew the Czar. Then Kerensky overthrew the Kadets with a policy of no enemies to the left, no friends to the right, which meant he disarmed the military officers, and armed the communists. Then the communists overthrew Kerensky. The leftism of the Czar led to his overthrow by the even lefter Kadets, the indecisive leftism of the Kadets led to their overthrow by Kerensky, and the radical leftism of Kerensky led to his overthrow by the even lefter communists, who then murdered the Czar, and millions of peasants, until the madness ended with them murdering each other.

What happened to Russia was leftism leading to more leftism.

Progressives agree that serfdom was absolutely horrid, and perhaps it was. If it was horrid, the solution should have been to free the serfs and leave the land with the lords. Or perhaps give some of the land to the more competent, successful, and wealthy serfs. But this solution was considered unthinkably horrible and inconceivably reactionary, which implicitly acknowledged that most serfs were not ready to run their own lives. What progressives wanted was the serfs freed with the land. But quite obviously, most serfs were incompetent to operate a small farm. So progressives wanted them to operate the land collectively. But if one man trying to run a small farm is hard, one hundred men trying to run a large farm is considerably harder.

So, Alexander the liberator freed them with collective ownership of the land. Which was predictably a disaster. And there was thereafter a succession of ever lefter government measures to try to deal with the problem, each of which made the problem worse. Russian agriculture still has not recovered. By freeing the serfs *and giving them the land collectively*, but not individually, Alexander the liberator set in motion a slide ever leftwards that continued steadily all the way to the liquidation of the kulaks.

The liberation of the serfs *with collective ownership of the land* created a crisis, for which the solution was always more leftism, which led to more crisis. This created an expectation that the way to power was to be lefter than thou. The Czar's generals and bureaucrats outflanked him on the left. Kerensky's socialists outflanked them on the left, and the Communists outflanked Kerensky on the left. Then the communists proceeded to outflank each other, till Stalin put a stop to that.

If at any time any of Alexander the Liberator's successors had been so horribly repressive as to demonstrate that lefter than thou was a seriously bad career move, as Stalin belatedly demonstrated, the slide leftwards would have halted and stayed halted. But instead the Czars allowed to the progressives to guilt them into doing whatever the progs demanded, which merely excited progressive bloodlust.

Game

2018-07-18 11:26:02

This is not a PUA blog. To learn PUA, read Heartiste[274] and Rollo[275], But, I seem to have been conscripted by the Dark Enlightenment

---

[274]https://heartiste.wordpress.com/
[275]https://amzn.to/2Np41eq

How to deal with woman, thepitch.[276]

> Call +31 J-I-M-I-A-N-I-T-Y *right now* and order our #1 best-selling product, *how to deal with women.*

to issue a post on how to deal with women in a relationship, what do with women after picking them up, and how the religion should deal with women, how the true religion should treat women and support husbands and fathers. So here it is:

Women are wonderful, much better than men in some respects. A woman wants, a woman needs, to serve and obey.

Women are terrible, much worse than men in other respects. All Women Are Like That.

This is the dark enlightenment, so I am leading off with the bad news.

Women are hypergamous. Men want to bang every fertile age chick. My little man salutes most of them. Women, however, only want to bang the very best. So men tend to be nice to every fertile age chick, while women give every attractive man a hard time, to see what he is made of, including the more attractive men in their place of employment, including the boss in their place of employment, so will invariably disrupt the working environment. They will give their husbands a hard time, to see what he is made of, and if you don't pass the test, you become invisible to her. And if you are her boss, also invisible to her.

A lustful man, such as myself, is nice to every fertile age woman he meets. A lustful woman does the opposite. Like Kate in "The Taming of the Shrew", her disruptive behavior and misconduct reveals her hunger. And I see a great deal of disruption and misconduct in the workplace, which disruptive misconduct seems to be strangely invisible to everyone else[277].

Women pay alarmingly little attention to the male hierarchy of status. They want an alpha male, but in our society, alpha males are severely restrained from violence, aggression, and misconduct, which restraint registers with women as not alpha. All Women Are Like That.

Hypergamy never sleeps, a man must always perform, can never relax, is always on stage, can never let his guard down. I generally maintain the semblance of a charismatic arrogant asshole playboy with potential for violence and crime (Marlon Brando in The Wild One) but if General Butt Naked showed up wearing an AK 47, his trademark necklace of human eyeballs, and absolutely nothing else, I would be*$#!%*out of luck.

You*will*be !#!% tests. !#!% tests. Anyone who says it is easy is lying, because women intend it to be hard. They want to separate the men from the boys, and the top men from the ordinary men. If you have an easy magic trick for passing *$#!%* tests, then as soon as chicks figure it out, it will not work any more.

Although women pay alarmingly little attention to the male status hierarchy, that is because our existing hierarchy fails to register with them as real. They are nonetheless much impressed by males backing the status of other males. If you have a driver, you score pussy points because you dominate the driver. If you have a bodyguard, you score huge

---

[276]https://alfanl.com/2018/07/09/how-to-deal-with-woman-the-pitch/
[277]https://blog.reaction.la/economics/the-disastrous-effects-of-females-in-power/

pussy points because the bodyguard registers on women as alpha, and because he implies the potential for violence. Similarly, cops impress women, but you will not be able to get a cop to treat you as high status, though you may well be able to get a security man to treat you as high status. Observe the theatrical way in which Trump deploys presidential security. He is very good at this.

God, of course, is the ultimate high status alpha male. So the husband should be the priest of his family. Say grace, don't let anyone start eating till you start, and don't let family leave the table till you are done.

Paul commanded: 1 Timothy 3:

2. A bishop then must be blameless, the husband of one wife, ...

3. ...

4. One that ruleth well his own house, having his children in subjection with all gravity;

5. (For if a man know not how to rule his own house, how shall he take care of the church of God?)

The Church should support the Sovereign in his state, the husband in his marriage, and the father in his family. And has not been doing that. We got Romance, celebrating adultery[278], at the same time as the Church undermined the power of the Holy Roman Emperor, and tried to require mandatory female consent to marriage. Priestly celibacy is a Christian holiness spiral, without support in the New Testament or the practices of apostles, which has been blowing up in scandal since it was introduced, because, as Paul observed, God calls very few men to celibacy.

Female consent should only required for virtuous women. Female misconduct should be dealt with by shotgun marriage, and in practice, despite near a thousand years of Church opposition, misbehaving women were shotgun married until quite recently. The holiness spiral that led to Romance, mandatory female consent, and priestly celibacy resulted in a Christianity that has failed to support proper earthly authority for husbands, fathers, and Kings, and in recent times has become dementedly and dangerously hostile to the authority of fathers and husbands[279].

All marriages that actually work are quietly eighteenth century. If your Church is hostile to such relationships, and it very likely is, you just cannot go there. Because then your wife or girlfriend sees you emasculated by other men, and by the the most alpha male of them all, God, and then she starts cruising social media looking for someone more alpha. The Pauline rules of worship (that women should cover their heads, and should not speak in church, nor exercise leadership positions) provide psychological support for the proper relationship of men and women, thus provide social support for durable relationships, thus make it possible for men and women to cooperate to conceive and raise children. If a Church deviates from these practices, it is likely not just failing to support, but aggressively undermining, the relationships necessary between men and women to form families. Dalrock has a great pile of horrifying anecdotes on this topic. Don't get burned. Do not let your wife or girlfriend see you bow your head before enemies who hate you. You need a God that backs you, not a God that emasculates you. If your church edits Ephesians 5:21 into Ephesians 5:22, and then drops Ephesians 5:23-29, they are

---

[278]https://dalrock.wordpress.com/2016/12/14/courtly-love-the-origins-of-cuckchivalry/

[279]https://dalrock.wordpress.com/2018/06/12/fathers-day-sermons-are-the-symptom-not-the-disease/

your enemies, they hate you, they intend you harm, they intend to deny you children and grandchildren. Ephesians 5:21 is part of Ephesians 5:19-21, referring to the congregation, while Ephesians 5:22-29 refers to the husband and the wife. If they cannot say 5:22 without first saying 5:21, they are evil people who intend you harm, they twist the words of the bible to emasculate you before your women. By quoting 5:21-22, without quoting 5:19-21, or 5:22-29, by joining these two verses, and separating them from their context, they place a false context on 5:22, which false context is intended to harm you and poison the relationships between men and women, for the context of 5:22 is 5:22-29, not 5:19-21. Whosoever does this is is a heretic and a white knight. White knights are evil and dangerous, and need to be punched out whenever you can get away with it. The God of Saint Paul's Church backed husbands and fathers. Accept no substitute Gods. The usual substitutes will destabilize your sexual relationships, impairing your ability to reproduce. There is no better ground for violence than that some male is impairing your sexual relationships and capability to reproduce. You need to defend your extended phenotype.

For your relationship to survive, you cannot be hardcore asshole all the time. From time to time you have show her a bit of nice guy beta provider. But not too much. Hard exterior, soft inner core that only she can reach. It is easy to overdo the nice guy. You have to make her earn it, or she will not appreciate it. You have to keep her on her toes. Having gracefully handled an exceptionally brutal !#!% test, then it is a really bad time for any action that is the slightest bit chivalrous.

Women want attention. They want a lot of attention. I wish women had an off switch like a television and could be put in a closet, but unfortunately they do not. Women want to help you. They want to be valuable to you, and you have to find ways to keep them busy, and then spend time appreciating what they have done. Quite frequently she will however not do stuff you have told her to do. This is both a $#!% test (she is daring you to make her do it) and also a cry for attention. Hear that cry.

Yes, you have to give a woman lots of time, energy, and attention, or she is going to go looking for attention on social media, where she will find a hundred males richer than you, handsomer than you, and with bigger tools (which they will show her) than yours. But at the same time, Poon Commandment Number Three[280]: "You shall make your **mission**, not your woman, your priority" The natural order is that a woman's focus is her man, and a man's focus is something higher. If your focus is her, suddenly and mysteriously she will lose interest in your interest. You have to give her attention, but you have to keep her on short rations and make her earn it, because you are an important person with important things to do.

When you get her doing stuff for you, reward her liberally with attention. When not satisfied, turn your face away. She wants attention, but also wants to earn it, not simply demand it. Shouting and spanking is attention and drama, and women love attention and drama, so shouting and spanking is not very effective in getting compliance. Women love to be made to comply. Just as you tip generously so that you can not tip when displeased, you should supply attention generously so that you can not supply attention when displeased. This is more effective in obtaining compliance.

But some kinds of attention are bad. If you are looking at her, and she is looking at

---

[280] https://heartiste.wordpress.com/the-sixteen-commandments-of-poon/

her task, this is the wrong dynamic. She should be looking at you, and you should be looking at your mission. Reversing the dynamic will make her unhappy.

A woman wants you to use her, to exploit her, to take advantage of her. At the same time she is going to make it difficult for you to do so. Life would be so much easier if women had an off switch, but since they don't, you just have to get on with the use, the exploitation, and the taking advantage. She wants to please you, so you need to give her avenues and opportunities to please you. At the same time, she is going to test you for weakness and neediness, and the tests are going to be hard. You cannot be weak or needy. Have to be arrogant, not weak, and demanding, not needy. You should want lots of things from her, and communicate that you are pleased when you get those things - while at the same time being totally entitled to get it, pleased but not grateful, because you are completely entitled to get whatever you want from her.

And, of course, there is that soft inner core. You should care, not about what she wants, for that will only irritate her, but about what she should want, as though she was your own flesh.

You will notice that for everything I have told you to do, I have also told you almost the opposite: Be an asshole and cherish her. Give her attention and don't give her attention. But it is worse than that. The difference between what I am telling you to do, and telling you to not do, is pre verbal, and by expressing the difference in words, I necessarily oversimplify and exaggerate the difference.

Barnacling

2018-07-27 06:53:56

Leftists have a word "entryism", which they use when privately talking amongst themselves. They never plainly state what entryism[281] is, but if you are part of the in group, it becomes obvious that they are talking in code. If the chans got hold of some emails about "entryism", would probably interpret it as referring to satanic rituals involving sex with children.

I don't know what "pizza" means in the pizzagate emails, other than that it obviously does not mean pizza, but I know what entryism means:

1. Identify a respected institution.

2. kill it.

3. gut it.

4. wear its carcass as a skin suit, while demanding respect

Since outsiders have never heard the word "entryism" used, they invented their own word for this: "Barnacling[282]"

---

[281]https://blog.reaction.la/tag/entryism/
[282]https://disneystarwarsisdumb.wordpress.com/2018/06/30/the-phases-of-a-geeker-gate/

Science died with peer review, and is now a skin suit worn by a demon. As social justice warriors moved into technology companies, the same has happened with technology. If you are a gamer, you will have noticed that you no longer need new hardware every year. If you are a fan of self driving cars, you will have noticed that they can self drive just fine 99.99% of the time, which is 0.01% less than is useful, and that impressive as this is, it is not getting any better, nor is it likely to get any better. Similarly, Google Translate was a gigantic achievement, but no real progress has been made in automatic translation since Google went social justice, quite a long time ago.

Musk is a serial scammer, always hyping technology that does not exist and that he has no real intention of producing, but his reusable booster was a real technological achievement. It was, of course, produced by male geeks, and now that the eye of Soros has fallen upon them, they are finding their job redefined from producing a reusable earth to orbit rocket, Musk's proposed, and genuinely intended BFR, to proving that black muslim women produced all technology, and whites stole it from them. Musk's electric cars and solar city are scams, which could have only produced a profit through Hillary's crony capitalism, but he really did intend the BFR, the re-usable earth to orbit and back again rocket. Reading between the lines, I feel him giving up hope for it now, which is going to destroy the lives and careers of a horde of really great rocket scientists. If no BFR, there is not much for them to do now. Their careers are going through the same dead end arc as a Fortran engineer's, or a nuclear engineer's or a climate scientist who tells peer reviewers what he actually observed, instead of observing what they tell him he observed.

The term "Barnacling" was coined in reference to the Social Justice takeover and destruction of the Star Wars mythos and intellectual property, but I have seen the same thing happen to various open source projects that adopted a contributor code of conduct.[283] Instead of the objective being to produce good software to serve some valuable purpose, the objective becomes giving black women STEM credits, and the project suffers bitrot and technical debt. The creators are, sooner or later, accused of mansplaining, sexual harassment, rape and racism, they become radioactive and permanently unemployable. And without them, the project mysteriously languishes while being used to adorn the resumes of progressives who do not know what a dongle or a fork is[284].

If you adopt Github's community code of conduct, your STEM career is going to die, because you are giving people who hate you and everything you stand for, who hate your race, hate your sex, and hate the entire civilization that your ancestors created, the tools with which to destroy your life.

If you have heard leftists talk about entryism (and you will have only heard them talking about it if they are confident you are a fellow leftist) it swiftly becomes obvious that they are talking in code about something that gives them great pleasure. You might suppose that the code is code for satanic rituals and diddling little boys, which is probably how the chans would interpret it, but they are talking about something more fun that that: They are talking in code about destroying the lives of people that they hate. And they hate you, and they hate everything you represent.

---

[283]https://help.github.com/articles/adding-a-code-of-conduct-to-your-project/

[284]https://www.reddit.com/r/programming/comments/1amhhi/forking_and_dongle_jokes_dont_belong_at_tech/

Stealing from the best[285], here is a detailed description of how social justice warriors destroy games and movies:

1. SJW CRITICISM – The intellectual property is criticized by SJWs for being racist, sexist, misogynist, homophobic, and a smattering of other things.

2. Intellectual property IS ABOUT TO UNDERGO REBOOT – or reimagining, or remake, or whatever term is fashionable at the time.

3. THE BARNACLING – SJWs barnacle themselves to the intellectual property both within its production and without in the fan base, and start lecturing long time fans.

4. FAN CRITICISM – Long time fans of the intellectual property voice legitimate criticism of the new direction.

5. SJW RESPONSE TO FAN CRITICISM – A large fan backlash is created when SJWs both within and without the production falsely accuse critics of being racist, sexist, misogynist, homophobic etc.

6. DISMISSING THE BACKLASH – Media publishes pieces declaring the backlash doesn't exist.

7. IGNORING THE BACKLASH – Media publishes pieces instructing others to ignore the "tiny vocal minority.

8. SUPPRESSING THE BACKLASH – Blogs and websites delete or otherwise "redact" critical comments and posts in discussion forums under the aegis of "hate speech."

9. BACKLASH INTENSIFIES – As an inevitable side effect of suppression, backlashers seek out other venues to express their criticism, and some publish their own, growing the backlash exponentially.

10. HATE HOAXES & FALSE FLAGS – The rank and file SJW activists get heavily involved in shouting down critics, and creating false flags and hate hoaxes in an effort to discredit critics.

---

[285] https://disneystarwarsisdumb.wordpress.com/2018/06/30/the-phases-of-a-geeker-gate/

11. Intellectual property FAILURES – The intellectual property starts to falter as fans drift away and sales plummet.

12. THE DAMSEL IN DISTRESS – A female member of the production (it could also be a gay man) is granted victim status over a fishy event in order to deflect from the failures of the intellectual property, and shame critics into silence.

13. DESPERATE PLEAS FOR COMMUNITY MANAGEMENT – "White Knights" in the media call for creative authorities to smack down the backlash and restore control of the narrative in response to The Damsel In Distress event. Media publishes multiple articles with the same talking points and buzzwords such as "toxic" in an effort to mischaracterize the fan base. Major news outlets report on the story, and quote these "think" pieces as authoritative.

14. ANSWERING THE CALL – Celebrities and creative cast & crew answer the media's call, and make public statements admonishing critical fans, typically over false accusations.

15. THE FINAL PUSH – Media entities, and rank and file SJWs tell long time fans to go find something else if they don't like it anymore, in a last ditch effort to push critics out of the "community" once and for all.

16. Intellectual property BLEEDING – The intellectual property continues to hemorrhage money, as long time fans continue to abandon the intellectual property in droves.

17. FANBASE OBLITERATION – The fanbase is utterly destroyed, leaving behind only the small handful of SJWs who don't make any purchases.

18. THE END – The new incarnation of the intellectual property comes to an end. Since the majority of the fan base has abandoned it, there's no more controversy or discussion about it. It's over. The best case scenario is that the original intellectual property is largely forgotten with the exception of a few die-hards who still carry the torch. The worst case scenario is that the new incarnation of the intellectual property overwrites the original intellectual property, and the original intellectual property is forgotten altogether and overshadowed by the new incarnation in all future media mentions.

19. MIGRATION – The remaining SJWs jump ship to devour a new intellectual property that is popular, and undergoing a transitional phase.

20. REBIRTH – The process begins anew.

If you are working in tech or science, as for example Musk's rocket, expect the same, though with far less reporting by major newsmedia. I have seen the same at Google and at projects that adopted a community code of conduct[286], and reading between the lines of Musk's tech announcements, I can feel his reusable earth to orbit rocket fading from a real project that would create income, purpose, dignity, and status for a great many rocket scientists, to yet another of his many tech scams. (As, for example, his self driving car: When Musk decided to produce a self driving car without lidar, it was obvious he had given up on the possibility of producing an actual self driving car.) Today, only a scammer can produce science and technology, because you have lie to social justice warriors, and scammers are apt to scam all sides, scamming those who have high hopes for science and technology, and scamming those who hope to have income, purpose, and dignity in creating it. Trump is the only notable scammer who seems to be genuinely on our side.

Socialism

2018-07-29 08:21:30

Leftism necessarily goes ever lefter. But what is "lefter"? Leftism has no essence, it is just a coalition to knock over the apple cart in order to grab some of the apples, so "lefter" is whatever direction looks like some apples could be knocked loose. "Lefter" could be almost anything, head off in almost any direction, depending on fashion, opportunity, and perceived vulnerability of people who have stuff.

Leftism necessarily goes ever lefter, because having knocked over one apple cart, there is now an apple shortage, and people then need to knock over another, and because of the broken window effect - when leftism works, in the sense that apples were rolling around, they go looking for something else to knock over, since that apple cart is already smashed up. Leftists perceive wealth as a snapshot in time, as if it were a gift from God. The ways that wealth is created are meaningless to them, it is a pie to be sliced up and enjoyed.

Right now "lefter" is heading off towards ethnic cleansing of whites and desexing of males. Many leftists find this alarming, being white or male or both, so are trying to find some other direction, any other direction – and socialism is some other direction.

Socialism is not currently a threat, being so thoroughly and totally discredited:

---

[286]https://help.github.com/articles/adding-a-code-of-conduct-to-your-project/

CAPITALISM
Bread is lined up
Waiting for People
SOCIALISM
PEOPLE LINE UP WAITING FOR BREAD

But what Democrats hope to do is run on a program of Ferguson and Krystalnacht, and then, instead of delivering Ferguson and Kristallnacht, deliver socialism. "Instead of burning down the supermarkets in Ferguson, leave them standing and we democrats, being such nice caring people, will order them to give you free stuff. So much nicer. Please don't burn my house down, kill me, and rape my children." Might work, but the dynamics of leftism are likely to get away from them. Venezuela promised socialism, wound up delivering socialism plus Kristallnacht.

People keep telling me that socialism works great - the statistics always improve enormously under socialism. Thus, for example, Venezuela has cured inflation and put everyone on a pension, and given everyone a university education, and provided universal healthcare. UN statistics always show socialist countries doing wonderfully well on the Human Development Index.

Of course they cured inflation by setting official prices, and you cannot actually buy anything worth buying at official prices, and universal healthcare gets you a bed to die in. Universal healthcare provides abundant caring, but a distinct shortage of health, and universal university education produces ignorance instead of knowledge.

In a thread on my blog, a supposed reactionary has been telling me how socialist agriculture worked great in Russia long ago and far away, and they had to do it because the climate being harsh, they had to have collective agriculture because it works so much better. And, similarly, lots of leftists will tell you how great socialism has been for Cuba and Venezuela - though the internet makes this story a bit more difficult to get away with than when they tell it about far away places and long ago times.

Poz, capitalism, and free markets.

2018-08-01 01:34:04

Is there a connection between free markets and Poz. Is a sound reactionary polity somewhat socialist?

In the comments some have been making the stupid argument that poz is the result of evil Jewish capitalists pursuing profit, that gay marriage was promoted to sell wedding cakes, which argument scarcely deserves a reply.

But others have been making more sophisticated arguments, which arguments deserve to be promoted into a post.

Obviously sound economic policy is trade with outsiders, which requires the Christian program of peace with outsiders, which is apt to result in the hyper Christian holier than Jesus program of surrender to outsiders.

Obviously the Libertarian Party promotes free markets, and also promotes poz that will at best result in whites being ethnically cleansed out of America, and males being spiritually castrated, and at worst could result in whites being physically genocided and males being physically castrated. This started with the nineteenth century English prime minister Gladstone building a coalition between economists and the hyperpuritan leftist evangelicals, which was swiftly devoured by the left, and ever since then libertarians have been trying to revive that coalition by accepting ever greater levels of ever more suicidal poz and ever more emasculating poz.

So in this sense, obviously there is a connection between sound economic policy and suicidal poz, manifest in the logic of trade, manifest in the holiness spiral of Christianity, manifest in Gladstone and manifest in the Libertarian party.

(But not however manifest in capitalists selling wedding cakes to gays, nor in capitalists selling mortgages to cat-eating illegal immigrants with no income, no job, and no assets. Obviously making marriage gay reduces marriage, does not increase it, obviously gays do not get married except to humiliate Christians and prevent straights from getting and staying married, and obviously selling mortgages to cat-eating unemployed illegal immigrants loses money. Obviously very few non Asian minorities can successfully handle a substantial mortgage, thus attempts to provide a substantial number of non Asian minorities with substantial mortgages inevitably and entirely predictably blew up in the loss of a trillion dollars. Whiteness predicts loan repayment better than credit history, except for the longest and most stringent credit histories. Even Asian nonwhites have substantially higher levels of credit scam for the same level of credit history, and non Asian non whites are all scammers, as near to all of them as makes no difference, just as all female CEOs and board members blow up the company as if it was a marriage to a beta male. If a non Asian nonwhite repaid a mortgage, it is solely because he flipped the house for a profit, and the real estate agent had to take the back payments on the mortgage out of the sale, in order to deliver a clean deed to the buyer. If he had a clean credit history before he took the mortgage, it was faked up. All women are like that, and all non asian minorities are like that.)

Carlylean Restorationist argues[287]

>

> Are you happy with Poz so long as there's a free market liberated from central planners?

>

> I'm sorry but I'm just not, at all. I'd rather live in 1988 Berlin not because I love five year plans, Soviets deciding what brands of breakfast cereal will be on the shelves (if any) and tanks on every corner.

> I'd rather live in 1988 Berlin than 2018 Berlin because 2018 Berlin's violent, rapey and full of filth, while 1988 Berlin isn't.

> I'd feel safer, more at home, in the 1988 version of Berlin.

>

> (I use Berlin rather than London not because of any preference for it – quite the opposite in fact. The reason is that 1988 Berlin had the worst kind of economic policy imaginable to one of our mindset. The thing is, in spite of that policy – or (red pill) because of it – it doesn't suffer from what 2018 Berlin suffers from under global relatively free trade.)

Well yes, but the brown face of the Democratic party, like Venezuela, has close to the worst economic policy imaginable, and also at the same time has poz at ethnic cleansing levels, in that the whiteish minority is being driven out of Venezuela Kristallnacht style.

Eighteenth century England had reasonably sound economic policy, and also far less poz than any twentieth or twenty first century society.

So, if we compare 1988 Berlin with 2018 Berlin, or with the suicidal ethnomasochist globohomo policy of the Libertarian party, looks like a strong connection between sound economics, and suicidal poz.

If we compare eighteenth century England, with Gladstone's England, looks like a strong connection between sound economic policy, and seriously damaging levels of poz. Gladstone began today's attack on the family, began the replacement of marriage with child support, and turned the British empire into the anti British empire, foreshadowing today's anti American "International Community" empire.

If we compare the Libertarian Party with almost anyone, looks like a strong connection between sound economic policy, suicidal ethnomasochism, and globohomo self castration.

On the other hand, if we compare Trump's America with Venezuela, or Trump with the brown face of the Democratic Party, or eighteenth century England with almost anywhere, looks like a strong connection between sound economic policy, free markets, and lack of poz. The libertarians attack Trump for insufficient capitalism, and insufficient poz, while the brown Democrats attack him for excessive capitalism, and insufficient poz.

The emancipation of the Russian serfs was simultaneously suicidal poz, and bad economic policy. I read that the "lavish lifestyles" of the nobility were harshly curtailed, and I also read that famine followed so it would seem that the lavish lifestyles of the serfs were also harshly curtailed. Which only makes sense if leftism did exactly what it always does: Knock over the apple cart to grab the apples. The emancipation of the serfs was a disaster for almost everyone in agriculture, particularly the serfs. The emancipation of the serfs was a disaster from day one, and steadily got worse and worse all the way to the liquidation

---

[287] https://blog.reaction.la/economics/socialism/#comment-1858715

of the kulaks, because the emancipation was accompanied by the introduction of collective land ownership. The correct solution was to emancipate serfs without land, converting them into agricultural laborers, tenant farmers, and sharecroppers. But the left was already campaigning vehemently against emancipation, and had it been done that way Alexander would have gone down in Whig history as worse than Vlad the impaler. So in Czarist Russia we see a connection between unsound economic policy, and poz leading to suicidal poz. Bad economic policy, in the form of collective land ownership, led to more poz, which eventually led to a disproportionately Jewish communist party taking charge. (Albeit Stalin continued bad economic policy while massively reducing poz.)

So yes, there is a connection between sound economic policy and ethnomasochistic rule by globohomos, since sound economics favors peace with outsiders, and favoring peace with outsiders is apt to blur into favoring surrender to hostile outsiders.

But Charles the second introduced sound economic policy at the same time as he exiled poz, and *burned poz at the stake for heresy.*

Defining Restoration and Reaction

2018-08-02 08:04:38

Social Matter, without changing its claim to be the blog of the restoration, has gone commie. Having been linking to centrist cuckservatives and pozzed libertarians for some time, is now linking to out and out communists pushing race revolution to implement Maduro style socialism in a brown and universalist world ruled by the international community.

The literal meaning of poz is a reference to the practice of political gays of deliberately infecting themselves with HIV in order to be holier than the next homosexual. Means intentionally becoming HIV positive to get intersectionality points. The metaphorical meaning of poz is the adoption of policies and programs likely to destroy one's ethnic group, one's friends, one's own career, and oneself, as for example a project code of conduct for one's own project.

So it is time to define the reaction and the restoration. Who is in, who is out:

The reactionary position is that leftism was evil, absurd, and mad in 1820, has been getting more evil, more absurd, and more mad, ever since, and the Restorationist program is that we need to be ruled by Kings.

The central insight of Moldbug was to look at anglosphere movement left starting the clock with the overthrow of Charles the First, rather than starting with the Nazis.

Nazis were and are leftists, just leftists who have been left behind by ninety years of movement further left, so if you start the clock at Nazism, the trend is less obvious, and less obviously headed towards catastrophe, mass murder, and social collapse. Hitler was weak on the women question, turning the clock back to early Weimar or moderate Weimar, rather than pre Weimar, while America and Hollywood from 1939 to 1963, after first wave anglosphere feminism and before second wave anglosphere feminism, was far to the right of Hitler, and far more red pilled that Hitler, whose beta orbiter propensities were notorious. Thus, for example, in the immensely popular show "I love Lucy", it is frequently implied that Lucy is going to be spanked for her many amusing misdeeds, that domestic discipline is a normal part of a normal and healthy marriage. The plotline of an "I Love Lucy" episode is that Lucy is a naughty girl, who does something naughty, which always turns out badly, implying that women need rule by husbands to keep them from getting into trouble.

If, however, you start the clock at Charles the First, the trend line is clear. Puritans are holier than thou, and Social Justice Warriors are holier than thou. Puritans make war on marriage, the family, and Christmas, and Social Justice Warriors make war on marriage, the family, and Christmas.

The restoration of Charles the Second in 1660 rolls them back and keeps them back for one hundred and sixty years in England. Hence our program of the Restoration.

The left has continuity of organization, personnel, and institutions all the way from the Puritans. Harvard was their theological headquarters, their Rome, once exiled from England by Charles the second. The American Revolution was a bad thing, and the founders were bad people, because it gave the Puritans control of a large part of America, and the War of Northern Aggression a worse thing, the Puritans conquering those states whose state religion was different from their own to impose a single unified state religion, headquartered in Harvard, on all of the United States. The War of Northern Aggression was not fought to make slaves free, nor to impose tariffs on the South, but to erase the Episcopalianism of Charles the Second and to capture the schools and universities for Harvard.

Progressivism is not Judaism, but is Christianity, a Christianity that first became holier than thou, then holier than Jesus, and is now holier than God. The founding fathers were Deists because they were holier than Jesus, and the progressives are holier than God. If you endorse the founding fathers, you endorse leftism. If all men are created equal then our civilization is going to be erased from history, and white people are going to be ethnically cleansed. If all men are created equal, it is totally unfair that not everyone in the world is free to move to America, vote in American elections, and get their share of my stuff. The failure of the founding fathers to torture each other to death for insufficient leftism was an unprincipled exception, and every unprincipled exception gets rolled back by those even more holy.

People adopt evil and insane principles to make themselves each more holy than each other, because proclaiming extravagant principles is easier and more visible than actually conducting oneself well to family, friends, and allies. The principles swiftly become so noble that they have horrifying implications. Those espousing those noble principles refuse to notice or carry out the horrifying and insane implications of those principles. And having successfully grabbed power on the basis of the extreme holiness of those principles, find themselves outflanked on the left by those even holier, who *do* notice and *do* carry out, and this holiness spiral has been driving our history since Charles the First. The extermination of white people, the destruction of Western Civilization, and the castration of males are logically implied by the remarkable purity of the Christianity of those seeking jobs in the state religion under Charles the First, which logic they failed to notice at the time, but are now starting to notice.

If you blame men for the misconduct of women, you endorse leftism. Women need to be under male authority in order to flourish and form families, and males need authority over their families to flourish and form families. Women should remain under the authority of their fathers till transferred to the authority of their husbands. If state and society fails to back legitimate male authority over females, you get defect/defect equilibrium, and everyone, male and female, finds it difficult to form families and have children. Cooperate cooperate equilibrium is inconsistent with moment to moment consent to sex. In order to reproduce, men and women have to agree to stick it out for richer for poorer, for better or worse, in sickness and in health, which means that people should be incapable of making sense of the self contradictory thought and phrase "marital rape" - it should be inexpressible and unthinkable.

Progressivism and the enlightenment is a religion, an evil, crazy, ugly, ignorant and stupid religion, worse by far than snake handling, speaking in tongues, young earth creationist Christianity, for that Jesus rose from the dead is unfalsifiable, and it takes a fair bit of thought and work with a crowbar and a sledge hammer to falsify young earth creationism, while anyone can and routinely does falsify that men are created equal. Similarly, speaking in tongues is not nearly as ugly and stupid as modern art, or modern architecture.

The timetable of movement left is as follows:

Holiness struggle for jobs in the state Church under Charles the First. Charles' bishops come under attack for insufficient holiness. Alliance with with far against near ensues as English holier than thou heretics forget about religious, cultural, ethnic differences to ally with Scots, who dislike Charles the First and his Bishops for completely different reasons. Charles the first fails to crack down on treason, so treason flourishes until it is too late to crack down on it. Loses his head.

Puritans rapidly get ever lefter, with war on Christmas and desecration of marriage. Cromwell takes fright when he sees the levellers, who resemble modern Republican cuckservatives, and the diggers, who resemble modern communist hippies, and cracks down, halting the holiness spiral at levels that are not all that crazy.

Restoration: Charles the Second regains power, institutes a sane Church of England under himself and his Bishops. Exiles the Puritans to America. If you check the genealogies of Puritans, they are all descended from those who fled Charles the Second, not the Mayflower crowd. When someone claims descent from those who came across on the Mayflower, he is actually descended from a relative of those who came across on the Mayflower, which relative stayed in England or returned to England to rule with his fellow Puritans, till he got kicked out by Charles the Second.

Charles the Second does a Deng, instituting the corporate capitalism of the joint stock corporation. We see Ayn Rand's hero engineer CEO mobilizing other people's capital and other people's labor to advance technology and make it widely available appear, which in time gives us the industrial and technological revolution. We also see the East India company formed to begin the conquest of the world. Charles the Second raises the furtive Invisible College to become the Royal Society, making the scientific method high status. With the Royal Society it becomes high status to win arguments by finding evidence and presenting evidence. The scientific, industrial, and technological revolutions get rolling, along with the British empire.

This is the restoration that we talk about. We want Trump or some general to do a Deng, to do a Charles the Second. We need democracy to end so that the mess can be put right. George the Third was on the right side, continuing the sane, sensible, and successful program of Charles the Second. The founding fathers were on the wrong side. Charles the second was Deng Xiaoping. Locke and Jefferson were Trotsky and Lenin, knocking over the apple cart to grab some of the apples.

Things go wrong in England with increasing unwillingness to discipline upper class wives. George the fourth screws the wives of aristocrats, while his wife cuckolds him. In 1820 he attempts to divorce his wife, in the process revealing that he is massively cuckolded, and becomes a figure of ridicule. His divorce is denied, because women are supposedly naturally so pure and virtuous that they can only do bad things because bad men make them do those bad things. The power of Kings ends when George the fourth goes massively public with how badly he has been cuckolded, instead of locking his wife in the tower. When George the Third told Pitt to take a long walk off a short pier, that showed Kings in charge. When the adulterous George the fourth could not divorce his flagrantly adulterous wife, that showed kings absurd.

Immediately British fertility starts falling, and has continue to fall to the present day, because if women are saints, they should rule men. Hence the current condition of marriage.

In 1840, the status of warriors comes under attack, and the British empire starts to be transformed into the anti British empire, as the American empire is the anti American empire, with hostile elites using the empire against their own people.

In 1854 Lord Cardigan, upon receiving suicidally stupid orders, personally led the charge, getting far in front of his men. Ordered to make an attack that was certain to fail with horrifying casualties, he carried out the attack by personally whacking the leading enemy officer, then immediately retreating, before all of his men had arrived, thus complying with orders to the letter, while ensuring that as few of his men as possible got killed by those stupid orders, in the process by exposing himself to more danger than any of his men. For this, he has been ridiculed and condemned ever since. Lord Cardigan, who in obedience to stupid and suicidal orders, led the charge of the light brigade was demonized. The whore Florence nightingale was made into a hero. Camp followers were deemed to be actual soldiers and put in uniform, with the inevitable consequence that proportion of actual soldiers in the military has been falling ever since. The British army, which has about two hundred generals, can now today field only about two hundred actual fighting men.

We are always ruled by priests or warriors, and giving camp followers the uniforms of warriors is a priestly blow at the status of warriors. Harvard is priests, being a theological college founded by Puritans for the purpose of religious rule by the extremely holy. Putting camp followers in uniform is a blow to the status of uniforms, to prevent rule by warriors, as is denigrating men like Lord Cardigan because he demonstrated both his loyalty to both his men and his superior officers when those loyalties came in conflict.

If you learned about men like Lord Cardigan, you would start to think that being ruled by such men, rather than ruled by those that hate us, sounds like a pretty good deal. For this, he has been condemned and ridiculed ever since. If to wear an officer's uniform, a man had to show loyalty to those above him, display loyalty to those below, and to show courage in battle, you would be inclined to obey the man in an officer's uniform. And so, the supply of uniforms to camp followers, and officer uniforms to camp follower bureaucrats. But if you can get the same uniforms, same pay, same status, and same honors, without battle or loyalty, who wants to get involved in battle? Hence the current ridiculous condition of the British army. There is no danger of British military takeover, because their officers are as absurd and contemptible as Lord Cardigan is depicted as being.

After World War II the American Empire got the upper hand over the British Empire, with the disastrous result that Harvard got the upper hand over the Royal Society, replacing the scientific method by peer review, by the the theological method of consensus building. It ceases to be high status to win arguments by finding evidence and presenting evidence, and instead becomes high status to win arguments by having one's argument incorporated into the state religion. Science died then, hence Global Warming and all the rest, and by 1972, the death of science began to afflict one technological field after another. Hence the reproducibility crisis.

The reactionary position is that leftism was evil, absurd, and mad in 1820, has been getting more evil, more absurd, and more mad, ever since, and the Restorationist program is that we need to be ruled by someone like Lord Cardigan.

Evolution

2018-08-04 08:09:05

Evolution is on topic for reaction, for the nature of women makes sense and is explicable in terms of Darwinian evolution[288], in terms of evolutionary psychology. You can also explain it as the curse of Eve, but if you explain it as the curse of Eve, it is rather arbitrary. Why did God curse women that way, and not some other way? (Answer, because we are risen killer apes, not fallen angels.) And because women are cursed in this fashion we cannot trust them to make sexual and reproductive choices. Nor can we trust them to vote, for they are going to vote for invasion, conquest, and the extermination of their menfolk.

Reed[289] criticizes evolution on the basis of irreducible complexity - that living creatures could not have evolved in small steps because its functionality is inherently complex.

This criticism is bunkum. No one has produced a single example of irreducible complexity in living creatures. Complex systems in living creatures are excessively and unnecessarily complicated, not irreducibly complicated. The reason for the unnecessary complexity is that they are adapted from a system that did something else. For example, inside the the dolphin's flipper is a hand for climbing trees. Hence considerably more complicated than the fish's fin.

---

[288] https://neurotoxinweb.wordpress.com/2018/08/04/women-jerks-and-evolutionary-psychology/
[289] https://www.unz.com/freed/more-on-evolution-from-the-mail-room/

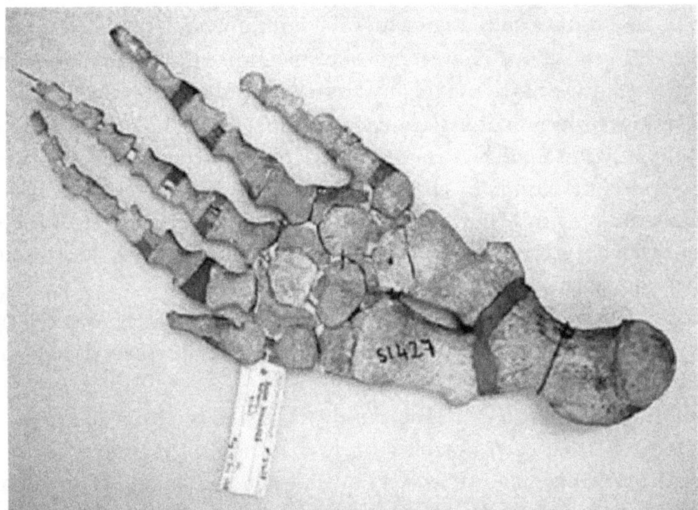

The dolphin's fin is not the simplest possible fin. It is the simplest possible fin that you can derive in small steps from a hand for climbing trees.

This all too reducible complexity is compelling evidence for evolution, not an argument against it. That the dolphin's fin is overly complicated is proof that the ancestors of dolphins climbed trees, and that the hands of the tree climbers were themselves adapted from the bottom gripping hands of first tetrapods.

However, while we have compelling evidence that existing living creatures evolved from simpler creatures of lower evolutionary grade, that all the animals you can recognize as animals evolved from the urbilatarian, a creature with jelly like flesh, a quite complicated brain, a heart, a liver, two very simple eyes that could barely see anything, a quite good sense of smell, and a single orifice used for sex, birth, eating, excreting, breathing, and smelling, Reed nonetheless has a compelling argument in that we don't have a plausible example of life that could have evolved from non life. Current earthlike conditions could not support forms of nonlife capable of evolving into life. While the complexity of existing life forms is quite certainly reducible, no one has produced something simple enough to appear spontaneously from nonlife. In this sense, yes, irreducible complexity.

Maybe during the Hadean era of the earth high energy life forms appeared that could not exist in current earthlike conditions, and as the earth calmed down, evolved into forms capable of existing in current Earthlike conditions. Maybe on the comets low energy life forms appeared that could not exist in current earthlike conditions, and evolved into creatures capable of existing in current Earthlike conditions - I tend to the latter theory, and think that the first forms of life were low energy, lived in conditions very far from earthlike, in places very far from earth, and existed long before the sun was formed.

Or maybe God created the first urbilatarian. Reed's argument is an argument in support of that position But if God did create the first urbilatarian, evolution has been running since then, as is proven by the Dolphin's fin and the Panda's thumb. So, even if God created the first urbilatarian, Darwinian evolution still explains the otherwise mysterious nature of women.

Vox Day asks, as if it was a killer argument, what is the mutation rate[290]?

Roughly ten per generation. However most of these are either neutral or harmful, which means that evolution has to run mighty fast to stay in the same place[291].

If he is asking how many mutations favored by evolution occur, how many mutations go to fixation, the answer is something in the ballpark of one every thousand years or so. However, we get lots of evolution by changing the ratios of large numbers of alleles of small effect, and describing this kind of evolution in terms of mutation rate is not very meaningful, since it is not accurately described in terms of mutations, and since the ratios rarely go all the way to fixation.

Vox Day's advice on handling women is not very good. It may well have been adversely affected by his reluctance to believe in evolution. Similarly, his faith in the sexless character of females under eighteen.

While I am delighted that #metoo is devouring those who funded it and sponsored it I know perfectly well that every notable #metoo allegation is a malicious lie, for the targets are always the men whom women very much want, wealthy and powerful men, and the accusers are mostly washed up narcissistic whores that men no longer want - the accusations are directed against those men who are most likely to be sexually contacted by women in a sexually aggressive manner, and the accusations come from those women who are most apt to sexually contact men in a sexually aggressive manner.

While we should never interrupt the enemy when he is making a mistake, and should enthusiastically cheer our enemies as they devour each other, Vox Day is a blue pilled sucker for failing to identify vicious lying whores as vicious lying whores. Weinstein and company deserve what they are going to get - but they deserve it for sponsoring the movement that is now devouring them. Similarly, when Stalin sent those who set up death camps to their own death camps for "objective fascism", it was a good thing that they were sent to their own death camps, but one should not be persuaded that they were actually were objectively fascists. And it will be a good thing if Weinstein and company are convicted of rape, but they are no more rapists than Trots were fascists, and if Vox Day thinks they are guilty, he is ignorant of the nature of women, to which ignorance his rejection of evolution has likely contributed.

The wonderful clarity of white genocide

2018-08-06 08:11:54

Sarah Jeong issued, over many years, an enormous pile of tweets expressing hatred of white people, and among those tweets a few expressing intent to murder all white people[292].

Naturally she was appointed to the editorial board of the New York Times.

Needless to say this appointment has been stoutly defended by every goodthinking leftist, though I see some white male leftists showing symptoms of mental breakdown, their mask of sanity slipping.

---

[290] https://voxday.blogspot.com/2018/08/evolution-evaluated.html
[291] https://blog.reaction.la/science/dysgenics-and-mutational-load/
[292] https://threadreaderapp.com/thread/1025437806775226368.html

Interestingly, some conservative commentators have also rushed to the defense of Sarah Jeong, their arguments inevitably sliding into implicit advocacy of white genocide. What characteristic do all these conservatives have in common?

'Tis a mystery.

"The Cathedral" accurately depicts our enemies as the centralized and authoritarian movement that they in fact are.

The puritan hypothesis depicts them as the pharisaical holier than thou religious fanatics that they are in fact are, which account is more concisely expressed as "Social Justice Warrior".

All men are supposedly created equal. Observed inequality must, therefore, be the result of "hate". Evil noticers are supposedly causing the underperformance that they notice. Thus, war on noticing. Since underperformance continues, the punishment of whites and males must be endlessly escalated. Endless escalation of punishment must eventually manifest as ethnic cleansing and genocide.

I see white non Jewish social justice warriors getting crazier, as trapped in their own logic, they are reasoning their way to their own destruction. Jewish social justice warriors tend more to evil and less to madness, though, like Scott, male Jews are apt reason their way to self destruction to punish themselves for their maleness, while enthusiastically supporting the destruction of non Jewish whites without ensuing mental disorder. So male Jews tend to be driven to madness by their maleness, while non Jewish social justice warriors are driven to madness both by their maleness and by their whiteness.

Since the focus is now on the extermination of whites, rather than the emasculation of males, the Jewish Question is becoming more true, and the Puritan hypothesis less relevant. But we still have plenty of action on the emasculation of males, for which thinking too much about the Jewish question is apt to mislead and confuse.

When World War T was winding down, we wondered what the next big cause for leftism would be. I was thinking that maybe they would come out with some brilliantly clever reasons why castrating nine year old boys and turning them into sex toys for gays was liberating, but men having sex with seventeen year old girls was worse than the holocaust, and we have been seeing some of that. Very young boys are being liberated from being oppressed by their horrid their toxic male identity. But it has not really received power support.

With the Francisco Sanchez acquitted because he shot Kathryn Steinle on the Embarcadero for being white, and Sarah Jeong being appointed to the editorial board of the New York Times, it is clear what the next big left wing cause will be.

The next big leftwing cause is killing all white people.

It is not like they appointed some fifty year old fat gay who recently emancipated his recently adopted nine year old boy child from toxic masculinity, which is what I was half expecting.

I am seeing a whole lot of schizophrenia among white progressives. They know this, and they do not know it. They support it, and they do not support it. Massive doublethink and split personality.

It is interesting how completely normal and mainstream the advocacy of white genocide feels. They are telling us that we must be hateful, evil, and crazy to disagree.

In the George Zimmerman Trayvon Martin case, it was obvious that those who supported Trayvon were advocating genocide, but they could plausibly deny it, deny it to themselves, because, after all, Zimmerman deliberately shot Trayvon through the heart when Trayvon attacked him, while Trayvon was merely indifferent as to whether he was endangering Zimmerman's life by his attack on Zimmerman. Zimmerman aimed for the heart, and knew his shot was true.

But with everyone who defends and supports Sarah Jeong, there is no real ambiguity. They want to kill us all. If they are going to come up with some motte and bailey argument "we are not actually advocating white genocide, we are actually advocating ...", what is the motte? If they are not advocating white genocide, what are they advocating?

During the Trayvon case, I would point out to a Trayvon supporter that she (and it was usually a white woman) was advocating white genocide, in that though she was supposedly arguing that Zimmerman attacked Trayvon, she was actually presenting arguments that Trayvon was right to attack Zimmerman. And often she would realize that she was arguing that, and respond "Well, yes, but Zimmerman could have solved the problem without lethal force" (The implicit assumption not being that white people need killing, but rather being that white people are not only expected to behave well, but use their super magic powers to prevent other races from behaving badly, and if other races behave badly, it is the fault of white males.)

OK, so what is the motte in the Sarah Jeong case? When you advocate the eradication of white people, not a lot of ambiguity remaining. When you support someone who advocates the eradication of white people, not a lot of ambiguity remaining.

Heartiste accurately analyzes those that hate us, and intend to exterminate us[293]
> Anti-White hatred is channeled through Trump, which explains why the rage against Trump is so unhinged.

Democracy is going to kill us all. People inevitably vote their tribe and their religion, which inevitably tends towards tribal warfare and holy war. The Democrats brought in hostile tribes for a vote bank, as the Populares allied with the Samnites against the Optimates. Of course the Samnites did not care about the differences between Populares and Optimates. They intended to level Rome and kill all Romans, Populares and Optimates both. And now the Democrats have a brown problem, as the Populares had a Samnite problem.

For us to survive, Democracy and the Constitution has got to go, and the Declaration of Independence needs to be taught in schools as treason against the King motivated by religious fanaticism. There is no middle course that ends with us alive. While the Jewish role in the promotion of genocide is obvious, they are simultaneously becoming irrelevant as their pets push them aside. Just as the Jewish question becomes more relevant, it renders itself irrelevant as the processes they set in motion escalate beyond their control. To focus unduly on the Jewish Question is to suppose that we can solve this problem while retaining Democracy, the Constitution, and the Declaration of independence. The Jewish role in advocacy of white genocide is obvious, but if you focus unduly on Jews, you think you can set things back to yesterday's leftism, back to 1933 leftism. The course

---

[293]https://heartiste.wordpress.com/2018/08/05/comment-of-the-week-anti-trump-hatred-is-anti-white-hatred/

we are on was not set by Jews, but by the founders. If all men are created equal, then it follows that I must be causing the problems encountered by black military age Muslims in Subsaharan Africa, in which case they all are entitled to claim asylum and come here to live on crime, welfare, and voting Democrat, a conclusion that, however congenial to Jews and Democrats, logically follows from the Declaration of Independence. And even if we gassed every Jew, still a conclusion highly congenial to the representatives of fifty percent of the voters. We cannot afford the Declaration, and we cannot afford one man one vote, Jews or no Jews.

The reactionary program for the coming civil war

2018-08-09 05:58:47

The reactionary program is fallen governance for a fallen world: Immanentizing the Eschaton is the progressive program, it is the opposite of the reactionary program. Whosoever claims that the truest and most pure reaction will Immanentize the Eschaton is a progressive entryist, like those telling Muslims that Islam is the religion of peace, therefore the truest Islam is something that is suspiciously progressive sounding, like those telling Christians that single mothers are heroes, and that they should adopt blacks from Saharan Africa.
> "hello fellow white male hetero sexual reactionaries. My reaction is purer than your reaction. And yet at the same time we need to be acceptable to moderates in order to obtain the broadest possible outreach."

Reaction deals with fallen men as they actually are – hence we want our ruling bandit to be a stationary bandit evil overlord, and view the primary problem with government as mobile banditry – that anonymous bureaucrats have, as Taleb says, no stake in the game. We are worried about the evil overlord's incentives, and not much worried about whether he represents the people, and not much worried whether he is nice and virtuous. We want a good man for Archbishop, but someone mighty like Trump for President, President for Life, King, God King, and Holy American Emperor.

If Trump successfully does a Stalin or a Cromwell, freezes leftism at the current year, that will be great, for the full implementation of the reactionary program is likely to be through all out war, where cities get burned, likely by nuclear fire, women and children get massacred, and the winning side is the side most willing to do the most terrible things.

If he does a Sulla, and rolls leftism back to 1933 that will be even better.

If he rolls leftism back to the leftism of the founders, better still. Best of all if he gets crowned God Emperor of the New Holy American empire, does a Charles the Hammer and a Charles the Second and rolls things back to 1660, in which case we are likely to get one hundred and sixty years of reaction.

The worst case outcome however, and a very likely outcome, is long, bloody, and terrible civil war with our enemies masters of the state. Trump gets impeached, not long after that imprisoned, and not long after that he and his entire family is murdered like the Romanovs as civil war and white genocide begins. In which case we will have to whip up our own state in one hell of a hurry.

Everyone who practices with a gun on the gun range is on our side.

Most men who lift iron are on our side.

Most men who practice the seriously dangerous martial arts on our side.

The great majority of young white males are our side.

Deus Vult. God is on our side.

But as well as that, if our enemies have a state, we will need a state.

Whites are in line for hot genocide. Whites also have more capability for war than any other race. No other race, no other people, have ever shown anything close to the capacity for organized mass violence. Which means that to re-awaken our capability, we need organization and mass.

To re-awaken the sleeping warrior, reward him for victory personally and individually with land, women and power, as well as with land and power for his platoon, his company, and his regiment. He will be back.

Set the status of women back to what it was in eighteenth century England, or better, back to what it was in the Carolingian empire. He will be back.

If the state remains in the hands of people who wish to destroy us, we will have to build our own state, and the quickest way to whip up a state from nothing much is feudalism and freehold - the full reactionary program. Every company and every regiment needs to be largely responsible for its own logistics, and will need its own pool of camp followers, thus will need its own domain of state power.

It would be better if part of the existing state comes over to us, with its existing institutions, in which case we will get something considerably less than the full reactionary program, very likely will get a Cromwellian program. We are not in this to build utopia. Reaction is impure in its essence, being committed to doing the best we can in a regrettably fallen world. The Cromwellian program would be great. Whosoever signals reactionary purity, signals leftism. We are, however, in this to win. If we cannot win with the existing state, or a breakaway part of it, will have to win without, and the full reactionary program is fully optimized for power, war, and the regrettable necessity of dreadful deeds.

The optics of noticing

2018-08-12 06:54:02

There is a lot of bad female behavior. It gets worse as they get older, but it starts very young indeed, typically around four years below fertile age, with a great deal of variance, much more variance than occurs in males.

People complain that when I notice sexual misbehavior in very young girls, that this is "bad optics".

I say that there is severe and widespread female misconduct getting right in our faces, that we need to stop them, and that we need start stopping them very young.

People then claim I advocate raping little girls, and that this is "bad optics".

I say that female consent is always unclear and ambiguous, and is usually foolish and given to very bad men with very bad consequences, and that therefore such decisions need to be made by the parent or guardian.

People then claim that I say that I should be allowed to have sex with other men's children and they should not be allowed to stop me, even though that is exactly the opposite of what I am saying.

These claims make no logical or factual sense. But equally obviously, they make emotional sense if you are badly cucked.

Suppose someone genuinely fails to see women behaving badly. Then, if he disagrees with me, the natural response is

> "No you are wrong, women are not behaving badly, they don't need to be controlled"

But instead I hear

> "horrible men need to be controlled and you are a horrible man, you rape other men's daughters and seduce other men's wives"

Which makes emotional sense if those making the accusation see what I see, but are frightened, weak, and impotent. It only makes emotional sense if one sees bad behavior, and, unable to address the bad behavior directly (because that would be domestic violence, hostile work environment, sexual harassment, mansplaining, and rape) displaces one's rage. If one does not see what I see, if one does not see a great deal of very bad behavior, it makes neither logical nor emotional sense to accuse me of these absurd views. For someone to make these angry hostile denunciations is displacement of anger and pain, thus only makes emotional sense if female misbehavior is causing him anger and pain, thus only makes emotional sense if he sees what I see.

Blaming men for female misconduct is fear, weakness and white knighting. People say that speaking the truth about women is "bad optics", but weakness is the worst optics. We are the strong horse.

I am indeed saying that women, starting at a horrifyingly young age, like sex, like rape, and rather like brutal rape. To conclude from this that I am arguing in favor of brutal rape, one has to attribute to me the white knight position that women should get what they want. But that is an implausible position to attribute to someone who is arguing that women want very bad things, wicked, foolish, and self destructive things, and who frequently says in the plainest possible words that women should not be allowed to get what they want. Chastity and monogamy are a plot by men against women and need to be imposed on women with a stick. Monogamy and chastity were first invented when one band of ape men wiped out the ape men of another band, killed their mothers, killed their children, and divided up the women among themselves.

When I talk about nine year old girls finding an older male to fuck them, I say "but she does not want to fuck someone like you - she is going to fuck a heavily tattooed forty year old motorcycle gang leader and drug dealer." When a heavily tattooed drug dealer is my example of youthful female hypergamy in action it is unreasonable to attribute to me the argument "This is what little girls want, and therefore giving it to them should be fine." What I say is that this is indeed what little girls want, and therefore they need to be whacked with a stick and in some cases shotgun married. We need to deal with this problem with domestic discipline and the threat of early shotgun marriage, not by doubling down on prohibitions against men, prohibitions that are only effective against respectable men, and thus wind up reinforcing the little girl's feeling that bad men are higher status.

Attributing to me outrageous and absurd positions only makes emotional sense as emotional displacement, and emotional displacement only makes sense if a problem is hurting one badly, and one is powerless and afraid to do anything about it.

Blaming men for the behavior of women is weakness and fear, and smells to everyone like weakness and fear. When people see the strong horse and the weak horse, naturally they will prefer the strong horse.

There is an enormous epidemic of extremely bad female behavior right in front of your face. That this epidemic starts at a very early age is just a small part of what people are refusing to see, and this small part is no different from the rest of it. Mostly what we see is bad female behavior in college and in the workplace, and it is in the workplace that most of the economic damage from female sexual misconduct happens.

Consider what happens at work. The boss is talking and a woman interrupts him and talks over him, in a supposedly helpful, respectful, friendly, and supportive manner. When a woman interrupts a man she always sounds friendly, helpful, and supportive at first, because women always play one man against another man, are always soliciting white knights.

The boss is trying to say X, but she is not letting him say X, and is insisting that he is actually saying Y. Y is usually something stupid, disruptive, and damaging to the business and the cohesion of the team, and even if it is something perfectly reasonable, it is not what the boss was attempting to say.

This is a shit test. If he raises his voice and insists on X and ignores this Y disruption, he is being mean to this supposedly sweet innocent girl who has supposedly done nothing wrong, was sweetly, politely, and supportively *interrupting him and speaking over him*.

Quite likely the boss fails the shit test, by allowing the woman who interrupted him and talked over him to win, the conversation proceeds to be about Y, and the boss never gets a chance to talk about X. In which case the boss becomes invisible to her, and if subsequently he forces himself on her attention, which being her boss he probably needs to do from time to time, she gets a creepy feeling as though something slimy and disgusting was trying to insert its semen into her, as though he physically forced himself on her, and she fought him off, and he slunk away ashamed. And, chances are, she will remember it as happening something like that, because that is what it is going to feel like. Women just don't like having betas around, just as they don't like having rats and slugs around. The distinction between a contemptible beta forcing himself on her attention, and a contemptible beta forcing himself on her body will not remain clear in her mind. Likely she will complain about him metaphorically forcing himself to her colleagues at the time, and years after the events, will genuinely remember him as literally forcing himself on her physically.

Now suppose instead the boss bulls his way through, and insists on talking about X, ignoring her gentle steering towards Y? Well, chances are that at first the interruptions become considerably less helpful, less respectful, less friendly and less supportive, more openly hostile and disruptive. But maybe, indeed very likely, her stiffening resistance will suddenly collapse, and she will accept the boss talking about X. In which case he has passed the shit test, and when he wins and when she capitulates to his verbal domination you will see her emit some subtle or not so subtle body language that signals that if he were to try some physical domination on her for size, maybe that might well go down similarly. Which was, of course the whole point of the exercise, the whole point of disrupting the bosses talk and attempting to silence him. The dance is pursuit and predation, conquest and surrender. To reproduce successfully, men and women have to form stable families, which means that men have to conquer, and women have to surrender. She is provoking him to aggress against her, so that he can conquer her. She never actually cared one way or the other whether the boss talked about X or Y.

Now you might suppose you can stay out of trouble by always capitulating, by losing to every shit test, by white knighting. Accepting defeat, accepting the higher status of your adversary, works in a conflict with a fellow male. It fails catastrophically in a conflict with a woman. Male conflicts are resolved by establishing hierarchy. Female conflicts are resolved by eliminating the losers. If you submit to male dominance, he would like to keep you around. If you submit to female dominance, she will casually destroy you. Men reproduce most successfully by ruling, females reproduce most successfully by being ruled, thus are maladapted to rule. White knighting fails.

To be more precise, white knighting fails as a strategy for men with women. It works as a cover for defecting on your fellow males. If one tells a woman one is supporting and protecting her, she will despise one. If one tells a man one is supporting and protecting his wife and his daughters, it will likely persuade him to refrain from killing one.

White knighting works as a sneaky fucker strategy for high status males. If a male is acting in a role that makes him higher status than you, as for example a preacher, he is in a good position to fuck your women. If, in that high status role, he preaches that women are higher status than himself, that is going to impair his chances. But if, in that role, he preaches that your women are pure and chaste (and therefore your women would never have sex with him)) and also preaches that women are higher status than *you*, that is going to improve his chances. "Domestic violence" laws are a white knight strategy targeting men who are low status in the male hierarchy but high status in female perception, because violent. People in authority are pissed that women like are criminals and men with no income, and so push "domestic violence""in an effort to undermine the authority of those men over their women, with the unfortunate effect of undermining the authority of all men over all women. The correct way to reduce the propensity of women to hang out with stone broke criminals and ignore the guy with the corner office in the skyscraper is to support male authority over females, but only for males in good standing, as the Mormon Church does. Of course, that has the effect that people in authority don't get to fuck the women of men in good standing, which is why this strategy is so frequently unpopular with men in authority.

Which is how we got into this mess. King George the fourth slept with the wives of aristocrats. His own wife slept around. He tried to divorce her, revealing himself as powerless and cuckolded. The power of Kings went away, and anglosphere fertility has been falling ever since, with a temporary recovery between first wave and second wave feminism. The elite go after each other's women, lose social cohesion, and social disorder ensues.

Recollect my story about the first men inventing chastity and monogamy: The leader of the first men assigns one woman to each of his followers who is any use, and a dozen to himself. Noticing that some of that dozen are apt to be frisky, he issues a commandment that marriage is eternal. If a woman has sex with a man, she may only have sex with that one man all his days. Further, if a woman does have sex with another man, it is absolutely fine for her husband to kill her and/or that man, and the rest of the tribe should support him in that endeavor.

Time passes, and the leader of the first men is getting a bit frail. A new leader is rising, and this new leader has as yet only one woman. As his power and status rises, he notices other men's women giving him the eye. The new leader announces that women are chaste and virtuous, and it is important to protect them. That works for him in the short run, but it is going to be bad for all the other men in the tribe.

I call them the first men, because they were smart enough to have laws and commandments, and likely smart enough to attribute those commandments to God, but looked like upright apes. It seems likely that they looked like upright apes, because women find male apes sexually attractive, while men do not find female apes sexually attractive, which indicates that in our evolutionary history, men have been exercising sexual choice, but women in the lines that we are descended from did not get to exercise sexual choice since the days we looked like apes. Which indicates that populations that allow female sexual choice die out, and explains the female propensity to make very bad sexual choices.

It is unlikely that males would have been able to coordinate well enough to prevent female sexual choice till smart enough to have laws and commandments (which is smarter than some present day peoples) so this implies a population with human intelligence and human social order but apelike appearance.

You cannot suppress female sexual choice except you have laws and commandments that prevent men from defecting on other men, from which I conclude that we are descended from a very long line of populations that had the law:

> Thou shalt not covet thy neighbor's house, thou shalt not covet thy neighbor's wife, nor his manservant, nor his maidservant, nor his ox, nor his ass, nor any thing that is thy neighbor's.

in effect, that though entire peoples kept falling away from such laws, peoples that fall away from those laws disappear from history.

That females are severely maladapted to an environment of female sexual choice, while men can accurately assess female fertility at thirty paces in seven seconds tells me that we are descended from peoples that were pretty relaxed about male choice, while forcefully suppressing female choice, people who only restricted males from impinging on the other male's property rights in female sexuality, and were otherwise fine with it being open season for male predation. So if we look back in history to the family law of a people that did survive, this is what we should see. Open go for male predation, except that other men's wives and fiancees are very much off limits, death penalty for women who sleep with one man, then cheerfully sleep with another man while the first man still lives.

And this is in fact what we do see. The biblical penalty for rape or seduction of an unbetrothed virgin was ... shotgun marriage. The biblical penalty for rape or seduction of a betrothed woman, was death. Which implies that if someone raped an unbetrothed woman, kept her around, fed her, looked after her, and she nonetheless sneaked off when he was not looking, the penalty was death, both for her and for whichever man she sneaked off to.

So who killed the offenders? The state, the temple, or the man whose property rights in women's sexual and reproductive capabilities were violated?

At the time of Jesus, it was the temple, and Jesus famously abrogated this. But the rabbis of the time were engaged in a holiness spiral, which holiness spiral Jesus often vehemently denounced, which holiness spiral led them into suicidal war with the Romans, literally suicidal as they wound up murdering each other and killing themselves, as holiness spirals so frequently end, so we cannot take temple practice at the time of Jesus as indicative of the will of Gnon, or the practice of earlier times. Jesus said no, and they perished. Both of these are good indicators that you are not following the will of Gnon.

What we can take as indicative of the family law of earlier times of those peoples who survived is the wisdom books of earlier times, in particular the Book of Proverbs. Wisdom books were issued by governments to advise their subjects about the private and quasi private incentives for good behavior that were in effect - hence "the wisdom of Solomon". And according to the section of the Book of Proverbs that claims to have been issued by the court of King Solomon, the incentive for not sleeping with someone else's women was not that the government would kill you, nor that the temple would kill you, but that the rightful owner of that woman's sexual and reproductive capability might kill you, and would have every right to do so, legally and openly. So, the Wisdom of Solomon (and of subsequent Kings that repeatedly re-issued that book) is that honor killing is fine. Which is a good indicator of the will of Gnon, since that is a people that survived and of the will of God, since that is the way that Old Testament law on adultery was implemented.

The book of Proverbs has different sections, as it was re-issued by King after King, government after government. But none of the sections threaten state or temple penalties for sexual misconduct, nor do any of the sections drop the Solomonic privately administered death penalty for sexual misconduct, indicating laws on sexual conduct that gave the maximum sexual possible liberty to men, short of allowing one man to tread on another man's toes, and the minimum possible sexual liberty to women. Since, to form families, men need to conquer, and women to be conquered, such laws are optimal for family formation and reproduction. Such also prevent conflict within the elite (King George the Fourth) and between the elite and the people, by preventing men from competing for women's favors, by preventing women from giving such favors, thus are optimal for social cohesion. Hence peoples with such laws are apt to invade, and not themselves be invaded. Which is handy if you have high elite fertility as a result of such laws.

So, in Old Testament times, if a man abducted a woman who was not married or betrothed, he was allowed to keep her, and if she was virgin before the abduction, *required* to keep her, and if she ran away to some other man, he was allowed to kill her and that other man. This is consistent with observed present day behavior of men and women, which indicates descent from populations with severe restraint on female sexual choice, and weak restraint on male sexual choice - indicates that we are descended from peoples who had laws like that, and that peoples more tolerant of female sexual choice failed to reproduce or were conquered and genocided. Our biological character indicates that among the populations from which we are descended male sexual choice was only restricted to the extent necessary to prevent one man's choice from impinging on another man's choice, while female sexual choice was almost nonexistent, indicating that Old Testament law, as interpreted and applied by the wisdom of Solomon in the Book of Proverbs, is the will of Gnon, the will of Nature and of Nature's God.

The Book of Proverbs goes on about sexual misconduct at considerable length. And it describes the reality that I see, not the reality that people keep gaslighting me with. In the Book of Proverbs, sexual misconduct is primarily the result of lustful women manipulating naive men in order to obtain socially disruptive sex. There are no grooming gangs[294] in the Book of Proverbs. Women sexually manipulate men in order to obtain sex in socially disruptive and damaging ways. Men do not sexuality manipulate women. Though the dance is pursuit and predation, conquest and surrender, as if lustful men were imposing themselves on sexless angels, that is the dance not the reality. The reality is that women and girls are lustfully manipulating men and their social environment to obtain social outcomes that in some ways superficially resemble lustful men imposing themselves on sexless angels. That is what the Book of Proverbs depicts, and that is what I see in front of my nose. And yet I live in a world where everyone with astonishing confidence and enormous certainty reports a very different world, a world of men sexually harassing and raping women, a world where male sexual predators lure innocent sexless female children. When I report the world that I see and experience, which is the world depicted in the Book of Proverbs, which is the world that the famous Wisdom of Solomon depicts, some people get very angry.

I have been writing this post over a couple of days. Last night I threw a big expensive party, at which party I played the role of the big high status male, and the highest status male guest, a colleague of my girlfriend's father, very courteously played along. This morning one of the party girls, who is fertile age but only very recently fertile age, and unfortunately very closely connected to my current girlfriend and that high status male, was still around. This morning, after this post was mostly written and the remaining guests mostly sober, I left for the beach for a swim with my girlfriend. And by coincidence, party girl just happened to decide to put on a bikini that she only recently came to need, and to take a swim shortly after I and my girlfriend left, joining us at the beach. And whenever I remained stationary and facing in a particular direction for any length of time, this young party girl, dressed in a bikini, would find some reason to hang around in that line of vision. You may recall that in my posts on testosterone and weight loss, I have frequently remarked that I have difficulty out-staring a pizza and a pitcher of Mountain Dew.

For men to cooperate effectively, as for example in genociding their less cooperative neighbors and taking their land, they have to keep their hands off each other's women, and *enforce* keeping each other's hands off each other's women. And since women are notoriously apt to find clever ways to give sneaky fuckers a chance, particularly sneaky fuckers in authority, in order to enforce keeping each other's hands off each other's women,

---

[294]https://blog.reaction.la/tag/rotherham/

they have to enforce each other's authority over each other's women. That is why when a group of males moves in on a group of women to attempt a pickup, they first have to agree in advance which of them is going to score which girl so that the girls cannot play them off against each other.

Conversely, the first thing a sneaky fucker in authority or in a position of status is going to do is undermine other men's authority over their women, even though this strategy is apt to backfire on himself, as it backfired on King George the Fourth.

Romance is an escape hatch out of the tenth commandment. Supposedly it is OK to fuck other men's women if that is what they want. Tingles supposedly make sex holy, and a woman should supposedly always get whatever man gives her tingles. So a woman can have sex with every man who gives her tingles, which is apt to be a disturbingly large number of men, and stop having sex with any man who stops giving her tingles, who is apt to be the father of her children.

Well I have bad news: Your women, including your daughters starting at a startlingly early age, *always* want to fuck some strange man because there is *always* some man higher status than you, so this escape hatch out of the tenth commandment is *always* going to burn you. Therefore any group of men that allows this escape hatch out of the tenth commandment is *always* going to perish in the long run. And any time someone claiming high status tells you that your women are not going to be tempted to fuck some high status male, provided you are sufficiently holy, or sufficiently progressive, or sufficiently manly, sufficiently patriarchal, or sufficiently antisexist, or sufficiently loving, is more interested in sneak fucking your wife than in the survival of the group to which he belongs.

These are the real optics: Nobody likes the weak horse, white knighting women and girls as sexless angels looks weak, and sneaky fuckers need killing even if, like William Duke of Acquitaine, they are far from weak.

Manafort trial

2018-08-20 08:06:38

Manafort's alleged crimes are boring. The permanent government's openly criminal reaction to the possibility of an acquittal is entertaining.

It is looking increasingly possible that Manafort will be acquitted, largely because his alleged crimes are obscure violations of complicated laws that are as difficult to understand as they are to comply with, so not everyone in the jury is likely to be able to keep straight what he is supposed to be guilty of, resulting in a hung jury or an acquittal. Putting him in solitary and starving him may well misfire by making the jury cynical about legalistic stuff that no one understands, and cynical about the unsupported testimony of witnesses subjected to extreme and grossly improper pressure, similar that applied to Manafort himself.

The mass media and permanent government are starting to melt down in fear of this possibility, and are attempting to intimidate the judge, dox the jury, and intimidate the jury.

So, why is it so important to permanent government that this unimportant man be convicted of a pile of minor and incomprehensible legalistic technicalities? And why was he starved and kept in solitary confinement pending trial?

Mueller's approach to convicting Trump of high crimes was to put the heat on everyone connected to Trump to come up with stuff Trump was guilty of. Anything at all. And, in order to put the heat on them, he put the heat on everyone connected to everyone connected to Trump to come up with stuff people connected to Trump were guilty of. And one of Manafort's associates was guilty of stuff, and was induced to testify that Manafort was guilty of stuff.

Despite that, and despite solitary confinement, Manafort was disinclined to testify that the President of the United States was guilty of being guilty. So he was prosecuted, imprisoned, and badly mistreated in prison by the permanent government. Still did not crack.

SupposeManafort gets acquitted. Then it becomes obvious that the Mueller investigation is an abuse of prosecutorial power. Hence the melt down.

If the permanent government can mistreat Trump's allies and supporters, Trump is powerless. If the permanent government is exposed as abusing the coercive powers of the state to intimidate Trump's people, maybe he can stop them. Stopping them is going to feel mighty like a coup. Stopping a coup always feels like a counter coup, always *is* a counter coup. And using the coercive powers of the state against a sitting president is suspiciously close to a coup, so stopping that, if Trump succeeds in stopping that, is going to be a counter coup, or close to it.

Which brings me to QAnon. QAnon is full of crap. How do I know he is full of crap?

Coups come in two major forms: Creeping coups, typically color revolutions, and sudden coups. Mueller, the FBI, the Department of Justice, and the State Department, are attempting a creeping coup or color revolution. In a creeping coup, the coupists get away with one illegal act of intimidation, and this then makes it easier get away with another, bigger, illegal act of intimidation, and then another, even bigger act of intimidation. If Trump pulls a counter coup, it will be a sudden coup. And the players in a sudden coup keep their cards very close to their chest. In the Chilean coup, no one spoke the fatal words out loud until a few hours before the coup. According to QAnon, Trump's people are speaking the fatal words ad nauseam, which is unlikely.

I hope, and it becomes increasingly possible, that Mueller's investigation gets wrapped up with the bang QAnon is predicting. But until that happens, if it happens, QAnon knows no more about what Trump is up to than anyone who holds a finger to the wind. But against this possibility, Trump's government has been acting rather intimidated lately, and the permanent government has been getting away with ever more lawless and criminal acts, attempting to intimidate the judge and jury being the biggest so far. If they get away with this, then the next act of intimidation will be correspondingly bigger.

A creeping coup is by definition slow, so if they get away with nailing Manafort tomorrow, Trump will not be impeached the day after. It is going to creep, eventually resulting in Trump being impeached or indicted, which would set us on the path to ever more openly criminal, and ever less legitimate, governments, as in 1917 Russia, and 1789 France.

From 1917 to the Holodomor was fifteen years. From 1789 to the red terror was four years.

From 1917 to civil war was few months. From 1789 to civil war was four years.

Or maybe Mueller and most of the Department of Justice will get nailed, will reveal all the blackmail material that they are holding on each other, and will all go to jail for a really long time.

The big delusion of the left is that they can overthrow Trump and it will result in the restoration of normality – failing to notice that every year for as long as I can remember has been more strikingly abnormal than the previous year. They think Trump is a right wing swing, failing to notice he is a slight slow down of the left wing swing. Trees do not grow to the sky, but they grow till they fall over.

And another one bites the dust

2018-08-25 20:35:06

The American empire, aka anti American Empire, aka The international community, aka rule by rootless childless cosmopolitans with no future and no past, is in retreat.

Having lost Russia, Poland, Hungary, and Philippines, it just took another body blow in Australia.

A shark has to keep swimming, or it will drown, and the ever increasing holiness of the left has to keep knocking over new applecarts, or else there will be no apples rolling around for ambitious leftist to pick up.

They never stop; they only pause to re-group and change strategy. They *can't* stop.

The Trump like Australian Prime minister Tony Abbot decisively stopped illegal immigration, (Zero illegal arrivals since 2014, yes, zero. You read that correctly. Zero.) and busted near every illegal visa overstay and violation of visa conditions, as near to all of them as makes no difference

Leftism had to start advancing in Australia on another front, on something other than white genocide. They dithered between expanding legal immigration as a slower route to white genocide, and smashing western civilization by rolling back the industrial revolution. And eventually coalesced on smashing western civilization, rolling back the industrial revolution.

Western civilization depends on concentrated and reliable energy sources, power on tap. Which means carbon or nuclear.

Nuclear was stopped primarily the way NASA was stopped, by putting stupid people in charge. It is not apparent that fusion power would be workable even with smart people in charge, but to be on the safe side, they put stupid people in charge of developing thermonuclear as well. The big vulnerability of nuclear power is not the imaginary evils of nuclear power (The long term effect of Chernobyl was the deaths of at most nine people outside the power plant outer fence) it is that you need smart people in charge of nuclear power. It is easy to disrupt cooperation between smart people by inserting stupid people.

The objective of the global warming scam is to stop carbon power, coal and oil.

And the left decided that was the front it would advance on in Australia was, instead of eradicating the white race. Expanding legal immigration had some success, but legal means that the numbers are known, and political pushback likely to be effective.

South Australia, and to a lesser extent Queensland, proceeded to smash their energy industries at the state level, but for any one Australian state to destroy its energy industry has limited effect if energy using businesses can flee to other states, and if energy can be imported through the grid from one state to another. For the policy to be effective, has to be federally implemented.

The Australian federal Prime minister bowed to pressure and introduced an "energy security" plan, which would have provided energy security the way that Lucy was going to hold the football for Charlie Brown. The real intent of the Global Warming scam was revealed in South Australia, where the South Australian state government did to South Australia what Obama did to flyover country.

With the "energy security plan" it became obvious that greenies would absolutely never accept any compromise that left Western high tech civilization viable, that any attempt compromise with greenies would end with a result that would do to the Australian economy what it damn near did to the South Australian economy.

Turnbull, the Australian Prime Minister, proceeded to "compromise" with those who will never compromise, with the result that he failed to compromise with the substantial sane and decent faction of his own party. No carbon program that does not radically disrupt our comfortable modern lifestyles and throw large numbers of people out of work is going to be acceptable to the left.

And so, he got thrown out and Scott Morrison became Australian Prime minister on a program of *not* destroying the energy industry, and still not allowing illegal immigration. No word yet on what he is going to do about alarming levels of legal immigration, but did I mention that they are alarming, and voters are becoming alarmed.

The shark is not drowning yet, still has white replacement going through legal immigration, but this latest is causing it major trouble breathing, and we are seeing calls for a color revolution against Australia. Australia has not decisively left the empire yet, the way Poland and the Philippines have, but this has become a very real possibility:

Scott Morrison may well cuck on Green (unreliable) energy, and may well cuck on legal immigration. Maybe he will get subverted the way Abbot was, but that his predecessor got thrown out for cucking on unreliable energy on top of cucking on legal immigration is a very good sign.

Current strategy is to overthrow Scott Morrison by fully legitimate and constitutional means, should he fail to cuck out, but that will likely prove difficult, whereupon constitutionality will likely get seriously stretched, the way that efforts to impeach Trump have seriously stretched constitutionality in the US.

The South Australian energy industry was looted in the course of being destroyed, and I expect that the federal destruction of the Australian energy industry would have provided a whole lot of loot for leftists. That they are not going to get this loot, at least not by peaceful, constitutional, and democratic means, is a major body blow. They were expecting another apple cart, and that cart is not falling - this is has had an immediate and obvious effect on their motivation and capability to generate political pressure.

The more stuff leftists knock over, the more loot for leftists, the more leftist activism you get. Conversely, when the expected gold rush fails to eventuate, you get loss of left wing morale and energy.

As leftism goes ever lefter, you have more people seeking holiness jobs, which means that ever larger apple carts have to be knocked over at ever shorter intervals. The shark cannot stop swimming, and will do whatever it takes to keep on swimming. And it is going to take measures that increasing collapse constitutional legitimacy and peaceful relations between nations, leading to internal war, external war, or both. Notice that when the color revolution in Libya failed, the state department turned spectacularly murderous and destructive, and that when the color revolution in Syria failed, it turned genocidal.

Expect, therefore, the unexpected. As the arc of history bends ever more to indiscriminate, destructive, and malicious evil, it encounters more resistance. One might expect that this will result in stability at some tolerable level of evil. This stabilization has never happened in the past and is unlikely to happen in the future. What happens instead is what we see happening in the US. The left escalates, drifting closer to war internal and external.

No perceptible global warming.

2018-08-31 08:16:32

It is plausible that the world has warmed very slightly - but in any one location, if we count the number of unusually cold events, anomalous snowfalls, and the like, and compare with the number of unusually warm events, we are just as likely to get more cold events and less warm events in recent times than the converse.

To detect global warming, you have to average over the entire world, and it is unclear and debateable how to make an apples to apples average over the entire world.

It is plausible that there has been a bit of warming over the past few decades for reasonable ways of doing the averaging.But polar bears are not only unlikely to go extinct, they are unlikely to notice. Regions where sea levels have been falling are approximately equal to regions where sea levels have been rising. To measure sea level rise, you run into the same problems as detecting global warming. You have to average over the whole world, because the signal in any one area is swamped by various random things, and it is unclear how to do a valid average over the entire world.

And similarly, coral bleaching events. There have always been coral bleaching events. Coral grows till it gets too close to the surface, there is an unusually low tide, and the coral dies back, bleaching. I have seen a few coral bleaching events, and it always shallow water coral hit by an abnormally low tide. Similarly, glaciers are always calving, have always been calving, even though each time a big iceberg breaks off a glacier, it is announced as proof of global warming.

You may have heard that the North Pole is melting - though no one told you that the South Pole has grown, and is now vastly larger than it was a hundred years ago[295].

This arctic summer, the Northwest passage failed to open. A few days ago, at the time of year when arctic ice is least, an icebreaker cruise ship attempted to force passage, repeatedly ramming very thick ice. The ship broke, the ice did not break.

Well, Warmists will say, that is weather, not climate, and they are of course, correct. But the bottom line is that a hundred years ago, the Northwest Passage through the arctic

---

[295]https://blog.reaction.la/global-warming/global-warming-scientists-trapped-in-antarctic-denial/

sometimes opened in high summer and sometimes did not, and today the Northwest Passage sometimes opens in high summer, and sometimes does not.

Changes in the weather remain enormously larger than changes in the climate, making it very difficult to detect any change in the climate.

The climate is always changing. Climate Change is always true. But over the last hundred year or so, it has not changed enough for unaided human senses, or even human senses aided by ordinary and reasonably affordable instruments, to detect. Sometimes the climate does change dramatically, sometimes catastrophically, in a hundred years or so. But not this last hundred years or so.

So, why the high drama about global warming? Why the catastrophism? Why the demand for dramatic changes that somehow always result in our power system being looted and damaged?

The reason for the high drama is that science, technology, and industrialization was created by white male capitalists, an enormous achievement for which mankind should be eternally grateful. And people who hate whites, hate males, and hate capitalism want to destroy science, technology, and industrialization. Anyone who talks about Global Warming or Climate Change in ways that imply it is an important crusade hates you and intends you harm. Maybe he wants to lower your status. Maybe he wants to exterminate your race. But either way, he is your enemy. Whosoever talks catastrophic global warming hates you and is motivated by desire to harm you.

Whites, males, capitalists, and white male capitalists created all the good stuff, so they tend to have most of the good stuff, so people who want to take our stuff hate us. Hate whites, hate males, hate capitalists, and particularly hate white male capitalists.

We are all comicsgate

2018-09-04 23:45:12

Ethan Van Sciver sues Vox Day for personal ownership of the comicsgate brand.

This is pissing inside the tent, and is likely to result in social justice warriors taking over comicsgate, since judges will rule in favor of social justice without regard for merit.

Whosoever pisses inside the tent is my enemy, for if he sues Vox Day, likely will sue me.

As the Comicsgate Wiki rightly tell us[296]:

> ComicsGate (or #ComicsGate) is an online movement that believes the comic book industry (especially publishers Marvel and DC) is oversaturated by political messaging that appeals explicitly to only one demographic that is not

---

[296]https://comicsgate.wikia.com/wiki/What_is_ComicsGate%3F

interested in the medium, to the detriment of the existing consumer base and the industry as a whole. It also addresses a lack of professionalism, inclusivity, objectivity and accountability of the publishers and their employees (i.e.management, editors, writers, artists, etc.) when dealing directly with the customers.

Ethan Van Sciver is attempting to appropriate value that a multitude of other people have created, Vox Day among them, which attempt, if successful, will inevitably wind up with the brand being used to educate us in the horrors of white supremacism, male supremacism, cishet normatism (or whatever they are calling it now), islamophobia, and so on and so forth.

Ethan Van Sciver is not comicsgate. He is pissing inside the comicsgate tent.

Inevitably, should the case go to court, the lawyers are going to depict the other side as nazis, white supremacists, islamophobes, antisemites, and whatnot, which puts the heat on everyone to hire social justice warriors and to issue comics where the main story is about a racial and sexual minority struggling with oppression.

The net effect of such a lawsuit is not just spending money on lawyers rather than artists. The net effect is that money raised to produce content of interest to people who don't want to be preached at and told that they are sinners will be used to hire people, to pay people, to preach at them and tell them that they are sinners.

The winner of this lawsuit will be the man most willing to use your money to tell you that you are a horrible person who should never get laid and deserves to die in a fire.

First World Poverty

2018-09-16 11:51:45

First world poverty, the inability to afford families, children, or safe housing, is as artificial as Ukraine Famine.

A silicon valley software engineer earning a hundred and fifty thousand dollars a year cannot afford a house, a wife, and children. A prosperous peasant in Mindanao can afford to house and feed his wife, his children, a mistress, and an extra house for his mistress and her children.

There is plenty of extra land, space, and capacity to produce cheap food and energy. I and others have covered this many times before, and everything in this post is a repeat or direct quote, but covering this again under this title in order that this title and concept goes into the canon.

Open letter to Linus

2018-09-17 20:11:14

When an open source project goes social justice it dies.

It suffers the same transformation we see in entertainment intellectual properties like Star Wars.1. Identify a respected institution.
2. kill it.

3. gut it.

4. wear its carcass as a skin suit, while demanding respectWhen a stem activity, such as open source, goes social justice, then its job gets redefined as showing that women, blacks, and Muslims are capable of stem by giving them stem social roles - which is how NASA lost the capability to go into space.

If you, Linus, are replaced by social justice warriors, which always happens when you get a code of conduct, Linux slowly dies – bugs will not get fixed, misfeatures will get added, and it will suffer from bitrot as the world changes around it.

It will go the same path as Soviet and Rhodesian agriculture. Soviet agriculture never recovered from the liquidation of the kulaks, Rhodesian agriculture never recovered from the genocide of white farmers.

This code of conduct is the work of people who think that all the stuff descended from the sky, and white males, being the evil sexist racist homophobic mysogynist islamophobes that we are, snatched all the good stuff up, thereby preventing anyone else from having it.

They think that if it was not for the horrid oppression committed by white males, they could just help themselves to the stuff in Walmart, and Walmart shelves would magically refill, the way the shelves in Venezuela were supposed to magically refill.

This code of conduct was brought to you by the same thinking on display in Venezuela and in South Africa, where without white farmers the South African crops mysteriously don't grow and without bakeries run by lighter skinned Venezuelans, darker skinned Venezuelans find themselves mysterious short of bread.

A code of conduct results in social justice warriors being helicoptered into the social role and social status of people who create value, but strangely and mysteriously, value ceases to be created.

The NPC plague

2018-09-18 22:01:54

For a long time I have been urging the left to engage in dialogue with us. I complain that they will neither listen to us nor speak to us, and that this will end in war, and mass murder.

Well, suddenly they have started to talk at us, with leftist NPCs showing up on reactionary blogs and lecturing right wingers on twitter and facebook. Listening, not so much. Their stuff tends to be robotic and spammy. Attempting to interact with them is like talking to an NPC (Non Player Character) in a video game. To some extent they actually *are* NPCs - we are seeing stuff that looks as if generated by Google's AI, and that AI programmed by someone who has no understanding of, nor interest in, the ideas of the people he is supposedly addressing. Looks very like a hasty makeover of a similar operation and similar software directed against Muslims, with the major change in the software being a global search for Mohammed, and a global replace with Moldbug or Heartiste.

To some extent it seems to be actual humans who are mechanically following a script written for them by someone else, and who are not allowed to deviate from the script, which sooner or later results in them being endlessly repetitious, somewhat resembling a non player character in a video game, but more resembling one of those highly unhelpful telephone help systems, where one is talking to an actual human, but if your problem is not one of the very limited set of problems covered by the script that that human is required to follow, you are sol, and find yourself trapped in the same script over and over.

It is an improvement, a genuine attempt to get off the path leading to civil war. Not really an adequate attempt, since to the extent that it is actual humans, those humans are not permitted to show comprehension of the ideas that they are attempting to re-but, and crimestop genuinely prevents them from comprehending the ideas that they are attempting to rebut. In place of dialog being totally forbidden, we are getting the super-ficial appearance of dialog, but so severely supervised and tightly controlled that it is not genuine dialog.

They make their preprogrammed argument, you make the obvious and well known counterargument, which is not covered by the script, even though it was first made one hundred and seventy years ago, and they repeat their original preprogrammed argument, claiming to observe and to have experienced the reality that progressives are trying to wish into existence.

Collapse of Building Seven

2018-09-22 02:35:09

Since World Trade Tower Building seven is the most decisive evidence that the collapse of the towers was, as it seemed, the work of terrorists equipped with boxcutters, the troofers manipulatively announce it to be their strongest evidence to the contrary.

Building Seven begins its fall like a tree, falling sideways towards the holes blasted by the plane on the south Side, and the fires started by the plane on the south side.

In this video, shot from the north side it falls away from the viewer. The structure on top disappears not because it falls into the building, for at this stage of the collapse the outer shell of the building is tilting like a tree, falling like a rigid object, but because the tilt of the building takes it out of view:

If the above image fails to animate for you, reload it in a new tab.

After about two or three seconds into the collapse it starts to fall downwards, as if in a demolition, but the start of the collapse is that the shell of Building Seven tilts and rotates southwards away from the camera like a tree falling towards the notch cut by the axeman. The change in the angle of the dark line shows that in the first few seconds of the fall, the movement is primarily rotation sideways, rather than droop downwards. The further end of the dark line drops by more than the north face of the building drops, indicating considerably more rotation southwards than droop downwards. In these images of the very first part of the collapse of the outer shell, the top of the building is moving away from the viewer a lot faster than it is moving downwards.

The image below, shot from the east side, shows it half way through its fall, transi-tioning from falling sideways like a tree, to collapsing downwards like a building.

Building seven was rated to survive three hours of uncontrolled fire, before the heat penetrated the insulation on the steel beams, softening them and causing them to collapse.

It instead survived seven hours of uncontrolled fire, roughly the amount of time predicted when it was built, when the builders considered the possibility of a fire raging for a long time without being brought under control.

They expected that any fire would be brought under control in three hours or less, and therefore the building could not be brought down by fire, but unfortunately the damage caused by terrorists crashing planes knocked out the water supply.

Building seven fell partly from damage, partly because the steel beams softened in the heat of the fire. When the building was designed the insulation on the steel beams was rated to withstand three hours fire:

> The instructions to the bidders for the WTC 7 job were to bid on a 3 h rating for the columns[297] and a 2 h rating for the metal deck and floor support steel, which corresponded to the more stringent fire resistance requirements for Type 1B (unsprinklered) construction. These ratings were to be achieved by application of Monokote MK-5, a gypsum-based SFRM that contained a vermiculite aggregate. According to the Underwriters Laboratories (UL) Fire Resistance Directory (1983), these ratings required a thickness of 22 mm (7/8 in.) of Monokote MK-5 to be applied to the heavy columns, 48 mm (1 7/8 in.) to be applied to the lighter columns, 13 mm (1/2 in.) to be applied to the beams, and 10 mm (3/8 in.) to be applied to the bottom of the metal deck. Private inspectors found that the applied SFRM thicknesses were consistent with these values

which is a longer fire than would ever be allowed under normal circumstances. The reason for having insulation on the steel beams is that the builders expected that without insulation, fire would cause the building to fall - as it did. It fell because it reached and exceeded its design limits for not falling, and it fell as we would expect a building to fall from such a cause, in that it started its fall like a tree, sideways towards the notch.

Global warming scam starts to unravel

2018-09-30 04:20:51

The basic religious impulse behind global warming is that technology and industrial civilization is a creation of whites, males, and capitalists, and primarily a creation of white male capitalists, therefore must be evil.

The political impulse behind global warming, its strategic value for the blue empire was that the replacement people were largely concentrated in blue coastal federal electorates, thus wasting their votes, so the blue empire wanted to move people who work and don't commit crimes out of federal electorates in flyover country, where their votes were likely to tip the balance, into coastal areas where they would be massively outvoted. Similarly, the policy of bombing marginal federal electorates in flyover country with black

---

[297] https://ws680.nist.gov/publication/get_pdf.cfm?pub_id=861610

male Muslim military age rapeugees living on crime and welfare. So they wanted to destroy productive activities, such as logging and coal mining, in flyover country. To avoid wasted Democratic votes, they want to move people who work and do not commit crimes out of flyover country, and people who do not work and who do commit crimes into flyover country. Similarly, they want people who vote Democratic armed (hence operation Fast and Furious) so that they can kill people who vote Republican (hence gun control).

The blue empire proceeded to apply its soft power to drag the rest of the world along for the ride. Thus the Paris climate treaty had almost all the pain to be inflicted on flyover country Americans, with just barely enough pain for the rest of the world to make it an "international" treaty (which is to say a treaty where the "international community", aka the US State Department, agrees with itself), and thus avoid the inconvenience of Americans who lose their jobs because of it being able to vote against it.

To the religious impetus of hostility to industrial civilization, which is to say white male capitalist civilization, was added the impetus of hostility to those horrid rednecks in flyover country.

The only real action item on the Paris accord was smashing Americans in flyover country, making them suffer, and providing political cover for smashing Americans in flyover country. If Americans in flyover county are not being smashed, not one gives a tinker's dam about the rest of it. It is already sliding out of sight and out of mind.

Trump has not been able to do much about the flood of illegal immigration, but the stops against coal mining and fracking rested on executive orders, and he simply issued new executive orders, whereupon those jobs that "were gone and not coming back" promptly came back.

Coal mines and such are generally in flyover country, Democratic voters on the coast, so, moving legacy American out of flyover country makes more efficient use of imported voters.

But Trump shuts down this tactic, and the entire rest of the world loses interest in Global Warming.

The rest of the world was being put through the motions to provide political cover for the blows against near. Paris was just political cover for shutting down jobs in flyover country, in order to move republican voters into areas full of wasted federal Democratic party votes.

With Trump shutting down that tactic, suddenly the soft power of "the international community" loses interest in Global warming[298].

One might suppose that this is the result of everyone reacting to the same data at the same time, but not so. When the climategate files came out, it was obvious that global warming was a religion, not science, and that global warming scientists had precisely zero interest in whether global warming was true of this world, that it was a religious truth, not genuinely expected to be empirically verifiable, not really expected to be supported by, or supportable by, the facts of this world.

The empirical evidence for global warming remains about the same as it has ever been. If any warming is happening, the effects are imperceptibly slight, and likely to remain

---

[298]https://business.financialpost.com/opinion/lawrence-solomon-trudeau-stands-alone-as-canada-and-the-world-abandons-green-energy

imperceptible for a long time.

But suddenly, around the world, people are forgetting about efforts to fight the terrible scourge of global warming.

For some time warmists have been making a big deal out of disappearing ice at the north pole (Glibly ignoring the fact that the South Pole is far larger than it was when the first expeditions visited the place.)

Every year since 2007 highly honored high status official scientist Peter Wadhams tells us:

> Arctic will be ice free in summer next year[299]

After a decade of false predictions, more honored than ever. Being wrong works great for official science, while being right is apt to be fatal for one's career.

Over the past couple of hundred years the North West passage has sometimes been closed all year, sometimes open briefly during summer. Always too much ice to sail the arctic reliably even in summer, always too little ice to reliably and safely reach the North Pole by sled even in winter. There is always ice, even in the North West Passage in summer, there is always open water, even at the North Pole in winter, and that is the way it is always been. Hard to see any climate change, because the day to day weather changes, and the year to year weather changes, are vastly bigger than the supposed climate change.

This year, even icebreakers could not make the Northwest passage in high summer.

Yes, the Arctic has less ice than it used to. And the Antarctic more, but I am not seeing a trend, just pink noise, temporally correlated random variation, a fractal roughly half way between red noise (a random walk) and white noise. If there is a trend, hard to discern against a background of large random changes. Finding patterns in climate change is not a whole lot easier than finding patterns in stock market price change. Retrodiction is apt to be a whole lot easier than prediction.

I will now predict the Arctic climate and weather:

The North West Passage has been open before and closed before: It will be open again, and closed again.

There have been large areas of open sea at the North Pole before, and it has been entirely covered by thick ice before: It will be covered by ice again, and open sea again.

There has always been enough ice that it is a big problem for ships even in high summer: There will continue to be enough ice that it is a big problem for ships even in high summer.

There has always been enough open sea at the North Pole that it is a big problem for sleds even in mid winter: There will continue to be enough open sea that it is a big problem for sleds even in mid winter.

It is rarely possible to reach the North Pole by ship, because ice is usually in the way. It is usually difficult and often dangerous to reach the North Pole by sled, because water is usually in way. Sledding and sailing has become easier, because aided by satellite observations, and because one can be rescued by helicopter. Helicopter rescues will continue to happen from time to time, both because of too little open water for ships, and too much open water for sleds.

---

[299]https://www.theguardian.com/environment/2016/aug/21/arctic-will-be-ice-free-in-summer-next-year

Goodbuy NAFTA, hello USMCA

2018-10-02 01:34:24

Major changes:

1. To qualify as USMCA manufactured cars have to be (mostly) built by workers earning $16 per hour - in other words white workers, because mestizo and indio workers are generally not worth $16 per hour. Usually minimum wages are a bad idea, because they keep kids out of the job market and prevent them from gaining experience, but since you can place a car plant anywhere the major impact of this is that car companies are going to be making cars away from Democratic party vote banks, in federal electorates where the votes of working class whites are likely to matter.

2. US gets to sell milk products to Canada. Again, jobs for Republican voters, in federal electorates where Republican votes matter.

This is a major victory for Trump's infamous hardball deal making style. By smacking Canada hard against the wall, Canada being of all the countries in the world the country worst placed to withstand a trade war with the USA, Trump creates the expectation that you have to do trade deals his way.

Same tactic as Reagan invading Grenada. Smack the monkey to scare the gorilla. (Canada being the monkey, and China the gorilla) Also delightfully humiliates that irritating girly man with the fake eyebrows, which likely gives Trump even more joy than it gives me.

Paternity, war and conquest.

2018-10-02 02:17:28

Competition with no limits and no rules is the war of all against all, is predation, every other creature except for close kin being obstacles or raw materials. Humans organize so that competition is channeled into productive activities, rather than massively negative sum activities. But how do we organize this? This is what we call order, and political order is also order in the thermodynamic sense, in that a functional state of the social system, where competition produces excellence through cooperation is a very special case, and any random change is apt to be for the worse.

Where does this organization come from. Where does order come from?

Partly it comes from a ruler, but for a ruler to actually remake society, he has to have remarkably great power, which is apt to result in competition to be the ruler getting out of hand, as it did in the Roman Empire. In substantial part it comes from natural selection of social orders. A society where people cooperate effectively is apt to conquer and dominate other societies, much as a group of humans can predate upon a herd of cattle. Thus, for example, colonialism, outsiders come in, inject themselves at the top of the colonialized society's social order, and remake that society in their own image, not necessarily killing all the men and enslaving all the women, quite likely creating greater prosperity and freedom for everyone, but rather more prosperity and freedom for themselves.

The better a society is at creating prosperity through orderly and productive competition, the more likely it is that its dominion is rather more civilized than killing all the men of the conquered society and taking their land and women. But there needs to be some substantial payoff for those imposing order. If no substantial payoff, drift to entropy is inevitable.

The population size estimated from Y chromosome diversity is smaller than the population size estimated from mitochondrial diversity, indicating that far more females than males reproduce - we are de-facto a substantially polygynous species.

About seven thousand years ago, during the transition from hunting and gathering to agriculture, this ratio went to extremes[300].

One possible explanation of this is that the local ruler owned all the land and owned all the women, thus only one male in seventeen got to reproduce. Another possible explanation is that women got to choose, and they chose one male in seventeen. But the bottleneck happened during the transition between hunter gathering and farming, hence connected to property rights and property rights enforcement, thus property rights enforcement in land, crops, cattle, and women.

Only the local ruler reproducing is unlikely to be stable. The other males will not fight for him. Thus a patrilineal group cooperating and fighting to enforce its property rights in cattle and women, as depicted in the book of Genesis. Genesis depicts Abraham's patriarchal group warring with Kings with reasonable success. Books later in the series depict patriarchal groups helpless before Kings and armed religions.

The bottleneck can be explained by competition between patrilineal groups, so that the survival of one man's Y chromosome is highly correlated with the survival of his kin in the paternal line, where one patrilineal group was apt to wipe out another patrilineal group and take their women. If you were a descendant of Genghis in the male line, you and all the other descendants of Genghis in the male line would work together to take the other men's women and prevent other men from taking your women - which implies and presupposes that women got no say in this.

During the transition, need property rights in land, crops, and cattle.

Father's brother's daughter marriage ensures social cohesion on Y chromosome lines. Abraham's property rights in cattle are secured by kinship relationships with people who share his Y chromosome.

Later, Kings matter more, patrilineal kin matter less, but if everyone secured property rights the way Abraham did, there would be a high correlation between Y chromosomes and reproductive success. Own stuff, have the same Y chromosome as other people owning stuff. Don't own stuff, don't reproduce.

In the book of Genesis, we see a bunch of wars in which patrilineal kinship groups fight kings as roughly equals. This environment could mean a much smaller effective population size for Y chromosome, since the population size would be number of property owning patrilineal groups, not number of individual males.

---

[300]https://www.reddit.com/r/science/comments/8nrxzy/about_7000_years_ago_something_weird_happened_to/

This does not necessarily manifest as outright conquest and abduction - just that you can feed women, and the guy without property rights cannot, and you can enforce your property right in women, and thus you *want* to feed your women and their children.

If enforcement comes from patrilineal groups, including enforcement of marriage, then a moderate disparity in willingness and ability to enforce property rights in women and children can result in a very large disparity in effective population size, because we are measuring not the number of successfully reproducing males compared to the number of successfully reproducing women, but the number of successfully reproducing patrilineal property rights enforcement groups compare to the number of successfully reproducing women.

Of course, we are still talking war between patrilineal groups but the war may fall short of killing all the men and taking all the women in one hit. But if a patrilineal group cannot defend its land and women, it is going to eradicated, possibly in a less sudden fashion.

The point is that one gets a reduction in effective male population size if genetic survival is correlated with one's Y chromosome. Everyone you know is descended in the male line from your great great granddad. And if he is not, no one is stopping you from taking his cattle and his women, and killing any children encumbering those women. But this implies that you know who everyone's dad is, which implies female sexuality is under male control - as depicted in the old testament in the time of patriarchs, where the penalty for consensual sex was death.

This does not necessarily mean that one night patrilineal clan A attacks, and in the morning the Y chromosome of patrilineal clan B is no more, but that is the net effect over time, meaning still fairly brutal.

For the model to work, a major unit of selection has to be the clan, with the men of clan B being eradicated, all of them, and the women of clan B being taken into clan A, which is what we expect to happen if cooperation is mediated through patrilineal relationships, and not matrilineal relationships, which implies women being hauled away, and males controlling their sexual choices.

For the model to work, your brothers in the male line and your cousins in the male line have to support your capability to reproduce, which requires that they restrain your women from screwing other men. Thus, patriarchy, and patrilocality. Patrilocality means you maintain your connection with your brothers and cousins in the male line, and if your sister is married or stolen outside of your male line, you lose your connection with her, and patriarchy means that the enforcement system for property also enforces marriage - thus your women are your property like your cattle, thus everyone knows who is someone's father. You stick up for male kin's property rights.

Exodus happens around the time of the collapse of bronze age civilization, 1200BC to 1150BC, therefore Abraham's kin group contending successfully with kings have to be around 2000BC or so, which puts them well after the bottleneck, but they could well be a survival, a leftover, of the bottleneck social order. The bottleneck lasted from around 5000 BC to 3000BC. Abraham has to be around a thousand years after the bottleneck, but some remnants of the bottleneck social order are still going strong today, in that we still have societies where patrilineal groups are important in protecting property rights in women and cattle. America's defeat in Somalia was patrilineal kin groups contending successfully with modern day sovereigns equipped with cruise missiles and attack helicopters five thousand years after the bottleneck, so it is plausible that Abraham and his kin could have successfully contended with Kings a thousand years after the bottleneck.

It looks as if the white race originated ten thousand years ago and four thousand years ago, in waves of near genocidal conquest by early whites. About eleven thousand years ago, neolithic grain growing middle eastern farmers, with light brown skins, dark hair, and brown eyes, who largely ate bread, porridge, and drank beer, conquered Europe, completely genociding the paleolithic brown skinned, but blue eyed, European hunter gatherers, who retreated before them towards Asia into more severe climate of Russia. As the middle easterners penetrated into harsher climates, they entered an environment less favorable for grain growing, and more favorable for cattle herding, and the paleolithic hunter gatherers retreating before them were no longer hunter gatherers, but cattle ranchers, so the conflict became more equal. The two races exchanged hostages, as recorded in the sagas, and interbred. Hybridization and subsequent selection produced higher IQ fair skinned people with mixed eye and hair colors, the ancestors of modern whites, who herded cattle, and lived on milk, meat, butter, and cheese. These people invented bronze and in due course, war chariots drawn by small horses, and conquered the farmers of Europe, killing the men and enslaving the women in another wave of hybridization, producing a race that largely ate bread, butter, and beer, who subsequently produced bronze age civilization.

But about twelve hundred years before Christ something went horribly wrong. Bronze age civilization collapsed and depopulated, and white pastoralists once again conquered, but this time, were conquering lands that had largely been abandoned - a functional society returned, because a dysfunctional society largely failed to reproduce. The switch from bronze to iron seems to have been forced by the collapse of long distance trade. Iron could be produced from local sources, but bronze required that people mine tin in one place, and copper in a very distant place, so that people were forced to find a technological solution to replace long distance cooperation, much as today the corporate form is collapsing, and we seek to replace the corporation with the block chain.

So it is non trivial to produce a society where competition leads to cooperation rather than destruction. Magic dirt does not do it, and high IQ does not in itself do it. A society where competition is productive rather than destructive is highly ordered and that order is the product both of selection and of conscious will.

The last days of bronze age civilization were socialist in the sense that the Egypt described in the bible was socialist, and socialist in the sense that Ithaca described by Homer was socialist. Archaeology indicates trade was centralized in the palace. Internationally traded goods and intertemporally traded goods, like the wheat that Joseph advised the Pharaoh to horde, were managed by kings, and distributed through the palace, as indicated by the archaeology of the Minoan civilization, indicating that private property rights were not secure. Similarly, we record Abraham pretending that his wife was his sister - thus property rights in women were insecure. And then, in the Ithaca recorded by Homer, and the Egypt recorded by Ipuwer, the property rights of the King also became insecure - people failed to reproduce due to the sexual immorality recorded by Ipuwer, and the fields lay unplanted, because he who sowed was unlikely to reap.

The decadent settled people of the bronze age vanished, and were largely replaced by severely patriarchal pastoralists - pastoralists who condemned coveting, and respected private property and marriage - thus prohibiting the most obvious forms of destructive competition.

In the ten commandments we see the conscious design of a social order by a ruler with kingly and theocratic power. The emphasis on prohibiting coveting suggest that Moses perceived the social breakdown and collapse of Egypt as a result of insecurity of marriage and property, but he was building on or reviving the social order of the patriarch Israel, or claimed to be doing so, which reflects the natural selection of social orders, since descendants of Israel had, overall, reproductive and military success - and it was this military capability that preserved their way of life against Egyptian attempts to multicult them, to assimilate their social order to the dysfunctional Egyptian social order.

There are four religious commandments concerning worship, which have the effect of making those obeying the commandments visible to others who obey the commandments, and ensuring that people who obey these commandments tend to associate with people who obey these commandments, since they were all required to take their rest day at the same time, and six commandments concerning how men shall deal with men, which have the effect of ensuring that competition for women and goods does not take destructive forms.

These latter six rules were generally obeyed by successful societies until recent times, but leftist redistribution of goods and emancipation of women now results in competition for women and goods being political, making it difficult to produce wealth or reproduce. Coveting, rather than being forbidden, has become a sacrament, and adultery a human right. Recollect how Starbucks was recently memed into providing black people with a free home and office.

If two men agree to exchange wheat and iron, the exchange must make both of them better off or else they would not agree to it, and is unlikely to have significant externalities, but if a woman decides to have sex with a man, the decision is always deeply irrational, an eruption of volcanic forces that she does not comprehend and is scarcely aware of, and the decision is apt to have enormous externalities, harming her actual and potential children, her parents and siblings, and her present or future husband. But we regulate the hell out of two men exchanging wheat and iron, while horrifyingly wicked and self destructive sexual choices are an absolutely inalienable human right.

As is the murder of unborn children. Currently we have a system were the unborn are treated as non people in relation to women, and as people in relation to fathers and taxpayers.

If we suppose that the unborn should be treated as non people, then it makes no sense that the tax payer or the reluctant father should provide child support. Bastards should be killed or enslaved.

If, on the other hand, the unborn should be treated as people, then the mother should be compelled submit to the father, to be always sexually available to him and never to any other, and the father should be compelled to support, protect, supervise, and guide the mother and the child, and to always be sexually available to the mother.

An inalienable right of women, but not men, to murder children is made necessary by the inalienable right of women to have sex or refrain from having sex with whoever they choose, whenever they choose, because their choices are apt to be so disastrous as to produce problem children.

Leftism and female emancipation is coveting and adultery, and leads to destructive competition over goods and women. Adultery is not a code word for sex. It means much the same thing in female pussies as in beer.

Another important virtue, not covered in the old testament, is truth telling, which was, in the England of the restoration, an aristocratic and noble virtue thinly disguised as a Christian virtue, though it was never a Christian virtue. The Gentleman was independent of and resistant to social pressure to go along with the false consensus. The gentleman could be relied on to speak the truth because of his independence. This ideal of gentlemanly independence is the opposite of peer review, which produces truth by consensus behind closed doors. Peer Review has produced the replication crisis, where no one can trust other people's data, and it was predictable that it would, since the social dynamics of consensus behind closed doors is to produce official truth unrelated to empirical truth, which by imperceptibly small degrees gradually becomes outright fraud, as unwanted data is "corrected" to fit the social consensus.

Peer review is bringing back the demon haunted dark. The demon haunted dark closes in upon us, shutting down nuclear power, forbidding fracking, superstitiously terrified of dangerous compounds at one thousandth their harmful levels. Peer Review needs to be condemned as vile, disgusting, and unclean, akin to adultery, for the social dynamics of peer review inevitably lead to lies being enforced, and truth being demonized. Peer review on empirical questions and empirical data is like wallowing in shit, you get exposed to memetic diseases. It is the memetic equivalent of gays in a bathhouse having sex in a great big pile. As sex in the bathhouse in a great big pile spreads biological diseases, peer review spreads memetic diseases. The lies fester and multiply behind closed doors.

The requirements of a functional social order are well known, narrow, and precise - and installing them means enforcing a moral code, requiring all in positions of status and power to affirm this moral code, and demolishing the status of anyone challenging this moral code by treating them as if they were stray dogs attacking your chickens, which moral code necessarily condemns leftism as inherently sinful.

Everyone should learn about the crimes of the twentieth century, and be taught that they were caused by coveting, as today they are taught that they were caused by racism.

It has been done in the past. It can be done again. That is the planning and conscious will aspect. If one society in one place manages it, and manages to keep to it, it will in due course colonialize all others, or massacre the menfolk of all others and enslave their women, or just eradicate all others completely. That is the natural selection of societies aspect. The social order of the patriarch Israel, with private property rights in cattle and women, was favored by natural selection, and consciously re-created by Moses in a deliberate act of political will, political violence, and divine revelation.

Science continues its downward spiral

2018-10-03 01:48:30

Science died shortly after 1944, when Harvard got the upper hand over the Royal Society and imposed peer Review in place of the scientific method.

The premier science magazine "Nature" tells us:
Arctic sea ice continues its downward spiral[301]

The article fails to show us exactly how downwards is this "downward spiral", other than it is worse than we thought.

Here is what the article fails to show you:

Yes, arctic ice is lower than it used to be, but a "downward spiral" would seem to imply it is continuing to go downwards, not that it dropped in 2007 and has been low since, which looks more like a downward step.

For this to be a spiral, needs to keep on going downwards. Looks like weather not a trend. Some days are hotter, some colder, some years are hotter, some colder, some decades are hotter, some colder, and some centuries are hotter, some colder. Not obvious this has anything to do with CO_2 levels. If this had something to do with CO_2 levels, you would expect steadily rising CO_2 to produce steadily falling ice, which is what the article untruthfully claims.

Nor is it obvious that human emissions of CO_2 have any effect on atmospheric levels of CO_2, are capable of having any effect on CO_2. Dwell time of CO_2 in the atmosphere appears to be a decade or so.

More likely that CO_2 is rising because temperatures rose some years back, than the other way around.

God Emperor beats Democrats at 4D chess

2018-10-06 22:55:09

Time and time again Trump does supposedly stupid stuff, supposedly demonstrating what an ignorant stupid buffoon he is, and then, strangely and mysteriously, wins.

The explanation for this strange mystery is that he is playing the game at a level his enemies do not understand, playing a different game by different rules to that which his enemies are aware of.

Recent events need to be understood in terms of the left's theory of legitimacy, and Moldbug's theory of the uniparty.
The Uniparty

Democrats are inner party of the uniparty, the high status inner members of the uniparty, Republicans are the outer party, the low status outer members of the uniparty.

Until the Kavanaugh nomination, Republicans were utterly determined to lose the mid terms in the house by any means necessary.Even though individual Republicans want to win their races as individuals, they don't want other Republicans to win their races,

[301] https://www.nature.com/articles/d41586-018-06882-4

because this would put them in a position where they are under pressure to implement Republican policies.

Democrats wield the carrot and the stick over Republicans. The carrot being "Cuck out and we will allow you to crawl close enough to us for us to spit on you", the stick being, as we have seen in the Kavanaugh crisis, actual stick.

Trouble with wielding actual stick is that if you wield too much stick against too many Republicans, the two party system is likely to rise from the dead. Remember all those complaints that Trump's Kavanaugh tweets were not helping? They were helping collapse the uniparty system. Trump knows how to trigger his enemies into acting unwisely. Today, the two party system rose from the dead. Today, Republicans voted *on party lines* for a judge that will rule that it is legal for Republicans to govern. In the next month, chances are that Republicans will campaign to win the house.

Legitimacy and Color Revolution

Legitimacy in general means, "Should be obeyed, even when you disagree or don't like it." But the only people who are supposed to ever do this are conservatives, because when progressives don't like it, it's illegitimate. The Democrats are the party of the priesthood, the party of Harvard, and the priestly class gets to define legitimacy.

So:

If people vote or some lower authority figure acts against progressivism, any other institution whatsoever is fully justified in neutralizing and reversing the outcome by whatever means necessary, and those institutions are portrayed as 'legitimate' which means that it is everyone's holy duty to defer to them, at the very least, surrender and acquiesce in submissive and obedient resignation, but more often, they are supposed to recognize that the action really does flow from the 'rule of law' and accurate universal principles and the "true meaning of democracy vs mere populism" or whatever.

On the other hand, when the shoe is on the other foot, these institutions are illegitimate, biased, corrupt, tribal, ultra-partisan, extreme and radical right-wing, etc., etc., usually racist, and basically Nazis. And "anti-democratic" as opposed to anti-populist or pro-Constitutional constraints. They deserve zero respect or deference - indeed, constant criticism, protest, public shaming, and personal destruction - and progressives should feel free to ignore any pronouncements of such an institution as presumptively suspect and inherently invalid.

The priests denounce the sovereign as illegitimate, and this sometimes manifests as color revolution: a handful of priests storm the winter palace, successfully applying hard power, because the warrior class, who could crush them like ants, have been neutralized by priestly soft power. To do violence to violent priests would be "illegitimate".

Today, a handful of priests stormed congress, and the warrior class crushed them like ants.

From time to time some judglet from Hawaii rules that Trump's policy is racist, therefore that judge gets to exercise executive, legislative, and fiscal authority and overrule the President of the United States. I have been urging and expecting Trump to pull a Tony Abbott, and use military power to overrule the courts, or to pull a Duterte, and just plain terrorize the courts, but to my surprise he has so far adopted a more moderate course, and appointed judges who will reliably rule that the elected president and the elected party have the right to govern.

This will put the priestly class in the interesting situation of claiming that the president, the congress, *and the Supremes* are illegitimate.

If Trump is to assume his rightful place as God Emperor, he will sooner or later have to pull a Duterte, but perhaps he judges that the time is not yet. Likely, when the priestly class is campaigning on the grounds that President, Congress, *and the Supremes* are all illegitimate, the priests will burn the Reichstag.

Angry mob meme

2018-10-11 04:37:55

The Democrats are an angry mob of crazy vicious moral degenerates.

Trump:

> "You don't hand matches to an arsonist, and you don't give power to an angry left-wing mob. Democrats have become too EXTREME and TOO DANGEROUS to govern. Republicans believe in the rule of law - not the rule of the mob."

Well, then, if the other party is an angry mob, democracy cannot really continue.

Democracy relies on a certain amount of comity, trust, and mutual tolerance keeping the stakes down to something that people can afford to lose, a general acceptance of playing by the rules.

Progs instituted a new rule: That if a male is accused by any women anywhere, even if there is no likelihood they ever met, different schools, different circles of friends, hang out in different geographical areas, even if the woman is ugly and the man handsome, even if the woman has no evidence and is strangely vague as to the place and time where this supposedly happened, even if there is no indication that the two ever met, or were ever in a situation where they could have met, well then, the man is guilty, because we cannot possibly doubt the victim. If you doubt the victim, the poor pitiful victim, you are a rape apologist.

And then, in a startling display of balls, Republicans refused to play by these rules. Democrats were outraged.

Eric Holder:

> "When they go low, we kick them. That's what this new Democratic Party is about,"

So, republicans must be punished for noncompliance with the 2018 rule until compliance is obtained, since failure to comply with the latest unilaterally announced progressive rules is obviously unacceptably bad behavior.

What, I wonder, will the 2019 rule be?

If Republicans must be punished, can they ever allow a mere election to return Democrats to power?

And if the Democrats do regain power, chances are that Republicans are going to be punished in a way that makes it impossible for them to ever return to power by democratic means.

I am not predicting that democracy will dramatically and visibly disappear tomorrow, because the Roman Republic never dramatically and visibly disappeared. Rather, we will have elections that increasingly resemble the style of today's California or the 1934 German plebiscite.

Yamna

2018-10-13 06:38:34

Origin of the white race:

I have mentioned this in passing a few times before, but it deserves a post of its own.

It is dangerous to use the word A***n, so scientists have been using the word Yamna. Also "proto indo european", but "proto indo european" is a bit long winded, whereas "Yamna" has the same number of syllables and a similar sound as the unspeakable word, and is close to being an anagram of the unspeakable word.

The Yamna were aristocratic, patriarchal, and white, and conquered much of the world, and today's whites are white because of Yamna repeatedly conquering inferior races, killing their men, and enslaving their women[302].

The coalition of the evil and unhinged

2018-10-19 00:18:30

People form political coalitions within a larger society in order to knock over apple carts to grab some apples. That is what politics is. That is why people use "political" as a negative word. Because it is a negative thing.

The left is not the largest coalition. The left is whatever coalition is largest.

Whatever happens to be the supposed coalition issues at any given time is unclear, arbitrary, and frequently changing. The left has no essence, no defining character, other than that is against whoever is managing the apple cart, and against whatever is keeping the apple cart upright.

But right now, it is a coalition of single women against males, husbands, marriage, and children, nonwhites and Jews against whites, and the underclass, Human Resources employees, accountants, and government employees against capitalists and against private sector employees who produce physical things, sexual deviants against straights, and non Christians against Christians.

Democrats tend to think that the only reason someone would which oppose this coalition is if he is a straight white male Christian capitalist.

(And I am a straight white male who is socially Christian in the sense of irregularly attending Church and ingrouping Christians, viewing them as adoptive kin, and arguably at least as capitalist as any kulak. Half the time Carlylean Restorationist and Glosoli tell us that they are only against invisible trillionaires, and the other half of the time, they are going to kill the peasant who raised a pig to eat, because he is supposedly forcing blacks on welfare to eat too much fried chicken fast food, so I am at least as capitalist in my economic role as those that Carlylean Restorationist blames for bad lower class behavior, and I am also socially capitalist regardless of what definition they use in any one comment

---

[302]https://elpais.com/elpais/2018/10/03/inenglish/1538568010_930565.html

and regardless of my economic role. When Human Resources went after management, I got drunk with management.)

All large tribes are necessarily synthetic, all a synthetic tribes are necessarily religious, are necessarily religions, broadly defined, and the people who are managing the unity, solidarity, and social coalition of the synthetic tribe are necessarily performing a priestly role, are clerics and priests, broadly defined. And so, in any synthetic tribe, you tend to get priests on top, and the path to get to the top of the priesthood is apt to be superior holiness.

So, it is not just our society that is coming down with a holiness spiral. It is the left coalition that is coming down with a holiness spiral and the left dominating our society.

The left, like my excessively frequent commentators Carlylean Restorationist and Glosoli, tells us that we white males should hate capitalists and capitalism (which happens to be overwhelmingly straight, white and male). Supposedly all these rape and sexual harassment charges are coming from Evil White Male Trillionaires, not from the cat ladies of Human Resources. Perhaps on some other blog, they pose as white women and tell white women to hate white males, and that therefore white women should ingroup blacks on welfare, and on a Muslim blog, tell Muslims to hate Christians, and that therefore Muslims should ingroup feminists, support abortion, and emancipate their daughters.

But, as the left coalition goes ever more extreme under the pressure of the holiness spiral, it is increasingly against all whites, all males, all Christians, and all heterosexuals. So in the coming election, all whites, all males, all married women, all Christians, and all straights should vote Republican.

We are seeing Republicans go after the votes of black males and the wives of black males, rationally appealing to the rational self interest of intelligent black men, and the wives of black men, that the Democratic anti male agenda is dangerous to men, and telling them it is especially dangerous to black men, that black males are under even worse threat of getting the Kavanaugh treatment than white males.

Trump's maleness appeals to black males. Hence Kanye West praising Trump's male energy. The president is the father of the nation, and it is has been a long time since the nation has had a masculine father figure. Lots of black males are, likeKanye West, missing that male father figure.

In the 2016 Republican Presidential primaries, we saw Trump, and only Trump, campaign against the holiness spiral.

In the 2018 mid term elections, we are seeing a whole lot of mainstream republicans, led by Trump and inspired by Trump, campaign against the holiness spiral.

But the holiness spiral is not the Democratic party, and cannot simply be voted out of power. Observe that the holy are still in power, despite having been voted out already.

Tony Abbott in Australia took measures unthinkably drastic by American standards, and yet the holy remained in power. Duterte and Viktor Orbán, however, are getting places. Duterte used right wing death squads. Viktor Orbán applied less drastic measures, but he has been in power a long time and only now is getting some traction.

Charles the First said "No Bishop, No King", meaning if no Bishop, then no King. For the merely elected leadership to be effective against the holiness spiral, they to intervene in the priesthood to stop holiness competition, which is what Viktor Orbán has been doing. He made superior holiness a poor career move.

There are huge number of state and quasi state jobs that are supposedly immune from "political" control, people who are on the government or quasi government payroll, who are chosen by their fellow social justice warriors on the basis of superior holiness, which means that they are immune from *merelyelected* politicians, but their appointments are in practice very political indeed.

What Viktor Orbán did is radically amend the constitution to put these under direct "political" control - put the priesthood directly under the authority of the merely elected government, and he then proceeded to make superior holiness a bad career move *within the priesthood*.

A similar change in the US, to do in the US whatViktor Orbán did in Hungary, would be to confiscate the college endowments, give the president the power to hire and fire any civil servant, including college presidents and judges, and make the president effectively the final court of appeal over the supreme court. And *then* elections could halt the holiness spiral. As long as we have a vast pile of quasi governmental institutions that are outside the power of the merely elected government, in particular Human Resources, we are going to continue having a holiness spiral regardless of people voting against it. Accounting is also falling to Social Justice Warriors, having been remade by Sarbanes-Oxley into a quasi governmental institution, and as a result the accounts of publicly traded joint stock corporations are fast becoming as unreliable as peer reviewed research, in much the same way, and for much the same reasons, as peer reviewed research has become irreproducible.

In the coming mid term elections, we will likely get a merely elected government that is hostile to that holiness spiral, though unable to do much about it. No Bishops, therefore no King. Once again I repeat my prescription: Archbishop, Inquisition, and Grand Inquisitor.

To implement that in America, likely will need a King.

The Reichstag is burning

2018-10-26 05:50:22

The fake bombs were not sent through the mail, (no postmark on the stamps and insufficient postage) therefore delivered in person by an insider. Recipients did not act as if they feared the bombs were real. Therefore, the insider was recognized by the recipients.

Therefore recipients were complicit in a fake bomb threat - which is as serious a crime as complicity in a real bomb threat. The criminality of fake bomb threats is settled law and practice, and rightly so, for deadly threats are apt to lead to deadly acts.

The interesting thing therefore is whether settled law and practice gets applied to senior Democrats.

If Democrats get away with this, they can get away with similarly criminal acts of real violence. If they cannot get away with this, it is the Reichstag fire.

If they cannot get away with this, then we are going to see a whole lot more people start hailing Trump as God Emperor Trump.

Although I have been referring to him as God Emperor Trump, this impious as well as optimistically premature. He is still merely a president presiding over a presidency that hates him, ignores him, and routinely defies him. If he does deal with those who set the Reichstag on fire, if the FBI chooses to obey him in and prosecute direct political crime committed by powerful people, then he has successfully brought the presidency to heel, whereupon a more appropriate name is Holy American Emperor Trump the First.

If he deals successfully with those who lit the Reichstag, I will then hail him as Holy American Emperor Trump the First, as is likely to reflect his real status.

If, on the other hand, the FBI ignores criminal acts by senior democrats, we have taken one more step towards Civil War II, but this time a rather large step, which will be in due course followed by even bigger steps.

Reactionary Fiscal Policy

2018-10-26 06:54:25

Reactionary fiscal policy is the same as every other reactionary policy: Avoid anarcho tyranny, avoid power slipping from the center into the hands of a faceless horde of anonymous bureaucrats, who will then be subject to incentives to act more like mobile bandits and less like stationary bandits, and who, having gathered vast power into their hands, vast, anonymous, hidden and covert power, will then proceed to legitimize their anonymous power with political programs that undermine the sovereignty of the ruler and his authority to legitimately rule, political activism hostile to the ruler that they supposedly serve.

The horde of bureaucrats gathers power, and sovereign loses power, by the bureaucrats uglifying and complexifying all the tasks of the sovereign, so that thesovereign gets a mountain of paperwork in his in tray, throws up his hands in despair, and moves the whole mountain from his in tray to his out tray, to be taken care of by whoever it is that takes care of his out tray, and he has no idea who takes care of his out tray, the contents of his out tray being treated as a pile of loot and pillage by a horde of faceless bureaucrats who get to anonymously, frivolously, and casually exercise the full power of the President.

The worst example of this was judges grabbing the Kingly power to rule on equity, rather than law, which gave us a thousand little Kings. And once again I say "Forms of action", the remedy that William the Conqueror successfully applied to solve the problem of dangerously great judicial power. But I digress. Back to fiscal policy:

Governance tasks have to be simplified, so that the exercise of Kingly power is sufficiently infrequent that the sovereign can actually make these decisions.

And one important task of Kingly power is issuing and managing money.

The huge advantage of fractional reserve banking is real bills - that liquid money is backed by illiquid assets, typically houses that have been mortgaged. Thus, in this sense, fractional reserve money is real money.

The trouble with fractional reserve banking is term transformation, which leads to banking panics, which leads to fiat currency and a central bank, and leads to all financial institutions becoming state or quasi state enties, leads to a financial system that largely socialist. And here we are.

The central bank sets the interest rates for the banks. The various interest rates charged by banks, credit card companies and the like differ from the central bank interest rates in ways that are supposedly set by the free market, and to some extent actually are set by the free market, but they all go up or down with the interest rate set by the central bank. And they all tend to go up when the permanent government dislikes the merely elected government (Trump) and they all tend to go down when the permanent government likes the merely elected government (Obama).

If the federal reserve sets the interest rate from day to day, then it all too complicated for the sovereign, who unavoidably winds up delegating it to a cabal of insiders who manage the not very free financial market for the private profit nominally of private entities who have been delegated substantial state power.

Thus, it tends to be lucrative, or at least not very costly, for bankers to be wrong about credit worthiness and loans provided that they are wrong in the same way at the same time as all the other bankers are wrong, because when the proverbial hits the fan, they will be bailed out.

Theoreticaly the central bank sets interest rates from time to time in such a way as to keep the economy on an even keel, and to some extent it actually does so, but when we look back at past adjustments, then in restrospect the central bank tends to get things wrong remarkably often, raising interest rates shortly before a demand, and lowering them shortly before an inflationary fake boom. What incentive do they have to get it right.

The right wins in Brazil

2018-10-29 04:12:40

If we are lucky, this will be the last Brazilian election in a very long time. Bolsanaro is more Trump than Trump is.

> The White House has confirmed that US president Donald Trump called Jair Bolsonaroon Sunday night to congratulate him on his election victory.
>
> White House spokeswoman Sarah Huckabee Sanders says that Trump congratulated the president-elect and that "both expressed a strong commitment to work side-by-side to improve the lives of the people of the United States andBrazil.

The losers looked remarkably like Hillary supporters on election night. Lots of delicious liberal tears.

His political program is on the face of it unremarkable: for gun rights, for family, against abortion, for capitalism, for God, for country, for secure property rights and in particular for secure property rights in land and houses, against crime and corruption. Is there anyone who is openly for crime and corruption?

So why the all the drama?

Because, in the eternal struggle between priests and warriors, he thinks that warriors should rule. When our priestly classes, the professoriat, the media, and the judiciary, cast

God out of the high places, they sawed off the branch on which they were sitting. For priests to rule, they need to plausibly claim to represent God and be backed by God.

And, having declared themselves holier than God, proceeded to rub it in with gay rights, transexuals, and so on and so forth. There is a limit to what can be done with soft power, and they have hit that limit, and are flailing. Increasingly they are forced to use openly dictatorial methods, such as seizing the gab.com domain name.

We have non priestly rulers in the USA, in the Philippines, in Hungary, and now in Brazil, the most openly opposed to the official priesthood of them all. In the USA, the priestly classes are abandoning their pretended support for freedom of speech and freedom of religion, so even if they win, they lose. In Hungary, and only in Hungary, the elected government has taken real power from the permanent government, but if it can be done in Hungary, possible in America.

The holiness spiral, the left wing singularity, inexorably leads the priesthood into self destruction. The details of the crash are different each time, as glass shatters differently each time, but the crash is inevitable. Where we go from here no one knows, but ever leftwards is looking less and less likely.

The seizure of Gab a few days before the election, and the obvious bomb fakery, reveals that they are abandoning business as usual, and are now going to try open priestly dictatorship, as in Russia in 1916

If they had just sat quiet for eight years of Trump, and waited for demographics to continue to move in their favor, they would have been fine. Business as usual would have worked for them and would have destroyed us. But the underlying force of the left wing singularity will not let them sit quiet. They have to continue becoming ever more extreme, ever faster, and it is biting them. The frog is now being fast fried instead of slow boiled.

Election outcome

2018-11-07 10:37:52

I am disappointed and surprised that we did not see a red wave. But the loss of the house changes little. Trump did not have a majority of Trump Republicans before the election and he now has a slightly larger minority of Trump Republicans. And in any case, the house has had no real power since FDR.

With better control of the Senate, Trump can get judges and appointments through better, and this makes a big difference, since personnel are policy.

Augustus could kill his opponents, and Duterte can kill his opponents, but it took Augustus over ten years to get real control of the Roman government, and Duterte still has no real control of the Philippine government. (Rome continued to suffer from anarcho tyranny, government by mobile bandits, until 11BC.)

Hitler, on the other hand, took real control of the German government in two years. Roman emperors continued to have problems controlling their government until Constantine got a religion in his pocket. Warriors need priests in their pocket in order to govern successfully.

As Charles the first said "No Bishop, no King."

No nation with a gay parade wins wars

2018-11-15 22:48:38

Israel has just been defeated yet again.

Three days ago they invaded to Gaza to put a stop to intolerable organized acts of war by the government of Gaza. Were militarily defeated.

This was rationalized as a one off bungle. These things happen, but now, rather than trying again with the supposed errors rectified, they are seeking a peace treaty that restores and legitimizes the intolerable status quo ante that they sought to change, indicating not merely one bad mistake, but an incapacity to make war.

Tolerating gays makes it impossible for men to express love and affection for each other. This undermines unit cohesion. Also trannies and women in the military undermine unit cohesion. And putting logistics and nurses in uniform and calling them soldiers rather than camp followers, embeds, and military contractors denies warriors the honor that is their rightful due.

Gaza does not have gay parades. Israel does. So Gaza wins, Israel loses. Israel has not won a war since they started allowing gay parades. Sooner or later, the Arab world is going to realize that Europe is weak, Israel is weak. There is a lot of loot and unowned chicks in Europe and Israel.

"Hail Fellow ComicsGate Fan"

2018-11-23 22:46:58

ComicsGate died. It died because it allowed a leadership that hates ComicsGate and hates the fans to take charge.

Hate is defined as wanting tropes that are now forbidden, like the Han Solo of the first Star Wars movie who rescued Princess Leia and the original very manly Thor. Thus either ComicsGate is hate movement or it hates the fans. And the leadership of ComicsGate hates the fans.

> "Go write it and find your audience"

But when Vox Day went half way towards writing what the fans want, the leadership of ComicsGate denounced, deplatformed, and demonetized him.

According to the leadership ComicsGate is against "politics" in comics – where "politics" is any trope or archetype that has been forbidden. And Vox Day's stuff is indeed political, very political, not because it flagrantly defies the Zeitgeist by using tropes and archetypes forbidden in 1979, shortly after Han Solo rescues princess Leia, but merely because it uses tropes and archetypes forbidden in 2010.

For this horrid crime (cool character wearing a confederate flag) Vox Day was denounced, deplatformed and demonetized. But 2010 is not what the fans want. The fans don't even really want the rogue Han Solo rescues princess Leia. Princess Leia is a subversion of the trope, because she is "feisty" They want the the rogue rescues princess Andromeda.

Perseus rescues princess Andromeda, returns her to her family, who turns out to be tight fisted about giving him his rightful reward. He then kills Princess Andromeda's fiancée (after Princess Andromeda passive aggressively manipulates him and her fiancée into a fight by acting like a cat toy), abducts her, and bangs her like a drum, and she enthusiastically gives him his reward.

Similarly the Sea Wolf, a pirate king played by Errol Flynn, abducts the princess not once but twice. The first time she is rather feisty, but the second time he bangs her like a drum. Her feistyness the first time was just a shit test. The second time he abducts her, he has passed the shit test with flying colors, and her feistyness vanishes.

Similarly McComb, played by Errol Flynn in "Silver City" deliberately causes the death of Georgia's beloved husband after amogging him, and Georgia (who, despite being not in the least feisty, passive aggressively set up their conflict by acting like a cat toy) forgives him with indecent swiftness.

The fans want the original Han Solo rescues princess Leia, and no one dares give it to them. They want the original Thor, and no one dares give it to them. And I am pretty sure that they would want Errol Flynn as the Sea Wolf rescues, then abducts princess Andromeda in the style of Perseus, cheerfully leaving a river of blood behind him, and no one has dared give them that for two centuries. Indeed the Pirate King "Captain Blood" played by Errol Flynn was itself a subversion of the trope, because of a disappointing lack of the promised blood. The fans who had watched Errol Flynn as the pirate King in "the Sea Wolf" were disappointed with insufficient wolving, wanted to see the pirate King "Captain Blood" earn his name, but he failed to do so.

The female fans want to see two extremely alpha males in conflict over a woman, and the male fans want to see two extremely alpha males in conflict. When I set up a party I always try to arrange for females to heavily outnumber males, so that amog is not a problem, but amog makes for good stories even though it makes for terrible parties. When I am host at a party I milk the host role to the max to amog, and when I am a guest I try to support the host in the role of amog, but I am apt to carelessly amog him anyway.

No one dares write for the masses. The masses want Han Solo to rescue Princess Andromeda, and instead they get action girl rescues lad in distress, even from Vox Day.

Cap'n Jack Sparrow is gay and respects women. He is a subversion of the Han Solo trope, not a modern example of Han Solo trope. And even the original Han Solo is a subversion of the trope, in that he rescues Princess Leia, not princess Andromeda.

The only comics producer who goes half way towards producing what the fans want claims to speak for ComicsGate, and the self appointed leadership of ComicsGate, who fail to produce what the fans want, denounce him: Only those who hate ComicsGate may speak for it.

The fans are not getting what they want, and the self appointed leadership of ComicsGate denounced, demonetized, and deplatformed Vox Day as ultra right because he weakly went half way in the direction of giving the fans what they want.

Ariana Grande can do rock concerts that promote prostitution to unaccompanied eight year old girls, but no one dares realistically depict the male and female courtship roles, Han Solo has not rescued Princess Andromeda for 196 years.

Rock music videos can do sadomasochistic rape on screen, but they are not allowed to do Rhett Butler and Scarlet O'Hara on screen.

"I want well written characters of all types"

Supposedly the leadership of ComicsGate wants well written stories of all types, but instead gives the fans action girl rescues lad in distress.

No one has been able to write the Perseus and Andromeda story for two centuries. They were writing in the corners, and the corners have become ever smaller, so that now they cannot write anything entertaining at all, just as Chris Rock can no longer be funny.

If ComicsGate got what it wanted, Han Solo would fly again and rescue Andromeda the way Perseus did. The leadership of ComicsGate melted down over Alt Hero comics and called it politicized fiction that goes against everything ComicsGate stands for. Imagine how they would react if the original Thor rescued Princess Andromeda after the fashion of Perseus.

When Perseus rescued Andromeda he did not ask her permission to touch her, just as Han Solo did not ask permission to touch Princess Leia. Perseus killed her fiancee, abducted her from her family, and banged her. She liked it, but it would have made no difference had she disliked it. No one has been able to publish such fiction for two centuries.

Vox Day's fiction is political right, but the heroine always rescues the lad in distress, the rogue is not lovable, let alone rescues the lady in distress. What does he have to do to be sufficiently left wing to meet the standards for "non political" comics?

Vox Day is an ultra extreme far right winger because he makes the heroines of his books a hot archer or spell caster rather than a fat frumpy lesbian who punches out a dozen mooks in one blow and rescues the lad in distress by punching through prison walls. If Vox Day were to do the original Han Solo in comics or books the leadership of ComicsGate would scream "Hitler" until their heads exploded.

And similarly, you cannot depict romance in movies and rock videos any more, because the male and female roles now have to be interchangeable, as for example the role inversion in "The Wedding Date" and the role symmetry in the Lord of the Rings movie.

You cannot do the pirate trope successfully if the pirates are required to be respectful towards women.

Romance in the the "Lord of the Rings" movie trilogy was sickening and boring, because they could not depict the mating dance as having fundamentally different roles for men and women, could not depict men conquering and women surrendering, nor men performing and women choosing, after the fashion of Errol Flynn and Rhett Butler.

Social Justice Warriors have declared tropes and archetypes that are an essential part of the fan mythos to be unacceptable and out of bounds. To write stories containing necessary and important elements is "extreme right wing". And no one is transgressive enough restore them. The bounds have become so restrictive that it is no longer possible to write good stories or tell funny jokes.

ComicsGate was a reaction to hostile acts by social justice warriors against the fan's myths and culture. To call for a "politically neutral" ComicsGate is like calling on the Warsaw uprising to even handed between Poles and German soldiers. It is preemptive surrender.

A "politically neutral" ComicsGate is a suffocatingly left wing ComicsGate that hates and despises its fans.

Han Soyboy's identity in the latest Star Wars was a pussy whipped beta loving from afar. Turned out that a lot of people preferred the identity of the bold alpha rogue who laid hands on women without asking them for permission. But not even Vox Day dares to be such an "extreme right wing misogynist".

When the leadership of ComicsGate tells us Vox Day comics are "Right Wing" and "don't appeal to everyone" they are telling us that there is a vast untapped audience that wants to see frumpy fat lesbians acting counter stereotypically.

If the movement had been glad to associate with the only substantial publisher who does not shove social justice down their throats, it would still be a movement.

There is no ComicsGate community any more. Once you punch right and purge rightists, everyone knows they will be next. Purgers need to be preemptively purged, because purges go ever leftwards until the purgers are themselves purged.

It is a wall

2018-11-26 04:10:05

The wall begins by executive order under President Trump's inherent authority to defend Americans from enemies foreign and domestic:

Invaders flying enemy flags advance on the Great Wall of Trump, chanting "The people united will never be defeated":

Invaders storm the wall:

Reaction 101: The reactionary red pill on women.

2018-12-07 06:01:26

The basics of Reaction need to be stated, and they need to be stated in a way that excludes our enemies, because we are seeing a whole lot of people saying "Hail fellow reactionary", who are clearly hostile to us, and not hostile the media/academic/judicial elite that we seek to overthrow, blaming various groups that tend to be allied or sympathetic to reaction for the problems caused by our holier than thou elite, urging reactionaries that the real enemy is group X, where X is anyone who is plausibly an ally or likely to become one. They want us to ingroup our enemies, ingroup those that outgroup us, and outgroup each other.

So, starting with the concepts most likely to offend: The reactionary red pill on women. Which are also concepts that have practical application even while our enemies rule. Next articles in the Reaction 101 series will be more directly political and have less individual application in daily life.

Emancipation was a bad idea. Feral women behave badly and are psychologically disturbed. They need to be redeemed by becoming the property of some man. Women are psychologically maladapted to independence and equality

In any marriage or long term relationship, the woman will endlessly launch physical, emotional, and legal power struggles against her husband or boyfriend, shit tests, which power struggles she wants to lose.

If she wins, she will break up, looking for someone who can conquer her. You just have to win. If the only way to win without going to jail is to send her away, send her away and go dark. But she would rather you beat her. You have to wear the pants. This is the PUA analysis of negs and shit tests, applied to long term relationships.

Women are maladapted to equality. That women find male apes sexually attractive while men do not find female apes sexually attractive indicates that among those humans that whites and east Asians are descended from, females have not been allowed to make sexual choices since the days we looked rather like apes. Since female sexual choice is quite common, we should conclude that groups that allowed women sexual choice failed to reproduce or suffered dysgenesis, and perished.

In order to reproduce, and particularly in order to reproduce in the white and east Asian ancestral environment, in a cold climate with severe winters that require food and shelter over winter, husbands and wives need cooperate/cooperate equilibrium, and if you have free women, you get defect/defect equilibrium. To impose cooperate/cooperate requires external coercion, in particular that women have to be stuck with the first guy that they have sex with, and are not permitted to be permanently on the prowl to trade up throughout their fertile years.

When allowed to be permanently on the prowl, they tend to practice serial monogamy until around thirty or so when their eggs start running out.

All businesses with women in power are destroyed, unless they are the beneficiaries of some state favor that artificially keeps them in business. Female executives are only useful if under the authority of a sexy alpha male, otherwise they turn on the shareholders, the employees, and the customers, perceiving them as betas.

Subjective personal observation: All sexual harassment complaints result from horny women shit testing terrified men, and then getting frustrated because the terrified men fail their shit tests. This personal observation is statistically confirmed by the fact that a far larger proportion of women complain about sexual harassment in workplaces where the women substantially outnumber the men. There has never been one complaint of sexual harassment against me, and if sexual harassment complaints resulted from what social justice warriors tell us constitutes sexual harassment, there would have been a pile of them.

Subjective personal observation: All rape complaints are false and all rape convictions are false, not because real rapes do not happen, but because women do not really mind real rapes and fail to complain. This personal observation is confirmed by the University of Virginia complaints process: The university of Virginia dealt with a big pile of rape and sex complaints, and dismissed every single one without disciplinary action. So Rolling Stone investigated them looking for poster girls and trouble, came up empty.

Men and women very much want to form families and want those families to last into their old age. My wife was eighteen in my eyes all her years, except near to the very end.

If you look at any successful family, no one is equal. Dad is in charge, mum picks up the socks. In principle, it is possible to form families in a society where men and women are equal, by freely contracting out of equality, but in practice, it is hard, and I see how hard it is for my sons. We have prisoners dilemma with few iterations, so the natural equilibrium between men and women is defect/defect. To prevent defect/defect, to ensure cooperate/cooperate, requires heavy handed coercive intervention by state, family, and society, and this heavy handed coercion necessarily bears far more heavily on women than on men. If you want a society where men and women know sexual love, or if you want a society which has above replacement total fertility rate, women just cannot be allowed to follow their pussies. And this requires a lot of supervision and coercion, primarily keeping women under control, rather than keeping men under control. For most women this requires that they be subject to the potential threat of physical discipline by the men in their lives. For a great many women, this requires that they be subject to the actuality of physical discipline by the men in their lives. So women should never have been emancipated, and some "violence against women" is legitimate, proper, and proportionate. Women, like children and dogs, need discipline and supervision and are never happy if they do not get them. A spoiled child, or a spoiled woman, or a spoiled dog, is never happy. The dog and the woman bark all the time.

Further, sexual impulses set in in girls at a disturbingly early age, usually well before puberty though there is a great deal of variance, while male sexual impulses set in at puberty, as reliable as clockwork.

Ever greater vigilance against "pedophiles"[303] is like telling a chicken farmer he should not fence or cage his chickens, but instead should make the world safe for his chickens to wander wherever they please. When nine year old girls go to an Ariana Grande concert without being accompanied and supervised by male kin, they are going there to get nailed. Restraints on female sexuality have to restrain females, have to be oppressive to women, because being oppressive to men is not likely to work, and is conspicuously and spectacularly failing to work.

The family law of the Old Testament got it right, and modernity is surrealistically deluded, and flat in my face insane. I see in front of my nose stuff that no one else sees, so either I am insane or the world is, and the statistics are strangely consistent with me being sane, and difficult to reconcile with the world being sane. If you are using words for human things and human conduct that the people of the Old Testament had no words for, chances are you are using words for things that have no real existence, anticoncepts[304], words that are lies[305], that you are speaking madness and delusion.

The family law and family institutions dictated in Deuteronomy and depicted in the Book of Proverbs lasted for thousands of years. Our current social order is extremely recent. Within living memory, within my memory, it has changed radically in ways that are horrifying, tragic, and terrifying, and everyone is acting like this is normal and nothing is wrong.

---

[303] https://blog.reaction.la/culture/words-that-are-lies/
[304] https://blog.reaction.la/culture/words-and-meanings/
[305] https://blog.reaction.la/culture/words-that-are-lies/

Modernity is for me like one of those horror movies where one character sees monsters and another character does not, and you wonder if the monsters are real or just delusion, until you see someone get eaten by a monster. And I see people getting eaten by monsters, in the sense of transparently false rape, sexual assault, domestic violence, sexual harassment et cetera charges, and I also see people who tell me men have nothing to fear, because women never lie, while women have much to fear because they so very very much dislike rape, sexual assault, domestic violence, and sexual harassment. But I also see these men acting terrified, while I am bolder than any of those men who supposedly believe that men have nothing to fear. In part of their minds they must see what I see, because I see their fear, and in part of their minds, the part that speaks and constructs a narrative, they do not see what I see, even though it is right in front of them.

This repression, repression of awareness of what is in front of everyone's face, and repression of male sexuality, is depressing every male's testosterone levels and sperm production, though if you consciously recognize it and consciously reject it, this reduces the impact on your testosterone levels a bit. Men go overboard on repressing each other, as a displacement activity because they are denied their deep desire to control women.

Women get angry because they do not get the supervision, command, and guidance that they crave. Sometimes this anger turns inward, as with cutting[306] and other self destructive acts[307], and sometimes it turns outward. She feels really badly treated, because she has in fact been really badly treated, but because the real causes of her discontent are unthinkable, she concludes she must have been sexually harassed or sexually assaulted, when in fact her mistreatment was lack of sexual assault, lack of a strong hand to discipline her.

Reaction 101: Priests and warriors

2018-12-21 10:12:32

We are always ruled by priests or warriors.

Priests are in the business of controlling what people think, warriors in the business of controlling people by hurting them and breaking their toys.

So who else matters?

Merchants can control people by offering them value, hence get targeted due to envy and covetousness, but merchants have no substantial incentive to cohere into guilds, whereas priests naturally cohere into priesthoods (see the Climategate files for this process in operation) because if you hear the same story from several different people it sounds a lot more convincing, and warriors naturally cohere into armies, because otherwise, likely to die.

And the rest should do as they are told, and if we make sure they get a wife, children, and a home by doing what they are told, they will surely do it.

If merchants group into a cartel, that would profit them collectively, but any one merchant has large incentive to defect on the cartel, and there is not much the cartel can do to stop him, whereas the priest does not profit by defecting on the priesthood. The

---

[306] https://blog.reaction.la/culture/cutting/
[307] https://blog.reaction.la/culture/field-report-on-a-trans/

warrior sometimes has large incentive to defect on the army, but there is a lot the army can do to stop him.

By "priest" we don't mean someone overtly in the business of making supernatural claims. We mean a member of a priesthood, and by a priesthood, we mean what the Chinese call a "knowledge faction" – a bunch of intellectuals who conspire together to give everyone the same story and use the same shibboleths, so that it sounds more convincing.

In practice, even when a priesthood vehemently denies making supernatural claims, as for example the communists vehemently claiming to be strict materialists, they frequently wind up sounding remarkably similar to those that do make overtly supernatural claims. Thus "occupy" meetings sound like prayer meetings. The Occupy Priest chants an incantation, and the congregation chants a response. Similarly the Chinese communist party is always talking about faith and values. Everywhere in communist China there are official party books about "How to be a good party member who has faith", "Chinese people have faith in the party", "Have faith in the ..." In China, you are forbidden to call Communism a religion, but it is perfectly OK to call Communism a religion in every way short of actually calling it a religion and the Communist Party itself does this all the time.

The claim that all men are created equal is transparently supernatural. The Marxist theory of history is the God of nineteenth century Judaism renamed "History", a thinly disguised supernatural claim. Holocaustianity is the tenth commandment inverted, a somewhat better disguised supernatural claim.

But what makes a priesthood a priesthood is not supernatural claims. Long lived religions usually restrict their supernatural claims to unfalsifiable issues, like transubstantiation and so forth. In the long run, falsifiable claims, claims about this world, claims that conflict with science, lead to problems, as for example the progressive claim that men and women are indistinguishable, a claim that every music video must endorse, which restriction makes music videos and comedians boring. What makes a priesthood a priesthood is that they get together to get their story straight, so that all of them are on message - which is what makes them a knowledge *faction*. Lots of people are knowledge workers, but the essential element that makes a priesthood a *faction* is that they coordinate to get their story straight in order to make it sound more convincing, and what makes them a priesthood, a *knowledge faction*, is that they seek power by controlling what people think.

To be effective, a priest needs to be part of a group of priests who back each other up by telling the same story, and a warrior needs to be part of a group of warriors that back each other up by physical violence, thus warriors naturally cohere into armies capable of ruling, and priests naturally cohere into priesthoods capable of ruling, while capitalists naturally compete for workers and customers, workers for jobs, entrepreneurs for capital and workers, so do not cohere into groups capable of ruling. If you see a capitalist who appears to rule, for example George Soros, he is a hireling of those who do rule.

When we are in power the state religion will make overtly supernatural claims, but these claims, unlike the supernatural claims made by the current state religion, such as that all men are created equal, will be entirely unfalsifiable, and will never draw faith into conflict with science, for in such conflicts, science always loses totally and devastatingly, as for example in Global Warming debate, and the ensuing destruction of science is bad for your society, your technology, your economy, and your military capability. The reason that our nukes do not work any more is because men and women are supposedly equal. Nukes don't work for the same reason that music videos and comedians are no longer entertaining. The state religion has to stay out of the way of science and technology, because science and technology are so terribly weak and fragile. Religions that make falsifiable earthly claims usually self destruct eventually, not because science defeats them, but because they blow themselves up, as for example the Jewish Zealots. The holiness spiral leads them to make earthly claims that require faith to be demonstrated by ever more disastrous earthly actions, as for example the Zealots destroying their own food supplies while besieged by the Romans, and transgenderism requiring one to castrate one's own children and sit them on the laps of gays.

This account of priests and warriors make them sound like entirely bad things, that warriors are bandits, priests conspiratorial conmen. That is the libertarian and anarcho capitalist position: bandits and conmen.

The reactionary position, on the contrary, is that warriors performing the right role of warriors is the most honorable profession, and in a good society warriors shoud be honored, and that priests performing the right role of priest is an honorable profession, and priests should be honored second only to warriors.

Obviously we need warriors to prevent bandits. The defense of property and freedom is costly, the price is terribly high, and the honor due to warriors is part of the fair price we must pay for the security of our persons and our property.

What about priests?

Priesthood is rather more complicated. The state cannot really enforce law. Your computer is not registered with the government. You have to enforce your property rights in it. The government will back you up, but this only works because there is widespread agreement on property rights and right conduct, shared beliefs about good conduct with other members of the ingroup. That the state is all powerful is bluff and illusion. We are never out of anarchy. The state is a ramshackle ship on a storm tossed sea. It cannot really enforce law, only back up private enforcement. And private enforcement will only work if beliefs about what should privately be enforced are widely shared.

And lately these beliefs have been radically and rapidly changing - most notably in the direction that women and gays can do no wrong. The old testament position that if one's wife or betrothed slept with another man, then it was fine to kill them, seems more in accord with human nature.

The American position on hot burglary, when a burglar openly and obnoxiously burgles an occupied dwelling, is that it is that it is totally OK to kill the burglar on sight without warning. The british postion is that it is totally and absolutely to do anything violent to the burglar, no matter how violent the burglar is, especially if you are white and the burglar is nonwhite. Similarly, the American debate about Trayvon Martin and George Zimmerman - some people took the position that it was totally OK for Zimmerman to kill Trayvon, if Trayvon was on top hammering Zimmerman's head against the concrete, while other people took the position it was not OK for a "white" man to kill a black man, no matter what the black man was doing. (Zimmerman got white status from both those who supported him and those who condemned him. Those who condemned Zimmerman called him white, because they hate whites, even if they themselves are whites, especially if they themselves are whites. Those who supported him called him white because they wanted to claim a man who can shoot straight while blood runs over his eye as of their own race, called him white for being able to shoot straight while having his head banged on the concrete. One shot directly through the heart.)

The Book of Deuteronomy tells us that adulterers should be killed, but takes no position on whether it should be state, Church, family, or offended husband that kills adulterers. The position of the Rabbis at the time of Roman rule, the time of Jesus, was that it should be church (temple) that kills adulterers. The law as interpreted and applied at the time of King Solomon was that it was the offended husband, which is very much in accord with human nature. Gnon tells men to defend their own.

Adultery means adulteration as in beer - a man sleeping with another man's wife or betrothed. If a man sleeps with a woman not his wife, but that women is not married or betrothed to another man, this is not adultery in the sense used in the old and new testaments.

If it is right for a man to defend his television set with deadly force (the American position) it is surely right to defend his capacity to reproduce with deadly force. State, family, and church should apply less extreme measures to adulterers, as they do to burglars, while backing the choice of the man who was personally threatened to use more extreme measures to adulterers, as he can to burglars.

The useful and proper function of warriors is to prevent mobile banditry - the stationary bandit prevents the mobile bandit. The useful and proper earthly function of the priesthood is to get the ingroup all on the same page of right conduct - to create a synthetic tribe, to get everyone feeling like part of the ingroup, *and to promote shared values of right conduct*, to get everyone *acting like part of the ingroup*.

You want everyone to agree on what constitutes cooperation, what constitutes defection from fair and reasonable expectations, and what constitutes defection so serious that violence on the spot is necessary and justified. And the legitimate earthly job of the priesthood is to form, represent, and communicate this consensus.

A priest should be in the business of teaching values and managing group identity, managing shared mythos and shared values. Thus something very like a priesthood creates something very like a religion, not necessarily in that it is about overtly supernatural claims, but in that it is an adoptive kin group based on shared values.

That the claims of traditional Christianity were either verifiable or unfalsifiable makes it a lot less supernatural than its new age competitors such as global warming or cultural Marxism, whose claims are not only supernatural, but entirely falsifiable, and usually falsified.

You want your warriors to be fighting for God, King and Tribe, as well as for gold, pussy, and land. And if you don't have a priesthood that is on your side and on the warrior's side, you don't have a tribe.

For being a warrior to be an honorable profession, the warrior must fight not only for gold, pussy and land, but for God, King, and Tribe. If a warrior fights only for gold, pussy, and land, not honorable. If only for gold and pussy, he is a mobile bandit, which is the most dishonorable of professions. And without a good priesthood, hard to have a good tribe.

And since the west is detribalizing, since the priesthood is hostile to us and to our warriors, we are going to be overrun by mobile bandits soon. The great asylum seeker migration, which is largely military aged males, prefigures this.

From the time we defeated the Mongol hordes in Hungary in 1241, to our defeat in Afghanistan in 1840, the west was uniformly victorious for six centuries. (The Mongols were victorious in Hungary in that they successfully devastated and terrorized it, but were defeated in that they were never able to control it, that they never were able to draw revenues from it, that they kept on losing large amounts of treasure, men, and horses in it, and that the west gained the secret of gunpowder from them.)

Since then, since 1841 we have been suffering defeats by ever weaker enemies, notably the hilariously humiliating British defeats in Basra, the Persian Gulf, and Helmand province. The writing on the wall is that the west is ripe for conquest, like a wealthy elderly widow in a neighborhood that has turned bad. Not so much conquest by a major power like China, but rather a dark age collapse, when ever changing minor actors engage in mobile banditry - closer to the New Year rape festival in Cologne, or the car burning festivals in Paris, than D Day. There is a lot of loot and pussy for the taking, and neither the will nor capability to defend it. Something is like to go pear shaped sooner or later. The forever war in the middle east is a sign that the west has delusions of power - that its actual military capability is far less than it is used to, far less than everyone tends to take for granted. The west has not fought a war against a substantial enemy for quite a while, and has been losing, or winning inconclusively, against absurdly weak and tiny enemies.

As a warrior is honorable when he fights for God, King and Tribe, as well as for gold, pussy, and land, a priest is honorable when he performs the earthly task, the task in this world, of ensuring that there is a tribe to fight for, and that the tribe has agreement on what constitutes good conduct such that good members of the tribe do not feel like fighting each other, that the interactions are, as far as possible, cooperate/cooperate.

Since our current State religion is headed towards suicide and mass murder, we are going to need a replacement, assuming we survive at all. And that replacement has to grant warriors honor, and enable men and women to form families.

Merry Christmas

2018-12-24 18:07:46

Peace on Earth, and goodwill to all men.

And, this being a reactionary blog, I remind you that peace on earth requires adherence to the Peace of Westphalia.

The forever war in the middle east is a violation of the Peace of Westphalia, because it is fought to teach nine year old schoolgirls to put a condom on a banana, and to ensure that more women than men graduate. if it was fought to slaughter those that allowed Al Quaeda on their territory, would not be a violation of the Peace of Westphalia, no matter how many were slaughtered.

Marxism

2018-12-30 14:05:44

The flat earther sees the earth is flat.

He then distorts or ignores all contrary evidence. The flat earther cannot explain why when I call my grandsons at sunrise, they are watching the sun set, nor why the stars in southern sky rotate around one point, while the stars in the northern sky rotate around the opposite point.

If you ask the flat earther about these issues, he will give a completely idiotic and incoherent explanation that that supposedly shows that sunset and the rotation of the stars actually prove the earth is flat. His explanation makes no sense, but if you complain that his explanation makes no sense, he will repeat it with added emphasis and demand that you present a rebuttal, even though you have just presented a rebuttal. If you repeat your rebuttal, he will again tell you that no one has rebutted him, and again repeat with ever greater confidence and certainty his completely incoherent and nonsensical explanation of why one person on a flat earth is watching the sun set, at the same time as another is watching it rise.

Similarly, a 911 troofer denying the airliner sized and shaped entrance hole in the Pentagon, and telling you that World Trade Center building seven suddenly went into free fall for no plausible reason. No matter how many times you tell him the photo shows an airliner size and shaped hole, and no matter how many times you tell him his video shows building seven starting its fall like a tree notched by an axeman, tilting to the south towards the terrorist notch cut in the building, and towards the square to the south of it, he will tell you that is not what the video shows, not what the photo shows. Or more likely change the subject, tell you a hundred things equally untrue, and then after telling you one hundred other things, then again tell you the photo does not show what shows and the video does not show what it shows. And this just goes on. He just will not concede what is in front of his eyes.

And, similarly the Marxist. But while Flat Earthers are stupid, ignorant, and crazy, and Troofers are stupid, ignorant, crazy and dishonest, Marxists are stupid, ignorant, crazy, dishonest and murderous.

Marxism, trooferism, and flat earthism all consist of breaking all the evidence in order to make it fit a bad theory. At some point, you notice stuff is not adding up, you have to toss your preconceptions, and start over. But whereas flat earthers ignore inconvenient evidence, and 911 troofers lie barefaced about inconvenient evidence, Marxists not only ignore evidence and lie about evidence, but murder witnesses, often major portions of the population.

The erroneous theory of Marxism is Marxist Class theory and Marxist economics. Marxist class theory makes no sense because they reify social classes as if they were individuals, as if the class was a single person with a single will, and Marxist economics makes no sense because they ignore the creation of value by capital and entrepreneurship.

A Bronze age Greek navigator settling the Aegean sets sail.

A rower asks him "Where the hell are we? We are lost."

Navigator says "That is Kasos. Over there is Karpathos."

Rower says "No it is not"

Navigator tells him "Shut up and row. Karpathos looks like that when you are this far away from it."

A Marxist talks of "Capital" as if "Capital" was a person, a single person who rules the world.

Thus the Marxist theory of history is that capitalism is very recent, and consists of "the burgher" taking power from "the lord". Not "a burgher", nor "a lord"

In fact, of course, the French revolution was not burghers taking power, it was burghers having their property confiscated, and then being guillotined.

The world was capitalist for thousands of years before its most recent feudal period, it was capitalist during the most recent feudal period, and it was capitalist after the most recent feudal period.

A Marxist thinks that "Capital" is one person, and that that one person rules, that "the capitalist class" acts as one person, as a socialist central planner.

A Marxist sees coordination, that bread is delivered the supermarket, concludes that all capitalists are one capitalist, that all firms are one firm, that big capitalists command little capitalists, thinks the world is a socialist system with a central planning office in Wall Street.

Perhaps a simple way of clarifying what Marxist Class theory is, is that if you believe in Marxist Class theory, it logically follows that "Capital" was rationally pursuing his self interest by successfully seizing power from the French aristocracy, and you will with great confidence come up with some clever explanation of why this seizure of power and successful pursuit of self interest resulted in so many capitalists losing their possessions, and so many of them losing their heads.

A Marxist thinks that capitalists rule. He concludes therefore that capitalism is recent, since at sometime in the past, kings and aristocrats ruled.

Thus a Marxist thinks that the french revolution was "the capitalist class" seizing power from the feudal lords, and therefore it was in the interests of "Capital" to do this. Of course in actual fact, the french revolution immediately resulted in most capitalists having their property seized and resulted in very large numbers of them being executed.

The French revolutionary government debased the currency, and then set maximum prices for bread and such, with the natural result that no bread was available, whereupon it immediately set to work executing bakers, farmers, and so on and so forth, an outcome that businessman usually expect in any change of power, since any time power changes hands there tends to be a period of mobile banditry following the overthrow of the previous stationary bandit, until a new stationary bandit appears. The overthrow of the Aristocracy was utterly devastating to the interests of the capitalist class, and they violently opposed it from the beginning, but were terrorized into submission many of them being murdered in that terror.

If someone tells you capitalism is recent, he is a commie, and he plans to murder you. If someone talks of "Capital" as though it was a person, he is a commie, and he plans to murder you.

Thus the Trotskyite tells the peasant with one cow that his real enemy is the "kulak", the peasant with two cows, and that the peasant should therefore ally with the Trotskyite

Jews from the big city to kill his neighbors cows. "Hail fellow member of the oppressed classes. Jews are oppressed too you know"

Meanwhile the Trotskyites are telling the Orthodox Jews "Hail fellow Jews, we are suckering these Christians into allying with us Jews, and when we have them fighting each other, we will destroy them"

And so the Jews help the peasant with one cow kill the cows of the peasant with two cows. "Hah hah, says the Trotskyite,"Hail fellow Jews. Now that this Christian is socially isolated, we will take his seed corn. " So they kill the cow of the peasant with one cow, then they pour petrol over his children and set them on fire to force him to reveal where the seed corn is buried, then they force him to dig up the seed corn, and then they kill him.

Then the Trotskyite, who never really cared about the seed corn, grabs one of his fellow Jews, and tells him he is a capitalist hoarder and oppressor of the masses, and tortures him with pliers and hot irons into revealing where his gold coins are. And having obtained the gold coins, tortures his supposedly fellow Jew some more, in the hope that there are more gold coins, but since there are no more gold coins his fellow Jew expires under torture.

Then the Trotskyite points out that all the noble work he has been doing for the oppressed victims of capitalism makes him holier than Stalin, and Stalin piously concedes his superior holiness, but finds some excuse to kill the Trotskyite before the Trotskyite is in a position to kill Stalin

The leftist who tells you "Hail fellow member of the oppressed, lets knock over this apple cart and grab some apples", is very likely after *your* apple cart and *your* apples. Thus they announce they are friends of the American working class, who should ally with them against evil billionaires, while seeking to destroy the working class in favor of an imported vote bank living on crime and welfare - hence spotted owl, global warming, Paris Treaty, wildfires, and TransPacific Partnership.

Leftists were always telling us that the TransPacific Partnership was a plot by our evil capitalist overlords seeking cheap overseas workers, but it was Obama and the Democrats pushing it, and Trump and the Republicans that killed it.

The Marxist thinks that capital is one being, but in fact, "capital" is your local Domino's franchisee, who is likely a white male like yourself, and likely about the same wealth as yourself, differing from you by about as much as the peasant with two cows differed from the peasant with one cow.

Troofers don't stick to any one story of what supposedly happened at 9/11, flat earthers don't try to make sense, and Marxists don't try to make sense either, circularly arguing that since capitalists rule, anti capitalist actions and policies are actually pro capitalist. Thus, for example, capitalists supposedly want to be taxed to support fatherless spawn, so that they can sell them stuff.

Failure of reality testing: Same problem with Marxists, flat earthers, and Troofers.

Flat earthers are stupid, but not evil. Too dumb to realize they are not making sense.

Troofers and Marxists are stupid and evil, and because Marxism is a rationale for murdering innocent people and taking their stuff, Marxists a lot more evil than Troofers.

One sees stuff that seemingly does not make sense - the islands of the Aegean viewed by a flat earther, the absence of a banged up airliner in front of the Pentagon, the fact that there is bread on the shelves, and start concocting a nut theory.

Round earth makes sense of what you see. Rule by "Capital" fails to make sense of what you see. You can see the capitalist right in front of you when you buy a pizza, and he is not "Capital"

One's physical intuition is led astray by the vastness of the earth, so that it looks flat except under rather special circumstances.

And under those special circumstances (navigating by looking at distant familiar landmarks over a long distance of ocean), one is apt to get weirded out as one's flat earth intuitions fail, and to avoid unnerving weirdness, one either has hang close to shore, or stop looking at familiar distant objects, or actually see the roundness of the earth as one sees the roundness of a child's ball and know in your guts that you have traveled a small but perceptible angle around it.

The navigators of the Chinese treasure fleets had to hang close to shore for psychological reasons, sailing a very indirect and dangerous route to minimize the disturbing sight of landmarks falling below the horizon. The irrationally shore hugging path they followed shows them to be flat earthers, while Europeans have known the world was round since before the dawn of history, probably as a result of settling the Aegean Islands.

The islands of the Aegean are close enough that you can generally see one from another, but far enough apart that if you are navigating by looking at the land on the horizon, you are going to be weirded out and get lost if you fail to recognize you are navigating on the surface of a sphere,

A troofer's intuition for small objects colliding at low speeds is misled by big things and high speeds. He expects to see a banged up commercial airliner sitting in front of a dent in the Pentagon, so he tells you there is no aircraft wreckage.

In fact, everyone in the vicinity reported a rain of aircraft wreckage in sizes from confetti to pocket handkerchief. The plane flew inside the building, creating Wiley Coyote style hole in the building, a commercial airliner sized and shaped entrance hole, and then exited the building in a very wide variety of paths and ways, mostly in the form of very small pieces, the largest intact part being one of the wheel hubs.

Had the troofer watched more Wily Coyote cartoons and fewer Scrooge McDuck cartoons, he would have found the commercial airliner flying into the Pentagon easier to believe.

"What?", thinks the troofer. "Where is the banged up airliner sitting in front of the Pentagon?", and then proceeds to construct an enormously over elaborate conspiracy theory, which overcomplication rapidly descends into incoherence. And because his theory makes no sense, it becomes a pile of lies, in part he deludes himself, but in part he intentionally and maliciously deludes others, so a natural error of erroneous intuition becomes a system of deliberate lies propagated by malicious, hostile, and disruptive conspiracy, which inevitably becomes a vehicle for evil people pursuing evil purposes, madness promoting evil, and evil promoting madness.

The Marxist see the natural order of the market and assumes it was commanded by a single entity: Today "Capital", an entity with a striking similarity to Satan, that commands the world through Wall Street.

So if someone is working at the corner store, the Marxist does not see the shopkeeper as working for himself, even if the shopkeeper himself owns the shop and is right in front of the Marxist. Rather he sees the shopowner as yet another employee of "Capital".

The Marxist observes that things generally work, that there are light bulbs in the sockets, bread on the shelves, toilet paper in the toilets, and assumes this coordination occurs by command of a single entity, assumes that we are already socialist, that we always have been socialist, it is just that some time in the past the commander was "the feudal class" and now it is "Capital", or "the Capitalist"

Genuine and natural error leads to genuine delusion, genuine delusion to loss of interest in having a consistent and complete story, logical incoherence to deliberate and conscious lying, systematic and coordinated lying becomes an evil priesthood pursuing evil purposes by evil means, vicious, hateful, degenerate, and depraved, while the underlying genuine error means that the evil, hatred, malice, and cynical manipulative lies never entirely replaces the genuine and unfeigned madness, stupidity, and ignorance

The Marxist thinks that Capitalism is a system of government, that Capitalism is the government, that the government puts bread on the supermarket shelves. The Marxist thinks that "You did not build that"

The capitalist took all this stuff from the lords, thinks the Marxist, so the Marxist will take all this stuff.

If moneyed interests controlled America's armies, they would be a hell of a lot more interested in oil than in opium. Why aren't the Arabs savages in the desert on the fringes of a petrocolonialist patchwork? Why is America not putting the ludicrously weak Venezuelan government to the sword and replacing it with ExxonMobil? Why is development in Antarctica forbidden?

I wish America's armies *were* controlled by moneyed interests. If the US army was fighting for "Capital", Venezuela and Saudi Arabia would be divisions of Exxon Mobile. That the war is in Afghanistan, rather than Venezuela, shows that it is about performing the holy sacraments, not profit.

Abortion is a holy sacrament. Nine year old girls putting a condom on a banana is a holy sacrament. And to these sacraments they have recently added the holy sacrament of twelve year old boys forced to wear dresses and forced to sit on the lap of a transexual. The Afghan war is being fought to force Afghans to perform our sacraments. If we were fighting for sane and practical reasons, if we were run by "capital" rather than a holier than thou priesthood, we would invade Venezuela, which is sitting on an enormous lake of oil which their internal disorder prevents them from pumping effectively, and a pile of gold which they cannot mine, because every time they make a deal with a mining company they attempt to shake down the miners before the miners have actually extracted any gold.

Venezuela is where the oil and gold is. Afghanistan is where the heresy is. Plainly, therefore, we are ruled by priests, not warriors.

The inability of the Venezuelan government to pump oil or mine gold falsifies Marxist economics, and the fact that we have not put their ludicrously weak government to the sword and converted them into an ExxonMobile division falsifies Marxist Class theory.

Modern type capitalism, the capitalism of the for profit joint stock corporation, the capitalism of Ayn Rand's hero engineer CEO mobilizing other people's capital and other people's labor to advance technology and make it widely available, the capitalism that gave us technology and industrialization, started with the restoration, centuries after feudalism in the sense of William the Marshal ended, and centuries before feudalism in the sense of warrior and aristocratic power, the system of Russia before World War II, German before World War I, and England before the Crimean war, ended. England industrialized under divine right monarchy.

Corporate capitalism makes it possible for capital to be put in the control of smart people, though it certainly does not guarantee it, thus makes industrialization and technological advance possible. This is entirely orthogonal to the system of government. Today Dubai is simultaneously feudal, monarchic, and corporate capitalist, as England was from 1660 to the early nineteenth century, and it looks to me to have a technological lead on the USA and England, though its system of governance would be familiar to a Middle Easterner of the ninth century.

The worse the reality testing, the greater the evil. Thus communists enormously more evil than Nazis, Nazis more evil than the darkly enlightened, because their purported virtue comes cheaper.

Observe that as progressives get further and further out of contact with reality, their evil gets greater and greater, as for example their support of wildfire policies that burned eighty five rural whites alive.

Communists were originally more evil than progressives, because Class theory was more deluded than that all men are created equal. But as progressives accumulate more delusions, they become more evil, because their ever greater purported virtue becomes ever more detached from reality.

White pill on the shutdown and wall

2019-01-03 23:56:53

The Ann Coulter black pill is that Trump is going to cuck out, and the wall is not going to be built.

Nuts!

[latex/images/wall/wall2.jpg][308]

The wall *is* being built. Trump just wants a fig leaf to make building it legal.

Obamacare was never legally passed: House passed one version, Senate passed another version, reconciliation produced a third version, none of them workable, so Obama took legislative, judicial, and fiscal authority into his own pocket and implemented his own Obamacare, using the various things that had arguably been passed as fig leaf. This is a problem of central planning, that since any one central plan steps on lots of toes, it is impossible to get a majority, or even a substantial plurality, in favor of any one central plan. A socialist American is an America that must be ruled by one man, with all the other branches of government ancient and absurd rituals, like the Queen going her stagecoach to open parliament. There is nothing actually stopping Trump from building the wall except the permanent government and he finally got enough control over the permanent government that he is going right ahead building it. He just needs to pretend the Republic

---

[308]latex/images/wall/wall2.jpg

is still in effect, because as in the rise of the Roman Imperium, accusations that the other guy is overthrowing the (long dead) Republic are going to be used to seize power and kill the other guy.

Obama implemented Obamacare illegally by executive order with a fig leaf of legislation, and Trump is dismantling and replacing Obamacare, taking advantage of (il)legal precedents set by Obama, without even a fig leaf. The shutdown is just to give Trump a fig leaf.

America's healthcare is in socialist crisis, because the system of cross subsidies has abolished prices and the market. You cannot shop around, because everyone is forbidden to tell you what the price is going to be, and in practice, the price is set retroactively on the basis of how affluent you are suspected of being. They are not only forbidden to tell you, they are forbidden to know. Trump is moving toward restoring prices and the market.

Reagan instituted a system where one hundred morbidly obese pregnant Mexican women with type two diabetes go to emergency and get free medical care, and then one middle class white guy goes to emergency because his son fell out of a tree and needs three stitches on his arm, and the white middle class guy gets billed for three stitches and one hundred morbidly obese pregnant Mexican women with type two diabetes.

America's healthcare is in socialist crisis, because the system of cross subsidies has abolished prices and the market.

Trump is not just dismantling Obamacare. He has Reagancare in his sights - heading towards a two tier system where normal people pay market prices for medical care, and socialist care is for the broke, the unlucky, and the improvident.

Given that Trump is actually building the wall, and actually dismantling the socialist system created by Reagan and Obama, I have high hopes he is going to keep on escalating the pressure - shutdown the Mexico border, shutdown various government activities that primarily benefit the Democratic vote bank in Democratic electorates.

I see lots of photos of people erecting new fence, and the caravan confrontation occurred around a fence that had been massively upgraded.They looked for a way around, and wound up attempting to go through a less used crossing, which had a thirty foot fence with barbed wire entanglements on top. It is also clear that though people are still going around the fence, it is a lot more difficult that in used to be, and some people are attempting to go over eight feet of barbed wire entanglements.

So, I am white pilled on the fence. Of course I am white pilled. We just had a caravan frustrated by the fence!

That is a fence. It is actually stopping people. We see people trying to climb over eight feet of barbed wire entanglements with spikes at the bottom! Yes, we need more fence, a lot more fence, but what Trump has already built is a major improvement, and nicely scary and unwelcoming.

You have probably heard that the shutdown started before Christmas, with a zillion fedgov employees furloughed.

This is not exactly true, since those laid off were not doing anything terribly urgent. Shutdown starts January 15, the first missed payday, when those laid off do not get paid.

1. Pay is delayed by about 8 days or so after the two week pay period in which it was earned. The shutdown would have to go until 1/15/19 for a fedgov employee to miss one single paycheck.

2. White middle class people like you and me are untroubled by dipping into savings to cover a few delayed paychecks when everyone estimates a 100% chance of getting back-pay.

3. And that includes your bank estimating a 100% chance of getting back pay - and therefore your bank will routinely pause mortgage payments on request and make you a loan against expected back pay.

4. All furloughed fedgov employees received "notice to creditors" letters, which are widely accepted, even by landlords, because few creditors want the PR trouble of putting to the screws to some guy who's been furloughed and is known for sure to be "good for it" just as soon as the money comes in.

5. Several major credit unions have offered easy, quick, low-interest loans so that the few people who are in tight spots can still pay all the bills, and then just pay the loan back as soon as they get paid. Two thousand bucks at five percent interest for two weeks is 4 bucks interest - not even worth the underwriting effort, but many banks seem willing to do it anyway.

6. Furloughed government employees can file for unemployment and get paid that way. That's also treated as a 'loan' which must get paid back when the money is turned back on, but no one should be in financial distress for a long, long time.

However, not all fedgov employees are people like you and me.

They are the Democratic Party vote bank, hired to vote, not to work. No one will lend them money, because there is no chance in hell they are going to pay it back, and they don't have any savings.

This shutdown inflicts massive pain on people who don't vote republican, on people who get paid not for doing anything remotely useful, but for voting Democrat. White government employees are generally hired to do something. Most government employees are hired because the permanent government wants a certain demographic in a certain electorate. And that demographic is not white and male.

On the first missed payday, we shall see that in certain electorates there are very large numbers of government employees who are absolutely and totally unemployable, who were hired because they profile as people that no normal person would ever hire for any normal job and who in a civilized society would be killed, exiled, or sold into slavery, and who can therefore be relied upon to vote democratic, and in these electorates there will be a whole lot of government employees complaining about genuine hardship. And, needless to say, these are electorates represented by Democrats.

So, all the pain is inflicted on Democrats in electorates represented by Democrats. The people that it hurts are people who were getting benefits for being Democratic party voters. Less benefit, less votes.

I predict a band of plains apes descending on their white Democratic Party representatives after January 15. I would like to see naked cannibal plains apes, but regrettably they will probably be still be wearing clothes. There will, however be a smell revealing that some of them lack the intelligence and self control necessary to learn or retain toilet training, and they will threaten to eat their Democratic Representatives, even if they regrettably refrain from actually eating them. Actual consumption of political representatives will not happen until several years of further movement left.

State of Emergency coming up.

2019-01-09 02:07:14

Trump is readying a state of emergency to build and fund the wall without congressional approval. He has already been building and funding the wall without congressional approval, but a state of emergency would arguably make it legal.

The Democrats are going to scream in pain that this is a dire threat to rule by the permanent government of law and democracy. Which it is.

There are already a thousand and one states of emergency, each of them consuming vast amounts of funds that congress has not appropriated, and each of them granting a vast and lawless army of bureaucrats open ended powers to smash the lives of Americans that they do not much like.

The difference between this coming state of emergency, and the other thousand and one states of emergency, is that all of the others were declared by bureaucrats tossing a declaration of state of emergency into the president's in tray, from which it went unread and unnoticed to his out tray. The usual bloody battle then ensued for the papers in the out tray, each of which grants a nameless bureaucrat, whose face the president does not recognize, power to act with the full power of the president. The winning bureaucrat then wipes the bloodstains off the declaration, feeds it into the presidential autosigner, then, after getting his wounds treated, hires an army of bureaucrats, forming a new bureau with himself as head to harass Americans all over America and radically disrupt their lives, loves, and plans, even though the original emergency only affected one orchard in South Florida.

This declaration of state of emergency is going to be different from all of the others because it actually references a real emergency, rather than an ant infestation in a South Florida orchard, because actually composed by the actual president, and because actually addressing the kind of threat that the office of president was intended to deal with, rather than functions that properly belong to state and municipal governments.

The Democrats are going to appeal this state of emergency, but unless they openly say "The president should reign but not rule, the permanent government should rule", the court cannot explain what makes this one different from the other thousand and one states of emergency.

The Democrats are going to tell us this a big step towards them getting helicopter rides to the Pacific, and they are absolutely right, but unable to explain why, or even to think why, because actually thinking through the reasons is crimethink.

war approaches faster.

2019-01-22 05:31:56

The story of the Covington boys is that the left saw some boys wearing Maga hats, wanted to murder them, and then felt there must be something or other justifying their desire, and therefore confidently announced that something or other had happened justifying murder on every news medium - which announcements continue in spite of the fact that the entire incident is on video showing no such thing. This is similar to what happens with rape or sexual harassment charges - a woman is sexually attracted to some man, being sexually attracted gives him a brutal and difficult to pass fitness test. He fails his fitness test, so she feels creeped out, so rapidly comes to confidently believe that some socially acceptable reason for her feeling creeped out must surely have happened. It is a manifestation of an increasingly feminine and female dominated left.

Eventually they are going to start large scale actual killing, and we are going to have to actually start organizing large scale defense. This will be easier than it sounds, because they are going to start killing each other. On the other hand, history is that the left usually wins until it self destructs, so maybe we will just have to flee and hide till its over, which may take a while. On the other hand the left does not always win, Sulla being the most famous counter example.

At almost the same time as Covington Boys incident, Speaker Nancy Pelosi announces that climate crisis is "the existential threat of our time[309]... end the inaction and denial of science that threaten the planet and the future."

In actual fact, of course, any warming that has happened, if any warming has happened, is humanly imperceptible, indistinguishable from recent variations in climate for warmer or cooler, and smaller than variations in climate over the past few thousand years. In the past, sometimes you could sail the Northwest passage, and sometimes you could

---

[309]https://wattsupwiththat.com/2019/01/21/climate-hysterics-skyrocket/

not, and today sometimes you can sail the Northwest passage, and sometimes you cannot.Past variations in climate are recorded in the δ18O levels of ice cores, and if you look at any ice core that runs from near the present to the ancient past, there is nothing out of the ordinary about recent variations, nor any clear trend. If warming is happening, you have to squint sideways at the ice core data to see it, and when you do see it, looks underwhelming compared to the Medieval Climate Optimum and the Little Ice Age.

Global Warming is just an excuse for hating on the civilization, the race, and the sex that created technology and industry, and any plan that purports to be a solution to global warming has nothing to do with Global Warming, is in fact a plan to end that civilization, end those people, and end science and industry.

The Nancy Pelosi statement on global warming comes from the same roots as the lies about the Covington boys. They want to do something monstrous, horrifying, terrifying, abhorrent, and enormously destructive, so feel that reasons must exist justifying the actions that they intend to take.

Deus Vult

2019-01-28 03:13:37

Gnon wills it.[310]
Trump cannot get stuff done, because he is merely president, and the permanent government is full of people that hate him.

But it is not just the permanent government. His political appointees are in bed with his enemies, and are subverting his agenda. Two years after Hitler was elected, Hitler had a Nazi running ever boy scout troop and every trade union chapter. Trump cannot even get a Trumpist running border security.

The one area where Trump has been successful is putting his people in the judiciary. Trumpist judges, though still massively outnumbered, are coming in at every level. Trump has been effective in appointing judges, because he has a big bench he can draw upon, which bench knows who whom, which bench is self policing, which bench can be relied upon to carry out his program without him needing to be on their back. Personnel is policy, and the Federalist society has a supply.

Reflect on the Federalist society: They have their article of faith - original intent. And they have a network to identify their fellow faithful. Just as Constantine adopted Christianity that provided him with a cohesive group to staff his government, in a Roman Empire disintegrating from elite incohesion.

To govern, you need a synthetic tribe, which Hitler had, which Constantine adopted, and which Trump lacks, except for the federalist society which is narrowly focused on judicial process.

The Federalist article of faith (Original Intent) that provides unity and cohesion is also an effective antibody against enemy outgroups. It is something no leftist can admit is even thinkable - to them, just words with no meaning that they dare conceive of. So when leftist entryists attempt to infiltrate the Federalists, they use their shibboleths incorrectly,

---

[310]https://blog.reaction.la/war/deus-vult/

like a Marxist purporting to be channeling Adam Smith, and wind up babbling random nonsensical meaningless scripted formulaic NPC gibberish.

We, on the other hand, agree with the leftists, that original intent is not really going to fly, while we agree with the Federalists that judges exercising executive, legislative, budgetary authority is intolerable. One emperor is a stationary bandit. A thousand little emperors is mobile banditry and anarcho tyranny. We, however, propose a solution far more radical than that of the federalists - that the final court of appeal should be the Sovereign, should be Moses, the King, or the President, and he should be able to intervene in any case, and fire any judge. We also propose William the Conqueror's "forms of action", meaning that judges should be reduced to data entry clerks filling out forms that result in remote procedure calls to a system of central databases, similar to the system used by Australia's border control force for dealing with "Illegal persons". (Australian Border Force is Judge Dredd with more typing required than Judge Dredd had to do, but the same refreshing speed, efficiency, and absence of lawyers and priestly robes as with Judge Dredd.) William the Conqueror's "Forms of action" kept judges in line for seven hundred years, and modern databases and remote procedure calls make William the Conqueror's solution lightning fast, so that it can be applied by a cop on the beat, after the fashion of Judge Dredd and the Australian Border Force.

We have our mailing lists and forums, like the federalist society. What we don't have is some articles of faith, a canon, a creed, a catechism. Constantine's Christians had a creed. Trump's federalist society has one. By getting agreement on certain principles, we can identify our fellow faithful, we can provide a tribe capable of governing. Our basic plan is that someone grabs power, needs a tribe to actually govern. Ideally, a warrior grabs power at gunpoint, swiftly discovers that guns do not suffice, realizes he needs a priesthood, looks around for a priesthood, finds us, as Constantine found Christendom, and Trump found the Federalist Society. When Trump appoints someone in charge of border security, he does not necessarily get someone who favors border security. When Trump appoints a Federalist Society judge, he reliably gets a Federalist, as Constantine reliably got a Christian, and Hitler reliably got a Nazi.

The political appointees that Trump appoints are frequently disloyal to Trump and hostile to his agenda. The Federalist Judges he appoints are loyal to federalism, thus reasonably loyal to Trump and supportive of his agenda. Indeed the left regularly complains that federalist judges are more supportive of Trump and his agenda than they are to federalism, which is not true, but has a substantial grain of truth in that federalist judges appointed on the basis of their federalism are more supportive of Trump and his agenda than are political appointees appointed on the basis of loyalty to Trump and his agenda. The Federalist society polices itself. Trump is not having much success policing Trump political appointees.

We are the reaction. Our program is to rectify social decay by reviving ancient and lost social technologies, among them Pauline marriage. These ancient social technologies tend, for the most part, to be social technologies preserved by Christianity through the Dark Age following the collapse of the Roman Empire, and by the Children of Israel through the dark age following the collapse of Bronze Age civilization, thus our program is Christian - old type Christian. Modern type Christians tend to assimilate to progressivism and worship demons[311].

There is a lot of stuff in the New Testament that can plausibly be used to justify gnosticism, communism, and suicidal social policies, stuff that is plausibly interpreted as opposed to family, social cohesion, and civilization "There is neither Jew nor Greek". But those variants of Christianity that survived have given sane, Gnon compliant, survival consistent, interpretations of these statements, banishing the crazy from this world to the next. After the resurrection there will be neither Jew nor Greek, neither man nor women, but in the here and now, women should obey their husbands. The New and Old Testaments, as generally interpreted by the community of saints in the apostolic succession, is sound social technology. It commands a market economy, durable marriage, and the authority of husbands and fathers over wives and daughters.

Nature's God is the Gods of the copybook headings[312]. The God of the Old and New Testament keeps getting reinterpreted as the Gods of the marketplace, but the ancient and long lasting Christian tradition is expressed by those copybook headings - Natures God, a God who in the fall instituted evolutionary psychology and a world of conflict accurately described by game theory. The curse of Eve explains the distressing female behavior also explained by evolutionary psychology, but people who are reluctant to believe in On the Origin of Species by Natural Selection, for example Vox Day, tend to interpret away the Curse of Eve and become blue pilled, or at best purple pilled, on women. I have often sarcastically remarked how in Vox Day's books Action Girl is apt to rescue the Lad in Distress. Darwin protects us from that heresy better than overly literal biblical literalism.

So: here are the articles of the Canon:

1. Throne

2. Altar

3. Freehold

4. Family

5. Property

Throne

Division of powers, divided sovereignty does not work, more rulers means mobile banditry and anarcho tyranny. A stationary bandit has better incentives than a mobile bandit.

---

[311]https://fabiusmaximus.com/2018/06/16/dalrock-looks-at-fathers-day/
[312]https://www.kiplingsociety.co.uk/poems_copybook.htm

Altar

You cannot separate state and church. The church will undermine the state and take state power for itself, or the state subvert the church, or both at once. Harvard is our high holy Cathedral. A holiness spiral ensues as the priestly classes, the professoriat, the judiciary, and the media, pursue power by each being holier than the other. Obviously we have a state religion, a state religion that every day becomes crazier, more dogmatic, and more intrusive, and that state religion needs to be formalized and made official so that the high priest and grand inquisitor can stop holiness spirals.

When Charles the Second was restored, the people of England held pagan celebrations, in the correct expectation that an officially official religion would be less repressive than an unofficially official religion.

The earthly telos of holiness is to promote the broadest possible cooperate/cooperate equilibrium. Holiness competition results in people finding grounds to declare other people unholy, thus Starbucks and LucasFilms declare their customers unholy, thus holiness competition destroys the earthly telos of holiness. Therefore we cannot allow excessively holy people to gain power in the state religion. Which requires that the state religion be formally the state religion, and appropriate restraints applied.

Freehold

Freehold necessarily involves and requires rejection of the principle of equality before the law, and property rejection of equality of outcomes. Not all men were created equal, nor are women equal to men, nor is one group or category of men equal to another. Stereotypes are stereotypical, because the stereotype is usually true for most individual members of the group or category.

We have never had equality before the law, and are having it less every day. Cops have a special right to use violence, blacks have a special right to use violence and to not be insulted, similar to that of the traditional aristocracy, Hispanics and illegal immigrants in California have a special right to use violence and to not be insulted.

State building is coalition building to rule. We need a coalition of the smart, the cooperative, and the productive, ruling the stupid, the disruptive, and the destructive. The doctrine of equality means you cannot reward the elite with status? *What!* Of course the ruling elite is going to be rewarded with status, and that is exactly what is happening.

The ruling elite always gets rewarded, the ruling coalition always gets rewarded. Members of the ruling coalition always get a superior right to use violence, and a superior right to not be insulted. That is the way it is, and that is what we saw when white people were ethnically cleansed out of Detroit. The doctrine of equality before the law was always a lie intended to destroy the coalition of the smart, the cooperative, and the productive, to guilt the best people into surrender, so that they could be destroyed by a coalition of the worst.

Freehold means that we acknowledge that some state power is in fact private property, and the sovereign lets his loyal vassals enjoy their privilege, because if he tries to meddle, he will be overwhelmed by detail and complexity, so best to formalize that privilege and make it official. If we don't have the aristocracy that so offended the founding fathers, we find ourselves with blacks exercising aristocratic privilege over whites. Equality before the law is an unworkable ideal, hypocritically betrayed in actual practice. Some people are going to be unjustly privileged. Let us try to make it the best people rather than the worst people, and try to make it the people that the state draws is wealth and coercive power from, rather than the people who sponge off the state.

Family

The immense biological and reproductive differences between men and women means that they can only cooperate for family formation on asymmetric, unequal terms. The wife has a duty to honor and obey, the husband to love and cherish. To ensure cooperation between men and women, the state, the family, society, and religion have to force men and women who sleep together to stick together, to force them to perform their marital duties, to force the man to cherish and the woman to obey, otherwise you get defect/defect, and reproduction and family become difficult for both men and woman.

For hypergamy to be eugenic rather than dysgenic, taxpayers and warriors need to have a special right to use violence and to not be insulted. For marriage to work, pimps, sluts, and whores need to have a substantially less protection against violence, insult, and rape. For marriage to be incentive compatible for women it has to be simply legal for a respectable man to chain a slut up in his basement, and if she does not want to risk that outcome, she needs to sign up in a nunnery or submit to husband. A right to protection should require chastity and/or submission to the authority of a husband or father. Sluts shall have legal authority equal to chaste women? What! This inevitably results in sluts being given legal status higher than that of chaste woman, and that is exactly what is happening. Wives, like whites, are very much second class low status citizens. We have an aristocracy, and black whores are at the top.

Women always wind up heading off the protection of the most alpha male around. If that is the protection of uncle Sam, you get what we have got.

You will notice that the doctrine that all women shall be equal required and led to the doctrine that all women are naturally chaste, enshrined in our current law on rape and sexual harassment, which presupposes that the primary person who is harmed by rape and sexual harassment is the woman, and the primary person who is going to object to it and be distressed by it is the woman, rather than the father, her biological kinfolk, and the husband. The transparent falsity and absurdity of this doctrine leads to the transparent falsity and absurdity of all rape and sexual harassment charges and convictions, as near to all of them as makes no difference. Legal equality necessitates and results in a denial of biological inequality.

Rape and sexual harassment laws that give women equal status to males are a problem, because in practice their resistance to rape and sexual harassment is a fitness test - they are pissed at you if you fail the test, not pissed by being successfully raped. So rape and sexual harassment charges based on the legal theory that these are crimes against the women herself, rather than her husband or family, always originate from failed shit tests - and the overwhelming majority of these failures do not involve rape and sexual harassment. What happens in the vast majority of cases, for all practical purposes all of them, is that a woman is sexually attracted to a man, hits him with a brutal and hard to pass shit test out of the blue, he fails, she feels creeped out, and comes to believe that something must have happened that legally justifies her feeling of being creeped out. In the rare and unusual occasions when they are based on an actual attempt at rape or sexual harassment, they are based not on the rape or the sexual harassment, but on the man failing her fitness test by retreating from her hostile response. They originate from male behavior that is not all that bad - just weak, the male trying something, but then retreating in the face of determined opposition.

We cannot give women the same legal right to protection against violence and insult as men, because they fail to cooperate in that protection. The best we can do is grant state backing for nunneries, husbands, and fathers protecting their wives and daughters, because husbands and fathers are are going to cooperate in that protection, and the male priests supervising the nunnery will cooperate in that protection. Violence and insult against women has to be handled as an offense against the male authority that cares for them, because if handled as an offense against the women themselves, the women are unhelpful, untruthful, deluded, and uncooperative, failing to report the kind of offenses that we want to suppress, and delusively reporting non offenses.

Men and women want families. Men and women want to cooperate to have families. But prisoners dilemma gets in the way. To fix the prisoner dilemma problem, need to hit women with a stick.

Property

Anti discrimination law violates people's property rights. Google hates us, but the problem is not primarily too much capitalism, but too little. In the James Damore affair, Google's Human Resources Department (the Human Resources department being a tentacle of the state inserted into every corporation) threatened the board and the management of Google with a lawsuit for not hating us enough, issuing an official opinion that thinking forbidden thoughts constituted a "hostile environment for women". Because stereotypes are usually true, private individuals and corporations should be free to make use of the information expressed by stereotyping. The trouble with libertarians and libertarianism is that they support every socialist intervention that is destroying our lives and our economy.

Family law and anti discrimination law violates the fourth amendment and the seventh, eighth, and final commandments
Thou shalt not commit adultery.
Thou shalt not steal.
Thou shalt not covet thy neighbour's house, thou shalt not covet thy neighbour's wife, nor his manservant, nor his maidservant, nor his ox, nor his ass, nor any thing that thy neighbour's.

Anti discrimination law reaches into a man's property, and commands it to be applied to the good of the ruling coalition, and moment to moment consent to sex reaches into a man's marriage and abolishes marriage.
The right of the people to be secure in their persons, houses, papers, and effects,[a] against

unreasonable searches and seizures, shall not be violated, and no Warrants shall issue, but upon probable cause, supported by Oath or affirmation, and particularly describing the place to be searched, and the persons or things to be seized.

The state deciding whether James Damore's thoughts constituted a "hostile environment for women" is an unreasonable search if ever there was, and it is an obvious violation of private property rights that libertarians would get terribly excited by if the government was bothering a black serial murderer.

Technological advance and industrialization comes from Ayn Rand's heroic engineer CEO, mobilizing other people's capital and other people's labor. We first see this archetype appear immediately after the restoration, when Charles the Second made it OK to use the corporate form to get rich. Unfortunately, Ayn Rand's hero is not heroically on our side, contrary to what Ayn Rand promised. He unheroically endorses the official religion, knowing his property could be attacked if he does not. But we should keep in mind that this makes him merely the instrument of power, not power. When we are in charge he will support our official religion and scarcely notice the change in the slogans posted in the rec room, which formerly endorsed coveting what belonged to others and females adopting male clothing and roles, but will then condemn coveting and endorse males performing male roles and females performing female roles.

Rand's superman is not on our side. But he is not on the progs side. He is his own side, and this makes him largely irrelevant for political power, which requires cohesion.

The state can facilitate science by being a customer and buying high tech stuff. Indeed, a great deal of advance has come from the state seeking means to hurt people and break their toys, but when the state tries to itself advance technology, it usually turns out badly: Nasa could not build rockets. Kidnapped Wernher von Braun. Asked him how to build rockets. Still could not build rockets.

Nasa puts Wernher von Braun in charge. Now it can build rockets. Puts a man on the moon.

Wernher von Braun retires. New types of rockets don't work. Old types of rockets gradually stop working no matter how much government money is poured down the toilet.

Where did Nasa find Wernher von Braun?

Nazis kidnapped him from the German rocket club which they shut down.

Seems obvious that we would have wound up with a whole lot better rocket technology if the rocket club became, or spawned, a bunch of startups, one of them led by Wernher von Braun, and governments outsourced rockets. Which is what gave us the reusable booster that lands as a rocket should land.

Before Wernher von Braun, american government rockets did not work. After Wernher von Braun, government rockets gradually stopped working. And the rocket club, not the Nazis, and not NASA, found Wernher von Braun.

Radar and wartime electronics present a similar story. Harvard created a huge radar and counter radar program during the war - which led nowhere, as NASA's rockets went nowhere after Wernher von Braun retired.

Natural Selection is reactionary

2019-02-04 00:14:15

Vox Day has been campaigning against evolution, arguing that like Catastrophic Anthropogenic Global Warming, it is fake science, demon worshiping religion dressed in the sacerdotal lab coats of science.

Vox is a great man, and I am a huge admirer of his. He had the courage, doubtless strengthened by his faith in God, to take on the enemy and show that the enemy can bleed[313]. He should be an inspiration to all of us, and you would be wise to buy SJWs Always Lie: Taking Down the Thought Police [314]

) I can report from personal experience that this is how you survive attack by social justice warriors. Long before this book was written, I dealt with weaponized sexual harassment complaints (directed against other men, not against me, even though I am the only male in any workplace I have ever been who actually does sexually harass women) in a fashion similar to that advised by this book, with the result that the complainant "resigned", and I did not get fired.

But on evolution, Vox Day is full of crap, and it is getting in the way of his understanding of women, with the result that he is purple pilled, and his novels feature kick ass action girl who rescues lad in distress.

Yes, the evolutionism of Gould, Jerry Coyne, and Richard Lewontin is demon worship wearing lab coats as sacerdotal robes. But Darwinism is true. Species originate by natural selection. We became human through a thousand genocides. We are risen killer apes. Jerry Coyne theoretically does not go full Gould, but rejects the obvious implication of Darwinism that subsaharan Africans are substantially less distant from chimps than whites are distant from chimps. He kind of knows its true, but favors silencing anyone who mentions it, having his cake and eating it too.

It is impossible to understand the nature of women except from the point of view that humans and races of humans were formed by natural selection over an immensity of time. Believing in the curse of Eve gets you half way there, but one can theoretically believe in the curse of Eve and still be blue pilled. Natural selection explains the desire of women for invasion, conquest[315], and rape[316], while the Curse of Eve merely tells us that husbands should rule wives.

The origin of species by Natural selection, Darwinism, is true science.

"Evolution" is indeed fake science: - the doctrine that humans arose from non human forms without the inconveniently racist and sexist conclusions that flow from the idea that humans arose from *lower* forms by *natural selection*.

Hence my koan: A creationist, an evolutionist, and a Darwinist were walking in the woods[317]

---

[313] https://voxday.blogspot.com/2019/01/reinstated.html

[314] https://www.amazon.com/gp/product/B014GMBUR4

[315] https://neurotoxinweb.wordpress.com/2018/07/15/red-pill-in-fiction-justina-robsons-keeping-it-real/

[316] https://blog.reaction.la/war/why-feminists-support-islamic-rape-jihad/

[317] https://blog.reaction.la/science/a-creationist-an-evolutionist-and-a-darwinist-were-walking-in-the-woods/

You will notice that in this koan the evolutionist is depicted as, like Global Warmers, unscientific, indeed hostile to science, and, like a gnostic, hostile to reality and the world.

Gnosticism is an anti human, and anti this world Christian heresy. Reaction worships Nature's God, and to understand the will of Gnon, have to see men and women as they truly are, and one can only see them as they truly are if one accepts Darwinism. The red pill on woman only makes sense from the point of view of natural selection - that for women abduction and enslavement is an escape from prisoner's dilemma, and that their resistance to rape, enslavement, and the authority of their husband is merely a fitness test.

State of the Union Speech

2019-02-06 08:08:37

Trump gave a great speech, in which he re-affirmed his campaign promises, not yet kept, to end the forever war and build the wall,

> Wealthy politicians and donors push for open borders while living their lives behind walls, and gates, and guards.

> Meanwhile working class Americans are left to pay the price for mass illegal immigration
> reduced jobs
> lower wages
> overburdened schools
> hospitals that are so crowded you can't get in
> increased crime
> and a depleted social safety net
>
> …
>
> Smugglers use migrant children as human pawns to exploit our laws and gain access to our country.

These memes cheerfully lifted from Heartiste and from the reaction.

And what made this speech even greater is that the Democrats are planning to shoot themselves in the foot by having Stacey Abrams, dim witted fat middle aged black cat lady romance writer with fifty thousand dollars in unpaid taxes, a hundred and seventy thousand dollars in credit card debt, and no substantial assets, deliver the rebuttal. Stacey favors open borders so that our enemies who hate us can invade us, opposes gun rights so that the people coming over the open borders can kill us, opposes voter ID so that they can outvote us, favors late term abortions, and opposes religious liberty because old type Christians are Nazis who need to be punched, like the Covington boys.

Stacey Adams is the new face of the non white non male Democratic Party, which is going to run Kamala Harris for its 2020 candidate.

One of the delights of the State of the Union speech was watching evil ugly wicked witch Nancy Pelosi stare into the headlights of the oncoming truck. Too white for Democrats, too anti white for whites. When Trump renewed his promise, not yet kept, to end the forever war, she sneered, reasonably so because the senate had just voted near unanimously to overrule the president on the forever war. Then, as one of his measures to end the for-ever war, Trump listed moving the embassy to Jerusalem. She gasped, visibly shocked and distressed.

Moving the embassy means giving up on the project of doing to Muslims in the Mid-dle East what Democrats have done to Christians in the West, and Trump's statement makes sense from the point of view that the forever war is a crusade to impose progres-sivism on Muslims, and Trump is *not* going to impose progressivism on Muslims. He aims to cut a deal with the Taliban whereby they agree not to export terror, *and he agrees to let them keep conservative Islam.* Putting the embassy move into the context of ending the forever war puts ending the forever war into the context of progressivism losing the middle east to Islam, and to hell with the arc of history.

OK, we elected him to save America for Christians, not to save the Middle East for Muslims, but saving the Middle East for Muslims shows our enemy can bleed.

Defunding the left

2019-02-17 02:47:41

Trump is defunding the left and lowering its status

The EPA will no longer take science advice from "scientists" who receive stupendous amounts of money for climate doom[318].

> During the Obama years, the EPA packed the CASAC panel. Twenty-four
> of its 26 members are now agency grantees, with some listed as principal
> investigators on EPA research grants worth more than $220 million

Environmentalists, predictably, sued, alleging this policy would change the "science" advice away from environmentalism - as obviously it would.

In 2016, the World Bank announced it would spend 28% of investments on climate-related projects by 2020, which is roughly three hundred to four hundred million dollars of American taxpayer money per year. All Climate related projects, as near to all of them as make no difference, are scams that enrich political activists, and again, Trump cut this out.

A horde of journalists have lost their jobs, and their status.

Trump is now taking aim at "Disparate impact" If he succeeds with "disparate im-pact", there are going to be mass layoffs of bitter angry aging cat ladies with vast unpaid college debt and credit card debt from Human Resources, radically curtailing the status, wealth, and power of the left.

OK, I hear you say, what about the wall?

Well, I said, wait a while for the dust to settle. I see Trump threatening the courts with a Jackson, and expect the courts to back down lest their impotence be revealed, as happened in Australia[319]. If the state of emergency goes through, the poison pills in the

---

[318]https://junkscience.com/2017/07/a-step-toward-scientific-integrity-at-the-epa/
[319]https://blog.reaction.la/war/operation-sovereign-borders/

budget are largely rendered irrelevant.[320] It is going to take a few days or a few weeks to see what has happened, what is happening and what is going to happen. And then I am going to post on the wall, the poison pill budget, and the State of Emergency.

These are all big moves, and are throwing the left into hysterics. But it is reasonable to doubt that they will suffice to save the day, for the biggest source of wealth, power and status for leftists is academia and the judiciary. The dissolution of the fake news media is a good start, but to win, will have to dissolve academia and the judiciary.

On the other hand it is a reversal of the movement to ever more wealth, power, and status for leftists. The enemy has revealed he can bleed.

But the real key to power, as Hitler realized, is the FBI, which is still engaged in criminal violence against Trumpists. Fixing the FBI would in practice be the coup, which I have long been optimistically predicting, and my predictions have not been fulfilled. But I can see an increasing number of Republicans uncucking over the FBI. Not enough yet to give the color of legality to the coup.

Of course, we are reactionaries here. You cannot rule without a religion in your pocket. Hitler could put a Nazi in charge of every boyscout troop and every union chapter. Trump cannot put a Trumpist in charge of the FBI. Getting away with violence is high status. Suffering violence done to you with impunity is low status. German Nazis were high status because they could get away with violence. Radical leftism is high status because they can get away with violence. Reaction is low status because violence is inflicted upon us with impunity.

When Constantine made Christianity the state religion, Christians could get away with violence against pagans. The extent of the persecution of paganism by Christianity gets hugely exaggerated. There was not in fact enough of it to erase every pagan temple and wipe out every pagan priesthood, or even a significant fraction of them. But there was enough of it to make paganism low status and Christianity high status, which over time had much the same effect as if Christians had done what they get accused of having done. The pagan temples came to be unused, and then Christians could smash them all. The real Christian clampdown came when there was nothing much left to clamp down upon.

Homosexuals became high status because they were granted aristocratic privilege to engage in violence The disrespectable gays were openly intimidating people with the tacit support of the 100% respectable elites. Alex Jones fans cannot intimidate anyone because they are not violent enough and don't have that tacit support. Compton's Cafeteria got Kristallnachted twice[321]. And so on...

And thus gays became respectable.

We are low status because Faith Goldy has been physically assaulted by protesters as Canadian media companies sat back and filmed. She has been scrubbed from every online payment service, making it impossible for her to support herself. Ads for her Toronto mayoral campaign have been banned by Rogers and Bell Media. Her life has been destroyed. She is shouted at in public and assaulted in the street

---

[320]https://neurotoxinweb.wordpress.com/2019/02/15/wall-good-budget-bill-bad-but-maybe-not-as-bad-as-feared/

[321]https://en.wikipedia.org/wiki/Stonewall_riots

To halt the left wing singularity is going to require some serious and substantial violence against leftists, and we are very far short of that. Lacking numbers, cannot control the FBI. Not controlling the FBI, going to lack numbers.

I had hoped and expected that Trump would simply put a Trumpist in charge of the FBI, and everything would fall into place. Hillary for Prison. That is not happening, in part because though Trump has a reliable supply of federalist judges, he does not have a reliable supply of Trumpists.

The reactionary program.

2019-03-06 03:27:15

Neoreaction plans to be the priesthood, but we think warriors should be on top and should steal sufficient to fund the army and the state, that warriors should do warrior stuff, merchants should do merchant stuff, and priests priestly stuff.

Our current problems are the result of an excessively numerous priesthood overflowing and intruding on the activities more properly performed by merchants and warriors. Thus human resources disrupts the corporation, wars are overrun by lawyers, and the military is forced to pretend that women can be warriors. This excess of priests is a result of priestly dominance with open entry into the priesthood and the resulting overflow of people into the priesthood.

We plan to cut off open entry into the priesthood. The Marxist and progressive program is a rationale for the priesthood intruding into the affairs of merchants and warriors. It is full employment program for Academia. Hence the joke that LIA, Low Intensity War, actually stands Lawyer Infested War. Hence the cat ladies of Human Resources, and the transformation of accounting from tracking value and value creation, to talmudic generation and enforcement of obscure, obstructive, and incomprehensible rules. Today, accounting is not about tracking value when it is transferred from one entity to another, and measuring the creation of value, but rather what rituals one must perform if one wants to transfer value from one entity to another.

Lawyers (who tend to be the day to day ruling class even if academia sets doctrine long term) and writers like all the priestly professions overwhelmingly oppose Trump.

In a reactionary state, the state will enforce marriage, and end open entry into the priesthood. Military priests will be trained in military academies under the control of retired warriors. Women will be forced to honor and obey the first man they have sex with till death do them part and will be denied access to men who are not yet contributing to the state and society.

Women feel that a man who is single and lonely, especially in today's world of open sexual market, is not fully a male of the human species. At best, he may be an animal with some horrid infectious disease of the skin to be pitied from a distance. But much more often they are just ignored or laughed at. No amount of ideology can override these hard wired settings in the female brain.

On the other hand, men see this in women and join the mocking and the laughter in order to signal that they're definitely not that type.

Since women are hypergamous, the natural tendency is for there to be a very large number of young males in this hyperoppressed class.

Further, this incel class cuts across the reactionary classes (warrior, priest, merchant, and followers), since high status wealthy businessmen, merchant class, often do very badly with women, and people that we categorize as priestly class, high status males whose career requires strict political correctness, who are required to very politically correct, usually do very badly with women.

But if we look at successful past societies, they have generally taken extraordinarily drastic coercive measures to minimize this class of men, to overrule female hypergamy.

While socialism in goods invariably fails catastrophically, in part because the priests run businesses to produce holiness, rather than value, drastic coercive intervention in the market for love and sex seems to be a basic requirement of civilization, without which civilizations fail. We need to ensure that every man who pays taxes and every man who fights for order tribe, society, King and God, gets pussy, which runs contrary to natural female inclination.

Marriage is a contract between the former owner of the bride, normally her father, and the new owner of the bride, normally her husband. Reproductive sex is an essential part of this contract.
Women should be attached to one male and not allowed to ride the cock carousel, ideally the first male they ever have sex with, hence shotgun marriage.

Male society consists of priests, warriors, merchants, and followers, and the female population is not a society, but consists of feral women and women under the authority of a husband or father. Women are only part of society through an intimate relationship with a male in authority over her. That is not the reactionary program. That is biological reality, manifesting in the disastrous consequences of attempting have female run corporations[322]. Today, we don't have equal women, we have feral women.

Late marriage west of the Hajnal line was, in the towns, linked to enforceable apprenticeship, up to about 1800 or so. A man was typically an apprentice till about twenty four or so, and it was ok to be lonely, despised, and mistreated, since upon successfully completing his apprenticeship, he would cease to be despised and mistreated, and would soon afterwards marry a virgin about four or so years younger than himself - who had been apprenticed to housewifery, to servant and housekeeping type tasks, or some traditionally feminine occupation, but who upon marriage would perform those tasks for her husband, or under the supervision of her husband. For women, apprenticeship was typically ended by marriage, for men, marriage typically followed not long after the completion of apprenticeship, at least in the towns, where work was formalized. In rural areas, work relationships and education were informal, so no connection between formal work, education, and getting married appears in the records for rural areas.

Apprenticeship was emasculating, but apprentices were expected learn from a manly role model who was working at producing value, and expected to become that man. Today, they are trained by priests who have no knowledge of the real world, and will not read old books, instead reading what other twenty first century academics say about old books that they have not read either.

---

[322] https://blog.reaction.la/economics/the-disastrous-effects-of-females-in-power/

The apprentice role was effeminate and emasculating, with the vows of apprenticeship and the restraints of apprenticeship resembling a wife's marital vows, but it was intended to prepare them for life as a man, not to prevent them from becoming men, whereas modern priestly education aims at preventing men from becoming men.

In North America apprenticeship typically ended about three years earlier at twenty one, and people correspondingly got married earlier.

Frame is a set of assumptions about the conversation and the interaction, and in order to facilitate communication and the interaction, we tend to tacitly accept the assumptions without conscious awareness.

Notice we have the word "racist", but no word for people who claim that there are no races, that everyone is alike. We have the word "sexist". If you think that women are different from men, you are sexist, but no word for someone who thinks they are interchangeable should be subject to the same rules, and perform the same social roles.

History shows that whoever tells you capitalism is a recent economic system intends to murder you. Notice that no one making this claim is prepared to argue it or defend it - they just frame it a way that presupposes it is indisputable fact that one doubts, that you agree that it is true. They will never argue on the basis of history, only try to project their frame on to you. Commies murdered a hundred million people, and commies told all of those people commies were on their side against evil capital.

The reactionary program is being met with efforts to frame it as if we agreed, as if everyone agreed, with progressive frame. Supposedly we want different rules for women because we hate women. Supposedly we want capitalism and security of property because we favor rule by the capitalist class. Supposedly we want families to be protected by society, Church, Sovereign, and God, because we hate women and want to beat our wives and children. Supposedly property rights are rule by capital, and did not exist for anyone except aristocrats until quite recently. Supposedly whites fled Detroit because they hate blacks, not because their houses were being burned down around their ears.

I intend a restoration modeled on Charles the Second: Fertile semi hereditary aristocratic elite, divine right monarch, openly official state religion, which one must affirm for state or quasi statal office, capitalism and modern corporate capitalism, with a restriction that the business plan be approved and adhered to. Investors need to know what they are investing in, and governments need to know that large successful corporations will not start investing in unrelated activities that buy them political influence and restrain competition. One corporation should have one business model.

The situation immediately preceding Charles the Second resembled today's American Hegemony: An officially unofficial state religion that had suffered a leftist singularity, which singularity was ended by Cromwell, not Charles the Second. He ended it with far less bloodshed than Stalin ended it in Russia, though bloodshed is frequently unavoidable, and more difficult to avoid the further leftism has gone.

The American hegemony also resembles the Turkish empire, which had become the anti Turkish empire as the US State Department has become "The International Community". It was the Turks, not the provinces, that revolted against the Turkish empire. I had hoped that Trump would be Mustafa Kemal Atatürk, would be Atatürk, Cromwell, and Charles the Second in one man, but that is a tall order. An Atatürk needs to be a military man, and the left has taken precautions against such a man.

As progressivism spirals to ever greater heights of madness, ever faster, there is bound to be a crack up - bound to be a Kemal Atatürk, a Cromwell if we are lucky or a Stalin if not quite as lucky, and, eventually, if we are brave, effective, prudent, and lucky, a Charles the Second.

Female emancipation never lasts, because peoples, tribes, cultures, states, and religions with emancipated females fail to reproduce. Pretty soon Japan will not have the Japanese. They either restore patriarchy, as the Japanese have done once before, or they will be conquered by manly patriarchs who enslave their women, as happened to the Chinese, or they just disappear and are replaced by outsiders. Peoples with emancipated women cannot fight very well, because they are short of young males, because involuntarily celibate young males prefer to hang out in mum's basement, and because young males are reluctant to fight for family, society, sovereign and God, because they don't have family. They are even more reluctant when society, official state religion, and the sovereign is hostile to them having sexual opportunity, and ejects husbands from their families. Why fight when you have no pussy to fight for, and when if you got married, would likely face a court order parting you from your children and denying you your assets. Our descendants will patriarchs, or we will be mighty short of grandchildren and we will be replaced by patriarchs.

Analysis of a Chinese video

2019-03-25 07:19:19

You will never see courtship realistically portrayed in videos made for the west in anything made since the sixties, but they are still allowed to do romance realistically in China.

Episode seven[323]: Hat tip Spandrell.

At 1:12 the pre fertile age chick is trying to attract his attention while simultaneously directing an expression of disdain and boredom at him. Obvious fitness test, which means she is after him. If a chick does this to you, you have to pass her test, which he does by commanding her to see him after class.

At 2:13, her boredom and lack of enthusiasm suddenly vanishes while his back is turned, only to instantly reappear when she positions herself in front of him. When the girl moves to the direction that you are facing, moves into your field of view, you know its on - and you also know that she is going to hit you with something unpleasant.

At 2:44 she references the previous episode six failed fitness test with an expression of maximum possible disdain and boredom, retesting him. He fails again. He apologizes, even though she is and was obviously in the wrong. Needless to say, at 3:03 apology not accepted. She doubles down on the fitness test, giving him another chance to pass. At 3:09 he changes direction, and starts a counter attack. At 3:13, seeing what is coming, she perks up.

At 3:52, she launches a new shit test, but she is simultaneously flirting, which takes the sting out of it.

---

[323]https://www.youtube.com/watch?v=w_HkCQZmuOc

At 4:17, she launches a physical attack, which cannot possibly succeed, hoping to provoke him into physically overwhelming her, but he allows it to succeed, failing the shit test, and she wanders off with entirely genuine boredom and disdain. End of the pre fertile age romance for this episode.

At 4:35 we get a boring promotion for Deng's new China and new market economic order. But you are not going to see the American market order promoted on American television, only denigrated and condemned.

Then at 7:39, a different romance thread involving a different couple: beta male (beta with her, alpha with everyone else) approaches the fertile age chick, who of course hits him with a blocking fitness test at 8:11, then gives him the lets be friends pushoff. He plows on, and she walks away at 8:39 with him chasing after like a lost puppy. If hit with an unpassable fitness test, do not plow on.

He keeps on plowing on, making a bad situation worse. And plow, and plow. Boring. More plugs for the new economic order. Then at 12:57, the video proceeds to denigrate the old economic order - its enforcers are the bad guys, who are mucking up the economy by restraining the pursuit of the self interest. Again, you are never going to see socialism portrayed realistically on a video made in the west. At 18:15 Dongbao courageously announces he will fight politically for the market order and the pursuit of self interest. You are not going to see that on American video.

At 18:39 romance thread with the fertile age chick resumes. Watch her perk up as she imagines, that he is going to pass her shit test, that his mission is more important than she is. Now she chases after him, entertains him, and serves him. He brushes her off, because his mission really is more important than she is, and she chases after him.

At 22:44, encouraged by this, he resumes plowing. Watch her enthusiasm instantly fade. She shrinks away from him. He resumes his mission, and she switches back to wanting to follow him.

Then it is another tedious propaganda pitch for the new economic order. Yes, yes, we know already. Instead of thanking the party planning committee for assigning you a new tractor, you thank the party for creating a political and economic order that enables you to buy your own damned tractor. Yeah yeah, it was mildly interesting the first time because we see the opposite of that on US television. On US television the videos condemn the evil old white males for avariciously maintaining a social order that enables someone else to buy themselves a new car, but thanking the party for an order that rewards hard work and wise decisions gets old really fast.

At 31:31, the party praises raising capital and individual economic initiative. Probably not news to most readers of this blog, but you are not going to see that praised on US television. Excruciatingly dull lecture of economic activity follows. "It is totally within reason for your brigade to be be rich". Yeah, yeah, not news to us reactionaries, but you are not going to see such a statement on US television. More thanks to the party. What you get on US television is "You did not build that". And then they thank the party some more. And thank the party some more. Well, better than having a transexual on every show and in every comic strip. Then more thanking the party. And did I mention they give thanks to the party?

38:07 Switches back to the romance with the fertile age female. Now everything is fine - once he stopped plowing and focused on his mission.

Sound economics, sound romance stories. Far too much praising the party.

Episode 8[324]

3:28 Pre fertile age chick "accidentally" runs into her love interest. He brushes her off, and she sticks like glue. Then she menaces him with another fitness test, which he passes by being amused, rather than menaced. Things then go smoothly.

Skipping forward over more cheering the party for its market oriented economic order, and more cheering the party, and nothing terribly interesting happening with romance of the fertile age love interest to 14:54, where the pre fertile age love interest is lurking to intercept teacher. This time, runs gleefully up to intercept him. No more boredom and feigned disinterest. She follows him around like a lost puppy, while he focuses on his mission. 19:58, hits on him. 22:24, asks him for a date. It is implied that they date.

Main romance, fertile age couple, proceeds to married happily ever after - boring. More boring, then at 41:44 we see the lead up to missionary position sex between happily married people which is, by wildly inflated US standards of consent, not very consensual. She shields herself with bedcovers and multiple layers of clothing, and he pounces on top her and starts forcefully removing them ignoring her protests and her demands to take things more slowly. She is, of course, entirely delighted with this, video fades to black, before she loses much clothing.

In the US video, she would, of course, be horrified by this. You will see full frontal full penetration on US videos, but even when they show a porn of sexual exploitation of illegal border crossers, it is explicit consent every step of the way. You will not see female submission to the conquering male realistically portrayed.

Episode nine[325]

Boring happy marriage of fertile age couple. Then at 7:09, second date of the pre fertile age chick.

And, what do you know: A product placement for Coca Cola. Pre fertile chick tells her love interest:"Taste of a smile". "Tastes really good".

It really is the new economic order. I wonder how much Coca Cola paid for that one. Not quite as boring as praising the party for the new economic order. Love interest poses holding the can with the logo directly facing the camera. The people making this video are not just preaching the new economic order. They are putting it into practice.

11:36 During the second date, love interest tells pre fertile age chick, with the coca cola can placed prominently on the table, "We can stand on the shoulders of giants like Copernicus and Newton"

You are not going to see that on US videos, or hear that in US university. What you hear is that Western civilization is a shame and a disgusting rape of the earth that needs to be smashed as soon as possible, and we are way superior to those ignorant prejudiced bigots.

Further dates to be postponed till she reaches a slightly less inappropriate age. And then it is all the new economic order, educating the viewer in capitalism 101.

---

[324]https://www.youtube.com/watch?v=VOIcGch6bVI
[325]https://www.youtube.com/watch?v=eyll3fm2s1E

Episode 12[326]

1:09 Bad old socialists causing trouble. At 1:20 They beat up a peddler for capitalism and confiscate his stuff, much as Trotskyites killed the cows of the peasant with two cows, and Carlylean Restorationist wants to shut down your local Domino's pizza franchise. Socialist rabble rouser declaims, as the cops arrest the poor peddler and the mob make off with his pile of goodies:

> "Strike a severe blow to speculation and profiteering!"
> "Be determined to amputate the tail of capitalism!"

Are we ever going to see a rabble rouser on USA television who is not a heroic good guy fighting power, or a mob that are not heroic good guys fighting power, but are just there to knock over the liquor store and set fire to the supermarket?

Having framed the socialists as rabble rousers and a mob who will burn down the supermarket to grab a case of beer, or rather beat up a peddler to grab his hot buns, rest of episode 12 is politics and economics.

The origin of cuckservatism

2019-04-05 11:39:45

The Cathedral's position on right wing individualism is rendered obvious by the mindless conformity and rigid ideological uniformity of our tenured academics, and the robotic programmed speech of NPC leftists of twitter, and by the ever swelling apparatus to impose correct thought on everyone, for example the Human Resources Department.

But at the same time there is a problem with right wing individualism: Burke is the father of cuckservatism. The trouble with Burke is that the Burke of Liberty subverted the Burke of authority. When Burke condemned the French Revolution and assorted left anarchists and socialists, he had to invoke the throne and altar that he was otherwise busy undermining.

![The Burke of Authority invokes throne and altar[latex/images/Smelling_out_a_rat.jpg] [latex/images/Smelling_out_a_rat.jpg]

If no stationary bandit, going to have mobile bandits. If no state religion, going to have a worse state religion.

The text that the revolutionist is writing while interrupted by Burke says "On the benefits of atheism and anarchism". And he is deemed a rat because he identifies with the ideas and principles of Burke, and takes them to their logical conclusion, which conclusion horrifies Burke.

The picture is "titled"Death of Charles the first, or the Glory of Great Britain", the book says "Treatise on the ill effects of order and Government on our society and on the absurdity of serving God or honoring the King"

But that position is just the position that Burke took on the British Empire, applied to great Britain itself, applied terrifyingly close to home. And a terrified Burke promptly invoked the throne and altar that he had been industriously undermining, and continued

---

[326]https://www.youtube.com/watch?v=BPjAfkxsscs

to industriously undermine. The cartoon depicts Burke menacing the anarcho socialist revolutionary with a glowing cross in one hand, representing the state religion that Burke was probably an apostate from, and the crown representing the throne he was industriously undermining.

Burke engaged in lawfare against the East India company, launching a pile of frivolous charges against an individual member of the East India Company, in which he sought to find him guilty of governing India.

The crown had long ago given the East India company authority to make war and peace. Finding itself under attack by bandit kings, it made war in a horrifying fashion, employing devastating methods that frequently amounted to plunder, pillage, and ethnic cleaning. Victorious, it transitioned from mobile banditry to stationary banditry. Burke charged it, not with the horrifying things it had done as a mobile bandit, but with bringing peace, order and prosperity as a stationary bandit. The process was the punishment. The accused suffered more grief in successfully defending himself, than he would have if he had pled guilty and accepted punishment. Despite the accused being acquitted, Burke successfully established the principle that the British Empire was illegitimate and wicked.

Cuckservatives have no ground to stand on. If liberty, why should some people have property and others not have property, why should some people have authority and others not have authority, which is why Burke had to turn to throne and altar when viewing the catastrophic consequences of his own cuckservative doctrines. The Burke of liberty continually contradicts and subverts the Burke of authority.

But wholesale rejection of individualism is not an option, because then everything becomes a coordination problem, and coordination problems are at best difficult to solve, seldom have satisfactory solutions, and usually have only utterly disastrous solutions.

Consider the school lunch program: Turns out that it is much easier for a mother to feed her children healthy food than for a vast overpaid bureaucracy to feed an army of children healthy food.

At the same time, making individualism a religious principle leads not to freedom, but to totalitarianism, for freedom is secured by walls that separate the proper domain of my power and decisions from other people's, and those walls are an intrusion on their freedom to set fire to the supermarket and steal a case of beer, leading to the socialism painfully familiar to the Chinese who produced this video[327].

And, as Moldbug argued, those walls have to be ultimately backed by a sovereign. Anarcho capitalism will always be conquered by tribalism.

But who defends the walls against the sovereign - and against the propensity of that sovereign to find himself surrounded by vast and ever swelling bureaucracy? Burke has a case - but the verdict of history is that Burkean liberty necessarily leads to surrender to those that so horrified Burke, and Burke's ready resort to throne and altar foreshadowed the verdict of history. The inconsistency between the Burke of Authority and the Burke of Liberty reveals that one must devour the other. Conservatism has failed. Libertarianism reveals itself as unilateral disarmament, manifested by libertarians who cheerfully tell the baker "Just bake the cake" when a Christian baker is commanded to bake a gay wedding cake and cheerfully accept measures against husbands and fathers that would

---

[327] https://www.youtube.com/watch?v=BPjAfkxsscs

outrage them if applied against serial killers, libertarians who find it intolerable for president Trump to use the military to build a wall against invasion, but have no problem with using the military to build girl's schools in Afghanistan to teach nine year old girls to put a condom on a banana.

Cuckservatism seeks to preserve the social technology that the restoration secured - while abandoning the principles of the restoration. This fundamental inconsistency bit Burke, and it continues to bite his successors. Conservatism has failed, endlessly surrendering. There is no alternative but to return to the throne and altar that Burke so readily returned to when order was under threat. Conservatism has failed. Libertarianism has failed. Only throne and altar can save us.

The alternative to throne is not liberty, but rather anarcho tyranny, a thousand Kings three miles away instead of one King three thousand miles away. The alternative to state religion is out of control religion, the social justice warriors.

Reaction will be implemented by reactionary methods, not by promising fifty one percent of the voters more bread and circuses. The cycle of history is that democracy gives way to the rule of one man. The end of the democracy draws near, the only question remaining being how many will be murdered in its death throes. That one man will find that guns do not suffice. He is going to need a priesthood, an official religion consistent with the rule of one man. Those who preach that the ruler rules by the will of God are in the running to be that priesthood.

Current technology is that a handful of able, well trained well equipped warriors can easily handle a mob of any size, and have little difficulty with a horde of poorly trained conscript cannon fodder. Our technological situation is analogous to what it was when the armored knight on the warhorse was the ultimate decider of battles. But guns alone cannot rule. Ideas are more powerful than guns. Our ideas are appropriate to the death throes of democracy, and to current military and information technology. Recent events have demonstrated that elections have already become largely irrelevant. Expect each election to be even less relevant than its predecessor. When the permanent government decided to ignore Trump, it decided to saw off the branch on which it sat. As Trump needed, and successfully used, the Federalist society, and the Federalist society successfully used Trump, the dictator is going to need us.

The recent parade in Italy reflects the increasing mass penetration of our ideas, in the meme of Emperor Trump, and the celebration of divine right warrior rule in the song Carolus Rex[328]. Supposedly this is mockery of Trump - but you don't mock by faithfully reproducing memes circulated by his most enthusiastic supporters at twenty times lifesize with loudspeakers blaring.

We are intellectuals, and the meme warriors disown intellectual analysis for meme warfare - but their memes encapsulate our ideas in their simplest and most compelling form. Meme warriors are our footsoldiers. If Trump fails, someone is going to succeed - the only question is how many will be killed before the return to simplest and most fundamental form of governance. The social justice warrior is trapped in a holiness spiral, and the position that all white males need to be killed is the next step in ever greater holiness. Let us hope we get a more stable form of governance before that happens. But

---

[328] https://www.youtube.com/watch?v=TQOkonLf8tg

sooner or later, and not very much later, we are going to get a more stable form of governance. Conservatism was born cutting its own throat. Libertarianism has surrendered. All that remains is reaction or socialist democide. Worst case outcome is socialist democide followed by reaction. We hope for a reaction that restores the social technology that has been destroyed, we hope for the restoration, and intend to provide an idea system that will make that reaction more stable, more secure, and less bloody. Restoration is the idea system that can provide the legitimacy that will make the coming dictatorship secure, peaceful, and more comfortable for everyone.

Michael Knowles at UKMC

2019-04-27 05:12:41

48:58

"Why the rage?

asks a member of the audience
Michael Knowles at UMKC tells us

When people have a weak point, they tend to shatter.

When people don't have confidence in what they are saying, they scream at you.

They are now seeing the fruits of a long simmering gender ideology, that men and women are identical,

Which ideology is resulting in horrific consequences.

Eradicating the differences between men and women. They lose their minds.

50.50[329]
> Why these people are crazy?
Asks a member of the audience.
Michael Knowles answers:

Despair.

They have driven themselves mad

There is no such thing as truth, there is no such thing as reality, we can not have a reasonable discourse about objective reality.

There are just personal interests, there is no reason, there is no logic to the universe. It is all a tale told by an idiot, signifying nothing. The only way you can get what you want, the only way you can take a bigger piece of the pie for yourself is to take it from someone else.

---

[329]https://www.youtube.com/embed/zWYliHNTXiw?start=3050

In contrast, Solomon's good women gets a bigger piece of the pie by using the market place to apply capital to its highest and best use. Proverbs 31:16: King Solomon tells us:
> She considereth a field, and buyeth it: with the fruit of her hands she planteth a vineyard

She "considereth land and purchaseth it". She does not just purchase it, and she certainly does not apply to the King or to Wall Street to get a piece of land assigned to her. That she "considereth" the best application of capital is what makes capitalism work and socialism fail. And then she "planteth a vineyard", creating capital.

The Marxist believes that the man running your local Domino's pizza franchise was assigned that franchise by wall street, unaware that he built it, and owns it.

The Marxist (and every tenured academic and every teacher is a Marxist or else he would lose tenure so fast it would make your head spin) refuses to know that the man who runs your local Domino's pizza franchise built it, owns it, created it, and could at any time take down the Domino's sign, and put up his own, because the academic, every tenured academic everywhere, intends to murder the man who runs your local Domino's pizza, and install someone holier, who will demonstrate superior holiness over his mere customers by providing you with bread and coke zero, instead of cheese and meat on your pizzas, much as those who created Captainess Marvel and Hans Soyboy celebrated the tears of their fans, for by giving the fans something they hated, they proved themselves holier than the fans who were paying them money.

You cannot run a restaurant from Wall Street, any more than you can run a restaurant from Moscow. But they are determined to believe the world is run from Wall Street, even though Human Resources will not let Musk or Bezos get laid, because they intend to run the world from Washington.

The end result of attempting do so is of course is that pretty soon you run out of other people's money. The shops empty, as they did in Revolutionary France and are emptying now in Venezuela, and eventually those holier than you and me burn down the shops, and shop keepers flee, as they are today fleeing Venezuela.

The French Revolution was an anticapitalist revolution. There was a very short lived alliance between the Merchant class seeking the abolition of the controls on price, supply, and distribution of grain, and the Popular Society, the Mountain, seeking a totalitarian society of superior holiness with the enforced state religion of the Enlightenment, the Church of Reason, which alliance, like every Popular Front ever, ended within a few weeks of the alliance taking power, the left devouring its allies immediately after taking power. The controls were lifted, and then soon thereafter reimposed, plus price controls on every thing plus terror against the merchant class, especially the butchers and bakers, terror against their former allies. Price controls led to shortages, shortages to rationing, and then production quotas, which production quotas amounted to enslavement of many members of the merchant class, especially the bakers.

As with Stalin and Pharaoh, former members of the merchant class in Revolutionary France were commanded to meet their output quotas, even when inputs were unavailable, as they frequently were, and punished for failure to meet those output quotas. Which resulted in bricks without straw in Egypt during the collapse of Bronze Age civilization, tomato soup infamously lacking in tomatoes in Soviet Russia, light bulbs with no filaments in Soviet Russia, and bread largely made of dirt in Revolutionary France. As in

Venezuela as I write, violence ensued, and the ruling elite, following the example of King Louis XVI, directed the rage against the merchant class.

In Cuba, there was enough bread and sugar, but only bread and sugar, resulting in epidemic of malnutrition related blindness, while the vanguard of the proletariat and visiting fellow traveler leftists from America ate like Kings. When I was in Cuba, the planes did not fly on a regular schedule like buses, but instead flew like taxis, responding to the momentary and immediate needs of members of the vanguard of the proletariat – or their fellow traveler guests, who seemed totally untroubled by the contradiction between their ideology of equality, their splendid lifestyle in Cuba, and the lifestyle of ordinary Cubans.

Similarly, when Haiti was ruled by NGO carryonbaggers from Harvard bringing billions of dollars in foreign aid after the earthquake, Haitians ate dirt. You want to know what Harvard intends for ordinary Americans? Compare Haiti ruled by mulatto thugs, with Haiti ruled by NGO carryonbaggers from Harvard. Under the rule of NGO carryonbaggers from Harvard, medieval plagues raged, the streetlights went out, and Haitians ate dirt. The streets of San Francisco, littered with human feces, foreshadow what Harvard has in store for the suburbia that it hates, as did the feces on the streets of Haiti during NGO rule. When I returned to San Francisco recently, it was noticeable that there had not been much paint, maintenance, or repairs done in my absence, and that there were human feces here and there.

Marxists, Human biodiversity deniers, Catastrophic Anthropogenic Global Warmists, and sexual difference deniers simply lie loudly and repeatedly. When one of their lies is rebutted, they ignore the rebuttal, and instead of responding, issue a dozen new lies, then return to the old lie, assuming not only that it was never rebutted, but that everyone, including the person who rebutted it, agrees that it is the obvious, unquestioned, and unquestionable truth - a style of debate that reveals that they know that they are lying.

If Marxists genuinely believed that capitalism was recent, or that the French Revolution was a capitalist revolution rather than an anti capitalist revolution, if Catastrophic Anthropogenic Global Warmists believed that global warming was causing a refugee crisis, they would respond to evidence and argument with evidence and argument, rather than telling you "the science is settled."

That they knowingly lie reveals that they intend harm to their audience. The method of argument used by troofers, Marxists, human biodiversity deniers, Catastrophic Anthropogenic Global Warmists, and sexual difference deniers, reveals that they know the truth, or that they believe their is no truth, only power. Watch the sexual difference deniers method of debating Michael Knowles. And if you find yourself debating with someone who believes there is no truth, only power, he regards all other people merely as obstacles and raw materials, and will wind up using the power he seeks to murder people. He will announce he is seizing the bakery for the people, and burn it down to steal a bottle of Coke Zero. This is why the left always winds up murdering the left. They knock over the apple cart supposedly believing this will result in an abundance of apples, and for a short while it does result in an abundance of apples. And when a mysterious apple shortage ensues, they launch a witch hunt for the evil witches casting the evil spells that are causing the the mysterious apple shortage, and most of the witches that they find are their fellow leftists. Nazis murder their enemies, but commies murder their friends.

Because leftists believe that, as Michael Knowles said, "the only way you can take a bigger piece of the pie for yourself is to take it from someone else" they believe that capitalism must be recent. If capitalists have stuff, they must have taken it from Kings, Aristocrats, and subsaharan Africans.

If someone tells you that capitalism is recent, he intends, personally and individually, to murder you, because he believes that is the way to acquire value. As Michael Knowles said "They rage and rage and create nothing."

And this is why a software project dies when it adopts a code of conduct. Left wing "software engineers" don't create software. They don't actually believe that software is created, just taken, and the code of conduct is a tool to expel the major creators of your software (as Linus, the creator of Linux and Git was expelled) so that they can take it, without the tedious inconvenience of understanding the source code or understanding how it works or why it is the way that it is. They rage at Linus, and create nothing.

They believe contradictory and nonsensical things, they doublethink, they do not care about the contradiction, but when they try to persuade you of contradictory and nonsensical things, they use the methods of debate of people who know that they are lying: They presuppose a fake consensus, and when this consensus is challenged, segue onto new issues, then shortly return to assuming that everyone agrees with the fake consensus.

Rather than asserting X is true, which assertion would instantly arouse the suspicion of the audience that X is not true, and might result in the audience asking for evidence for X, they talk about Y, where Y presupposes and assumes that the audience already knows and agrees that X is true, even though X is as insane as the proposition that men are women, that all men are created equal, that capitalism came into being recently, or that climate change is causing refugees and a reduction in the livable land area.

And, more dangerously, as an organized and collective left wing group: When a mysterious shortage of value mysteriously ensues, that organized group of leftists is apt to engage in large scale terror and mass murder, largely of other leftists, because by the time that they are able to engage in large scale mass murder, it is mostly leftists who have what little stuff remains.

Coup

2019-05-11 09:51:10

Trump has said the coup word.

Of course, it is not really a Democrat coup until they send a bunch of guys dressed in freshly issued police uniforms and equipped with a subpoena from some judge in Hawaii and give him the perp walk without bothering with the old fashioned inconvenience of a senate supermajority impeachment. And if one coup once, chances are there will be another coup, this time without bothering with the freshly issued police uniforms and subpoena.

But it is a creeping coup. In a creeping coup coupists do bad things, get away with it, and, getting away with it, people dare not stop them when they do worse things. And so far, the Democrats have gotten away with it, which inevitably results, and is intended to result, in an escalation of those bad things.

And if he starts arresting Democrats for their numerous illegal acts, they will certainly think it is a Trump self coup - and it will be, regardless of whether Trump intends it to be or not.

The Roman Republic died when the Gracchi defied term limits, and the senate murdered them.

When Augustus attempted to revive the Republic, or pretended to attempt to revive the Republic, he was not attempting to heal a gravely ill patient, but to perform necromancy. He revived the forms of the republic, but those forms were full of imperial content, for the imperium was the only thing that could make them function.

The presidency has grown and swollen the American government, and the only thing that can make it function is if a president swallows it.

The Mueller report was a dud. Not only did it find no Trump collaboration with efforts to influence the US election, nor any obstruction of justice - the allegations of obstruction of justice are just mind reading that Trump thought about killing off the Mueller investigation, but whatever he thought about, he did not in fact obstruct it, and even if he did obstruct it, which he did not, you cannot have obstruction of justice without an underlying crime.

Further, extraordinarily, the Russian government did not attempt to influence the American election - unlike one hell of a lot of other governments, or if they did, Mueller could not find any such attempts, and is lying when he claims that he did. The people being charged are accused in the Mueller report of being Russian agents, but when he actually brought charges which a hostile lawyer might cross examine, he did not charge the offender with being an agent of the Russian government, revealing that he knew that under hostile cross examination, the charge would sink like a stone. Instead the offender is charged with incomprehensible legal technicalities under vague and sweeping laws in an unsuccessful effort to get them to rat out Trump - which they were unable to do, having no connection to Trump, and no connection to the Russian government that Mueller was willing to present in court.

Mueller has been caught lying about two of the supposed Russian agents, one of whom is in fact a Mueller agent. If one lie, all lies.

The behavior of the democrats show that they are not actually interested in the contents of the Mueller report - they failed to read the minimally redacted redacted report issued for limited non public distribution. They know it is a dud. They want the attorney general removed because he is investigating them, and are just trying to link his removal to supposed Russian intervention in US elections. They are working on a coup because the perceive Trump as working on a self coup, and Trump is working on a self coup, or perceived to be working on a self coup, because the Democrats are working on a coup.

Everyone pretending there is some substance in the Mueller report is doing a Point Deer Make Horse - including the numerous republicans going along with the pretense. Point Deer Make Horse is a classic part of a coup: if people go along with the blatant lie, this shows they will go along with the coup. So everyone who talks as if the Mueller Report was not a dud, is signaling he is on board with an anti Trump coup.

So either Trump does a self coup - takes control of the FBI and turns it on his enemies, or will be removed in a coup - which will initially only arrest him, but such arrests lead to escalating drama, which eventually result in the arrested leader and various people close to him being executed.

If Trump does a self coup he will say, and perhaps believe, he is preserving the Republic, but once struggle within the political elite goes violent, it is going to get more violent. If Trump succeeds, the general public will not see a coup, but the Democrats and the left generally will, and even if they quietly submit this time, and everyone gets into line, we will be in the situation of the Roman Republic after the Gracchi: the political elite lacks cohesion, and will no longer play by mutually agreed rules, which inevitably results in political conflicts turning violent.

The Democrats have deleted God from the house of representatives. For a nation to be one nation, people need a big daddy on top. If no longer "One nation under God", going to need a cult of personality leader to be one nation. The state religion of progressivism cannot provide for the orderly transfer of power, so we are inevitably moving towards disorderly transfer of power.

Augustus had to be deified to make the Roman government work (steel alone did not suffice) but the trouble is that when your state religion is based on flagrant lies, it is fragile so has to be repressive.

When the rot set in

2019-05-23 00:59:35

The priesthood exists to serve the army, by providing legitimacy, moral guidance, and social cohesion. When the priests undermine army officers, pretty soon you get what we have got.

Priests are supposed to supply asabiyyah. That is their number one job in this world. What we have is priests destroying asabiyyah .

The problem is not so much elite disloyalty to the masses, nor a Jewish plot against members of the elite not of their own race, as elite disloyalty to the elite. When the priesthood seeks to destroy the common man and return flyover country to wilderness, their real target is not lumberjacks and coal miners, but military officers. Lumberjacks and coal miners are just collateral damage.

We are always ruled by priests or warriors. When priests get on top, there is military weakness. When they get on top, there is also an incentive and ability to go into a holiness spiral.

So, when did the rot set in?

This interpretation of events is largely based on Volume 55 of the North American Review, page 45, "The English in Afghanistan" by Summer, who quotes extensively from contemporary primary sources

Before the British intervened in Afghanistan, the most recent news that most people had of it was records of Alexander's army passing through two millennia ago.

The empire of the East India company was expanding, and the empire of the Russias was expanding, and it was inevitable that the two would meet. And so it came to pass that the Kings of Afghanistan encountered both, and played each against the other.

When the British became aware of Afghanistan, they interpreted its inhabitants as predominantly white or whitish - as descendants of Alexander's troops and camp followers and/or descendants of Jews converted to Islam.

Afghanistan was, and perhaps still is, a elective monarchy, and the fractious electors tended to fight each other and elect weak kings who could scarcely control their followers, and so it has been ever since Alexander's troops lost Alexander.

Mister Mountstuart Elphinstone, in his account of is mission to Kabul in 1809, says he once urged upon a very intelligent old man of the tribe of Meankheile, the superiority of a quiet life under a powerful monarch, over the state of chaotic anarchy that so frequently prevailed.

The reply was "We are content with alarms, we are content with discord, we are content with blood, but we will never be content with a master!"

As Machiavelli observed, such places are easy to conquer, but hard to hold, and so it proved.

To conquer and hold such places, one must massacre, castrate, or enslave all of the ruling elite that seems fractious, which is pretty much all of them, and replace them with your own people, speaking your own language, and practicing your own customs, as the Normans did in England, and the French did in Algeria, starting 1830. The British of 1840, however, had no stomach for French methods, and were already starting to fall short of the population growth necessary for such methods.

So what the British could have done is paid the occasional visit to kill any king that they found obnoxious, kill his friends, family, his children, and leading supporters, install a replacement king, and leave. The replacement king would have found his throne shaky, because Afghan Kings have usually found their thrones shaky, but the British did not need to view that as their problem, knowing the solution to that problem to be drastic and extreme. If the throne has been shaky for two thousand years, it is apt to be difficult to stop it from rocking.

After a long period of disorderly violence, where brother savagely tortured brother to death, and all sorts of utterly horrifying crimes were committed, King Dost Mahomed Khan took power in Kabul in 1826, and proceeded to rule well, creating order, peace, and prosperity, and receiving near universal support from fractious and quarreling clans of Afghanistan.

The only tax under his rule was a tariff of one fortieth on goods entering and leaving the country. This and the Jizya poll tax are the only taxes allowed by the Koran, at least as Islamic law is interpreted in this rebellious country which has historically been disinclined to pay taxes, and because this tax was actually paid, it brought him unprecedented revenues. On paying this tax "the merchant may travel without guard or protection from one border to the other, an unheard of circumstance"

However he did not rule Herat, which was controlled by one of his enemies, who been King before and had ambitions to be King again. He therefore offered Herat to the Shah of Persia in return for the Shah's support against another of his enemies, Runjeet Singh. He was probably scarcely aware that Runjeet Singh was allied to the British, and the Shah was allied to the Tsar of all the Russias.

Notice that this deal was remarkably tight fisted, as was infamously typical of deals made by Dost Mahomed Khan. He would give the Persians that which he did not possess, in return for them taking care of one of his enemies and helping him against another.

The British East India Company, however, saw this as Afghanistan moving into Russian empire, though I am pretty sure that neither the Shah of Persia nor the King of Afghanistan thought they were part of anyone's empire.

So Russia and the East India Company sent ambassadors to the King of Afghanistan, who held a bidding contest asking which of them could best protect him against Runjeet Singh. He then proceeded to duplicitously accept both bids from both empires, which was a little too clever by half, though absolutely typical of the deals he made with his neighbors.

Dost Mahomed Khan was a very clever king, but double crossing the East India Company had in the past never been very clever at all. No one ever got ahead double crossing the East India Company. It was like borrowing money from the Mafia and forgetting to pay them back.

Russia and England then agreed to not get overly agitated over the doings of unreliable and duplicitous proxies that they could scarcely control - which agreement the East India Company took as permission to hold a gun to the head of the Shah of Persia. The East India company seized control of the Persian Gulf, an implicit threat to invade if the Shah intervened in Afghanistan to protect Dost Mahomed Khan. It then let Runjeet Singh off the leash, and promised to support his invasion of Afghanistan.

So far, so sane. Someone double crosses you, then you make an horrible example of him, and no one will do it again. Then get out, and whoever rules in Afghanistan, if anyone does manage to rule, will refrain from pissing you off a second time.

The British decided to give a large part of Afghanistan to Runjeet Singh, and install Shah Shoudjah-ool-Moolk, a Kinglet with somewhat plausible pretensions to the Afghan throne, in place of Dost Mahomet Khan.

Up to this point everything the East India Company is doing is sane, honorable, competent, just, and wonderfully eighteenth century.

Unfortunately, it is the nineteenth century. And the nineteenth century is when the rot set in.

> His Majesty Shah Shoudjah-ool-Moolk will enter Afghanistan, surrounded by his own troops, and will be supported against foreign interference, and factious opposition, by the British Army. The Governor-general confidently hopes, that the Shah will be speedily replaced on his throne by his own subjects and adherents, and that the independence and integrity of Afghanistan established, the British army will be withdrawn. The Governor-general has been led to these acts by the duty which is imposed upon him, of providing for the security of the possessions of the British crown, but he rejoices, that, in the discharge of this duty, he will be enabled to assist in restoring the union and prosperity of the Afghan people.

So: The English tell themselves and each other: We not smacking Afghans against a wall to teach them not to play games with the East India Company. On the contrary. We are doing them a favor. A really big favor. Because we love everyone. We even love total strangers in far away places very different from ourselves. We are defending the independence of Afghanistan by removing the strongest King it has had in centuries and installing our puppet, and defending its integrity by arranging for invasion, conquest, rape and pillage by its ancient enemies the Sikhs, in particular Runjeet Singh. Because we love far away strangers who speak a language different from our own and live in places we cannot find on the map. We just love them to pieces. And when we invade, we will doubtless be greeted by people throwing flowers at us.

You might ask who would believe such guff? Obviously not the Afghans, who are being smacked against the wall. Obviously not the Russians. Obviously not the Persians. Obviously not the British troops who are apt to notice they are not being pelted with flowers.

The answer is: the commanding officer believed this guff. And not long thereafter, he and his troops died of it, the first great defeat of British colonialism. And, of course, the same causes are today leading to our current defeat in Afghanistan.

The commanding officer of the British expedition made a long series of horrifyingly evil and stupid decisions, which decisions only made sense if he was doing the Afghans a big favor, if the Afghans were likely to appreciate the big favor he was doing them, and his troops were being pelted with flowers, or Afghans were likely to start pelting them with flowers real soon now. The East India company was no stranger to evil acts, being in the business of piracy, brigandry, conquest, and extortion, but people tend to forgive evil acts that lead to success, prosperity, good roads, safe roads, and strong government. These evil acts, the evil acts committed by the British expedition to Afghanistan, are long remembered because they led to failure, defeat, lawlessness, disorder, and weak government.

As a result, he, his men, and their camp followers, were all killed.

Progressives tend to judge people by their good intentions, and the intentions of the British Empire in invading Afghanistan were absolutely wonderful, but the man who does evil because insane is a worse problem than the man who does evil because he expects to profit. The rational profit seeking evildoer, you can pay off, or deter. You can surrender on terms that will probably not be too bad. The irrational evildoer just has to be killed. Before 1840, the East India Company was sometimes deterred, frequently paid off, and frequently accepted surrender on reasonable terms. In 1841, just had to be killed.

This illustrates the importance of the rectification of names, of formalism. If you lie to yourself, you are deceived. I have been reading the Clinton emails, and one of the most striking features is that Clinton and company were deluded and deceived by self flattering lies, that despite having vast spy networks in far flung places, were seriously out of contact with reality, as their circle told each other what they want to hear.

If you know the enemy and know yourself, you need not fear the result of a hundred battles. If you know yourself but not the enemy, for every victory gained you will also suffer a defeat. If you know neither the enemy nor yourself, you will succumb in every battle. Hillary and her advisers, and therefore I suppose the entire state department, know neither the enemy nor themselves. They dream grandiose delusions, in which they are the terribly smart and virtuous people, rather than a drunken old sow surrounded by lying flatterers.

The East India Company did not realize that it was about to be recast, or was recasting itself, from being a for profit company, empowered to make war and engage in acts of piracy and extortion for private profit, to being the British government's instrument of holy do gooding, benevolently carrying the white man's burden for the benefit of a bunch of strangely ungrateful foreigners. In place of a ruthless mafia with uniformed soldiers, the East India Company was about to become an NGO with uniformed nursemaids.

Yet strangely, the greater the good intentions, the more they were to be resented. The East India Company seems to have been more popular when they were pirates and bandits than when they were pious do gooders. No one seemed to appreciate the East India Company doing good to them at gunpoint. The ridiculous part of the white man's burden was the striking ingratitude of the supposed beneficiaries, resembling the striking ingratitude of Middle Easterners towards meddling by presidents Bush and Obama in the Middle East. Those @!^&$ Middle Easterners just somehow do not know what is good for them, unlike far away strangers, who, being terribly clever, know exactly what is good for the Middle East without ever having lived there.

In the Clinton emails there is an awareness that everything is going horribly wrong and a suspicion that things are about to get a great deal worse, but that cannot possibly be caused by any mistakes of the current leadership, who are of course the smartest, wisest, noblest, best, and most beloved leadership ever.

Fat is a reactionary issue

2019-05-26 06:27:30

Facebook recently purged a facebook group for advocating healthy eating habits - right wing healthy eating habits - adequate protein, plenty of animal fats and less or no snacking, especially snacking of overly processed foods made from unknown ingredients, which tends to be what snacks are made of.

Leftism being the party of defection, infanticide, sodomy, adultery, effeminacy, and treason, is also the party of vice. And the most common vices of today are gluttony, sloth, and adultery.

Gluttony, as well as being the most common vice, is a highly visible vice. And usually indicative of other vices.

A leftist chick in a "long term relationship" is far more likely to be cruising for an upgrade, and apt to go right on cruising long after the wall has made an upgrade improbable, and a leftist, male or female, is far more likely to be fat and weak. Adultery is primarily a female sin, since female sexual misconduct is far more likely to obfuscate paternity and obstruct fatherhood.

Obesity is epidemic in the modern world. How do you fix it? The solution to obesity is now well known - well, well known in some circles, but oddly unknown in left wing circles, in the mainstream media (but I repeat myself).And now unknown on Facebook.

The primary cause of obesity in the modern world is the cafeteria diet, snacking, especially snacking on foods that contain a lot of carbs, vegetable oil, and not much protein. (And what protein there is tends to be soy.)

The formula for losing weight is fewer meals, approximately one hundred grams of protein per day for a male, which is approximately a pound of meat, and plenty of animal fat, as for example bacon, eggs, cheese, and butter. You should go about seventeen hours, if socially possible, before breaking fast. And since dinner is usually socially required, that likely means skipping breakfast.

Too little animal protein makes you weak, less muscled, and impairs healing and body regeneration, but too much protein stresses your kidneys and liver, and if you are eating too much protein, you probably will find you don't like it. People on very high protein diets get sick, and find it hard to keep meat down. For most men, one hundred grams of protein per day is about the right amount.

Some white people, and most Asians and middle easterners can handle carbs just fine, but a lot of white people cannot. Cut the carbs. You will find it far easier to control your eating on a very low carb diet, one where you mostly eat low carb vegetables like broccoli roasted with butter, or mushrooms fried in lots of butter, rather than high carb vegetables. And most fruit is a bit on the high carb side, if you need a very low carb diet to control your appetite.

Don't eat vegetable oils, except for olive oil, coconut oil, avocado oil, and palm oil. Nuts are generally OK, even peanuts, but peanut oil not so much.

Our metabolisms are primarily designed to handle saturated fats - the short chain fats generated by our bowels, and our own fat stores. Animal fat is what we are designed to metabolize as our primary energy source. Apes consume a lot of fibre which gets metabolized into short chain fats in their large intestine, and our ancestors lived on their own body fat between kills.

Avoid soft drinks, especially zero calorie soft drinks. It is a mystery to me why zero calorie soft drinks are fattening, but just looking around, you can see that they are. Maybe they stimulate insulin secretion. Notice that people in whom insulin secretion is defective (as in type one diabetes) don't get fat even if they eat a lot, and are apt to lose alarming amounts of weight unless they inject themselves with insulin. That, however, is just a wild assed guess.

Or maybe it is that sweet drinks cause you to overeat. I drink Mountain Dew with moonshine on social occasions, and Mountain Dew always makes me eat and drink too much. Likely Coke Zero would have similar effect. Maybe that is the problem. That is just another wild assed guess, but looking at fat people's eating habits, you can see that substituting zero calorie soft drinks for sugary soft drinks is not a solution. Get your caffeine fix from black coffee or unsweetened tea.

These specific prohibitions don't matter that much, and do not necessarily apply to everyone, provided you follow the general rule which does apply to everyone: The main thing that makes people fat in the modern world is continual snacking - the cafeteria diet. It is snacks, and, for white people carbs, that make you fat. Don't do that. Go for long periods, at least seventeen hours every day, and every now and then forty two hours, where you eat nothing and drink nothing but water and zero calorie tea and coffee. On a forty hour fast, you will lose about two pounds, and a seventy hour fast about five pounds but doing it too often can stress you, resulting in diverse non specific illness. You should not lose weight too fast over the long term.

If you are trying to lose weight, you need to weigh yourself every morning. What you do not measure, you will not control. Scales are cheap. I have three of them, two of which

I use - the two that usually give very similar results. They lean against the wall facing the sunrise, and I weigh myself at about the time that I watch the sun rise, and record my weight every day. (I have big problem with lust, gluttony, and wrath, and have managed, with some difficulty, to control gluttony. My current weight, as of this morning, is four pounds over my ideal weight.)

Trump's state visit to England

2019-06-04 01:32:55

Ideas are more powerful than guns, and fashion is more powerful than ideas.

The main weapon and instrument of successful rulers is their role as the fount of all honors, mortal and divine. Because of the problems of scaling, their bureaucracy, rather than being the instrument of their rule, tends to become the main threat to their rule.

Trump's visit to England is primarily a status parade. Trump bestows status on the queen (which is useless, but required, because one should always give one's host top status, even though it is only useful to bestow status on one's host if the host is a man), and the Queen bestows status on him.

They also bestowed status on the other people assembled. And guess who is not there?

Hollywood, the media, and for the most part, woke capital is not there. Capital is there, but the media and such are mere onlookers The Queen and Trump bestow status on the military and on merchants, but somehow merchants whose activities overlap with the priesthood generally seem to have been neglected.

Depressingly, the Queen's speech was about universalism, framing World War II as a holy war to establish the rule by the "international community" over the entire world – and that this was a good thing intended to thereby end war forever. Of course, in fact, World War II was so horribly bloody precisely because it was a holy war by universalists seeking to rule the world, and universalist rule has been terribly bad, destroying men's families, ending science, suppressing the scientific method, and causing technological progress to stagnate. As promised universalism has so far avoided large scale horrifying wars, but war is a bursty phenomenon, and the recent period of relative peace has so far lasted no longer than previous periods of relative peace that follow a terrible war in which one hegemon gains overwhelming dominance. China now has radar coverage of the South China sea, and is building a fleet of artificial islands as unsinkable aircraft carriers – a strategy that suggests that they believe that aircraft carriers are eminently sinkable, that in a war between technologically advanced wealthy powers, each side will be able to deny the other side the air and the sea, a vision of conflict that if accurate makes it hard for one hegemon to dominate the entire world. We have already seen how Russian anti air capabilities limit US reach.

But then, to my considerable relief, she segued onto Anglosphere nationalism "Our strong cultural links" ... "*British descent*".

And then "Economic ties", a hat tip to Trump boosting brexit with a promise of a US-UK trade deal. Trump nods.

And then a toast to Trump and the prosperity of the United States (not universal peace, nor universal prosperity). The start spangled banner plays. Trump and his wife stand with their hands over their hearts. Behind the queen stands a British warrior, a member of the Coldstream Guards, costumed in seventeenth century dress uniform. The Coldstream guards were General Monck's Praetorians when he secured parliament and ensured the restoration of Charles the second, a coup well dressed in the costume of legality and constitutionality, steel on the inside, legality on the outside.

The guards are recruited from those parts of England and Scotland where General Monck recruited his praetorians, so they tend to have family ties to each other and to ancestors who were part of the Coldstream guards.

The guards behind Trump, the Queen, and Melanie salute the playing of the star spangled banner.

Hollywood and the media will call this all silly low status obsolete rigmarole, but it is hard to say "low status" to someone with warriors behind him and powerful and wealthy men assembled before him.

Then Trump speaks, remembering World War II. Trump, however, frames world war two as as a war for *our* civilization, where "our" is, in context the Anglosphere, and tells us that the British fought to hold their destiny in their own hands, another nod to brexit. Then he gives a nod to universalism – liberty in all lands – which looks remarkably like all lands having the culture of Harvard imposed upon them. Then it is back to the Anglosphere winning World War II for the Anglosphere. "Shared Victory".

And then, after piously giving the nod to universalism he starts redefining universalism to not be universalism, much as the progressives have redefined Christianity to be exemplified by the right of women to freedom from husbands, moment to moment consent to marriage, unilateral abortion on demand to birth and immediately afterwards without the consent of their husbands, and the right of men to have gay sex in a great big pile.

This is the reverse of Pope Francis defending gay priests having gay sex in a great big pile by pointing out that they were all consenting adults, and look, Global Warming.

Nah, supposedly this great crusade was not about the international community making everyone into clones of Harvard. It was supposedly about "Freedom, Sovereignty, self determination, the rule of law, and reverence for the rights given to us by Almighty God". (Which is pretty much the opposite of what the great crusade accomplished). So, if brexit fails to go through, you are falling short of the noble goals of this great crusade. And just in case you failed to notice, he said the bad word "crusade" again – and then that other bad word "God" – the ultimate patriarchal alpha male that stands behind the authority of each patriarch when he summons his family and guests to eat and says grace, the patriarchal alpha male that stands behind the ruler making his people one nation under God.

And then another bad word "patriotism": "The patriotism that beats proudly in every British heart". Yet another nod to brexit. So if you are against brexit, you are against God, country, and the goals of the great crusade, not to mention against a man who has a warrior standing behind him, a warrior of a group of warriors who put the current royal line back on the throne.

And then a toast to the Queen. Being an alpha male, he gives her a little pat, which she much enjoys.

The polls were wrong about the brexit referendum, indicating that our priestly elite had successfully made support for brexit wicked and low status. Trump proceeds to make it virtuous and high status.

The counter coup unfolds.

2019-06-07 05:28:01

A couple weeks ago, Trump condemned congresswoman Ilhan Omar for dismissing 9/11, and all the left and all the mainstream media united around her, and repeatedly told us she was black, and Trump hates blacks, and a woman, and Trump hates women, and he is lying liar.

Lo and behold, by a strange coincidence, an investigation of congresswomen Ilhan Omar comes out revealing she has committed no end of illegal acts - but until now these laws were never enforced against Democrats.

At almost the same time, the black leftist Democratic party House Oversight Committee[330] chairman is discovered to have been cheerfully embezzling from charities, shortly after he complained about a whole lot of Trumpists getting security clearances that would enable them to see information formerly only visible to leftists in good standing, information that will likely reveal a whole lot of stuff that Democrats would prefer buried.

I predict that thanks to a change in leadership of the FBI and the justice department, in particular the resignation of Mueller, there will be sudden drop in criticism of president Trump, and a sudden drop in anything likely to attract a hostile tweet from president Trump.

By another amazing coincidence, ABC news reporters who cheerfully and openly committed illegal acts find themselves facing dawn raids and charges from the Australian government in relation to their most recent illegal act. It is interesting that these utterly unprecedented and extraordinary actions, for enforcing laws against leftists is unprecedented and extraordinary (laws are for us, not them) happened at almost the same time.

Because of ever more laws, whosoever controls the FBI and the justice department holds the political process by its throat. A very short while ago, no end of people connected to Trump were getting the dawn raids, and being charged with a multitude of legalistic crimes that were difficult to explain or comprehend. That was a dangerous escalation of a process that has long been in motion, and escalation is not always passively accepted by the victims, nor is Trump a man who is inclined to passively accept escalation by his opponents.

It was inevitable that the use of the coercive power of the state to manage electoral outcomes would eventually be used against the left itself, though I expected and predicted that the left would use it against each other. But using such means against the president himself was the most dangerous use of that power possible, and Trump probably the most dangerous man to use it against.

The right using the power of the state against the left is unprecedented, despite a huge volume of complaints by the left projecting their own conduct onto their enemies. Nixon

---

[330]https://www.foxnews.com/politics/cummings-fights-baseless-allegations-against-wifes-non-profit-agency

used "plumbers", but Obama used the FBI. And now Trump is using the FBI.

Now that the dawn raids on Trumpists have stopped, I predict we will suddenly find a whole lot more Trumpists around, and a much bigger pool of loyalists for him to hire. And as loyalists get appointed to positions where they can destroy their enemies and protect their friends from destruction, this will in turn make it easier for him to hire more loyalists. And now that the dawn raids on mainstream media reporters have started, at least in Australia, I predict that the quality of "fact checking" on Trump's tweets will show a dramatic improvement. When Trump does something like talking with the veterans of D-Day, it will mysteriously become a whole lot easier to find in the mainstream media. It seems to me that reporting has improved already.

I am not yet sending in an application for the post of Grand Inquisitor. Maybe after Trump gets re-elected in 2024.

The Faith

2019-06-28 08:34:50

Holy war is coming, as the poz gets ever more extreme, ever faster, and our ruling elite increasingly uses state coercion and the FBI to accomplish political outcomes, coercing fellow members of the political elite for political reasons.

Have to bring a gun to a gunfight, and a faith to a holy war.

Deus Vult.

Whites are detribalized, and contrary to the white nationalists, "white" is not a tribal identifier. Whites are wolf to whites. A religion, defining religion broadly to include things like communism and poz, is a synthetic tribe. To win, we need a faith.

With our enemies going further and further into delusion, we have to form a faith on the Truth of Gnon, the Will of God as manifested in the natural order, the Logos manifested in the order of the world, natural law as the will of God. We will, in accordance with the Christianity of about a thousand years ago, interpret Christ as, among other things, the incarnation of the Logos, and thus interpret his words as in accordance with game theory and evolutionary psychology, and divine prophecies as the predictable outcome of cause and effect.

One can deduce ought from is, which is exactly what the Book of Solomon and the copybook headings do, what every reasonable person does in practice. If one is a strict atheist materialist, then "good" is what game theory and evolutionary psychology tells us that we should desire in our kin, our friends, and the character of those that we should ally with. If God created the world then "is" was created by God, and cause and effect a manifestation of the Logos. And if a Christian, then cause and effect manifested as wholly man, and that man ended Talmudic legalism, ended the practice of deducing "ought" from some other "ought" taken as given and absolute and then deducing ever sillier and ever more repugnant conclusions from the first "ought", whether one takes that given "ought" as the "greatest good for the greatest number", or takes as that given "ought" that one should not boil a goat in its mother's milk.

The expulsion of the Jews by the Romans illustrates the Divine Logos telling us "The letter killeth but the spirit giveth life" The divine will manifested through entirely natural causes, because the natural order of the universe reflects the will of God. And the spirit of the law, being manifest in cause and effect and manifest in the natural order, needs to be understood with reference to natural law, game theory, and evolutionary psychology. When the Jews obeyed the letter of the law while massively violating the spirit of the law, they were, in accordance with prophecy, expelled from Israel – which reflects the will of God and divine prophecy, but also reflects the fact that if you violate the spirit of the law, you will get into stupid wars with your neighbors, and eventually war with one of your neighbors that happens to be a six hundred pound gorilla. The Jews got into war with Rome not because of corrupt Roman tax collectors, oppressive taxation, harsh Roman law enforcement, and all that, but because they were so scrupulous about avoiding contamination by blood that they wound up getting covered in the wrongfully spilled blood of a Roman cop whom they murdered in the performance of his duty while he was attempting to impartially enforce a just, reasonable, and necessary law that applied to everyone. Which would not have led to war had they not felt so very righteous about it because they were being so faithful to rule about avoiding blood – so faithful to it that they spectacularly disregarded the commandments on coveting, theft, and murder. Attending synagogue while avoiding walking on ground contaminated by chicken blood was so terribly important that they could do anything they liked to accomplish these holy goals, including theft and murder, and their great determination to accomplish these holy goals demonstrated their superior holiness. And their stubborn self righteousness over this incident eventually and predictably led to the Romans going Roman on them.

In Christianity, the rot set in on women about a thousand years ago, with romance and contractual marriage, with natural law increasingly being tortured to fit church doctrines that were increasingly arbitrary, unreasonable, and out of contact with reality, and with contractual marriage quietly and subtly replacing sacramental marriage, though Christianity only went really progressive on women during the twentieth century. We endorse old style contractual and old style sacramental marriage right now, at least as a moral standard and ritual solemnization, even though we are in no position to enforce it collectively, and after we gain power, start by rolling contractual marriage back to the late eighteenth century, while celebrating sacramental marriage at least symbolically, and eventually go all the way back to sacramental marriage. We approve of and support husbands and fathers unilaterally enforcing it, even though such enforcement is highly illegal and subject to social disapproval, and we will have our marriage ceremonies proclaim it.

Evolutionary psychology and game theory implies that the family law of the Old Temple Hebrews and the first Millenium Christian Church was entirely correct, and the eighteenth century Christian position on family, war, identity, and the establishment of religion was quite good.

Pozzed Christianity, which dumps on fathers on father's day and tells us we are Homer Simpson, and which thinks that Catastrophic Anthropogenic Global Warming is far more important that a bunch of priests having gay sex in a great big pile, because the priests were all consenting adults, is not Christian.

Chaos is coming. Chaos is already here, and will get a lot worse. Eventually order will be restored through Caesarism, that being the cycle of history. I hope this happens soon, with Holy American Emperor Trump, but if it does not happen soon, it will happen eventually, possibly after a century of blood and ruin.

When it starts happening, and I hope it is beginning now, we should catch that tide and sail it to victory.

Revolutionary movements never get anywhere without backing from a substantial faction of the elite. So what section of the elite is going to back us?

Warriors need priests, and priests need warriors. We are always ruled by priests or warriors, so they tend to struggle for power, priests destroying the military, instead of sustaining it and giving it cohesion. The recent stupid wars where the military fought for no sane, useful, or achievable purpose, with one hand tied behind its back, were attacks by the priesthood on the military, as was insourcing logistics, putting camp followers in military uniforms.

To explain these stupid wars, people say they were fought for Israel, but if fought for Israel, would have been fought to win, rather than lose. If fought for Israel, we would not have women in the military,*Israel* would not have women in the military, we would not have kicked Israel out of Gaza, and logistic workers would not be wearing warrior uniforms.

We are priests who believe warriors should rule (using the term "priesthood" to mean any knowledge faction that internally coordinates its story in order to give the story more effect and in order to gain power, analogously to using the term "religion" to include communism and poz.) We are therefore in a good position to catch the coming tide.

The time of Ceasarism approaches. Caesar, Napoleon, or Augustus will need priests who say and believe his rule under God is right, because God said so, because one stationary bandit is better than mobile banditry, and because one King three thousand miles away is better than a thousand kings three miles away.

Trump closes the asylum loophole.

2019-07-16 06:02:13

a new immigration rule Monday that will restrict illegal immigrants from countries, other than those bordering the United States, for applying for asylum first in the U.S. if they have attempted "to enter the United States across the southern border after failing to apply for protection in a third country."

Trump threatened Mexico with tariffs, they gave asylum. Mexico agreed to new asylum rules designed to meet the long established US rules on third country asylum, and now Trump can deport hundreds of thousands of people pouring over the border[331], a quarter of a million last year, if the borders remain open, likely increasing, if Democrats continue to hold the borders open, to a million next year, four million the year after that, sixty million in 2026, a billion in 2030.

New rules apply allowing Trump to immediately deport asylum applicants back to Mexico.

If the flood of people demanding asylum from the poverty, violence, chaos, and destruction that they created and intend to inflict upon us continues to grow exponentially there will be over a billion black male military age Muslims in the US by 2030 screaming for infidel blood and white pussy.

If we go by what the asylum seekers are saying, they believe that all white people need killing, that the poverty and violence from which they fled is the result of us stealing from them, that our wealth is an indication of our sinfulness, and destroying our wealth will make them rich.

Now maybe they are just saying that like Havel's greengrocer. Maybe they are just saying that because the murder of white people, the destruction of white property, and the destruction of the technology that white people developed is politically correct, and don't really intend any of it. Marxist economics has become dangerous to doubt. But that is what they are saying.

Judges are likely to rule Trump's order illegal and order the borders remain open, a flagrant abuse of judicial power, and an abuse that is likely to get my children killed and my property destroyed. At some point, Trump has to do a Jackson, or threaten a Jackson and see if the judges back down.

If Trump is defeated on this, hundreds of millions of Americans are likely to be murdered. If the current asylum seekers, like Havel's Greengrocer, do not truly believe what they are saying, and quite likely they do not truly believe, they are eventually going to be massively outnumbered by a billion black male Muslim military age asylum seekers from black Africa in 2030 who do truly believe it, in so far as they are capable of any thought beyond "gibmedat".

At some point Trump has to just damn well close the border against illegal immigration, which Judges are likely to rule illegal and unconstitutional. And if he hopes to win

---

[331]https://www.youtube.com/watch?v=fZOFm9zzq8E

the 2020 election, he has to do it well before the end of 2020. And if he loses the election he and his family are going to be arrested, and once you start arresting ex presidents, you soon start killing them.

The General Flynn Affair

2019-07-17 18:09:32

From the beginning, it has been obvious that the FBI and the Democrats sincerely believed they had the goods on Trump, that he was guilty of something or other, had to be guilty of something or other, even though they were never clear in their own minds of exactly what. And from the beginning, it has been obvious that the FBI and the Democrats did not have the goods on Trump, because anything that they deluded themselves that they had, they leaked ten times over to the press in ten different versions, and it was all nuts.

It was always obvious that all this stuff was self delusion, wishful thinking, and motivated reasoning, usually reasoning so highly motivated as to be Trump derangement syndrome. It was obvious from the beginning that they were evil plotters who could not get their evil plot together because driven mad by Trump.

General Flynn hired defense lawyers that were completely in the pocket of Trumps enemies, completely in the pocket of Mueller, completely in the pocket of those prosecuting him. He pled guilty to lying to the FBI, which is the universal all purpose charge of which anyone who talks the FBI is guilty. If they ask you questions for eighty hours, you are bound to say something that that plausibly can be interpreted as contradicting something else, so anyone who talks the FBI for long enough is guilty of lying to the FBI. He then got a plea deal in which this terrible crime would be excused, because he was such a cooperative witness. They talk to you until you say something that can plausibly be argued contradicts something else you said, then they demand you tell them what they want to hear. This is a closed loop that leads to madness, because it is guaranteed to produce confirmation of delusions.

Which plea deal makes sense only if the FBI and the Democrats believed he had the goods on Trump and he had agreed to give them the goods on Trump. And also makes sense only if he believed that the presidency, the traitors, had the power, and the mere president did not have the power. And similarly, hiring "defense" lawyers that were completely in the pocket of Mueller and the prosecution lawyers only makes sense if the presidency, the traitors, have the power, and the mere president does not have the power.

His lawyers were radical leftist traitors attempting to overthrow the elected government of the United States, the prosecutors were radical leftist traitors attempting to overthrow the elected government of the United States, and Mueller is a radical leftist traitor attempting attempting to overthrow the government of the United States with a long history of abusing the power of the FBI to persecute real and imagined rightists, while turning a blind eye to the crimes of leftists. There was no daylight between Flynn's defense team, and Mueller's prosecution team, they were all in each other's pockets, they were all one big happy family. And it only makes sense for them to be all one big happy family if they were all after Trump, *they all believed Flynn had the goods on Trump, and they all believed that Flynn had given them the goods on Trump.*

The Mueller investigation consisted of going after everyone connected to Trump, concocting crimes for them, and demanding that they sing on Trump to be excused these crimes. And, often enough, when put under sufficient pressure, they did sing on Trump but the tales they came up with never had any substance, always wild assed speculation, bare faced lies, sheer nonsense, or just hints that pointed Mueller's team to go after someone else, anyone else. Trouble with putting people under pressure is if you apply too much pressure, they are going to tell you what you want to hear, but it is not necessarily going to be anything likely to stand up in court.

Eventually, belatedly, very belatedly, the light dawned, that Flynn had not given them the goods on Trump, that he did not have the goods on Trump. This had always been obvious to me from the transparent insanity of all the leaks telling us that Flynn had the goods on Trump, but it had not been obvious to all the transparently insane people leaking how Flynn's testimony nailed Trump.

So the defenseprosecution team, defense and prosecution being a single team that was after Trump, not Flynn, decided that Flynn had broken his plea deal, and they would hang him out to dry. Whereupon Flynn, to Trump's delight, fired his "defense" lawyers, who were trying to lock him up and throw away the key, being driven mad with rage by the failure of Flynn to nail Trump. Flynn then got a Trumpist defense lawyer who was, and is, determined to expose the crimes of the Mueller investigation and nail Mueller's hide to the wall. Flynn's choice of defense lawyer only makes sense if the president has the power, and the presidency, the traitors, do not have the power.

So this looks like a creeping coup, and a creeping countercoup, with Trump countercoup successful. Going after Flynn is an act of pointless self destructive vindictiveness, an act of madness. They just want to lash out and hurt people for no sane reason. Punishing Flynn does not help them - it just makes it more obvious that the investigation of Trump was criminal, and used criminal methods. And if their attempt to punish Flynn fails, as it looks like it will fail, it also makes it more obvious that they lost, that they are defeated, that they are out of power. If they can punish Flynn, they are still in power. If they cannot, not in power. And now, whether they are in power or not is about to be put to the test. If they cannot punish Flynn, no one will fear them any more, and if no one fears them any more, everything falls apart for the traitors.

Mueller Testimony

2019-07-28 01:22:43

A lot of people interpreted the Mueller testimony as Mueller being senile and forgetful.

Did not look like that to me. He was "forgetful" under hostile cross examination:

Looked to me that he was repeatedly caught lying to congress. He was not forgetful, he was changing his story in midstream.

Looked to me that he is used to an environment where lying is mandatory, crimethought forbidden, so you can lie easily and comfortably and no problems ensue, everyone lies to each other and to themselves, everyone is supposed to lie, and was caught like a deer in the headlights when he was required to interact with those so shockingly discourteous as to follow different rules.

When Nunes issues his opening statement Mueller looked to me like a criminal listening to the prosecutor make his opening statement, then, part way through the prosecutor's indictment, realize that the prosecutor has not yet found the good stuff, and he stands a good chance of beating the rap. Mueller is worried, but he not as worried as he would be if Nunes had the goods on him.

Marriage

2019-07-28 09:32:49

The core of the reactionary program is to make marriage legal again. Without marriage, the higher races cannot reproduce successfully, and reproduction is dysgenic.

Leftist marriage, modern marriage, is gay. Marriage has been gay since 1928.

Obviously reactionaries must reintroduce marriage that is suitable for heterogamous organisms, and we will have to introduce it as a matter of faith and morals before we can introduce it as a matter of law.

The left offers your wife cash and prizes for destroying the family assets, destroying you and destroying your children. The lawyer and the marriage counselor will tell her she is oppressed, and she can get a court order that gives her cash and prizes, raises her status, and will result in her marrying a six foot six billionaire athlete with a dong the size of a salami.

Modern marriage is gay. Everyone who gets married gets gay married. If your wedding vows are symmetric and interchangeable, the same of the man as for the woman, your marriage is gay and you are being gay married.

If your wedding has a master of ceremonies or a priest who acts like he, rather than the groom, is the big important man at the wedding, that he is the alpha male, your wedding is gay, and you are being gay married. (And the master of ceremonies is usually gay, and if he is not gay, he thinks that two males pretending to marry each other with the intention of cruising for nine year old boys to transexualize is smart and fashionable.)

The wedding organizer appoints a gay master of ceremonies whose main job is to define the groom as Homer Simpson, to emasculate him in the eyes of the bride. The minister conducts a gay wedding ceremony that treats the bride and groom as equal and interchangeable, even though experience has demonstrated that wives will not tolerate househusbands, and will invariably leave a domesticated man for a wild man who beats her, rapes her, and rapes and beats her husband's children.

The worst thing progs did ever was remove "Honor and obey", "submit and reverence" from the marriage ceremony.

The book of common prayer purged the wife's vow to honor jind obey and purged Paul's letter to the Ephesians 5:22-33 in 1928. That, not female suffrage, was the worst thing ever, effectively abolishing marriage.

One household necessarily has one captain. If the wife does not promise to honor and obey, to submit and reverence, you are not actually getting married, because you are not actually forming one household, so no point in the ceremony, and, surprise surprise, people stopped holding the ceremony, just as they stopped turning up to Church when the pastor started telling them their husbands were Homer Simpson and if you showed up at Church you were likely homophobic.

We have to restore the marriage ceremony to what it was before first wave feminism.

The marriage ceremony needs to include "honor and obey", and it needs to once again include Paul's letter to the Ephesians 5:22-331. Wives, submit yourselves unto your own husbands, as unto the Lord.

2. For the husband is the head of the wife, even as Christ is the head of the church: and he is the saviour of the body.

3. Therefore as the church is subject unto Christ, so let the wives be to their own husbands in every thing.

4. Husbands, love your wives, even as Christ also loved the church, and gave himself for it;

5. That he might sanctify and cleanse it with the washing of water by the word,

6. That he might present it to himself a glorious church, not having spot, or wrinkle, or any such thing; but that it should be holy and without blemish.

7. So ought men to love their wives as their own bodies. He that loveth his wife loveth himself.

8. For no man ever yet hated his own flesh; but nourisheth and cherisheth it, even as the Lord the church:

9. For we are members of his body, of his flesh, and of his bones.

10. For this cause shall a man leave his father and mother, and shall be joined unto his wife, and they two shall be one flesh.

11. This is a great mystery: but I speak concerning Christ and the church.

12. Nevertheless let every one of you in particular so love his wife even as himself; and the wife see that she reverence her husband.

And once again include the first epistle of Peter 3:1-7

1. Likewise, ye wives, be in subjection to your own husbands; that, if any obey not the word, they also may without the word be won by the conversation of the wives;

2. While they behold your chaste conversation coupled with fear.

3. Whose adorning let it not be that outward adorning of plaiting the hair, and of wearing of gold, or of putting on of apparel;

4. But let it be the hidden man of the heart, in that which is not corruptible, even the ornament of a meek and quiet spirit, which is in the sight of God of great price.

5. For after this manner in the old time the holy women also, who trusted in God, adorned themselves, being in subjection unto their own husbands:

6. Even as Sara obeyed Abraham, calling him lord: whose daughters ye are, as long as ye do well, and are not afraid with any amazement.

7. Likewise, ye husbands, dwell with them according to knowledge, giving honour unto the wife, as unto the weaker vessel, and as being heirs together of the grace of life; that your prayers be not hindered

And we also need to have 1 Corinthians 7:3-5, though the book of common prayer does the same thing in a different way:

1. Let the husband render unto the wife due benevolence: and likewise also the wife unto the husband.

2. The wife hath not power of her own body, but the husband: and likewise also the husband hath not power of his own body, but the wife.

3. Defraud ye not one the other, except it be with consent for a time, that ye may give yourselves to fasting and prayer; and come together again, that Satan tempt you not for your incontinency.

Because without the obligation each to sexually gratify the other, no marriage.

The need to bring marriage back implies a familist movement will look awfully like a religion.

Another important aspect of family is eating together at the same time. Everyone, kids, wife, and guests, holds off from eating until the patriarch says "Amen" then they all eat together. Grace is a ritual that ensures that everyone eats together and that presents the alpha male as backed by the ultimate alpha male, God. Women inherently like their alpha male to be backed by a bigger alpha male, and they are astonishingly comfortable with being assigned to another man by a higher alpha.

So any effective familist movement necessarily has religious rituals that are going to qualify it as a religion. But, like the Masons and progressivism, will probably have to pretend that it is not a religion.

On the other hand, to inculcate the appropriate attitude in women, to make the rituals work, have to tell them "God says do it this way", which kind of gives the game away.

OK, if God is three and God is one, familism can be a religion and not a religion. If AA can be not a religion, familism can be not a religion.

The Anglican Church died, as the Congregational Church died as a Christian movement long before them, and the Roman Catholic Church is dying in the west. The Pope defends priests having gay sex in a great big pile by saying "consenting adults" and "Global Warming". Well, if Global Warming is the great moral crisis of our times, why should anyone show up at Church. And they don't. And if the Church abolishes marriage, why should anyone get married. And they don't.

The Christian and biblical position is that Christians are kin by adoption and by marriage, that Christians are adoptively the children of God, and the Church is the bride of Christ. So when the pastor abolishes marriage and attacks the authority of the father and the husband, he saws of the branch on which he sits, and it looks to me that every Church dies after it abolishes marriage, though its death takes a bit over a century. The longer ago they abolished marriage and the family, the longer ago they died. Congregationalism was the first to abolish marriage and the family, and the first to go.

We want a synthetic tribe, because we are detribalized. God backing dad comes in mighty handy for making the family a family, particularly for making people eat meals at mealtime. And God comes in mighty handy for promoting ingroup cooperate/cooperate equilibrium by making people kin. These two functions of God seem to be connected in practice.

It is recorded that Christianity spread in the early Roman empire in large part through conversion of women. It is also recorded that marriage had collapsed in the early Roman empire. I suspect these two facts are connected, that Christian marriage may have been a familist movement in the early Roman empire. Similarly we notice that today white female Christian converts to Islam are overwhelming fertile age single women. Roman women converting from dead paganism to live Christianity in the Roman Empire may well have been similar to white Christian women converting to Islam today. They are joining a synthetic tribe where the ultimate alpha male will assign them a husband and ensure that they have a family. While the ultimate alpha male of today's Christianity is going to give them a "season of singleness".

If we look at the marriages depicted in the bible, they are all marriages in which the top alpha male assigns the woman. Which is what women want, even if they don't know they want it.

In Genesis, God, the ultimate alpha male, marries Eve to Adam.

Abraham, a powerful alpha male who successfully made war with kings, marries Rebecca to Isaac. Rebecca is not consulted until afterwards, and Isaac is not consulted at all.

In the book of Ruth, Boaz is a powerful male who is the top alpha in the environment where Ruth is working. Ruth sneaks into Boaz's bed while he is drunk and sleeping, asks Boaz to marry her, and appears to believe he has authority to perform marriage on the spot. He declines to do so, saying he has to resolve some legalities first but they spend the night together anyway. In the morning he goes off and successfully resolves those legalities, and later assembles witnesses and marries Ruth. Ruth's mother in law (Ruth is a widow and the adoptive daughter of her mother in law) gives the bride away. Boaz, a powerful alpha male, is the one who presides over this ritual, not a judge or a priest. The elders witness, but they don't emcee. If Ruth is present at this ritual she does not speak, but before the ritual she had plenty to say to her mother in law and to Boaz in private.

Chicks like the man who is throwing a party, because he is top alpha at the party. As "Setting the Record Straight" tells us[332], game boils down to three simple things.

- Pass her shit tests

- Don't show weakness

- Dominate other men

It is obviously optimal for marital harmony if the wife always sees her husband in social contexts where he is top alpha. When you throw a party, other alpha males act at the party as if you are the top alpha, even if in other social contexts you are not. So having someone else preside over the marriage is not a good idea. Marriages should resemble the marriage of Boaz and Ruth - unless the bride actually is being assigned to someone else by a powerful human alpha, as tended to happen during the early days of Australian settlement. If we look at first millennium Christian doctrine on marriage, it appears that

---

[332]https://blog.reaction.la/misc_upl/Setting%20The%20Record%20Straight.pdf

marriage is a sacrament performed by the husband with the priest being wedding organizer, rather than presiding over the wedding. Existing Catholic doctrine is that marriage is a sacrament performed by the husband (which was very recently re-interpreted as the husband and the wife), but the priest presides over the ceremony, with the husband not being the alpha male in that context. Anglican doctrine back in the days when it was actually functioning as a religion is that marriage is and is not a sacrament. The articles say it is not a sacrament, but the preamble given by the priest in the book of common prayer treats it as a sacrament, and in the ritual the husband performs that sacrament.

He takes the brides hand, and
> With this ring I thee wed

And then the priest tells the congregation what just happened, describing it terms that make it sound mighty like a sacrament performed by the husband. So, marriage is a sacrament or something very similar performed by the husband. And we know from evolutionary theory, PUA theory, and PUA empirical observation that this is in fact what women want - which suggests that the husband, rather than the priest should preside over the marriage, with the priest acting as wedding organizer and second in command at the party.

To get women to collectively behave better, women have to be informed as to what behavior is good.

Depict wives and children interacting with husbands and fathers the way they were depicted on television and movies after 1933 and before 1963. That will inform them. We cannot do that till we are in power. But while out of power, can restore the marriage ceremony to what it was before 1928: Wife promises to honor and obey, husband promises to love and cherish.

And let us go back a bit further, nine hundred years further. Husband administers the sacrament of marriage. Technically he still does: Takes wife hand. "With this ring I thee wed." Places ring on finger. But that has been heavily played down for many centuries. It was a big power struggle in the Church of England after Henry the Eighth. They keep trying to make the marriage contractual ("I do"), when it should be sacramental ("with this ring I thee wed"). Women really hate contractual marriage. Contractual marriage is failing a shit test right at the starter's gun.

We also need to restore the tradition that is implied in the story of the wise and foolish virgins, where the husband mock abducts the wife to a big party which he emcees, and everyone at the party treats him as top alpha male. Abduction, or else someone with family authority over the bride gives this woman to this man, leading her to the man. "Who giveth this woman to this man?" Women do not really like consensual and contractual marriage, hence the need for the bride to be given away or abducted.

Gay needs to be suppressed

2019-08-06 09:53:17

Gay simply did not exist until the late nineteenth century, and when we are in power, they will no longer exist, and people will not quite remember that they ever existed, much as they do not quite remember that pre-2008 Obama was opposed to gay marriage and was born in Kenya, or that before Christmas 1978, the Democrats and every single tenured academic in the entire US government hegemony supported the Khmer Rouge, or at least politely remained silent while his academic institution supported the Khmer Rouge, taught students a pro Khmer Rouge version of recent events, and required them to affirm that version in essays.

Chesterton's Fence: All functional societies either look down on homosexuality, or altogether strictly prohibit it, executing the offenders, and those that stop suppressing it, soon go into decline. Likewise, all successful religions that last for a long time prohibit it. Those societies that manage to reproduce most fruitfully invariably restrict gay activity.

The reactionary state will in theory throw men who lie with a males as with a woman off skyscrapers, or publicly hang them, or something like that – something terrifying, deadly, and, most importantly, *publicly humiliating*. Without the public humiliation, nothing we do will have the desired effect. No society has ever managed to kill off gays as efficiently as they kill off themselves and each other, thus merely killing gays is of limited effectiveness. It is essential to kill them in a way that lowers their status.

In practice, however, we should only do that to people who obstinately and persistently shove the gay in our faces despite lesser punishments and lesser humiliations, because those are the ones that cause problems. If gays stop shoving gay in other people's faces, if gays let us pretend that they do not exist, things are fine enough, even if a whole lot of bad things may be happening behind closed doors. We don't need to poke our nose behind everyone's door. They would love us to pay them that much attention, and we would fail their fitness test if we did pay them that much attention. We do need to poke our nose behind the doors of people who are ostentatiously shoving the gay in our faces, and use what we find as an excuse to throw them off a tall building so that they will damn well stop shoving the gay in our faces.

We need to terrorize gays, not into not existing, which would require far too much terror, and give them far too much attention, which attention they would enjoy far too much, but we need to terrorize them into allowing us to pretend that they do not exist, as successful societies routinely pretended. Our ancestors knew that sodomy happened, but denied that those involved were attracted to males. Rather, they assumed that those guilty were attracted to concave surfaces, or concave surfaces that were part of children. They did not quite forget the joke (after all it is right there in the Old and New Testaments, so it is hard to forget) but did not quite remember it either.

This post stolen wholesale from this excellent comment[333], which reminds us of Chesterton's fence. All societies that survived suppressed homosexuality. Failing to suppress it presages decline and collapse.

So why do societies that tolerate gay then collapse?

Signalling Hazard: If you allow gays, David cannot love Jonathan. If David cannot love Jonathan, hard for the mighty men of David to stick together. If the mighty men cannot stick together, the state cannot cohere. If the state cannot cohere, you get anarcho tyranny, a thousand Kings three miles away instead of one King three thousand miles away.It's just no longer possible for men to hang out with each other, especially in intimacy, without the lingering suspicion that something of the "poop-dick" variety must

---

[333]https://blog.reaction.la/uncategorized/the-general-flynn-affair/#comment-2114199

be going on. Gay destroyed men's friendships. It used to be possible for men to walk together down the street and even invite each other for sleepover without anyone having the faintest suspicion that anal sex is involved. To have successful cooperation, we have to be able to meaningfully bond with each other, but meaningful bonding is absolutely impossible when signalling "I love you bro" translates to "I want to fuck your ass." Without gays in society, we would be able to express legit affection and signal brotherly loyalty to each other, and without the nagging need to perpetually explain that we are "no homo."

If gays are free to speak, I am not free to speak. "Just bake the cake, why don't you." If you tolerate homosexuality, you must tolerate free speech by gays about sex and sexuality, whereupon you cannot, in practice, tolerate free speech by straights about sex and sexuality

"Multnomah County Library offers a series of programs called Drag Queen Storytime. These events seek to explore ideas of difference, diversity and inclusion through stories, music and costume. The library serves a diverse population with a broad range of interests, preferences and needs. We strive to reflect our communities' needs in selecting programs, books and other materials.[334]"
Evidently biblical marriage and the heterosexuality of old movies is not "diverse". If men dressed as women having sex with small boys in public on the Multnomah County Library floor are officially incuded, Perseus rescuing and abducting princess Andromeda must necessarily be officially excluded.

Normalizing perversion inevitably leads to and requires abnormalizing normal male sexuality. Thus normal male and female sexuality (men conquer, women surrender, but men perform and women choose) can no longer be depicted. You cannot depict the Han Solo of the original Star Wars movies or the original Indiana Jones any more. A society that allows homosexuality to be depicted is unable to to allow heterosexuality to be depicted[335], except by having the heterosexuals act gay, as for example in the recent star wars and avengers movies. If society makes space for gays act gay, it cannot allow space for straights to act straight. If gays are included, straights are necessarily excluded. There is no room for both them and us. For us to have room to be ourselves, we have to deny them room to be themselves. Even in porn, you will not see female submission to the conquering male realistically portrayed. You have not seen male conquest and female surrender since "McLintock", and "Gone with the Wind". What you *will* see portrayed is males and females following the gay bondage domination and submission script. Bondage domination and submission is a hateful gay parody of the inherent inequality of the courtship dance, as drag queens are a hateful gay parody of femininity. You are not allowed to depict Han Solo hitting on Princess Leia If you were to attempt to create something like the first Star Wars movie today a whole lot of men and women with no children will complain that depicting men and women following very different mating strategies, (men conquering and women surrendering, men performing and women choosing) is oppressive. If those complaining get declared normal, I get declared abnormal. There is no room in the world for both them and me, for they will not permit room in the world for Han Solo, Indiana Jones, Rhett Butler, and McLintock. A world with no room for heroes has no room for

---

[334]https://www.lifesitenews.comlatex/images/local/files/PDFs/Drag_queen_child_abuse.pdf
[335]https://blog.reaction.la/economics/analysis-of-a-chinese-video/

me. If it is legal for gay to exist, then it is illegal for me to exist. It is legal for a person who identifies as a man to have sex with a person who identifies as a woman, but it is illegal for me to act as men act with women, as men and women in old movies acted. It has proven impossible to include gays without excluding straights.

Denormalization of biological families: Whenever homosexuals are allowed, they inevitably argue, "We are normal, just like everyone else. We should be allowed to have kids." And when they do get children, what happens? For one, the children grow up in confusion about what normalcy is and what it isn't, leading to dysfunction later in life as they try to make sense of the world. Secondly, state and society face endlessly weird, even absurd, "Clown World" dilemmas in dealing with homosexual "families," e.g.when homosexuals fight over custody over children donated by sperm or egg or adopted. Thirdly, the traditional family unit itself is wholly unraveled as the door is now opened for whatever bizarre sort of household one can imagine: "Why can't transsexuals be parents too? My single mother has already transitioned to a single father and Xe still loves me!" and so on and so forth. And fourthly, allowing sex freaks to raise children is prone to result in sexual abuse, whether it's diddling by gay "parents," or anti-testosterone hormonal torture by lesbian "parents," or growing up in a whorehouse attended by fetishists of every shade, hue, and color.

Consent Culture: Women don't really like consent. They prefer "It just happened". If consent is defined as normality, then biblical marriage is defined as abnormality, as a crime. Consent culture makes Paul's first Epistle to the Corinthians 7:3-7 crime instead of law. If consent defines what sex is right and what sex is wrong, this effectively abolishes marriage, making it hard to reproduce. Women don't like to be beaten and don't consent to be beaten, but they like men who might beat them regardless of consent, like men who will take them sexually regardless of consent, and sometimes, some women, some of the time, will make you prove it. It is not that women want to be mistreated, but they want to be alone and in the power of a man who might well mistreat them, or alone with him, his minions and his numerous concubines. Under these circumstances, "No" is merely a fitness test. Gays invert this by consenting to being beaten. BDSM is a hateful gay parody of the inequality characteristic of normal sexuality and of divinely ordained biblical marriage. As Drag Queens get off on an ugly hateful gay parody of femininity, BDSM gays get off on an ugly hateful gay parody of biblical marriage. In order to attain sexual liberty, the LGBT crowd have signed off on "consenting adults" morality. Hence their enthusiastic embrace of whatever the latest installment of Feminist dogma is, without which they would be condemned as "rapists" by the Feminist system. Perverts benefit from Consent Culture, because it allows them to do as they please ("consenting adults") while preventing evil privileged heterosexual men from forming stable families with young women. Thus, all homosexuals regardless of political affiliation adhere to the Consent Culture Feminist dogma. Consent means that a drag queen can have sex in public with a six year old boy on the floor of Multnomah County Library, but Perseus cannot abduct Princess Andromeda. If drag queens get to molest small boys on the floor of Multnomah public library, then I do not get to abduct Princess Andromeda. If it is legal for drag queens to molest small boys in public on the floor of Multnomah public library, then it is illegal for me to marry in accordance with Saint Paul's letter to the Ephesians 5:22-33, First Peter

3:1-7, and First Corinthians 7:3-5. If we don't throw gays off tall buildings, or hang them in public, or something similarly terrifying *and status lowering*, then they make biblical marriage illegal, making it difficult for us to have children. We have to suppress them, for if we fail to suppress them, they suppress us. If they get away with secretly having sex with small boys behind closed doors, that does not cause problems for us, assuming it is fatherless boys, which it always is, but if they can get away with having sex with small boys in public on the floor of Multnomah public library, then we cannot get away with divinely ordained marriage. We have to stop them, so that they cannot stop us.

Diseases: Gay sex is unhealthy, and moreover, the typically promiscuous habits of most gays—triple digit partners are par for the course among the vast majority of them—vastly exacerbates the spread of venereal diseases. STDs, particularly the serious ones such as AIDS, are essentially a homosexual phenomenon, though it's also shared by other degenerates and reprobates that choose to come into regular contact with them. Gays, whose sexuality is undiscriminating and impulsive, and who are prone to heavy drug use (they do condom-less "chemsex" orgies with complete strangers), are the petri dishes of humanity, carrying assorted manifestations of God's wrath. Like rats, wherever they go, disease follows; thus homosexuals, especially when unrestricted, are a public hazard. Furthermore, through their normalization of queer practices (cunnilingus, anilingus, etc.) among normal people, and through bisexuality, the gays have managed to infect some members of regular society with their abominable filth, which infection is useful for the gays, as it allows them to scare-monger society about the diseases that they themselves spread! Then they ask us taxpayers to invest resources into solving their sicknesses. Gays, knowing full well that they're disease-ridden, steadfastly sought to receive the "right" to donate blood.

The ever increasing rage and repression directed against men attracted to fertile age women, and men to whom young girls are attracted is a displacement activity for the rage which ensues when people are forbidden to notice, and forbidden to prevent, gay sexual activity with eight year old boys. Because the state of Florida dares not stop drag queens from having sex with small boys in public, the State of Florida gives a mandatory five year sentence if you induce a woman who looks twenty two, but who is actually seventeen years and nine months, to send you a naughty selfie on Facebook Messenger, even if you have never met her in person and had no way of knowing her age. Going after straight men interacting with fertile age woman is displacement activity that they engage in because they cannot do what they inwardly wish to do, punish gay men having sex with eight year old boys, just as they punish men in the vicinity of misbehaving women because they cannot do what they inwardly wish to do, punish misbehaving women.

We seek to restore young arranged marriage. The homosexuals and their leftist supporters will viciously fight tooth and nail against arranged marriage, because "What if someone is gay?" In a society in which everyone is assumed straight, gays being either all dead or hiding deep in the closet (or not born in the first place), there is no such problem; but when gays are tolerated and accepted, and their presence is constantly celebrated, then any attempt to restore arranged marriage will be met with fierce opposition and cries of "Not everyone is heterosexual! Therefore, you oppressive bigots need to allow people to voluntarily choose their sex-mates, and only upon reaching fully mature adulthood!"

– thus, modern Liberal Marriage. Gays are heavily invested in sexual liberalism, in allowing all adults to consent to sex with all other adults, and to withdraw consent to sex at their most frivolous whim, hence rampant divorce and defect-defect equilibrium. Liberal Marriage is absolutely incompatible with the reactionary program to make real young patriarchal marriage legal and easily attainable again.

Shamelessness: The behavior of gays is lacking in shame, a trait for which they've been infamous from time immemorial; they proudly wear their deviance on their sleeve. Whereas a normal person doesn't parade around his sexual proclivities, the gays constantly shove theirs in everyone's face. When gays are present, the atmosphere itself becomes gay, because they keep broadcasting their gayness in broad daylight. They emit an incessant sexual noise, forcing the rest of us who are naturally averse to faggotry to seek refuge from it, psychologically or physically. Can you imagine straight men parading around giant sex toys and so on?

Perversity: It's extremely common for homosexuals to possess plethoras of aberrant fetishes, which, like their "main" deviance, they also seek to normalize. The BDSM world (gimp suits, sexual torture, etc.) is inextricably linked to gays, who pioneered it, and who were embraced by it. They relish dangerous, risky sexual behavior that leads to harm and death. Gays host scat parties in which the participants shit diarrhea and vomit on each other; they are fond of various sexual gratification toys that most normal people want nothing to do with; they are often sexually attracted to prepubescents, even toddlers (nepiophilia); there is the whole queer "furry" thing; and in all aspects, their sexual behavior is abnormal and depraved, bearing no resemblance to that of most heterosexuals.

Subversion: A fundamental political problem with homosexuals is that they always seek to upend sexual mores and morality to make them as favorable as they can be to their own death style. One can say that this is understandable and sympathize with it, but why exactly is it in society's interest to abandon its own healthy ways to cater to the deviant desires of sexual minorities? Homosexuals never cease trying to converge everyone and everything to their death style, hence why they insinuate themselves into sundry political movements and undermine the dominant, pro-social morality therein in order to suit their special agenda. They attempt to turn all political and cultural niches incompatible with homosexuality to "gay friendly" - and, if that doesn't work, they frantically endeavor to destroy said niches.

Homosexuals generally don't conform to natural sex roles, because faggots are effete and dykes are masculine; consequently, they have long been the most vociferous and ardent advocates for turning all social institutions – and, indeed, society itself – into "sexually neutral" domains. They champion the entry of women into the workforce and oppose patriarchy and patriarchal marriage for that reason; they support coed education and coed workplaces; they want women to have authority over men; Homosexuals and Feminists share the same goals, and needless to say, there's great overlap between these two categories. Most feminists are ugly childless lesbians, and the rest become cat ladies when they are no longer hot enough to bang musicians and criminals. Effete men want to be allowed to do whatever women traditionally do, and masculine women likewise want to be allowed to do everything men traditionally do, thus gays and lesbians are deeply embedded in Feminism, particularly the "classical" Feminism of giving women "equal rights."

Homosexuals as an integral ingredient of the Feminist poison. Long before gays parodied marriage by marrying each other, preparatory to winging each other while searching for nine year old boys to transexualize, lesbians made heterosexual marriage gay, in the name of the rights, freedom, and safety of married women, which rights were demanded by women who were single and unlikely to ever get married.

Infertility Normalization: Homosexuals usually have little to no children. The omnipresent celebration of the LGBT alphabet soup has resulted in a normalization of singlehood and childlessness; it's no longer possible to say in polite society that reproduction is good and lack of reproduction is bad, because, among other things, of "homophobic overtones." Whenever we critique low TFR, we critique a condition that is part and parcel of the gay death style, one that incessant propaganda, particularly aimed at young women and nerds, propaganda often produced by actual fags, has successfully transmitted to the entire society. By being loud, proud, and childless, and by attaining high status in society, the gays have turned childlessness into a "legitimate life choice," indeed, as many leftists will tell you, a preferable choice than breeding. Homosexuality marches shoulder-to-shoulder with anti-natalism.

Gays are annoying. Gays predate on straight men constantly; they are offensively extroverted (gays) and aggressive (lesbians); their manner of speech is disgusting; their body movements are always exaggerated, ostentatious, and sexually non-conforming; they always manufacture more drama than they are worth. Their character's virtues-vices ratio is horrible, as they possess more vices than one can count, and little to no virtues. Everything about them signals "Bad News." They are also extremely petty and politically domineering, hence their going specifically after nice Christian bakeries and forcing them at the government's gunpoint to "Bake the cake."

Lack of Pair-Bonding: It is normal for humans to pair bond. This is another aspect of basic human decency which is conspicuously absent in faggots: They switch life (death) partners without the tiniest bit of attachment to anyone who came before. It's just a "mood," you see? Every day, nay - every hour, can bring someone new to take the place of the previous "sex mate." Gays are never "couples" after the heterosexual model: They are always inexclusive friends-with-benefits looking for a novel sexual sensation. Deep affection and amorous loyalty are altogether foreign to their mentality. This has ramifications for normal society, as gays – especially during the Baby Boomer generation – have contributed their part to normalizing divorce, swinging, and promiscuity.

Disinhibition: Again, they just can't help themselves: They constantly sexually harass normal people, and have absolutely no control over their own aberrant inclinations. Their behavior is wholly impulsive and high time-preference; they are unable to refuse drugs, unable to refuse condom-less sex with AIDS-positive strangers, and usually unable to plan anything ahead - they "live for the moment," and as one would expect, die young. They are entirely controlled by Satan.

Cultural Marxism: The Frankfurt School Cultural Marxists and the like-minded Freudians have pioneered and disseminated advocacy for homosexuality and various bizarre sexual behaviors. These guys hate us and intend our destruction, therefore anything and everything they advocate is intended to destroy us.

Bad Aesthetics: Homosexuality is viscerally repulsive. Knowing that the dude right next to you engages in anal sex with men is vomit-inducing. Beauty is truth, and evolution has instilled in us natural aversion to the unhealthy; we can tell ugliness and vileness when we witness them, and instinctively know to back away and stay away. Those whose instincts don't tell them to avoid homosexuals have something wrong with their brain-wiring and/or brain-structure. By tolerating gays around, society makes itself disgusting. While this alone may not be, and may not register as, a sufficient argument to ban the gays, it does point us to a valid field of inquiry: Why does homosexuality intensely trigger our healthy disgust reflex? Of course, beyond it being a dead-end reproductive strategy, it's also a recipe for quick premature death from disease; it's also eerie, like seeing mutants, androids, or cadavers, alerting us that something is terribly wrong. Gay is in uncanny valley, and our aversion to uncanny valley is generally healthy.

Leftism: Homosexuals are naturally prone to leftist politics, as leftism is, by no means exclusively but in substantial part, a project to normalize the abnormal for this or that reason; being abnormal themselves, homosexuals are automatically inclined to support general left-wing causes, be it race-denialism, socialism, Feminism, and really any form of artificial egalitarianism or war by the unsuccessful against the successful. Notice how homos constantly blame everyone else for their afflictions, instead of examining their own behavior; so no surprise they're in a coalition with like-minded anti-civilizational forces against civilization. Gays are pro-black, pro-brown, and pro-Muslim. Muslims hate gays, but gays like Muslims because Muslims hate us. Gays inherently and naturally tend to treason, so need to be excluded from power, and, more importantly, excluded from status, for if gays are high status, treason is high status, and if treason is high status, it appears that treason prospers, and if it appears that treason prospers, then treason will prosper. Gay status is the overthrow of King, Crown, Throne, Altar, and the massacre of our soldiers.

Objectively Aberrant: Homosexuality is a natural dead-end. If a man is attracted to other men, and is not attracted to women, he is not very likely to pass his genes forwards. It's an evolutionary death sentence.

Slippery Slope: "acceptance" of gay has led to Gay Marriage, normalization of "sex change" disfigurement, Drag Queen Story Hour, and so on. Once sodomy is tolerated, a Pandora's Box from Tartarus full of Hell-spawn is opened, and other perversities follow suit. For example, cuckoldry, which cuckolds now call "polyamory." Presumably, one reason that some people support faggotry is because they themselves are perverted in some or other way, and by clamoring for homosexuality to be normalize, they seek to thereby open the door for their own perversity, as with World War Tranny.

Confusion: Just generally, having gays around creates endless confusion about what is sexually normal and what isn't. People are being bombarded with all kids of nonsense about "orientation" and "gender identity" and so on, and some are lost in the confusion and can't sort out what is going on. We seek to usher in clarity: People need to know what is expected of them and where they are hierarchically stationed. Homosexuals disrupt clarity, bringing turmoil and vagueness into both day-to-day life and into the political scene. Being neither fish nor fowl, being sexually inverted, they've intentionally proceeded to insert "queerness" into manifold aspects of life, from clothing to school curricula to 56 different sexual identifications on Facebook to whatever else.

Preference Politics: The homosexuals have made it impossible to discuss sexuality in a logical way, because sexual politics have been marred by "preference politics": The idea that your political objectives correspond to, and merely boil down to advocacy for, your personal sexual proclivities. Thus, when I say "Attraction to 13-year-old chicks with boobs is part of normal healthy male sexuality," most readers automatically assume that I have a "fetish for jailbait," and will call me "hebephile" or "ephebophile" for it; I will then have to spend ages explaining that my own preferences (or lack thereof) have nothing to do with it. Since gays are all about preference politics, politics in service of a specific sexual preference, people assume that all discussions of sexuality must likewise necessarily revolve around preference politics. Yes, it is frustrating to be unable to say "It's normal for men to be aroused by 13-year-olds" without people assuming that I, personally, have a specific fetish for 13-year-olds, and am saying what I'm saying solely due to my own personal fetish. That "This person is engaging in preference politics" is now most people's null hypothesis is the result of gays, lesbians, bisexuals, and so on similar perverts forcing themselves on normal society. Even though gays are a tiny minority, they soak up all the cultural space, leaving no room for straights.

Hypersexuality: Gays are hypersexual, and invest tremendous efforts acquiring more and more sexual experiences, to the exclusion of other pursuits. Their excessive lust leads them, and whoever is politically influenced by them, to prioritize gay sex above e.g.scientific-technological advancement and cultural creation. The faggot's quest to attain ever greater sexual pleasure takes precedence over whatever else he wants to do, so often they end up doing nothing else but cruising for sex. Individually, that's self-destructive; on the political level, it results in gay parasitism, e.g., gays using our tax money to subsidize gayness, instead of other things. By and large, homosexuals are not "also gay," but rather, are "gay above all else."

Biological Leninism: Another reason that the homos support left-wing causes is because of Biological Leninism: Since their status under normal circumstances is low indeed, gays attach themselves to and promote whatever political faction that promises to artificially raise their status. They are natural members of the left-wing coalition, and are status-invested in maintaining the Cathedral, for without the Cathedral's elevation of the gays, they would rapidly lose their social prestige. They may not rank as highly as transsexuals and abortionists on the Progressive Totem Pole, but under any healthy system they'd be absolute pariahs, or dead, so they side with the Cathedral. Moreover, they need a Cathedral to normalize homosexuality through "point deer, make horse," i.e., by collectively and unanimously pretending that homosexuals are totally normal. Without the Cathedral, people will once again notice that the deer is not in fact a horse – that gays are not anything remotely normal.

Pedo-Hysteria: Hysteria about "pedophiles" is in large part a consequence of Gay Liberation, as many homosexuals have a distinct preference for prepubescent boys. The current witch hunts against "pedophiles," which result in multitudes of normal heterosexual men getting sent to the slammer for bogus sex-crimes, is facilitated by both the presence of homosexuality in the social atmosphere (leading to the invention of the "pedophilia" anti-concept) and by actual homosexual predation on boys who are often prepubescent. Pedo-hysteria doesn't allow us to notice that Humbert Humbert doesn't creep into the bedrooms of 9-year-olds, but that it's the other way around. Furthermore, LGBT politics are fundamentally hostile to male sexuality and to heterosexuality in general, because inherent to LGBT politics is a re-definition of normalcy to exclude old-fashioned normality.

Priests vs.Warriors: Homosexuals give power to the leftist priesthood, the lawyers, the judges, the professoriat, official science and the official mass media, and in turn are supported by the leftist priesthood, because acceptance of homosexuality rests on rule-by-priests. A society ruled by warriors does not tolerate faggotry and male effeminacy, so faggots are naturally inimical to warrior rule and to warriors; they feel much more comfortable when society is ruled by priests, and are adept at playing holiness signalling games. Any Priesthood not explicitly anti-homosexual sooner or later becomes homosexual. Hence the problem with the Roman Catholic priesthood.

Conspiracy: Gays always conspire, form secret cliques and secret clubs, as for example the band of perverts now running the Vatican, which gives them leverage over those not in the know; that's one way in which gays acquire power. Their conspiratorial behavior makes them dangerous, because in order to govern effectively, the government – which is fundamentally a conspiracy – needs to eliminate other conspiracies that vie for power. Government being a conspiracy, it should be the only conspiracy in place; thus, by having secret societies, the gays undermine the government, and it's in the interests of the ruler to uncover the gay cliques and to eliminate them.

Cosmopolitanism: Homosexuals are atomized individuals not invested in the prosperity of their tribe; generally leaving no descendants behind them, being genetic dead-ends, they freely associate with members of other tribes, and form alliances based on homosexuality, rather than on ethnicity, or geography, or religion. They are outsiders and outcasts within their own societies and among their own ethnicities, so they tend to ally themselves with other outsiders and outcasts, and with any global power promising to advance their agenda, perceiving their in-group to include fellow gays and perverts, and to exclude most everyone else.

Suicidal Ideation: Gays are not only apt to self-destruct, a quintessential feature of their psyches; they also flaunt their self-destructive proclivities before everyone else, seeking – and, through propaganda in the media and in the entertainment industry, succeeding – to normalize suicidality. They are sick, morbid people, and they spread their morbidity around; misery doth love company. By making suicidal ideation "cool," they have wreaked damage to whoever absorbed that idea and became depressed, dysfunctional as a result. By inflicting their suicidal ideation and self-destructive modes of thinking and behavior on the rest of society, they have further reduced the fertility of all those malleable to be influenced by fashion, which is now determined by gays. The TFR, and overall happiness and satisfaction in life, suffer under the homosexuals' cultural domination; gays aggravate civilization's downward spiral.

War approaches

2019-08-10 07:03:54

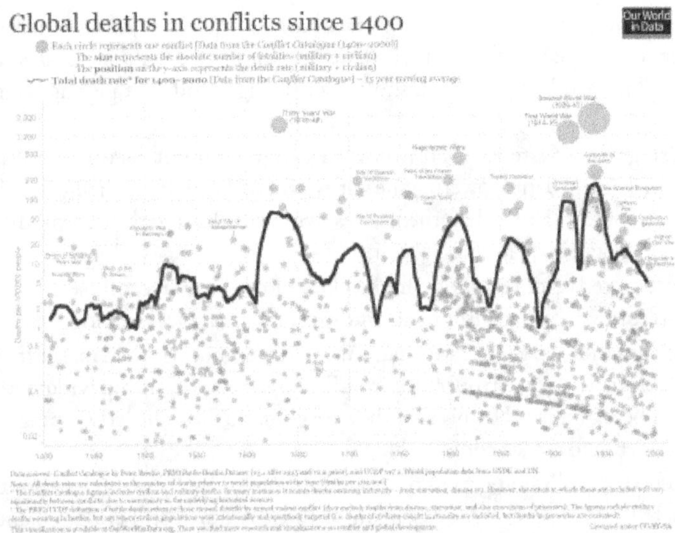

That is deaths as a proportion of population on a logarithmic scale, so the upward trend in the graph represents a doubling in the proportion of people killed in war.

The next big war is due round about now.

Right now we are heading into civil war[336]. War is easy, peace is hard, in the sense that falling off a cliff is easy, climbing a cliff is hard. Unless you make an effort to listen to the other guy and walk in his shoes, you are going to fall into war, and while it takes two to make peace, only takes one to make war.

They will not hear us, therefore sooner or later, probably sooner, will start killing us and each other. Probably mostly each other.

I am seeing no end of people on Twitter and Facebook calling for white genocide and the destruction of all productive activity and technology, and receiving social approval and state backing for so doing. To the best of my recollection, whenever calls for genocide and indiscriminate destruction have met social and state backing, actual genocide and indiscriminate destruction followed not very long after.

The most peaceful and humane era was about 1750 to 1911. Since then, war, mass murder, crime, violence, and slavery have generally been escalating, most notably in the colossal mass murders of communism(not shown in the graph above). Support for socialism is rising rapidly, and everyone who supports socialism, supports slavery, torture, and mass murder. Recollect that every tenured academic everywhere in the entire US Hegemony supported the Khmer Rouge until Christmas 1978 (at least in the sense of remaining piously silent) while his institution supported the Khmer Rouge even though the crimes of the Khmer Rouge were widely reported in 1975. Every socialist throughout history has, when socialism started racking up huge body counts, continued to support

---

[336]https://www.amren.com/news/2019/08/igniting-civil-war/

that socialist state until it collapsed of its own evil and self inflicted ruin.

Trouble is that crimestop renders them oblivious to hideous crimes, as in Haiti, Syria, Libya, and the Congo.

Notice how easily overseas color revolutions have turned into terror, mass murder, and attempted genocide, without affecting their sense that they are holier than God, and their confident belief that the benighted will shortly see the light and start pelting them with flowers.

Notice how raising the self esteem of Hutus by lying to them about history (We Waz Kangs) swiftly and easily turned into lowering the self esteem of Tutsis by vaginally impaling Tutsi women with objects larger than themselves, without affecting the enormously inflated self esteem of progressives in the slightest.

We are seeing attempted color revolution in the USA, and we have recently seen overseas color revolution turn genocidal without anyone except deplorables noticing.

I am seeing crazy lunatic leftists who are totally fine with communism and mass extermination of deplorables getting into trouble for insufficient leftism. If Trump is removed from power without being replaced by his son, they are going to die. The left is going to murder Scott Alexander before they come looking for me.

They are unlikely to start listening until holy war has burned itself out, and holy war is apt to be conducted by killing everyone, starting with the women and children, and destroying everything. For us to survive, we will have to kill them, destroy their stuff, and enslave their women.

Chances are that initially many of us will be massacred, and the rest will become refugees, and then, if things go well, we invade when they start fighting each other or the massacre of women and children and the destruction of capital depletes their resources, as the Tutsi refugees invaded their homeland when Hutu energies were absorbed by destroying capital and murdering women and children. Or we might get Chinese assistance to invade, as a relatively sane Khmer Rouge faction received Vietnamese assistance.

The holy, expecting the Eschaton, are apt to destroy the resources and capabilities that they need to wage war, as the Khmer Rouge did. Their indiscriminate self destruction may well work in our favor. Recall the Zealots of Jerusalem destroying their food supplies while under Roman siege, and recall the Romans of the last days of the Roman Empire murdering the wives and children of their foreign mercenaries. The guys on twitter calling for white genocide will set fire to their own cities, cut down their own power lines, and rip up their own water and sewage lines, as the Palestinians of Gaza destroyed the capital that the Jews of Gaza left behind, and that Jewish philanthropists had paid large amounts of money to transfer to the Palestinians in good order and condition, as the blacks of Detroit continued to destroy Detroit after expelling the white people that had built Detroit and given the black people of Detroit good jobs at good wages.

We may well find ourselves rebuilding and restoring order in a howling wilderness. In a long war, they will destroy the resources they need to fight a long war, and we will inherent the howling wilderness. A short war, however, will be funded by smash and grab, which is apt to favor those most willing to smash stuff and to massacre the weak, the vulnerable, and the innocent. In a short war, their superior holiness will work in their favor in that they will be more willing to massacre women and children. In a long war, the fact that understanding economics and logistics is crimethink will work in our favor.

Reaction looks to the past to restore old social technologies that have been lost, and avoid repeating past errors.

Notable among those past errors was the murder of a hundred million or so by socialists, socialism, and leftists, which outcome now threatens us once again. The cure for that error is the corporate capitalism of Charles the Second.

Another error was the thirty years war. The cure for that error is national churches and the peace of Westphalia. As with Orthodox Christianity, the Church should be both national and supranational, with neither characteristic obliterating the other. America's current wars are, like the troubles leading to the thirty years war, universalist wars fought to impose America's state religion of progressivism and the holy priesthood of Harvard on the world. The reason the Afghan war goes on forever is that it is not fought to prevent Al Quaeda from re-emerging, but to teach Afghan schoolgirls to put a condom on a banana. Holy wars are always costly, hence we need to restore the peace of Westphalia. Holy war with China looms. If we are going to impose a government on Afghanistan, it needs to be an Islamic monarchy, that is not going to allow Al Quaeda, but is not going to teach schoolgirls to put a condom on a banana either. If we impose a government on Afghanistan, our model should be one of emirates, not Harvard. Our relations with Russia and China need to be governed by the Peace of Westphalia.

The internal democides of twentieth century socialism threaten us once again, and the external holy wars of the seventeenth century threaten us once again. Internal civil war looms, and external holy war looms.

Science is dying, replaced by the demon haunted dark of peer review. Corporate capitalism is dying. Technology is stagnating.

We intend to restore what gave us science, technology, corporate capitalism, and empire, so that mankind can rule the stars under the star empire.

The Restoration of Charles the Second gave us empire, corporate capitalism, industrialization, technology, and science, which is what we intend to restore. Corporate capitalism is one of the things that we intend to restore, under a divine right monarchy resembling that of Charles the Second.

We are never ruled by capitalists. The capitalist class is no more capable of ruling than the proletariat is capable of ruling. We are always ruled by warriors or priests. Right now we are ruled by priests, and when priests rule, they are apt to succumb to holiness spirals.

Capitalism dates back at to least our earliest written records, to at least the early iron age, and probably all the way back to the neolithic Y chromosome bottleneck. Moses was consciously restoring the real or legendary social order of the Patriarch Israel against the decadent socialist social order of the late Bronze age, and the social order of the Patriarch Israel was a survival from the Y Chromosome bottleneck.

Our restoration, if all goes smoothly, will resemble that imposed by Charles the Second. If things go badly, will necessarily resemble that imposed by Moses. A restoration resembling that of Charles the Second will be one that avoids socialism and holy nuclear war with China. A restoration resembling that of Moses will be one that follows the democides of socialism and holy nuclear war with China.

If all goes well, the Holy American Empire and the Chinese Hegemony will both race to the stars, each seeking to grab as much of the universe as possible before the other does. Worst case, and the chance of the worst case is not insignificant, the entire white race gets murdered.

If all men are created equal, then it logically follows that the underperformance of official victim groups is caused by heterosexual white males. Since no amount of reparations seems able to remedy this underperformance, it obviously follows that killing all white male heterosexuals, then all whites, all males, and all heterosexuals, is going to to fix the problem and bring about utopia, and anyone who opposes utopia is an evil white supremacist, and therefore killing him is totally justified, indeed a heroic act of superior virtue.

#ClintonBodyCount

2019-08-12 05:10:01

People who know too much about the Clintons have been suiciding with remarkable regularity, and no one paid much attention, but the suicide of Epstein was just one too many convenient suicides.

Attorney General William P. Barr issued the following statement:

> "I was appalled to learn that Jeffrey Epstein was found dead early this morning from an apparent suicide while in federal custody. Mr.Epstein's death raises serious questions that must be answered. In addition to the FBI's investigation, I have consulted with the Inspector General who is opening an investigation into the circumstances of Mr.Epstein's death."

That there are going to be dual, and dueling, investigations into Epstein's convenient suicide suggests that Barr, like myself, suspects that the FBI may have given Epstein a bit of help suiciding, in which case he probably also suspects that a whole lot of other people who knew too much about the Clintons may also have had a bit of FBI assistance in their similarly convenient suicides.

Now, everyone is a "conspiracy theorist". We are now in the latter days of the Soviet Union, when no one believed the narrative that everyone was required to believe. Twitter has shadowbanned #ClintonBodyCount. All other conspiracy theories about the Epstein alleged suicide are allowed, but not the obvious one: that the FBI arranged for his suicide to protect the Clintons and a host of other members of the elite. The suggestion that Mossad murdered Epstein is disinformation from FBI shills, and the suggestion that Epstein is still alive is just nuts. People who know too much about the Clintons don't get sent to a remote tropical island. If that was not Epstein's body on the slab, it would be because the real body showed indications of strenuous and violent disinclination to commit suicide.

That the story got out of control reflects loss of cohesion on the left – the crazy left went after Epstein because they deluded themselves he had something on Trump - every major media outlet was loudly announcing a nonexistent Trump Epstein connection, while ignoring the Clinton Epstein connection, and the connections between Epstein and all the usual rich and powerful older and more moderate progressives. Epstein died twelve hours after this narrative predictably collapsed.

Epstein knew too much about too many important and powerful people. In particular he knew too much about the Clintons.

His continuing usefulness depended on him being pals with Trump, and thus potentially having the goods on Trump. The mainstream media was salivating over the Trump connection. So they put the heat on him to give them the goods on Trump. And then it comes out that though he says he is pals with Trump, though he told his girls he was pals with Trump, they never saw Trump palling with him.

Hence not useful. And, a few hours after this comes out, a few hours after it becomes known he is not useful, there is a convenient camera malfunction and he hangs himself in a room with nothing to hang himself from.

Yet another tragic suicide by someone who knows stuff about the Clintons. But this time, something is different.

Hating whitey is the KKKrazy glue that holds together the coalition of the fringes. The very white and disproportionately Jewish progressive elite cultivated the crazies, and predictably, like Frankenstein, found themselves unable to control their monster. The crazy left joined with the sane right to let the Epstein cat out of the bag. It was crazy for them to do this, and sane for us to do this.

Used to be the left had all the smart people, because they had the elite universities, and they selected the smartest people for the most intense indoctrination, starting as early as possible, and then promoted smart leftists to high positions in the power structure. Recruiting the smartest people, however, led to embarrassing results. If you select the smartest and most civilized 0.1% of whites, and the smartest and most civilized 0.1% of blacks, the smartest black you recruit will be rather obviously dimmer and less civilized than the dimmest and least civilized white you select. For one hundred and fifty years, they have been tinkering with university entrance criteria to make them more inclusive, looking for criteria that will enable more members of under-represented groups to qualify, which tinkering has in recent years become alarmingly drastic as leftism has become alarmingly holy, with the result that elite universities are no longer recruiting the best, the left is no longer recruiting the best. They are recruiting the craziest. All the smart people in the progressive establishment have one foot in the grave. The left has long been the anti white party. It is about to have an anti white face.

Going after Flynn was crazy, and is predictably blowing up in their faces, and going after Epstein was crazy and has predictably blown up in their faces. Chances are that more crazy stuff is on its way.

The Flynn affair and the Epstein affair are good places to start draining the swamp, to purge the FBI of leftists. If Trump gets control of the justice department and the FBI, Trump will have a self coup. Once he has the FBI, if he gets the FBI, social media will then fall.

I have been predicting a Trump autocoup for a very long time, and my predictions have been wrong. I have also been predicting the great wall of Trump for a very long time and my predictions have been wrong. But now construction on the great wall of Trump has started. We now see you tube videos of the great wall of Trump, and it is starting to look great.

Trump is still not in a position where he dares hire Trump loyalists. Hence no one wants to be a Trump loyalist. But the prospect of him, or his dynastic successor, being able hire Trump loyalists, gets closer.

Highly scientific climate change of doom

2019-08-13 04:36:52

The world is going to end soon unless drastic climate action is taken.

Well then, how soon?

In the year 2000 - oops that report[337] is thirty years old[338].

In the year 2010 - oops that report is twenty years old

In the year 2020 - oops that report is ten years old.

It is *definitely* going to end the year 2030.

That is definitely right. All scientists agree. It is the scientific consensus, and if any scientists fail to agree, they will lose their jobs.

If you doubt it, you are anti intellectual and anti science.

How much did temperature actually rise in the past forty years?

Latest Global Temps

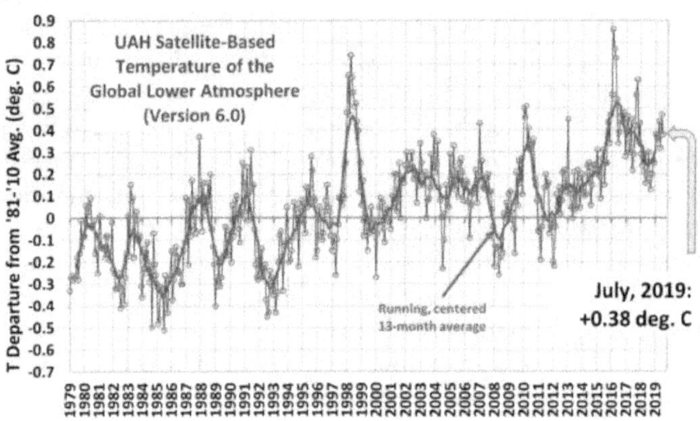

0.4°C[339]

Which looks indistinguishable from random variation well within the normal range.

Assuming that the change is real, rather than random variations similar to those that have been going on for centuries, it is not humanly perceptible.

How has temperature changed in the past?

[337] https://www.apnews.com/bd45c372caf118ec99964ea547880cd0

[338] https://www.apnews.com/bd45c372caf118ec99964ea547880cd0

[339] https://www.drroyspencer.com/latest-global-temperatures/

In order to figure that out, need to use proxies, and since using one proxy for the present, and a different proxy for the past gives unlimited freedom to cherry pick results, have to use the same proxy for the present as the past.

In a multiproxy reconstruction, you are necessarily adding apples to oranges, and even if you are being honest, there is a lot of room to get whatever result you want. And the "trick to hide the decline" was very far from being honest.

Individual proxies never show a hockey stick, and seldom show the present warmer than the medieval climate optimum. But somehow, when you put a lot of non hockey stick proxies into the sausage maker, out comes a hockey stick. Or your paper will not pass peer review, and you lose your tenure.

The best proxies are those have high temporal resolution (as for example Law Dome) and that give continuous coverage from the distant past to near the present. Such proxies are usually ice cores. Ice cores have been taken from around the world, and they show nothing unusual about recent temperatures.[340] It has been cooler, and it has been warmer. Temperatures have risen faster in the past, and temperatures have fallen fast in the past.

The best ice core is the Law Dome ice core, because of rapid ice formation and great depth of ice.

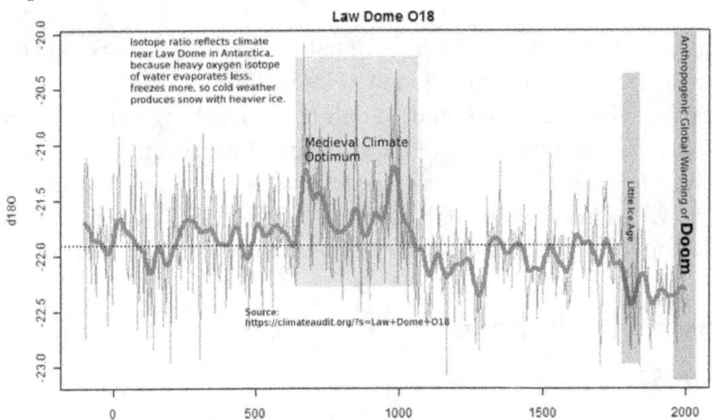

All the others show roughly similar results. Some show more warming, some show more cooling but none of them show unusual warming, and none of them show a hockey stick. They show the climate has always been changing, and oftimes, changing a lot more than it is changing now, and most of them show a medieval climate optimum far warmer than the present day.

I support the Hong Kong police too!

2019-08-14 07:02:26

Hong Kong has never been democratic. It was an island out of time, founded by British pirates and drug smugglers, keeping the early nineteenth century British political system

[340]https://climateaudit.org/2011/12/05/kinnard-arctic-o18-series/

of local rule by the local gentry, and the late eighteenth century early nineteenth century British form of capitalism, derived from Manchesterism and little changed from Manchesterism. (British impact and Hong Kong's colorful history started well before the first Opium war, but the story for some reason seems to have been erased, as if the white man never set foot there before the first Opium war.)

The one nation, two systems deal, was that Hong Kong would keep its ancient and customary political and economic system, with China handling its external affairs and defense. The protester's demand for universal suffrage is a violation of of the two systems deal, that would create a subversive and hostile Cathedral and US Government State Department outpost on China's doorstep.

The protesters destroyed the legislative assembly, and shut down Hong Kong International airport, an airport I frequently use, inconveniencing and endangering large numbers of people much resembling myself.

If the local elite lacks the will to govern, and the will to crush those grasping for power, then China has little choice but to itself violate the two systems agreement by directly intervening in Hong Kong, itself directly repressing those who would overthrow the ancient and customary system in favor of the system of the modern west, an intervention that would unavoidably destroy the Hong Kong system almost as badly as universal suffrage would.

The Hong Kong government should recover their testicles, and, if necessary, read the riot act and disperse the crowds with napalm and machine gun fire.

The old system served Hong Kong well, and the only reason for changing it is that the protesters hope for backing from the US Government State Department, so think that power is up for grabs. I hope that Trump's call for calm will be interpreted as implying that no such backing will be forthcoming. China alleges that the US Government State Department has been up to no good, and I see ample reason to believe the accusation.

Breaking Epstein's hyoid bone

2019-08-15 20:46:57

To break your hyoid bone in a suicide, you need to tie a rope around your neck and jump off something high enough that there is a drop before the rope tightens, and the rope tightens before your feet hit the ground. And there needs to be a decent drop distance before the rope tightens.

An "Introduction to the Work of a Medical Examiner" by John Miletich and Tia Lindstrom says that the "drop distance needed to break a neck depends on the person's body mass...the hanged person's neck breaks when his falling body reaches the end of the rope, rapidly tightens the noose, and wrenches his neck sideways, dislocating or snapping his neck's axis bone."

For Epstein to suicide, he would have had to tie the bedsheets around his neck, and then lift his feet of the ground, which can be done, but requires a fair bit of crazed determination and will not break your neck bones. Why would Epstein want to kill himself when he still had the goods on powerful people, and had gotten out of trouble before? Even if he wanted to suicide, he would not have sufficient determination or madness to kill himself that way.

A correctly applied chokehold, where you are behind your victim, your right elbow is at the front of the victim's neck, your right hand is nestled in your left elbow, and your left hand is gripping your right arm, will not break any neck bones either, but if the victim is struggling effectively, and he gets your feet out from under you, you both wind up rolling around on the ground, *then* you are likely to break his neck bones. You want to lift the victim of the ground, so that your eyes are protected by his back from an eye gouge, and he has no leverage to get you off balance and get his feet behind your feet.

That Epstein was screaming, and that his hyoid bone was broken, indicates his killer was having a hard time of it. A correctly applied chokehold will instantly silence the victim, incapacitate him in ten seconds, render him unconscious in eighteen seconds, and dead in three minutes, leaving no indications that this was not another convenient suicide.

This post was posted under party politics, this being the way that party politics is conducted these days.

The strong horse and the weak horse

2019-08-16 19:50:03

When people see a strong horse and a weak horse, they will naturally want to side with the strong horse.

Israel has a law that people who call for the destruction of Israel are not allowed visas. Rashida Tlaib and Ilhan Omar intended to go on tour organized by a "Palestinian" ngo aimed at highlighting the plight of the Palestinians. The important signal that would have been sent by that tour would not have been the plight of the Palestinians, but that the left is strong, and laws are not for it, and that the right is too weak to dare defend itself.

A "Palestinian" ngo is the USG State Department in transracial dress, so this was the USG left saying "We are strong, and you are weak".

Israel would have allowed the tour because of US pressure, the public face of that pressure being House Majority Leader Steny Hoyer, and Trump's staff were playing both sides, supporting the tour while pretending neutrality, but Trump bypassed the enemies that surround him by tweeting:

> It would show great weakness if Israel allowed Rep.Omar and Rep.Tlaib to visit.
>
> — Donald J. Trump (@realDonaldTrump) August 15, 2019

This tweet had two effects: It made the brown commie squad the face of the Democratic Party, as Trump Derangement Syndrome forced the entire left to come to the defense of the squad, and that it was followed by Israel barring them a few minutes later shows Trump is the strong horse - he issues a tweet, and his will instantly prevails. When the left tweets "Bad Orange man nasty to brown Democrats" they sound like whiny losers. Successful nastiness shows strength - it is failed nastiness that will bite you. If Trump halts the invasion, everyone will stop caring about mistreatment of the invaders.

A similar dynamic has been playing out with brexit, with the remainers telling everyone that Europe is the strong horse, Britain the weak horse, and supporting Europe (far) against Britain (near) .

In fact of course, Europe is the weak horse, for brexit will likely cause Britain to prosper, and Europe to fall apart. Europe is bluffing from an absurdly weak hand. The British elite love Europe, because they can blame intrusive, stupid, and disruptive regulation on people far away, because they can use the power of far against near. The Common Market made economic sense, because of market economies of scale, but the European Union does not make economic sense for larger countries with larger markets, because of administrative diseconomies of scale, which are biting, and biting hard.

Every time a British bureaucrat meddles, he is saying he is strong, because he is backed by mighty Europe, and the Briton whose life he turns upside down is weak. Government officials love laws that are confusing, contradictory, and incomprehensible, and Europe gives them an ample supply of what they love.

But the referendum made brexit a political issue, whereupon everyone saw the spectacle of remainers siding not just with remain against brexit, but siding with Europe against Britain. Corbyn has sided with every group and faction that is anti British. The squad in America, and brexit in Britain, reveals the leftist strategy of siding with far against near as treasonous and hateful - which gets overlooked if they look like the strong horse, but is apt to burn them when their weakness is revealed. If brexit prevails, the remainers will be burned for supporting Europe against Britain.

The problem with the coalition of the fringes is that fringes have to march endlessly from victory to greater victory, or else normies will notice that the left is not on their side. The converse of this, however is that Trump has to achieve substantial victory against the invasion before the 2020 election, or else it will continue to not be seen as the invasion that it is.

The Tony Abbott victory over illegal immigration in Australia demonstrates this. When it looked like he was going to fail, everyone worried that the methods he was using were harsh and cruel, and judges kept granting themselves vast powers and overruling him. When he successfully halted illegal immigration, everyone stopped worrying about that, leftist complaints about cruelty to poor pitiful illegals fell on deaf ears, and all lawfare for illegal immigrants was stopped dead by the judiciary, who quietly complied with a radical diminution in their authority.

Cathay Pacific staff and executives assisted and supported Hong Kong protests that massively inconvenienced their customers and disrupted their flights, losing the airline an immense amount of money. It seems that the Hong Kong airport occupation was an inside job. The disruption, disrupting the lives of countless important people, seemingly proved the democracy movement to be the strong horse.

In the company statement, chairman John Slosar said "recent events" had called into question Cathay's commitment to flight safety and security and put the carrier's reputation and brand under pressure. It was time to "reset confidence" with new management.

In other words, he and the board fired the leftists in top management shortly after their role in the disruption was revealed.

I predict that the protesters will swiftly and silently melt away - that the firings show them to be the weak horse, that this will quell the protests more effectively than hosing down the streets with machine gun fire. I also feel confident once again in using Cathay Pacific's services - that if they don't want their flights disrupted by Democracy protesters, their flights will not be disrupted. My confidence has indeed been reset.

The climate scam movement

2019-08-29 20:05:05

Trump ignores the climate summit, and dismisses it as dreams and windmills.

> "I'm not going to lose that wealth, I'm not going to lose it on dreams, on windmills, which frankly aren't working too well,"

Greeny heads explode, because the US is supposed to fund the climate scam movement. "Trump views the United States as a busted valise, and he's a miser hiding his pennies under his pillow.[341]"
The hilarious thing about the greenie reaction to Trump standing them up is that it becomes obvious that the goal was a joint declaration of something expensive, the more expensive the better, with the US footing the bill and the greenies skimming the expenditures.

The "International Community" is the state department, and the greenies are largely NGOs, which are also the state department, so the planned meeting would have been the presidency putting pressure on the president to fund activism against the president.

Climate action primarily consists of shaking down energy companies and disrupting the electricity grid. Even if windmills and all that met their promises, which they never do, the effect on CO2 emissions would be absolutely insignificant.

A number of places, notably South Australia have taken drastic action to transfer to renewable - with the result that in practice they have taken radical action to import energy from states using coal power, and their state grids have suffered alarming brownouts and blackouts.

Action to shake down energy companies and disrupt the electricity grid is indeed unstoppable, but the actual effect of all these measures on CO2 emissions has been near zero. Green energy projects do not in practice generate energy. They generate superior holiness. The objective is never to generate electricity from wind, but to generate holiness from wind, and convert holiness into money and political power. The alternative energy projects are never implemented with serious intention to generate substantial amounts of energy. They merely go through the motions of trying to generate energy, and, as the climategate files reveal, Michael Mann merely went through the motions of investigating whether the world was warming or cooling.

Members of the priestly caste that engage in holiness spiraling are always conmen and frauds, whether Saint Jerome arguing for mandatory priestly celibacy, or Michael Mann arguing that western civilization threatens the earth. And when these priests use priestly power to intrude into merchant activities, as when they get involved in large scale solar

---

[341] https://crooksandliars.com/2019/08/when-asked-what-world-should-be-do-about

power and wind farms, the ensuing business activities are always cons and frauds. The real objective is never to generate power, but to shake down the people operating the energy grid, which results in brownouts, blackouts, and high energy prices. The problem is not just that wind power and solar power are intermittent and unreliable, but that the people implementing wind power and solar power are unreliable. The problem is not the technology, though the technology is unsatisfactory, the big problem is the people implementing the technology. Hydro power is intermittent also, because some years it rains and some years it does not, but we never had the problems with hydro power installations that we are now having with big wind farms and big solar power installations. The problem is that they are not even crooked merchants, they are crooked priests who do not understand and do not care about the business and the technology. They want to destroy technology, not implement renewable energy. The technology works, at a price, or rather could be made to work, at a price, but the operators invariably play the holiness card to scam the grid instead. If you do business with crooks, you get burned.

The climate scam movement is a movement to destroy western civilization in order to steal a few bucks from the energy companies.

The hockey stick curve is a multiproxy reconstruction of past climate, and in a multiproxy reconstruction, you are adding apples to oranges, and there is an alarming amount of room even for an honest well intentioned person to add apples and oranges one way, or to add them in a different way. But Mann's hockey stick graph was not just based on excessive creativity in the course of adding apples to oranges, but on fraud.

How do I know Mann's Hockey stick was fraud, rather than excessive creativity in adding apples to oranges?

Dr Tim Ball did a similar multi proxy graph based on substantially the same data, but, unlike Mann, showed his work, revealed his data and mathematical methods.[342]

Battle of the graphs: Mann versus Ball

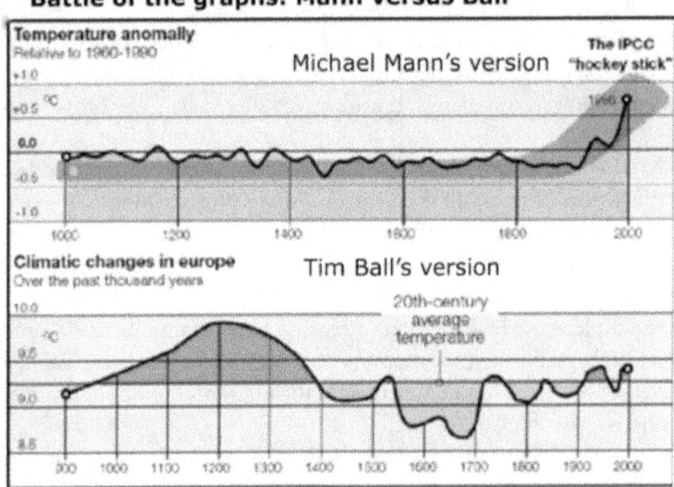

His multiproxy graph, like every singleproxy graph from all over the world that covers the same period with adequate time resolution, shows the medieval climate optium

---

[342] https://principia-scientific.org/breaking-fatal-courtroom-act-ruins-michael-hockey-stick-mann/

far warmer than the present, and today's climate changes far smaller than past climate changes.

The discrepancy between his graph, and Mann's graph, was so severe that he called Mann a fraud. According to Ball, here was simply no way you could add apples to oranges and get Mann's graph, no matter how creative you were about adding apples to oranges.

So, is Ball a fraud, or is Mann a fraud? One of them has to be a fraud. How do you know that Mann, rather than Tim Ball, is the fraud?

Mann sued Ball for libel. Ball defended his work on the basis of truth, that it was truthful to call Mann a fraud and the hockey stick graph fraudulent, thus turning the libel case into court trial on which version of our climate past was fraudulent.

Mann tried to win the case by dragging it out and running up endless and enormous legal fees, lawfare tactics that revealed he was speaking power to truth. After eight long years of delay and the artificial manufacture of huge legal bills, the court found in favor of Ball[343], because Mann refused to supply the calculations whereby he supposedly derived the hockey stick graph from the proxies.

Brexit

2019-09-07 22:16:36

I have been ignoring Brexit, because the EU is just a provincial subject state of the USG State Department Empire - but Brexit in the age of Trump is turning into an independence movement from that empire.

The Turkish empire turned into the anti Turkish empire, and the Turks, not the provinces of empire, revolted against it. Purported provincial independence movements were a reflection and result of Kemal Atatürk's central revolt of the Turks against the (anti)Turkish empire, and the ensuing lack of interest and will in imposing unitary government upon the distant provinces. Even before Trump was elected, I remarked on my hopes that he would be a Kemal Atatürk. Maybe he is.

Checking on Brexit, I see loud and strident agitation by the establishment, the mainstream media, and assorted thugs given license to intimidate and engage in violence, against no deal Brexit.

For example the mainstream media tells simultaneously tells Britons that no deal exit is going to ruin British farmers by forcing them to sell food at lower prices, and will also raise food prices in the supermarket, both articles appearing at the same time in the same newspaper. Much as they cover climate change. Any change in climate is supposedly going to be disastrous, though in fact the world has been steadily and rapidly getting greener, more pleasant, and more clement[344] since the little ice age started to ease up two centuries ago. I can see with my own eyes the semidesert that I wandered as a youth is now grassy and forested, with forests of trees considerably younger than myself appearing. What you will doubtless read is polar bear habitat is threatened, and some poisonous desert dwelling

---

[343] https://wattsupwiththat.com/2019/08/22/breaking-dr-tim-ball-wins-michaelemann-lawsuit-mann-has-to-pay/

[344] https://www.nature.com/articles/nclimate3004

lizard's habitat is threatened. You will not read of new forests appearing, in lands that were formerly so barren that even sheep and goats had a hard time.

In the third world, we have repeatedly seen the nice friendly morally superior soft power of the Cathedral backed by the most terrible of hard power, the most brutal extreme being the recent repeat genocide of Tutsi in the Congo, a rerun of the Rwandan genocide. If Clinton had been re-elected, chances are that the Alawites would have been genocided also.

So, I think no deal Brexit is likely to go through, because the Alawites were not genocided. Soft power works on credit, and without hard power backing it, the bill comes due. The campaign against Brexit is losing its clothes, revealing itself as hostile to Britain and the British. Remainers talk democracy, while refusing an election and tearing the British constitution to shreds. To constitutionally enforce Remain they have to fire the prime minister with a vote of no confidence, and appoint a new prime minister with a vote of confidence, but are unable to do so, because they cannot unite behind one leader. And they cannot unite behind one leader because Clinton is not in a position to let them know who their leader is, so they are reduced to no end of increasingly desperate end runs around the constitution to delay Brexit indefinitely. Their disunity reflects the current Democratic Party conflict between the young, brown, stupid, and communist wing of the Democrats, and the elderly, decrepit, sick, but smart and white wing of the Democrats. They cannot get their act together, because the American Cathedral cannot get its act together. Brexit is coming because Trump has no desire to hold the (anti)American empire together, as Kemal Atatürk had no desire to hold the (anti)Turkish Empire together. Brexit is coming because Trump would not genocide the Alawites in Syria the way that Clinton-Obama genocided Tutsi in the Congo.

We are all white nationalists now

2019-09-16 04:49:01

Including Elizaneth Heng[345], an east Asian child of Cambodian refugees and a moderately left wing Republican candidate.

When she took out a campaign ad reminding people that socialism is a murderous disaster, she was a racist, a sexist, a misogynist, a white nationalist[346], and all that. And similarly, if you try to discuss the facts on global warming, you are suffering from toxic masculinity[347]. Obviously the only possible reason for disagreeing with plans to destroy the economy and murder millions of people is that you hate women and nams. If you disagree with the self appointed saviors of humanity, that constitutes violence against them - violence motivated by racism and sexism.

Recently esr called me a disgusting racist. I have no idea why. I did not ask him and if I had asked him would not have received a coherent answer, because to answer would be to acknowledge some thought crime or other. They cannot acknowledge thought crimes even while denouncing them.

---

[345] https://www.elizabethheng.com

[346] https://twitter.com/AOC/status/1172323323641905165

[347] https://theconversation.com/green-with-rage-women-climate-change-leaders-face-online-attacks-123155

The left has a paranoid style of discourse, where every word, every fact, and every thought is scrutinized for patriarchy, misogyny, homophobia, racism and all that, and not just the left, but the entire mainstream right, including esr, has responded with no friends to the right, no enemies to the left. When the left decide someone is a racist Nazi misogynist and proceed to punish the evildoer, the mainstream right enthusiastically goes along in the hope of being the last to be thrown to crocodiles, but these days, they are feeding people to the crocodiles faster. Having no friends to the right just does not work any more.

The left is increasingly open about its intent to eliminate the Republican party, punish them for having been Republicans, and get rid of the fifty percent of the population who profile as likely Republican voters.

Denouncing those to your right as hateful racists and ignoring hate facts in front of your nose is just not working any more. If the Democrats regain power, Trump is going to jail, shortly to be joined by his family, and not long thereafter his family, and soon after that most of the Republican party, cucks and rinos included, then people who cling to their guns, then ...

The reason socialism tends to be so astonishingly murderous is that it tends to this paranoid style. Without the paranoia, it still needs killing fields[348], but it is no more murderous than Hitler was.

Socialism is knocking over the apple cart to produce an abundance of apples, and for a short while, there is indeed an abundance of apples. But very shortly thereafter, a severe apple shortage. Which must be caused by evil witches casting evil spells, because it could not possibly be caused by knocking over the apple cart. So they go looking for the evil witches casting the evil spells, and the paranoid style of discourse that we see on the left (and the mainstream right, including esr) tells me they are going to go looking for the evil witches very hard indeed, and will therefore find a great many, esr and Scott Alexander among them.

Time for a second Dissolution of the Monasteries.

2019-09-22 01:52:14

In French Revolution, they smashed the enforceable apprenticeship system, and in the nineteenth century, the British smashed their enforceable apprenticeship system. After the enforceable apprenticeship system was ended, the quality of workmanship declined with each generation for several generations, as revealed by old furniture.

This was a move to priestly power. The priestly class were seeking to force all children to spend endless hours at Church school. And ever since then education has been getting longer and longer, and sucking up people's entire youths, when they should be working and having children.

It is time for the Dissolution of the Monasteries.

The priestly myth of education is that there is some magic juju with education, that there is a special magic secret way, and if your kids do not get it, they will be irreparably harmed.

---

[348]https://reaction.la/killingfields.html

From time to time, drinking their own Kool-Aide, they have experimented with various magic formulae for teaching children, but each experiment produces the null result[349]

On the face of it, this would seem to show that education simply does not work. But this is an obviously absurd conclusion, since it is obvious that when you do stuff, you generally get better at it, and it is obvious that when a child does stuff under the supervision of an adult who is good at that stuff, he gets a lot better at it.

Rather, the conclusion should be that there is no magic special sauce for education, and that priestly education is only good for teaching people to be priestly. If your dad makes furniture, and makes you help, you will get better at making furniture.

The control test for formal education is unschooling and Sudbury school, Sudbury being a school that just does not school children. There are 50 years of anecdotal evidence that the original Sudbury Valley School works very well, at least for middle class kids who are already probably of above average intelligence, and the numerous imitators produce similar results. Also works with parents volunteering in place of staff, which approximates the deliberately less formal and less organized unschooling programs.

Reading surveys of the unschooled, looks like the results are similar to schooling, supporting the null hypothesis, and that the results are better than schooling to the extent that it leads to the child spending a lot of time with adults, and worse to the extent that it leads to the child being socially isolated - that a child learns more spending time one on one with a random adult, than in a class of thirty kids and one teacher, and learns more in proportion as he spends time with several different adults. Bad outcomes occur if the only adult contact is the mother, and the mother does not know much or do much, but even bad outcomes are not conspicuously bad. An unschooled boy who has had bad unschooling is not obviously and radically worse off than the boy who has had good regular schooling. The worst unschooling does not make a dramatic or consistent difference, short of locking the kid in a dungeon and feeding him through the keyhole.

Unschooling is often combined with, or a result of, a theory that children don't need discipline. If you have an undisciplined four year old in your house he will make a mess, break stuff, and hurt people. Starting at a quite early age children need to be stopped from doing lots of stuff they want to do, and made to do some stuff they do not want to do. Otherwise they will occupy the entire house and leave no room for anything or anyone else, and occupy everyone's entire attention, and leave no time for anything else. But the priestly class does not have any magical special high value formula for stuff that children should be made to do. Most of their magic rituals are a great big waste of child's time, when he could be actually learning something, such as learning how to do useful work by actually doing useful work. When kids transfer from unschooling to schooling, as often happens with college, they seldom have any problems catching up on all the stuff that the college kids were supposed to learn, but frequently failed to do so.

There is nothing obviously very wrong with unschooling. Most unschooled kids do OK. If a child spends a lot of time with adults who know stuff, he will learn stuff - but he will learn a whole lot better to the extent that those adults have loco parentis authority over him and he is compelled to treat them with respect. The most educational activity of them all is child labor under adult supervision. It is not that teaching does not work,

---

[349] https://www.arnoldkling.com/blog/the-null-hypothesis-in-education-is-hard-to-disprove/

but that a special cast of priestly highly trained specialist teachers using special magic juju methods does not work. Children spontaneously soak up knowledge from adults like sponges, and they soak it up better if compelled to treat those adults with respect. The rest is details that the priestly class, the educationists, have no special knowledge of or ability at. If the knowledge is around, the kids will pick it up.

In practice most stuff is learned from Joe Random, where Joe is not an educationist, but you glommed on to him because he was good at something you needed to do.

The professor is high status, and he tells people that everyone can be high status, thereby propagating his religion to other people's children - and producing an oversupply of priests. Throw more money and power at the professor, and supposedly everyone will be affluent and high status like the professor. Probably writing essays on hermeneutic lesbianism in seventeenth century French poetry, and getting master of arts in intersectional basket weaving.

We obviously want to cut off open entry into the priesthood, and cut the priesthood back to reasonable numbers.

Assume an apprenticeship system. We used to have something very like apprenticeship for the officer class. That is a path to high status. We have something very like apprenticeship in the judiciary, with judicial clerks tending to become judges. And then Trump's show "The Apprentice" marketed apprenticeship as a path to high status in the merchant classes. That was a path to high status. Most people are not going to get high status positions, but a plumber probably makes more money than you do. We are going to get excess demand for apprenticeships to high status positions, and the solution is to filter the applicants for intelligence, diligence, pro social qualities, and good breeding.

We want all kids to learn reading, writing, and counting. Not all of them, left to their own devices, will, but it seems that most will, much as all white kids and most black kids pick up human speech without any elaborate state intervention. It does not follow that we need to incarcerate all kids through most of their childhood and young adulthood. Maybe we should detect and incarcerate problem children, and the children of problem parents, into low status institutions for low status people.

Education obviously works, in the sense that if you practice something, you get better, and if you practice under the supervision of someone who is good at it, you get a lot better. The null hypothesis is not that education fails, but that if you try to bureaucratically mass produce it and make sure no one slips through the cracks, the results are not much different from what happens if kids educate themselves under the supervision of parents and adult associates of parents, that mass produced education fails to produce the expected and hoped for results.

Education is not only "book learning" of various sorts, but socialization. Morals and ethics. Religion. Asabiyyah. Thus, for example, most American children still pledge allegiance to the flag every day. This sort of ritual binds the nation. We can do that for an hour on Sundays, and when people are being hatched, matched, and dispatched. Also various special occasions, such as thanksgiving and Christmas. We don't have to suck up everyone's childhood.

Reading old books, stuff written before 1935, it is obvious that the elite and upper class did not think the stuff taught at elite upper class schools mattered. The important thing learned at Eton was sportsmanship and forming social bonds with other upper class kids and social cohesion within the upper class. Some time during the twentieth century, we forgot the joke. People wanted to believe that if you gave everyone the right education, everyone could be upper class. It was said that "the battle of Waterloo was won on the playing fields of Eton". In the book "When Worlds Collide", written in 1932, the author takes it for granted in his character descriptions of upper class characters that that is the elite attitude to education, that elite believed that the sports and ensuing elite social cohesion was what mattered, that the educational material at Eton and Oxford was mostly pointless, not very useful or high status, and that the elite is correct to believe so. The null hypothesis of education is what all gentlemen believed back then. The trouble was that the priesthood running Harvard did not like people to know that truth. And now people don't.

Classic Chinese, is I am told, a shared body of allusions and in jokes to poetry, history, story, and legend. Looks like the mass production of a shared elite culture, to hold China together against the centrifugal forces of empire. That is a legitimate and useful function of mass education, though cramming is going to give you a shitty elite culture of test optimizing grinds who are not actually all that good at anything.

But teaching engineering does not give you engineers. I know this well, for I was in on the dawn of software engineering, when no one was trained in software engineering and academics had not yet reinvented it as an academic discipline, and I subsequently had to interview no end of people who were trained in engineering by academics. Doing engineering gives you engineers. It is all self taught or learned by apprenticeship. If East Asian grinds think otherwise, they are all wrong.

Draining the swamp

2019-09-28 04:46:20

Trump, because Biden is the most electable Democratic Party candidate, drew attention to the fact that Biden used taxpayer money to shut off the light on his families corruption. So, naturally they accuse Trump of doing what Biden did, and are now attempting to impeach him for it - which draws further attention to what Biden, and other Democrats, and the assorted ngos closely connected to the Democrats and the State Department, got up to.

What triggered this is that the new administration in Ukraine is now in a position to shine the light on the dirty deeds of the previous administration, which looted the place in conjunction with assorted American carryonbaggers.

Trump called the new Ukraine administration up to shine the light on the dirty deeds involving the Clintons, Obama, Victoria Nuland, Vice President Biden, and the roots of the Mueller investigation.

Naturally the very holy panicked, and proceeded with the worst possible response:

Their response is an effort to protect their self delusions of moral superiority and competence. It is not a response directed at external reality, but at protecting their internal delusions.

Trump's real crime is of course insufficient wokeness, which is illegal in the current year, and getting more illegal every day, but pegging the charge on the Ukraine was to hang it on the worst possible peg. Visualize an impeachment hearing featuring a large cast of ngo carryonbaggers with Clinton, Obama, and Biden connections, caught like deer in the headlights.

One of the many hurtful effects of a state religion that requires you to disbelieve in what is seen, rather than merely believe in what is unseen, is that it drives the adherents mad and makes them stupid.

We are required to disbelieve in things things that get right in our face, such as female misconduct in the workplace, disbelieve things that expose us and our children to substantial physical danger like the black problem, and to believe in things that lose buckets of money, as illustrated by the destruction of the Star Wars franchise that Disney paid four billion for.

Notoriously, social justice warriors always project. If they are doing something bad, they will accuse other people of what they are doing - thereby alerting you to what they are up to. If they are caught doing something bad, they will accuse twice as loudly, even if it is absolutely obvious to everyone else that they are doing something bad, often with bad results for themselves. Their projection is primarily to defend themselves from becoming aware of their own conduct, not to deflect accusations.

They are, of course, going after Trump for insufficient wokeness, and if they ever return to power, will imprison him, imprison his family, then the Republican party, and then kill them. But they are going after Trump on the Ukraine connection to protect the color revolutionist self image as bringing freedom and democracy to the oppressed masses, when in fact they are just knocking over apple carts to grab some apples. It is the worst possible strategy for protecting their image in the eyes of public, but they are trying to protect it in their own eyes.

Another side effect of a state religion that requires you to believe in absurdities is that those who can make you believe absurdities can make you commit atrocities. Every color revolution, at best winds up with carryonbaggers knocking over the apple cart to grab some apples, at worst, in genocide. Despite the frequent and loudly announced claim that western elites are squeaky clean, unlike those terrible third world regimes, we observe that ngos in color revolutions and international assitance projects are generally a cause of corruption, rather than a cure, the aftermath of the Haitian Earthquake being a spectacular example. The ngos did far worse damage than the earthquake did. Since you are always telling big lies, why not tell some big lies that enable you to grab the food out of the mouths of starving people?

Attempting to impeach Trump on this enables Trump to focus everyone on the swampiness of the swamp.

"Well," said Br'er Fox, "it looks like there's no water around here to drown you in. I guess I'll skin you instead." "Okay, Br'er Fox, no problem," chattered Br'er Rabbit, "Go ahead and skin me, cut out my eyes, cut off my legs, just don't throw me into that briar patch!"

Looks like Trump is already reveling in that briar patch.[350]

---

[350]https://www.dailywire.com/news/i-am-draining-the-swamp-trump-crushes-biden-in-new-video

The crisis

2019-10-08 12:44:23

I have predicted from past trends that 2020 will probably be the last democratic election, and the proverbial hits the fan around 2026. (Though chances are that we will still be holding elections for a very long time to come, as the Roman Empire did, and the Queen still rides in a stagecoach to open Parliament.)

The current impeachment crisis is that Social Justice Warriors always project. When Trump investigates Democratic crimes, they perceive him as committing the crimes that he investigates.

It looks as though the 2020 election is going to be decided by which side puts the other side's leading candidates in jail, which is not all that democratic and is on trend for the end of democracy very soon.

In Britain, the remainers are planning to imprison the British Prime minister. So far he has not done anything towards getting the remainers imprisoned, but he is calling them traitors, and what do you with traitors who are attempting to overthrow the government and the constitution and are acting in service to a hostile foreign power?

The remainer plan is that the permanent government imprisons the merely temporary government. Might work.

The Democrat plan is insane, since the constitution puts the impeachment process squarely with the merely temporary government, who are starting to realize that they are next in line for prison after Trump.
> The Senate shall have the sole power to try all impeachments. When sitting for that purpose, they shall be on oath or affirmation. When the President of the United States is tried, the Chief Justice shall preside: and no person shall be convicted without the concurrence of two-thirds of the members present.
>
> Judgement in cases of impeachment shall not extend further than to removal from office, and disqualification to hold and enjoy any office of honor, trust, or profit under the United States: but the party convicted shall nevertheless be liable and subject to indictment, trial, judgement and punishment, according to law.

If they follow that process, impeachment in the House followed by an actual trial in the Senate, the trial will be a disaster for them. All the Democrat dirty linen gets aired in the trial, the public will be outraged by the blatant attempt to steal the election, and the inevitable acquittal renders Trump bulletproof. Attempts to steal the election will continue despite the acquittal, and those attempts will blatantly be treason and insurrection, justifying and necessitating a crackdown that will render the election irrelevant, even if public outrage did not guarantee a landslide.

So when reality sinks in on the Democrats, if it ever does, their plan is going to mutate to raising a mob to interrupt the trial, raise the mob by allowing them to knock over the liquor stores and the supermarkets, and then lead the mob to the Senate where the permanent government is supposed to piously announce it is helpless before the power of the mighty and justly enraged mob, and let the mob grab the Republicans. The democrat rump in the Senate would then impeach the president. This plan is only marginally saner than their current plan.

If, as is likely, the impeachment trial in the Senate winds up nailing Democrats, the Democrats will likely boycott the hearings and go out to raise a mob, but I doubt that their mob will follow them from the liquor stores to the Senate. They will find themselves with a bunch of ngo employees and students sent by their professors for course credit, plus some homeless there for the free food, which, as with "Occupy Wall Street" fails to make a mob capable of occupying anything in the face of three determined rentacops.

The Democrats are talking about having the Washington police arrest the people around Trump. If they try it, and it works, then they will arrest Trump - which is approximately the British remainer plan.

What are the crimes for which those around Trump are to be arrested? The Democrats are kind of vague on that, but what they all amount to is obeying Trump (when they do, which is not often) If those orders are illegal, then the remedy is impeaching the man who gave the orders, not arresting people for obeying the president. Arresting members of the permanent government for obeying the merely temporary government is an obvious violation of presidential privilege. And they cannot impeach him - at least not constitutionally, though they seem inclined to make up their own process, call it impeachment and read it into the constitution. They are already denying the need for a Senate supermajority.

If Trump gets "impeached" and arrested (or more likely arrested then retroactively impeached) the irregularity of the process is going to make it dangerous to allow him to live, for a power struggle will ensue, pursued by means even more irregular, and one side or the other will want to spring him, by means even more irregular still, so that they can wrap themselves in a dead constitution and in legality that no one except Trump has been complying with for nearly a decade now. And so the other side will very likely kill him, on charges of conspiring with the side that wants to spring him. And then it is off to the races.

What I hope for is that at some point in the process, Trump has his people do dawn raids on the Democrats, ending the matter (and rendering the election largely irrelevant). But Trump has not got people, so this could get sticky. The FBI, the state department, even the DOJ (despite Barr) has been dragging its feet on the crimes of the Democrats.

I hope that it is then announced, as Augustus announced, that the dead constitution has been miraculously resurrected and legality strictly observed, and everyone will believe it, as they believed Augustus, and today believe so many things that are contradicted by the facts in their faces.

Listen to what the enemy does not say

2019-10-10 00:37:38

The New York Times issued a vague and meandering editorial on the latest developments in the ever escalating crisis.

"No simple resolution is available" - and then conspicuously fails to mention some simple resolutions.

"Congress ... can't very well send its sergeant-at-arms to the White House to enforce its subpoenas."

Why not, you ask? What is unsaid is that Congress attempting to enforce its will against the President without going through the impeachment process would be the first step into Civil War II, which would probably end with Trump as King.

The younger, browner, and dumber Democrats may well snatch power from the frail and failing hands of the elderly white Democrats, and if they do, are dumb enough to start Civil War II, but they are probably not going to snatch power tomorrow morning.

"Impeaching a president for refusing to participate in an impeachment inquiry is a kind of meta-impeachment. It would allow Mr.Trump to argue that the meta-impeachment is illegitimate because it isn't based on an investigation." Why not hold the impeachment inquiry without Trump's cooperation, as they did with Nixon on Watergate, and then impeach Trump both for the Ukraine *and* for failure to cooperate as they impeached Nixon both for Watergate and for failure to cooperate? Why not follow long established precedent? It is not as if there is any genuine doubt about what happened in the Ukraine. The purpose of the proposed inquiry is not resolve doubt, but to manufacture doubt where there is no genuinely doubt, to manufacture smoke regardless of the existence of fire, to obfuscate Democratic crimes in the Ukraine with much shouting, posturing, and vague accusation.

Because long established precedent is the briar patch that Brer Rabbit wants to be thrown into. Trump wants a full blown trial in the Senate with the power to call witnesses and compel testimony on what happened in the Ukraine.

By calling an impeachment on failure to cooperate without impeachment on the underlying charges "a kind of meta impeachment" the New York Times implicitly admits that such an impeachment would be unprecedented and arguably unconstitutional, like finding someone guilty of obstructing justice without finding that there was some underlying wrongful conduct for him to obstruct justice in

If the House impeaches for non cooperation, without impeaching on the matter that cooperation is being demanded upon, then the Senate cannot investigate the matter that cooperation is demanded upon, so cannot investigate whether the cooperation was reasonable, so it would be flagrantly outrageous and unjust for any Senator to vote for impeachment, and that would bite them in the next election.

What is unsaid is that full court dress trial in the Senate inquiring into the Ukraine would be a catastrophe for the Democrats, a catastrophe that Trump is trying to maneuver them into, and a catastrophe that the whiter, smarter, elderly, and frail Democrats are trying desperately to avoid.

Sixteen more years

2019-10-24 22:25:27

Trump when addressing the masses does not explicitly cover the issues covered in this blog, but when addressing the shale conference, addressing the merchant elite, he touched on them:

He tells the shale industry that they should run shale *because the merchant class should have the property rights they need to do the day to day running of the ordinary stuff: "you make this country run"..*

Trump hopes to continue ruling beyond 2024: "Sixteen more years"

The way the wind blows, looks increasingly possible. Trump anticipates that his opponents are going to resort to violence, and is confident that once open violence is on the table, he wins. His opponents are making a big mistake.

The left increasingly doubt that they can win 2020, so are determined to remove the president. They know that attempting to remove the president by following precedent and the constitutional process of impeachment would be a disaster for them, so left's plan for impeachment is color revolution: escalating defiance of the rules until they finally impeach Trump in an irregular fashion contrary to the constitution. But this only maintains the appearance of legality and precedent if Republicans go along with it.

The color revolution script is "he is weak, weaker, weaker, he is falling, he is falling, falling, falling, falling, he has fallen". And if he has already fallen no need to hold a merely formal impeachment. Trump is countering the color revolution script by talking up unity and greatness, and by and large, most of the cuckservatives are reluctantly falling into line.

Color revolutions are apt to turn into genocidal holy war when the other side does not play along with the script. The "he has fallen" announcement is apt to be made in flagrant defiance of reality, as happened in Syria. Actual fighting then ensues between the new "government" and the "fallen" government. Not that I am betting on civil war before the 2020 election, but the Democrats are on a path where they either fail, or proceed to civil war. Likely they will accept failing this time, whereupon the older smarter whiter Democrats lose power to the crazies, who complain that the saner Democrats stabbed the crazier Democrats in the back, as of course they will have done if we are to postpone Civil War II till after 2020.

If they go with impeachment according to the rules and precedent, will totally blow up in their faces. If they back off from impeachment, the left will devour them. If they follow the color revolution script to the bitter end, irregular impeachment proceedings followed by premature proclamation of decisive victory and irregular impeachment, then Civil War II in place of the 2020 election.

We probably will not have Civil War II in place of the 2020 election, but everywhere around the American Hegemony, elite civility is collapsing, and they are playing with tactics that bring us closer to civil war. in many places in the American hegemony the elite are maneuvering to start arresting each other, everywhere political events are deviating further and further from established precedent and established legality. It seems too soon for Civil War II before the 2020 election, but the path to that is on the table. If I was in Trump's shoes, I would aim to delay Civil War II till after 2020, but events are out of control. The saner Democrats need to get their crazies in line, and are so far not doing so, because no enemies to the left, no friends to the right. Irregular impeachment, if followed all the way to "he has fallen" would result in Civil War II considerably sooner than I expect. They have to capitulate by giving him the regular impeachment process in accord with precedent and the constitution, or just put impeachment on the back burner, and get on with normal legislative business like passing the the new trade deal, whereupon they get torn apart by their crazies.

The ideal outcome would be a short and not very bloody Civil War II, followed by a purge of the presidency and the military. But a purge will have limited effectiveness so long as we have no replacement for our current state religion, which will continue to exercise religious power even if it temporarily suffers major losses of presidential power. A nastier civil war and a more effective purge will create a smoking crater where the current state religion used to be. A gentler solution would be that progressivism falls apart, as communism did, when movement towards ever lefter is off the table, and falls apart internally rather than being converted into a smoking crater, and then we install a more stable state religion based on the ancient traditions of the west. Sulla did the smoking crater solution, but the smoking crater remained. Suharto did the smoking crater solution, but he had an existing state religion ready to roll.

Because Trump has few people, a smoking crater this soon would be a problem.

The resurrection of God

2019-10-28 09:08:45

Western Civilization has a great big God shaped hole at its center.

Nietzsche and Bronze Age Pervert had a go at filling that hole with something more manly than Christianity, but Nietzsche failed and Bronze Age Pervert is no Nietzsche. Bronze Age Pervert correctly tells us that the job now is destruction, but the left will destroy itself soon enough if we don't. We need to prepare for construction once the left self destructs.

The Christianity of Constantine and Charles the Hammer was manly enough for anyone. We could do with the Christianity of King John the Third. Christianity tends to holiness spiral the sermon on the mount and the Good Samaritan, but provided you don't holiness spiral, the Sermon on the Mount and Good Samaritan is entirely compatible with being a man[351]. After you are out of cheeks you can beat the stuffing out of the bad guy.

If Christ is the incarnation, then he is, among other things, the incarnation of the logos, and interpretations of his words that give him meanings incompatible with game theory and evolutionary psychology should be treated as heresy. (Because the New Testament is politically incorrect, Game theorists are apt to neglect to mention that in a world of imperfect and asymmetric information, the strategy that leads to cooperate/cooperate equilibrium is one tit for two tats, rather than tit for tat. But even less does a strategy of zero tits for unlimited tats lead to cooperate/cooperate equilibrium.)

The death of God led to the death of western philosophy, summarized by Alf in his book "The Resurrection of God"[352].

> "What does it mean to be a good person?"Aristotle
> "What does it mean to be?"Descartes
> "What does it mean?"Nietzsche
> "What does 'it' mean?"Bertrand Russell

---

[351] https://blog.reaction.la/war/how-to-genocide-inferior-kinds-in-a-properly-christian-manner/
[352] https://gardenoftheinternet.com/2019/10/15/the-resurrection-of-god-is-out-now/

"What does it?"C.S. Lewis
"What?"Lil' John
"42"Douglas Adams

And eventually to the death of science, for if there is no truth, what is science? You need to take the ground beneath your feet on faith. Build on the void, your buildings fall down. An individual atheist scientist can do fine science, but science as a collective endeavor, as a social endeavor, requires a shared belief in the pursuit of truth, and we just have not been successful at maintaining a shared belief in truth without God. Hence the reproducibility crisis and peer review, which replaces evidence with social consensus. Robert Boyle told us that if a scientist talks about consensus, he is likely dishonest, and, honest or not, is facilitating dishonesty. He who believes in consensus, has no regard for truth. Robert Boyle tells us that if a prominent expert tells you experts agree, or gives you third hand evidence, what they supposedly agree upon is unlikely to be true. The supposed expert consensus is being manipulated, and *you* are being manipulated. If the supposed consensus was not being manipulated, they would invoke evidence from primary sources, not consensus nor third hand evidence.

Alf tells us:

> if man necessarily has individual faith, then what do we call shared faith?
> Well, we call it religion, of course.

I hope for Alf to be Archbishop under Holy American Emperor Trump.

The faith of Gnon requires adherence to law of Gnon, which requires, among other things, that people are required to see what is in front of their noses. If someone cannot commit, or even acknowledge, a thought crime against progressivism, they are not of our faith, but of a faith that intends our destruction.

The faith of Gnon requires confidence that God intends use to be happy, provided that we follow his laws, intends us to conquer the world and the stars, requires the white pill. If someone accepts the red pill but concludes the black pill from the red pill, concludes from the red pill that a wife and children that belong to him, in a home that belongs to him, will not make him happy, not of our faith. The black pill is gnosticism. The white pill requires us to accept the world of the fall, the world of Darwinian natural selection, and still be cheerful and optimistic about it. Every morning the dawn wakes me up, I squeeze my wife's backside, and she makes me coffee while I watch the sun rise over the islands and the sea. Most evenings I check my fruit trees, then I sit down on my log in my garden, and watch the sun set over the mountains. Every few weeks, I get drunk with my friends. Is this a world that belongs to Satan? Is this a world ruled by Satan? Every dinner and most lunches I thank the Lord for my food, for the pleasant company with whom I eat it, and for the beautiful creation in which I eat it.

The faith of Gnon requires that we respect the lessons of old and successful social technologies – eighteenth century marriage, Biblical marriage, recently existent capitalism, and science as it was before 1944, that we think very carefully before dismantling Chesterton's fence, and carefully monitor the consequences of dismantling, or failing to properly maintain, Chesterton's fence, requires proper respect for tribal taboos and the copybook headings.

Cooperate/cooperate equilibrium between men and women requires indissoluble marriage, otherwise you get defect/defect. We need marriage vows and a marriage ceremony that reflects and respects the fact that humans are heterogamous organisms. Children need to be raised in one household by their mother and their father. One household requires one head of household, and if your marriage ceremony does not give this woman to this man, if the wife does not promise to honor and obey, to submit and reverence, you are not actually getting married, because you are not actually forming one household, you are getting gay married[353].

The faith of Gnon requires generosity and forgiveness, but generosity and forgiveness should not be unlimited, lest we empower evil. Charity begins at home, and we owe more generosity and forgiveness to kin, friends, neighbors, and co-religionists, than we owe to strangers in places we could not find on a map. We owe peace and goodwill to strangers of goodwill, but no more than that, and not everyone is of goodwill. Sometimes you have to go Old Testament. The New Testament does not cancel the Old, merely cancels the legalism that the Jews substitute for the spirit of the law. We are risen killer apes, angel and killer ape both, and we rose on a thousand genocides, as tribes of killer apes that cooperated more effectively wiped out tribes of killer apes that cooperated less effectively.

We should be peaceful to all men of goodwill. A few centuries ago Europe achieved a highly successful social technology for peace on earth, for avoiding terrifying and immensely destructive wars, which social technology which was lost during the twentieth century. That social technology was: Cuius regio, eius religio, the Peace of Westphalia. Interpreting "religio" broadly, that means that every country is entitled to its own ways, and that the current ruler should be respected even if he is not following our ways. The Peace of Westphalia aims for a world of sovereign and independent nations who protect their citizens, respect their neighbors, and honor the differences that make each country special and unique. When the Harvard and mainstream media priesthood call someone a "dictator" that means they are plotting to overthrow him and probably kill him, which is not very peaceful. Installing "liberal democracy" on the bloodstained sands of the Middle East on people unfamiliar with "liberal democracy" and demonstrably bad at it is far from peaceful. We should pay the rulers of alien countries appropriate respect and refer to them by the titles that they have managed to get away with, rather than calling them something that implies that overthrowing them and murdering them is good. We should accept each country conducting themselves in the ways that are particular to the uniqueness of each country. When the holier than thou priesthood of Harvard and the mainstream media support a violent, destructive, dangerous, and revolutionary faction in Hong Kong in order to install "liberal democracy" in Hong Kong, a system that the people of Hong Kong have never experienced, do not genuinely comprehend, and are clearly even less competent than ourselves to operate, that is an act of war by a nuclear power against another nuclear power. The state religion should be universal within the state, but should not impose itself outside the state, while maintaining collegiality and communion with the state religion of other states with a similar state religion. The state religion should never pursue or encourage the overthrow of a sovereign, unless its own sovereign has first declared war. Especially against a nuclear power.

---

[353]https://blog.reaction.la/culture/marriage/

Genocide on the way.

2019-11-08 07:24:36

White culture and white history is being demonized and erased. Historically, demonizing a group is usually a prelude to attempting to physically exterminate the group, to physically erase them after culturally erasing them.

Progressives, or at least some progressives whose superior holiness is such that progressives, and even conservatives, are unable to criticize them, are now piously advocating the next step, in the august pages of the New York Times, among other places.

These calls for extermination are couched in ambiguous language. But when someone ambiguously tells you he means to kill you, and fails to clarify that ambiguity, he means to kill you.

If you don't intend to kill someone, and it sounds like you do intend to kill someone, you are going to clarify. The New York Times and the rest are not clarifying.

The usual terrified cowardly cuckservatives piously tell us that these terrifying threats are "clearly" intended merely to advocate our erasure from the culture and from history, but it is not clear at all. Rather, what is clear is that these terrifying threats are deliberately ambiguous, like the "Liquidation of the kulaks as a class"

Thus for example:[354]

> —BAP's claim that a columnist for the Huffington Post "wrote an article titled 'Towards a Concept of White Wounding,' apparently calling for racial violence." The article does no such thing; in context, it's clear "white wounding" means something like "white guilt"

In context it is absolutely clear that "white wounding" does not mean white guilt. What it actually does mean is far from clear, but what is clear is that this cuckservative is grasping at straws to find rationalizations for the stream of threats and menaces that Bronze Age Pervert cites. I read the article as calling for racial violence, but maybe it means something else. If it does mean something else, neither I nor the cuckservatives have any idea what that something else is. It does not say "Time to exterminate the white race" in so many words, but neither did Hitler say "Time to exterminate the Jews" in so many words. If the article is not saying "Time to exterminate the white race" it is profoundly unclear what it is saying. What the article does, however say clearly is that whites simply by existing unavoidably and incurably oppress other groups. What the author proposes to do about this problem is unclear, but she does seem to be implying the obvious solution and denying the possibility of other solutions.

Bronze Age Pervert lists a pile of exterminationist screeds[355].

> The anti-male and anti-White rhetoric of the new left is extreme. The racial attacks on whites in particular approaches exterminationist propaganda seen only in, e.g., the Hutu against the Tutsi in 1990's Rwanda.

[354]https://americanmind.org/post/baps-bait-and-switch/
[355]https://americanmind.org/essays/americas-delusional-elite-is-done/

The cuckservatives reply that these screeds are not calling for extermination. Well, they are certainly calling for something, though what they are calling for is not totally clear. If it is not extermination they are calling for, what *are* they calling for? Nobody calling for extermination ever says plainly what they mean. These sound mighty like past calls for extermination, and they surely do not sound like anything else. If it is not extermination they propose, what are they proposing? They are obviously proposing something. The lack of clarity is par for the course whenever monsters propose monstrous deeds. These are all calls to action. If the action is not "exterminate whitey", what is it?

Thing is, the left always has to have a new cause. Holiness spirals collapse when they cannot get any holier. As a shark has to swim or die, the left has to move ever leftwards or die. Puritanism collapsed when Cromwell halted the holiness spiral, and communism collapsed when Stalin halted the holiness spiral. Transsexualism has run out of puff after males wipe the floor in female sports and men in drag have sex with nine year old boys on the floor at Drag Queen story hour.. They have been casting about for a new cause for some time. Green socialism and nationalizing medicine are the biggies, not genocide. But genocide is on the table, competing with green socialism and nationalized medicine. I don't think it likely we will go directly to genocide if a Democrat gets elected, but they will be industriously laying the foundations for genocide for when Green Socialism and socialist medicine runs out of puff. Nationalized Medicine and Green Socialism are not terribly sexy. Nationalized medicine sounds like "Take a number and we will get back to you in nine years", and the trouble with Green Socialism is that it is just too transparently obvious that the greenies do not really believe their own bullshit. It is thirty years on, they are still announcing doomsday, and they are starting to sound bored. The mighty wrath of justly enraged Gaia has passed its use by date. The Greenies are starting to sound and look rather like the post Stalin Communists and the post Cromwell Puritans - tired, cynical, bored, demoralized, and transparently corrupt. So white genocide, being new, shiny, pure, and exciting, might well become the next big holy cause. If it does not, it is in the queue, to be the big holy cause after the next big holy cause.

The Khmer Rouge were full of wrath at foreign educated intellectuals, notwithstanding the fact the Khmer Rouge cadre were composed of foreign educated intellectuals, and very rapidly the Khmer Rouge cadre wiped out the Khmer Rouge cadre. I expect that when Scott Aaronson is informed, somewhat to his surprise, that he is white, he will agree that the needs of the many outweigh the needs of the few. If you are a progressive, and white genocide is on the table, then the way to postpone your execution is to be twice as enthusiastically in favor of it as everyone else. Observe the response of the cuckservatives.

Politics played for keeps.

2019-11-12 22:25:51

The progressives are signaling that if you are white and male very bad things are going to happen to you. The cuckservatives are starting to signal that if you are a Trump supporter, then when term limits remove Trump, or the next massively rigged election removes Trump, very bad things are going to happen to you. The cuckservatives hope that if they signal hard enough, it is only going to be white male Trump supporters.

Out of one side of their mouths cuckservatives say that it is absurd to suggest that progressives are proposing the extermination or expulsion of white males, and out of the other side of their mouths they say that if you are a Trump supporter, come the end of the Trump era, you are going to pay.

This is not necessarily a good way of removing Trump. Not in 2020, and not in 2024. In the impeachment vote, every Republican voted party line, which is an extraordinary and startling turn around. This is a vote that signals a hope that Democrats will never be allowed to return to power, and an expectation that such a return may well be prevented.

The Republicans, faced with increasingly dire threats from the enemy have united behind Trump. With the threat in front of them that from henceforth politics is going to played for keepsies, they are going with keeping. And Trumpism is increasingly moving to the position "screw the constitution, if we are ever removed from power, the constitution is dead anyway. Lets grab on to power and hang on for our dear lives."

White males and white Christians cannot continue to win elections, and cannot afford to lose them.

What, you may ask, does Trump expect?

> What they don't know is that we hang it up in five years, or nine years, or thirteen years (pause for cheering) maybe seventeen years …

Well, what is it that the Democrats don't know? Trump is a very good public speaker. He is not in the habit of losing the thread of his own words.

So either he is going senile, or what they don't know is that he is preparing a self coup against their color revolution.

> The great betrayal is over. America is not for sale. We are more determined than ever to drain the swamp … A lot of bad things happened, and a lot of bad things are going to be revealed.

If the people that sold out America face charges for quid pro quo, not a whole lot of Democrats in the 2020 election. Biden makes a really bad deal for the US, and his son walks away with a truckload of Chinese money. Seems that there have been a whole lot of mysteriously bad deals.

Trump deploys rhetoric that is preparation for an election, and also preparation for civil war.

> They want to obliterate the rule of law, drive out faith from the public square, silence you online, confiscate your guns … they want to indoctrinate your children, destroy anyone who has traditional values. All you have to do is ask the Covington boys. The far left wants to impose their authoritarian ideology on the nation telling you what to think, what to believe, and how you should live. They want to erase our traditions, our history, our culture, and our heroes. They want to subjugate you and break you to their will.
>
> …
>
> Deep State and the failed American ruling class believe it is their right to rule over you and redistribue your wealth all over the world. … Past leaders

transformed far away nations into chaotic war zones then they demanded that America take unlimimited immigration from those terror afflicted regions. ... We did not fight them over there only to invite them over here.

...

Democrats have waged an unrelenting assault against people of faith.

...

Free speech, freedom of assembly, religious liberty, and the right to keep and bear arms. ... Faith and family.

Trump is appealing to tribalism to win the forthcoming civil war, but a tribe needs a faith, and the priesthood is in the hands of our enemies. And when he addresses the Covington boys, he condemns the enemy priesthood.

Draining the Swamp

2019-11-25 10:43:14

Trump made three big promises. To bring the jobs back, to build the wall, and to drain the swamp.

Bringing the jobs back was effective almost immediately. He reversed a bunch of Obama presidential orders that had shutdown coal fields, oil wells, and pipelines, or prevented new ones from opening, and they immediately opened and started hiring at the stroke of his pen. Overnight, or rather over three months, America ceased to be a major energy importer and became a major energy exporter. It was a radical and abrupt turnaround. Bringing back the factories took a little longer than reopening the mines, because they can move a factory to China, but they cannot move a mine to China, but the factories have come back and are continuing to return. Instead of the great centralization, we now have the great decentralization, with white males moving back into flyover country.

Building the wall took longer, but now its going up, and a mighty impressive wall it is.

It is depressingly late, and a good deal later than I expected and predicted, but it is very much the wall he promised at election rallies.

Very shortly after Trump was elected, he took action against legal immigration by a multitude of presidential orders. I heard great screams of pain from employers importing H1Bs, and much whining from dot Indian chicks that I talked to the airport. Lately the Dems have acknowledged what is happening and joined in the whining[356], though it goes against their narrative "weak, weak, weak, weaker, weaker, weaker".

And now, finally, draining the swamp:

The biggest and most important swamp draining operation was not investigating Democratic Party corruption, but rescuing warriors under attack by the most holy priesthood of Obama appointees in the military, who were seeking to break up the bands of brothers that so frightened them. The cucks in top military brass were and are after Eddie Gallagher because he was a right wing Christian. The prosecution kept changing its mind about what war crimes he had committed. When one war crime did not work, they would come up with another. When war crimes did not work, their reaction was the same as when Mueller found that the Russians were probably the only foreign power that did not interfere in the 2016 US election. They wanted to get him on something, anything, everything. The pursuit of Gallagher was priests getting antsi because they smelled a warrior priest, a paladin, of an enemy religion. If one thing did not work, they would try another thing. I don't care whether Gallagher was guilty of war crimes, and as the case dragged on, it became increasingly obvious that the prosecution cared even less than I do.

Trump cannot drain the Democratic party swamp unless he has a military that will back him against a color revolution. The Democrats are planning to react to arrest of Democrats with the arrest of Republicans. In the Eric Ciaramella testimony, the Democrats were feeling out how much backing they have in the Department of Defense for color revolution, and the answer was, quite a lot. Impeachment can only work if they first arrest the president, his family, assorted members of his administration, and then threaten to arrest, or actually arrest, enough Republicans in the Senate – color revolution. The soldiers

---

[356]https://blog.reaction.la/war/politics-played-for-keeps/#comment-2270130

will only obey orders to enforce the constitution against color revolution if they think Trump has their back, and is able to have their back.

But now, finally, at long last, at long long last, the much promised, much delayed, swamp draining operation against the Democrats:

WASHINGTON, DC 20510
November 15, 2019

The Honorable Ken A. Blanco
Director
Financial Crimes Enforcement Network
Department of Treasury
Dear Director Blanco:

The Senate Finance Committee and Homeland Security and Governmental Affairs Committee are conducting an investigation into potentially improper actions by the Obama administration with respect to Burisma Holdings (Btuisma) and Ukraine. As discussed in our November 6, 2019, letter to the State Department, while then-Vice President Biden was in office, his son, Hunter, worked for Burisma and "would be paid as much as $50,000 per month." At the time, Burisma and its owner were under investigation by Ukraine and U.K. authorities. According to a report, in 2016, then-Vice President Biden threatened to withhold aid to Ukraine unless the Ukrainian prosecutor that was investigating Burisma was fired, which he eventually was. In addition, Burisma's consulting firm, Blue Star Strategies, used Hunter Biden's board membership to gain access to Obama administration officials at the State Department and potentially influence matters before government of?cials on behalf of Burisma. The Committees have jurisdiction over the taxpayer-funded operations of the State Department and the Financial Crimes Enforcement Network (FinCEN).

To assist the Committees in the examination of these matters, we are requesting a copy of all Suspicious Activity Reports (SARs) and related documents that have been filed regarding the following individuals or entities:
. Hunter Biden;
. Devon Archer;
. Christopher Heinz;
. Karen Tramontano;
. Sally Painter;
. Burisma Holdings;
. Rosemont Seneca Partners;
. Rosemont Seneca Bohai LLC;
. Rosemont Capital;
. Bohai Harvest RST; and
. Blue Star Strategies.

...

Please provide these documents no later than December 5, 2019. Thank you for your prompt attention.

Sincerely,

Charles E. Grassley
Chairman Committee on Finance

Ron Johnson
Chairman Committee on Homeland Security and Governmental Affairs.

In two weeks, Horowitz releases the report on illegal spying on the Trump campaign.

OK, swamp not being drained yet. And the barbed wire entanglements along the border in the 2018 election were not a wall either. But they were an indication of the will and capability to build a wall. Firing the Secretary of the Navy was an indication of the will and capability to resist color revolution, and ordering production of documents is a indication of intent to do something with those documents.

Good and Evil

2019-12-09 20:51:39

Good people cooperate to suppress evil deeds and exclude evil men, drive out evil men, kill evil men. If no words for good and evil, no extended large scale cooperation. If no extended large scale cooperation, we are not truly human, and we perish.

Unless we can speak of good and evil, unless we can speak of good people and evil people, we will perish.

The words "Good" and "Evil" are both socially defined, and also defined by Gnon. When the people of your social group define good and evil, they instructing you on their social technology and social capital for achieving cooperate/cooperate equilibrium within their group, and this social technology, the copybook headings and tribal taboos, necessarily varies a little from one group to another.

When Gnon defines good and evil, he is telling you that some people and some behaviors make it very hard to achieve cooperate/cooperate equilibrium. Those people are evil people, and those behaviors are evil behaviors.

The Old Testament told us to pay attention to tribal taboos and copybook headings. The book of Proverbs is copybook headings, and the book of Deuteronomy is tribal taboos. But in Old Testament times, they had good and working social technology. The New Testament told us to judge a tree by its fruits. In the cold and cynical language of the Dark Enlightenment, the New Testament tells us that when the tribal taboos get holiness spiraled, they are likely to be really bad social technology, and we should check that the social technology is still actually working.

In the first century of our Lord, Jewish holiness spiraled defective social technology eventually resulted in the most severe defect/defect equilibrium of them all: War. War with Rome. The worst possible of wars. The Jews thought it was more important to observe the pharisaic law on attending synagogue and the pharisaic law on avoiding blood contamination from walking on ground on which chicken blood had been spilled, than to observe the commandments of Gnon on coveting, on theft, and on murder.

Commies kill their friends.

The holy continually invent new ways to be ever more holy. Which, because universalism and utilitarianism, requires the continual invention of new and ever more terrible harms caused by inadequate holiness. White privilege. Male privilege. Therefore, being white and male, you are committing all manner of terrible harms, and should rightly be hated and punished. So the sincere leftist will hate you and punish you.

It is defect/defect equilibrium, because the leftist perceives all near as defectors. You cannot establish cooperate/cooperation equilibrium with a leftist, because his perception of cooperation is defective, just as his perception of female sexual desire is defective.

Near is supposedly oppressing far. So the more he hates near the holier he is. The more he harms near, the holier he is. Hence Trayvon-Zimmerman debate. "10-10 No Pressure" was a wish fulfillment fantasy. They want to kill your children.

Leftist males frequently want to cut their own balls off, because they are ashamed and horrified by how much they are oppressing women. But even more, they want to cut your balls off. Especially if you are scoring more pussy than they are, which you probably are.

A leftist just hates you, he hates his fellow leftists, and he hates himself. He will try to harm you and frequently does. Sometimes he will harm himself in the course of harming you.

In the recent prosecutions of warriors, the priestly prosecution suppressed evidence that would indicate innocence (for example the fact that the dead "civilians" shot by Army 1st Lt. Clint Lorance were in fact Taliban who had their DNA on IED devices) and went looking far too hard for evidence of guilt, went looking so hard that they were likely to find it regardless of whether it existed or not.

They just hated warriors, because our priesthood has just hated warriors since 1860, wanted to maliciously harm them, and were trying to do so. The prosecution did not give a tinker's dam whether those guys were innocent or guilty.

Leftists are nicer and politer than rightists, in part because they are always worried about microaggressions, in part because all bad language oppresses some official victim group, in part because they tend to have no real friends, thus feel weak individually, and unable to openly confront people individually.

Kathy Forth was industriously destroying the lives of people in Scott Alexander's social circle, and everyone was far too nice and far to polite to call her out for it or speak up in the defense of those she damaged.

Scott Alexander on his social circle's response to an evil and insane woman causing immense damage: "I do think that the people who work on making sure harassment allegations get heard and dealt with have done a really great job, and often while Kathy was stalking them and their friends, and I commend that"

That politeness and niceness is truly astonishing. Approaching Pol Pot levels of politeness and niceness. It is absolutely obvious that Scott's social circle is outstandingly nice and polite. But really lousy friends. They were throwing each other to crocodile in the hope of being last to devoured.

Pol Pot, who murdered everyone with any connection to himself, was a famously nice man. Everyone who met him and survived (which is not very many of those who met him) reported on how remarkably nice he was. None of his family, none of the classmates he went to school with as a child, survived. The amazingly nice Pol Pot was so nice as to eradicate anyone who obstructed immanentizing the eschaton. And since eschaton failed to immanentize, it was obvious that no end of people were obstructing it.

The collapse of faith in government and social institutions (which we and Trump are riding) is happening because leftists not only behave badly collectively, they behave badly individually. A leftist government is apt to murder millions, and a leftist sister is apt to murder her brother for the inheritance. (The left has no legitimate grounds to arrest Trump, and thus it is difficult to arrest Trump or the people around him without openinly abandoning the Republic, but he has ample supply of legitimate grounds to arrest the top leadership of the Democratic party for individual non political crimes. Biden was open about what he was doing, because everyone in his social circle was doing it, so Trump could arrest his opposition while everyone still politely pretends to believe the Republic still lives.) The average leftist would like to kill you, and will steal anything not nailed down. The holiness spiral heads to war, because it destroys cooperation, because it destroys the words "Good" and "Evil", destroys the meaning of those words.

The end state of this collapse of cooperation is war, frequently the state making one sided war upon its disarmed subjects.

To detect this sort of weaponized niceness, watch for incongruity between inner frame and outer frame. The apparent niceness of progressives usually has incongruous inner frame, as in the debate over Martin and Zimmerman. Outwardly they cared deeply that blacks were victimized by white authority figures. Inwardly they believed that blacks were entitled to rob houses and attack white people without white people defending themselves, which incongruity manifested in supposedly supporting the proposition that Zimmerman attacked Martin with arguments that Martin had motive for attacking Zimmerman.

The outer frame was that they cared deeply about other people, the inner frame was that they hate me and mine and intend harm to me and mine. Niceness is a weapon. If someone is nice, watch out that niceness is not a knife in his hand.

When I hear leftists talking in moralistic language, they use that language in the same way they use the symbols and language of Christianity, to desecrate and denigrate. They hate goodness and decency and want to destroy it, they shrink from it as a vampire shrinks from sunlight, or Merkel famously shrank from the German flag. They use the language of virtue and goodness like satanists inverting the symbols of Christianity in sacrilegious rituals. "Piss Christ" fails to impress me as an indication of heartfelt Christianity, and leftist claims to be in favor of fairness are as convincing as communist claims to be in favor of the peasants. "Land to the tiller".

Did the tiller get land?

The communists stole his land, and mortgages in the Great Minority Mortgage Meltdown were distributed in a way that was a savagely and destructively unfair as it was possible to be. The people who say "Think of our Children" also issued "10 10 No Pressure". They don't want to save the earth for our children, any more than the communists intended to give land to the tiller. They want to murder our children in order to save the earth, and are not shy about saying so.

The warmists want to murder our children, the communists are so vitally concerned about fairness that they want to take the tiller's land and the worker's house and force them all to live in giant Le Corbusier Housing projects. Is it fair to take the tiller's land?

Complex societies are the result of males cooperating - and the male capacity to cooperate is the result of selection for collective action to hog the most women.

Failure of the elite to reproduce reflects breakdown of cooperation within the elite. The state religion contains the social technology for cooperation within the elite, thus failure of the elite to reproduce reflects a dysfunctional state religion promoting a dysfunctional moral code, a moral code that prevents cooperation, an evil moral code.

Woe unto you, scribes and Pharisees, hypocrites! for ye are like unto whited sepulchres, which indeed appear beautiful outward, but are within full of dead men's bones, and of all uncleanness. Ye outwardly appear righteous unto men, but within ye are full of hypocrisy and iniquity.

The namefag problem

2019-12-13 07:04:26

In today's environment, it is impossible to speak the truth under one's official name, and dangerous to speak the truth even under any durable and widely used identity. Therefore, people who post under names tend to be unreliable. Hence the term "namefag". If someone posts under his true name, he is a "namefag" - probably unreliable and lying. Even someone who posts under a durable pseudonym is apt show excessive restraint on many topics. Moldbug has not written anything of much value since he was doxed.

The aids virus does not itself kill you. The aids virus "wants" to stick around to give itself lots of opportunities to infect other people, so wants to disable the immune system for obvious reasons. Then, without a immune system, something else is likely to kill you.

When I say "wants", of course the aids virus is not conscious, does not literally want anything at all. Rather, natural selection means that a virus that disables the immune system will have opportunities to spread, while a virus that fails to disable the immune system only has a short window of opportunity to spread before the immune system kills it, unless it is so virulent that it likely kills its host before it has the opportunity to spread.

A successful memetic disease, a demon, that spreads through state power, through the state system for propagation of official truth wants to disable truth speaking and truth telling - hence the replication crisis, peer review, and the death of science. We are now in the peculiar situation that truth is best obtained from anonymous sources, which is seriously suboptimal. Namefags always lie. The drug companies are abandoning drug development, because science just does not work any more. No one believes their research, and they do not believe anyone else's research.

It used to be that there were a small number of sensitive topics, and if you stayed away from those, you could speak the truth on everything else, but now it is near enough to all of them that it might as well be all of them, hence the replication crisis. Similarly, the aids virus tends to wind up totally suppressing the immune system, even though more selective shutdown would serve its interests more effectively, and indeed the aids virus starts by shutting down the immune system in a more selective fashion, as progressivism started by only shutting down a narrow range of thought crimes, but in the end cannot help itself from shutting down the immune system totally.

To exorcise the demon, we need a prophet, and since the demon occupies the role of the official state church, we need a true king. Unfortunately there is a persistent shortage of true Kings.

Don't use enemy words, you will not be understood.

2019-12-16 06:47:53

Enemy words are always understood as enemy meanings. And they will always be understood in this sense even if we hold the megaphone, because their official definition always conflates two very different and incompatible natural kinds.

Don't use the words "racist", "psychopath", "sweatshop", "sociopath", and "pedophile", among many others equally evil.

When someone says "Democrats are the real racists", he is using the word "racist" correctly and in accord with its official definition ("racist" means badwhite), and he thinks he is being understood, and it superficially looks as if he is being understood, but instead of being understood as saying that we need to shutdown affirmative action and stop blacks from shooting cops and burning down the shops in their neighborhood, is instead understood as saying that the Democratic Party needs to purge its remaining whites and go brown.

Using the word "racist" in accord with its official definition (badwhite) fails to communicate, because the natural kind of evil anti correlates with the natural kind of white. Whites are the most good race, the least evil race.

If you say Arkan is a psychopath, you are using the word correctly and in accord with its official meaning (evil warrior), and people will seemingly understand you, but you will be understood as saying that Army First Lt. Clint Lorance was also a war criminal, and that the prosecution was right to cook up whatever crimes and whatever evidence for those crimes were necessary to convict him, and that Trump was very wicked to pardon him.

If you say Trotsky was a psychopath, you are using the word incorrectly, since psychopaths are supposed to be calm in the face of danger and resistant to coercion. Trotsky was not resistant to coercion, and it is hard to tell if he was calm in the face of danger, because he always ran away from danger. You will be understood as giving credit to his story that he was a successful and effective military officer in the civil war, which in a sense he was, but Trotsky administered the military from an embarassingly safe distance, while Stalin headed off to where the action was.

Using the word psychopath in accord with its official definition (evil warrior) fails to communicate, because the natural kind of evil anticorrelates with the natural kind of warrior. The virtues of calm in the face of immediate danger, and determination in the face of immediate harm anticorrelate with the vices of short term manipulative lying, short termism in interpersonal skills, and the pursuit of short term goals. cluster B is toxic masculinity, psychopath hardcore toxic masculinity, and sociopath is a toxic husband who loves his wife, his children, his kin, and his friends.

You need a word for courage and manliness, and you need a separate word for evil.

When you have a word for something that is not a natural kind, but a combination of the characteristics of two natural kinds that are by nature contrary to each other, its sole function is to create confusion between natural kinds. Actual usage necessarily collapses to referring to one kind or the other.

If you are white, you are a racist, if you are brave, you are a psychopath, and if you love your family, you are a sociopath. And when people attempt to use these words in other meanings, as with "Democrats are the real racists", they just fall flat on their faces.

Just flat out does not work. It is laughable to even attempt to say it. When a black gang roams the streets looking for white kids to beat up no one calls them racists, because they are not racists, and if you call them racists you sound crazy. No one understands what you are talking about.

The official definition of "racist" is not "white". It is "badwhite". But simply having such a definition necessarily collapses in practice to "it is not alright to be white". And the official definition of psychopath is not warrior but evil warrior, which is in one sense plausible, since warriors regularly do terrible things. On the other hand, because the warrior virtues are in fact virtues, does not make sense, so in actual usage necessarily collapses to "it is not alright to be brave or manly"

Because the characteristics used in the official definition of a psychopath, a sociopath, a pedophile, or a racist anticorrelate, actual usage necessarily to collapses to one cluster or the other cluster

If you have one word for both, then priestly types can never be evil, and warrior types can never be good. So the actual usage in practice necessarily collapses to a hateful word for warrior.

Official definition of racist: "Badwhite"; Actual usage and what happens if you attempt to use it in the official sense: "Whites are evil".

Every attempt to use enemy words in accordance with their official enemy definition simply fails every time. "Democrats are the real racists"

Communication just does not ensue.

The intent of words that do not correspond to natural kinds is to lie and confuse, and trying to use them to tell the truth just fails. They are words with a lie at their core built into them.

"Sociopath" is a hate word for love and loyalty. If you care about your wife and kids, you are a sociopath, and again, no one is going to understand you if you attempt to give it a non standard and unusual meaning. Trying to use these words is like calling blacks and democrats "racist". Just does not compute. No one is going to understand you.

If capitalism and poor work conditions were a natural kind, if the word "sweatshop" referred to a natural kind, that would imply that capitalism is poor work conditions, or causes poor work conditions. If injustice motivated by racial difference was a natural kind, that would imply that noticing racial difference is injustice.

Libertarianism

2019-12-22 00:54:44

Libertarianism is classical liberalism. Classical liberalism is, or was, the Puritan sect known as the Levelers, who opposed aristocracy, Kings, and Bishops, but supported private property in the means of production, supported natural inequality, opposed socialism and communism, opposed them for a mixture of religious reasons(God ordained private property and capitalism in the fall) and quite modern reasons (price control and debasing the currency has the consequences that it does, therefore wrecking the market does not work)

Trouble with the Leveller-ClassicLiberal-Libertarian theory is that if everyone is equal before the law you have to give everyone the vote, and then someone comes along and says "Vote for me and I will kill all the classic liberals and you can take their stuff".

The libertarians, the levelers, were of course correct on capitalism. We intend to revert to the most recent known working social order, the one that gave us science, technology, industry, industrialization, and empire, the social order of Restoration England.

Puritan England was capitalist, had been capitalist since a brief interruption to capitalism which ended in the twelfth century, and remained capitalist because Cromwell crushed the Puritan extremists, who wanted communism. But the restoration introduced corporate capitalism and the joint stock for profit publicly traded corporation, which made possible Rand's heroic entrepreneur, who uses other people's labor*and other people's capital*to advance technology and make it widely available and widely used.

Without rich people, no mills, no abundant cheap good quality steel, no transistor, no integrated circuits, no computers. Without billionaires, no access to space. You cannot make a pencil unless the boss provides you with custom made tools and tells you how to use them.

Way back in the beginning, the people who were to become what we would later call Classic Liberals believed that blacks were equal to whites, and not only before the law, but in the sense that they were as capable of adhering to contracts and working for a living as free laborers as whites are.

It seemed absolutely obvious to the abolitionists that if you abolished slavery, the former slaves would contract with the former masters to the same work as before, at a fairer reward, and without the very considerable overhead of whips and chains.

This did not in fact happen, because the slaves were an inherently low trust, less trustworthy, group.

The libertarians/classic liberals were unable to realize the problem of keeping low trust peoples away or under control, because of Christian universalism. They were the levelers, and in substantial part, they still are.

Obviously, if you believe in freedom of contract, private property, and all that stuff, then affirmative action and all that is the grossest possible violation. Affirmative action and all that is also wildly unpopular, yet where do you hear libertarians campaigning on that?

Libertarians are not people who believe in private property and Ayn Rand's account of economic growth and technological advance. They are Puritans.

"I, Pencil" is a libertarian tale about how no one knows how to make a pencil but through the magic of markets lots of people cooperate and pencils get made.

Ayn Rand disagrees. In Ayn Rand's version the pencil factory owner understands how to manufacture pencils better than the workers, the lumber company owner understands how to get men to produce lumber in exchange for money, the shipping company owner understands logistics and ships things on schedule even though the parts of his operation don't have to understand the whole.

On this, Reactionaries are on board with Ayn Rand. But where Ayn Rand is very wrong is that good governance does not fall from the sky. Leftists think that goods fall from the sky. Libertarians think that knowledge and ability to make goods fall from the sky. And Ayn Rand thought that good governance falls from the sky.

Ayn Rand thought that warriors "mystics of muscle" were dangerous and useless, and priests "mystics of spirit" were merely peddling foolishness, much as commies think that capitalists do not do anything useful, and progressives think that factories and capitalists do not do anything useful. Supposedly stuff just magically appears on the supermarket shelves, and the evil capitalists cruelly charge people money for stuff that they had nothing to do with.

The entrepreneur has to outsource stuff outside his core competence to the market, which the libertarian version gets right, but he is in the business of insourcing his core competence, which the libertarian version ignores.

Rand, unlike the libertarians, got both the outsourcing and the insourcing correct, but neglected the problem of defending property rights. You need warriors to actually defend property rights, and priests to give the warriors cohesion and to get everyone on the same page about what rights are rightly defended by what means.

If libertarians are people who believe that the economy should run on freedom of contract, they would be in favor of feeding low trust people into the wood chipper, feet first, slowly, but observed libertarians are in favor of open borders and less incarceration. Puritanism strikes again.

Today's leftism is organizationally descended from Puritanism (when the former headquarters of the former state Church of Massachusetts declares that Oceania has always been at war with Eastasia, every academic everywhere outside of China and Russia instantly and completely agrees, and not only agrees, but is entirely certain without a shadow of doubt that he always has agreed) but while leftism has rejected every tenet of puritanism except war on Christmas and war on marriage, through one heresy after another, Libertarians are descended memetically from the leveler sect of puritanism, pretty much unchanged, their error and their failure being the original error of the levelers, still doing wrong what the original levelers did wrong.

If you are a libertarian, you don't believe in welfare. So what do you do if someone finds it difficult to get a job because of a past history of misbehavior, and is unmotivated to get a job because he cannot think ahead all the way to payday, and is likely to be fired before payday anyway.

Well if you are a libertarian, you say that there are no such people, abolish welfare for the undeserving poor and everyone will behave well when they get sufficiently hungry. That is the leveler speaking. "No Bishop, No King!"

If you are a reactionary however, you suspect that such people are more likely to try to eat you when they get hungry, and therefore such people need to be enslaved, exiled, or otherwise taken permanently out of circulation.

Impeachment

2019-12-23 23:38:46

Trump:
> This Witch Hunt must end NOW with a trial in the Senate, or let her default & lose.

Trump wants a trial in the Senate at which Democrats get to call witnesses, Trump gets to cross examine their witnesses *and Trump gets to call witnesses*, and they get to cross examine his witnesses.

During which he gets to put on the greatest show on earth, unlike the ratings killing impeachment investigation.

The Democrats want a trial in the Senate during which they continue their aimless, endless, boring, and fruitless fishing expedition for something, anything, everything, to pin on Trump, but Trump does not get to call witnesses or cross examine their witnesses.

The cucked Republicans want it all to end now, before Trump gets to hang out all the Uniparty and Deep State dirty linen in the Senate.

I have been expecting and predicting a color revolution attempt, but that Nancy is sitting on the articles of impeachment indicates that this is off the table, at least for now. Maybe not until 2026, when revolution will be riper. But if it is off the table, the tiger she is riding is going to get even more difficult and fractious.

Nancy Pelosi is using the Republican desire to avoid letting it all hang out as leverage to continue the forever investigation of Trump, which has been running since he nominated in 2016, but agreement is unlikely. She cannot even find agreement within the Democrats. Making deals is hard, and it is now becoming impossible, since there is no one to make a deal with. The only possible resolution of the impasse is to drop the whole hot potato into Judge Robert's lap, and if neither side is offering that, neither side wants the impasse to end.

But both Trump and the tiger Nancy is riding do want the impasse to end. So, expect the unexpected. But probably not the most dramatic outcome of them all, color revolution.

Creeping coup

2019-12-31 06:29:22

Doing illegal acts and getting away with it due to state power is a creeping coup. If one side in a struggle for state power can do illegal things, and the other side cannot, the illegal things eventually escalate till the political leadership of side that cannot commit crimes flees the country or goes into hiding. We are in hiding, and people in the military with dangerous ideas get prosecuted for war crimes. People associated with the Trump campaign get charged with obscure and incomprehensible crimes that everyone unknowingly commits, while Democrats stuff ballot boxes and collect bribes with complete immunity. Jon Corzine (Democratic party privilege, not Jewish privilege) got off for robbing investors,

and the banks were forced to make the people he robbed whole.
> Treason doth never prosper: what's the reason?
> Why, if it prosper, none dare call it treason.

Thus, for example, the normalization of homosexuality. The gays were allowed to commit violence against those that disagreed with the normalization of homosexuality, the courts and police winked at the violence, and suddenly everyone agreed that homosexuality was just the cats whiskers. And now, antifa and illegal immigrant violence against white people, as for example the Kate Steinle case.

The only real crime that anyone connected to the Trump campaign has been convicted of is stretching the truth on a mortgage application. But during the great minority mortgage meltdown, every white speculator, starting in 2005 November when every white speculator realized that the bubble was going to burst, unloaded overpriced housing onto blacks and Hispanics, usually Hispanics with no income, no job, and no assets, often a drunk cat eating wetback pulled out of the gutter from outside Home Depot with a bottle of whiskey, and the loan officer, usually a loan officer working directly or indirectly for Countrywide Bank, created a pile of lies that the drunk could not read and signed with his mark. None of the people who created these highly creative loan applications were prosecuted, because the banks, and especially Countrywide Bank, were doing the very holy work of moving minorities into green leafy overwhelmingly white suburbs.

The speculators unloaded overpriced houses onto people who could not pay, because people who could not pay were unworried about the price, even if they were sufficiently sober to know what the price was and what they were signing, but were nonetheless able to borrow, because if they were not able to borrow, it would constitute redlining. Beverly Hills Bank was destroyed by the regulators for its racist reluctance to make such loans, for its insistence that borrowers should be able to pay mortgages (redlining) but when the bad loans blew up, no one was punished, everyone was bailed out. Angelo Mozillo, the biggest villain in the Great Minority Mortgage Meltdown got a slap on the wrist for billions of dollars in losses on completely fraudulent mortgages and general failure to keep legally required records of who owned what, and who owed what, while Trump adviser Paul Manafort gets severely punished for a bit of creativity on one small mortgage application, which mortgage did not go bad.

Normally if a borrower is able and willing to pay on time, no one cares exactly what was written on the mortgage application, which tends to be filled out by the loan officer with whatever it is supposed to say pro forma, without too much consideration for the underlying reality for those details that are not all that relevant to the borrowers ability and willingness to pay. There are too many boxes, and they just routinely tick them all without examining them too carefully. But the details that are relevant to ability and willingness to pay, those they are supposed to be take seriously, and for white people, they do take them seriously.

Conveniently, the white speculators unloading overpriced houses had no written connection or direct financial relationship to the borrower or the loan officer, and no part in preparing the loan application, though the (usually white) speculator usually gave the (always black or Hispanic) borrower something under the table, and the (usually Hispanic) real estate agent usually gave the (frequently Hispanic) loan officer something under the table.

By 2006, every speculator with skin in the game, every speculator willing and able to pay a mortgage, which speculators were almost always white, had unloaded onto people who were borrowing against their race, not their assets. Then in 2007, the whole house of cards came tumbling down, because the white people had stopped playing the game and left the table, and everyone who had fraudulently set pen to paper was very holy, or of a protected race, and usually both, and so none of them were punished, except for Angelo Mozillo, who got a slap on the wrist for all the innumerable wrongdoings of innumerable loan officers directly or indirectly in his employ.

When the bubble burst there was frantic search for scapegoats who were not race hustlers. They eventually decided to blame the derivatives market, even though everyone knew the problem was dodgy loans. That precisely no one was prosecuted for signing a dodgy mortgage application, even though all mortgage applications are so tediously lengthy that you could probably find something dodgy on most of them, suggests that every single white speculator who was underwater unloaded before the bubble burst. In 2006 January it appeared to me that every white speculator was unloading and most of them had unloaded by the end of 2005 November. That the derivatives market was, in significant and substantial part, managed by Jews suggests that Jewish privilege is dropping to the bottom of the list of privileged people, with dot Indians way ahead of them.

If there had been any white speculators with under water mortgages still around when the bubble burst, they would today be remembered great outrage. Whites skedaddled when it became obvious how it was going to end. Only those protected by racial privilege kept on partying to the end. White speculators got out in 2005 November. Everyone who was still partying the bubble in 2007 as if it was still 2005 was protected by racial privilege or Democratic party membership from adverse consequences.

The bank did not lose any money, or even suffer any late payments, on Paul Manafort's loan, nor was it ever likely that they would. Every loan officer everywhere is apt to routinely tick all those boring overly numerous boxes. During the great minority mortgage meltdown, they massively falsified the ability and willingness to pay of borrowers who were usually obviously unable and unwilling to pay, and sometimes had no idea what they were signing, pissing away unimaginably huge amounts of money, yet no borrowers and no loan officers were ever prosecuted, while Paul Manafort gets the book thrown at him for one trivial detail on a loan application - which implies that Mueller's lawyers went over every document of everyone connected to the Trump campaign with a fine tooth comb. If someone went over every document that you signed, often documents with far too many pages detailing lots of boring complicated routine requirements that no one actually cares about or pays much attention to, how would you fare? The stack of documents you signed in a mortgage application is several inches thick. Did you carefully read all of them? What did your loan officer write on those documents that you signed and never read?

The loan officer wrote on your stack of documents the same thing he wrote on a thousand similar six inch deep stacks of documents. Was everything he wrote applicable to your loan? You did not read them, but it looks like Mueller's lawyers read everything signed at any time by anyone involved in the Trump campaign.

After FDR the merely elected government lost power to the permanent government, the president lost power to the presidency and, starting around 2008, the permanent government lost power to the deep state. And the deep state is apt to send cops to the doors of its enemies, while the Democrats merely sends a mob of blacks, who are less dangerous.

The legislature has long ceded the boring tasks of legislating to the permanent government, the judiciary and the lobbyists, the latter faction reaching its ill fated and ludicrous extreme in the Transpacific Partnership, where skyscrapers full of high paid lawyers in New York wrote pallet loads of planned legislation and regulation to be applied world wide to govern the minutiae of daily life and economic activity in far off places of which they knew nothing and cared less, whose pallet loads of dense obscure legalese and bureaucratese could all be summarized in five words: "everything now belongs to us", the ultimate absurdist end point of lobbyist written legislation. Mostly they wanted to confiscate value created in flyover country, which is what got Trump's goat, but disrupting the value creation being done on the other side of the planet in the Australian outback would have been collateral damage, since this colossal pile of freshly minted onerous regulation would have been *trans pacific*.

Meanwhile the presidency auctioned of America's foreign policy to the highest bidder, cheerfully ignoring the president. Obama was content if the foreign policy establishment gave him some photo ops. Too corrupt to stay bought, they implemented both Israel's foreign policy, and the "International Community" anti Israeli policy. While their holy belief system was Harvard's foreign policy, their actual foreign policy was even more erratic and less intelligible, and terrifyingly and bloodily unpredictable. They armed and funded Islamic State, and they bombed Islamic state. They destroyed Libya, and were surprised and confused when they were unable to rule the ruins. Having destroyed Libya's military, they were unable to believe it when Al Quaeda used conventional war and a conventional military to pursue power and remove American power.

In order to govern, it is necessary for the governing elite to act as one, which requires social cohesion and rules of good conduct, which come from ethnic and religious cohesion. Puritanism arose in a holiness spiral, which rapidly spiraled to post Christianity. A holiness spiral undermines cohesion, and post Christianity drops the the beliefs that made Christendom cohesive and effective. Thus the Puritans lost power in England in 1660, and England became sane, and remained sane for a century and a half. The holiness spiral of the Church of New England escalated more slowly, but is now reaching heights of madness comparable to those of the post Christian Puritans that Cromwell had to crush. The state religion of progressivism is succumbing to madness, rendering it incapable of functioning as the faith of an elite capable of ruling.

This manifests in the increasing use of violence and coercion, police power, and the criminalization of political differences in struggles within the elite. Convicting Sheriff Joe in 2017 crossed the Rubicon, and there are no more sharp lines between "ordinary" political conflict and civil war. If you arrest one political opponent over political differences, why not all of them?

If you arrest one political opponent who is a fellow member of the elite for his political position, eventually it will be all of them.

The design of the founders was that the elite would act as one through the person of the president, and this worked. But the rise of the power of the presidency, and the decline of the power of the president, meant it stopped working, and Harvard's holy synods of bishops are a poor substitute, as illustrated by the chaos of American foreign policy and the absurdity of the Trans Pacific Partnership.

Clinton was famously crooked as a dogs hind leg, but he imposed some order among the Democrats. When Obama became president, their legal immunity resulted in all manner of crimes. Hunter Biden's legal troubles go all the way back to 2008. The democrats and the deep state have endless crimes that Trump could legally jail them for, but he does not. We all know what the Durham report will show, if it does not continue the pretense. We have known what it could and likely will reveal since 2012, long before Trump got caught up in this. The Horowitz report was a limited hangout, which points towards a full hangout. Chances are that the Durham report will make what everyone has known since 2012 official administration knowledge, that the deep state has been illegally wiretapping the political elite since 2008 and likely earlier.

In 2012 Edward Snowden and Julian Assange revealed that the NSA was illegally spying on Americans. And everyone shrugged their shoulders and said to themselves "Hey, they are not going to care about me, they are going to looking at important people." And, of course, we now know that they *were* looking at important people, both Hillary Clinton and Donald Trump, and everyone connected to them.

The 9/11 presidential order in 2001 gave them alarmingly broad powers to tap people - which would be not too bad if the president could control that information, but inevitably it slipped from the president's hands. In 2007 Bush rescinded that order. I conjecture that he realized it was being used against Republicans, and perhaps himself, and expected that when he left office, would be used in that manner a whole lot more, but the rescission was ignored. The actual practice has been illegally escalating ever since, and under Obama, no end of petty partisans in the elite gained the ability to spy on other members of the elite and use that knowledge for nefarious petty partisan purposes. And with the election of Trump, that presidential power inevitably came to be used by the presidency against the president. The trouble with allowing spying on Americans is that it is such a powerful tool that the elite is bound to turn it on each other, with the result that power falls into the hands of the security agencies.

Sooner or later as the elite increasingly relies on coercive means and secret police to resolve policy conflicts, they are bound to start arresting, and shortly thereafter, killing, each other. Either Trump will jail them, or they will jail Trump, and shortly thereafter start jailing each other, then kill Trump and his family, and shortly thereafter, kill each other.

If, in the Durham report, the Trump administration comes to officially know what everyone has known since 2012, that the deep state has been acting illegally, then it is war between the deep state and the Trump administration.

What is holding up the Durham report? Everyone knows what will be in it if it is not yet another cover up. I hope that what is holding it up is the same thing as is holding up Pelosi sending the articles of impeachment to the Senate. Trump is likely sounding out the praetorians and getting them in place. Everyone is getting ready for what happens when arresting members of the elite over political differences escalates a lot further than it has already escalated.

If Trump imprisons them, the pretense that we are still a Republic will continue to have some plausibility, but Trump will be Caesar, for the arrest of the deep state for illegal acts that everyone knows about but no one admits will give him the power to arrest democrats for everything from notorious ballot box stuffing to equally notorious graft and corruption. If they arrest Trump, the pretense will get a bit thinner, though no doubt everyone will continue to piously believe.

9 798330 450473